NO NAY NEVER

BLACKBURN ROVERS v BURNLEY

Published by
Legends Publishing

E-mail david@legendspublishing.net
Website www.legendspublishing.net

"This book is dedicated to all Clarets' and Rovers' fans, past, present and in the future who, having chosen their football club, have stuck with it through thick, thin and everything in between. You are the life blood of the game, the real football heroes. Now, irrespective of the colour of the shirt, having remained steadfast to the cause, you have won the right to join in the chorus of that great American folk song, "We shall not, we shall not be moved".

CONTENTS

Introduction

Once upon a time, as all good stories begin, there was a much respected and extremely experienced footballer who had spent most of his career at Sunderland, regularly going into battle in the North-East derby. This is still one of the greatest of its kind, a veritable hot bed of passions, emotions and deep antagonism from both sets of supporters. By his own admission, he loved a scrap but his career was inevitably winding down and he arrived at Burnley Football club for one last spin on the merry-go-round which is modern day professional football, prior to finding a final resting place for his boots. He was sadly expecting a more sedentary experience with no bruising derbies to look forward to..... and then it happened. Even with all his experience of the vitriol, the rancour and often sheer brutality of the game, he was totally stunned by what went on when the Rovers met the Clarets.

You can read more about Kevin Ball in the following pages of what is a chronicle of football's longest existing professional derby, born on the cobbled streets of Victorian East Lancashire. At times it has not been for the faint hearted but this is far more than a book based solely on the unacceptable face of football. It is a celebration of two small town English football clubs, tucked away in an often forgotten spot in the backwoods of Lancashire. Here, in spite of being dwarfed in so many different ways by multiple giants of world football within an hour's drive, they have continued to joust with the best, to hold their own in a now scandalously money-orientated game and occasionally risen to the top of the pile.

As an East Lancastrian born and bred, closing in on seventy years of supporting Blackburn Rovers but with a genuine admiration and fondness for Burnley FC, it has been my pleasure to delve into the history of this rivalry. Words such as "see-saw" and "bragging rights" are woven into the tapestry as I recount so many memories of watching games at Ewood Park with friends and family and swapping banter with numerous Burnley fans who are also my friends and in-laws. Coming right up to date, it is a magnificent story and on whichever side of the fence you genuine footballing men and women sit, there are so many ups and downs but ultimately so much to make us all proud.

Michael Hodkinson

And they're off!!! Escorted Burnley fans leave
Turf Moor en route to Ewood Park in March 2013

The Combatants

Neighbours,
Should be there for one another,
That's when good neighbours become good friends
Written by Tony Hatch and Jackie Trent
Recorded by Barry Crocker, 1985

The public being frog-marched on to buses by the police and convoyed across the border. Squad cars on every motorway bridge. Seats being ripped up and thrown. Stewards guarding stands in case any foolhardy individual should risk clambering on to the roof to hurl down tiles. Police on horseback holding back rival groups. Police on foot armed with batons charging into the fray. Small groups arriving in taxis at a pub about a mile away and marching down the road, ready to take on anyone who should stand in their way. A train full of returning supporters being hit by an onslaught of bricks and stones as it passed through rival territory. A coach being guarded by six police outriders, one racing ahead to each junction to check if all was clear. Was this Belfast during the troubles in the 70s, the race riots in Birmingham, Alabama in the 50s or a Hong Kong student rebellion in recent times? Well, actually it was on the 18th of October 2009; the date of a football match at Ewood Park in Blackburn and the border was an imaginary line in Accrington.

But this was no ordinary football match. It was the East Lancashire Derby, the first to be staged at the highest level in English football since 1966 and, apart from an FA Cup tie in 2005, the first Burnley versus Blackburn Rovers game since April Fools' day 2001. For many years, this had been a regular fixture, but with the changes in fortune of the two clubs over the previous 40 years, almost approximate to the up and down movement of a see saw, "derbies" were something of a rarity. And the fewer there were, the more actual assaults and public disorder became common place on match days; animosity ruled, all fired up of course by hatred, vitriol and no little consumption of alcohol. No wonder tensions were high.

From 1882 until the end of the Fifties, there was undoubted rivalry between the sides whenever they met. This occasionally spilled over to include conflict between the fans, but there was little evidence of the hatred which the last 50 years has brought. There were bragging rights of course, and throughout the quarter of a century from 1924, they rested firmly at Ewood Park with the exception of two seasons. There was little of the Schadenfreude mentality however in those days, where genuine pleasure is obtained from the misery and misfortunes of the other club. It was banter, mickey taking, having a laugh

Police horses outside Ewood Park ahead of the 1913 derby FA Cup clash

when "our lot" won and "t'other lot" lost, but the moment quickly evaporated. Unfortunately, at times in recent years, it almost seems more important, to certain fans of one or other of the protagonists, for the enemy to lose whoever they are playing; the more heavily the better.

For Rovers fans pre-Second World War, and equally for Clarets supporters from 1947-8 onwards until the mid-seventies when the tables had completely turned, the mentality was far more of the "live and let live" variety. The four FA Cup ties between 1952 and 1960 may have begun to sow the seeds of genuine hostility, but in a strange sort of way, the period from 1966 to 1976, which signalled the start of a 33 year Burnley decline, was probably more instrumental. In the 35 seasons between 1966 and 2000, the clubs only clashed ten times, leaving a total of 30 separate years without a derby game. Some may find it hard to imagine how the rivalry continued with so little opportunity to test the clubs' respective skills, but continue it did.

Festering is probably the most accurate adjective. The dictionary definition of the verb to fester is "a negative feeling... becoming worse or more intense, especially through long-term neglect." There is no apt cliché to use which sums up the situation. It was not "out of sight, out of mind" and it certainly was not "absence makes the heart grow fonder." In fact, it was the extreme opposite in both cases. "Gone but not forgotten" is probably the most appropriate glib phrase. It was at this point that the relationship changed and although there has been a lull in the storm, caused by Burnley's superiority league wise, one dreads to think what the atmosphere will be like when the clubs face up to each other in the Championship during the 2022-23 season.

The rivalry for some is sporting but, for many, the hatred is so ingrained that sharing a pint with, or swapping a joke with, is completely out of the question; simply taboo. Even walking on the same side of the pavement provokes a response; spitting in the gutter being one. Rivalry between organisations, whether sporting, political or religious, is nothing new in this area and has existed throughout the ages. I know of two examples from within my family. I had a Liberal voting great grandma who would not even look at her Tory voting best friend on the days either side of the local Council Elections. But for many supporters of the two clubs, the dislike is permanent, it is life long and to an extent becomes woven into their personalities.

So has the anti-Blackburn/anti-Burnley feeling replaced the religious bigotry which certainly existed from the days of Henry VIII, through the Victorian period and only faded away in the modern Elizabethan age? In particular it dominated any decision making on the choice of spouse. An attractive looking young lady, a relation of mine, was brought up as a strict Methodist and was secretly "courting" a Roman Catholic for perhaps four years before her father found out. "You stop seeing him immediately or never set foot in this house again" was his edict and she did. Sadly, she died a few years ago, well into her nineties, having never married.

Now I am sure that the inter-town rivalry has yet to reach that limit of personal tragedy, but I heard a story the other day about a conversation in a pub. It went something like this.

"She has a new boyfriend."

"Where's he live?"

"He's from Burnley."

"Good God, he's a Dingle."

And apparently there was laughter all around.

Now it was only banter of course, but in the cold light of dawn, it does show how the fierce football rivalry has become all-compassing, extending to all aspects of life in the two towns. There is nothing wrong with banter of course, providing it is harmless and equitable, but it does indicate the power of football in the nation's psyche.

The nickname "Dingles" has been in circulation since the down at heel family descended on our TV screens during the nineties in ITV's long running soap, "Emmerdale". It is uncomplimentary, a down-right insult, but with a touch of humour; albeit of the dark variety. Burnley has a much longer running barb aimed at the opposition. It is "Bastard Rovers", lacking in subtlety but straight to the point. Natalie Smith, a young lady from a family steeped in the tradition of following the Clarets, gives a female perspective to this.

"I was much younger than my two brothers who, along with my dad, were season ticket holders at the "Turf". I suppose my parents wanted to bring me up as a nice, polite girl and so swear words were banned in the house. When they wanted to talk about the Blackburn team, they had to say, "Basket Rovers" in my presence."

According to the AA Route Map, it is 11.8 miles in an easterly direction from Ewood Park, the home of Blackburn Rovers since 1890, to Turf Moor, the residence of Burnley FC from 1882. The route in this day and age is mainly along the M65; in Victorian times it was on the A679 via Accrington. It is the distance that friends will travel on a weekend afternoon to visit those for whom they care, friends through thick and thin. There ought to be celebrations for each other's achievements, commiserations when disappointments come their way. But this is football we are talking about. This is tribalism, this is the closest we come to civil war and although the Clarets and the Rovers may well be neighbours, "friends" is something they are certainly not.

For supporters of Burnley FC, there would only be one local rival. For a very short period of time it could have been Accrington, but when that club dropped out of the league in 1893, it had to be Blackburn Rovers. To the north of both Blackburn and Burnley, the nearest professional club is Carlisle United, approximately 90 miles away. To the east of Burnley, Halifax Town was the nearest port of call (20 miles). Bury to the south was the nearest club in that direction (21 miles), which meant that the Rovers were by far the closest. For the Ewood Park club, there were alternatives. Preston North End and Bolton Wanderers (in the days that they played at Burnden Park) were both exactly 13.5 miles away, so either could easily have been the derby of choice. So why was it Burnley? I suspect that the decision was made by the Burnleyites. The Rovers were their adjacent club which became their closest rival because in the early years, they occupied the same division, the clubs became evenly matched and the Blackburn side was an extremely big fish; one they wanted to batter.

With pressure coming from the east of the county, the Ewood fans were only too happy to accept Burnley as the one they always had to beat. I have long felt that Burnley fans are not only more vociferous, but have more passion for their club than the supporters of their immediate neighbour. There is no measuring tool available which can back up this assumption, but a win over the Rovers always appears to be that little bit more important to the Clarets' fans. They give the impression of being the underdog, the one who is forced to fight that little bit harder even to achieve parity, particularly following the Premier League success that the Rovers had in the 1990s.

Yet for my generation growing up in the fifties, it was the Blue and Whites who had to accept the supremacy of the Claret and Blue shirt and I wonder if the generation of school children, being new to the game from 2012 until 2022, will have seen it in exactly the same way. In particular, for the six seasons that Burnley occupied a place in the Premier League, when the Blackburn side was at best, performing as an average Championship club, a trophy for Sean Dyche's side would have cemented their place as East Lancashire's top dog and erased the hurt of thirty odd years of being in the shadow of their rival. But the relegation in 2022 has levelled the playing field and we wait with baited breath for the next twist in the story.

In spite of so many apparent differences, historically speaking, Burnley and Blackburn have so much in common. Although there is evidence in both towns of Anglo-Saxon settlements with each community developing close to a river, there were precious few inhabitants in the region from Norman times until the start of the 18th century. The local industry was hand loom weaving, initially wool followed by cotton. Then local inventors mechanised the industry, large factories were built with rows of terraced houses alongside each other to accommodate the work force and from the late 18th century, cotton became "king". An industry required fuel to power it and coal mines were developed in the Burnley area.

The manufacture of weaving looms (the "Burnley Loom" being recognised as one of the best in the world) also helped to diversify employment to the east of the county, whereas Blackburn on the other hand was known by many as the cotton weaving capital of the world. The Industry needed to move its manufactured goods and the towns benefitted from various transport revolutions. The Leeds-Liverpool Canal, developed towards the end of the eighteenth century, runs through both town centres and in 1848, the towns were linked on the completion of the East Lancashire Railway. Nearly a century and a half later, the M65 was completed to serve the needs of both communities.

Immigrants have been the life blood of the area and it will be difficult to find anyone now living in these parts that is not from immigrant stock. The opportunity to work and the monetary rewards which accompanied it, attracted the Scots and the Irish; the latter famed for their construction skills. The work was tough, the living conditions desperate but anything was better than trying to survive the Irish Potato famine of the mid-19th century. These immigrants stayed, marrying into local families and being eventually subsumed into the local culture. In the second part of the 20th century, the population again grew rapidly with the emigration of so many families from the Indian sub-continent. They too will stay and eventually be considered as "Blackburnians" and "Burnleyites", just as the Scots and Irish before them. Now working immigrants from Eastern Europe are adding to the indigenous mix, raising the population in Blackburn to 117,963 according to the 2011 census whilst the population of Burnley was indicated as 87,059. The political preferences also express a similarity between the towns.

Blackburn has been represented by a Labour member of parliament since 1945 and in Burnley, Labour has generally been successful in elections since 1935 until the "Johnson wave" swamped the north at the end of 2019. After Local Government Reorganisation of 1974, each annexed a small neighbouring town. Padiham has become part of the District of Burnley whilst Darwen is now within the Blackburn and Darwen Unitary Authority. Interestingly from a football perspective, these two small towns were prominent in the early years of organised football; in fact, they were the first prominent team in their respective areas and both appeared in the FA Cup. Darwen reached the semi-final in 1881 and Padiham the 3rd Round in 1884.

With such similarities and so much in common, they are virtually twin towns. Geographically Burnley is closer to the Pennines and somewhat hillier but the most important common link is that they are both East Lancashire communities, hardy working-class folks, Lancastrians to the core who ought to be Brothers in Arms; good neighbours and good friends.

The fact that they are certainly not, especially with regard to football, is the subject of this book which compares their histories, looks at the rivalry (the incidents on and off the pitch) and which attempts to work out why such deep, underlying hatred can be caused by sporting competition between the towns.

Which teams do we support and more importantly... why?

"What is a football club? It's the noise, the passion, the feeling of belonging, the pride in your town or city. It's a small boy clambering up stadium steps for the very first time, gripping his father's hand, gawping at that hallowed stretch of turf beneath him and, without being able to do a thing about it, falling in love."

Sir Bobby Robson – Newcastle: "My Kind of Toon"

Sometimes I wonder if football is as important as we think. The sports pages of daily newspapers would have me believe differently, being so dependent on the action and even more so the gossip. Whole industries have been developed to produce football statistics and programmes such as Talk Sport and Sky Sports News give the impression that nothing counts more in the whole wide world. Certainly the round ball game accounts for more than 50% of their output, leaving other sports to fight over the scraps of time on their schedules. The majority of folks will say that they support such and such a team but further conversation reveals huge gaps in their knowledge as well as a lack of interest in talking about the subject. That of course is their prerogative. I, given like-minded company, can talk about the game for hours but I do speak to many people for whom it has less than a passing interest. There are those who give the impression that "having a club" is a status thing. For many celebrities, it is definitely "de rigeur" to drop the name of their team into the conversation during interviews. Inevitably it is usually an A list side and much as I wait for someone to say they have supported a Rochdale or a Cheltenham Town all of their life, I am so often disappointed.

My mother never watched a professional game in all of her 94 years, but each Saturday she would ask "how have the Rovers gone on today?" That was as far as her interest went. There were no follow up questions, only occasional comments such as "they are doing well at the moment" or "they're a real load of rubbish, aren't they?" My wife displays a similar disinterest and often never even puts the question when I walk through the door. "Do you want to know the result?" I ask. "Don't need to," she responds. "I always know by the look on your face." I suspect that this type of conversation is commonplace in many

IN LOVING MEMORY
OF

BLACKBURN ROVERS

Who met their death at the hands
of Burnley, March 8th, 1913.

Boldly to the match they went,
Their hearts on winning the Cup were bent;
But with sad hearts they came away,
they found their masters at the play

'Twas two good teams that played that day,
But the best team won with grand display;
And their death, 'twas lamenting hey!
They'll lie down till resurection day.

of our households. And there are many men who likewise show little interest and fair enough. Football has no divine right to be worshipped by the whole population. We all have our passions, our interests and our hobbies and just because ours happens to be football, it should neither place us on a pedestal nor particularly make us stand out in a crowd.

But for those who are genuinely interested, it can become an everlasting love affair; a weekly event which tempts and torments the soul, bringing joy and misery often in equal measures to our evenings or afternoons. This book centres on the football supporters of two East Lancashire teams, so why do we support the team we do. Now this is something bordering on personal and may entail searching deeply into our own souls. So why do I support the Rovers?

Geography obviously played a part. I was born and raised just 3.7 miles away from Ewood Park in the adjoining small town of Darwen and the majority of my friends at school all sported the blue and white scarf. My family was also an important influence. My grandfather on my mother's side had supported the Rovers all of his life and he was stood on the terraces at Ewood Park in 1929 when 62,793 were packed into the ground to witness the FA Cup 4th Round tie v Bolton Wanderers. He sadly died when I was three so I only know about his interest in the game because my mother regularly reminded me, but in spite of being a fairly tall man, he apparently saw very little of the action on this particular day, relying on information from an extremely tall friend who gave him a running commentary. I also learned that he could not obtain a ticket for the 1928 final when the Rovers defeated Huddersfield Town at Wembley. My father on the other hand could but at the age of twelve and the depression looming, his parents refused to allow him to travel to London on both safety and economic grounds. He also was a Roverite and a regular on the ground whenever he was able to escape briefly from his commitment to the family fruit, vegetable and flower business.

But probably the greatest influence on my early interest in the game came from my maternal great grandfather. As an old man in his eighties, he lived with us and he told me lots of footballing tales. He told me that he had been a centre forward in his younger days, renowned for his heading ability which ultimately caused his baldness but his "piece de resistance" concerned an away game at Turton, possibly in the late 1890s. He allegedly scored the winner in the dying moments and on exiting the field, discovered that the crowd had raided the "dressing tent" and thrown their clothes into a stream which ran behind the pitch. They hauled them out, no doubt dripping wet and bolted down the road towards the railway station in their football kit, pursued by an angry mob. My mother later told me that her grandmother, wife of this early Alan Gilzean, had no recollection of this event but apocryphal or not, it certainly whetted my appetite for the game. He talked to me about the top teams of the early fifties and we used to listen to the results on Sports Report. I distinctly remember him tuning into the 1952 FA Cup Final on the wireless in our living room and he showed me the "News Chronicle" newspaper on the day. It had a special pull out illustrative section, pictures of how Newcastle United and Arsenal had reached the final. One was of the semi-final where the Geordies had beaten Blackburn Rovers at Elland Road in a replay, following a goalless draw at Hillsborough.

This was my first recollection of seeing the Rovers in print, but I began to follow their progress in the Northern Evening Telegraph from then on. The 2nd Division became the focus of my attention in the following season, although I was considered too young to actually attend a match, my mother perhaps being a little precious concerning the safety and welfare of her only child. Looking up the league tables on the internet from various weeks in that season confirms my memories. They were struggling, third from the bottom at the end of November 1952 following a defeat at Bury. It was then that they swooped to sign Tommy Briggs and Bill Smith from Birmingham City and there was a huge upturn in their fortunes. They slowly climbed the table, finishing in a respectable 8th position. To add to my joy, my dad promised that he would take me to a game the following season.

To quote our good Queen, the 1953-54 season was my "annus horribilis". I was beset by a stomach ailment which at the time was labelled acidosis. Putting it simply, whenever I ate anything "fatty", I was sick. It took a long time for my doctor and a specialist to finally diagnose the root cause, but from January until mid-March, I spent two weeks in Blackburn Royal Infirmary followed by a seven-week sojourn in a Children's Convalescent Home in Southport. As you can imagine, it was a difficult period in my life. I was restricted in my attempts to follow the football scene but the children's para-

A young Burnley fan, comforted by his father, now understands what losing to the enemy is all about

dise that was Hesketh Park was just across the road from the Home. There the nurses encouraged impromptu games of football. I quickly discovered that I was never going to realise my ambition to make it as a goalkeeper but that I did have sufficient ability to hold my own as an outfield player. The biggest regret however was that my introduction to the delights of Ewood Park was put on hold. Because my dad worked most Saturday afternoons, it had to be a game on a public holiday. My mother however allowed me to travel down on the bus to the Anchor Ground at the other end of town to watch Darwen play a couple of Lancashire Combination games, with older boys from around our streets in attendance. I don't remember the opposition but I loved the experience and it served as an aperitif to my first ever "proper match". I cannot begin to match the majesty of the words of Sir Bobby Robson at the start of this chapter but suffice it to say, one of this nation's most loved football characters has hit the nail bang on the head. Fast approaching was a defining moment in my life and I suspect many of you can tell a similar tale.

And what a way for an eight-year-old to lose his football virginity!! Good Friday 1954 was the day my dad took me to my first professional game. It was in Division 2 at Ewood Park, Blackburn Rovers v Leicester City. The two sides were tussling at the top of the division, two teams battling to regain their status amongst the twenty-two elite clubs in the land. To my eternal joy in this landmark event of my life, the Rovers won 3-0. I was one of 45,521 spectators that day and although a tiny boy, I missed not a moment's action because between them, my dad and my Uncle John supported me as I sat on the top of a crush barrier on the Riverside. The magic of that first game made it a racing certainty. From that moment on, there was only one shirt for me; the blue and white halves.

Could it have ever been another club? There is something heart-warming about supporting your local team, although that would have been a foreign concept to me as an eight-year-old. But as I reached secondary school age and I no longer needed my dad or a relative or a friend of my dad to take me, it was so easy to jump on a bus at the bottom of my street and disembark outside the Rovers' ground. Being able to watch your team play regularly is not necessarily obligatory but it certainly helps. There were men who lived in our district who were Bolton Wanderers supporters, only a "Ribble bus" ride away, although it was perhaps a thirty-minute ride instead of the twenty to Ewood. The much older brother of one of my best mates was an avid Wanderers fan, but it never crossed my mind that they could be my team. Burnley of course seemed so far away, but I did have one link with the Clarets. An uncle of mine became proprietor of what you would now call a Convenience Store (Corner Shop in the early 50s) and this was situated at the top of Brunshaw Road in Burnley, the main road which runs straight into Harry Potts Way where Turf Moor is situated. He must have had customers who were well in at the club. One day he called round to our house with an autograph book signed by each of the first teamers. This was from my first full season as a regular spectator at Ewood Park, my coming out year of 1955. I found it again not too long ago and gazed at the names of Claret legends of the day, Cummings, Adamson, Holden, McIlroy, McDonald, Pilkington etc. I was proud of this and it stimulated an interest in both Burnley and autograph collecting. It coincided with the amazing 1955-56 FA Cup 4th Round tie when Burnley were matched with Chelsea, reigning 1st Division Champions. They played the tie five times, before Chelsea finally won 2-0. I supported the Clarets in this particular tie and was sorry when they finally lost, but my mother quickly put me back on track. She knew someone who knew someone and within days, there was another page in the book, full of different signatures; Tommy Briggs, Eddie Quigley and Ronnie Clayton et al. No longer did Burnley FC cross my horizon, At this time, Blackburn and Burnley were in different leagues and I automatically believed that Burnley was the bigger and better club. And in those days, there was no talk of a hostile rivalry between the clubs in our house, amongst family or school friends.

But Clarets' fans have become equally fanatical. Mick Duffy has been obsessed with the round ball game for virtually all of his seventy plus years. He has played, managed, refereed, been a league secretary and then turned his attention to running schoolboy football in the Red Rose County. He was secretary of Lancashire Schools' FA for nigh on thirty years but none of this deflected him from his first love, watching Burnley Football Club. Here is his story.

"My affair with Burnley follows a circuitous route. From the age of about six I was a Nelson supporter, standing on the cinder mound in a corner of Seedhill near the corrugated iron shed that served as a toilet. With my grandfather and his mates, we would walk down to the ground through the side streets, stopping at a quaint shop called the "Slip In"; really no more than a converted front room in a terrace. Coltsfoot rock, sarsaparilla tablets, pear drops or liquorice torpedoes would be the pre-match treat, lasting till about half-time.

Although I did not know it at the time, this was, apart from the ten Football League years in the twenties and thirties, a golden era for Nelson. The club was Lancashire Combination league and cup champions in 1949-50. In 1950-51 they were runners-up, only losing on goal average, though they did retain the Combination Cup. Joe Fagan became the player-manager in 1951. He had left Manchester City and was cutting his teeth in management, an apprenticeship that would eventually take him to the top with Liverpool. What I also did not know at the time was that Nelson was the first team to beat Real Madrid on their home ground – a 4-2 score line back in 1923.

From 1951 to 1954 they finished second, champions again, fifth and then third. In 1954-55, my final year as my grandfather's companion and Nelson supporter, they won the Lancashire Challenge Trophy at Ewood Park, beating Lancaster City 3-0. This was my final regular Nelson game. By that time, I was at St Mary's College in Blackburn, the only Nelson boy in my year, though the Burnley boys soon became my companions on the Longside at Turf Moor. That cup final was accompanied by a detention as I was caught in a Maths lesson writing out the Nelson side in a notebook.

The first visit to Turf Moor of which I can remember having memories is attending a game with my father. I was sitting on a crush barrier at a corner of the Bee Hole End and held by my father. This must have been in the 1953-54 season.

With regard to Burnley v Blackburn meetings, it was not until 1958-59 that the clubs met whilst I was a fan. I recall little of a 0-0 draw at home but recoil at a 4-1 defeat at Ewood Park when Ray Pointer opened the scoring after 20 minutes only for newly promoted Blackburn to hit four in reply. In the FA Cup that season, an abandoned 0-0 stalemate at half time at a frozen Ewood Park was eventually played later that January with McIlroy and Robson scoring in a 2-1 win. Burnley finished seventh for the third or fourth time, perhaps signs of better things to come.

Oddly enough when Burnley became champions in 1959-60, Rovers won 3-2 at home, a Pilkington goal and a Bryan Douglas own goal our only consolation in a defeat, which was offset later in the season when Jimmy Robson scored the only goal at Turf Moor. I could not get to the game at Maine Road when on the last game of the season; Burnley clinched the title with a 2-1 victory. By now, the Clarets side that is etched in my memory was in full flow. The team was Blacklaw, Angus, Elder, Adamson, Cummings, Miller, Connelly, McIlroy, Pointer, Robson and Pilkington. Gordon Harris came into the side after Pilkington was transferred to Bolton. Our main opponents at the time were not the Rovers but Tottenham Hotspur and I recall some classic encounters between the two clubs in the League and sadly in the FA Cup defeat in 1962.

In the sixties, my active support of Burnley was intermittent due to my playing in amateur leagues in Lancashire, three years studying in Manchester and then a five year stay in Canada. Even in the outback of Canada I managed to tune in to the football scores which were always preceded by a tune that still haunts me – the Elizabethan Serenade.

My return to work in Burnley in 1974 was hardly a triumphant return; for the fan or the player. There was the shock of the cup defeat by non-league Wimbledon and at the end of the decade, I had broken my leg in a game and was confined to spectating at Burnley in the 2nd and then the 3rd Division. A season ticket in the cricket field stand for me and my son was the "reward" for eighteen months of non-playing.

Since that time my support has been consistent but the performances far from it, that is until recent years. My attendance was curtailed by other footballing affairs – managing school and amateur sides, refereeing for several years and scouting for Everton. The nadir was the 1986-87 season when I could not face going to Turf Moor for the Orient game, instead listening nervously on the radio as a 2-1 victory ensured Football League survival. It took until 1992 for Burnley to escape from the basement division. Two years later we gained promotion as the sixth team in the second division; twelve points behind Stockport, the team we eventually beat at Wembley in the play-off final.

A year is a long time in football but our stay in Division 1 was just one year in 1994-95. It took until 2000 for the team to return to Division One (later the Championship), second placed to Preston North End. The encounters with Rovers in Division One were far from happy – a 0-2 at home and a 0-5 away set back as the Rovers finished second; Burnley back in seventh.

That fine line between success and failure in football is ironically best defined by the history of the two clubs since the millennium. That fine line has kept the clubs apart for most of recent seasons. Rovers' success in the topflight was matched by Burnley in the doldrums of lower divisions, until the wheel of fortune strangely virtually reversed the situation both on and off the field. As Rovers' fortunes faded, Burnley's were suddenly on the rise. Then the long-awaited win by the Clarets came after 35 years when a 2-1 victory led to two more wins in 2015-16.

"Hope for the best, expect the worst" has always been my motto for Burnley. The euphoria of a rise to the Premiership, the set-back of dropping from the topflight after one season was followed by an immediate return the next year as the Burnley Board wisely retained faith in the manager. A wonderfully successful second season in 2017-18 ensured that Burnley would be in the Premiership for a third tilt whilst the Rovers have returned to the

Championship. Mid-table finishes by both clubs have guaranteed a status quo situation for the 2020-21 campaign. How long it will be and in what league the two will renew acquaintances is debatable."

So, it appears that the team you support is either local or has family ties or of course both. But I have no antipathy with those who support teams for other reasons. It has nothing to do with me and I genuinely respect those who support a side through thick and thin. Being a fan has no legal binding such as a marriage or civil partnership, but I do believe it is about "for better for worse, for richer or poorer till death us do part". I am less inclined to be charitable to those who chop and change, often depending on the success that a side is currently experiencing.

The North West is full of professional teams playing in the four top leagues in England; seventeen at the last count. All these clubs have their supporters, but I have lived in Darwen, Hyndburn, the Ribble Valley, South Ribble and South West France and always bumped into many Manchester United fans. They are a great club with a wonderful post war history, but as tragic as it was, I do believe that it was the Munich Air disaster which catapulted the Stretford Enders into an international commodity. There is no doubt that the Old Trafford side was potentially the best in the world under Busby and in later years, their success has added to the legend, collecting new batches of supporters day by day. I have a story which may add weight to my argument.

Following straight after the disaster in 1958, they were pitted against Bolton Wanderers, local rivals from down the A666 in the FA Cup Final. Now Bolton is the nearest large town south of where we lived and you would imagine that many Darweners would have supported Nat Lofthouse's side. But nothing of the sort! It was a case of unless you hailed from Bolton; you were desperate for the Red Devils to win. There is of course always an exception to the rule and in this case, it was yours truly. To this day I do not understand why I supported Bolton Wanderers in that final.

At 12 years of age, I watched the game on a black and white television set and was so pleased when the Wanderers won. On the Monday morning, there were a number of long faces on the top deck of the bus travelling to Darwen Grammar School. Being a spirited first former, I reminded the older boys that I had predicted a Wanderers win and as one, they dragged me off the seat and proceeded to sit on me, generally roughing me up.

It was horse play of course and I was none the worse for what the legendary rugby union commentator Bill McLaren would have referred to as a good "scragging". But what this episode did show was the tremendous feeling of sympathy and affection for the red side of Manchester, an affection which gave birth to what became a massive fan base throughout the world.

I know several friends and acquaintances in the Blackburn area whose grandchildren are being brought up as 3rd generation fans. None of them live in the Manchester area, but I can accept that, so long as they don't change their affiliations should the fortunes of the Old Trafford side diminish; now that would be unacceptable to me. I am also reminded of an age old saying from the Roman Catholic religion. "Give me a child until the age of eight and I will show you a Catholic for life" was the mantra; one which could easily be associated with football clubs. Interestingly in the last couple of years, conversations with friends and acquaintances have revealed that three of their boys support Manchester City. One of them is from a family with strong City connections going back to the 1930s, but the other two neither live anywhere near the city of Manchester nor have any historical family links.

The Etihad club has now been crowned Premier League champion six times in eleven years and there now is a phenomenon similar to what occurred in the 1980s when virtually every youngster you spoke to supported Liverpool. However, the swings and roundabouts of the professional game have seen a massive Anfield revival so who knows which club the next generation of fans will support. Children are the most impressionable members of society and they will want to be associated with success. I can imagine that any ten year old boy saying that he supports Morecambe could be the victim of verbal abuse in the playground, hopefully only of the light hearted variety, but it can be no fun going into school every Monday morning, knowing that your side has lost yet again and is still rooted to the bottom of their league. At that age it must be easier to switch your allegiance to one of the two Manchester or Merseyside giants... and quite understandable I suppose.

I cannot remember coming across anyone that has passionately supported more than one club in modern times, but there are stories around suggesting that up until the sixties, it was not uncommon for football fans to watch a certain club one week and a neighbouring club the week after. This could be easily facilitated because even now, clubs such as Blackburn Rovers and Burnley never play at home together on the same weekend in scheduled league fixtures. Paul Cox told me that until 1960, it was a regular occurrence in Haslingden for the locals to visit Turf Moor one week and Ewood Park the next.

Such was the disgust however over the distribution of Wembley Cup Final tickets by the Blackburn club that so many in the area chose to forget the Rovers and become regular Clarets. Doug Hargreaves, now an avid Blue and White supporter, told me that when he was a boy growing up in Accrington, there was never a Saturday that his father did not take him to a game. It could be the Stanley or either of their two bigger neighbours. When the Accrington team folded in 1962, it was either the "Turf" or Ewood. There is a fondness in East Lancashire for the "Stanley", that phoenix club of all phoenix clubs. Forced to leave the Football League in 1962, the apocryphal tale tells of how the League (and possibly both the Clarets and the Rovers) refused to loan them the cash to pay their electricity bill. Bob Lord, the Burnley Chairman of the day, was perhaps unfairly cast as the villain in this sorry saga, but there were other debts as it turned out to the Inland Revenue and for the unpaid transfer of players. The good folks of Accrington rallied to their cause and Accrington Stanley 1968 was formed. The revival made slow progress up the long and winding road of the football pyramid before to the surprise of everyone south of the Mersey, Stanley were crowned Conference Champions in 2006, re-appearing in the 4th Tier of English football in League Two.

They arrived as something of a Music Hall joke, but they have stubbornly held their place for 16 seasons. It is literally a miracle. They are regularly short of cash and their gates are consistently the second lowest amongst the 92 professional clubs. Now entrenched in the third tier of English football, it is impossible for anyone in East Lancashire not to have admiration for them. I was suddenly reminded part way through the 17-18 season by my older son Stephen who always considers himself to be an "Accy lad" but a Rovers' supporter, that no status quo lasts for ever.

The Rovers had momentarily dipped into the third tier of football when he said... "If Stanley go up this season and the Rovers don't achieve an instant promotion back to the Championship, which side am I going to support next season?" It was a very valid point. "Let's hope they both go up" was my reply and thankfully they did.

We have determined that the majority of us who support football teams do so for genetic and/or geographical reasons. Plus there are also those of course who simply want to be associated with, and therefore support, a successful team. Paul Cox's story however is linked to a fourth category .... let us call it "random". Haslingden is almost equidistant to Turf Moor and Ewood Park, but let him tell the story.

"I suppose it all began with my parents moving from the City of Derby to Lancashire, my father having found work in the mills of the North West as an electrician in the early 1970's. I was two years old when we made the move. My parents were both Derby County fans, having followed the club during the greatest era of its history when Clough and then McKay led them to 1st Division titles followed by European football. The problem for me was that we had moved from a one club city to a small town bordering two teams. Supporting "The Rams" was something that did not go down well at school.

There was a large group of boys in my class. Those who didn't understand football and the glory hunters all supported Liverpool. It was the late seventies / early eighties and if it had been the nineties, this group would have all followed Man Utd. Then there was the group that really did love the game. This group was split into two; Blackburn or Burnley and it was a choice that I just had to make, because you either picked or you just drifted off. I chose Blackburn, somewhat strange because my best mate at the time actually preferred Burnley. So that was that. You made your choice and you stuck to your choice.

Of course these were the pre 'football TV saturation days'. Then, for me, it was reading the back of the Evening Telegraph during my paper round that fuelled my interest and kept me up to date with the Rovers. The only

A young Rovers fan shouts for his team on derby day

football on TV was 'Football Focus' and trying to stay up for 'Match of the Day'. As we grew older and we started going to pubs, the split was still there. Often you would walk in a Pub and you would say "look it's so and so, he's Burnley" or "it's Joe, he's Rovers". Certainly, living in the Helmshore/ Haslingden area often created a few issues. The town was pretty much split 50-50 between the Rovers and Burnley. I can still remember being sat in the 'Tack' in town having an early beer with two of my mates, saying "let's go Rovers this aft". So off we set in my Ford Capri to Ewood, queueing up to pay £5 on the turnstile and then straight in. I vividly remember my mate Paul borrowing his mum's car because they had gone on holiday. We picked up 3 more of our friends then drove to Brighton one Saturday to watch the Rovers. It was only recently he told me she never knew he'd taken the car and he was "bricking" the fact she would notice almost 800 extra miles on the clock when she came home.

There have been many stories and many away days and as we have always said, "another great day out only ruined by the football". Twice in recent years it was a case of "no football" ruining the day as we travelled to both Newport County and Gillingham only to find that the weather had caused a postponement on both occasions. And all this has come about because of an almost random decision I made thirty odd years ago. I chose 'Blue and White' over 'Claret and Blue' for no particular logical reason. That decision has taken me to many places; given me so many exciting times, caused delight and depression in almost equal measures but always making me believe that I made the right choice. Over the years I have detested all things Turf Moor related but, as time (dare I say) makes me wiser, I have to admit, albeit somewhat reluctantly, that choosing Burnley would have given me similar feelings, similar experiences and an equally strong love affair that lasts forever."

Damian Hartley is a Burnley fanatic, but he could quite easily have supported the Blue and White halves, had fate not played a hand. Here is his story.

"I was born in Oswaldtwistle, much nearer to Ewood Park than Turf Moor, but my father had no interest in football. My family was extremely musical and at the age of seven, I was starting to learn to play the piano. At the same time we moved close to the centre of Accrington and although much younger, I tagged along with my elder brother who quickly found new friends. In our neighbourhood there were two fathers who used to take a car full of kids to Turf Moor. One of these dads was Jimmy Mulkerrin, a Scottish centre forward who had struggled to get into the great Hibernian side in the early fifties. He came down to Accrington and played for the Stanley for a couple of seasons, scoring thirty six goals in seventy appearances. His family settled in Accrington after he retired and one day in the summer holidays of 1976, he was taking my brother and mates down to Ewood Park to watch a pre-season derby game in the Anglo-Scottish Cup. They squeezed me in the van as an afterthought and I was open mouthed as I watched swathes of supporters, all wearing their scarves around their wrists and chanting the name of their club. I was told I had to support the Claret and Blue shirts but I couldn't remember the score, so I have since looked it up. It was a 1-1 draw but I do remember the smallest player on the pitch. It was Brian Flynn and he scored Burnley's goal. I was also small for my age so he became my first ever football hero. On the way home, Mr Mulkerrin asked me if I had enjoyed the game and I remember telling him that it was better than learning the piano. So that was it. I was a Burnley supporter.......for life. But I do often wonder how many other Clarets' fans saw their first ever game at the home of the enemy.

It is also an interesting topic of conversation with ex-professionals. I am certain that for the length of time they are at a club, that is the team to which they give their everything, but you often hear them say on retirement that such and such a team is the first result I look for. I spoke to Craig Short, an ex-Rover who also played with distinction at several other clubs, but he had a different take on the matter.

"I was born in Pickering in North Yorkshire, miles from any professional club. My father was from Bridlington, close to Hull and the "Tigers" were his team. But when I was small he was posted to Germany and I was effectively brought up there. In the late seventies, there was only one team that counted in England and that was Liverpool. My only contact with home sport was through "Sports Report" on the radio each Saturday afternoon and so inevitably Bob Paisley's side became my team, Graeme Souness my favourite player. When we finally returned to Pickering, I had trials with a number of clubs, but the only one interested in me was Scarborough, newly promoted under Neil Warnock into the Football League. Since then as my confidence and physical stature grew, I played at Notts County, Derby County, Everton, the Rovers and Sheffield United and I have to say that I now regard them all as my clubs, following their results every week. I probably enjoyed my time at Ewood the most but I have such fond memories of all the clubs that I have to say that I now no longer support any one of them in particular. All of the above mean a great deal to me."

Graham Alexander sees it slightly differently.

I was born in Coventry and lived there with my parents until Scunthorpe United took me on as an Apprentice. I followed Coventry City from being a small boy and was at Wembley when they defeated Tottenham Hotspur 3-2 in the 1987 FA Cup final. At that stage I could never see me supporting another club. Slowly it all changed as I spent a number of years at four different clubs, Scunthorpe, Luton Town, PNE and Burnley. When you are a pro, there is only one side that matters, the one where you are at that moment, and I have since developed relationships at clubs I have managed, Fleetwood Town, Scunthorpe, Salford City and now Motherwell. Instead of it being Coventry or nothing, I now have strong feelings for the above clubs, but as I was at Preston for nine and a half years and considering that we have lived in the town for twenty years, I suppose that is the club I would choose if I was to retire now. Completely different is my allegiance to a country. I have only lived in England, but my father was Scottish and he drummed it in me that Coventry was my club, Scotland my country. So it became obvious that my number one football ambition was to wear the blue jersey of Scotland. I was thirty when I was first chosen and I honestly thought by then that it would never happen. When it finally came, there was no prouder parent than my dad and playing for my country is the highlight of my career.

Perhaps not so much now, but certainly in earlier years, there were players who had been born in the town, supported the club from childhood and played there for the whole of their career. One such example is Bryan Douglas. He told me this story when I interviewed him.

"I was born in a street just to the side of the Fernhurst pub, less than a quarter of a mile from Ewood Park. I attended St Bartholomew's Primary School which has since been knocked down to make way for the official car park which was even closer to the ground and I played on Ewood Park as a schoolboy in the local schools' finals and for the Town Team. But also as kids, we used to play in the ground. I was brought up during the Second World War and the Government used the Darwen End of the ground to store Ammunition Boxes. We would climb over the wall, clamber over the boxes, make camps and dens and have the time of our lives. We were always being caught there and kicked out, but we would always try to sneak back in on the following days. So when my ability came to the notice of the clubs, it was inevitable that I would try to play for the Rovers. My parents wanted me to have a trade so at fifteen, I started work at the Corporation Bus and Tram depot in Intack, a district of Blackburn. But the Rovers kept inviting me to play in matches for the B Team on a Saturday in the Blackburn Combination. I was about four foot six and we were playing against big hard men from clubs such as Oswaldtwistle Immanuel and the R.O.F. and they used to knock me about. My first game was at Rishton and I was selected as Reserve. One fellow didn't turn up until very late and so they pushed me in. The lad who was late was Ronnie Clayton. There had been a muddle over bus times coming from Preston and this was the first time I ever met him. Ronnie had to catch three different buses to get to many of our games, so no wonder he was sometimes late. Because the B Team changed its personnel weekly, we often lost heavily, This was the case at Rishton where we lost 7-1, although I scored our goal. There was also a Thursday League which all the local professional clubs used to play in such as Preston, Bolton and Burnley. They used it mainly for triallists, decent amateurs and sometimes the pros returning from injury. Almost every week, I was having to go to the manager to ask him for the Thursday afternoon off. He eventually got fed up with this and asked me to make my mind up whether I wanted to be a mechanic or a football player. My dad met up with the Rovers manager Jackie Bestall and I was signed on to the "ground staff", training with the players every morning, running their errands at lunch time and then sweeping the stands or replacing the divots in the afternoon. We were dogs bodies as all apprentices were then and both Ronnie and I did this at the same time. My career developed from there. Within three months I was playing for the A Team but because I was still on the ground staff, I had to continue cleaning the boots of the professionals. Willie Kelly's boots were on my list of those to clean. He was a tough centre-half and he and the others each paid me one shilling a week for my work. One time he forgot to pay me so I didn't clean them the following week. When he asked me why I had left his muddy, I cheekily told him that until he paid me the money, I was not cleaning his boots. It was not a smart thing to do or say. The result was predictable. He grabbed hold of me and knocked me round the changing room, so I never gave cheek to him or the other senior pros again. Quite quickly I was being chosen for the Reserve team, but this coincided with me having to do National Service. I was sent to a barracks near Grimsby, but they would release me each Friday at about 5.00 pm to travel home to play football. The problem was that it took about five hours for me to reach Manchester by train but the last one to Blackburn had left by the time I got there. So I had to find accommodation in the city but I had so little money. I stayed every Friday in a "doss house" for three shillings and sixpence a night. A lot of the other guests were tramps so you could imagine how awful it was. But it toughened me up and I was lucky enough to stay at the Rovers for the whole of my professional career. I still carried on watching them when I retired and when the ground was redeveloped with its reception rooms and suites, they named one of them the Clayton-Douglas Room. I have a table for myself and a couple of guests for lunch at every home game. So you could say that Blackburn Rovers has been my only team for eighty five years.

We all think that we have a special reason for supporting "our" club, but they don't come much more special than Gary Bowyer's.

"My dad was a professional footballer and my first memories are of him playing at Nottingham Forest. He was part of the great Brian Clough side that won the European Cup twice and he jokingly reminds me that they were won back to back. I was too young to go to Munich for the 1979 final but the following year at the age of eight, I was sat in the Bernabeu Stadium in Madrid watching my dad win his second medal when they defeated Hamburg (Kevin Keegan and all) 1-0. Brian Clough signed me at the age of eighteen from Hereford United where I had actually played in the same team as my dad. I was a left back or a centre mid-field player but it was difficult breaking into such a strong side and I eventually joined Rotherham United, managed by ex-Forest stars Archie Gemmill and John McGovern until I was seriously injured and had to retire from the game at the age of twenty-five. So as you can tell, Notts Forest had a big influence on both my upbringing and my footballing career. One of my fondest memories of being a manager was when the Rovers won 3-1 at the City Ground in October 2014."

For someone who has been a hero in Blackburn and an absolute villain in Burnley, David Dunn surprisingly has had links with both clubs. I first came across him as an Under/9 playing for the Hyndburn Primary Schools' Town team. He was two years younger than the majority on the pitch, an enormous gap at that age, and he was such a tiny boy but it was obvious that he knew how to play the game.

"I was invited over to the Burnley Centre of Excellence and I stayed there for a year before I moved to the Rovers. Great Harwood where I lived was a mixture of Blackburn Rovers and Burnley fans, but my grandad, who ran me everywhere, was a Rovers man. From then on the Rovers were my team as I progressed through the schoolboy ranks and into the professional set-up. As a local lad, there is a tendency for the club to overlook you and the lads who came from a distance seemed to get all of the perks whereas I had to work hard for mine. I presume they believed the local boys would stay and did not need pampering. Eventually I signed Schoolboy forms for two years with a two year YTS added on."

Steve Kindon was brought up playing rugby and again, he has a different take on which club he has always supported.

"When I was young, it was all rugby and I didn't have a favourite club. During my professional career I have played for Burnley (twice), Wolverhampton Wanderers and Huddersfield Town. I now support each one equally and each one has a local derby match against the club that the fans hate. So at Burnley it is the Rovers, at the Wolves it is West Brom and at Huddersfield at that time it was Barnsley. So when I do look at the results, these are the clubs I want to win every game and if any of their unfriendly neighbours lose, I cannot help having a little smile, getting some satisfaction from the result."

For the many who earn their living in the game and I suppose for those in other walks of life who move around regularly because of work, their choice of club can be quite random and can change. But for the majority of football followers, the norm is to follow the mantra "Club X 'till I die". But who do you support if you have been born in or hail from some out of the way spot like Penzance down on the tip of Cornwall for example?

There is no professional club in that county, so Plymouth Argyle, a two-hour drive away, is your nearest port of call. If you are looking for a club with prospects, Bristol City is over three hours away by road. You could support Penzance FC but they play down at Tier 11, not the most exciting of prospects. But people do loyally support these lowly ranked clubs and I am reminded that I am a Darwen boy and they were the first team I ever saw in action. But embarrassingly, I have to report that I have not been to watch them play for many years. Perhaps I was a "Glory Hunter" at the age of eight when I began to follow the Rovers, even though for many of the subsequent 66 years, fighting relegation or being satisfied with mid-table mediocrity has had the loosest of loose connections with "glory".

But when I occasionally look down my nose at the supporters of "Man United", Chelsea and Arsenal, mentally accusing them of only supporting the club because they win trophies and making snide comments such as "he must be a United fan, he lives south of Watford", should I not take a look in the mirror and ask myself why I never go down to the Anchor Ground in Darwen? But as I have already stated, the club you follow is your own personal choice and no-one has the right to question you.

Derbies and Rivalries

"A derby is a sporting event involving teams
from the same area or city."
Collins English Dictionary

The origin of the word "derby" in a sporting context may well be lost in the mists of time. One possible explanation comes from the staging of football matches between local villages back in the Middle Ages on religious holidays. The goal posts were several miles apart, one in each village, and the number of competitors unlimited. The tradition slowly died away except for in Ashbourne in Derbyshire where the annual Shrove Tuesday game still continues. Thus the link to the word "derby" may have been derived from the name of the county where the game was played.

A perhaps more plausible explanation is that it may have a connection with the Epsom Derby. It was first run in 1780 and organised by the Earl of Derby, hence its name. Since around 1840, the word "derby" entered the English language, simply meaning any type of sporting contest. The word "local" began to be attached to it if it was between competitors from the same area but I have the impression that "derby" and "local derby" now mean the same thing. Allegedly, the first printed citation which mentioned the word in a footballing context was in the Daily Express in October 1914. "A local Derby between Liverpool and Everton" was the headline. It was not the first game between these two sides but the first to have been titled as such.

It is true to say that a derby is a rivalry, but a rivalry is not necessarily a derby. During the Ferguson/Wenger years, the Manchester United v Arsenal games were eagerly awaited. It was a massive rivalry but the distance between the sides made it impossible to use the word derby. Likewise, the Gary Neville and Jamie Carragher inspired United and Liverpool sides served up some mouth-watering, often "X rated" delights, rivals to the bitter end but they still could not have the "derby" appellation. Thirty-three miles is too much of a distance between the grounds in a region packed with other professional clubs. So just how close together do two grounds have to be to be awarded "derby" status? There are no specific rules but the most obvious ones are those within the same city or town. Thus in England there are definitely derbies in Liverpool, Manchester, London, Bristol, Sheffield and Nottingham. London can be geographically divided; Spurs v Arsenal is the North London derby and recently we have seen a variety of West London derbies involving Queens Park Rangers, Fulham and Brentford in the Championship.

The Fylde Coast derby is a recent addition with Fleetwood and Blackpool a mere tram ride apart. Until the end of the 2017-18 season, Rochdale played four such fixtures, Bury home and away in the M66 derby and likewise against near neighbours Oldham Athletic in what is comically becoming known as the "El Flatcapico". The game between Norwich City and Ipswich Town features two clubs 43 miles apart, a massive distance in the more congested parts of England but the East Anglian derby is an acceptable label because of the sparsity of professional clubs in that area of the country.

Newcastle United and Sunderland, just 14 miles apart in the North East have a rivalry which is generally full of bad intentions but certainly the "baddest" derby in the United Kingdom is that staged at least four times a season by the banks of the River Clyde. There is genuine hatred between the supporters of the two Glasgow giants, Celtic and Rangers, often ignited by differing religious beliefs and all police leave is automatically cancelled on the day of the match.

And so the list goes on, but perhaps the world's most prestigious derby matches were the UEFA Champions' League finals of 2014 and 2016, both contested by Madrid sides. On each occasion, the Cristiano Ronaldo inspired Real defeated their cross-city rivals Atletico, the great man notching a penalty in each game. The stadia of these two sides in the Spanish capital are just 4 miles apart, but because of the competition regulations which decree that the final venues are chosen several years before, the games were played in the Estadio da Luz, Lisbon and in the San Siro Stadium, Milan.

The world's first competitive football matches were staged in England. The FA Cup was first held in the 1871-72 season and here we have a possible contender for the first ever derby. In Round 1, all the ties were played on November 11th and Maidenhead beat Marlow (seven miles away along the River Thames to the west of London) by a 2-0 margin. This has to be the world's first ever competitive derby game, the venue being York Road in Maidenhead. The ground probably holds the record for the world's oldest senior football ground continuously used by the same club (from 1871). Turton near Bolton has made a similar claim but these records are difficult to authenticate.

If however, we look for the world's first ever derby match in a league game, the picture is somewhat different. Professional football was embraced in the North West and the Midlands whilst the rest of the country was still playing the amateur game and the English Football League kicked off on September 8th, 1888. Once again, England organised the first ever League with its Scottish counterpart following two years later. The other major European professional leagues, Serie A, La Liga, Bundesliga and Ligue 1 arrived on the scene at much later dates. Of the original twelve clubs, the closest neighbours were West Brom and Aston Villa, Burnley and Accrington, Blackburn Rovers and Accrington and Burnley and Blackburn Rovers. Consequently, the first ever League derby game was played at Leamington Road in Blackburn on September 15th of that year when the Rovers were held to a high-scoring 5-5 draw against Accrington. Sadly the "Owd Reds" left the league at the end of the 1892-3 season and folded in 1896. As a result, the first ever derby between sides still playing against each other 130 years later took place at Turf Moor in Burnley and resulted in a 7-1 victory for Blackburn Rovers, Jack Southworth scoring a hat-trick. Thus the great rivalry was born. At times in the past it was given the title of the "Cotton Mills" derby and recently some refer to it as the "M65" derby, but I believe that the "East Lancashire derby" is the correct and most accurate name. Did the original players realise that a further 100 games and counting would be completed or that the rivalry would become increasingly bitter? Probably not and certainly Southworth and co would never have dreamt that their margin of victory would still be a record for an away win in this fixture. As time has moved on, games have become much more competitive than on that November day in 1888.

It is interesting to listen to the professionals. In some respects they have little say concerning the club they play for. You can only play for a club which needs you. When you are surplus to requirements or bigger clubs are fighting for your services, off you go. As a result you have a nomadic existence. And when you arrive at a club, you quickly have to learn all of its quirks, all of its traditions, its local rivalries and are often taken by surprise. Kevin Ball, hero or villain in East Lancashire depending on the shirt you support, has a fascinating tale to tell.

> "I was born on the south coast in Hastings, but I played the majority of my football in the north east at Sunderland. It was there that I found out what derbies were all about. Some say the clash between Celtic and Rangers is the world's tastiest local derby but I know that the North East confrontations take some beating, having been involved in a number in the Nineties. I finally arrived at Burnley via Fulham, in my mid-thirties but still fit enough to do a job for Stan Ternent. Having only played against Burnley at the "Turf" once before, I looked forward to seeing what the passion was like from the Burnley fans as that was what I thrived on, being the style of player I was. My first game at the Turf was a pre-season friendly against Newcastle United. It was also an eye-opener. Having been at Sunderland for nearly ten seasons, I was ready for the Geordie travelling fans to have a go at me, but I was largely ignored. What I did notice though was that the home fans booed the Newcastle striker every single time he touched the ball. Back in the dressing room at half-time, I asked why. "It's Kevin Gallacher" was the response. "So?" I said and was told that he was an ex-Blackburn Rovers player. Again I questioned why this should matter and it was then that I learnt about the long history and ill-feeling between the clubs. So having just left an area where you were either friend or foe depending on the colour of the shirt you wore, I found myself back in a bear-pit again and looking forward to it!"

Andy Payton also can talk with experience of derby duels.

> "When I was at Middlesbrough, I heard that Liam Brady wanted to sign me for Glasgow Celtic. You didn't say no to a move like that in those days and I was fortunate to score in an Old Firm derby. The funny thing was that when

Tommy Boyle's headed goal gave the Clarets a 1-0 win at Ewood Park in 1913

I was at school in Padiham, I had collected Trevor Steven's autograph. As I walked out and we were hit by a wall of screams, cheers, applause and boos, I looked over at the Rangers' line up and saw Steven there. I thought about telling him I had his autograph but then I thought better of it. Up to then, this was the most terrifying atmosphere I had played in until the 2000 derby game at the "Turf". I am not saying the atmosphere was more intimidating, but it was on a par and for a local boy, it had even more of an effect on me. You simply could not escape the noise, but that could act as a positive. As a seasoned pro you thrived in these situations and I was proud to play in them. On the days before such a fixture, there was something a little different at the Training Ground. As in Glasgow, I could feel the nerves until the whistle went and the butterflies disappeared. But the one big difference concerned the fans. I don't know if it happens anywhere else, but away supporters are bussed to the ground from their own ground in this one. You cannot get to the game any other way and this all adds to the drama. It certainly doesn't happen in Glasgow. For the southern boys, it was probably nothing special but for me, being the only local lad apart from John Mullin who was on the bench for the first game, it was one of the games of my life."

Mickey Mellon was another seasoned pro who had been round the block a couple of times, so playing in the East Lancashire derby was nothing new to him.

"Having started my career at Bristol City, I was aware of the animosity amongst the crowds whenever we played Bristol Rovers and when I was at West Brom, the Black Country derby against Wolves was another laced with

Burnley versus Blackburn 1983

atmosphere. The 2000 derby at Turf Moor was the equal of these two. With this deep feeling of aggression and animosity amongst the crowd, the Police told us before the game that we had not to run off the pitch if we scored. There was also a helicopter which continuously circled the sky during the game, adding to the tension. There was so much noise from the crowd and you really felt it on the pitch, although for most of the game, the players seemed to cope with it."

Paul Weller arrived at Burnley as a sixteen year old, took part in trials and was taken on as an Apprentice. Having travelled 300 miles from home in Brighton, he had no inclination that there was a serious rivalry in this part of the world but he soon learnt all about it from the other youngsters.

"I immediately discovered that we had to meet at Accrington College every Thursday for the education segment of the Apprenticeship and being taught in the same classroom were the kids from Blackburn Rovers. Some of their lads were local, some of ours were local and they all knew about the ill-feeling between supporters. Very quickly there was ill-feeling between our two groups and we totally disliked each other. There was a smouldering aggression throughout, glaring at each other, making nasty comments about each other. I was so glad when, at the end of the year, the Rovers group moved to a new venue at Ewood Park. Within weeks of our second year starting, there was a serious incident at the College with one of our group and we were all kicked out. Our education had to carry on and although none of us could believe it, we were sent down to join the Rovers group at Ewood. Parts of the ground were being rebuilt, but you could tell it was going to be a big club again. Jack Walker had recently taken charge and this was the time that Dalglish was buying star players all of the time. We really felt like second class citizens plus we had to put up with their Apprentices being so cocky. Part way through that year, we were drawn against them in the Youth Cup at Blackburn. FA Youth Cup games had to be played on the main grounds and so we turned up at Ewood expecting a very small crowd. The spectators from the Rovers were few in numbers but there must have been 1,500 wearing Clarets' scarves. They never stopped singing throughout the match, even though we lost. They also ripped up some seats and let everyone know that they were Burnley supporters. I knew then that this rivalry was for real. I had witnessed it at first hand and I was totally shocked. I had never played in an atmosphere like that before."

Steve Davis, the one who was at the club for three separate spells and who racked up 321 league appearances in the Claret and Blue shirt, knew that derbies were not unique to East Lancashire.

"I grew up in Hexham, a small town in the north-east which splits its footballing loyalties about 50-50 between Sunderland and Newcastle United. Because my father followed Sunderland, I automatically followed them and I can remember how the atmosphere would become quite fraught in the school yard in the week before a derby. I moved to Southampton at sixteen as an Apprentice and their local rival from just along the coast was Portsmouth. I was shocked to find that even when playing in Reserve team games against Portsmouth, there was a different attitude on the pitch than in other games. Players would really get stuck in and tough tackles were the order of the day. Between stints at Burnley, I was at Luton Town for three seasons and I played derby games against Watford. So when it came to the derby at Turf Moor against Blackburn Rovers, I thought I would be prepared for an increase in tension on the pitch. But possibly because the two sides had not clashed for eighteen seasons, the crowd in the home sections could not wait for the kick-off. You could sense the atmosphere was brewing to a fever pitch and we all knew we had to raise our game. In a derby game, a shot, a good save, a strong challenge and a hard tackle all lift the crowd even more. It was clear that this was the big one and we had to impose ourselves on the opposition and of all the 500 plus league games in my career, this was the one with the most intensity."

If fans from either club were asked to name a player with whom the derby games were synonymous, Simon Garner would certainly be on the list. Surprisingly, he only played in three, as Burnley slid down the leagues during his twelve years of playing first team football in East Lancashire. His memories of the passion generated by this rivalry make for interesting reading.

"I only played once at Turf Moor for the Rovers and once for West Brom, but I was lucky to score each time. In those days there was a long stand the length of the pitch where everyone stood. The home spectators appeared to occupy half of it and the visitors the other half. So if you scored and ran to the fans to celebrate, you were actually extremely close to the Burnley lot. And they hated it, calling you the worst names imaginable, the language the worst you could ever hear.

Nowadays the players are warned not to further ignite the situation and so players do not race towards the visitors and do not respond to whatever is said to them. In my day it was different and when the Burnley crowd started making rude gestures to me, it seemed ok to do it back. It may have been for this reason or because I always scored against them, but for whatever reason, they hated me. It was common knowledge within football and when I was at West Brom, the Chairman called me in and said that under no circumstances was I to over-celebrate if I scored at Turf Moor. Of course I couldn't resist and I whipped my shirt off in front of them when I scored. There was a rumour going round that I wore a Rovers shirt under my West Brom shirt but as amusing as it would have been, it is totally untrue.

I then finished my career at Wycombe Wanderers and thoroughly enjoyed my time there. After my retirement I settled in that area and Wycombe found themselves in the same league as Burnley, The southern club invited me to make the half-time draw when Burnley came down to Adams Park. As ever they were well supported on their travels and probably made up half of the crowd. There were scarcely any police in the ground, it was mainly stewards and when I came out, I was instantly met with a torrent of boos. The locals could not believe what they were hearing and then some of the Burnley fans tried to invade the pitch to get to me. The local stewards, unused to this, had to really struggle to keep them at bay.

On another occasion, I was the "guest of honour" at an Ewood derby and it was proposed that I should make the half-time draw. The Police emphatically vetoed the idea. It was hard enough for them without any further provocation that my appearance would have created. I must however dispel one rumour that refuses to go away. I had absolutely nothing to do with the aeroplane which flew over Turf Moor. I don't hate Burnley, it's a club I admire and I have to say that I totally loved the rivalry when I was playing up there. I think most footballers enjoy the stick they receive from the visiting supporters. It means that they must be doing something right and it motivates you even more."

Lenny Johnrose was a Preston boy who represented Lancashire Schools with distinction before becoming an Apprentice with Blackburn Rovers straight from school. He started twenty first team games and came on as a substitute twenty-two times, scoring eleven goals. His career took him to Hartlepool United and then on to Bury where he played 188 times for the Shakers under the managership of Stan Ternent. When Stan moved to Burnley, he bought Lenny for £225,000 and although now playing as a defensive midfielder, he gave the team that extra backbone required to win promotion from Division 2 and then stay in

Rovers fans celebrate with Franco Di Santo after he'd scored his side's second goal against Burnley at Ewood Park in 2009

Division 1. He is one of very few players who have represented both the Clarets and the Rovers in derby matches, although his appearance for the Blue and Whites in a Manx Cup game in 1988 is not recognised as an official game as far as career statistics are concerned. Here are his thoughts:-

"I loved playing in local derbies, I was very aware of the rivalry between Burnley and Blackburn, having joined Blackburn as a 16-year-old in 1986. My abiding memory of the first of such derbies was in a pre-season friendly. There used to be a tournament called the Lancashire Manx Cup, where the winners would go to the Isle of Man the following pre-season to play in another tournament. We won at Turf Moor and after the game, our team bus was attacked by a number of Burnley supporters.

From a playing point of view, I wouldn't necessarily say that I wanted to win those games more than any other, but I perhaps looked forward to them a little bit more. I don't think I played in many Burnley/Blackburn games, although I do remember playing for Burnley when Kevin Ball was sent off for a very late tackle on David Dunn. The atmosphere of the game was toxic, and I think I'm right in saying that the underpasses in Burnley town centre were vandalised after the game by the Burnley fans.

I can't really say that I am into all that rivalry stuff, it just goes too far, for me. In truth, I have never understood how you can hate another team to the point where you become abusive and violent. But then, I suppose I am not a supporter of any one team. I know I am one of a few players who have played for both clubs in derby games but I have never really thought that it is a big deal playing for both teams, My job was always to give my everything to the team that I was playing for at that time and I like to think that I did that. Supporting one or the other has always meant a lot more to the sup-

Danny Ings expressing strong emotions to the TV camera at the end of the derby day clash in 2013

porters. I love the atmosphere and the intensity of a derby match, but I'm not really a badge-kissing sort of guy. So yes, while it is quite rare, to me it is just football."

Managers also have their take on derby games and it would have been so revealing to talk to Harry Potts. He actually scored in a wartime derby in 1944 and played in both of the 1947-48 versions. His first derby as manager was in the 1958-59 season and he went on to be involved in twenty-four such affairs, the final one being in 1979. This is not just a record for the Burnley club, it is a record for both clubs. Harry's daughter Linda married Philip Webster, a local lad from the Cliviger area and knowing Harry well, has been able to talk to me at length about the great man.

"I wouldn't say that he took derby games any more seriously than others such as Wolverhampton Wanderers, Tottenham, Man United or Liverpool. This was because he approached every league game as if it were the most important game ever. When Linda and I were going out with each other and in the early days of our marriage, we were regularly invited to her parents for a meal on a Sunday. At that time there were no Sunday games and if they had won the day before, he would be relaxed and good company. If they had not performed well, the atmosphere would be completely different. In fact there were occasions when her mother would ring and cancel because his mood was so foul. He lived and breathed for Burnley FC, it was his life and apart from his family which he was devoted to, football was his only interest. So it was obvious that the result from the day before would affect him so much. He certainly did not hate Blackburn Rovers; in fact he had respect for them, but there was one incident in a derby match which caused him so much pain and grief. I was still a boy then and have no first-hand knowledge of how it affected him, but Linda and her mother often referred to it, as he did himself. It was the FA Cup tie against Blackburn in 1960 and it was not just the eventual result that so upset him. He felt that the Clarets' display over the seventy five minutes was exceptional. Then came the penalty given against Alex Elder; a decision so unjust in his opinion that it haunted him for years. He also could not accept how and why his team suddenly caved in. It had been 3-0, it was now 3-1, but this was the best side in the country. Surely they could defend a two goal lead for a little over ten minutes. He reluctantly accepted the defeat in the replay but he really struggled to come to terms with how the club had let down the fans. In total over 100,000 had watched the two games and half of those must have been Burnley supporters. He knew they deserved better and he carried that upset with him throughout the rest of his life. I am not saying that he would not have been upset if it had been another club which had beaten them in this manner, but he knew what the fans thought about Blackburn Rovers. The anger and frustration he felt as a football manager was the norm, but when he took on board the grief of virtually the whole town, it became a massive cross to bear. Thankfully the Clarets went on to clinch the First Division title, but he never forgot that day in March 1960. As a post script to this, I have just been reminded that when the Rovers played Wolves in the final, Bob Lord and his wife and Harry and his wife Margaret were actually invited to the Rovers' after match banquet. The Lords went but Harry and Margaret went to the Wolves winners' banquet. It was understandable as Harry had spent three years at Wolverhampton as Head Coach to Stan Cullis prior to taking the Burnley job, but relationships with Ewood were a little strained after this, especially as Burnley won the league game at Ewood 4-1 a few months later. I am fairly certain this was the game Alex Elder sat on the ball when Burnley had the game won, taking the mickey and proving their supremacy. Whether Harry orchestrated this I don't know, but it went down well in Burnley."

You can add the name of Graham Alexander to the long list of players who played in the East Lancashire derby who knew nothing of its existence before joining either of the two clubs.

"I was twenty-seven when I arrived in the North-West at Preston and was surprised by the number of clubs in such a short proximity. I learned that traditionally, the club's fiercest rivals were Blackpool and Blackburn Rovers, but in my first eight year stint, we scarcely played against either of them. The shortest trip therefore was to Burnley and it was fascinating that the two clubs fighting over my signature when I left Luton were PNE and the Clarets. For each of the eight seasons that I was at Deepdale, the two clubs were in the same division and when I finally transferred to Turf Moor in 2007, the clubs were rivals for the next two years. So for me, the greatest rivalry I played in was between these two old Lancashire clubs. They were really competitive on the pitch, more so than any other fixture at this time. The games pulled in large crowds and Preston generally had the better of the games. The Rovers were a division above Burnley for two seasons when I arrived there so there was little mention of the East Lancashire derby, but from the moment we came off the pitch at Wembley having beaten Sheffield United to gain promotion to the Premier League, all you ever heard anyone talking about was the Blackburn game. I very quickly learned the traditions and how important the game was in the area."

The aspect of the Rovers v Burnley derby games which most surprised Gary Bowyer was the lengths the Police went to in order to protect the players in transit.

"We have had other Police escorts, but nothing quite like the one that protected us on the journey to Burnley in September 2013. We must have had six outriders on their motor bikes surrounding the coach and on every motorway bridge we passed under, there was a Police presence above it to

A police Inspector takes Burnley manager Frank Casper to the trouble spot at Ewood Park to appeal for calm in April 1983.

Pascal Chimbonda smashes the ball past Brian Jensen to give the Rovers a 3-1 interval lead in 2009

make sure no-one threw anything at the coach. As we approached any junction, one of the riders would accelerate at tremendous speed towards it, again checking that everything was clear. Some of our younger players had never seen before what was going on yet they loved watching the sudden acceleration. One of our members of staff actually told me that he would love to be a Road Traffic officer for a day because it must be such a thrill to ride at that speed. We were surrounded by uniformed police when we arrived at the ground. There was no way that the Burnley fans could have reached us. It may have been exciting to the younger element but I just sat there thinking that this was England in 2013. How had the country come to this, just for a team to travel for a game of football?"

Graham Branch, undoubtedly a "Scouser" if I am allowed to use that phrase, knew all about derbies when he arrived at Turf Moor in 1998. They are the meat and drink of football in the bustling conurbation which is Merseyside. When he left nine years later, he certainly knew that they were equally massive up in the backwoods of East Lancashire.

"I knew absolutely nothing about this derby when I was transferred from Stockport County. The ferocity immediately shocked me but I think the comments made by Graeme Souness after the 2000-01 season best sum it all up. 'I have played in the Merseyside derby, the Glasgow derby and the Istanbul derby {that's Galatasaray v Fenerbahçe; Editor} and I have never seen a rivalry as fierce as this'. It's when you talk to the supporters that you feel it most. The defeats when I was there really hurt them. Many have so much hatred for Blackburn and nobody has fully explained to me where it actually came from, where it really started. You cannot play for Burnley and be unaware of the rivalry."

Derby games are the most anticipated games on a fixture list but unfortunately, they have a habit of displaying all that can be wrong in life; the bias, the hostility and the lack of respect for marvellous institutions and generally wonderful men and women. I have a quote from Paul Fletcher which, in an ideal world, ought to summarise the derby.

"We should only be enemies on a Saturday afternoon. The rest of the week should be spent celebrating the great big family of football."

The Early Days of East Lancashire Football, 1875-88

"Five days shalt thou labour. As the Bible says,
the seventh day is the Lord thy God's.
The sixth day is for football."
Anthony Burgess 1917-1993
Mancunian author

Organised ball games slowly became popular in the 19th Century but they were very much the preserve of the wealthy. And as their male off-springs attended public schools and the majority of these establishments were in the south of England, it was inevitable that the clubs that made their mark in the early days of both organised football and rugby were to be found south of the Midlands. Traditionally the working week for the working classes had been six days of work with the Sunday being the rest day. Sometime during the 1870s, it became accepted that the working week should be shortened. Although Sunday was universally accepted as the day that the populace attended church, there were others who looked upon it as a day to forget the trials and tribulations of work and "get drunk". As a result, there were many a number of workers who would arrive late for work on the Monday morning, badly hung over and unfit for anything remotely manual. Therefore the employers began to compromise with the work force. "We will give you Saturday afternoon off if you promise to arrive on time and fit for work on a Monday morning". Saturday became recognised as the "big night out" but it also freed up the Saturday afternoon and into the vacuum arrived organised football. It was football to play and of course football to spectate.

The FA Cup, first played for in the 1871-72 season, was the only national competition in those days, but in 1877, the Lancashire FA had been founded. It offered more competition and local clubs mushroomed, as if from nowhere. In the 1877-78 FA Cup, Darwen first appeared. In the following season, the club from the Lancashire mill town made substantial progress, but it was then discovered that playing for them were two of Scotland's standout players, Fergie Suter and James Love. It was obvious that they were being paid by the club as they had both been transferred from Partick Thistle in Glasgow. There was outrage amongst the wealthy amateurs within the southern clubs who found it abhorrent that anyone should be paid for playing football. A proposal was made to the FA that "no side which does not consist entirely of amateurs, as defined by the rules to be drawn up by the committee, be entitled to compete in the Challenge Cup competition". As the proposal included the words "rules to be drawn up"(presumably soon in the future), there was an implication that Darwen had not yet broken any legislation and the proposition was defeated. Although it cannot ever be validated, it is virtually certain that Suter and Love were the first two professionals in the whole of the football world and that Darwen was the first club to play professionals.

Four years previously in 1875, Blackburn Rovers had been formed. This was very much an amateur team and in spite of Blackburn being full of working-class young men working in the cotton industry, it was started by ex-public school and grammar school boys living in the town. These young men had progressed from public schools to the finest universities in the land and the choice of strip, light blue and white halves, was heavily Cambridge influenced. The club first entered the FA Cup in 1879-80, losing 5-0 to Nottingham Forest in Round 3, but Darwen reached the semi-final the following year, losing 4-1 to Old Carthusians at Kennington Oval, the Wembley of the day. In the 1881-82 season, the Rovers went one better, storming through to the Final where they narrowly lost 1-0 to the Old Etonians. En route they had defeated Blackburn Park Road, Bolton Wanderers, Darwen, Wednesbury Old Athletic and in the semi-final, The Wednesday after a replay.

The Blackburn Rovers 1882 FA Cup Runner-Up side v Old Etonians was: Roger Howarth, Hugh McIntyre, Fergus Suter, Fred Hargreaves, Harry Sharples, John Hargreaves, Geoffrey Avery, James Brown, Thomas Strachan, Jimmy Douglas, John Duckworth.

This was the final year of ex-public school dominance as Blackburn Olympic, a team based at the top of Shear Brow on land now occupied by St Mary's College, won their way to Kennington Oval the following season where they mastered the Old Etonians 2-1. The Olympic was very much a working-class outfit, no doubt paying their players, albeit unofficially, as professionalism came to be accepted but they were unable to keep pace financially with other local clubs and they folded shortly afterwards.

Meanwhile, whilst all this was going on, the strong, athletic men from Burnley were busy playing rugby. The two codes developed at a similar pace at the same time and whereas the Blackburn, Accrington and Bolton areas were almost exclusively football, further up the valley, the initial preference was for rugby. Burnley Rovers was one of the stronger fifteens but as the 1880s appeared, the pendulum was swinging towards football across the whole industrialised north. It must have been a frenetic time for the game with clubs springing up all over the area. Padiham just down the road was the leading exponent in the Calder valley, but it was no surprise when towards the end of 1881, the members of the Rovers (that is the Burnley variety) also began to talk about switching codes. Following a meeting at the Bull Hotel in the centre of

BLACKBURN ROVERS, 1884-5, 1885-6.

H. Arthur. Sowerbutts. Suter.
Turner. J. Forrest. Jas. Brown (Capt.) H. Macintyre.
Douglas. Lofthouse. Fecitt. G. Howarth.

the town on May 16th, 1882, the club which was to be known simply as Burnley FC was formed. Within a short period of time, a liaison was set up with Burnley Cricket Club and the two sports began to use Turf Moor. They quickly began to play friendly fixtures, but after a number of defeats, they began to invest in players from further afield.

The Rovers' were now playing at a newly purpose-built ground on Leamington Road which included a 700-seater stand costing £500. The Darwen v Rovers clashes had been the scenes for East Lancashire's first stormy encounters with a fever pitch rivalry between the clubs both on and off the field. When the Blackburn club poached Fergie Suter from Darwen, it was probably the catalyst for the abandonment of a "friendly" at Barley Bank; arguably the world's first occurrence of football hooliganism. It could also have been the first instance of money talking in the sport, proving as we all now know that currency is king. It was in the 1883-84 season that Blackburn Rovers became a by-word for football across the land. Queens Park, Scotland's top club, entered the FA Cup at the time, reaching the 1884 and 85 Finals, each time against the Rovers. But on each occasion, the English style of play prevailed. The Blackburn side won 2-1 in 1884. Southport, Blackpool South Shore, Padiham, Staveley and Upton Park were all put to the sword in the early rounds before Notts County provided stubborn resistance in the semi-final. The Rovers eventually came through 1-0 before goals from Joe Sowerbutts and James Forrest proved just enough to bring the trophy to Blackburn against the Scottish side.

The Blackburn Rovers 1884 FA Cup side that defeated Queens Park (Scotland) 2-1 was as follows: Herby Arthur, Fergus Suter, Joe Beverley, Hugh McIntyre, James Forrest, Joe Lofthouse, Jimmy Douglas, Joe Hargreaves, James Brown, Joe Sowerbutts, John Inglis.

In 1885, Rossendale were hammered 11-0 before Blackburn Olympic gave them a tough time in the next round. The Rovers eventually won this local derby 3-2 and followed it up with wins over Witton, Romford and West Bromwich Albion. Old Carthusians were easily defeated in the semi-final, the last hurrah for the public schools and goals from James Brown and James Forrest at Kennington Oval returned the FA Cup to the north.

The Blackburn Rovers 1885 FA Cup winning side that defeated Queens Park, Scotland, 2-0 was: Herby Arthur, Richard Turner, Fergus Suter, George Howarth, Hugh McIntyre, James Forrest, Joe Lofthouse, Jimmy Douglas, James Brown, Joe Sowerbutts, Howard Fecitt

In 1886, Blackburn Rovers reached the Final yet again. Clitheroe Central, Oswaldtwistle Rovers and Darwen Old Wanderers all succumbed to the wave of attacks from the pale blue and white halved shirts and then it was the turn of Staveley again, Brentwood and The Swifts to fail to prevent the Rovers reaching Kennington Oval for the fourth time. The Final produced a dour goalless draw against West Bromwich Albion but in the replay staged in Derby, the Lancashire side was an easy 2-0 winner. Sowerbutts opened the scoring for the Rovers and according to Spartacus Educational...

> "In the second-half James Brown collected the ball in his own area, took the ball past several WBA players, ran the length of the field and scored one of the best goals scored in a FA Cup final".

The Blackburn Rovers 1886 FA Cup Winning side that defeated West Bromwich Albion 2-0 in a replay, following a 0-0 draw was: Herby Arthur, Richard Turner, Fergus Suter, Joseph Hayes (Nat Walton in replay), Hugh McIntyre. James Forrest, Thomas Strachan, Jimmy Douglas, James Brown, Joe Sowerbutts, Howard Fecitt.

So for three successive seasons, they carried off the FA Cup. The amateur club the Wanderers had won three on the bounce in the mid-1870s and the Rovers equalled this feat. Since then, no other team has managed to match this performance. The FA had still not fully accepted professionalism but neither were they particularly proactive in punishing the top North West and Midland clubs which were definitely paying their players. Somehow the Rovers managed to stay beneath this particular radar, despite playing Scots born stars of the day such as Suter, Douglas, McIntyre and Inglis. There was no way that they would travel from across the border to play at Blackburn for nothing; in fact they lived in the town and the club would find them well remunerated employment, whether they turned up for work or not. But Burnley had their wings clipped in 1886, being forced to field an all amateur eleven for their FA Cup tie against Darwen Old Wanderers, a game they lost 11-0.

For whatever reason during this period, Blackburn Rovers made all the correct decisions off the field whereas the fledgling Burnley FC seemed to stumble from one crisis to another. The club was in the "bad books" of the FA from the very beginning and whereas the Blackburn club had appeared in four FA Cup Finals, winning three by the end of the 1886-87 season, the Turf Moor club, still embroiled with the authorities over allegations of professionalism, had failed to proceed beyond Round 1. In the final year before the formation of the Football League, they managed to reach Round 2, but lost 3-2 to Accrington at Thorneyholme Road. And yet Burnley had acquired good players who were handfuls on the pitch.

Although the FA Cup and the Lancashire Senior Cup merited most attention, the clubs played many friendly fixtures, often necessitating long trips to Scotland and occasionally to the south of England. From the commencement of the 1878-79 season until the formation of the Football League ten years later, Blackburn Rovers played over 350 of these matches. As an example, between Christmas Eve and January 2nd of the 1881-82 campaign, they played at Nottingham Forest followed by successive home games against Scottish opposition in Dumbarton, Queen's Park and Third Lanark. So, when Burnley was formed six months later, they had to play a game of catch-up. In their first full season they managed thirty-four friendly matches, all within a very local radius. Two seasons later, that number had doubled. There were a number of clubs in the Burnley area and this was the time for them to prove they had the local bragging rights. Blackburn Rovers, no doubt at this stage feeling somewhat superior to virtually every club on the planet, would send along a "Blackburn Rovers select eleven" for fixtures against local opposition, blooding younger players and giving a game to their reserves; in other words saying to clubs like Burnley that the result did not really matter.

There was no doubt that Burnley were closing the gap on their rivals, with rumours sweeping the town that the top players were being paid as much as £2 per week. A number of these were brought in from a distance away, some as far as Scotland. It was very much back pocket and under the table payment, but the club was pursuing a professional route, although the Football Association had yet to rubber stamp the decision to allow professionalism, even in a diluted form. There is a belief that this was the basis for the first falling out between the two East Lancashire clubs. The Rovers was the longer established club, they were the ones known nationally and they undoubtedly had influence at the Lancashire FA. They probably moaned about what was happening at Turf Moor and, albeit hypocritically, presented themselves as whiter than white. The FA finally ruled that professionalism was legal, but only if a player had been born in the district or had lived there for two years. This immediately ruled out the Scottish contingent from cup games. The fans no doubt looked down the road and asked why the Leamington Road club had this reputation and was able to regularly win the only competition that really mattered whilst they could not even win a single game when medals were on the line, even though they had exceptional players like Scotsmen Danny Friel and Alex McClintock, England former international Alf Jones and the Clitheroe born Jack Keenan. For friendly games, no-one was exempt and from the 1885-86 season, the rivals clashed fourteen times in friendly fixtures over a three-year period, Burnley winning seven with two draws. It could be argued that the Rovers had slipped slightly from their position of total dominance, but nonetheless, the "Turfites" were a top-quality side... but who outside East Lancashire actually knew. By this stage, other quality players such as William McFetridge and Pat Gallocher from Scotland, plus ex Padiham stars David Waugh and William Bury were making their mark at Turf Moor. Walter Place (Senior), [pictured right] who would play for the next ten years, scored their first ever FA Cup goal against Astley Bridge from Bolton.

PRE-FOOTBALL LEAGUE DERBY FRIENDLIES

Date	Home Team	Away Team	Ground	Score	Scorers
27 09 1884	Burnley	Blackburn Rovers	Turf Moor	2-4	Gemmell 2 A Birtwistle, J Brown, Harper, H Fecitt.
23 03 1885	**Burnley**	Blackburn Rovers	Turf Moor	5-1	D Friel, Strachan 2, o.g. Kennedy J Brown.
03 10 1885	Blackburn Rovers	Burnley	Leamington Road	2-2	J Sowerbutts, J Douglas. Woods 2,
19 10 1885	Burnley	Blackburn Rovers	Turf Moor	1-1	Scrimmage, Unknown.
14 12 1885	Blackburn Rovers	**Burnley**	Leamington Road	0-2	Howell, unknown.
06 02 1886	**Burnley**	Blackburn Rovers	Turf Moor	1-0	Unknown,
15 11 1886	Burnley	Blackburn Rovers	Turf Moor	0-1	W Whitehead.
22 01 1887	**Burnley**	Blackburn Rovers	Turf Moor	4-0	J Abrahams, D Friel 2, P Gallocher.
24 01 1887	Blackburn Rovers	Burnley	Leamington Road	1-0	J Sowerbutts
02 04 1887	Blackburn Rovers	**Burnley**	Leamington Road	0-2	W McFetridge 2
18 04 1887	**Burnley**	Blackburn Rovers	Turf Moor	2-1	P Gallocher, Howarth. W Rushton
10 09 1887	Blackburn Rovers	Burnley	Leamington Road	3-2	E Chadwick, W Rushton, J Heyes. D Waugh, R Elston.
28 04 1888	**Burnley**	Blackburn Rovers	Turf Moor	3-1	Holden, F Poland, Howarth E Chadwick

The world's first International had taken place in 1872, Scotland and England fighting out a goalless draw, but there were no players from the North West of England on view. All England sides were selected by the London based FA for many years, giving an obvious advantage to the amateurs from the south, but as the clubs from the industrial North and Midlands began to dominate the FA Cup, East Lancashire's finest could not be ignored. Burnley players however were slow to catch the eyes of the national selectors (possibly because so many were Scottish) and not a single representative from Turf Moor wore an England shirt prior to the formation of the Football League.

The story at Blackburn Rovers was somewhat different. In the years prior to the commencement of league football, eight representatives of the Blue and White halved jersey earned International caps. Joe Lofthouse, who had previously played once for his country whilst playing for Accrington, was capped a total of seven times whilst at the Rovers and the Hargreaves brothers, Fred and John, as well as Doctor (his Christian name and not his title) Greenwood gained England selection in 1881 and 1882. Jimmy Brown, the great goal scorer from the 1886 Cup Final, was capped on six occasions. Joe Beverley, signed from Blackburn Olympic, was selected three times at left back and another local man was goalkeeper Herbie Arthur, one of a number who gained three FA Cup winners medals. He was selected for duty on seven occasions, but eclipsing them all was Jimmy Forrest. The Blackburn born wing-half was a multiple FA Cup winner, being the youngest to play and also to score in this iconic competition. He was selected for England and was officially the first professional to be capped by his country, although the Rovers had to promise not to pay him the week of the International game. Altogether he won eleven England caps, a club record that stood until Bob Crompton came along.

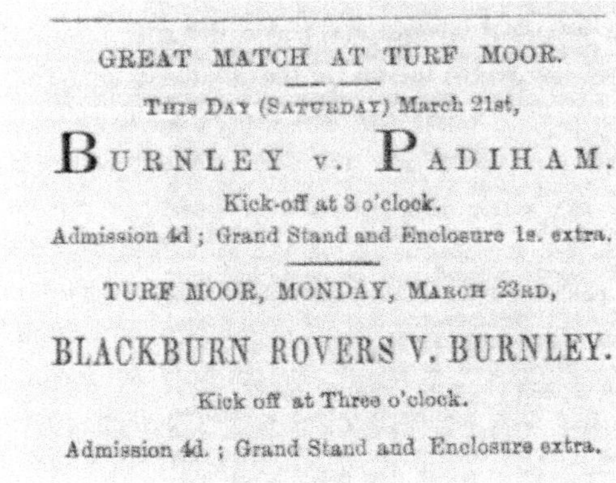

GREAT MATCH AT TURF MOOR.

THIS DAY (SATURDAY) March 21st,

BURNLEY v. PADIHAM.

Kick-off at 3 o'clock.

Admission 4d ; Grand Stand and Enclosure 1s. extra.

TURF MOOR, MONDAY, MARCH 23RD,

BLACKBURN ROVERS V. BURNLEY.

Kick off at Three o'clock.

Admission 4d. ; Grand Stand and Enclosure extra.

[Left] A local newspaper advertising the Rovers v Clarets match, which took place on March 23, 1885.

It's time for change so let battle commence: League Football begins, 1888 – 1900

"As the present now will later be past, the order is rapidly fadin'...
for the times they are a changin'."
Bob Dylan, "The Times they are a changing 1963"

The concerns over professionalism cast a long shadow over football as a whole. It was now clear that a new elite had not only sprung up in the game but was there for the long haul, causing the old guard to be under enormous pressure. It was simply a case of who was going to control it. In March 1888, William McGregor, a draper from Birmingham but more importantly a Director of Aston Villa, wrote a letter to what he considered to be the five foremost professional football clubs in England. They were Aston Villa, Blackburn Rovers, Bolton Wanderers, Preston North End and West Bromwich Albion. His suggestion would allow the FA to continue to run football but would form a competition for professional clubs to play each other on a weekly basis, without the geographical and birth restrictions regarding payments to players.

In a nutshell, he wanted to bring some shape to English football; clubs agreeing to a full set of home and away fixtures and then honouring them throughout the season.

Ten clubs turned up at the initial meeting, none from the south of England. It has been suggested that the strength of the London FA had much to do with their absence. They were strictly amateur and totally inflexible. No club with links to professionalism could partake in their competitions. The North-West was well-represented and Bolton Wanderers were steadfast in their support of Burnley in spite of their less than auspicious FA Cup record. McGregor was adamant that only one team per town could take part and Blackburn Rovers was given the nod over Blackburn Olympic. It would be known as the "Football League" and would kick-off in September 1888. There would be many in the country who would question Burnley's inclusion, but those in the North West knew their strengths and would hear no criticism. The initial 12 team League consisted of six Midland

and six Lancashire clubs, a symmetry that appealed to McGregor, the ultimate diplomat. The twelve successful clubs were as follows.

Accrington, Aston Villa, Blackburn Rovers, Bolton Wanderers,
Burnley, Derby County, Everton, Notts County, Preston North End, Stoke,
West Bromwich Albion, Wolverhampton Wanderers

From this point on, rivalry between Burnley FC and Blackburn Rovers would be formalised. Friendlies would no longer have kudos; league position would be the ultimate indicator. But one thing would be very much self-evident over the next decade. The haphazard state of football nationally had become a well-oiled machine. The times were definitely changing.

1888-89

Team	Pos	Played	Won	Drawn	Lost	GF	GA	Pts
Blackburn Rovers	4	22	10	6	6	60	45	26
Burnley	9	22	7	3	12	42	62	17

Blackburn Rovers		Burnley	
Most Appearances	Jimmy Douglas, Willie Almond, Jack Southworth (all 21)	Most Appearances	Danny Friel 22
Most Goals	Jack Southworth 17	Most Goals	J Brady 7

As the countdown to the first ever Football League season began, the League fixtures for the 1888-89 season had been published in advance. No doubt the fans who could read poured over them, shouting out the important fixtures to others less well educated than themselves. Games against the two previous FA Cup winners Aston Villa and West Brom, and dark horses Preston North End were eagerly awaited and of course everyone was looking forward to their local rivals arriving in town. Accrington was geographically closest to both Burnley and Blackburn, but there had been some extremely competitive friendly fixtures between the Turfites and Rovers, so the early November game at Turf Moor was possibly the big one in the calendar.

In their first ever League fixture, Burnley travelled westwards across the county to Preston. There they met with a hefty 5-2 defeat; North End immediately setting down a marker of intent to the rest of the league. Pat Gallocher, a signing from Padiham although he was Scottish, scored Burnley's first ever league goal, and they recorded their first league win the following week with a 4-3 away victory at Bolton Wanderers, William Tait scoring the club's first ever hat-trick. The Scotsman, with a penchant for alcohol, was allegedly sacked shortly afterwards for persistent drunken behaviour having made only five appearances for the club. The only positive to come out of this first fully professional season for them was the selection of Jack Yates to represent England.

The winger played against Ireland at Anfield at the end of the season, scored a hat-trick in the 6-1 hammering of the men in green and was never picked again. The Rovers played Accrington in their debut game and this match at Leamington Road produced a sensational result. After a hard fought ninety minutes, the English Football League's first ever local derby ended level at 5-5. As a sign of things to come, Jack Southworth scored the Blue and Whites first ever league goal and Billy Townley later scored twice. The Rovers finished fourth with Burnley having to go cap in hand to the Annual General meeting and seek re-election from its peers. Southworth notched two hat-tricks during the campaign, plus a four timer against Notts County and it was no surprise that he and Billy Townley, both names that will forever remain in the annals of Blackburn Rovers, were capped by England this season.

The derby games

Below is part of the report of the first ever League derby match between the Rovers and Burnley. It was printed in the Lancashire Evening Post (extra football special) at 8.00 pm on the evening of the game, November 3rd, 1888.

> Played at Burnley in drizzling rain before about 3,000 spectators. Burnley kicked off with the incline and Yates kicked out two yards wide. After Arthur had sent the sphere to mid-field, the Rovers rushed up, and Beresford on the point of "centreing", made a false kick........ After eighteen minutes, the right wing (Beresford) scored, and one minute later, Forrest scored with a long shot... and Fecitt scored a third in quick time. Yates (Burnley) made a grand run and centre, from which McKay scored, amid cheers. Just before half time, Walton worked up the ball, and made a stinging diagonal shot, which passed under the cross bar, and an appeal that it had passed through was disallowed. (No nets and certainly no VAR then). A minute later Southworth from a scrimmage put the ball through as he was standing behind the backs; and an appeal for offside was disallowed, half time arriving with the score Rovers 4-Burnley 1. About ten minutes before time Southworth got the sphere from Abrams and McFetteridge, and a long shot hit the upright, and passed in before Poland could reach it. (Southworth scored again four minutes later but there is no reference to it in this report) Immediately afterwards Southworth made a dashing run and a quick cross, Fecitt scoring amid cheers. Result Rovers 7-Burnley 1

When it came to the turn of Burnley to visit Leamington Road, the game was played on the first Monday in February and the attendance, was estimated at 2,000. I can think of no special reason why it took place on a normal working day, except that the First Round of the FA Cup was played on the previous Saturday with the replays scheduled for seven days later, but Burnley put up more of a fight this time. It was to no avail however and the Blue and Whites finished the season with a 4-2 victory to complete a tasty double. As an example of the calibre of the Rovers' side, three internationals shared their goals. Inevitably Southworth was on the mark twice and Townley and future international Walton completed the scoring. But there was talent further back in the side. Full back Joe Beverley, goal-keeper Herbie Arthur and Jimmy Forrest, probably England's finest half back of his generation, had worn the three lions badge on their white shirts. Burnley, with their proliferation of Scottish players, had yet to produce their first international, but the Scotland FA policy certainly did not help. They refused to select players from English clubs. Had they done so, surely the great Danny Friel, the resolute Sandy Lang and the top marksman Pat Gallocher would have sported the "red lion rampant" badge on the dark blue shirt. This is probably one of the reasons why Burnley folded so quickly in the first two derby games. Having mixed with other international players, the likes of Forrest were battle hardened and five of them had played in the 1886 Cup final, the replay and the preceding rounds. They had learnt and now understood the mentality required for the big games, whereas Burnley, with no cup runs behind them, were novices at this level.

Date	Home Side	Away Side	Score	Scorers
03 11 1888	Burnley	Blackburn Rovers	1-7	J Southworth 3, J Beresford, H Fecitt 2, J Forrest. W McKay
04 02 1889	Blackburn Rovers	Burnley	4-2	J Southworth 2, W Townley, N Walton P Gallocher, A Brady.

The Blackburn club failed to reach the Cup Final, losing out to Wolverhampton Wanderers after a replay in the semi-final, but their performance in the last eight was the talking point of the nation. Drawn at home to an Aston Villa side that actually finished second in the table, they crushed the pride of the Midlands 8-1. Southworth [pictured] was again unstoppable, helping himself to four goals and Robert Haresnip, who was actually transferred to Burnley in the forthcoming close season because the Rovers had sufficient talented forwards, scored a hat-trick. Burnley, having scraped through Round 1 against Old Westminsters, staggered out of the competition in Round 2 (last sixteen) after being thrashed 5-1 at West Brom.

1889-90

Team	Pos	Played	Won	Drawn	Lost	GF	GA	Pts
Blackburn Rovers	3	22	12	3	7	78	41	27
Burnley	11	22	4	5	13	36	65	13

Blackburn Rovers		Burnley	
Most Appearances	Tom Brandon, John Forbes, Harry Campbell, Jack Southworth (all 22)	Most Appearances	Bill Bury 22
Most Goals	Jack Southworth 22	Most Goals	Robert Haresnip 6

Burnley had survived the vote at the AGM, thus retaining their place in the League, but it was even worse this time round. They finished last but one, fielding twenty-six players in just twenty-two games, an indication of the lack of quality amongst the talent at the club. Only eighteen goals were scored in their first seventeen matches, winless for thirteen months and languishing at the foot of the table. Then, as if a steam train had suddenly arrived at Burnley Central from Glasgow, half a team of Scottish stars disembarked.

These included Claude Lambie, Alex Stewart and James Hill and together they spearheaded a most unexpected but welcome turnaround, the last five games producing four wins, a draw and eighteen goals. It was a comeback worthy of Lazarus, enabling them to leap-frog Stoke who failed to escape the re-election axe. The FA Cup started too early to be affected by Burnley's surge in form and they were defeated 2-1 at Turf Moor by Sheffield United.

The Blackburn side would finish third, a performance which would not be matched for another twenty years. They were the most prolific scorers in the league with seventy-eight goals. As is virtually always the case, successful sides have settled elevens and nine of the outfield players were regulars. But it was the FA Cup which brought the loudest cheer, the Rovers reaching the Final for the fifth time where they produced the greatest performance in the history of the club. Against The Wednesday, Football Alliance champion club from Sheffield, the Blackburn side was simply unstoppable.

Billy Townley became the first player to score an FA Cup Final hat-trick and together with goals from Lofthouse, Southworth and Walton, a 6-1 victory resulted. No other side has scored more than six in an English final. Philip Gibbons wrote a book entitled "Association Football in Victorian England". His comment about the Rovers in the final of 1890 was praise indeed.

> "The Blackburn side has given one of the finest exhibitions of attacking football in an FA Cup Final, with England internationals Walton, Townley, Lofthouse and John Southworth at their peak."

The Blackburn Rovers 1890 FA Cup Winning side v The Wednesday W 6-1: Johnny Horne, James Southworth, John Forbes, Jack Barton, Geordie Dewar, James Forrest, Joe Lofthouse, Harry Campbell, Jack Southworth, Nat Walton, Billy Townley (pictured).

So many Scotsmen earned a living in England in these early years. For Burnley's last five games, their only successful run, they fielded thirteen different players. Four were locally born, nine were Scots. The Rovers included three, but Forbes, Dewar and Campbell were three of the finest. When you consider how many players from north of the border currently play in the Premier League, what has happened to Scottish football?

The derby games

The Rovers inevitably completed the double over Burnley, Walton and Henry Campbell each scoring twice as the league strugglers' were humiliated 7-1 at Leamington Road. Completely shot of confidence in front of 4,000 spectators, Burnley's last win was way back in January and the Blue and Whites, in the form of their lives, had knocked seven past Aston Villa just seven days before. So outclassed was the Turf Moor side that with a score line of 7-0 after seventy minutes, the home eleven inevitably took their feet off the gas, enabling Campbell, a close season signing from Darwen, to grab a consolation goal. It was a much closer affair at the "Turf", as the influx of Scots began to make a difference. The winless streak had now reached eighteen but at least Lang and his fellow defenders kept Southworth quiet. A crowd of 7,000 attended the game, particularly high considering that the home side was currently bottom of the league, and they rejoiced mightily as Stewart gave them an early lead. But there was still a quality gap and goals from Walton and Townley sent the locals home, fuming at the result and the referee. Unbelievably, bizarrely and downright stupidly, the Football League had appointed Richard Horne to officiate the match. The Blackburn goalkeeper was John Horne and yes, you have guessed it. The two were brothers, although there was no indication that any dishonesty had prevailed.

26 10 1889	Blackburn Rovers	Burnley	7-1	J Southworth, H Campbell 2, N Walton 2, o.g. Unknown. J Campbell.
22 02 1890	Burnley	Blackburn Rovers	1-2	A Stewart. N Walton, W Townley

1890-91

Team	Pos	Played	Won	Drawn	Lost	GF	GA	Pts
Blackburn Rovers	6	22	11	2	9	52	43	24
Burnley	8	22	9	3	10	52	63	21

Blackburn Rovers		Burnley	
Most Appearances	Johnny Forbes, Geordie Dewar (both 22)	Most Appearances	Archie Kaye 22
Most Goals	Jack Southworth 26	Most Goals	Claude Lambie 16

Leamington Road was simply too small for one of the country's elite clubs and the Rovers moved into the former athletics track and sports ground at Ewood Park on the southern outskirts of the town. The Rovers lacked the consistency of the previous two seasons, finishing sixth and scoring fewer goals, although Jack Southworth was the country's leading scorer. He notched exactly half of the team's total goals, this in spite of missing the last four games. He is one of only five Ewood Park marksmen to top the national list in the first tier of football; Harper, McEvoy, Shearer and Sutton have since followed suit. Southworth's five hat-tricks was also a club record, an effort since equalled by McEvoy and Shearer. Joining the ranks of Internationals were Jack Barton and Nathan Walton , both signed from the Blackburn side Witton.

Over at Turf Moor, there was rejoicing with eighth place and a relaxed AGM for the club representatives, finishing just three points behind their less than friendly rivals. Exactly half of the twenty-four players used were born north of the border and their two strikers, Lambie and McLardie notched sixty per cent of the goals. Lambie hit three hat-tricks and one four timer and his partner was close behind with fourteen. And in their return game with Preston North End towards the end of the season, Tom Nicol also scored a hat-trick on his debut, the first and only "Turfite" to achieve this distinction. The Football League AGM was, for once, a comfortable place to be.

The derby games

The Burnley club's Directors may have sat comfortably at the AGM, but the fans were still irked by the complete domination that the Rovers had over them. In the first three seasons of the Football League, the Ewood Park club had netted thirty-one times in six derbies, including eleven this season. And this time it had not been all about Southworth. The centre forward only contributed three times but the Blue and Whites were superior in every department. Even in those far away days, when goals were more commonplace than now and tactics were not designed to defend from the front, conceding fives and sixes was not the norm. The II-3 aggregate score equalled the record, shared with the 1888-89 season. The opening game at the "Turf" had echoes of the very first official derby, the Rovers gaining early dominance, Burnley reducing the arrears before the Blackburn side accelerated away to a 6-1 victory. Jack Southworth and his partner Nat Walton at number eight must have been difficult opposition. They were both on the scoresheet again at Ewood where, as in the previous campaign, the Rovers came from behind. Place (Senior) and McLardie giving the visitors a two goal interval lead but once they restarted, the Rovers were unstoppable, and it was yet another Burnley bashing.

18 10 1890	Burnley	Blackburn Rovers	1-6	A McLardie. N Walton 2, J Southworth 2, J Barton, J Lofthouse.
22 11 1890	Blackburn Rovers	Burnley	5-2	W Townley, N Walton 2, Unknown, J. Southworth. W Place senior, A McLardie.

JAMES H. FORREST (Left Half-back).

The FA Cup Final was played once again at Kennington Oval. After two attempts to eliminate Middlesbrough in Round 1, it was plain sailing until the semi-final. West Bromwich Albion were certainly one of the country's best clubs and it was equally tough this time. The Lancashire side however could still compete with the best, winning 3-2 to qualify for the final. There Notts County proved easier opposition and with goals from Southworth, Townley and centre-half Geordie Dewar, a 3-1 win gained them their fifth trophy. Forrest's achievement was far short of the Alfred, Lord Kinnaird's record of nine finals for The Wanderers and Old Etonians in the earliest days of the competition, but the Blackburn born former cotton mill tape sizer must have been some player. The Rovers had equalled The Wanderers' record of five wins and Forrest had played in all of them, equalling the record jointly held by Kinnaird and Charles Wollaston, also of the Wanderers. In recent times, Ashley Cole of Arsenal and Chelsea has raised the bar somewhat, playing in seven FA Cup winning sides. Burnley squeezed their way into Round 2, beating Crewe Alexandra at home 4-2 after extra time. But Notts County, en route of course for the final, proved too good for them.

The Blackburn Rovers 1891 FA Cup Winning side v Notts County, W 3-1 was: Rowland Pennington, Tom Brandon, John Forbes, John Barton, Geordie Dewar, James Forrest, Joe Lofthouse, Nat Walton, Jack Southworth, Coombe Hill, Billy Townley.

1891-92

Team	Pos	Played	Won	Drawn	Lost	GF	GA	Points
Burnley	7	26	11	4	11	49	45	26
Blackburn Rovers	9	26	10	6	10	58	65	26

Blackburn Rovers		Burnley	
Most Appearances	John Forbes, Harry Campbell, Jack Southworth (all 24)	Most Appearances	Jack Hillman, Sandy Lang (both 26)
Most Goals	Jack Southworth 22	Most Goals	Tom Nicol 17

For Burnley supporters, it was a case of everything comes to those who wait, as there was further improvement at Turf Moor and a further slight deterioration down at Ewood Park this season. As a result, and for the first time, Burnley could proudly claim to be East Lancashire's finest. The "Turfites" completed the season in seventh place, their best ever league showing.

They had unearthed a giant in the goals, literally and metaphorically. Jack Hillman, originally from Plymouth, ranks alongside other luminaries such as Dawson, McDonald, Stevenson, Heaton and Nick Pope for ability. Unfortunately, his behaviour was on a much lower plane.

There were two embarrassing defeats, 5-1 at Preston and 6-1 at Aston Villa, but many of the games were close affairs and the Turf Moor side certainly held their own. They twice hammered the hapless Darwen side, initially a 9-0 victory at Turf Moor, still to this day a record league home win. A 6-2 thrashing at Barley Bank followed. Both Nicol and McLardie scored a trio of goals in the 9-0 drubbing and a double each in the slightly more competitive away encounter.

The FA Cup had for once seemed promising for Burnley after a 3-1 win at Everton in Round One but Stoke, who would be relegated with Darwen, surprisingly triumphed 3-1 in Lancashire to send them packing in Round Two. But the best news of all was that they finished above the Rovers.

The Blackburn club had players who were reaching their "sell by" date. Injuries, particularly to the likes of Forrest, Lofthouse and Southworth, were also difficult to deal with and they finished in ninth spot, safe from relegation but their worst league showing thus far. Southworth, with twenty-two goals and an inevitable hat-trick against Bolton Wanderers, was once again in a class of his own when it came to converting chances.

There was to be no third consecutive Cup Final appearance for the boys in blue, being eliminated in Round 2 by the eventual winner West Bromwich Albion. In fact in the subsequent one hundred and thirty years and counting, they would only twice more contest a Final. The club in general was on its way to becoming known as a well-established but a rather ordinary member of the footballing elite.

The derby games

There was little to choose between the two local sides and the first derby game of the season at Ewood Park illustrated that point. It was an early season encounter at the end of September and the Rovers rocketed into a two goal lead within ten minutes with those twin strikers Southworth and Nat Walton being on the mark. Slowly but surely, the away side assumed control and by the time the clock was ticking down to the final whistle, goals from Lang, Nicol and McLardie had put them in touching distance of a first ever derby win. But with three minutes to go, Southworth (who else) slammed in the equaliser and the Burnley lads returned home, at least celebrating their first point.

The following report of the Turf Moor game, Burnley's first ever league derby victory, is taken from the Lancashire Evening Post's 'Today's Football' section on December 12th, 1891... the headline read, 'Extraordinary Scene On The Ground'.

> The match was played at Turf Moor, Burnley, before 5,000 spectators. For three hours previous to the match snow had been falling heavily, and the field was covered with a shallow layer of slush. The game commenced in a blinding snowstorm. Stewart (the Burnley captain) won the toss, and chose to have the driving snow behind his men... Nicol missed a fair chance, and the game went in favour of the Turf Moor combination, who, after some good pressure, scored with a scrimmage seven minutes from the start. (The goal was later accredited to Nicol). At the other end Lofthouse, having time to take aim, made a wide shot, amid ironical laughter. The visitors were handicapped by the blinding snow, which came down without cessation... After half an hour's play McLardie scored amid renewed cheers... The ball and the field were very heavy... This made fast play impossible. A few minutes from the close Galbraith with a long shot scored a third goal. Half Time Burnley 3 -Rovers 0. After a long interval Burnley turned out in clean jerseys... The referee penalised Lofthouse for tripping Laing. An extraordinary scene took place, which caused great uproar. Lofthouse and Stewart came to blows opposite the Grandstand... Stewart and Lofthouse had come into collision several times. As Stewart was taking the ball down the field, Lofthouse appeared to kick Stewart, who seemed to retaliate with his foot. A fight followed, and the Referee went up to the offending players and ordered them both off the pitch. The Rovers immediately after created a scene in a body and left the field at cheerful speed amid a great uproar, the only one of their players remaining being Arthur. After waiting some time, the referee ordered Burnley to recommence play... (and then) Arthur appealed for offside which was granted... As the Rovers did not reappear, referee blew his whistle and stopped the game... Only fifteen minutes were played in the second half. Result Burnley 3 - Rovers 0.

The FA stepped in and severely censored the Rovers, awarding the points to the Turf Moor side. This was the first account of controversy in the fixture, but there would be many more to follow, on and off the field.

26 09 1891	Blackburn Rovers	Burnley	3-3	J Southworth 2, N Walton. S Lang, T Nicol, A McLardie.
12 12 1891	**Burnley**	Blackburn Rovers	3-0	T Nicol, H Galbraith, B Bowes*.

* Some sources give the Burnley second goal to A McLardie

1892-93

Team	Pos	Played	Won	Drawn	Lost	GF	GA	Pts
Burnley	6	30	13	4	13	51	44	30
Blackburn Rovers	9	30	8	13	9	47	56	29

Blackburn Rovers		Burnley	
Most Appearances	John Murray, Geordie Dewar (both 30)	Most Appearances	Tom Nicol 30
Most Goals	Bill Sawers 11	Most Goals	Robert Buchanan, Billy Bowes (both 8)

Southworth, having scored 97 league goals in 108 league appearances, was sold to Everton at the end of the campaign for £400. Was he as good as Shearer? Their records were similar, but we must be careful not to denigrate football in the early days because it was often as difficult to score in late Victorian times as it is now. Then there was also far less protection for anyone on the field. Big, brawny centre halves considered it a badge of honour to kick lumps out of the opposition's "shooter", but "Iron Jack" missed just fifteen games in five seasons, with no substitutes to bring respite after seventy minutes. When he left Ewood Park, I am certain that Burnley supporters of the day would, albeit through gritted teeth, have given him the finest possible reference. After all he did score twelve times in the ten games when facing "the enemy" and he failed to complete two of them; once because the ten outfield players walked off and once because he was dismissed for fighting. Just prior to his departure, he gave a master class when the reigning champions Sunderland were defeated at Ewood Park in the last eight of the FA Cup. A record crowd of 28,000 packed the ground, bringing in gate receipts of £760, but the majority expected an away victory. They reckoned however without Southworth who scored twice as the Rovers went on to triumph 3-0. Scottish international John Murray, ex-double Division 1 medal winner for Sunderland, had signed for the Rovers and played regularly for the next four years. They reached the semi-final, losing 2-1 to the eventual winners Wolverhampton Wanderers. But this was another year during which the Blackburn club failed to compete with the best in the league, finishing in ninth place once more.

It was an incredibly tight campaign for Burnley who finished sixth, one point above the Rovers. This was the Turf Moor side's best ever showing to date, but they depended on a cast-iron defence as not one of their forwards achieved a double figure haul of goals. Lang, yet another Scot from Bridge of Weir just south of Glasgow, was Burnley's original solid rock; a Mr Consistency and ever reliable, He had been originally signed from Padiham in 1885 and was one of those who played in both the pre-Football League days and then continued their careers into the world's first professional league. He was never one to shirk a challenge and he certainly had his moments in these derby clashes, being initially involved in the Lofthouse-Stewart incident which caused the abandonment of the 1891 fixture and of course being sent off after the brutal confrontation with Southworth this season. Records do not conclusively show how many times he represented Burnley prior to 1888, but he certainly made 122 Football League appearances until finally being released in 1895 when his career came to a close. Burnley had still to make any sort of impression on the FA Cup, this time losing 1-0 to The Wednesday in Sheffield in Round 2.

The derby games

In early December, the two sides had fought out a goalless draw at Turf Moor. This was probably the biggest indicator yet that there was absolutely nothing between the teams. There had been a couple of draws in friendly fixtures and the classic 3-3 clash at Ewood Park the previous year, but this was the first stalemate in a league fixture. Now that these two traditional fixtures were becoming far more competitive with an expectation on both sides that a win was a possibility, the more likely it would be feisty. It was in this season that crowd trouble became a serious issue in the derbies. The Ewood game was marked with unacceptable behaviour and the following report is from the Lancashire Evening Post of December 17th, 1892.

> Played at Blackburn before 7,000 spectators. Great interest centred on the game..... Several hundreds of people came from Burnley, the railway company having run three or four specials...... The Rovers continued to press, and delighted their supporters by the vigour of their attacks. The visitors' defence was admirable...... Campbell, after a good deal of finicking with the leather, at last got an opening, and he brought Hillman to the ground. After half an hour's play Bowdler took advantage of an opening given by Matthews and Nicol falling over each other, sending a terrifically fast shot. Hillman, though he just got the tip of his fingers to the ball, had hardly a ghost of a chance of stopping it...... Some hot scrimmaging in front of Hillman created great excitement just before the close of halftime. Chippendale smartly centred and Southworth beat Hillman a second time. Half-time Rovers 2-Burnley 0...... Chippendale cleverly dodged the backs, but only to be more cleverly robbed by Hillman. Who gave a corner which came to nothing. Immediately afterwards Hillman saved in fine style...... The Rovers continued to have the best of the play, but it was difficult to see in the waning light. Just before the whistle blew Southworth and Lang got at loggerheads, and were both ordered off the field. Result Rovers 2-Burnley 0

At the final whistle, the Rovers' supporters attacked the Burnley players. This was not only a verbal assault. Mud and stones started to be thrown and it had become an extremely serious situation. Possibly the Southern based ruling body at the time gave a shrug of their shoulders, a tacit acknowledgement that this is what life was like in the less civilised north but it was an unedifying spectacle and it was clear that the ill-feeling between both players and supporters was degenerating from banter into something far more serious. An underlying viciousness was beginning to appear, perhaps symptomatic of an age where women were just beginning to assume a more dominant role and men felt the need to prove their masculinity, but it was a precursor to much that followed over the next century.

03 12 1892	Burnley	Blackburn Rovers	0-0	
17 12 1892	Blackburn Rovers	Burnley	2-0	J Bowdler, J Southworth.

1893-94

Team	Pos	Played	Won	Drawn	Lost	GF	GA	Pts
Blackburn Rovers	4	30	16	2	12	69	53	34
Burnley	5	30	15	4	11	61	51	34

Blackburn Rovers		Burnley	
Most Appearances	Harry Marshall 29	Most Appearances	John Espie 30
Most Goals	Harry Chippendale 14	Most Goals	Peter Turnbull 15

In a season containing a degree of irony for the "Turfites", Burnley produced their best League performance to date. Unfortunately they lost their position as East Lancashire's cock of the walk, their great rival pipping them to fourth place. Harry Chippendale, who had taken over the mantle of main goal scorer from Southworth, gained his solitary cap against Ireland. The household names were now drifting away from Ewood Park, although Forrest played for much of the season. Consequently, this season has to be rated highly in the annals of the club and it would be another sixteen years before this result was improved upon. In fact, in the one hundred and thirty seasons of league football, this performance has only been bettered seven times. For those further obsessed with statistics, only in the 1914-15 campaign, when the Rovers finished third and Burnley fourth, have both clubs finished in the top four. In this season, they both occupied top five spots, making it the second best combined season for the two clubs on record. Heady days; how we now yearn for them?

Probably Burnley's first real star player hit the national headlines this season. Jimmy Crabtree was a locally born wing half, a tough tackler and a clever distributor of the ball. He gained International recognition, winning the first of his three caps whilst at Burnley in a 2-2 draw against Ireland in Belfast in March 1894. But as a forerunner of what was to happen so many more times at Turf Moor over the ages, a big club came in waving pound notes the following year and he was off to Aston Villa. There he finally gained fourteen England caps and was one of the stars of their double winning side of 96-97. Crabtree, possibly with the exception of Bob Kelly, had to be ranked number one for Burnley in the middle of the park until Jimmy McIlroy arrived on the boat from Belfast fifty-six years later. Peter Turnbull, signed from Third Lanark, also deserves a mention, having topped the scoring charts here at Burnley this season and then moving a few miles west to become leading scorer in a blue and white shirt two years later.

The derby games

The points were shared, Burnley's Scottish left winger James Hill scoring in both games. As was becoming the trend, they were both extremely close confrontations. Geordie Dewar, Billy Townley and Forrest, the only remaining stars from their days of glory, turned out in the blue and white halved shirt in both games, contributing to a cracker of a contest at Ewood Park. The home side led 2-0 and then 3-1, but the visitors plugged away, only just failing to grab the equaliser. The third and crucial goal scored by Townley was his fourth derby goal, not a bad return for a winger. The other Burnley goal has been attributed to "scrimmage". This was not unknown at the time as mauls and scrums and goodness knows what else used to develop near goal lines, but it is hard to imagine that no-one on the pitch knew who made the final contact. Then again, there would be no countless replaying of the goal on TV and no post-match interviews in those days, so if the reporter could not work it out, the local newspaper would award the goal to the mysterious "scrimmage". This was the third time this occurred to Burnley in the season plus two of the goals in their 3-3 draw at Derby County had been credited to "unknown". The Turf Moor encounter was heading for another stalemate until Hill stepped in with a goal on the hour mark. The Scot, who would have been a shoe in for a place in the Scotland side but for their policy of not selecting "Anglos", had certainly added a touch of class to the Burnley line-up since arriving in December 1889.

18 11 1893	Blackburn Rovers	Burnley	3-2	H Chippendale, J Whitehead, W Townley. J Hill, scrimmage.
23 12 1893	**Burnley**	Blackburn Rovers	1-0	J Hill.

Once again, the Blue and Whites closed in on another FA Cup Final but were defeated 1-0 in the semi-final by Notts County, the eventual winners, at Bramall Lane. This followed wins over West Brom, Newton Heath and Derby County. Burnley were also knocked out by the Nottingham side, predictably for the era in the First Round.

1894-95

Team	Pos	Played	Won	Drawn	Lost	GF	GA	Pts
Blackburn Rovers	**5**	**30**	**11**	**10**	**9**	**59**	**49**	**32**
Burnley	**9**	**30**	**11**	**4**	**15**	**44**	**56**	**26**

Blackburn Rovers		Burnley	
Most Appearances	Adam Ogilvie, Harry Chippendale (both 30)	Most Appearances	Tom McLintock, Archie Livingstone, Billy Bowes (all 30)
Most Goals	Harry Chippendale 12	Most Goals	Tom Nicol 11

The season, which started so well for the Burnley club, eventually saw them commence a decline down the slippery slope which was to lead to their first ever relegation. Crabtree packed his bags to join the Villa at the end of the campaign, but Jack Hillman, one of the country's finest goalkeepers, had already left for Everton by then; surely the root cause of what was to follow. Hillman was a giant of a man but whichever club he played for, he always fell out with the management or the Directors. As a consequence he was forever on the move. For the first time, the club appointed a Team Manager, Harry Bradshaw stepping up from his role as Club Secretary. The derby games were once again shared and Tom McLintock, a Scottish left back signed from Kilmarnock, was on the score sheet. He was a fine servant for the club, making 233 League appearances over a ten-year period. Another stalwart of the Burnley side throughout this period was Scottish inside forward Billy Bowes. In his ten years at Turf Moor, he had started 269 league games and was on target on seventy-nine occasions. When he was finally released in 1901, he was the club's all-time leading goal scorer and appearance maker. Following the home victory over the blue and white halves, a top three finish was on the cards but anticipation quickly turned to despair as they gained one solitary point in their last nine matches. Fortunately the end of season arrived before the damage became terminal, finishing in ninth place but only two points clear of relegation.

Blackburn Rovers once again finished closer to the top than the bottom and without any particular player consistently setting the world on fire, they could feel pleased with a fifth-place finish. Harry Chippendale and Ted Killean both scored hat-tricks in the 9-1 annihilation of the Birmingham side Small Heath. A mainstay of the defence throughout this period was another Scot, Geordie Anderson signed from Leith Athletic. In seven seasons he made 178 appearances, always in the number 5 shirt. There were a number of talented centre forwards in Division 1 at this time and for Geordie to make the team for so long says much for his qualities. At this time, the Rovers defence was 100% Scottish, yet another example of the drift south by professional footballers eager to enhance their income in a more affluent area of the United Kingdom.......... relatively speaking.

The derby games

It was another season when the derby games ended all square, the Rovers winning at Ewood and Burnley at the "Turf". Sharing the spoils was a decent achievement for the Turf Moor club, having lost Hillman, an outstanding goal keeper, but they still had Crabtree to set up attacks from deep. The Ewood Park game was only decided in the seventieth minute with a strike from Harry Chippendale, yet another extremely useful left winger. A crowd of 7,000 poured into Ewood to witness this game but 10,000 were enticed to watch the return. Prior to the return game, both clubs had lofty ambitions for a potential podium finish.

First half goals from Bowes and McLintock steadied the nerves of the locals and made the half-time Bovril so much more enjoyable, but a goal from Killean, yet another local Blackburn man, with twenty to go certainly made for a nervy climax. Such an important win ought to have been the springboard for a final charge up the table for the Burnley side, but it was downhill for them from here. As for the Rovers, even with this defeat they were just above their rival in the table, but five points from the final seven games rather put the damper on their hopes also, even though it was sufficient to claim bragging rights.

17 11 1894	Blackburn Rovers	Burnley	1-0	H Chippendale.
12 01 1895	**Burnley**	Blackburn Rovers	2-1	B Bowes, T McLintock. E Killean.

In this season's EA Cup, Burnley, to use cricketing parlance, never troubled the scorers, losing 2-1 at Newcastle United, whereas the Blackburn side went out in the next round, losing 3-2 at home to Everton in a replay. The Blackburn side's domination of this event was no more. Since 1882, they had reached the semi-final on nine occasions, winning six of them. The next time they would reach this stage would be in 1911.

1895-96

Team	Pos	Played	Won	Drawn	Lost	GF	GA	Pts
Blackburn Rovers	8	30	12	5	13	40	50	29
Burnley	10	30	10	7	13	48	44	27

Blackburn Rovers		Burnley	
Most Appearances	Adam Ogilvie 30	Most Appearances	Tom McLintock 30
Most Goals	Jamie Haydock, Peter Turnbull, Harry Chippendale (all 7)	Most Goals	Hugh Robertson 10

The season saw East Lancashire's finest slide a little further into mid-table mediocrity. It is debatable which club emerged on top. Blackburn Rovers gained two more points and finished eighth to Burnley's tenth but there was embarrassment in the away derby and the Turf Moor side netted eight more goals and conceded six fewer over the campaign. To balance the argument, the Rovers had won the Ewood Park derby, but at the end of the season, success is judged on points gained and here the Blackburn side had outshone their rival , twenty-nine to twenty-seven. No-one came within a distance of hitting the double figure goal mark, They had made an impressive start to the campaign, only losing once in their first six starts which included a 1-1 draw with Aston Villa, the best club in the land. The end of the season was a disaster, one draw in the last five games with only two goals scored. West Brom at Ewood had come out of the hat in the 1st Round of the FA Cup. The two clubs had always produced close finishes and this time the honours went to the Midlanders by a 2-1 margin.

James Hill's career at Turf Moor was in its final stages, but he scored a hat-trick at Gigg Lane, spearheading a comeback as Bury were defeated 4-3. Signed as the decade had started from St Mirren, he completed 151 games in almost exactly seven years. A left winger with a knack for scoring goals, his contribution to the early days of the club's life was immense, captaining the side on numerous occasions. The Burnley side also lacked a prolific goal scorer, but for the first time ever in the FA Cup, the "Turfites" progressed further than their rivals, reaching the last sixteen before crashing out 7-1 in a replay at Stoke. In the First round, they had thumped Woolwich Arsenal 6-1. On the score sheet that day were two cousins, Walter Place and Walter Place, differentiated only by the suffix of "Senior" and "Junior". They were both well respected, each one completing over one hundred games for Burnley.

The derby games

Back in October the game at Ewood Park was so competitive. It took a Chippendale goal after half an hour to split the sides, his third in the derby in three successive years, and the Rovers managed to hold on for the two important points which, at the end of the season, would determine which of the two rivals could claim supremacy. The return game at Turf Moor came at the very end of the season and this account from the Liverpool Mercury of April 14th, 1896 gives an indication of the one-sided nature of the match.

> The game was played at Burnley in front of 4,000 spectators. After eight minutes' play Place Senior scored, Nicol getting a second easily a little later. Then Ogilvie had several times to save, having to run out a little later. Nicol got a third, Burnley leading at half time 3 goals to nil. After the interval Burnley soon became aggressive again, and Robertson score Burnley's fourth after Ogilvie had saved... Nicol scored a fifth close under the bar... Then the Rovers pressed for a time but Reynolds and McClintock defended well... then Robertson got a sixth.

This was to be the Turf Moor club's record win over the enemy, but as this was the final game of the season, they then had no chance to capitalise and chase down the Rovers in the league table. Nicol [pictured] had been signed from the Glasgow Junior club Mossend Swifts five years before and in spite of playing much of his career at right back, he certainly scored goals whenever he was given the chance to move forward. This hat-trick was scored in a twenty-nine minute period either side of half-time and with thirty-six minutes to play, the score was 5-0. The derby points had actually been shared but as the Rovers conceded six on their travels and scored only one at home, it would have been a difficult task to convince any Burnley fan anything other than their club was the top dog.

05 10 1895	Blackburn Rovers	Burnley	1-0	H Chippendale.
13 04 1896	**Burnley**	Blackburn Rovers	6-0	T Nicol 3, W Place senior, H Robertson 2.

1896-97

Team	Pos	Played	Won	Drawn	Lost	GF	GA	Pts
Blackburn Rovers	14	30	11	3	16	35	62	25
Burnley	16	30	6	7	17	43	61	19

Blackburn Rovers		Burnley	
Most Appearances	John Campbell 28	Most Appearances	Walter Place (Senior), Joe Taylor (both 30)
Most Goals	John Wilkie 7	Most Goals	Billy Bowes 11

This was a season where there was gloom at Ewood but doom at the "Turf". The Rovers' defence was sieve like, conceding an average of more than two goals per game. There were three disastrous results at Derby, The Wednesday and Sheffield United, but fortunately they secured three wins on the bounce in March, including the double over Everton. John Proudfoot, yet another Scot, this time from Partick Thistle, scored five of their goals on this short winning streak raising hopes of survival. And survive they did, which is more than manager Tom Mitchell achieved. To be fair, he had masterminded two FA Cup triumphs in nine seasons, but his time was up and he was succeeded by Joseph Walmsley. But it had been a cheerless season without anything like a regular goal scorer. A barely acceptable fourteenth-place finish was too close for comfort in a sixteen-club division and the club called time on the careers of Dewar, whose 174 appearances was a club record at the time and Chippendale.

Over at Turf Moor however, six wins from thirty games was totally unacceptable. They had to hope for salvation from the Test Matches, but this was not forthcoming. There was no reprieve after losing out to Newton Heath and Notts County and for the first time in their history, Burnley were relegated. The manager had used twenty-nine players and only the ever-reliable Billy Bowes looked like he knew where the net was. They were trounced 6-0 at Goodison, but they managed to complete the double over Liverpool and quite remarkably triumphed 3-0 at Villa Park, a performance akin to stopping an express train in full flight. But these were mere drops in the ocean and it is fair to say that they fully deserved last place. Next season they would be playing Darwen. Burnley's dismal form was carried over to the FA Cup, being eliminated the first time up by Sunderland who themselves had performed poorly throughout the campaign. The Rovers actually scrambled their way into the last sixteen with narrow, but most uplifting wins at Bramall Lane and Molyneux, before having to travel again to Everton, only to lose 2-0. It was the year that the nation celebrated sixty years of Queen Victoria's rule, but there were few celebrations in East Lancashire. It was indeed a dire time to support either the Turf Moor side or the Blue and White halves.

The derby games

It had been in 1890 when a double victory was last achieved in the derby, but the Rovers narrowly won home and away in this campaign, 1-0 at the "Turf" and 3-2 at Ewood. With both clubs performing badly in the league, it was these two victories which helped the Blackburn side to stay safe and above Burnley in the league. The first hour of the opening game played at Ewood Park was a carbon copy of the Turf Moor game two years previously. After an hour, the away side led 2-0, Bowes and McLintock once more on the score sheet. This time however, the 9,000 crowd roared on their team and gradually, goals from defenders Dewar and Anderson brought the scores level. With a quarter of an hour remaining, Harry Chippendale was not to be denied and the Blackburn club battled through to a hard earned victory. It was the winger's fourth goal in four consecutive seasons, a record for derby games, matched only by Jack Southworth and then Sid Puddefoot in the 1920s. The return game at Turf Moor, a matter of five weeks later was another close encounter. John Campbell, a winger signed from Partick Thistle at the start of the campaign, scored the game's only goal on the stroke of half-time.

03 10 1896	Blackburn Rovers	Burnley	3-2	G Dewar, G Anderson, H Chippendale. B Bowes, T McLintock.
07 11 1896	Burnley	Blackburn Rovers	0-1	J Campbell.

There was further evidence of the ill feeling amongst spectators of the two clubs in a story regarding Tom Nicol. The Scotsman had been an excellent servant of the club, and although still turning out regularly at Turf Moor, he and his newly married bride had taken over the management of a public house in Blackburn. As a consequence, there was a backlash against him from the Burnley supporters and the directors. Nicol could no longer stand the bile and vitriol, the criticism and barracking from the spectators and he left to join the Rovers in November, playing every game until the end of the season. It was unfair, it was uncalled for, but it shows that the hatred engendered by this particular football fixture has a long history.

1897-98

Team	Pos	Played	Won	Drawn	Lost	GFr	GA	Pts
Blackburn Rovers	15	30	7	10	13	39	54	24
Burnley	1	30	20	8	2	80	24	48

Blackburn Rovers		Burnley	
Most Appearances	Tom Brandon, Tommy Booth, John Wilkie, John Proudfoot (all 29)	Most Appearances	Joe Taylor 30
Most Goals	John Proudfoot 9	Most Goals	Jimmy Ross 23

There was an even bigger scare for Blackburn Rovers in the 1897-98 season when the club finished next to the bottom in fifteenth place. The Rovers were unequal to the challenge in Division 1. They could not close out games, leaving little for the Ewood crowd to feel optimistic about. Proof of this was that ten games were drawn, but goals were in short supply with no-one leading by example. Manager Joseph Walmsley started to blood younger players including Tommy Booth, capped against Wales this season, and local boys Fred Blackburn and a seventeen-year old right back called Bob Crompton were both thrown in at the deep end. If there was promise for the future, there was only desperation in the present, although the battle to avoid relegation must have been the tightest on record. Five teams all completed the campaign with twenty-four points and the unwilling participants in the "Test Matches" were decided on goal average. Preston North End, Notts County and Bury all lived to fight another day but the Rovers plus bottom club Stoke were thrown into the mix with Newcastle United and Burnley from Division 2.

The only way to follow relegation is to bounce straight back and Burnley did just that. Winning became a habit for Harry Bradshaw's boys, losing just twice and scoring eighty goals. Loughborough, Newton Heath, Darwen and Grimsby Town were all hammered, with Bowes, Place (Junior) and Tomin in particular all finding the back of the net on a regular basis. But Jimmy Ross [pictured], the veteran Preston North End goal scorer who was reaching the end of his career, immediately showed that he could still perform at this level. His twenty-three goals, including five against Loughborough, saw them to their first national title. Their home form was bomb-proof, completing the season without a single home defeat. Bradshaw was able to use just eighteen players and the trophy residing in the Board Room was ample proof that fielding a settled side brings its rewards.

The Burnley Division Two title winning squad 1897-98 (played over 10 games, max 30) was; David Haddow, Jeremy Reynolds, Tommy McLintock, Peter O'Rourke, Joe Taylor, Archie Livingstone, Tommy Morrison, Jimmy Ross, Wilf Toman, Billy Bowes, David Beveridge, William Ferguson.

The derby games

It had looked like a derby-free season, but the draw for the Test matches immediately paired the two clubs. Just because Burnley had topped the league, promotion was not automatic. In spite of the Blue and Whites occupying a place in the league above Division 2 where Burnley could be found, it was clear that the Turf Moor side had far more to offer and were the better team, the Rovers being bereft of confidence. The 3-1 win at Ewood Park sent a message around the footballing community that the East Lancashire club was back. They certainly had fire power up front, and after the local right winger Tommy Briercliffe had given the Blackburn side an interval lead, Toman destroyed the home side with an immaculate three timer. The second tie brought an equally comfortable win over their arch rival. Again it was the power and skill up front that brought the victory, goal scorer extraordinaire Jimmy Ross and Toman providing the goals in a 2-0 win. As could be expected of a team that was flying high, Burnley played the same eleven in both games but the struggling Blue and Whites made several changes, all to no avail.

When the Burnley v Stoke game ended in a goalless draw, principally because both sides realised the futility of attacking when this result would produce a place in Division 1 for both sides the following season, the Rovers were down. The footballing gods however were with them because at the AGM, it was decided to extend the League to eighteen clubs and the Rovers were saved. There is a wonderful touch of irony surrounding the decision. The previous season, in an attempt to save themselves from relegation, Burnley had proposed an extension to the number of league clubs, which was rejected.

This time, the Turf Moor directors felt obliged to "re-put" the proposition which was passed, a beneficiary being their neighbour. The quality Burnley side, too good for Division 2, fully deserved to be promoted, even though the shenanigans around the Stoke fixture (the ball was kicked over the stand by both sides on numerous occasions and there was no added time in those early years) provoked accusations of cheating. I am certain that it is legally incumbent on a side to play to win a game, but no doubt a referee will confirm it.

21 04 1898	Blackburn Rovers	**Burnley**	1-3	Test match T Briercliffe W Toman 3
23 04 1898	**Burnley**	Blackburn Rovers	2-0	Test match J Ross, W Toman

Because of the skulduggery in the Stoke v Burnley game, Test Matches, to decide promotion and relegation, became a thing of the past. When "Play-Offs" were introduced nearly ninety years later, there would be no mini-leagues, just straight knock outs. Burnley had the edge in the FA Cup but Everton eliminated both them and the Rovers, the Blue and Whites 1-0 in Round 1 and the "Turfites" 3-1 in Round 3. This was actually the best ever performance by the Turf Moor side, having defeated Woolwich Arsenal and Burslem Port Vale in the first two rounds.

1898-99

Team	Pos	Played	Won	Drawn	Lost	GFr	GA	Pts
Burnley	3	34	15	9	10	45	47	39
Blackburn Rovers	6	34	14	8	12	60	52	36

Blackburn Rovers		Burnley	
Most Appearances	Ben Hulse 34	Most Appearances	Tom McLintock 34
Most Goals	Danny Hurst 14	Most Goals	Wilf Toman 11

The momentum gained from Burnley's promotion charge the previous season was carried over to the next campaign and their third-place finish was their best so far. There was an alarming paucity of goals and it has to be an extremely rare event when a club finishes in the top three but scores fewer than it concedes. The start to the campaign was indifferent, twice conceding four goals to Stoke and the Villa. They then managed to compile several decent unbeaten runs as they arrived at Christmas Eve in second place. A 4-0 defeat to Everton took the wind out of their sails but the 2-0 derby win at Ewood Park in front of 20,000 spectators steadied the nerves and the final place on the podium was a scrap between them and Everton. It went down to the last day of the season when the Toffees turned up at Turf Moor. It was a tense ninety minutes but the Burnley defence held firm and the goalless draw secured a very creditable third spot. Wilf Toman topped the scoring charts with one more than the evergreen Bowes and Jimmy Ross continued his fine form, albeit more of a goal creator than scorer. His transfer to Manchester City in mid-February however was a contributory factor to the goal drought which produced just seven goals in the last ten games. Jack Hillman [pictured] returned, having failed to settle at both Everton and Dundee. He gained his only international cap against Ireland at Sunderland, generally being a lonely figure as his team-mates hammered the Irishmen to the tune of 13-2. The only shadow cast was at the end of the campaign when Woolwich Arsenal poached Manager Harry Bradshaw away from the club.

Although Blackburn Rovers had to abdicate all bragging rights to their neighbours, they had a much-improved term. A sixth-place finish and sixty goals scored exceeded all expectations. Ben Hulse, Danny Hurst and Tommy Jackson all reached double figures on the goal scoring list as Notts County were hit for six and Bolton Wanderers, Stoke, West Brom and Newcastle United all conceded four at Ewood. On the debit side, the Baggies from West Brom exacted revenge for their heavy defeat in Blackburn by crashing six past Jim Carter in the return game in the Midlands. The Bob Crompton era had now begun in earnest and Tom Brandon won a Scottish International cap, a fitting reward for the veteran full back who amassed 216 appearances in two stints at the club. Both sides crashed out of the FA Cup at the first time of asking, the first time this had happened. They each had a difficult draw, the Rovers losing 2-0 at Liverpool and Burnley sharing four goals with Sheffield United at Turf Moor before going down 2-1 in the replay. However, with regard to the area's top two clubs, this was their second best combined season, equalling the exploits of the 1893-94 sides who finished fourth and fifth.

The derby games

Not only did Burnley win both derby games for the first time in scheduled league fixtures, they twice kept a clean sheet. This was the most successful side to come out of Turf Moor since the commencement of league football, but it must be remembered that this was also a much improved Blackburn eleven. The opening game, played at the "Turf", was Bob Crompton's introduction to derby encounters, but a McLintock penalty and one from the ace goal-poacher Toman was sufficient to win the game and send Burnley into third place.

A crowd of 12,000 had been present but in the return at Ewood Park, 20,000 was the approximate gate. This was due in no small part to the fixture being played on December 26th. The Boxing Day derby was later to become a great footballing tradition in East Lancashire, but the sizeable home crowd could not roar home their favourites, the Burnley side once more proving their superiority with goals from Jimmy Ross and Toman again. This victory strengthened their grip on second place and at this stage they looked Aston Villa's strongest challenger, but it would sadly be their last victory in Blackburn for twenty years.

26 11 1898	**Burnley**	Blackburn Rovers	2-0	T McLintock, W Tomin.
26 12 1898	Blackburn Rovers	**Burnley**	0-2	W Toman, J Ross.

1899-1900

Team	Pos	Played	Won	Drawn	Lost	GF	GA	Pts
Blackburn Rovers	14	34	13	4	17	49	61	30
Burnley	17	34	11	5	18	34	54	27

Blackburn Rovers		Burnley	
Most Appearances	Bob Crompton 34	Most Appearances	Tom McLintock, Joe Taylor (both 34)
Most Goals	Arnold Whittaker 11	Most Goals	Edgar Chadwick 10

After the sunshine comes the showers, and although Blackburn Rovers just managed to dodge them, they fairly drenched Burnley. A late April 2-0 victory over fellow strugglers Notts County enabled the Ewood Park club to crawl over

the safety line, but for Burnley, a last match 4-0 thrashing at Notts Forest, saw them finish last but one. With no second chance through the Test match system, it was their second relegation in three years and this time there would be no instant return. At Ewood Park, Crompton played in every game and Arnie Whittaker [pictured] was leading goal scorer from the right wing. Their only conclusive victory saw them defeat a mid-table Stoke 3-0 at home in front of just 5,000 spectators, but away from home they conspired to lose every fixture; probably the low point being a 4-2 defeat at bottom club Glossop North End.

Burnley's name was besmirched when Jack Hillman, back at the club for a second spell, allegedly tried to bribe the Notts Forest players prior to the final game. If money changed hands, then Hillman was taken to the cleaners as the Forest banged four past him without reply. The keeper, whose heroics had done much to keep the Turf Moor side in contention throughout the season, admitted the offence but claimed he was only joking. The FA Committee banned him for a year, telling him in no uncertain terms that they were not joking. Edgar Chadwick, born in Blackburn, commenced his career at Blackburn Olympic, moved on to the Rovers and then became a star at Everton, winning seven England caps. He finally signed for Burnley and although past his best, he was still the leading goal scorer. As was the case in so many seasons, the defence held up fairly well. It was at the other end of the pitch where the problems often lay; only Glossop scoring less. In fact they failed to score on thirteen occasions. They won 1-0 at Anfield but were thrashed 6-1 by Notts County on their travels. Their home form almost saved them, a 1-0 win over Sheffield United in the penultimate game raising hopes, but the Forest defeat proved fatal, enabling Preston to edge above them.

Following manager Harry Bradshaw's departure to Woolwich Arsenal, Ernest Mangnall, who had been a Director at Bolton Wanderers, was appointed to the position. This was the era when the manager picked the team but left any coaching that there may be to the Trainer. Hence the manager would have as much knowledge of the office as the tactics on the pitch; a man more accustomed to wearing a three-piece suit.

The derby games

The derby games were shared, Billy Bowes winning the game for Burnley at Turf Moor and Tommy Briercliffe and Jack Dewhurst on target for the Rovers at Ewood Park. Dewhurst, born in Padiham, compiled a record of 43 goals in 169 games over a six-year period. The derby games certainly pulled in the fans, 12,000 being on the Turf with 3,000 more at the return game in Blackburn on New Year's Day. Going into the Turf Moor fixture, both teams were struggling. The Ewood side had collected four points from five games, the home side just three, but they managed to edge the game to stay unbeaten on their own "midden" as they used to say. Including "Test Matches", this was their fifth successive derby win. Burnley were still mid-table as the new century came in, but it was the Blackburn fans who were celebrating as their boys won comfortably. This was no surprise as the Blue and Whites were strong at home, they simply could not travel, It was their seventh win of the campaign in their seventeenth game, just about "safe from relegation" form and it enabled them to hold position just above their rival's. This fixture concluded the first chapter of matches in the derby saga. They had played each other twice in every campaign, the Rovers (thanks to their flying start) winning thirteen to their rival's nine with two draws. The fans would now have to wait fourteen years for the next league encounter.

07 10 1899	**Burnley**	Blackburn Rovers	1-0	B Bowes.
01 01 1900	Blackburn Rovers	Burnley	2-0	J Dewhurst, T Briercliffe.

Once again, neither of the two East Lancashire clubs made any impact in the FA Cup. Burnley fell at the first fence, losing 1-0 at home to eventual winners Bury and the Ewood Park side lost by the only goal of the game to Preston North End at Deepdale. They had previously battled their way through three ties against Southern League side Portsmouth, two draws and a victory at the neutral venue of Villa Park. Three games to beat a non-league side took some stomaching and PNE were a poor Division One side.

And n'er the twain shall meet ... for a decade or so, 1900 – 1911

"Oh, East is east and west is west,
And ne'er the twain will meet
Till Earth and Sky stand presently
at God's great Judgment Seat;"
"The Ballad of East and West"
Rudyard Kipling; 1892

For the second time, there was no schedule for the two to play each other. In the 1897-98 campaign, the clubs had been forced together at the end of the season by the Test Match system, but having been banned the following year, there was now no mechanism which could satisfy the appetite of those longing for derby matches. They could only resume with promotion for The Turfites or relegation for the Rovers. Kipling's poem (above) referred to the schism between British (Western) civilisation and Indian (Eastern), and for the fans of both the two Lancashire clubs, the first decade and more of the twentieth century similarly showed signs of a permanent divide between the two factions from the east and west of the area. "Permanent" and "ne'er"? Well not quite, but to impatient football fans, a gap as wide as thirteen and a half years before those to the east met up with those to the west in league encounters, seemed like permanent.

1900-01

Team	Pos	Played	Won	Drawn	Lost	GF	GA	Pts
Blackburn Rovers	9	34	12	9	13	39	47	33
Burnley	3	34	20	4	10	53	29	44

Blackburn Rovers		Burnley	
Most Appearances	Walt Whittaker, Bob Haworth (both 33)	Most Appearances	Fred Barron, Joe Taylor 34
Most Goals	Arnie Whittaker 8	Most Goals	Billy Bowes, Billy Jenkinson (both 9)

Once again, average is the word that best sums up the first season of the new century for Blackburn Rovers. A ninth placed finish was certainly an improvement on the relegation struggle the year before, but at no time did they look like a team of potential achievers. Tommy Booth and the lively winger Tommy Briercliffe were sold and time was called on two defenders who had given sterling service; Tom Brandon and George Anderson. Two Bobs, Crompton and Haworth replaced them, the former seemingly to play forever and the ex-Darwen centre half making 122 appearances before being sold to Fulham. Once again Arnold Whittaker was leading scorer but why was a right winger scoring goals? Surely he should have been providing them for a goal hungry centre forward, but there was no-one at the club that fitted that description. Woolwich Arsenal defeated them 2-0 in the FA Cup at Plumstead in South-East London in Round 1.

The average gate at Ewood Park in the 1900-01 season was around 7,500, the likes of Newcastle United, Preston North End and Manchester City attracting five figure crowds. But it has to be remembered that transport was far from easy in this period, no cars and coaches to speak of and a railway system that at best chugged along. This virtually ruled out away days. Within Blackburn and Darwen, steam trams had started operating in 1881 and by 1903 had all been converted to electrical power, making for a comfortable journey to the ground.

A current financial situation has always been a simple calculation between income and expenditure. Nowadays there are many ways in which a football club can generate income, but in Edwardian England, Rod Stewart and Elton John concerts, concessionary stalls, hospitality suites, replica shirts and other marketing ploys did not exist. Income was produced from gate receipts, selling players and whatever spare cash was found in the pockets of the Directors. But similar to today, the gate was dependant on the league you play in, the success gained in that season, the size of the fan base and the opposition. So many men were working on a Saturday morning, more often than not heavy manual work necessitating perhaps five hours of standing and to go down to the ground on a wet and/or cold Saturday afternoon was asking a lot of their potential supporters.

There were hopes in Burnley that this season would be an action replay of the 1897-98 campaign when the "Turfites" charged straight back to Division 1. For those at Turf Moor, the wind had been taken out of their sails by two relegations, so the number one priority was to prise themselves away from the also rans and join the big boys. Unfortunately, everyone would have aged considerably, the beards would have grown far longer and another decade would pass before these dreams would come close to reality. The first few years of the Edwardian era failed to excite even the most ardent of supporters. Not that by modern standards there were too many of them. In Burnley's first season following relegation, the average home crowd was around the 3,400 mark. And just to show that it was the derby that was the main attraction even in those far away times, the last one at the Turf in 1899 had pulled in 12,895, the return in Blackburn 14,000. But in this 1900-01 campaign, they won six out of seven at the start of the season and Turf Moor was a fortress as they were victorious in fifteen out of seventeen games, drawing the other two. Unfortunately, their performances away from home were once again their Achilles Heel and they slipped away on the run in and finished third behind the promoted Grimsby Town and Small Heath. Local born full back Billy Bannister represented England against Wales and they at least reached the 2nd Round of the FA Cup, courtesy of a 7-1 home win in a replay against fellow Division Two side Newton Heath, Irishman Morrison and Burnley boy Jenkinson each scoring twice. Any hopes of a run in the competition evaporated in the next round when Small Heath scored early in Birmingham and hung on to progress to the last sixteen. Ten more seasons would pass before promotion returned to the agenda.

W. BANNISTER.

1901-02

Team	Pos	Played	Won	Drawn	Lost	GF	GA	Pts
Blackburn Rovers	4	34	15	6	13	52	48	36
Burnley	9	34	10	10	14	41	45	30

Blackburn Rovers		Burnley	
Most Appearances	Bob Haworth, Jack Dewhurst (both 34)	Most Appearances	Henry Ross 33
Most Goals	Jack Dewhurst 16	Most Goals	Cornelius Hogan 10

For a time in this campaign, the Blackburn club chased eventual champions Sunderland before slipping down to a fourth-place finish; their best for eight years. Bob Crompton was reaching the peak of his form and as a natural born leader; he brought the best out of his team-mates. He won the first of his many England caps, playing in the Home International Championship alongside club mates Kelly Houlker (a left-Half) and Fred Blackburn [pictured]. All three were local boys, an indication of the talent developing via the impromptu street games which could be found all across town in the days before motor vehicles made it impossible to find a pitch outside your house. At last, they could field a number nine who played like a centre forward. Jack Dewhurst had been at the club for a couple of seasons but he suddenly began to appreciate what was expected of him and he cracked in sixteen goals. Notts County were destroyed 6-1 at Ewood, Hugh Morgan, Dewhurst's strike partner hitting a hat-trick. Derby County had twice been thumped 4-1 in previous FA Cup encounters but this time they travelled to Blackburn in Round 1 and cruised through to a 2-0 victory. Apart from this defeat, it had been a most successful season for the blue and white halves. Once more they were at the forefront of English football, the fourth best team in the land.

Burnley finished ninth, but light years away from the promotion spots. In fact, in spite of finishing half-way up the League, they were only two points clear of the re-election zone. It was by far their worst ever season and the Balance Sheet confirmed that the club was in a dire financial situation; one that could only be resolved by selling their better players. Understandably, Hillman was off to Manchester City, centre half Billy Bannister to Bolton Wanderers and Irish international winger Tommy Morrison to Manchester United. There were moments to excite the home faithful, but not many. Doncaster Rovers shipped seven goals and Gainsborough Trinity six at the "Turf", Matthew Brunton, signed from Accrington Stanley in the close season, and Cornelius Hogan, signed from Watford, each notching three timers. To add insult to injury, Burnley were forced to appear in the Final Qualifying Round of the FA Cup. They travelled to Bishop Auckland and scraped through via a Hogan double in a 3-2 victory. Walsall had failed to be re-elected to Division 2 the previous summer but although now in the Midland League, they were too good for the East Lancashire side who lost 1-0. It had been the club's third season in the wilderness in total and was the first time that they had not challenged for honours. The future was certainly not bright over Turf Moor, but by 1902, it was possible to board a tram in Padiham and travel all the way through to Nelson. Therefore internal transport within the Borough and surrounding areas certainly made visits to the "Turf" far easier for the locals.

1902-03

Team	Pos	Played	Won	Drawn	Lost	GF	GA	Pts
Blackburn Rovers	16	34	12	5	17	44	63	29
Burnley	18	34	6	8	20	30	77	20

Blackburn Rovers		Burnley	
Most Appearances	Sam McCLure, Arnie Whittaker, Jack Dewhurst (all 33)	Most Appearances	George Lockhart, Henry Ross, Fred Barron (all 34)
Most Goals	Arnie Whittaker 10	Most Goals	Cornelius Hogan 7

The whiff of corruption around the game centred once again on East Lancashire towards the end of the 1902-03 season. There was little to cheer for all football fans in this part of the county. The promise and optimism at Ewood Park simply disappeared. They struggled to hit the back of the net and local boy Arnie Whittaker was the only one to hit the double figure mark. With two games to play, they looked down and out, but comfortable wins over Everton at Goodison Park and at home to Newcastle United were enough to save the day. They had won one and drawn two of their first ten games and the arrival of Andy Bowman from

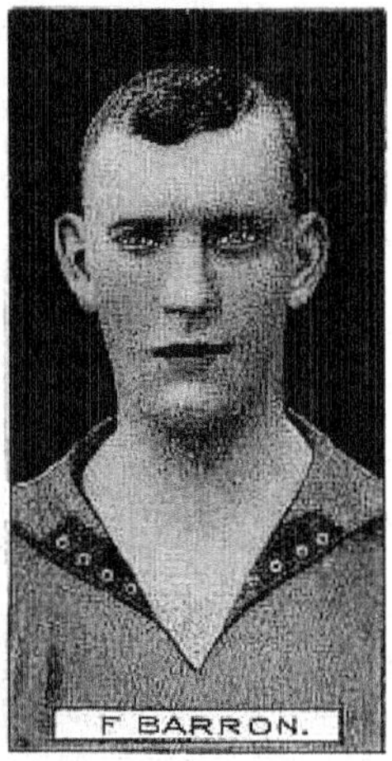

Everton in late March was their saviour. The number nine scored five times in seven games and there was a final margin of four points over the relegated Grimsby Town and rock-bottom Bolton Wanderers. And then came the news that Manager Joseph Walmsley had tried to bribe Everton players in the penultimate game. No money changed hands and there was no points deduction against the team, but the Rover's boss was banned sine die.

The sell to survive policy at Burnley could only end in disaster and sure enough, their next season-long performance was abject. The only reward for twenty points and thirty goals from thirty-four games was the wooden spoon. They were back canvassing for votes at the AGM in June and fortunately they succeeded in finding enough support, but if the Burnley fans had thought that it was a racing certainty that they would quickly return to rub shoulders with the elite (and of course their less than friendly neighbours), they had to think again. In fact, they had to become accustomed to life in a lower Division. Whereas the nation as a whole continued to respect the Rovers as a permanent top tier club, they began to accept Burnley as a Division 2 side. And yet after five games they were in fifth position, but one more win before Christmas saw a rapid descent down the table. The next twenty four games produced just four wins although they were never really trounced.. Defensively, there was a consistency of selection with a back five of Ross, Lockhart, Barron, Taylor and Dixon playing together in all but three games, but the problems were all further forward with no-one to regularly score goals. Neither had there been even a glimmer of hope from the FA Cup. A 1-0 defeat at Reading from the Southern League somehow summed up this woeful season. A bizarre twist at the end of the campaign saw Ernest Mangnall, not the most successful of managers at Turf Moor, leave to take up the same position at Manchester United. And so, the Burnley fans were pondering over who would be in charge of their fortunes next term and ironically, the Blackburn club waited to see which man would be brought in as their new manager. One thing both sets of fans were certain of was that the new appointments could not do any worse than the previous incumbents.

1903-04

Team	Pos	Played	Won	Drawn	Lost	GF	GA	Pts
Blackburn Rovers	**15**	**34**	**11**	**6**	**17**	**48**	**60**	**28**
Burnley	5	34	15	9	10	50	55	39

Blackburn Rovers		Burnley	
Most Appearances	Fred Blackburn 33	Most Appearances	Fred Barron 34
Most Goals	Lionel Watson 14	Most Goals	Henry Williams, Dugald McFarlane (both 8)

Life of course was somewhat different in the summer prior to the 1903-04 season. Whereas a club in the top tier in the modern world will search potential managers worldwide, Blackburn appointed RB Middleton, the ex-Manager of Darwen. Burnley likewise opted for a local man. Spen Whittaker had been in charge at Oswaldtwistle Rovers, also from the Lancashire Combination. A great honour bestowed on the Ewood Park club was when Bob Crompton was appointed England captain. It was unusual for the FA to proffer such an honour on a young man from a very working class background, often appointing Southern amateurs who could make a speech and talk to dignitaries. Crompton however was one of the new breed of professionals who not only made it to the top but stayed there for so long. Even with the England skipper in the side, the Rovers were dragged into another relegation battle, one they escaped by two points and two positions. Lionel Watson had been brought in from Manchester City and scored regularly from an inside forward position. Then from being an upper mid-table kind of side, just two games were won in the final four months. It was only a 2-0 away win at Middlesbrough that saved their skin, Watson and Bowman, the latter recently returned from a long absence through injury, scoring the goals. For the third consecutive year, the club was drawn away to Derby County in the FA Cup, and for the third consecutive time, the Blue and White side lost 2-1. Liverpool and Nottingham Forest had been put to the sword in rounds 1 and 2, with Dewhurst scoring four times in total.

Whittaker made a promising start and at one stage the Turf Moor side looked like promotion candidates, particularly after an unbeaten run from Boxing Day until the end of February. Then five consecutive defeats in March forced them down to fifth place. The one notable victory was when they knocked in five at Blackpool without reply, the Cumbrian born Dugald McFarlane scoring twice en route to being joint top scorer. But they conceded six in successive away games at Bristol City and Glossop and further humiliation was to be found in the FA Cup. Because of their poor performance in Division 2 the previous campaign, Burnley, now playing in green shirts, had to enter the competition at the 3rd Qualifying Round stage where they beat Keswick 8-0. The 4th Qualifying Round was staged at the home of Lancashire Combination hot-shots Darwen. The mill town's glory days were long gone, but they easily handled Burnley; the result a remarkably comfortable 3-0 victory. The new manager was highly dependent on Fred Barron. The Stockton born defender missed just twelve games in a run of a dozen years in which he made 400 appearances. He is still eighth on the all-time list, a testimony to his toughness and commitment.

1904-05

Team	Pos	Played	Won	Drawn	Lost	GF	GA	Pts
Blackburn Rovers	13	34	11	5	18	40	51	27
Burnley	11	34	12	6	16	43	52	30

Blackburn Rovers		Burnley	
Most Appearances	Jock Cameron 34	Most Appearances	Billy Green 34
Most Goals	Andy Bowman 12	Most Goals	Dugald McFarlane 13

Attendance figures slowly rose through the decade and with compulsory education being law since 1880, more and more members of the community had learned to read. Suddenly the press found a way to engage with the working man and the concept of a back page relating uniquely to sport was born. Probably as a result of this extra publicity, the crowd at Ewood Park averaged out at over five figures for the first time ever; 11,415 to be exact. It was a bizarre old campaign at Ewood, one which appeared to have no logic as tiny winning runs were wiped out by equally short series of losses. In the end, the Rovers only survived by three points in spite of their final thirteenth position. When the Champion's elect Newcastle United lost 2-0 at Ewood Park, relegation seemed impossible and so it proved to be, although the manager and players did their best to put the shivers up the spine of the fans by taking just one point from the last three games. Sighs of relief were heard from the locals who simply could not predict what the next score line would be. The Scottish centre forward Adam Bowman had proved to be an inspired signing, averaging almost a goal every two games and he topped the scoring chart once more. Centre-half Jock Cameron had been signed from St Mirren and he and Crompton helped to keep the ship afloat but this was the third consecutive season that the club had finished in the bottom quarter of the league. RB Middleton was proving to be no Moses who could lead them to the Promised Land. The FA Cup was a non-event, bowing out to The Wednesday in Round 1. The higher crowd figures had to have been because of the increased publicity for the matches; it certainly could not have been because of the results on the pitch.

All the optimism engendered by Spen Whittaker's first season quickly evaporated as Burnley lost eleven of their first thirteen matches. However, by dint of hard work, the manager eventually sorted the problems. A final position of eleventh place, albeit only three points clear of safety, was achieved. The

HUGH MOFFATT, Burnley.

attendances at Turf Moor certainly bucked the national trend and barely one thousand turned up to watch the Burslem Port Vale fixture. The club was being run on a shoestring and they were taking just the bare starting eleven to away games. Hugh Moffatt, a quality left-back signed from Congleton who chalked up 201 appearances, travelled separately to Chesterfield and missed a train connection in Manchester. He arrived after the final whistle but the ten men, defending heroically, salvaged a 1-1 draw. Whittaker's only first-rate purchase of the season was inside forward Dick Smith who shared striking duties with fellow Cumbrian McFarlane. He scored eight from 27 starts. The revolving door, which even to this day brings players to a club and then sees them depart, witnessed the farewell of Henry Ross. Aged only twenty-three, he had already played over one hundred league games at right back and was considered a star of the future. Ex-boss Harry Bradshaw, now in charge at Fulham, was quick to lure him Thames-side, a sad blow to the Lancashire club, but with it came a coded message. If you under-perform, you lose your better players. Burnley did not have to join the FA Cup competition until the Intermediate Round, the one before Round 1. Lincoln City, a mid-table Division 2 side visited the Turf, an encounter which ended with honours even, but Burnley lost 3-2 in Lincolnshire, having twice led.

1905-06

Team	Pos	Played	Won	Drawn	Lost	GF	GA	Pts
Blackburn Rovers	9	38	16	8	14	54	52	40
Burnley	9	38	15	8	15	42	53	38

Blackburn Rovers		Burnley	
Most Appearances	Bob Crompton, Billy Bradshaw, Arnie Whittaker (all 36)	Most Appearances	Hugh Moffat 38
Most Goals	Andy Bowman 15	Most Goals	Dugald McFarlane 10

With perfect symmetry, both Blackburn Rovers and Burnley finished in ninth position in their respective leagues. A Scottish/Welsh strike partnership of Bowman and Billy Davies contributed half of the goals as the Rovers put together a ten game unbeaten run mid-season. Davies had been bought from Wrexham for £150 and he eventually proved to be worth every penny, scoring in exactly fifty percent of the games at Blackburn, 66 in 132. The Rovers were particularly strong at home, losing only three times and also won 3-1 at Liverpool, Bowman and Davies inevitably sharing the goals. And once upon a time, particularly at Ewood Park, the onset of the FA Cup would provoke a spine tingling feeling around the town. Not any more, a 1-0 defeat to a poor Stoke outfit in Round 1 telling its own story.

Both Division One and Division Two had been extended to twenty clubs and Burnley's haul of forty goals from thirty eight games did nothing to excite the fans. Dugald McFarlane was once again leading scorer, but his season's total of ten goals was hardly headline making news. They were as high as fifth in November, slumped badly in the winter months towards relegation until a run of six unbeaten games took them to a season ending ninth. For the third time in four years, Burnley were eliminated by a non-league side in the FA Cup. In fairness, it was a former winner that did the damage as they lost 2-0 in London to Tottenham Hotspur in Round 1.

1906-07

Team	Pos	Played	Won	Drawn	Lost	GF	GA	Pts
Blackburn Rovers	12	38	14	7	17	56	59	35
Burnley	7	38	17	6	15	62	47	40

Blackburn Rovers		Burnley	
Most Appearances	Jimmy Robertson, Jack Martin (both 36)	Most Appearances	Fred Barron 38
Most Goals	Jack Martin 17	Most Goals	Dick Smith 16

A local businessman, Laurence Cotton by name, was now Chairman at Blackburn Rovers. A man with bold ideas but with his feet cemented firmly to the ground, he oversaw the building of the Nuttall Street Stand (now the Jack Walker Stand). Over 35,000 witnessed the 1907 New Year's Day 1-1 draw with Preston North End, proving that improvements to the ground and its amenities can help to pull in more spectators. The fare served up by the side in the 1906-07 campaign was still rated at somewhere close to mediocre but Jack Martin, signed from Lincoln City, found the net on seventeen occasions as the club comfortably avoided relegation in twelfth position. The Blackburn side actually played a total of five games in the FA Cup, but only progressed to Round 2. They drew 2-2 against Manchester City and won the replay at Maine Road 1-0. Three games were then necessary before a winner was found. Successive 1-1 draws at Ewood Park and White Hart Lane ensued before Tottenham Hotspur, the Southern League club that was good enough to be playing in Division One, progressed through 2-1 at the neutral venue of Villa Park.

Meanwhile down in Division Two, Burnley improved a touch, finishing in seventh place. They were a country mile away from catching the two promoted clubs, but they were comfortably mid table. And just for a change, there was an abundance of goals to celebrate. Dick Smith was leading scorer with seventeen to his name. All fine careers end eventually and Joe Taylor, the Burnley born defender, finally called it a day after making 329 appearances. Early on in his career, he was suspended by his own Board of Directors for a succession of reckless challenges but everyone had to admit that he was the original stick of Burnley rock. Break him in two and you would find Burnley FC embedded throughout him. Barrowford born defender Arthur Dixon, who made 175 appearances, moved on to Tottenham Hotspur, and was sorely missed. It was a tough FA Cup draw for Burnley. They were at home, but to the FA Cup titans Aston Villa who won 3-1.

1907-08

Team	Pos	Played	Won	Drawn	Lost	GF	GA	Pts
Blackburn Rovers	14	38	12	12	14	51	63	36
Burnley	7	38	20	6	12	67	50	46

Blackburn Rovers		Burnley	
Most Appearances	Bob Crompton 33	Most Appearances	Thomas Wolstenholme 38
Most Goals	Billy Davies 10	Most Goals	Dick Smith 24

SH. R. SMITH, Burnley.

The 1907-08 FA Cup was yet another episode in the ongoing saga of doom and gloom for the East Lancashire clubs. Both clubs fell at the first time of asking to lower opposition, Burnley at home to Southern League Southampton and Blackburn Rovers at Leicester Fosse from Division 2. Since last winning the trophy sixteen years before in 1891, the Rovers had won just fourteen cup ties. During the same period, Burnley had managed to win eight. In terms of the local rivalry, the Blackburn fans may have been encouraged by those statistics but to be frank, they were both dismal and both clubs could have and should have "done better".

The Ewood side limped in from well down the field in joint fourteenth position. The spectre of relegation had haunted them throughout and only a final four game unbeaten run saved the day. Bob Evans, a "custodian of the goal" to use a term favoured by early football journalists, had been signed from Wrexham in the 02-03 season and he became the first Rovers player to be capped by Wales.

Burnley's Dick Smith [pictured] helped himself to twenty-four goals including hat-ticks in consecutive weeks against Barnsley and Chesterfield. This set a club record, bettering Jimmy Ross' twenty-three goals ten years earlier. His goals kept this dysfunctional side away from the foot of the table and he went on to score 70 times in 174 appearances. It was hello to Cliviger born goalkeeper Jerry Dawson, a true legend in the making, a position he would hold on a regular basis for almost twenty years. There was a much more cavalier approach to the game from Whittaker's boys and although it was a second successive seventh spot, there was an improvement in both goals scored and points gained.

1908-09

Team	Pos	Played	Won	Drawn	Lost	GF	GA	Pts
Blackburn Rovers	4	38	14	13	11	61	50	41
Burnley	14	38	13	7	18	51	58	33

Blackburn Rovers		Burnley	
Most Appearances	Jimmy Ashcroft 38	Most Appearances	Jerry Dawson 36
Most Goals	Billy Davies 19	Most Goals	Dick Smith 13

W. BRADSHAW,
Left half-back.

The Football League came of age in the 1908-09 season, twenty-one and still counting. And although it was not exactly party time in Blackburn, there was much to excite the fans. A fourth-place finish was the best in seven years, although they were twelve points adrift of top spot. Billy Davies led the goal scoring chart with a total of nineteen. He failed to score a hat-trick but notched two four timers against Everton and Bristol City. The Welshman was capped nine times over a five year period. A number of players who would feature in Rovers' successes several years down the line were now at the club. Outstanding forwards such as Wattie Aitkenhead, Edwin Latheron and George Chapman, defenders Bob Crompton and Billy Cameron, half backs Billy Bradshaw and Albert Walmsley plus the recently signed winger Walter Anthony would all make a major contribution at the beginning of the next decade. There had been a mini-cup run by the Ewood Park club, but after a 2-0 away win over Division 1 side Notts County and a 2-1 home win over Chelsea, also from the top division, it all unravelled at Old Trafford where Manchester United thrashed them 6-1, still an FA Cup record defeat.

There were certainly no celebrations at Burnley with regard to their league performance, only sighs of relief that they had once more escaped seeking re-election, this time by two points in fourteenth place. They did have a habit of making things difficult for themselves, missing three penalties at home to Grimsby Town. They were actually awarded a fourth which Billy Abbott converted in a 2-0 victory. The FA Cup brought a glimmer of hope to the Turf Moor supporters and the last sixteen replay was a record equalling 9-0 home thrashing of Southern League side Crystal Palace, Smith scoring his fifth hat-trick for the club. Burnley came out of the hat against Manchester United in a last eight tie and with twenty minutes left on the clock at Turf Moor, and with the home side leading 1-0, it started to snow heavily. The Manchester players complained to the referee that they were struggling to see and he abandoned the game. Everyone connected with the East Lancashire side was up in arms about the decision and the annoyance turned to downright anger when the reigning Division 1 champions won the re-arranged tie 3-2. There were suggestions that the opposition had cheated their way to the semi-final, but on the positive side, the Turfites had equalled their best ever FA Cup showing.

1909-10

Team	Pos	Played	Won	Drawn	Lost	GF	GA	Ptts
Blackburn Rovers	3	38	18	9	11	73	55	45
Burnley	14	38	14	6	18	62	61	34

Blackburn Rovers		Burnley	
Most Appearances	Wattie Aitkenhead 38	Most Appearances	Jack Cretney 36
Most Goals	Wattie Aitkenhead 12	Most Goals	Benny Green 18

AITKENHEAD, BLACKBURN

Blackburn Rovers edged a step closer to the dizzy heights of League 1, finishing a record equalling third, five points behind Aston Villa. The Rovers crashed in seventy-three goals which included a 7-0 thrashing of Woolwich Arsenal in early October. Wattie Aitkenhead, a Glaswegian who had been signed several years before but who had patiently waited his turn before becoming an Ewood favourite, was the leading scorer with fourteen goals. The side accumulated a record forty-five points making it a season to remember. Bob Crompton was immaculate as he marshalled the defence which also included fellow England internationals Jimmy Ashcroft (a goal keeper signed from Woolwich Arsenal) and the Lower Darwen born left back Arthur Cowell. From October through to January, the blue and white halves topped the table but defeats on the road were their undoing. One indicator of a successful side is the number of players used in the campaign. During this particular season, Middleton used just nineteen players, a joint low record for the club. There was another mini-cup run, starting with a 7-1 thrashing of Accrington Stanley away from home. Then Aitkenhead's second double strike gave them a 2-1 win at Division 1 Bradford City but an on form Newcastle United proved too good in a 3-1 defeat in the North-East. The big question in East Lancashire was whether the Blackburn club was in a position to win the league. Five FA Cup wins were not to be sneezed at but the League Championship was beginning to have more kudos. Several clubs had by now won them both. For the Rovers to regain their position as one of the country's premier clubs, a league title was a necessity. Would it be next season?

It was status quo time at Turf Moor as Burnley finished in fourteenth place again, but this time they were eight points clear of re-election. All of this became irrelevant as the season drew to a close. Tragedy struck in early April as Whittaker was travelling to London by train to register a new signing (no fax machines in those days). He somehow fell out of the train on its way to Crewe and died the following day in hospital. He had given almost seven years to Burnley FC, keeping the club afloat through this period. He had been the club's youngest manager and the town rallied round to help his wife and young family. It had been difficult for him as can be seen by the fact that he had used thirty players the previous season and thirty-one this season. Burnley's principle concern was to find a new manager. They had refrained from doing so until the season ended as a mark of respect to a much-loved late manager, but it would have been foolhardy to start a new season without a replacement settled into the office underneath the stand. Only then could they dream about improvements on the field. Before the manager's tragic death, they had gained revenge over Manchester United, knocking them out of the FA Cup at the first hurdle, 2-1 at a joyous Turf Moor. Then, typical of the lack of consistency, they lost 2-0 at non-league Swindon Town in Round 2.

1910-11

Team	Pos	Played	Won	Drawn	Lost	GF	GA	Pts
Blackburn Rovers	12	38	13	11	14	62	34	37
Burnley	8	38	13	15	10	45	45	41

Blackburn Rovers		Burnley	
Most Appearances	Wattie Aitkenhead 35	Most Appearances	Benny Green 37
Most Goals	Billy Davies 17	Most Goals	Benny Green 11

In the run up to the 1910-11 campaign, the Burnley fans were expecting one change; a new manager but they were certainly not expecting a second massive change to the complexion of the club. John Haworth was chosen as the replacement for Spen Whittaker. He had connections with Accrington Stanley

A. COWELL (*Back*)
ENGLAND.

where he had been club secretary but moving to Burnley was one large learning curve. He quickly realised that green was not an appropriate colour for the team shirts. Like Don Revie, fifty years later at Leeds United, he had a theory. If you clothe a football team in the same colours as the best team on the globe, there is a chance they will play like them. Revie switched to the all-white strip of Real Madrid and John Haworth chose the claret and blue of Aston Villa. The theory certainly worked in Leeds and it worked also in East Lancashire. It did not take the fans long to pick up on a new nickname. "C'mon the Clarets" was the chant and ever since 1910, there has only been one name worth shouting. There was no instant revival, but an eighth-place finish was an acceptable start. After a sound start, John Haworth was making progress but the newly named "Clarets' fans" were still consumed by doubts caused by a pattern which had emerged during the first ten years of this new century. And the pattern, which sat uncomfortably with them, was that their nemesis was a permanent Division One club whilst they were certainly not.

There were great expectations around Ewood Park at the start of the season following their third-place finish. The 1910-11 league campaign however was so disappointing and a twelfth-place finish upset many fans. There was consolation however in the shape of a long FA Cup run. For the first time in seventeen years. Southend United, Tottenham, Middlesbrough and West Ham had all been brushed to one side before they reached the semi-final where they unexpectedly lost 3-0 to the shock winners, Bradford City. Injuries affected selection and both Cowell and Walmsley were missing for most of the cup run. Without doubt, RB Middleton, who had replaced the banned Joseph Walmsley eight years before, had planted the seeds of recovery and in spite of this momentary setback, they were beginning to flower.

With no derby games played in this period, the anxiety, agitation, acrimony and aggression never surfaced. There had been no opportunities, but had the passion in the towns died away? Without radio, television, texting, emails and social media, it is impossible to tell as letters to the editor of the local newspapers such as the Blackburn Times and the Burnley Express rarely referred to readers' comments on the absence of local football rivalry. However, the attendance of 48,000 at the first Turf Moor derby for over fourteen years on New Year's Day 1914 would certainly indicate that the both the faithful and casual supporters had certainly been missing the thrills and spills of derby football and the opportunity to let off steam.

Golden Years, 1911 - 1922

"Golden Years;- The period during which someone or something flourishes."
Dictionary definition Wiktionary

Until this era, both Blackburn Rovers and Burnley had produced good performances from time to time, particularly the Rovers in the FA Cup and certainly both sets of fans had been content with league placings on occasions. But this was the first time that both clubs had simultaneously put together runs which aroused the local supporters and reminded the nation that these were two of the original founder members, each with long histories. And for the next decade, they would make their mark on English football once more. It was the first "Golden Age" of football across East Lancashire.

1911-12

Team	Pos	Played	Won	Drawn	Lost	GF	GA	Pts
Blackburn Rovers	1	38	20	9	9	60	43	49
Burnley	3	38	22	8	8	77	41	52

Blackburn Rovers		Burnley	
Most Appearances	Albert Walmsley 37	Most Appearances	Jerry Dawson, Robert Reid, Billy Watson (all 38)
Most Goals	Wattie Aitkenhead 15	Most Goals	Bert Freeman 32

It was a long time coming but twenty-four years after joining the Football League as arguably England's finest club, Blackburn Rovers won the title. They were the country's tenth different champion and the eighth to now adorn their CV with League and FA Cup triumphs. The five FA Cup wins had been magnificent achievements, but just six wins would suffice whereas consistency over a thirty-eight game programme had to be accomplished to attain the top spot. The mean defence conceded just ten goals in nineteen home games. This was the key to success along with a level of consistency, so abjectly lacking the previous season. A long three-month unbeaten run took them to the top of the table and even with the odd hic-cup, they still had enough points in the bag to keep Everton at bay. The signing of English international right winger Jock Simpson from Falkirk had given the Blue and Whites more attacking options and Wattie

BURNLEY.
B. C. FREEMAN.

Aitkenhead was the top marksman for the second time, although the goals were shared around.

The Blackburn Rovers Division One title winning squad 1911-12 (started over 18 games, max 38) were; Alf Robinson, Bob Crompton, Arthur Cowell, Albert Walmsley, Percy Smith, Billy Bradshaw, Jock Simpson, Eddie Latheron, Wattie Aitkenhead, Joe Clennell, Walter Anthony, John Orr, George Chapman.

The name on everyone's lips at Turf Moor was Bert Freeman, bought from Everton at the prime of his career. His thirty-two goals set a club record as he dragged Burnley to the threshold of promotion with the considerable assistance of goal scoring partner Teddy Hodgson. Sadly, an unforeseen drop in form in the last five matches produced only three points and the Clarets ended two points short. Turf Moor proved a most difficult ground to visit, the Clarets remaining unbeaten at home. They had bought Tommy Boyle, the Barnsley centre half and formidable header of a football for £1,150, a fortune for a Division 2 club. The Yorkshireman went on to become a club legend, making 210 league appearances; a total which would have been much higher had the Great War not intervened.

In the FA Cup, the Rovers came through a last eight home replay, 4-2 against Manchester United. Talk of the double however was premature as following a goalless draw in the semi-final, they lost 1-0 to West Bromwich Albion in the replay at Hillsborough. The Ewood Park side was full of Internationals. Full backs Crompton and Cowell, plus wing half Billy Bradshaw shored up the defence. Simpson and Eddie Latheron were two English forwards and Aitkenhead from Scotland and the Welshman Davies were also prominent in attack. It had been Blackburn Rovers' best season ever to date and more was expected. Burnley had experienced their best season since 1901. They had an extremely competent manager and they had Bert Freeman. Surely promotion would be achieved the following year. An away trip to Fulham, well below them in the league, ought to have been the springboard to a decent cup run, but the Clarets could not hang on to an early lead following another Freeman strike and slipped to a 2-1 defeat.

1912-13

Team	Pos	Played	Won	Drawn	Lost	GF	GA	Points
Blackburn Rovers	**5**	**38**	**16**	**13**	**9**	**79**	**43**	**45**
Burnley	2	38	21	8	9	88	53	50

Blackburn Rovers		Burnley	
Most Appearances	Alf Robinson, Albert Walmsley, Eddie Latheron (all 36)	Most Appearances	Bert Freeman 37
Most Goals	Eddie Latheron 14	Most Goals	Bert Freeman 31

And it was the fans at Turf Moor who were shouting the loudest as the 1912-13 season drew to a close. It was not because Blackburn Rovers played poorly; the team had remained unbeaten until Christmas, finishing in fifth place. At times they were unstoppable moving forwards, but five successive defeats rather took the wind out of their sails. Middleton then made a decisive move into the transfer market, signing Danny Shea [pictured] from West Ham United for £2,000, breaking the British transfer record in the process. The Cockney was a wizard of the dribble, the most effective of goal scorers and Joe Hodkinson, an outstanding left winger was also purchased, this time from Glossop for £1,000, Both went on to represent England but alas they arrived too late in the campaign.

But if there was guarded satisfaction at Ewood Park, it was carnival time at Turf Moor. The locals became intoxicated on a surfeit of goals. Bert Freeman was the leading scorer in English football and the club's eighty-eight goals was also the highest in the land. The 2nd Division title would have been nice but the fans did not complain too much. The second-place finish propelled them into Division 1 for the first time in thirteen seasons. Billy Watson was established at left-half and manager Haworth bought the Scottish right-half George Halley from Bradford Park Avenue late in the term, shoring up the defence and keeping them in the race. Burnley had professionally played out the rest of the season and big-time football was back on the agenda. The league games had prompted a state of euphoria around Turf Moor, but cup fever was also in the air.

The Burnley Division 2 Promoted squad (finished 2nd) in 1912-13 (started over 17 games, max 38) was; Jerry Dawson, Tom Bamford, David Taylor, Jimmy Bellamy, Tommy Boyle, Billy Watson, Eddie Mosscrop, Dick Lindley, Bert Freeman, Teddy Hodgson, Billy Husband, Billy McLaren.

The derby FA Cup game

Both of the East Lancashire sides won through to Round 4, (the last eight in those days). The Clarets had seen off Leeds City, Gainsborough Trinity and Middlesbrough, the Rovers knocking out Northampton Town, Barnsley and Reading. Suddenly it happened!! The first name out of the hat for the 4th Round draw was Blackburn Rovers, followed immediately by Burnley. It was to be the first meeting of the rivals since New Year's Day 1900 and the first ever FA Cup pairing. For those desperate for a derby battle, the tie was a saviour. Tom Boyle's goal, which giave Burnley the victory at Blackburn was described in the Leeds Mercury on Monday March 10th, 1913, as follows:

> Burnley accomplished a big performance by beating Blackburn Rovers at Ewood Park by a goal to nil and delighted the twenty thousand enthusiasts who accompanied the team. The Blackburn goal had a very narrow escape in the first fifteen minutes when Husband sent in a splendid centre and Bradshaw cleared when Cowell was beaten. Later on the Blackburn forwards in their turn set up promising attacks, and good shots were sent in by both Latheron and Aitkenhead, Dawson cleverly clearing on both occasions. The game was fought out at a great pace... At the end of half an hour, however, Burnley gained what proved to be the only goal of the match, Boyle heading in from a corner kick... Shea looked like having a chance of scoring, when he was most effectively tackled by Bamford. A little later Shea sent in a fine shot, which Dawson saved... once Freeman got between the Rovers backs and Robinson only saved the situation by running yards out of his goal to rob the Burnley forward of the ball.

It had to have been the standout moment in the last thirteen years for the "Turfites", a win not only against one of the top five clubs in the land, but against the enemy. This win came in the middle of a fourteen game run by the Ewood Park side which had seen just one other defeat. The Rovers had a full strength eleven on the pitch; they were a formidable goal scoring machine so what a night they must have had in the local drinking hostelries in the Burnley area. Victory in the last eight meant a first semi-final appearance. Unfortunately, it was the mighty Sunderland that would provide the opposition at Bramall Lane. The Burnley eleven put up the fight of their lives, drawing the first encounter 0-0 in dreadful conditions, before going down 3-2 in the replay at St Andrews, the home of Birmingham.

Date	Round	Home Side	Away Side	Score	Scorers
08 03 1913	6	Blackburn Rovers	**Burnley**	0-1	T Boyle.

The football fans in East Lancashire could not wait for the commencement of the next campaign. The Rovers had outstanding players, Burnley were back

Burnley fans display a banner taunting Rovers manager Bob Middleton

Rovers take to the field before the derby FA Cup clash in 1913

in the top flight and to add the final layer of icing to the cake, there would be a resumption of the derby. Appetites were whetted, what a season it would be.

1913-14

Team	Pos	Played	Won	Drawn	Lost	GF	GA	Pts
Blackburn Rovers	1	38	20	11	7	78	42	51
Burnley	12	38	12	12	14	61	53	36

Blackburn Rovers		Burnley	
Most Appearances	Arthur Cowell 38	Most Appearances	Tommy Bamford 38
Most Goals	Danny Shea 27	Most Goals	Bert Freeman 16

Prior to this season, there had never been an opportunity for both sets of supporters to rejoice and there has been no occasion since, so 1913-14 was a unique season in the annals of the two East Lancashire clubs. And the return of the league derbies certainly added to the thrills and excitement on offer. It was a campaign that had everything. Winning the Football League was RB Middleton's main aim. Ewood Park, now providing extra cover for 12,000 on the River Darwen side of the ground, could now accommodate over 50,000 spectators. They were unbeaten for the first ten matches and with Bob Crompton; the Bobby Moore of his day, peerless at the back, the defence was strong throughout. But it was the scintillating form of Danny Shea that made the difference. He must have been "Messiesque" in the way he dribbled past defenders and stuck the ball into the net on twenty-seven occasions. The ever reliable Latheron contributed thirteen more, but one of the mainstays of the two championship wins was local boy Albert Walmsley. He often operated just below the radar but he made 272 appearances for the club at right half, in spite of losing four vital years because of the war. As April approached, the title was secured, Aston Villa limping in second some seven points behind. It was their second title in three years and they were once again the best in the land. The greatest ever Rovers' side? In terms of league football, definitely yes, the margin of victory being greater than in 1912 and 1995. Whether the 1886 side which romped to a third consecutive FA Cup triumph was better, it is so difficult to say. League tables make comparisons easy, cup triumphs less so, but a seven point winning margin wins the argument for me.

There have of course been more emphatic statements of superiority at the very top of the English football pyramid with Huddersfield Town (1924-26), Arsenal (1933-35), Liverpool (1982-84) and Manchester United twice (1999-2001 and 2007-09) having completed hat-tricks of Tier 1 titles, but the performance of the Ewood Park club in winning the supreme title twice in three years puts this particular eleven in a category just behind the above elite. It was somewhat appropriate that probably the Rovers' greatest ever season also saw the end of the international career of their greatest ever player. Bob Crompton played for England forty-one times. It is still the club record and was the English record until Billy Wright overtook it in 1952.

Crompton was thirty-five years of age when he played his final game, but if the war had not intervened, he could possibly have achieved even more. In those days, the international programme usually consisted of just three matches against Ireland, Scotland and Wales with the occasional summer tour to Eastern Europe. With the depth of qualifying games and tournaments in the modern game, it has been assessed that Crompton would have topped 120 caps had he played in more recent times. He also captained his country on twenty-two occasions, another record until the Wolverhampton Wanderers legend came along.

The Blackburn Rovers Division One Title winning squad 1913-14 (played over 16 games, max 38) was; Alf Robinson, Bob Crompton, Arthur Cowell, Albert Walmsley, Percy Smith, Billy Bradshaw, Jock Simpson, Eddie Latheron, Wattie Aitkenhead, Danny Shea, Joe Hodkinson, George Chapman.

Burnley's return to the highest level of English football was satisfactory in terms of their League performance. The Clarets finished twelfth, six points above the relegation spots. Burnley was not short of internationals either. Bert Freeman, Tommy Boyle, Ernie Mosscrop (bought the previous season from Southport) and Billy Watson all gained English recognition. Later in his long and illustrious career, goalkeeper Jerry Dawson would be capped by England. Bert Freeman was inevitably the leading scorer and defensively they were relatively sound.

The derby games

There were the derby matches of course with Blackburn Rovers undoubtedly the favourite. This was only the third game of the season, but two hefty home wins, 3-0 v Newcastle United and 6-2 against Liverpool, had sent alarm bells ringing across the country. This was a team hell-bent on regaining their crown. Shea had smashed in a four timer against the Reds and Latheron had notched three over the two games. The derby match was away from home and the fact that it was a derby with all of its unpredictability had to be factored in, but the 36,000 who packed their way into Turf Moor arrived more in hope than expectation. It was a tight encounter and the crowd was roused to fever-pitch when Freeman scored after four minutes.

Shea and Latheron failed to make the score sheet, but this was an eleven that could score from anywhere and it ultimately told. Centre-half Percy Smith a wonderful servant at Ewood Park through those glory years, having been signed from Preston North End in 1910, was on the mark just prior to the interval and centre forward George Chapman hit the target early in the second half to give the Blue and Whites a 2-1 win. The Clarets had been valiant in defeat, perhaps surprising a number of impartial observers and they upped their game even more on New Year's Day. Shea had scored seven in his last three starts, Aitkenhead three and apart from an injured Crompton, they were at full strength.

A crowd of 48,000 had crammed themselves into Ewood Park, a ground record at the time, hoping for yet more goals, but it was a strangely quiet game. Burnley had drawn their previous two matches, Sunderland and West Bromwich Albion being two of the country's foremost outfits, conceding just one goal. They were at full strength also and although the dull encounter may have sobered up many of the fans, they were left disappointed. The Clarets had managed to keep the reins on the Rovers' forward line and prevent them from scoring, but in fairness, the Rovers' defence was equally adept at controlling Freeman and Hodgson, a goalless stalemate ensuing. The Ewood side still topped the league and Burnley, in their first season back in the big time, held on to eighth place, so both sets of fans were ultimately content with the afternoon's proceedings.

08 09 1913	Burnley	Blackburn Rovers	1-2	**B Freeman,** P Smith, G Chapman.
01 01 1914	Blackburn Rovers	Burnley	0-0	

The FA Cup sent pulses racing after Sunderland were beaten 2-1 at Turf Moor following a goalless draw at Roker Park and the semi-final versus Sheffield United resulted in another goalless stalemate. After a titanic struggle in the replay, a place in the final was assured courtesy of another trademark Tommy Boyle header.

The town went down to South London in their droves to contest the Crystal Palace final with Liverpool and King George V himself was also making his cup final debut. It was not the most stirring of matches but Bert Freeman did what he did best; sticking the ball in the net and His Majesty presented the trophy to Burnley skipper Tommy Boyle. The winning goal was typical Burnley of the day. Billy Nesbitt knocked over a cross, Teddy Hodgson nodded it down and like all great strikers, Freeman was first to the ball, smashing it into the net. There was great rejoicing in the town as the news of the 1-0 victory filtered through.

Burnley had at last won a national trophy, thirty-two years after being formed and the crowds could not care less that the enemy down the road was Champion of the League. The only sad aspect of this memorable victory was the absence of Jerry Dawson between the sticks. Having strained his groin in the semi-final, Ronnie Sewell deputised in the replay. It was left to Dawson himself to declare himself fit or otherwise, but he made the sensible decision to sit it out and Sewell was the lucky beneficiary of an FA Cup winner's medal.

The double, (Division 1 and the FA Cup) was briefly on the cards at Ewood Park after an Aitkenhead hat-trick derailed Middlesbrough in Round 1 and a Shea double against Bury saw them safely into the last sixteen. Manchester City were a middle of the road Division 1 side at this time, but the Rovers failed to come through their third successive home tie, 41,250 watching them go down to the Sky Blues by a 2-1 margin.

The Burnley 1914 FA Cup Winning side that beat Liverpool 1-0 was; Ronnie Sewell, Tom Bamford, David Taylor, George Halley, Tommy Boyle, Billy Watson, Billy Nesbitt, Dick Lindley, Bert Freeman, Teddy Hodgson, Eddie Mosscrop.

It had been the most successful season in East Lancashire football history, both major trophies finding their way to the area. What no-one knew at the time was that over 100 years on, it would still be the ultimate year in the history of football in East Lancashire.

1914-15

Team	Pos	Played	Won	Drawn	Lost	GF	GA	Pts
Blackburn Rovers	3	38	18	7	13	83	61	43
Burnley	4	38	18	7	13	61	47	43

Blackburn Rovers		Burnley	
Most Appearances	Joe Hodkinson 38	Most Appearances	Tom Bamford 38
Most Goals	Percy Dawson 20	Most Goals	Teddy Hodgson 19

Britain declared war on Germany on August 4th and in spite of half a million young British men joining the forces in the first five weeks, the Football League pressed on with its plans to kick off the new 1914-15 season. Surprisingly, the season did start and it actually ran its full course, although there was criticism from many sources, some within the game itself. In normal circumstances, it would have been remembered as a humdinger of a campaign locally with two titanic battles between reigning league and cup winners, but in actual fact, it was understandably low key. Blackburn Rovers once more went goal crazy, the league's top scorers whereas Burnley were water-tight defensively more often than not. They both finished on forty-three points with the Rovers just holding on for third place against an unbeaten nine game final sprint from the Clarets. The margin of "victory" for the Ewood Park side was a superior goal average of a mere 0.07 of a goal. Both sides included a marksman who had an exceptional season. Percy Dawson, bought for a club record fee from Heart of Midlothian, scored twenty goals, one more than Teddy Hodgson from the rival camp. John Haworth's side had shown that they were a side capable of competing with the best and once the dreadful war was over, they made a point of proving it.

The derby games

Blackburn Rovers had not been short of goals as they cantered away with the league title the previous campaign, but looking ever forward as all well managed clubs do, they brought in Dawson for a fee of £2,500 to lead the attack. He had already hit the net on seven occasions prior to the first derby where he set a record which still stands. These two games were played out against the backdrop of the Great War. It was called the "phony war" at this stage, the horrific and tear-jerking incidents which wiped out whole regiments were still to begin. But everyone knew someone who had joined up and in the greater sphere of things, football meant very little.

Nonetheless, the prospect of a victory over the enemy up the road would momentarily erase the worry and stress for families fearing for the fate of loved ones, possibly why the government had been keen to see the Football League programme continue. But as true as these sentiments may have been, the reality was that the masses had more to worry about than the derby matches, a fact underlined by the much smaller crowds which attended; 21,000 at Ewood and more tellingly, as the war began to have more and more impact, 14,000 at the "Turf". Prior to the late November clash at Ewood Park, the home side was well in the hunt for further glory whilst the Clarets were making steady, if unspectacular progress in the middle of the pack. Neutrals expected a home victory, but no-one would have predicted the final score line. The Manchester Courier and Lancashire Advertiser reported on November 30th,1914:

> The Derby match at Ewood park provided one of the most sensational results of the day. One never imagined, writes "Onlooker" that the league Champions would beat the Cup holders by six clear goals, but so convincing was the display of the Rovers that it would not have surprised even the Burnley supporters had they secured victory by a larger margin. The injury to Boyle, which necessitated a re-arranged team, undoubtedly upset the calculations of Burnley, but... the understanding which existed amongst the Rovers' players was remarkable, although there was a total absence of what might be termed stereotypical methods... (Percy Dawson) In addition to obtaining four goals, he never neglected his colleagues, and his speed served him to a good advantage... Crompton was again in fine form and he completely mastered Mosscrop... Jerry Dawson was in no

> way to blame for the points scored against him... The (Burnley) halves gave a feeble display... Throughout the ninety minutes play they were unable to hold the Rovers' quintette. and they staunchly saw time out to record a memorable victory which catapulted them up the table; revenge tasting oh so sweet.

Dawson's four-timer is still a record for East Lancs derby games. Revenge must have been the motivating factor when the clubs next clashed at Turf Moor on Easter Saturday. In spite of being down in thirteenth place, the Clarets had beaten Everton, champs in waiting 2-0 on Good Friday at Goodison Park, with goals from Hodgson and the emerging young starlet, Bob Kelly. The Blackburn side had been neck and neck with the Toffees at the top of the table but a defeat at Aston Villa the day before may have caused the jitters to emerge. Bert Freeman gave Howarth's side the lead on the half hour mark but Latheron replied early in the second period. Hodgson, not to be out-done by his strike partner, put the "Turfites" in front once more and Mosscrop's seventieth minute strike seemed to have settled the game. But their rivals still had unfinished business and when Crompton smashed in a late penalty, it was Burnley's turn to encounter the jitters. In military terms, defensive kingpin Tommy Boyle led from the front and they staunchly saw time out to record a memorable victory which catapulted them up the table; revenge tasting oh so sweet.

28 11 1914	Blackburn Rovers	Burnley	6-0	P Dawson 4, o.g, E Latheron
03 04 1915	**Burnley**	Blackburn Rovers	3-2	**B Freeman, T Hodgson, E Mosscrop** E Latheron, R Crompton

Burnley had started well in pursuit of retaining the FA Cup, but a 2-1 home defeat by Bolton Wanderers brought them up short. Meanwhile the Rovers disappointed, shockingly losing 1-0 away to Southern League Swansea Town.

1915-19

Football during the war to end all wars.

And so, all serious football came to an end. Three notable careers would no longer proceed when football resumed. At Ewood Park, Wattie Aitkenhead who had scored seventy-five goals in 210 appearances, retired from football, but Edwin Latheron who had made 257 appearances, scoring ninety-four goals and making stacks of assists, was killed at Passchendaele, one of the bloodiest battles in history. It was also the last hurrah for the Claret's popular striker Teddy Hodgson. He survived the war and then at the start of 1919, he was posted to Turkey as part of a clean-up operation. There he contracted a serious kidney ailment and was transferred back home but to no avail, dying in hospital at the start

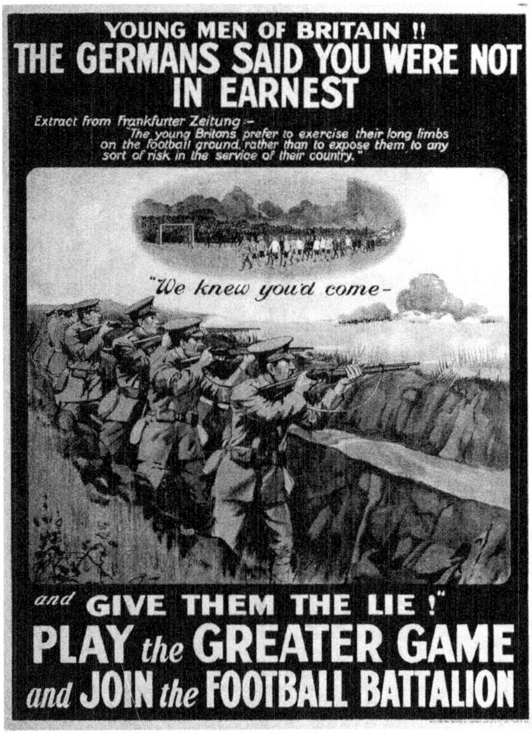

of the first post-war season. From the start of the 1915 summer, the war effort was the only thing that mattered and many, many players joined up. There is documentation to prove that well over two hundred professional footballers lost their lives in action. How many of the 950,000 soldiers and non-military personnel that died during the conflict were football fans is impossible to calculate but the figure must have been huge. Apart from Hodgson, several other ex-Burnley players also died in the Great War. These included goalkeeper Billy Green, defender George King and centre forward Wilf Toman. Many others fought, but even if they returned fully fit, they had lost what would probably have been their most productive years. It was 1919 before the competitions resumed and fans would have to become accustomed to a whole new generation of players turning out in the colours of their favourite team. There were wartime Regional Football Leagues of sorts, with players appearing for the team nearest to where they were stationed. There are statistics to show where clubs finished each season, the results of the games and who played where, but none of these are included in the official records.

1919-20

Team	Pos	Played	Won	Drawn	Lost	GF	GA	Pts
Burnley	2	42	21	9	12	65	59	51
Blackburn Rovers	20	42	13	11	18	64	77	37

Blackburn Rovers		Burnley	
Most Appearances	Ernie Hawksworth 41	Most Appearances	Len Smelt 42
Most Goals	Ernie Hawksworth 17	Most Goals	Bert Freeman 12

It was a new era, the guns had fallen silent, the "war to end all wars" was over and the Football League was back in business some nine and a half

months after the armistice was signed. The footballing authorities had plenty of time before the start of the 1919-20 fixtures to make any improvements, the principal one being to extend both Divisions to 22 clubs. Leading the league's chasing pack were Burnley who finished second, albeit nine points behind the leader. It was the Clarets' highest ever finish and Bert Freeman returned for a final curtain call, topping the scoring list with twelve to his name.

Len Smelt was signed from Gainsborough Trinity to play at right back and he went on to complete 229 appearances for the club. In terms of immediate impact, an even better buy proved to be that of Joe Anderson from Clydebank. With Bob Kelly now joining Watson [pictured] in the England side, there was no doubt that this Turf Moor side was on the verge of something special. Billy Watson, who remained at the club for seventeen years, became club captain and represented England on three occasions. He amassed a total of 346 league appearances, currently standing in tenth place in the all-time list. Burnley occupied second spot for a total of twenty-two weeks. The season was neither a Turf Moor goal festival nor a total defensive lockdown, but it was the Clarets' best ever finish to a campaign, hopefully a portent of what was to come. The 5-0 victory over Everton was all about Joe Anderson, a hat-trick hero in just his sixth game in Claret and Blue.

In contrast, Blackburn Rovers were a complete shambles. Bob Crompton played his final season, taking his league appearances to 530, but at the age of 40 years and 150 days when he made his last appearance against Bradford Park Avenue, his best days were behind him. Crompton and Arthur Cowell had been first choice full backs from 1905. Cowell gained just one England cap but was injured pre-season and never played again. Bizarrely in 280 first team appearances, he never scored a goal. The concept of attacking full backs had not been dreamed up at that time. The relegation tussle was played out until the very last day of the season. With four games to play, the Rovers were hot favourites for their first ever "drop", but Ernie Hawksworth, a signing from Rochdale, scored five times in the last four matches, steering them to safety. The manager gave a start to a club record of thirty-nine players and it could be claimed that he did not know his best team. But so poor were the players at his disposal that it could equally be argued that he simply did not have a best team. If there was heartache for the Blue and Whites on the field, there was equally bad news from the Boardroom as Laurence Cotton was elected to the position of Mayor of Blackburn, so he resigned as chairman of the club.

The derby games

With the quality levels between Burnley and Blackburn Rovers being poles apart, it was no surprise that the Clarets accomplished their second derby double. The matches were played on consecutive Saturdays in September and the Ewood Park encounter played in front of 20,000 spectators, was extremely close. Billy Taylor, deputising for Halley who still had not been demobbed, put the away side in front, but the Rovers hit back and took the lead through Dawson and a Levy Thorpe own goal. Boyle stroked home an equalising penalty as half time beckoned and the second half was a dog fight as each side tried to assert their authority. But it was Mosscrop who sent the Burnley fans home happy with a late winner. The following week with a similar gate, it was eventually easier for the home side at Turf Moor, but not before Hawksworth had given the visitors the lead. Kelly's equaliser on the stroke of half time settled the nerves and goals from Freeman and Nesbitt pushed the Blue and Whites closer to the abyss and the "Turfites into second place. These victories were met with glee on the terraces, confirming that Burnley now ruled the roost in East Lancashire football.

13 09 1919	Blackburn Rovers	**Burnley**	2-3	P Dawson, o.g. W Taylor, T Boyle, E Mosscrop.
20 09 1919	**Burnley**	Blackburn Rovers	3-1	R Kelly, B Freeman, W Nesbitt. E Hawksworth.

Blackburn Rovers could only draw 2-2 with Division 2 side Wolverhampton Wanderers in Round 1 of the FA Cup and lost 1-0 in the replay at Molyneux. Burnley made hard work of their initial tie, drawing 0-0 with Thornycrofts, a works team from the Southampton area in a game played at Fratton Park, the home of Portsmouth FC. Normal service was resumed three days later when a hat-trick from Lindsay downed the non-leaguers 5-0. Sunderland in Round 2 was a tough fixture but home advantage should have given the Clarets the edge, but the Roker Park side held them to a 1-1 draw before winning convincingly 2-0 in the replay back in the north-east.

1920-21

Team	Pos	Played	Won	Drawn	Lost	GF	GA	Pts
Burnley	1	42	23	13	6	79	36	59
Blackburn Rovers	11	42	13	15	14	57	59	41

Blackburn Rovers		Burnley	
Most Appearances	Levy Thorpe 42	Most Appearances	Billy Watson 42
Most Goals	Percy Dawson 17	Most Goals	Joe Anderson 25

The good news from the Football League was the formation of a Third Division for the 1920-21 season. It contained only Southern clubs, thus breaking down the barrier erected by the London FA over thirty years before. Not that the loyal supporters of Burnley FC cared. The side has to be the greatest ever in the history of the club. They were scintillating at Turf Moor, knocking seven past Oldham Athletic and Aston Villa. On Christmas Day, it was as though Santa himself was at the ground, his present being a whopping 6-0 victory over Sheffield United. Bob Kelly, against the Latics and Joe Anderson against the Blades, hit four timers, with the Scot notching five against the Villa.

Anderson was a hero of the Turf Moor faithful. He had been bought to replace Bert Freeman and he quickly stepped into the master's shoes, scoring thirty-one league goals. Freeman left behind a legacy of 103 Claret league goals including a record thirty-two in a season.

When the Clarets gained a point at Everton, they had won the title with three games to spare; the final winning margin being five points clear of Manchester City. The Turf Moor side had embarked on a magical run of thirty matches without defeat. This record stood for over 80 years into the twenty-first century before the "Invincible" Arsenal side stayed unbeaten for a full season in 2003-04. The Clarets thus became the twelfth different champion and the tenth to have collected both trophies.

The Burnley Title winning side 1920-21 (started over 16 games, max 42) was: Jerry Dawson, Len Smelt, Cliff Jones, George Halley, Tommy Boyle, Billy Watson, Walter Weaver, Bob Kelly, Joe Anderson, Benny Cross, Billy Nesbitt.

The supporters of Blackburn Rovers had to grin and bear it. The season was not disastrous, a much-improved eleventh place finish. Percy Dawson continued his goal scoring form to complement Hawksworth. Two players from Ewood Park represented Ireland this season, the right winger Pat Robinson and David Rollo filling the right back berth. There was another indicator of the supremacy of the Turf Moor club. Two of their cast offs had signed for the Rovers, goalkeeper Ronnie Sewell and centre half Levy Thorpe. Neither were poor players, in fact Sewell proved to be a most competent keeper, but the signings came with a subliminal message for the Blackburn fans. "We don't want them but they may be good enough for you." What an insult!! Both players actually made quite an impression. Between them, Sewell and Thorpe missed just one league game and Scottish centre-half Frank Reilly, signed from Falkirk part-way through the previous season, was a steadying figure at centre-half. But where were the international class players, the successors to those medal-winning pre-Great War icons? Hodkinson missed just three games, but his last international call up was two years before as his career slowly declined.

The derby games

Mid-January was the scheduled date for the first derby game of the season with the return one week later. The following report is taken from Yorkshire Post and Leeds Intelligencer on January 17th, 1921.

> Burnley in Form Against Blackburn Rovers: At Burnley with over 40,000 spectators. With their usual team in the field, Burnley easily overcame their neighbours from Blackburn, and thus materially strengthened their position at the head of the League chart. Burnley has the better of the early exchanges, and in twenty minutes, Cross opened the scoring for Burnley. The Rovers were dangerous occasionally, and Sandham equalised, but Kelly placed Burnley ahead again. Interval. Burnley 2 goals-Rovers 1 goal. The Rovers re-opened the game with pressure, and Burnley responded, play being keen and exciting, with Burnley the more dangerous. Cross placed Burnley further ahead, and Boyle followed with another goal from a magnificent long shot. Burnley had the better of play to the end.

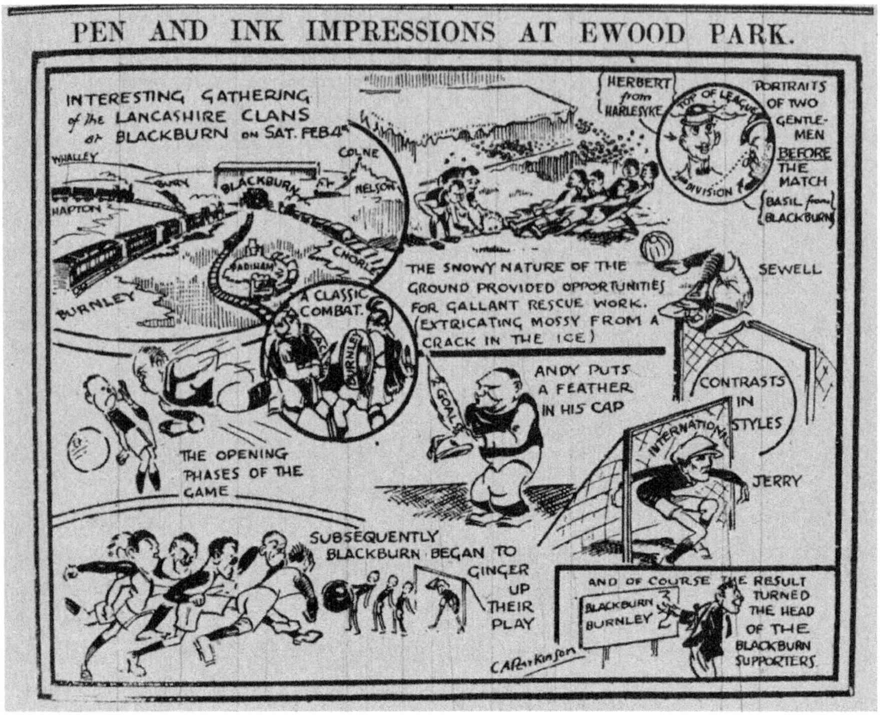

Burnley attack the Rovers goal at Ewood Park in February 1922

The Ewood Park fixture saw a similar score line. Kelly opened the scoring, and although Joe Hodkinson briefly raised the hopes of the 43,000 crowd with a thirty-eighth minute equaliser, Mosscrop was on target before the interval and Anderson's late effort made it a comfortable 3-1 win. For the second year running, Burnley had completed a derby double and having gone to the top of the table in November, these victories further convinced the locals that the title was on its way to their town. With an aggregate of 7-2 in the Clarets' favour, it was probably the most one-sided set of results since Jack Southworth and co dominated in the early years of league football. The Blackburn side were in the middle of a run of ten matches without a win, and although still well clear of the drop zone, there was certainly concern in the town about the direction of travel of the Blue and Whites. Putting a more positive spin on it however, the Clarets had completed the double over a number of sides, including Tottenham Hotspur and Newcastle United, both top six finishers. So perhaps this derby double defeat was not so much a disaster as had been first thought.

15 01 1921	**Burnley**	Blackburn Rovers	4-1	B Cross 2, R Kelly, T Boyle. W Sandham,
22 01 1921	Blackburn Rovers	**Burnley**	1-3	J Hodkinson. E Mosscrop, R Kelly, J Anderson.

Burnley travelled to Second Division Leicester City and won 7-3 in Round 1 of the FA Cup, Anderson scoring four. The Scot helped himself to a double in Round 2 as Queens Park Rangers were beaten 4-2 at Turf Moor but unfortunately he was injured when they crashed out in Round 3 at Hull City, their 3-0 defeat being the shock of the day. The mood at Ewood Park was sombre. It was not helped when they again failed to win an FA Cup game, drawing 1-1 at Ewood against Fulham from Division 2 and losing 1-0 in the replay in London. Following the war, the crowds had returned to football with so much enthusiasm and a staggering 45,000 arrived by tram to watch the Fulham game, but all must have journeyed home disappointed.

1921-22

Team	Pos	Played	Won	Drawn	Lost	GF	GA	Pts
Burnley	3	42	22	5	15	72	54	49
Blackburn Rovers	15	42	13	12	17	54	57	38

Blackburn Rovers		Burnley	
Most Appearances	Ronnie Sewell 41	Most Appearances	Len Smelt 41
Most Goals	Percy Dawson 12	Most Goals	Joe Anderson 20

The furore emanating from the north of the country was so loud that the "powers that were" instituted another Third Division, this one having the "North" appellation. Burnley made a lightning start to the thirtieth running of the Football League. Scoring goals was no problem and Joe Anderson was once more the leading scorer. Jerry Dawson was at last capped by England and a fellow international was his club mate Bob Kelly who, with eleven caps whilst at the club, is still Burnley's highest capped English player. They topped the league into December and even into the new year, Burnley and Liverpool were neck and neck. But where was their neighbour when they required a favour?

The two derby defeats dropped the Clarets off the Podium and although four consecutive wins brought them straight back, their title hopes had taken a tumble. To add tragedy to insult, their inspirational captain Tommy Boyle was carried off in early February and was on the treatment table for the rest of the season. Even at thirty-four he was still a formidable defender and Burnley simply had no replacement. They battled hard to the end of the season but a third-place finish was such an anti-climax. Nonetheless, four top four topflight finishes in four successive seasons was most commendable, one only the very best teams achieve.

In spite of the two derby victories, Blackburn Rovers' performance was generally poor. There was little fear from relegation as they finished six points from the drop zone in fifteenth place, but the team produced little else to shout about. Ronnie Sewell, once a regular in the reserves at Turf Moor, played in all but one of the Rovers' games. Percy Dawson was still banging in the goals. His three in two games ensured another double, albeit against a woefully weak Manchester United side. He was helped once again by the lightning left wing pace and measured crosses from the veteran Joe Hodkinson and the Scottish forward pairing of Jock McKay and Johnny McIntyre had arrived from Celtic and The Wednesday respectively. They would play their part going forward over the next few years. Robert (RB) Middleton was finally dismissed as manager mid-season. He had guided them to two Division 1 trophies in his nineteen-year tenancy at the club, but the directors felt it was time to change. He was replaced by Jack Carr. He was an ex-Newcastle United and England full-back and had been trainer for the North East side for 10 years.

The derby games

If anyone wanted a pointer as to how the fans expected the derby games to pan out, one needed only to look at the attendances. At a time when the gates at football matches were continuing to soar, only twenty thousand of mainly Blue and White fans bothered to turn up at Ewood Park. Over twice that number surged into Turf Moor and from a neutral's point of view, it looked like a certain derby double. And it was, but not the way the fans and pundits expected. For the first thirty-five minutes of the game in Blackburn, the players followed the script. Anderson had already netted twice for the Clarets and the Rovers had still to wake up. But wake up they did and Norman Rodgers, whose selection was as inconsistent as his performances but who often scored vital goals when given the shirt, hit the target twice. Dawson, of course, was never far from the action. He scored a third and Burnley had dropped from second to third. Exactly a week later they were fifth. No-one expected lightning to strike twice, but in retrospect, John Haworth's side had been together for years and the shelf life of several was coming to a close. The legendary half back line of Watson, Boyle and Halley would play their last game together in this second derby and for those two outstanding wingers Mosscrop and Nesbitt, this was to be their final full season. They were still a much more superior eleven than their neighbour's and the game was once more ever so close, but Dawson's goal gave the visitors a half time lead. Anderson's equaliser looked like saving the day, but Rodgers, as unpredictable as ever, nudged the Rovers in front with twenty to play. Burnley had dominated large chunks of the game, but they had nothing to show for their efforts and the Blackburn team and supporters floated home as on a cloud; two points and a derby double in their pockets.

04 02 1922	Blackburn Rovers	Burnley	3-2	N Rodgers 2, P Dawson. J Anderson 2.
11 02 1922	Burnley	Blackburn Rovers	1-2	J Anderson. P Dawson, N Rodgers.

Huddersfield Town defeated Burnley and Blackburn Rovers en route to the last ever FA Cup Final at Stamford Bridge, prior to the opening of Wembley Stadium, in Round 1 and Round 3 respectively. The Rovers had reached this stage with wins over Southport and Swindon Town and held Huddersfield to a 1-1 draw at home before capitulating to a 5-0 defeat in Yorkshire.

There's a Wembley win... but both clubs remain side by side in Division 1. 1922 – 1930.

Now, when they've all had their quarrels and parted
We'll be the same as we started
Just traveling along
Singing a song
Side by side..
Harry M Woods

Throughout this period, both East Lancashire clubs retained their places in Division 1. It was difficult at times because the competition was fierce from the big city clubs but ironically, Huddersfield Town (obviously not from a city) dominated the league, being champions for three successive seasons.

But the London clubs, particularly Arsenal, were beginning to be a force and after all, this was where the money was. But both small town sides could hold their heads high, compete with the giants and from time to time, make their presence felt. The Harry Woods song at the head of this page was a popular ditty at the time and the verse listed is the final one. Perhaps appropriately in a 1920s football context, the first line starts with.... "We ain't got a barrel of money." As a result, in spite of their rivalry, our two clubs could metaphorically link arms, glance at the league table and feel proud that side by side, they were in the same hallowed company. Whether the fans of the clubs ever did this is debatable. I suspect they were more concerned about "getting one over" on the lot down the road.

1922-23

Team	Pos	Played	Won	Drawn	Lost	GF	GA	Pts
Blackburn Rovers	14	42	14	12	16	47	62	40
Burnley	15	42	16	6	20	58	59	38

Blackburn Rovers		Burnley	
Most Appearances	Jimmy McKinnell 41	Most Appearances	Len Smelt, Benny Cross 42
Most Goals	Jock McKay 12	Most Goals	Bob Kelly 17

P. DAWSON

In the lower reaches of the League table of the 1922-23 season, there was a real scrap going on between Blackburn Rovers and Burnley. Ultimately the Blackburn club won this particular battle, finishing fourteenth, one place above their rivals. Any Rovers' fan desperately trying to find something else to shout about could point to an improvement of one league place, but in all honesty, this was the fourth successive indifferent season since the war. They did manage to score five at Ewood Park against Everton when the Scot, Johnny McIntyre helped himself to four goals. There have been greater goal scoring feats, but McIntyre's goals all came in a five-minute period. The club finally said good-bye to a great servant. Joe Hodkinson was capped by England either side of the conflict but he still managed to accrue 228 appearances in Blackburn. This was the final season for Percy Dawson [pictured], signed in 1914. He then missed four years at what should have been the prime of his life, but still managed to score 71 league goals in 140 league games, a scoring rate of plus 50%, the magic figure which is the yardstick by which all great goal scorers are measured.

The expectancy level had been low at Ewood Park of course but it had been much higher at Turf Moor, so a slump down to fifteenth took some stomaching. The Clarets had started like an express train and one of the early successes was when they smashed Nottingham Forest 8-2 at home. Benny Cross, who was an ever present, scored a hat-trick but from then on in, there was little to please the fans. So why did the form which had lit up the Division suddenly flicker and die? All great careers have to come to an end sometime; this time it happened to Tommy Boyle and George Halley. The club signed Irish international William Emerson from Glentoran to replace Halley and John Haworth spotted the danger signs before the end of the season and signed a centre forward from Chesterfield. The fans were crying out for the next Bert Freeman and a successor to Anderson who had suddenly lost his goal touch and returned to Clydebank. The Scot had 64 league goals in 121 appearances, even better than fellow Scot Dawson down the road. Would George Beel be the man to replace him? Fortunately Jerry Dawson was still going strong, fifteen years since his debut and with more still in the tank. Unfortunately he missed the last eleven games through injury and the loss of such an experienced goal-keeper would have also contributed to the disappointing end to the season.

The derby games

If you looked at the derby games after the season ended and studied the league table, you would not say that the derby games "went with form" this campaign because neither side had shown a great deal of form. This was actually not true at the time of the clashes, because Burnley were positioned in the top five when both these games were played, incongruously a week apart, some strange whim of the Football League during this immediate post-Great War period. The Rovers had not won in their last four games, so a home win was expected at Turf Moor.

It had been nine seasons since the Blue and Whites last won the title and the Claret and Blues had won the FA Cup but there were still several players around from that memorable year. Jerry Dawson, David Taylor, Billy Watson and Eddie Mosscrop started for the home side and still plying their trade at Ewood Park were Hodkinson and Dawson. The difference between the sides in the opening game was Bob Kelly. The consummate inside forward, along with McIlroy, the greatest play maker/goal scorer ever to don a Burnley shirt, was recognised as one of the top stars of his day and the Rovers' defence could not handle him. He knocked in an early penalty but the visitors hit back with a goal from the in-form McIntyre.

Cross regained the lead for the Clarets before half-time before Kelly finished what he started, putting the game out of reach with an eightieth minute strike. When the sides met at Ewood Park a week later, Dawson had sufficiently recovered from injury to lead the Rovers' line and he once more did not disappoint. He opened the scoring in the first half and right winger Dickie Bond extended that lead before Anderson's late strike raised the tempo of the last ten minutes without altering the result. Thus the derby games actually ended all square for the first time since war broke out.

21 10 1922	**Burnley**	Blackburn Rovers	3-1	R Kelly 2, B Cross. J McIntyre.
28 10 1922	Blackburn Rovers	Burnley	2-1	P Dawson, R Bond. J Anderson.

Burnley failed to clear the first hurdle in the FA Cup, losing to a very strong Sunderland side at Roker Park. The inconsistent Blackburn Rovers eleven had knocked Aston Villa out of the FA Cup, but then lost a replay in ignominious fashion to South Shields from the insignificant end of Division 2.

1923-24

Team	Pos	Played	Won	Drawn	Lost	GF	GA	Pts
Blackburn Rovers	8	42	17	11	14	54	50	45
Burnley	17	42	12	12	18	55	60	36

Blackburn Rovers		Burnley	
Most Appearances	Tom Wylie, Ted Harper 42	Most Appearances	Jack Hill, Benny Cross 39
Most Goals	Ted Harper 18	Most Goals	George Beel 19

Blackburn Rovers certainly showed some improvement in the 1923-24 season, even though the average attendance was slightly lower. Ronnie Sewell, the ex-Burnley veteran was able to show what a fine keeper he was, earning an England cap v Wales at the age of 34. Also capped against Wales, but this time for Scotland, was inside forward Jock McKay. An eighth-place finish was certainly acceptable to Jack Carr, their first top ten placing since the resumption of the game in 1919 and the Ewood crowd had a new scoring hero. Ted Harper, signed from non-league Kent club Sheppey United, knocked in 18 goals. He played in every game throughout the season and his was the best return at Ewood Park since Percy Dawson's 20 in 1914-15, being backed up in the goal scoring department by McIntyre and McKay. The full back positions were automatic choices, Irishman David Rollo playing on the right side and Tom Wylie, signed from Queen of the South, playing on the left. Jack Roscamp, legendary hero of the future 1928 FA Cup success, began his career at Ewood having been signed from Northern League club Blaydon as a right-half, but his centre forward days would arrive at a much later date.

Burnley failed to raise their game and ended in seventeenth place, six points above the drop zone but it was another disappointment for the fans. Beel was a rare ray of sunshine as he scored nineteen times including a hat-trick against West Ham United. They twice cracked in four goals against West Brom and Arsenal, both at the "Turf" with left winger Walter Weaver notching a brace against the Baggies. More pre-war legends said good-bye to the club. Left back David Taylor (221 appearances), that most consistent of wing halves Billy Watson (346) and flying winger Billy Nesbitt (172) had all reached the end of their careers but John Haworth had plunged into the transfer market to belatedly replace Tommy Boyle. Jack Hill, a mountain of a man, arrived from Plymouth Argyle with a £5,000 transfer fee on his head. He proved to be an outstanding centre half, one who would actually captain England later in his career.

The derby games

The two derby games, played yet again on consecutive Saturdays in November, gave more pleasure to Blackburn than Burnley who had been in the bottom two a couple of weeks before. The Rovers were looking down at them from a position just inside the top ten and Ted Harper had already been on the score sheet seven times. As in most levels of football, home advantage does count, so there was a general air of optimism around Ewood Park as the first derby of the season kicked off. It was tense, but it was dour and all the action was reserved for the last five minutes. Kelly had to be the man to break the deadlock, but with just one minute to play, Jock McKay delivered again, saving the day for the club and sending both sets of supporters home in a reasonably satisfied frame of mind. Having drawn away, it was logical for the Claret and Blue supporters to expect a Turf Moor victory the following week, but how rarely has logic applied in derby games? Ten thousand more Burnley folks turned out than did their counterparts at the Blackburn game (30,000 to 20,000) and George Beel was quickly on hand to score his first derby goal. Carr must have given his players a rocket at the interval, because within seven minutes of the re-start, his team was in front. Harper did the initial damage and then Johnny McIntyre, who was beginning to be a thorn in the side of the enemy, slipped in the winner. It was the Blackburn side's second win at the "Turf" in three years and Burnley were left to battle against relegation for the remainder of the campaign.

03 11 1923	Blackburn Rovers	Burnley	1-1	J McKay, R Kelly.
10 11 1923	Burnley	Blackburn Rovers	1-2	G Beel. J McIntyre, E Harper.

Burnley fans must have split their sides laughing on learning that the Rovers had fallen at the first hurdle, 1-0 to the non-league side Corinthian in the FA Cup. This London based club had no permanent home base, was a true-blue amateur side but included talented footballers who did not want to turn professional, usually because they were earning far more money from working in the city or from private incomes. They also gave their name to the expression "Corinthian Spirit" which describes the way that they played the game. The Clarets squeezed their way through to the 3rd Round by beating lower opposition. There they produced the performance of the year. A crowd of 54,775, a record that still stands to this day, witnessed a 1-0 win over the Division 1 champions-elect Huddersfield Town and they reached their third ever semi-final following a quarter final 3-1 replay victory over Swindon Town, Beel netting a double. Aston Villa were the opposition at Bramall Lane, but the legendary cup fighters were far too good on the day, easily winning 3-0.

1924-25

Team	Pos	Played	Won	Drawn	Lost	GF	GA	Pts
Blackburn Rovers	16	42	11	13	18	53	66	35
Burnley	19	42	11	12	19	46	75	34

Blackburn Rovers		Burnley	
Most Appearances	Joe Hulme 42	Most Appearances	Benny Cross 40
Most Goals	Jock McKay, Johnny McIntyre (both 12)	Most Goals	Tom Roberts 15

BOB KELLY

Relegation was never an issue for the two East Lancashire clubs in the 1924-25 season because the relegated Preston North End and Nottingham Forest were tailed off, but 16th and 19th respectively for the Rovers and Clarets was extremely poor fare. Only one point separated them but the Rovers had an extremely topsy-turvy end to their campaign. They achieved a rare double, the league's highest victory and largest defeat, thrashing Birmingham City 7-1 at Ewood in early April and being on the receiving end of a 6-0 thrashing by Bolton Wanderers at Burnden Park three weeks later. Harper somehow lost his form, unable to cash in on chances provided, so it was left to the two Macs, McKay and McIntyre, to take over the burden of goal scoring. There were three new faces, each of whom achieved so much in the game. Joe Hulme, a right winger, was signed from York City and he would later become part of one of the most famous front fives in the history of English football, lining up at Arsenal with the likes of Jack, James and Bastin. Sid Puddefoot, signed for a club record £4,000 from Falkirk and Aussie Campbell from a Durham village club, both stayed at Ewood until way past the '28 Cup Final where each in their own way, contributed so much to that victory.

Tommy Roberts was the Clarets' leading scorer with 16 goals in half a season. The former England international, who had been signed from Preston North End, had shown sensational form and his goals lifted them towards safety. He was then seriously injured in a home game against Tottenham Hotspur and he missed the rest of the campaign. Burnley however conceded seventy-five goals during the league season, five at home to their local rival and to Huddersfield Town and at Bolton and Arsenal. Injuries did not help with Hill, consistent right back Len Smelt and Bob Kelly each missing a fair number of games. But the fans had much more to mourn than a leaky defence. John Haworth had been manager for fourteen years, delivering a promotion, a Division 1 championship and an FA Cup victory. He is possibly the most successful manager that the club has ever employed but in December he contracted pneumonia and died at the age of forty-eight. Albert Pickles, already a director at the club, was given the task of stepping into the great man's shoes.

The derby games

For the first time since the end of the war, the fixtures were played at different times during the year, the first one in Burnley in mid-September where Blackburn Rovers were looking for their third away victory in four years

> Superb Rovers
> There were some startling changes in the match at Burnley, where Blackburn were visitors. The home team took an early lead, Hill getting a couple of goals and Freeman a third. Before the interval McKay and McIntyre scored for the Rovers. The forward play of the Rovers was superb after the interval. Hulme soon equalised, McIntyre gave them the lead, and Crisp found the net, and they won 5 to 3.
> Daily Mirror
> 15th September, 1924

This had been one of the most bizarre games in the lengthy history of East Lancashire derbies. After sixteen minutes, any knowledgeable bookmaker would have closed his book. Albert Freeman incidentally was no relation to Bert but a bit-part striker. Some sources attribute the final goal to McIntyre, thus giving him a hat-trick and the shocked, stunned and dismayed crowd trudged home, not believing what they had just witnessed. By the date of the return at Ewood Park, the Burnley side had fallen to twentieth in the table and the worried fans travelled west with little confidence. Once again there were goals, but it was a complete reversal of form. Tommy Roberts was on fire, continuing his scoring spree and netting twice. The ever-reliable Benny Cross was on hand with a third and Burnley cruised to a 3-0 victory. John Haworth, possibly looking down, would have been proud of them. This was the first time that both away sides came away victorious in the same campaign and it would not be repeated until the 1965-66 season.

13 09 1924	Burnley	Blackburn Rovers	3-5	J Hill 2, B Freeman. J McIntyre 3, J McKay, J Hulme.
17 01 1925	Blackburn Rovers	**Burnley**	0-3	T Roberts 2, B Cross.

In the FA Cup, Blackburn Rovers put their league form to one side and had a tremendous campaign. Goals had been hard to come by in the early rounds, winning 1-0 at home to Oldham Athletic in Round 1 and then taking three games to beat Portsmouth. Amazingly, in 300 minutes of football, the only goal scored was by left winger Jack Crisp in the second replay played at Highbury. Tottenham Hotspur were eventually beaten 3-1 in a 5th Round replay in Blackburn, each of the three newcomers Campbell, Puddefoot and Hulme bagging a goal. Over 60,000 witnessed the narrow 1-0 home win over Blackpool which saw them through to their twelfth semi-final, Puddefoot being on target once again and Cardiff City provided the opposition in the last four. Unfortunately this was the end of the cup run as they lost 3-1 at Meadow Lane, home of Notts County. Burnley had quickly lost interest in the competition, losing 2-1 away to Everton at the first attempt..

1925-26

Team	Pos	Played	Won	Drawn	Lost	GF	GA	Pts
Blackburn Rovers	12	42	15	11	16	91	80	41
Burnley	20	42	13	10	19	85	108	36

Blackburn Rovers		Burnley	
Most Appearances	Arthur Rigby 42	Most Appearances	Louis Page 41
Most Goals	Ted Harper 43	Most Goals	Louis Page 26

The off-side rule had led to stagnation as defences became extremely adept at using it to their advantage. The Football Association decided to change it and there was an immediate increase in goals scored, so for once; fiddling with the laws increased everyone's Saturday afternoon enjoyment. In the far east of Lancashire however it was a scrap for survival. With such a leaky defence, Burnley shipped 108 goals. What frustrated the fans most however was that they also scored 85, virtually half of them away from Turf Moor.

Louis Page, a Liverpudlian signed from Northampton, topped the scoring charts with 26 goals including six in one away game at Birmingham City; still a club record. The season had started disastrously when the Clarets travelled to Aston Villa and conceded ten goals without reply. Bob Kelly was sold to Sunderland for a record £6,500 fee and eight goals were shipped at both Manchester City and Bury. Relegation seemed certain, but they beat Tottenham Hotspur 2-0 at White Hart Lane and thumped Cardiff City 4-1 at Turf Moor to dive over the finishing line, safe from relegation for another year. Burnley had somehow survived a most traumatic season in Pickles' first full term in charge, so optimism was tinged with reality as the next season loomed.

The leading goal scorer in the country came from Blackburn Rovers for the first time since Jack Southworth back in 1890. Puddefoot setting up chances for him was just the incentive Ted Harper needed and he banged in forty-three goals, setting a league record which lasted just two years before Dixie Dean's sixty goal haul for Everton. No Rovers' striker has emulated this feat and an England cap v Scotland was his reward. Both Puddefoot and left winger Arthur Rigby also reached double figures and they scored seven at home to Manchester United and at Newcastle. But they lacked consistency and finally finished twelfth.

The derby games

No-one could deny that Blackburn Rovers were the better side this season, the derby games confirming that judgement. Burnley were rock bottom when they entertained the Rovers at Turf Moor and it showed. It was one-sided, Ted Harper rattling in three goals. Page reduced the arrears two minutes from time but by then, many of the 26,181 crowd had left. For once, there was a higher attendance at Ewood Park, 29,991 to be exact and they saw a most exhilarating game. Burnley were still bottom and were completely outclassed for most of the contest. They managed to keep Harper quiet for much of the game and for all their dominance, the Blackburn team had only a Puddefoot goal to show by half-time. Rigby scored a second ten minutes after the break and the game was petering out as the final fifteen minutes approached. Then all hell broke loose. Goals from Puddefoot and from Rigby went in as the Blue and Whites threatened to run amok, but it then suddenly became an even and open game. Five goals were scored in the last ten minutes, three to Burnley with a double from Percy Richards and one from Jack Bruton.

The Rovers also joined this crazy party. Harper was certainly not going to miss out, but he had to be content with a single strike while Rigby claimed the match ball as they cantered to a 6-3 win. If the first three years of the Football League are disregarded, the Blackburn club being streets ahead in ability at that time, the total of thirteen goals was the highest number scored in derby games per season to date. Not even the most partisan of Burnley fans dared to claim bragging rights.

31 10 1925	Burnley	Blackburn Rovers	1-3	L Page. T Harper 3
13 03 1926	Blackburn Rovers	Burnley	6-3	S Puddefoot 2, A Rigby 3, T Harper. P Richards 2, J Bruton.

Joe Hulme had left for Arsenal by the time the FA Cup came around and he was certainly missed when they played Preston North End in Round 3 (the previous Round 1). A crowd of over 40,000 filled Ewood Park but the Rovers could only draw 1-1 with Division 2 opposition. Back to their best in the replay, doubles from Rigby and Stan Dixon, a centre-half as a make shift inside forward, helped to thrash the once Proud Preston 4-1. Drawn against Arsenal in Round 4, the Blackburn side lost 3-1 in London. Burnley, as inconsistent as their neighbours, drew 2-2 at Cardiff City with Beel scoring twice, but lost 2-0 in the replay at home.

1926-27

Team	Pos	Played	Won	Drawn	Lost	GF	GA	Pts
Burnley	5	42	19	9	14	91	80	47
Blackburn Rovers	18	42	15	8	19	77	96	38

Blackburn Rovers		Burnley	
Most Appearances	Arthur Rigby 40	Most Appearances	Jack Bruton 42
Most Goals	Ted Harper 35	Most Goals	George Beel 24

It was all change in the 1926-27 season as Burnley moved up fifteen places to fifth and Blackburn Rovers slithered down to eighteenth, though fortunately well clear of the relegation places. The Rovers started well, winning 5-1 at West Ham, Puddefoot notching a hat-trick against his former club. This was surprisingly one of three occasions when they scored five away from home. Jack Carr was removed as manager to be replaced by a returning local hero, none other than Bob Crompton. There was a steadying of the ship and Harper was still knocking in the goals, another thirty five to enhance his reputation. There was some improvement under the new Manager, although nothing even bordering on satisfaction, but there was a feeling in the club that "Bob would eventually get it right". The end of season placing however was the lowest since 1919-20 and it ended a run of four campaigns where the blue and whites had finished above the Clarets. Looking forward, Tommy Mclean had been signed from St Johnstone, fullbacks Hutton and Jones had arrived from Aberdeen and Blackpool respectively and Jock Crawford was now the regular custodian of the goal posts. Could there be something special on the horizon for next season?

After a dire baptism into football management, this season must have brought a smile to the face of Albert Pickles. They conceded eighty goals but lost only once at home and a 5-1 victory at Newcastle, with a hat-trick from George Beel was some result. Beel's goals saw him back at the top of the scoring charts again and Louis Page played seven times for England. Jack Bruton was beginning to show his skill and pace, a provider for both Beel and Page. A fifth placed finish was a surprise to the fans, but it could have been far better. A 1-0 victory at Turf Moor against Manchester United on February 5th sent them to the summit with fifteen to play. Anticipation was high, but the subsequent eight defeats and two draws was nowhere near title winning form. Beel had scored 22 times in the first half of the campaign but managed a paltry two from then on in and several heavy defeats certainly dented their confidence. George

Waterfield, the Clarets' left back, made his solitary England appearance this season, but of far greater significance, centre-half John 'Jack' Hill captained England at Hampden Park, the first such honour for a Burnley player. Jerry Dawson finally hung up his gloves following a club record 522 league games, a true one club man.

The derby games

The previous season had been all Blackburn Rovers, but what a difference a year makes. Burnley sat at the top of the table going into the Ewood Park game and 42,898 spectators, no doubt remembering the goal bonanza of last season, waited in expectation. There were similarities to that memorable game, specifically with the events of the final ten minutes. On this occasion, Cross scored early, but a Puddefoot equaliser sent them into half-time all square. After eighty minutes, the sides were still locked at 1-1 and then the flood gates opened. McCluggage knocked in a penalty, Freeman quickly followed up with a third and Page netted twice more in the last five minutes. It had become a rout and the Rovers, falling like autumn leaves, had now played seven games on the bounce without a win. When the return game at Turf Moor came around, Burnley had slipped down a couple of places. The Blackburn side had found some form, Harper netting an incredible nine times as four wins from five games were recorded. Only 24,546 turned up and once more it was close for a while before Burnley's forward power came into play. Beel gave the home side the lead but Campbell responded shortly after the interval. With their two international defenders Hill and Waterfield keeping tabs on Harper and Puddefoot, the Burnley forwards saw far more of the ball and the derby double was achieved with Page and Cross both on target. Their 5-1 win at Ewood is still their record away victory across all official derby competitions.

16 10 1926	Blackburn Rovers	**Burnley**	1-5	S Puddefoot. B Cross, A McCluggage, B Freeman, L Page 2.
05 03 1927	**Burnley**	Blackburn Rovers	3-1	G Beel, B Cross, L Page. A Campbell.

Burnley had hinted at a good FA Cup run when comfortably disposing of Division 2 opposition in the shape of Grimsby Town and Fulham in Rounds 3 and 4, but Chelsea, another lower ranked side raced to a two goal lead at Stamford Bridge, and a solitary Cross strike was insufficient to turn the tie around in front of over 62,000 spectators. Not content with being humiliated by South Shields and Corinthian in recent Cup campaigns, Blackburn Rovers once again exited at Round 3, embarrassingly at Division 3 North Southport.

1927-28

Team	Pos	Played	Won	Drawn	Lost	GF	GA	Pts
Blackburn Rovers	12	42	16	9	17	66	78	41
Burnley	19	42	16	7	19	82	98	39

Blackburn Rovers		Burnley	
Most Appearances	Jock Crawford 40	Most Appearances	George Waterfield 42
Most Goals	Tom Mitchell 15	Most Goals	George Beel 35

Blackburn Rovers improved somewhat under Bob Crompton. They finished in twelfth spot but in the 1927-28 season in a closely contested league which had a difference of only sixteen points between top and bottom, they were only three points clear of the relegation places. Ted Harper had been sold to The Wednesday and Jack Roscamp, a Geordie wing half, was switched to centre forward as an experiment. As it turned out, the utility player will forever reside in the Pantheon of Blackburn Rovers heroes. Harper had scored a hat-trick immediately prior to his departure in a thrilling 4-4 draw at home to Birmingham, a feat repeated by Mitchell as Arsenal were beaten 4-1. Doubles by Puddefoot and Roscamp contributed to a 6-0 thrashing of Portsmouth, but they conceded that number of goals on three occasions to Derby County, Bolton Wanderers and Leicester City, the Bolton defensive disaster being at home.

Burnley were extremely fortunate to avoid relegation. Five successive defeats at the start of the campaign meant they were quickly playing catch up. They conceded 98 goals and fifteen defeats were suffered on their travels. Sommerville, the new Clarets keeper, was carried off with a broken collar bone at Bolton and with no substitutes in those days, a 7-1 thrashing was inevitable. In a division so concertinaed that at its conclusion, only six points separated fourth from the relegation places, Burnley found themselves in fifth place on St Valentine's Day. As the season came to a close, only a memorable 2-1 home win against the dual FA Cup and Football League runners-up Huddersfield Town saved them from relegation. It was George Beel's goal scoring ability which kept them up. He scored thirty-five times but to be fair, Louis Page's contribution of twenty-two goals was also a vital factor in clinging on to the safety of a nineteenth placed finish, one point above the relegated Tottenham Hotspur. Remarkably, seven clubs, including Burnley, finished on thirty nine points; it was one of those seasons. Andy McCluggage was capped by Northern Ireland. He went on to win eleven in total and make 204 league appearances for the Clarets.

The derby games

After two seasons of one-sided derby games, normality returned and the matches were far more competitive. The Ewood Park encounter was the opening fixture of the campaign and it was a home victory, the Rovers triumphing

2-1. In front of a crowd of 32,441, local boy Harold Hargreaves, who had actually been signed from Tottenham Hotspur two seasons before, gave the Clarets an interval lead, but with Beel missing through injury, they could not hang on to it. Puddefoot once more and Tommy McLean with his first derby goal, swung the game to give the home side the points. New Year's Eve fell on a Saturday and the 28,354 who came out to start the revelling early, went home celebrating a local win over the old adversary. It was a season's high crowd at the "Turf" and Beel and Page gave the home side a comfortable interval lead. The visitors came out strongly and Tom Mitchell quickly reduced the deficit before the home side were awarded a penalty. The dead-eyed McCluggage inevitably scored and he was on course to convert six such goals in eight derby games over a four-season period; the master from the twelve yards out. At the end of term, when all points are added up, these two points for Burnley were the difference between 1st and 2nd Division football the following season.

27 08 1927	Blackburn Rovers	Burnley	2-1	S Puddefoot, T McLean. H Hargreaves.
31 12 1927	**Burnley**	Blackburn Rovers	3-1	G Beel, L Page, A McCluggage. T Mitchell.

It was the FA Cup which proved to be the highlight of the East Lancashire season, certainly in the western half of the area. The Rovers hammered reigning Champions Newcastle United in Round 3, 4-1 at Ewood Park. Tom Mitchell, signed from Stockport County the season before, scored twice. He contributed 4 goals during the cup run, but missed out in the final two games, Crompton preferring to play George Thornewell, a conventional right winger. It was bad luck on Mitchell who topped the Rovers' scoring chart for the season. For the next three rounds, they struggled to edge home against Exeter City, Port Vale and a poor Manchester United side, before showing that they could scrap with the best of them against the highflying Arsenal in the semi-final. Jack Roscamp scored the only goal of the game. It was his fourth of the competition and the Rovers were in their first final since 1891. Burnley's cup run in contrast never got off the ground, losing 2-0 at home to Aston Villa.

Huddersfield Town provided the opposition at Wembley; consistently the best side in the country in the "twenties" and undoubted favourite. The side contained the ex-Burnley star Bob Kelly, the super-talented Scottish winger Alex Jackson who had torn England to shreds at Wembley and playing at centre-forward was George Brown, later to sign for Burnley in the mid-thirties. There was drama in the very first minute. In Roscamp, the Rovers had a centre forward with more brawn than brain but he quickly changed the predicted script by chasing a through ball and cannoning into the Huddersfield keeper as he grasped it to his chest.

By modern day rules, it was a foul but goal keepers in those days had little protection, and when the ball crept over the line, the goal was given. Inside left McLean added a second before half-time, rocketing a shot home from the

The Blackburn Rovers 1928 FA Cup winning side that beat Huddersfield Town 3-1 was: Jock Crawford, Jock Hutton, Herbert Jones, Harry Healless, Willie Rankin, Austen Campbell, George Thornewell, Syd Puddefoot, Jack Roscamp, Tommy McLean, Arthur Rigby.

edge of the penalty box and although Jackson pulled one back, Roscamp scored again to send the trophy back to Blackburn for the sixth and so far final time. For the next twenty-nine years, they shared the honour with Aston Villa for "most FA Cup wins". Crompton was given great credit for the win and this was an Ewood Park side with its share of internationals. The skipper Harry Healless finally totalled 360 appearances retiring at thirty-nine as an Ewood Park great. Left back Herbert Jones, left half Austen Campbell (by popular consensus the man of the match for his ferocious tackling), Syd Puddefoot and Arthur Rigby all represented England during this period and right back Jock Hutton was a regular in the Scottish side.

1928-29

Team	Pos	Played	Won	Drawn	Lost	GF	GA	Pts
Blackburn Rovers	7	42	17	11	14	72	63	45
Burnley	19	42	15	8	19	81	103	38

Blackburn Rovers		Burnley	
Most Appearances	Jock Crawford, Syd Puddefoot (both 40)	Most Appearances	Joe Devine 42
Most Goals	Jack Roscamp 16	Most Goals	George Beel 30

After the magic of Wembley, there was improvement from the Rovers in terms of league form. It was another congested league and although they fin-

ished just seven points from the summit, they were back in seventh place. Harry Healless continued to play his part, but injuries affected them defensively, the full back pairing of Hutton and Jones playing one game together. The main problem hitting the Rovers hit the rest of Lancashire, but the "cotton capital" suffered more than most from the "Great Depression". Many were laid off from work and at such times, money has to be spent on the bare essentials and not football. Roscamp, still on a high from Wembley, scored six times as they won four on the bounce in September, including victories over The Wednesday and Bolton Wanderers who, between them, hoovered up the two major trophies. Clarrie Bourton, signed from Bristol City, scored all four goals at Manchester United and Arsenal lost 5-2 at Ewood Park. A total of 11 draws did not help, although the goals conceded were the league's second lowest.

It was another stressful season for Burnley with a definite inability to manage games. They hit the back of the net on eighty-one occasions with four players, Beel, Bruton, Devine and Page, hitting the double figure mark, but with a defence that leaked a league high of 103 goals, they were once again fortunate to finish nineteenth and avoid the drop. They were actually top after 9 games which included a stupendous 7-2 win at Newcastle United, George Beel netting a hat-trick. There was no surprise when regular England international Jack Hill signed for Newcastle for £8,000 in early October. The team performed to a satisfactory standard at home but had several away defeats which made self-respecting Clarets' fan hide their heads. A 10-0 thrashing at Sheffield United was only marginally worse than the 8-0 loss at Anfield and the two lots of seven that they shipped at Huddersfield and Cardiff. George Beel's 30 goals was their saviour for the second year running and a seven point cushion over the relegated Bury was ultimately comfortable, but this was only achieved with a five game unbeaten run at the end of the campaign. They also provided two more international one cap wonders; Stanley Bowsher for Wales and the defender Hugh Flack for Northern Ireland.

The derby games

The first derby at Turf Moor in October drew a gate of 36,694. There was little between the clubs at this stage of the campaign, both being in the top ten. Jack Hill was playing his last game in a Claret and Blue shirt, but the Rovers

were twice ahead, each time with goals from Tommy McLean. But Burnley were not to be denied, twice pulling back the deficit with a McCluggage penalty and a late equaliser from Joe Devine. The Scotsman had arrived at the end of the 1924-25 season, signing from Bathgate, a non-league club north of the border and he contributed 27 goals in 114 appearances, helping the Clarets to remain in Division 1. Peter O'Dowd had played in the number 5 shirt for the Blackburn side in this game and a year later, he would become one of the few players to have played for both sides in derby games following his transfer to the Turf Moor club. Draws in East Lancashire derby games were a rare event and this was only the third one. The number quickly became four at the beginning of May. Both sides had nothing to play for except bragging rights, but the game was competitive. The Blue and Whites scored early through Puddefoot and Jack Bruton levelled the scores. This was the first season that both derby games had ended all square, a feat not to be repeated for another eighty-three years. Every picture tells a story and anyone looking round at the vacant terraces within Ewood Park would conclude that fixtures in May were unpopular. There was nothing to play for, therefore nothing worth watching. They had more important things to spend their few spare coins on and the current Burnley side was not worth leaving the house for. The crowd? A pathetic 5,461.

20 10 1928	Burnley	Blackburn Rovers	2-2	A McCluggage, J Devine. T McLean 2.
02 05 1929	Blackburn Rovers	Burnley	1-1	S Puddefoot. J Bruton.

Blackburn Rovers had another exciting FA Cup run. Barnsley were beaten 1-0 in Round 3 and for once they had the better of Derby County in this competition, winning 3-0 away in a Round 4 replay. A 1-0 home win over Bury led to a last eight tie against close neighbours Bolton Wanderers. It produced the biggest gate ever recorded at Ewood Park, 62,522 packed like sardines to witness a 1-1 draw. Home advantage however counted for the Wanderers in the replay, edging through 2-1. Burnley produced a promising performance in Round 3, beating Division 1 rival Sheffield United 1-0 at Turf Moor, but Division 3 South club Swindon Town sent Burnley packing, coming back from two goals down at the County Ground in a replay, winning 3-2.

1929-30

Team	Pos	Played	Won	Drawn	Lost	GF	GA	Pts
Blackburn Rovers	6	42	19	7	16	99	93	45
Burnley	21	42	14	8	20	79	97	36

Blackburn Rovers		Burnley	
Most Appearances	Herbert Jones 39	Most Appearances	Andy McCluggage 40
Most Goals	Clarrie Bourton 21	Most Goals	Louis Page 15

At the wrong end of the table, two of the twelve original members of the Football League dropped into Division 2. Inevitably it was Burnley and (for the first time in their history) Everton. This left just Aston Villa and Blackburn Rovers as the only two founding members never to be relegated. The Clarets had spent thirteen seasons at the elite level of English football, their best run so far, but as they had struggled over the last few campaigns, their relegation came as no shock. Such was the pressure on the finances that two of their best attacking players were sold, Jack Bruton to Blackburn Rovers and inside forward Joe Devine to Newcastle United. Unbeaten in their first four games, optimism abounded, but it was another of those incredibly tight seasons where almost anyone could beat anyone. Sheffield Wednesday had run away with the league, but between second and twenty second, there was a mere 15 points. Joe Mantle, Beel and Page all completed a double figure haul of goals, but they had the league's worst defensive record. With four points separating Portsmouth in thirteenth spot and Burnley in twenty-first, there was an almighty scrap to avoid relegation, but they fell into the drop zone after losing the penultimate fixture. And typical of this totally unpredictable campaign, they hammered runner-up Derby County 6-2 at the "Turf" in the final fixture, Mantle scoring a hat-trick. Sadly it was all too late and the fact was that they would be playing Division Two football next season.

Blackburn Rovers had a most respectable season, continuing the form shown since Bob Crompton's return. Their FA Cup winning side was breaking up, Campbell moving to Huddersfield Town and Rigby to Everton. Injuries also played their part and Bill Imrie, a Scottish international wing half, was signed from St Johnstone. The Rovers averaged over three goals a game during their home campaign, seeing in the New Year with a 7-0 blasting of Middlesbrough, eight against the Clarets and a crazy 7-5 encounter with Birmingham City when Puddefoot scored four, the highest ever aggregate score at Ewood Park.

All this enabled the side to achieve a sixth-place finish. This was their best performance since 1915, not to be topped until the resurgent side led by Kenny Dalglish finished in fourth spot sixty-three years later. The capture of England international right winger Jack Bruton for a record £6,500 was inspired and Clarrie Bourton was leading scorer, only the fourth Rovers player behind Southworth, Shea and Harper to net more than twenty in a season. In this free-scoring age, they failed by one to score a century of goals.

The derby games

Ultimately, football is about scoring goals. We have all celebrated when we knocked the ball between the coats in the school yard. This is why fans turn up so loyally, hoping for their favourites to hit the back of the net. And that is why, at the epicentre of the century's worst economic depression when the unemployed would stay in bed all morning because it saved fuel costs, 22,647 spectators filed into Ewood Park for the derby. The Rovers were twelfth, the Clarets seventeenth and for 30 minutes it was close.

Then Billy Down in the Burnley goal collided heavily with Arthur Groves. Without substitutes, he valiantly carried on, his movement being strictly limited. After the game he collapsed with a ruptured kidney, thankfully recovering. With a passenger guarding the nets, the game became one-sided. Groves completed his hat-trick, McLean and Roscamp each scored twice and Imrie grabbed the eighth. Although likely to concede further at any moment, the Burnley side never gave up. McCluggage had converted a first half penalty and he repeated the feat late on in the game, with Louis Page also finding the net.

It was the highest scoring game in the history of the derby, the only time that eight has been achieved. By the time of the second instalment, Burnley were deep in the relegation mire but the Rovers, having lost just twice in their last eleven games, were viewing a possible podium finish. But revenge was on the menu at Turf Moor on this mid-March day. There may have been more dramatic events carried out on the Ides of March, the famous day in the Roman calendar, but this was a thriller and the satisfaction felt by the Burnley fans when revenge was finally taken, must have matched that of Brutus and Cassius when assassinating Julius Caesar.

McLean had put the Rovers ahead, an own goal from goal keeper Cliff Binns drew the Clarets level but Bourton gave the visitors the interval lead. The second half belonged to Burnley and after just five minutes, yet another McCluggage penalty and one from O'Dowd, recently signed from Blackburn, gave them a lead which they clung to. Relegation followed, but the Burnleyites could boast for six years that they won the last East Lancs derby.

09 11 1929	Blackburn Rovers	Burnley	8-3	A Groves 3, J Roscamp 2, T McLean 2, W Imrie. A McCluggage 2, L Page.
15 03 1930	**Burnley**	Blackburn Rovers	3-2	o.g. A McCluggage, P O'Dowd. T McLean, C Bourton.

The FA Cup draw was difficult for Burnley, an away tie to the all-conquering Sheffield Wednesday. The Clarets gave it their best shot, but went down 1-0. Blackburn Rovers made more progress, consecutive 4-1 victories over Northampton Town and Everton, but who wanted to go to Villa Park in the 5th Round of the FA Cup. As feared, they returned home after a 4-1 defeat.

So, with the twenties left behind, the fans pondered on life since the end of the War. A title for Burnley and a Cup for the Blackburn side were stellar performances but football clubs cannot afford to look back. For the Rovers, there was hope of success under a manager they trusted but for many of the spectators of both clubs, there would be something missing; the opportunity to metaphorically thump their hated rivals. Since football had re-started after the Armistice, the Rovers had occupied the higher league position in seven out of the eleven seasons, but Burnley had won the title whereas the Rovers' best finish was sixth. The Blackburn side had won at Wembley and reached a semi-final, for the Clarets, one semi-final appearance. It was 10-9 to Burnley with three draws in the derbies so who had the bragging rights?

Rovers in charge .... then the unthinkable happens. 1930-1945

"Nothing in the world is permanent, and we're foolish when we ask anything to last, but surely we're still more foolish not to take delight in it while we have it."
W. Somerset Maugham

There had been an assumption on the part of the Blackburn Rovers fans that they were a First Division side and would always be a First Division side. They took great delight in the fact as of course they should. They knew it was difficult competing at the very highest level with their richer counterparts, but it was surely their divine right to stay with the elite. It had been for forty-eight years, why should it change?

At Turf Moor the attitude was somewhat more pragmatic. "We have had our good times, we can expect bad times but we will surely return". During the next nine years until football rightly took second place to the war effort, both sets of supporters had to scratch their heads and re-think their long held views. In Burnley, there was no indication whatsoever that the good times would return and in the summer of '36, it dawned upon the supporters of the Blue and Whites that nothing in the world is permanent; nothing lasts forever.

1930-31

Team	Pos	Played	Won	Drawn	Lost	GF	GA	Pts
Blackburn Rovers	10	42	17	8	17	83	84	42
Burnley	8	42	17	11	14	81	77	45

Blackburn Rovers		Burnley	
Most Appearances	Cliff Binns 42	Most Appearances	Peter O'Dowd 42
Most Goals	Jack Bruton 19	Most Goals	George Beel 25

This was a slightly better than average season in Blackburn, a tenth position but a distance from a top three place. Back in mid-table, there was even confusion for the fans with a pair of Brutons scoring goals. Jack was the outside right and playing centre-forward was Les signed from Raith Rovers; same name but no relation. At inside right was Puddefoot, still performing well although in his mid-thirties.

Two results stood out, albeit for the wrong reasons. They shipped eight goals at Sunderland and five more in a crazy 5-4 home loss to Middlesbrough. Bob Crompton had been manager at Ewood Park as football moved into the thirties and in the eyes of most folks, he would be there forever. In fact Blackburn Rovers without Bob would not be Blackburn Rovers. However the most astonishing aspect of this season was that he resigned his role as manager in February 1931. At fifty-one years of age, the "great one" probably felt as though he needed a rest from the internal politics and dressing room bickering that has always accompanied the game. There were rumours of player discontent. Even as a player, Bob was considered to be autocratic. He knew his own mind and rarely listened to others. He was stubborn and quite aloof. He was also on the Board of Directors and when he fell out with other members, he was voted off. As a result, he quickly resigned all other positions, resulting in the club being short of a manager. He was replaced by Arthur Barritt, but this new man at the helm was an administrator, having been the club secretary. Crompton had been involved in all of the Rovers' successes over the last thirty-five years. Was he irreplaceable? Yes, without a doubt. The Rovers reached the 5th Round of the FA Cup, having beaten Walsall after a replay and smashing Bristol Rovers 5-1. Les Bruton scored three against the West Country club, but Chelsea upset the form book and won 3-0 at Stamford Bridge.

All the fans at Turf Moor wanted was to bounce straight back. As a result, Burnley's eighth position in Division 2 was certainly disappointing. Goals were no problem, largely due to the renaissance of George Beel who found Division 2 defences more to his liking. He was leading scorer at the club for the fourth time and his hat-trick against Wolverhampton Wanderers was his eleventh for Burnley. The Clarets shocked everyone with a 3-0 win over the high flying Manchester City in Round 3 of the FA Cup, but a 2-0 defeat at Bradford Park Avenue crushed their hopes of further progress. The "ever revolving door" is a much used expression to describe players arriving and departing, but at Turf Moor, because of the fraught financial position, it was more a case of two doors; "Exit for good players" and "Entrance for those less talented". Andy McCluggage was a good player and he left for Dundalk after 204 appearances,

1931-32

Team	Pos	Played	Won	Drawn	Lost	GF	GA	Pts
Blackburn Rovers	16	42	16	6	20	89	95	38
Burnley	19	42	13	9	20	59	87	35

Blackburn Rovers		Burnley	
Most Appearances	Jack Bruton 42	Most Appearances	Jim Brown 41
Most Goals	Ernie Thompson 21	Most Goals	George Beel 12

This campaign brought the mire at the bottom of both leagues almost within sniffing distance. The Blackburn defence was in turmoil as 95 goals were conceded following the worst possible start, a 6-1 thrashing at Sheffield Wednesday. Arthur Barritt's most inspired signing was Ernie Thompson from non-league Bath City. He top-scored this season and in total netted 82 league goals in 171 appearances before being sold to Manchester United, his name appearing at number twelve on the all-time list of scorers at Ewood Park. Gate receipts continued to drop and there was less than ten thousand on the ground for seven of their home fixtures, but what could you expect from a combination of poor performances and a cotton industry declining rapidly. In the FA Cup, Burton Town were comfortably swatted away 4-0 in Round 3, Jack Bruton and Cunliffe scoring twice each, but although the same two wingers were on the score sheet in Round 4, Derby County netted three times and visions of Wembley were no more. Arthur Cunliffe, Chorley born, was the third Blackburn Rovers outside left to be capped for England in a decade behind Hodkinson and Rigby. The 1928 FA Cup winning side was slowly broken up and the magnificently named Syd Puddefoot was reaching the end of a sparkling career. He made exactly 250 appearances for the Blackburn club, scoring 79 goals before moving home to West Ham United. Jock Roscamp, the hero of Wembley, was also heading to the twilight of his football life at Bradford City, having completed 223 appearances at Ewood Park.

This was a season close to disastrous at Burnley. The Turf Moor crowd were in panic mode as the club plunged towards the relegation zone, but they battled away and eventually avoided relegation, completing the season in nineteenth place, just two points clear of the drop. Running a football club can be all about virtuous circles. If you win a few games, the attendances improve, more money is made available and you can buy better players. Unfortunately, the Clarets were deep into a vicious circle, losing games, losing supporters, losing money and ultimately having to lose their better players. These included the talented Peter O'Dowd (ex-Blackburn Rovers) to Chelsea and Louis Page, having scored 111 goals, to Manchester United. Everyone has to move on eventually and George Beel's time at the "Turf" had come to an end. In ten seasons, he had scored 178 league goals, a record which still stands. And there was no good news from the FA Cup. Derby County came to Turf Moor and won in a canter, 4-0; another blow to the fans of the Clarets.

1932-33

Team	Pos	Played	Won	Drawn	Lost	GF	GA	Pts
Blackburn Rovers	15	42	14	10	18	76	102	38
Burnley	19	42	11	14	17	67	79	36

Blackburn Rovers		Burnley	
Most Appearances	Jack Bruton 42	Most Appearances	Tom Jones 40
Most Goals	Ernie Thompson 17	Most Goals	Tom Jones 16

Defensively there was further deterioration in this campaign at Ewood Park as a record 102 goals were conceded. Goalkeeper Bill Gormlie must have put severe pressure on his back muscles, picking the ball from out of the net six times at Goodison Park and eight times at Highbury. An away tie in the FA Cup 3rd Round at Lincoln City brought some relief as Cunliffe scored twice in a comprehensive 5-1 victory, but Division 1 Birmingham away from home were a much different proposition and the Rovers' defeat was comprehensive, 3-0. Jack Bruton had been outstanding in Burnley and he certainly let no-one down in Blackburn, a great servant to both. He was in the process of putting together a run of 120 games, a remarkable sequence for a player not in his first flush of youth. Two Wembley veterans departed in 1933, left back Herbert Jones to Brighton after 247 league games and Bill Rankin, the Scottish tower of strength at centre half to Charlton Athletic.

After Burnley were thrashed 6-1 by Preston North End at Deepdale on the August Bank Holiday Monday, 1932, the average attendances dropped to around the 8,500 mark as survival continued to be the name of the game, narrowly achieving it again from nineteenth spot. The hot seat at Turf Moor was no bed of Roses. Arthur Pickles had taken the club down in 1930 and he struggled on for a further two years, somehow avoiding a further relegation before resigning. His replacement Tom Bromilow was the first boss at Turf Moor to have pedigree as a player, twice winning Division 1 titles with Liverpool and five England caps at wing half. There have been better times to take over Burnley, but he was quick to make his mark and he fought off the dreaded drop in his first campaign. It was the interestingly named combo of Smith and Jones joining forces to score sufficient goals in the 32-33 season to keep the club afloat.

The Welshman Cecil Smith, a Bromilow signing from Stalybridge Celtic, scored 47 goals in total before being sold to Cardiff City. Bromilow also managed a decent FA Cup run which gave the fans something to cheer. A win at Swansea and home wins over Sheffield United and Chesterfield gave them a 6th Round tie against Manchester City. Even with home advantage, it was a difficult hurdle to cross and so it proved, but not before the Clarets put up a performance to remember before going down 1-0.

1933-34

Team	Pos	Played	Won	Drawn	Lost	GF	GA	Pts
Blackburn Rovers	8	42	18	7	17	74	81	43
Burnley	13	42	18	6	18	60	72	42

Blackburn Rovers		Burnley	
Most Appearances	Jesse Carver 42	Most Appearances	George Bellis 41
Most Goals	Jack Bruton, Ted Harper (both 15)	Most Goals	Cecil Smith 17

This season somewhat lifted the spirits in Blackburn as they were the only team to stay unbeaten at home in the Division. Unfortunately, seventeen defeats away from Ewood Park meant that eighth position was their final destination. Ted Harper returned to the club in mid-November, sharing the scoring honours with Jack Bruton and adding a further fifteen goals to his scoring records at Tottenham, Preston and of course the Rovers. Manchester City were enjoying a good run around this time and it was a tough Round 3 draw which sent the Blue and Whites to Maine Road. The result, a 3-1 defeat, was not unexpected.

Tom Bromilow settled Burnley into mid-table. It was mediocre, but mediocre was an improvement on a relegation scrap. The triple whammy of dwindling crowds, dwindling finances and less than quality players made for a difficult life. Final positions in the mid-teens had to be accepted as the norm as falling into Division 3 could not be contemplated by a former FA Cup winner and Football League Division 1 champion. Bury were a useful team before the War and they finished one place above the Clarets this season. They also had the upper hand in the FA Cup, knocking the Clarets out of the competition, 3-2 after a replay at Gigg Lane. International caps were rare at Turf Moor in the thirties, but Northern Irish full back Tommy Willighan gained his second and final cap against Scotland this campaign.

1934-35

Team	Pos	Played	Won	Drawn	Lost	GF	GA	Pts
Blackburn Rovers	15	42	14	11	17	66	78	39
Burnley	12	42	16	9	17	63	73	41

Blackburn Rovers		Burnley	
Most Appearances	Jack Bruton 42	Most Appearances	Jim Brown, Percy Downes 38
Most Goals	Jack Bruton, Ernie Thompson (both 18)	Most Goals	George Brown 21

The eighth position the previous season was yet another false dawn as Blackburn Rovers slithered down the table to fifteenth place. Tommy McLean was the last of the Wembley heroes to say farewell to the Ewood Park faithful after 247 appearances, forty-four league goals and five in the Wembley run-in including a crackerjack of a shot at the Stadium itself. Jack Bruton, now into his thirties, once more played every game and was the joint leading goal scorer with Ernie Thompson. In the FA Cup, it was Birmingham that once again struck the final blow, winning 2-1 at Ewood Park in Round 5 after threats from Middlesbrough and Liverpool had been extinguished.

One interesting footnote to the season was that Walter Crook, a locally born left back, began his run of 208 consecutive league appearances, a club record. The only recipient of an international cap was the second string goalkeeper Jack Hughes who represented Wales v Northern Ireland.

It was moderate and it was again mid-table for Burnley. Ronnie Hornby, still a youngster but proving one for the future, had been signed from Stalybridge Celtic and he participated well in the FA Cup run which the Turf Moor fans needed as a distraction from the tedious league displays. And it did prove to be a wonderful tonic. Ted Hancock, bought from Liverpool, proved to be the unexpected star, scoring four times in four games as the Clarets showed the required grit and determination to reach the last eight. The clubs they had pushed to one side were Mansfield Town, Luton Town and Nottingham Forest and both George Brown, a veteran recently signed from Aston Villa and Cecil Smith were also amongst the goals.

It was Birmingham at the Turf in Round 6 and from a 2-0 deficit, a double from Hornby which sandwiched a goal from Hancock, cemented a semi-final

berth; their first for eleven years. Thousands travelled down to Villa Park; the opposition being Sheffield Wednesday, a top three Division 1 outfit. England international left-winger Ellis Rimmer had scored in every round and was not going to miss out this time either, scoring twice more as the Wednesday proved too strong, too experienced and ultimately too good. The unexpected run to the semi-final brought Bromilow's name to the attention of many clubs and he left for Crystal Palace in the summer. For the subsequent years including war-time football, a Selection Committee made up of Chairman Tom Clegg, Secretary Alf Boland and Senior Trainer Billy Dougall took charge. The end of the season was good bye time for two of their better players.

Loyal defender George Waterfield after twelve years and 371 appearances at the "Turf", still tenth in the all-time appearance list, moved to join Bromilow at Crystal Palace. Burnley's best performer at this time was wing half Jim Brown. Signed from East Fife, starting 228 league games in eight seasons, he moved on to Manchester United at the end of term.

1935-36

Team	Pos	Played	Won	Drawn	Lost	GF	GA	Pts
Blackburn Rovers	22	42	12	9	21	55	96	33
Burnley	15	42	12	13	17	50	59	37

Blackburn Rovers		Burnley	
Most Appearances	Walter Crook 42	Most Appearances	Alick Robinson40
Most Goals	Ernie Thompson 15	Most Goals	Cecil Smith 10

And then there were none! Of the original twelve clubs that formed the original Football League, only Aston Villa and Blackburn Rovers had never been relegated. At a stroke at the end of April, both dropped through the trap door. The Rovers were rock bottom on thirty-three points. The irony of the situation was that they made a lightning start, but good became indifferent and indifferent morphed into awful as only four of the last twenty-three games brought wins; two of them in the last three games being totally irrelevant.

And they certainly performed like relegation fodder, two 8-1 defeats in the West Midlands at Wolverhampton and West Brom plus shipping thirteen goals in two visits to the North East in Sunderland and Middlesbrough. These were grey days for the club and with them looking like dead ringers for relegation in

March, Arthur Barritt resigned after five years in the job – the Board of Directors assumed command of team selection. There were brief hopes of an FA Cup run with a win in a replay against Bolton Wanderers, Thompson grabbing a late winner, but Bradford City beat them easily in an away tie. Such a disappointment yet again!

At Turf Moor, Tom Bromilow's resignation made little difference to the team's performance, a three place drop down the table but late in the season came the one real highlight. Alf Boland blooded a young centre forward aged 16 years and 163 days. His name was Tommy Lawton, the club's youngest ever first teamer and five goals in his first seven games hinted at great things to come. But would the small mill town club be able to keep hold of such talent for long? The FA Cup was a case of "after the Lord Mayor's Show" for the Clarets, exiting at the first opportunity to Sheffield United albeit in the replay after a goalless draw at the "Turf".

The crowd numbers continued to fluctuate wildly in the thirties. For example, there were over 26,000 on Turf Moor for the successful 2-1 Christmas Day 1934 battle against Bolton Wanderers and a paltry 3,765 for the end of season 1-0 home win over Norwich City. The Christmas holiday game in 1931 drew a crowd of 40,059 to Ewood Park to watch Dixie Dean's Everton, champion in waiting, but only 3,624 were in attendance when Aston Villa came to town on April 29th, 1933. At that time, the December 25th afternoon game was as much part of the Christmas festivities as Santa Claus, Rudolph and a glass of sherry. Nowadays, if you are a season ticket holder, you are more likely to trek down to the match. Season tickets were far rarer in the thirties, possibly being one of the reasons for such fluctuations in attendance. The lack of derby games, almost always a guaranteed good fund of revenue, also made a difference. However with the relegation of the Blue and Whites, it brought the local derbies back into play. With Burnley appearing to be stuck forever in Division 2, the rivalry, the rancour and the recriminations would once more be part and parcel of life in the cotton mill towns.

1936-37

Team	Pos	Played	Won	Drawn	Lost	GF	GA	Pts
Blackburn Rovers	12	42	16	10	16	70	62	42
Burnley	13	42	16	10	16	57	61	42

Blackburn Rovers		Burnley	
Most Appearances	Walter Crook 42	Most Appearances	Gilbert Richmond 42
Most Goals	Jack Bruton 16	Most Goals	Charlie Fletcher 12

It was a case of the boys being back in town for the 1936-37 season, but sadly in the wrong town. All of East Lancashire would have looked forward to a return to the derby clashes in Division 1. Now if only it had been a Burnley promotion, but Blackburn's relegation meant that the rivalry continued, just at a lower level. The fans of both hues expected fireworks, but it was necessary to trawl down to twelfth and thirteenth spots to find Blackburn Rovers and Burnley...... in that order. It was a slight improvement for the Clarets, but rather embarrassing for the Rovers who would have hoped for a one year stay. In actual fact, the two clubs finished equal on points, divided only by goal average. The final placings swung on two late season results. The Ewood Park club hammered Nottingham Forest 9-1, Billy Guest, an outside left signed from Birmingham, scoring four goals, whereas the Turf Moor side lost 7-3 at Leicester City. Not on the score sheet for the Rovers against the Forest was Jack Bruton, but his measured crosses provided assists for six of them.

He did make up for it over the season as a whole however by topping the scoring charts, compensating for the loss of Ernie Thompson. Shortly after this outgoing transfer, the Directors relieved themselves of team management duties and offered the post to the Secretary Reg Taylor, a move which made little difference to their plight. The Blackburn side was forced to off load another quality player during the season. James Gorman had made 213 appearances at right back, but he became frustrated after the relegation fiasco and moved to Sunderland for £6,250. Crook, his full back partner remained, continuing to play in every fixture.

Just as the Rovers were losing their best defender, Burnley were also forced to sell the young Tommy Lawton. He had continued his goal scoring exploits, notching another eleven in eighteen games when Everton came knocking on the door, cheque book in pocket. On New Year's Day 1937, Lawton signed for the Toffees for £6,500, a lot of money for a seventeen year old. The honour of topping the scoring chart went to Charlie Fletcher and there were good players coming into the club.

Arthur Woodruff arrived from Bradford City, the commencement of a memorable career in defence. Jimmy Stein had arrived from Everton before Lawton's departure and he contributed well from the right wing. But this was now a well-established Division 2 side, a very ordinary Division 2 side and although there were solid and reliable members of the team, working their socks off every week, they were ordinary Division 2 players because anyone of any quality who came along would be sold. That was 1930s football in Burnley. Thirty different players ran out beind the skipper during the season, but few were regular starters throughout the campaign.

The derby games

For six and a half years, pent up frustration had slowly built up amongst fans desperate for derby matches and at last, here it was in late October at Turf Moor. It was watched by 32,567 fans, an exceptional crowd for a Division 2 game, all turning up to watch a goal spree. What they got was a painstaking goalless draw, not even Tommy Lawton could light up the crowd. There was no doubt that the Ewood Park side was going through a re-building process, one which would be totally decimated by the onset of war three years down the line. Burnley supporters, reading their match programme, would have struggled to have heard of a number of the opposition players. Apart from Bruton, only Gorman, Crook, Whiteside, Pryde and Thompson were remotely in the "household name" category. Blackburn fans were far more cautious in spending hard-earned money, particularly following the insipid nature of the first derby; 18,240 turning out. It was the fourth highest gate of the season, only the two Christmas games and a late season encounter with the soon to be promoted Blackpool topping twenty thousand. The bragging rights were riding on the return at Ewood Park, the Rovers having improved their squad with the arrival of Guest plus Len Butt and John Wightman from Huddersfield Town. Consequently, after an edgy start when Stein gave the Clarets the lead, goals from Bruton, Butt and Guest made it a comfortable home victory. Bruton's goal was of great significance, In fact it was unique at the time and still is over eighty years later. He had previously twice scored for Burnley in derby games before transferring across to Ewood Park. This particular goal gave him the distinction of being the only player ever to score for both clubs in East Lancashire derbies.

24 10 1936	Burnley	Blackburn Rovers	0-0	
27 02 1937	Blackburn Rovers	Burnley	3-1	L Butt, J Bruton, W Guest. J Stein.

If the Blackburn side had fractionally taken the local credits as far as the League games were concerned, Burnley certainly came out on top in terms of the FA Cup with the laughs undoubtedly on the boys in Blue and White. Accrington Stanley were paired with the Rovers at Ewood in Round 3. To the delight of everyone east of Blackburn, the clubs fought out a 2-2 draw and then came the shock result; a 3-1 win for Stanley in the replay. The Division 2 side had taken a risk in playing several reserves but this takes nothing away from the performance of the Peel Park team. Burnley played out of their skins in Round 3 to achieve a 3-2 victory over Aston Villa in Birmingham, the doyens of the FA Cup still coming to terms with life in a lower sphere. The Turfites then ran rampant over Bury and the home tie in Round 5 brought colour and excitement to the area as 54,445 packed the ground when Arsenal came to town. It was here that the Burnley cup run hit the buffers with an almighty bang. The Clarets were overrun as the Gunners, football royalty in the thirties, treated them to a lesson in the art of the game, winning 7-1.

1937-38

Team	Pos	Played	Won	Drawn	Lost	GF	GA	Pts
Burnley	6	42	17	10	15	54	54	44
Blackburn Rovers	16	42	14	10	18	71	80	38

Blackburn Rovers		Burnley	
Most Appearances	Walter Crook, Len Butt, Billy Guest (all 42)	Most Appearances	Bob Brocklebank 42
Most Goals	Len Butt 20	Most Goals	Bob Brocklebank 14

A. ROBINSON

There was no doubting which East Lancashire club made the most progress this season. Burnley improved some seven places to sixth, although they were thirteen points behind champions Aston Villa, a team on the fast track back to their spiritual home. The Clarets were strong at Turf Moor, losing just twice and conceding eleven goals in twenty-one games. Arthur Woodruff had settled into his defensive role and he would go on to play 271 League games for the Clarets, in spite of having a career decimated by the war. He was ably assisted in his duties by the skipper Alick Robinson, still going strong and well on his way to topping two hundred appearances for the club. Goals however were hard to come by, particularly away from the "Turf", but Bob Brocklebank, signed the previous season from Aston Villa, was the leading contributor. They defeated the champion as well as runner-up Manchester United at home and actually drew away at the Villa, but there were inconsistent performances such as losing at home to Chesterfield and Plymouth Argyle. They finished nine points from promotion and to be fair they lacked the strength, talent and most importantly the resources of the elite of the Division.

There were worrying times however for the supporters of Blackburn Rovers. Reg Taylor was working with a weakened squad and although they finished sixteenth, the gap to the relegation spots was a mere two points. Fortunately, a 2-1 home win over Tottenham Hotspur on the penultimate Saturday of the season moved them away from danger. Jack Bruton was playing his last full season as a professional footballer. He had of course been successful at Turf Moor and was an automatic starter for nine seasons at Ewood with 324 appearances and 108 league goals. Exciting it may have been for the fans as they cracked in seventy-one goals, Len Butt being leading scorer. The eighty conceded did however indicate the weakness in their line-up and towards the end of the season, Taylor was moved back upstairs and Bob Crompton returned yet again. He quickly concentrated on the defensive side of their game and the club was able to drag itself to safety, winning four and drawing one of their last eight games. The rescue act was due to Bill Guest in no small way, the outside left hitting the net seven times in the final six matches.

The derby games

Blackburn Rovers were mid-table when they hosted Burnley in the season's first derby game, two weeks before Christmas. Burnley, several places above in eighth, were therefore a slight favourite, but the game turned out to be a rip-roaring affair. Willie Miller, born in Falkirk but signed from Everton, put the visitors in front before half-time. Len Butt levelled the scores shortly after the restart, but Stein's penalty opened up a Clarets lead once more, a goal which was quickly wiped out by Butt's second of the game. Local winger Tommy Storey appeared to have given Burnley the points with a third only for Jack Bruton to break Burnley hearts with a late equaliser. The outside right had been idolised on both sides of the great divide and this was his last derby outing, such a fitting end to a great career. The return in Burnley on April 23rd was a vital game for the visitors, but not even the reporter in the Burnley Express could show any excitement when writing about this end of season game.

> Victory Without Effort
> It is sad to think that this was a "Derby" match, and to think that old and mighty rivals like Burnley and Blackburn Rovers could not attract more than 12,500 spectators, sad to think that on an occasion of this kind one side could become so completely masters of the situation that they could assume an attitude of tolerance, if not indifference, walk to the ball instead of run to it, pass it with a take or leave it style and still know that they were giving nothing away... There was a time in this remarkable match when it seemed that Burnley were simply giving an exhibition. The Rovers... started smartly enough... but when it came to finishing... They shot often enough but hopelessly... Burnley could not miss but take the lead after 21 minutes. Brocklebank (was left) completely uncovered to receive a perfect ground pass from Stein (and) when he did shoot there was no chance of Matier saving... Guest did better immediately after the resumption for he rattled the crossbar... (but) Seven minutes later Stein... sent in a curling shot which dipped over Matier's uplifted arms... Half an hour had gone when Brocklebank completed his side's scoring. He headed in from Miller's pass. Rover's went straight down and scored. Bruton made the initial running, and passed to Chivers, who squared the ball for Guest to score. Most matches end with a roar from the crowd, but this one ended with a comparative silence.
> Burnley Express 28th April 1938

11 12 1937	Blackburn Rovers	Burnley	3-3	L Butt 2, J Bruton. W Miller, J Stein, T Storey.
23 04 1938	**Burnley**	Blackburn Rovers	3-1	R Brocklebank 2, J Stein. W Guest.

The further you fall down the pyramid, the higher the degree of difficulty in the FA Cup games. Tottenham Hotspur were amongst the leaders in Division 2 when Blackburn Rovers were drawn to play them away in Round 3. It was one of the better Rovers' performances with Tom Sale, a centre forward sold to Stoke City shortly afterwards and Guest on the score sheet, but the Spurs found the target three times; an exit in two consecutive seasons at the first time of asking for the Ewood club. Burnley's first opponents were Sheffield Wednesday whose star had diminished in recent years. They were near the foot of Division 2 but the Clarets had to rely on a Stein last minute equaliser to take the tie into a replay at Turf Moor. Once more they conceded early, but a brace from Brocklebank and one from Ronnie Hornby comfortably saw them through to Round 4. Chesterfield were on a decent run in Division 2, but a number of places behind the Clarets. It started well with a Miller penalty putting the visitors in front, but the Derbyshire side replied with three goals and a last minute effort from Billy Robson could only reduce the arrears.

1938-39

Team	Pos	Played	Won	Drawn	Lost	GF	GA	Pts
Blackburn Rovers	1	42	25	5	12	94	60	55
Burnley	14	42	15	9	18	50	56	39

Blackburn Rovers		Burnley	
Most Appearances	Walter Crook, Jack Weddle (both 42)	Most Appearances	Ted Adams 42
Most Goals	Nobby Clarke 21	Most Goals	Jim Clayton 10

War clouds may have been gathering over Western Europe, but from out of nowhere, the 1938-39 season was close to perfection for Blackburn Rovers. With a goal difference of plus thirty-four, a bountiful number of chances were made and although both Sheffield sides chased them all the way, Bob Crompton found the right track to guide them to the Division 2 trophy. Walter Crook was still a quality performer, Pryde and Whiteside still totally dependable but Crompton knew he had to add depth to his squad. And so he signed the English international forward Jack Weddle from Portsmouth who eventually became first team coach at the club. Nobby Clarke, a striker from Birmingham who topped the goals table, was also signed and the Manager was also quick to spot the talent and blood the young Burscough winger Bobby Langton. Each of these three for-

wards comfortably broke the double figure barrier for goals scored, as did Butt and Billy Rogers. One of Crompton's unsung heroes was right half Arnie Whiteside. He was a one club man who played at Ewood Park for sixteen years, totalling 218 first team appearances. He actually played at Ewood throughout the war years, starting in 166 games during that time, but typical of so many of his generation, by the time "official" football resumed, he was nearing the very end of his career. Captain of this trophy winning side was Bob Pryde.

The Scot put in a long stint either side of the war, and even with a seven-year war time gap, he still notched up 320 appearances. He was a tall centre half who performed so well for so long. Perhaps the most salient statistic however concerned the number of players used by Crompton. It was a record equalling low of nineteen, but even more pertinently, the same eleven players turned out on more than thirty occasions. Managers dream of saying "same side again".

The Blackburn Rovers Division 2 title winning side of 1938-39 (started over 31 games, max 42) was; Jimmy Barron, Billy Hough, Walter Crook, Arnie Whiteside, Bob Pryde, Frank Chivers, Billy Rodgers, Jack Weddle, Nobby Clarke, Len Butt, Bobby Langton.

Burnley had definitely believed that this could be their year. They had shown improvement the previous season, now was the time to kick on. Unfortunately, it never happened and the fans were left to look at Tommy Lawton's progress at Goodison Park, once more Division 1 leading scorer. In comparison, James Clayton topped the Burnley charts with a meagre ten goals, as the Clarets finished in an inauspicious fourteenth place. Jack Billingham and Billy Morris, signed respectively from Bristol City and Llandudno Town, made their debuts in the second half of the season and both would go on to feature prominently in the successful early post-war side. But this season turned out to be another in the "might have been" category. After four games, they topped the table, their best start since before the 1st World War, but then the inevitable slump followed. The team was hard working, gave of its best but it lacked star quality. Even to this day, the clubs who break out of the second tier to play at the top level have a couple of players with that essential stardust, but anyone who had even given an inkling about possessing star quality at Burnley had been sold over the last few years. Burnley, as a club, had a Division 2 mentality and those they had bought had been struggling to find a place in a Division 1 starting eleven. Unless there was a massive sea change at the club, promotion opportunities would be rare indeed.

The derby games

Blackburn Rovers had made a flying start to the season winning six and drawing one of their first eight games, but then losing two on the bounce. Burnley had made a less encouraging start but were in eleventh place as the first derby game loomed at Turf Moor. It was obvious that Division 2 games no longer pulled in the large crowds that Division 1 derbies had and so 15,136 at the game was probably thought to be acceptable. It was however an extremely pleasurable afternoon for those sporting claret and blue scarves; the pleasure of watching the prospective champions lose 3-2. Jimmy Clayton had been bought from Aston Villa the week before and this was his home debut. And what a way to start. Within fifteen minutes, he had scored twice and a form book upset was on its way. But the Rovers' front line was loaded with fire power and they roared back after the interval. Nobby Clarke scored his eighth and ninth goals of the season and the impetus lay with the visitors. But up popped Ronnie Hornby, taking advantage of a scramble in the penalty area to net a late winner and the Clarets had moved into the top ten. As was typical of the derby games in the inter-war years, there was rarely much between the sides on the day, irrespective of league placings. When the action switched to Ewood Park in February, the Rovers were leading the pack with the Clarets still in mid-table. It ought to have been a home win and it was, but only after a hard fought encounter which was settled by a Billy Rogers first-half strike.

15 10 1938	**Burnley**	Blackburn Rovers	3-2	J Clayton 2, R Hornby. N Clarke 2
18 02 1939	Blackburn Rovers	Burnley	1-0	W Rogers.

Keeping a regular starting eleven only happens when everything is going to plan and it certainly had done for Bob Crompton this season. And when you are on a roll, somehow the games seem less tough, including those in the FA Cup.

They were too good for Division 2 Swansea Town in Round 3 and for Southend United from Division 3 South in Round 4. Division 1 Sunderland were not having one of their best seasons but the Rovers matched them all the way in Round 5, ultimately coming away from the neutral venue of Hillsborough with a 1-0 victory courtesy of Guest's winner in the second replay. A 6th Round away trip to Huddersfield Town was just as daunting but Rovers once more battled to a 1-1 draw. A crowd of 54,400 packed the Blackburn ground for the replay but unfortunately, a semi-final place was denied them. Len Butt scored against his old team, but the Yorkshire side showed sufficient quality to emerge as 2-1 winners. For Burnley it was a case of "Hello Cup, Goodbye Cup". Notts County were languishing in the Division 3 South and a trip there in Round 3 seemed like an away banker. It was nothing of the sort, the Nottinghamshire side cruising to a 3-1 victory.

1939-45

After just one week of games in the 1939-40 season (the two Saturdays and a mid-week fixture), Prime Minister Neville Chamberlain announced to the country, huddled round their wireless sets on Sunday lunch time, that "we are now at war with Germany". The Football League immediately cancelled all fixtures. Because there had been no immediate attempt at an invasion of the British Isles, they organised a "Football League Wartime Cup." It was played over three months from March 1940 onwards and the two finalists were West Ham United and Blackburn Rovers. The final was played at Wembley, watched by a 40,000 plus crowd in early evening, in spite of fears that the Luftwaffe may begin to bomb the capital at any time. The Rovers were at full strength apart from Bobby Langton, one of the first to be mobilised. It was a close encounter, the Hammers winning courtesy of the only goal of the game scored by Sam Small. Burnley had also entered and after defeating Chester, they lost to Blackpool by a 5-1 aggregate score line over two legs. During this season and the following six, there was a War Time Regional League, similar to what occurred in the First World War. Once again, scores and final league tables were produced, but none are included in the official statistics regarding either clubs or players. As the war turned serious, the country needed an antidote to the threat of injury, death and the very real fear of invasion, so Prime Minister Winston Churchill was in favour of football carrying on. Attendances were generally poor however, the last two matches at Ewood Park of the 1939-40 campaign brought in gates of 300 and 347, the opponents being Carlisle United and Rochdale. Not even Burnley could entice spectators through the gate for a derby encounter, only 1,233 attending the December fixture at Ewood.

The vast majority of footballers signed up to fight in the war and there were some who had to fight in the most dangerous of arenas. Others however had it far easier. Many were fortunate to be given the rank of PTI (Physical Training

Instructor) and they were based at large army bases such as Aldershot, ensuring that soldiers were fighting fit prior to being mobilised abroad. It was also possible to be in a regiment posted far away from the serious action. Bobby Langton, being a young man at the Rovers in 1939, was part of the first cohort to be signed up and he was quickly posted to India. Harry Potts, a similarly aged young man at Burnley, also spent most of the war on the sub-continent. Blackburn Rovers lost two of their regular first teamers. Centre forward Nobby Clarke was sadly killed on active service in France in 1944 and Frank Chivers, who had opted to be a "Bevin Boy", working down the mines, was actually killed in a pit explosion. Probably the most mourned wartime death at Ewood Park however had nothing to do with the war. On March 15, 1941, the Rovers had just finished a match against Burnley at Ewood Park, the result of the game being a 3-2 home win. Bob Crompton, still managing the side, had a heart attack. He died overnight at the age of sixty-one, a terribly sad but somehow appropriate way for such a footballing legend's life to come to an end. The irony of the opposition and of course the result would not have been lost on the locals. If such things are possible, a man of the calibre of Crompton would never have left life's stage on the back of a defeat to his club's greatest rivals.

There were many players of course who suffered from history drawing a veil over six years of football. There is no doubt that the war interfered with so many footballing careers; in fact, it is true to say that a number were actually ruined or never even started because they lost the opportunity to play at the highest of levels. They will never be remembered. But how many more caps would the likes of Stanley Matthews, Tom Finney and Tommy Lawton have won? Where would they now stand, not so much in the panoply of all-time greats (they are there already) but on the lists of most capped/highest goal scorers? We will never know and they could claim to be unlucky to have been born in that particular generation, but at least they came back to resume their careers. The Second World War claimed far fewer victims than its 1914-18 predecessor, but there are still thousands of graves both here and abroad containing the bodies of young soldiers killed in action or families wiped out by the German bombing raids on our large cities. Had the 21st century celebrity obsessed social media been around in those days, it would have bemoaned the fate of the "Super Star footballers", so unfortunate to be denied the opportunity to make more money and become even more famous through their chosen profession. But in 1940s working class parlance, they were "bloody lucky still to be alive".

But just briefly throwing out a few names of players with blighted careers, Harry Potts certainly comes to mind. He made his debut at the "Turf" in 1940 but was only able to make nine (non-official) appearances in the next six years. It is reasonable to think that in normal circumstances, he would have been placed towards the very top of the "appearances" and "goals" charts. Bob Brocklebank from a slightly earlier generation made 189 war time appearances and scored seventy-seven times during these turbulent times. Adding his pre-war contributions, his goal tally was 110 from well over three hundred starts. Arthur Woodruff, George Bray, Jack Billingham, Harold Mather and Billy Morris all played before and after the war in the Claret and Blue shirt and their final totals would have taken them close to such post-war luminaries as Adamson, Dobson and Miller in the all-time top ten had war time appearances counted.

Those who suffered most at Blackburn Rovers were the ones who played before and after the War. Bobby Langton's total of eleven England caps would have been much greater. Bob Pryde's 320 appearances would have certainly topped 500, bringing him close to Crompton in third place. Walter Crook and Arnold Whiteside, great defensive mainstays of the club, also turned out in the immediate post-war seasons and they too would have massively contributed to their official figures. Forwards Billy Rogers, Bill Guest and Len Butt would certainly have featured amongst the top twenty strikers at the club.

With the war ending in Europe on May 8th, 1945 but in the Far East on the 2nd of September, the Football League decided to postpone the commencement of the new season until September 1946.

Downs and Ups at Ewood... The Long and Winding Road at The Turf 1946 – 1958

That it's getting better.
Growing stronger,
Getting better every day, better every day.
Barry Mann and Cynthia Weil

There was something different about Burnley immediately after the war. For the previous ten seasons and more, they had resembled a ship without a rudder, never in control of their own destiny. Suddenly, to the delight of their loyal supporters, they had re-emerged as a club on a mission. Their days in Division 2 post-war were of the shortest possible duration, but unless they were a club which had inherited a fortune (or perhaps with a Brian Clough as manager) it was going to take time to climb the ladder to the summit of English football.

But a scatter graph showing performances in these twelve years would definitely indicate a slow but steady upward movement. It was progress exponentially to use an Economics expression. As this phrase is not usually part of my every day vocabulary, I like to think of Mama Cass, sixties Hippy icon, who repeatedly sang "it's getting better". It perfectly sums up the progress of the Burnley club, one which was pulling itself up with its boot laces towards a future with no boundaries. It was, to quote Paul McCartney from a similar vintage, "a long and winding road". This was no German autobahn, it was a country road with twists and turns, but Burnley knew where they were heading and as this particular period of time covered by this chapter ended in '58, there was no doubt that the East Lancashire club had become a contender and glory could be only a couple of years away.

1945-46

There was no official League programme in the 1945-46 season, but there was a twenty-two strong League North in which the Clarets finished sixteenth, the Rovers twenty-first. However, the FA felt that there was time to squeeze in their own Cup competition. This one had official status and is referenced in all lists of the FA Cup. It was a colossal effort by the FA, completing the Extra Preliminary Round on September 1st and all the qualifying rounds by November 3rd. These were contested by non-league teams but to provide extra revenue for the professional clubs, Rounds 1-6 were then played as two legged affairs; the first game on the Saturday with the second leg in mid-week.

BILLY MORRIS, Burnley's Welsh international inside-forward.

There was little excitement emanating from East Lancashire this season with regard to the FA Cup. In fairness, both Burnley and Blackburn Rovers were given difficult ties. The Clarets had to face a Stoke City side which included the "wizard of the dribble" and Stanley Matthews was certainly the most famous if not the best player in the world at this time. He led them a merry dance in the Potteries as Stoke won 3-1, Morris on target for the Clarets and although Burnley edged their way to a 2-1 victory at Turf Moor with goals from Harry Jackson and Peter Kippax, they lost 4-3 on aggregate. The Rovers came out of the hat with Bolton Wanderers, a tough Division 1 side. A 1-0 defeat at Burnden Park in the first leg held out hope of a potential victory at Ewood, but although Cecil Wyles, a guest player from Everton who would complete the season as leading scorer with sixteen goals, scored for the Blackburn side, the Wanderers comfortably went through 4-1 on aggregate.

Following the death of Bob Crompton, the Blackburn Rovers committee looked after team affairs for war time matches. Eventually they did splash out, announcing that Eddie Hapgood was to be their new man in charge. He had played at left back in all of Arsenal's Championship and FA Cup winning sides during the thirties, captaining the club as well as England in many of his thirty international appearances. He was in his prime at thirty when the war broke out. He came to the Rovers at the age of thirty-five and the fans must have believed that he could re-create some of the magic that the Gunners had possessed in the previous decade. Burnley staggered on during the war years without an appointed manager, but In May 1945 they announced that Cliff Britton had taken charge. He too was a former international, playing in the same team as Hapgood on a number of occasions, and he too had won the FA Cup; with Everton.

1946-47

Team	Pos	Played	Won	Drawn	Lost	GF	GA	Pts
Blackburn Rovers	17	42	14	8	20	45	53	36
Burnley	2	42	22	14	6	65	29	58

Blackburn Rovers		Burnley	
Most Appearances	Bob Pryde 40	Most Appearances	Jimmy Strong, Harold Mather, Alan Brown (all 42)
Most Goals	Jack Smith 12	Most Goals	Harry Potts (15)

And so, after a seven-year gap, league football returned to the country on a national and official basis. There would be no guest players but the fixture list, which had been issued for the aborted 1939-40 season, was re-released and for once, the pundits had little idea as to the direction the trophies would be heading. Many of the stars of the late thirties had reached their "sell by date", others had returned with injuries which would hamper them over the length of the season and there were the new kids. These had developed their skills when too young to join the conflict but would provide the next generation of top players.

For example, Burnley had only Woodruff, Bray, Morris and Billingham representing the club either side of the war. Blackburn Rovers were more fortunate. Pryde, Whiteside, Rogers, Guest, Butt and Langton all kicked off the new season. Also turning out was Walter Crook, in the process of setting a new club record of 208 consecutive league appearances. The Blackburn Rovers side that Crompton brought up from Division 2 in 1939 had some potential but seven years on, it was mainly a mixture of talented but ageing professionals plus others of far less quality that Hapgood brought into the squad. Money was scarce and they lost ten times at home; real relegation form.

The points they picked up on their travels however from eight wins and three draws saved the day. They were also helped by Brentford and Leeds United finishing well adrift. Hapgood became disillusioned with a Board which made decisions without always consulting him so he resigned at the end of February. Will Scott his successor, had been the trainer at PNE and he saw them over the safety line, finishing seventeenth, guaranteeing another season in Division 1. Jack Smith, who was at the club for just this season, hit a hat-trick against Everton in a 4-1 home victory. Fourteen years after first arriving at Ewood from Scotland, Bob Pryde managed to make forty first team starts.

Cliff Britton told the Burnley AGM that the club would be in Division 1 in fifteen months' time. "Sheer bravado" thought the critics, but ten months later, the Clarets had put together a sixteen-game unbeaten run. Then after slipping up at home to Nottingham Forest on Boxing Day, another twelve games without

A. WOODRUFF

defeat brought promotion into view. There were several bumps in the road but a strong finish ended with a flourish. Manchester City were beyond reach, but there was no-one in Burnley who was dissatisfied with a second place finish and Division 1 waiting.

Harry Potts and Jack Billingham hit the goals, Alan Brown was one of Britton's shrewd buys and he was immediately made captain. His strength and experience at centre half certainly instilled stability and confidence in the side. They conceded a mere twenty-nine league goals and their defence of Strong, Woodruff, Mather, Attwell, Brown and Bray became known as the "Iron Curtain". Inside forward Billy Morris was their only international, gaining his first Welsh cap. A new club record was set, eleven wins in twenty-one away games. Now the club could once more renew its rivalry with the "enemy" in Division 1.

The Burnley Division 2 promotion side (finishing 2nd) 1946-47 (started over 20 games, max 42) was; Jimmy Strong, Arthur Woodruffe, Harold Mather, Reg Attwell, Alan Brown, George Bray, Jackie Chew, Billy Morris, Jack Billingham, Harry Potts, Peter Kippax, Ray Harrison.

Britton believed in consistency when it came to picking the side. You needed the rub of the green with regard to injury, but the fans could arrive at the ground knowing the team. This was the norm in those days. There was no rotation and certainly no "Tinkerman" as manager. The game has changed since then. It is now far faster; the footballs travel much further and the players certainly run a much greater distance.

Back in the day, defenders rarely crossed the halfway line and attackers were not expected to race back to defend. With more space on the pitch with fewer players crowding the man on the ball, there was a limit to the amount of physical contact. On the other hand however, the pitches were often mud baths, the players were guaranteed far less protection by the referee and there was far more one v one tackling. Defending then was not about interceptions, keeping your shape or occupying a space. It was about wading into someone and trying to force the ball away from your opponent.

There were no dieticians, no strength and conditioning coaches and if a player sustained a serious injury, they would be out for a long time. Careers were often ended with a broken leg. There were also no substitutes, meaning that you had to play on when injured. If you could walk you had to go back on to the pitch. Rotating players is now seen as the way forward and I am not saying it is wrong. But the game then was just as exciting, enthralling and probably less predictable when a manager had eleven men and eleven men only at his disposal.

Burnley memorably defeated Division 1 Aston Villa, 5-1 at Turf Moor in the FA Cup. Meanwhile Blackburn Rovers could only draw 1-1 at home to Hull City but an improved performance in the replay gave them a 3-0 win, Rogers scoring twice. Port Vale were overcome 2-0 at Ewood and over in Burnley, the Clarets replicated the same score against Division 2 rivals Coventry City, both East Lancashire clubs being in Round 5 together for the first time since 1914.

It was a good omen for the Clarets as they beat Luton Town 3-0 at home in a replay, Harrison scoring all three. It was the end however for the Ewood Park side, narrowly losing 1-0 to Charlton Athletic at the Valley. Burnley made the trip to the North East in the last eight to take on Division 1 Middlesbrough.

The result was a 1-1 draw but the winter of '46 was the worst on record and the club was forced to dig many inches of snow from the pitch to enable the replay to take place on March 4th at the "Turf". A crowd of 49,244 witnessed the Tuesday afternoon replay as it moved into extra time, before the diminutive Morris scored the winner. Liverpool were the semi-final opposition, Ewood Park ironically the venue.

Again, there were no goals and so Maine Road, Manchester was the designated ground for the replay. The Merseyside club was champion elect of Division 1 and the double was in their sights but Ray Harrison scored the only goal of the game late in the second half to send the Clarets to Wembley Stadium for the very first time, meeting Charlton Athletic.

The final against an under achieving Division 1 side, albeit the runner up from the previous final, was certainly winnable. Until extra time, the highlight of the game had been the ball actually bursting during the game, but then in a very close affair, Charlton's Chris Duffy snatched the vital goal in the 114th minute. Burnley had given it their best shot, Potts hit the bar but at least it was back to Division 1

The Burnley 1947 FA Cup Runner-Up side that lost by a goal to nil after extra time against Charlton Athletic was; Jimmy Strong, Arthur Woodruffe, Harold Mather, Reg Attwell, Alan Brown, George Bray, Jackie Chew, Billy Morris, Ray Harrison, Harry Potts, Peter Kippax.

1947-48

Team	Pos	Played	Won	Drawn	Lost	GF	GA	Pts
Burnley	3	42	20	12	10	56	43	52
Blackburn Rovers	21	42	11	10	21	54	72	32

Blackburn Rovers		Burnley	
Most Appearances	Bob Pryde 40	Most Appearances	Jimmy Strong, George Bray (both 42)
Most Goals	Les Graham 15	Most Goals	Harry Potts 14

To the joy and surprise of the whole town, Burnley achieved a third place finish in Division 1. Goals were at a premium both home and away, Jack Billingham notching the only hat-trick in the home victory over Portsmouth. The defence, expertly marshalled by Alan Brown, was at its most miserly, conceding an average of just one goal per game, only Manchester United taking them to the cleaners by knocking in five in Manchester.

It was an exceptional performance from a Burnley team which had just been promoted. From the third game of the season, the Clarets lost just once until Boxing Day, that being a 1-0 home defeat to Arsenal. By now they were second in the league, just behind the front-running Gunners. There were occasional defeats from then on, but victories over Chelsea and Huddersfield Town saw them clinch a place on the podium, their best finish for twenty-seven years. Turf Moor saw its record league gate in October as the Clarets defeated Blackpool 1-0 in front of 52,869 spectators.

Another interesting feature during the immediate post war period was the regular inclusion of Peter Kippax, a pure amateur who would have been the first amateur to play for the England professional side since 1922 had he not been taken ill the evening before the game v France and had to withdraw. He actually played for Great Britain in the 1948 London Olympic Games, but as the son of a wealthy mill owner in Burnley, he chose to work in the family business, playing football as a hobby.

The Blackburn manager Will Scott became extremely ill in the early part of the new campaign. Local hero Jack Bruton had been appointed assistant trainer after the war and he stood in for Scott, eventually taking over in December. Scott eventually recovered and went on to manage Preston North End with distinction. The Rovers really struggled, winning only eight home games and had to suffer the ignominy of a 7-1 thrashing by a lowly Middlesbrough side at Ewood Park. It was downhill all the way from then onwards; just one win in their final ten games seeing them relegated alongside Grimsby Town, four points adrift of safety.

So, after just one season together in the same league, the Clarets and the Rovers were once more separated, this time for another ten-year stretch. Les Graham, in his first season at this level, was leading scorer, hitting a hat-trick at home against Sheffield United for a 4-1 victory. As usual in a struggling side, there were many team changes from week to week. Local born wing half Jimmy Baldwin was a regular in the side before being transferred to Leicester City.

The derby games

For all of this season, Burnley and Blackburn Rovers were almost a full division apart but typically, the derby games were exciting affairs. The October game was played at Ewood Park. The immediate post-war seasons were noted for the large crowds and the 41,635 attendance watched intently as locally born right-back Bob Tomlinson gave Burnley a fifth minute lead by scoring an own goal. It was another fifty minutes before Billy Morris increased their lead before Alec Venters, bought from Third Lanark, raised the hopes of the locals with a 63rd minute goal.

The Clarets however hung on to a win which kept them knocking on the Podium door. Early March was scheduled for the return game and the Rovers had suddenly put together a run of seven games with one defeat to lift them away from the relegation zone. The Burnley players had pushed themselves into second spot and so this was a game which both sides needed to win. It was another whopping crowd, 44,240 but they all left for home feeling disappointed. The goalless draw did neither side a favour, although the Ewood Park side was probably the happiest.

Only Pryde and Langton amongst the Blue and Whites had previously played in a derby game but for the Claret and Blues, Woodruff, Bray, Billingham and Morris had all played in the 1938-39 season. Up until this season, there had been head to heads in Division 1, in Division 2 and there were the years when all that Burnley fans could do was to look upwards and watch the Rovers playing all the big clubs. Suddenly there was a different scenario. Blackburn Rovers had been relegated to Division 2, Burnley were sitting proudly amongst the elite and now it was the turn of the Rovers' fans to look upwards with envy in their eyes. Au revoir once more to derby games.

18 10 1947	Blackburn Rovers	**Burnley**	1-2	A Venters. o.g, Morris.
06 03 1948	Burnley	Blackburn Rovers	0-0	

Burnley's 3rd Round exit from the FA Cup was inexcusable, losing 2-0 at home to Division 3 South side Swindon Town; a Wiltshire club usually playing one or two tiers below which had become something of a bogy side. Blackburn Rovers were left as East Lancashire's sole representative and they almost came down at the first fence, drawing 0-0 at home to the 2nd Division's West Ham United, but winning the replay 4-2. Charlie McClelland, a reserve inside forward who went on to have a long career with Exeter City, scored twice. Drawn away in Round 4 to Southampton, a leading Division 2 team, they gave it their best shot but went out by the odd goal in five.

1948-49

Team	Pos	Played	Won	Drawn	Lost	GF	GA	Pts
Burnley	15	42	12	14	16	43	50	38
Blackburn Rovers	14	42	15	8	19	53	63	38

Blackburn Rovers		Burnley	
Most Appearances	Bill Eckersley 42	Most Appearances	Jimmy Strong 42
Most Goals	Dennis Westcott 21	Most Goals	Jackie Chew 11

Burnley supporters had stars in their eyes as August 21st, 1948 approached. Not only would this signal the very first time that they were competing at a tier above Blackburn Rovers, but they had every right to gaze at the pinnacle of English football. And those eyes continued to sparkle as excitement grew, step by step. It is never easy for football fans to blend together patience and expectancy and to repeat the stunning performance of the previous season was not going to happen, particularly when they sold Alan Brown, the centre piece of the Iron Curtain defence, and manager Cliff Britton left for Everton; money talking in both deals. To lose Britton towards the end of September was a bitter blow. A promotion, a Wembley visit and then a top three finish indicated the ability of the man. The club appointed Frank Hill as the new boss. Capped by Scotland at right-half, he had won medals in the great pre-war Arsenal side and became player-manager at Crewe Alexandra from whence Burnley lured him. He built his sides on a solid defence and in six years developed the Clarets into an established Division 1 outfit. The initial fifteenth place was disappointing but they had survived what could have been a difficult season. In the FA Cup, the defeat at Wembley was avenged with a 2-1 home win over Charlton Athletic, Rotherham United were beaten 1-0 in Yorkshire and then unexpectedly, the poor Division 2 side Brentford beat them 4-2 in London in the 5th Round.

Relegated at the end of spring 1948, the whole of Blackburn expected a promotion charge in the lower league, but it was not to be. They finished fourteenth but too close to relegation in a congested division. Bruton signed Dennis Westcott, a prolific scoring centre forward from Wolverhampton Wanderers and the form of a young left back brought from amateur football in Southport really excited the crowds. Bill Eckersley [pictured] was a small man, but he was quick, could time a tackle to perfection and was completely at ease on the ball. Even though performing in Division 2, he began to attract the attention of the international selectors. There was a notable 7-1 win over Lincoln City, but it was no surprise when Bruton was sacked at the end of the campaign to be replaced by Jackie Bestall. Like his predecessor, Bestall had been capped by England, whilst at Grimsby Town. He had cut his management teeth at Doncaster Rovers as they stormed to the Division 3 North title in 1947. This season was the swan song for their rock-like leader, Bob Pryde. Bobby Langton, in his prime, had moved to Preston North End during the summer for £16,000 but Dennis Westcott saved the day with his twenty-one league goals. Eddie Crossan, a mercurial inside right bought from Derry City in 1948 for £3,000, played for ten seasons, managing a total of 73 goals in 287 games which ranks at fifteenth in the all-time list. Eric Bell started his ten year stint at left-half. Plucked out of non-league football in Northumberland at the age of twenty-five, he retired after 323 first team games in 1956. But life had been a struggle on the pitch and they crashed out of the FA Cup in Round 3, losing to Hull City.

1949-50

Team	Pos	Played	Won	Drawn	Lost	GF	GA	Pts
Burnley	10	42	16	13	13	40	40	45
Blackburn Rovers	16	42	14	10	18	55	60	38

Blackburn Rovers		Burnley	
Most Appearances	Eric Bell 42	Most Appearances	Jimmy Strong, Harry Potts 42
Most Goals	Dennis Westcott 16	Most Goals	Harry Potts 11

Burnley scored and conceded forty goals the following campaign; weak in attack but watertight at the back. It was nothing to send the supporters into ecstasy but tenth spot was extremely acceptable and with the young Tommy Cummings now an established player and Jimmy McIlroy signed from Glentoran for £7,000, being a Claret felt somehow comfortable. In the FA Cup, both Notts County and Port Vale were overturned before Arsenal had too much for them in Round 5.

Life was still dull at Ewood Park. "We cannot finish fourteenth again," thought the faithful and they were quite right. Blackburn Rovers completed the season in sixteenth spot, equalling the 1937-38 debacle as their lowest ever position. It was no fun being a Blue and White fan but Bill Eckersley made the England World Cup party and reserve team goalkeeper Bill Hughes won five Welsh caps. Westcott was transferred to Manchester City for a fee of £12,500 in February, but still managed to top the list of goal scorers. Ron Suart arrived from Blackpool in 1949 and made 176 starts at full back or centre half. Over 50,000 flocked into the ground to watch the Round 3 FA Cup tie versus Liverpool and they witnessed a goalless stalemate, but in the replay at Anfield, the Rovers went down 2-1.

1950-51

Team	Pos	Played	Won	Drawn	Lost	GF	GA	Pts
Burnley	10	42	14	14	14	48	43	42
Blackburn Rovers	6	42	19	8	15	65	66	46

Blackburn Rovers		Burnley	
Most Appearances	Jack Patterson 42	Most Appearances	George Bray 42
Most Goals	Les Graham 13	Most Goals	Bill Holden 12

"If you don't concede you can't lose" continued to be Frank Hill's dictum in the 50-51 season. The side had to work hard for their meagre total of 48 goals, the league's joint lowest as they finished tenth again and at the conclusion of their fourth consecutive season in Division 1, the fans were now becoming accustomed to seeing the elite of English football parading their skills at Turf Moor. Surprisingly however, Harry Potts, their most prolific and certainly most imaginative player since the end of the war, was sold to Everton. A total of 47 goals in 165 games was an excellent return for someone who was ostensibly a play-maker rather than an out and out scorer. The Burnley eleven that almost completed the double (FA Cup runner-up and second in Division 2) provided the back bone of the side, particularly defensively. Both Potts, and Brown two years before, has been sold for good money, but the others, such as the Oswaldtwistle born George Bray [pictured] who later served in a number of roles with the club, all virtually completed their careers at Turf Moor. Philip Webster, son in law of Harry, explained why Potts left.

> "Harry always used to say that he was happy at Turf Moor so I asked him why he left for Everton. It appears that the Burnley contracts at that time were for the football season only. They received no money during the summer months but they did at Everton. Also there was the suggestion that whereas the Burnley lads were on £11 a week, they could earn £17 at Everton. He had just turned thirty and knowing that a footballer's career was usually ended by their mid-thirties, he had to look after the interests of his family."

The faithful were shocked at this sale, but £20,000 for a thirty year old was good business for the club. Fortunately a star in the making had been a regular in the reserve side during the last few months of the previous season following his transfer from Glentoran in Northern Ireland. Once in the first team, Jimmy McIlroy quickly began to dictate the pace of play and set up the goals for the young Bill Holden. There was an early elimination from the FA Cup however when Aston Villa edged them out 1-0 in Round 3 down in Birmingham.

At Ewood Park, Jackie Bestall continued to offer encouragement to the crowds who, in spite of numerous setbacks at the club, were still flocking down Bolton Road to the ground. Over 44,000 saw them defeat Preston North End 2-1 in November. Sixth place was an improvement on the previous two seasons and there was an abundance of goals at both ends. In the last game of the season against Queens Park Rangers, a sixteen-year-old Ronnie Clayton made his debut at the end of a far more interesting and enjoyable campaign. There was a third successive Round 3 exit from the FA Cup, this time by a 2-1 margin at Bristol City. Continuity and commitment appeared to be absent at the club. It is difficult to point the finger at any one group; players, management or Directors and at such times, the loyal fan has to take it on the chin. Nonetheless, the feeling of frustration was high amongst those who cared for the club. Bill Eckersley was the outstanding player throughout the period, captaining the side, representing his country and being one of only six players to top the 400 mark in appearances made.

1951-52

Team	Pos	Played	Won	Drawn	Lost	GF	GA	Pts
Burnley	14	42	15	10	17	56	63	40
Blackburn Rovers	14	42	17	6	19	54	63	40

Blackburn Rovers		Burnley	
Most Appearances	Jackie Campbell 38	Most Appearances	Tommy Cummings 42
Most Goals	Eddie Quigley 11	Most Goals	Billy Morris 18

This was the season when Burnley and Blackburn Rovers finished the league programme with almost identical statistics. Both were placed fourteenth, they had equal points and conceded the same number of goals. There was one gigantic difference however. The Clarets were competing in Division 1, the Rovers a level below. Frank Hill's side were involved in two high scoring affairs. A trip to Newcastle United resulted in a 7-1 thrashing but when Middlesbrough paid a visit to Turf Moor, they returned home on the wrong end of an identical score line. Billy Morris scored a hat-trick in the demolition of the Teesiders and was also on target four times when West Bromwich Albion were thumped 6-1. Billy Elliott was signed from Bradford City for £23,000 and the left winger became the first Burnley player to be capped by England since Jack Bruton in 1928. He played five times, all in 1952 and was never on the losing side, scoring three times. Cummings, had taken over the captaincy and two lengthy

runs lifted them well clear of relegation to a season high seventh place but with eight of the last twelve being lost, it was another fourteenth place finish. Two Turf Moor stalwarts, survivors from the Wembley game, played at Turf Moor for the final time. Both defender Arthur Woodruff and half-back George Bray had played before the war and their final appearance total of 271 for Woodruff and 241 for Bray would have been so many more if war had not intervened.

The highlight of the Blackburn Rovers' 1951-52 season was the FA Cup run, but the league performance was disappointing. They won their first league game at the tenth attempt and were rock-bottom in mid-November. New blood was required and goalkeeper Reg Elvy from Bolton Wanderers and Willie Kelly, a centre-half from Airdrieonians joined the club. They were both moving towards the veteran stage, but each played almost two hundred games and were part of this most exciting side which eventually had fans flocking to Ewood Park. The gifted Eddie Quigley [pictured] from Preston North End was a good buy and for four seasons, he gelled so well with Briggs. His 92 goals from 159 appearances was extremely impressive. There was a rapid improvement in performance culminating in a fourteenth position finish. Round 3 of the 1952 FA Cup was successful for both East Lancashire clubs. Burnley beat lowly Hartlepools United 1-0 at the "Turf" and the Rovers accounted for Nottingham Forest at the second attempt. Both clubs came through 2-0 against Division 2 opposition in home ties in the next round, the Clarets against Coventry City, the Rovers against Hull City with goals from Nightingale and Wharton. Division 1 opposition bit the dust at both Turf Moor and Ewood Park in Round 5. Burnley deposed of Liverpool 2-0. Morris and Shannon being on target, the latter's second goal in this season's competition. The Blue and Whites eliminated West Bromwich Albion with the only goal of the game, a penalty from Bill Eckersley.

The derby FA Cup game

The Rovers were the first team out of the hat in the quarter final draw, followed immediately by the Turf Moor side. These were dizzy heights for the Ewood club and Burnley had become far more accustomed to playing at this level. It was previewed as a fascinating derby encounter, the first for four seasons. It was only their second FA Cup clash ever, the last one being a 1-0 victory for the Clarets in 1913. That too had been played in Blackburn, also in the quarter final, perhaps an omen for the Claret and Blues. The Burnley Express, partisan but generally objective, found it hard to believe that Burnley could lose against a team from the division below.

Burnley fade-out led to rout by Rovers: There is no excuse for this Cup-tie defeat. Blackburn Rovers hustled Burnley out of the competition exit door in a three goal rally after the Clarets had held the lead. After the opening fifteen minutes, Burnley looked to be well set for the semi-final, and it was a fair speculation, once Jackie Chew had given them the lead, as to how many times they would score... The turning point in the match however was in the 47th minute. Mr Bond... had ironically enough allowed time for injuries (particularly) when Billy Dougall had to minister to Elliott (injured in a clash of heads with Suart). Two Blackburn corners and then a third by Wharton which Glover turned into the centre for Nightingale to beat Strong... Burnley gave one of their most disjointed and discouraging displays of the season... and after 57 minutes Holmes headed through from Nightingale. After 82 minutes... Holmes beat the centre-half (Cummings) between the near post and corner flag and put in to Glover who was unmarked... By the end the Clarets were a well-beaten side... (the Rovers being) a keen, quick tackling opposition... a team of bonny cup fighters. By "Sportsman

Bill Holmes was an amateur who played in the number nine shirt for much of the season and the Rovers' reward was a semi-final pairing with Newcastle United.

08 03 1952	Round 6	Blackburn Rovers	Burnley	3-1	A Nightingale, W Holmes, A Glover. J Chew

Could it be their first Wembley appearance since 1928? The "Toon" were reigning cup holders but the Rovers showed great tenacity to hold their Division 1 opponents to a goalless draw at Hillsborough. Jackie Campbell, the ultimate utility man who started a total of 224 games in ten seasons, kept Bell out of side, with Ronnie Clayton occupying the number 6 shirt. In the replay at Elland Road the following Wednesday afternoon, Quigley was on target, but the Tynesiders were one of the country's best outfits and they came through 2-1.

1952-53

Team	Pos	Played	Won	Drawn	Lost	GF	GA	Pts
Burnley	6	42	18	12	12	67	52	48
Blackburn Rovers	9	42	18	8	16	68	65	44

Blackburn Rovers		Burnley	
Most Appearances	Reg Elvy, Ron Suart, Jackie Campbell (all 42)	Most Appearances	Tommy Cummings, Bill Holden, Les Shannon (all 42)
Most Goals	Eddie Quigley 18	Most Goals	Bill Holden 22

Burnley had a much improved season In 1952-53, finishing six points behind the leader in sixth position. Bill Holden scored four times in a 5-1 thumping of Sunderland. An eleven-game undefeated run from December into March was a signal to the rest of the league that this was an established top tier club. They topped the league for a couple of weeks and the title was in view but a poor finish burst that bubble.

Holden [pictured] was leading scorer, the first post-war twenty plus haul. Billy Morris and Jimmy Strong were the Wembley retirees this season, goalkeeper Strong after 246 starts and Welsh international forward Morris with 211 and 47 goals. Billy Elliott moved on to Sunderland for £26,000. He had impressed during his two year stay at Turf Moor. They reached the 5th Round of the FA Cup, going down 2-0 to Arsenal at the "Turf" after defeating Portsmouth and Sunderland, Holden notching a double against the Roker Park side.

Blackburn Rovers' start to the 1952-53 campaign was so disappointing and by the end of December, the club was again in trouble. They conceded six at Luton Town and with one win in twelve games, they needed a major signing. Tommy Briggs, arriving from Birmingham City was the answer. He scored goals for fun, a centre forward of his time with a rocket shot and good in the air; in other words quite a handful. Ultimately his 140 goals in 194 games (a 0.72 goal ratio) beggar belief, but his early goals, along with those of Eddie Quigley, turned around the fortunes of the side. Just three defeats in their last eighteen games saw them to the safe haven of ninth in the league. Manager Jackie Bestall, realising his unpopularity with the fans and players in his four year tenure, tendered his resignation at the end of the season. The Rovers had been hammered 6-0 at Luton Town earlier in the season and they returned in Round 3 of the FA Cup, hoping to show improvement. This time they scored but still conceded six again, their worst Cup debacle since 1909 at Old Trafford.

1953-54

Team	Pos	Played	Won	Drawn	Lost	GF	GA	**Pts**
Burnley	7	42	21	4	17	78	67	46
Blackburn Rovers	3	42	23	9	10	86	50	55

Blackburn Rovers		**Burnley**	
Most Appearances	Reg Elvy, Ron Suart, Willie Kelly (all 42)	Most Appearances	Billy Gray 42
Most Goals	Tommy Briggs 32	Most Goals	Billy Gray 19

THOMAS SMITH CUMMINGS - BURNLEY

Led by Tommy Cummings, Burnley continued to impress, particularly at home as they completed the 53-54 season in seventh place. There was an impressive 5-2 victory at Arsenal and sixteen victories at home regularly sent the faithful home happy. Billy Gray, a talented winger was signed from Chelsea and Chorley born Brian Pilkington, signed from Leyland Motors, established himself as the first team left winger this season, replacing Billy Elliott. The Clarets were amongst the promotion contenders for virtually the whole of the season and only three successive defeats as winter turned to spring denied them a podium finish.

Jackie Chew, the goal scoring right winger finally said goodbye, moving to Bradford City after making 225 appearances. As expected from a side in the top half of Division 1, international caps started to flow towards Burnley players. Brian Pilkington won a solitary English cap in 1954 and McIlroy was now a regular in the Northern Irish side. Jock Aird amazingly became their first Scottish capped player. He appeared in the 1954 World Cup (his fourth and final appearance) before emigrating to New Zealand at the end of the following season. Here he won international recognition once again, twice representing the Kiwis; a rare footballing dual international at senior level. There was a Fourth Round FA Cup reverse which Mike Duffy well remembers from this season.

> The first two games that stand out in what can sometimes be hazy recollections were in the post-Christmas period in the 1953-54 season. In the FA Cup in January, Burnley really turned it on to beat Manchester United 5-3 with goals from Shannon who scored twice, Holden, McIlroy and Gray. Later the same month my father who was from the North East wore two different coloured rosettes as Burnley played Newcastle United, Pilkington scoring in a 1-1 draw at the Turf. Sadly, the Round 4 replay ended in a 0-1 defeat.

The Blackburn Rovers Board gambled on a great player to replace Bestall, but one with no managerial experience. The Dublin born Johnny Carey was an outstanding right back at Old Trafford, captaining the club to FA Cup and Division 1 honours. On retirement, he came to the Rovers and how the Ewood crowd took to his attacking philosophy. Briggs found the net on thirty-two occasions and Quigley twenty two. The fixtures against Lincoln City achieved a remarkable swing of 14 goals in the two games, the Rovers winning 6-0 at Ewood Park, having gone down 8-0 at Sincil Bank early in the season; still their joint record league defeat. The Blue and Whites finished third, pipped at the post when Leicester City beat them 4-0 on Easter Monday and Everton won their final game. It was a valiant effort, achieved by just eighteen players, but expectations were now high in Blackburn. They looked east to watch the progress of Burnley, not so much jealous but with an eagerness to join their adventure. Bill Eckersley received his seventeenth and final English cap against the Magyar masters, the Hungarians smashing the hosts 6-3 at Wembley in a watershed moment for the English game and Eddie Crossan won his third Northern Ireland cap. Following a 1-0 home victory over Bristol Rovers, they reached Round 4 of the FA Cup but the 2-1 away defeat in the replay against an undistinguished Hull City side was disappointing.

1954-55

Team	Pos	Played	Won	Drawn	Lost	GF	GA	Pts
Burnley	10	42	17	9	16	51	48	43
Blackburn Rovers	6	42	22	6	14	114	79	50

Blackburn Rovers		Burnley	
Most Appearances	Ronnie Clayton, Eric Bell, Frank Mooney, Bobby Langton (all 42)	Most Appearances	Les Shannon 42
Most Goals	Tommy Briggs 33	Most Goals	Bill Holden 14

Burnley claimed their third consecutive top ten finish......just. There was a paucity of goals in their games; the only team in the league with goals for and against totalling less than 100. Frank Hill had accepted an offer from Preston North End and the Burnley Board brought back Alan Brown to replace him. His on-field influence had played a massive part in the glorious year of 1947, and he had been coach at Sheffield Wednesday. His three years at Turf Moor were ones of consolidation rather than success, but he was the master of the defensive game, guiding them to a respectable tenth place. The last of the team of '47 played their final games for the club. Reg Attwell (244 appearances) and Harold Mather (301) moved out of the professional game. It is easy to see the loyalty within the group, a loyalty which probably came from the feeling of contentment at such a homely club. Burnley fell at the first hurdle of the FA Cup, losing 1-0 at Sunderland to a side which would finish fourth in Division 1, ex Claret Billy Elliott scoring the goal.

The Blackburn fans were roused to a state of hysteria by the attacking fare laid before them in the 1954-55 campaign. A record 114 league goals were scored, 69 of them at Ewood Park. Middlesbrough conceded nine, Doncaster Rovers seven and Bristol Rovers eight. I watched all three matches, but the most memorable was the Bristol game when the visitors led 3-2 after 45 minutes. Tommy Briggs crashed in six after the break to add to his first half effort and his seven goals is a club record, just as the 9-0 win over Middlesbrough is still their record league win. Fascinatingly, all five Rovers forwards reached double figures for the campaign. They were defensively suspect however, which led to a disappointing sixth place, four points from promotion. Even more disappointing was the crashing out of the FA Cup at the first time of asking, a 2-0 home defeat to Swansea Town who finished well below them in Division 2.

1955-56

Team	Pos	Played	Won	Drawn	Lost	GF	GA	Pts
Burnley	7	42	18	8	16	64	54	44
Blackburn Rovers	4	42	21	6	15	84	65	48

Blackburn Rovers		Burnley	
Most Appearances	Ronnie Clayton 42	Most Appearances	Colin McDonald 42
Most Goals	Tommy Briggs 31	Most Goals	Peter McKay 25

Tommy Cummings had led the vanguard for the next wave of star players at Burnley and he, Jimmy Adamson and McIlroy played throughout the fifties; all with great distinction. A number of those who followed came off the Gawthorpe production line, some even brought in as school leavers and nurtured, coached and trained to the level expected of Division 1 players. As opposed to the subsequent Bob Lord era, the Clarets were still a buying club. In the fifties, money had been spent on Elliott, Les Shannon from Liverpool, Gray, McIlroy and Peter McKay bought from Dundee United. Those who made the journey from Gawthorpe to the first team included Roy Stephenson, Adamson, John Angus, Adam Blacklaw, Albert Cheeseborough, John Connelly, Walter Joyce, Brian Miller, Jimmy Robson, Bobby Seith and David Smith. Bill Holden followed Elliott to Sunderland, this time for £12,000. The Bolton born centre forward had netted 74 times in 187 appearances, but had lost his place to McKay. Burnley once again showed that they belonged in this company with a satisfying seventh spot, Seven narrow home defeats spoiled their season but on the credit side, there were seven away victories with a 3-1 win at Maine Road against a resurgent Manchester City being the pick of the crop. Peter McKay continued his goal scoring run from his Tannadice days, his twenty-five strikes being the best at the "Turf" since George Beel in 1931. Scotsman Bobby Seith at last was given a sustained run in the side and Colin McDonald had now become the number one goalkeeper, arguably the best prospect in the country. In 1956,

Burnley were given a home tie against reigning Division 1 Champions Chelsea in Round 4. And what a long, drawn out affair it proved to be. The Clarets, in fine form, were favourites. Initially there were 1-1 draws at Turf Moor and at Stamford Bridge. The clubs were then ordered to play the second replay at St Andrews in Birmingham where it ended 2-2. The FA, possibly lacking in basic geographical knowledge north of Watford, opted for Arsenal's Highbury Stadium for the next neutral venue. This time the clubs obliged with a goalless draw and so to even up affairs (he added sarcastically), Tottenham's White Hart Lane was chosen for the fourth replay. The game was finally played and it was the Londoners who triumphed, beating a no doubt tired and weary Burnley 2-0.

In the 55-56 campaign, Tommy Briggs blasted in another 31 goals for Blackburn Rovers and the main change was the sibling wing half pairing of Ron and Ken Clayton, the latter replacing Eric Bell. Ronnie made his England debut and he was such an inspiration with stamina to burn. My dad said that he covered every blade of grass on the pitch, such a strong compliment. Port Vale was the sacrificial lamb to the slaughter, losing 7-1 at Ewood; Crossan with a hat-trick. The Rovers finished equal on points to Liverpool, and the home game against the Merseysiders was a classic, Crossan scoring twice in a 3-3 draw. Ultimately however, the fourth place was good, but not quite good enough, finishing four points short yet again of promotion. National Service commitments made it difficult for Bryan Douglas to play for the first team and he was twenty-one before he became a regular, This is how he remembers that time.

"I did not know this at the time, but my rise to the first team was due to the influence of Ron Suart. He had been a good professional, playing at right back in the first team for years, but he was now taking his coaching badges and helping out with the Reserves. He apparently approached Johnny Carey and told him that I was ready for the first team. I was selected at inside left against Stoke City. We won 3-0 and I scored the second goal. It was the sort of goal you couldn't miss. Langton went past the full back and slipped it across and I scored from about three yards. I thought I was struggling at this level after playing twice more at number ten, but the next Friday I looked at the team sheet which had been pinned up and I was selected at outside right, replacing Frank Mooney. My dad rarely interfered with my football, but he did on this occasion. He asked me why I had stopped taking people on. "This is your game" he said. "Get back to doing it". So I went out against Bury at Gigg Lane and started to dribble again. We won 4-0 and I scored once more. This was a more satisfying goal as I burst through and dribbled round the goal keeper and tapped it in. The manager picked me at number seven for the rest of the season and I was suddenly capturing the headlines. But I still knew my place in the team. I was twenty-one and the rest of the front four, Crossan, Briggs, Quigley and Langton were all at least ten years older than me. Because I was small, full backs thought they could kick me and rough me up and on at least three occasions, I was dumped in a heap down by the corner flag as they tried to smack me into the wall on the other side of the grass. Each time Willie Kelly raced forward from the half-way line and screamed at me to get up straight away. "If you stay down, they will think you are soft, Don't show them you are hurt". It was good advice but not that easy to follow when you feel like your leg is broken. Another time, Bobby Langton came up to sit next to me at the break and took my face in his hands. He then smacked me across the face, not that hard but each smack was in tune with him saying "Pass-the-ball, pass-the-ball". It was their way of helping me to survive at this level. They were so experienced and I was the novice. But although I had so much skill, you also had to be smart, tough and street wise to be successful. I learnt all that from these veterans."

In the FA Cup, they reached Round 5 before going down 3-2 in the replay at home against a struggling West Ham United side. Both Northampton Town and Barnsley had been beaten in Rounds 3 and four and a satisfactory draw at Upton Park set them up nicely for the replay, but the result at home quite dismayed the Thursday afternoon crowd of almost 30,000.

1956-57

Team	Pos	Played	Won	Drawn	Lost	GF	GA	Pts
Burnley	7	42	18	10	14	56	50	46
Blackburn Rovers	4	42	21	10	11	83	75	52

Blackburn Rovers		Burnley	
Most Appearances	Bryan Douglas, Tommy Briggs 42	Most Appearances	Bobby Seith 41
Most Goals	Tommy Briggs 32	Most Goals	Jimmy McIlroy 13

Burnley once more furthered their reputation in the 56-57 term, only losing twice at home, both times at the feet of the Manchester clubs. It was another strong season, a consecutive seventh place and Colin McDonald was showing the nation how good a keeper he was. This was their tenth season in a row at the top level and they were looking like they were there to stay. Injuries gave the manager the opportunity to blood Angus and Miller and the only problem was at number nine. McKay could score goals, but he was a tiny striker who did little off the ball and Brown quickly shipped him off to St Mirren. At the end of the season, Billy Gray was allowed to move to Nottingham Forest for £4,500 where he went on to win an FA Cup winner's medal. Burnley brought their shooting boots to Turf Moor in the FA Cup, recording a resounding 7-0 victory over Chesterfield from Division 3 North. Those shooting boots were given an extra lick of polish for the visit of Lancashire Combination side New Brighton in Round 4. The gulf in class was enormous, Burnley scoring at will on their way to a record equalling 9-0 victory. The headline story concerned the young Burnley centre forward Ian Lawson. He made his debut versus Chesterfield and scored four times. Against New Brighton he notched a hat-trick as did Jimmy McIlroy. It was the stuff of comic strip heroes. Lawson was on target yet again in Round 5 at Huddersfield Town, a 2-1 victory. By the time the 6th Round draw was made, there was much excitement in the town. It was Aston Villa, and Alan Brown's side missed a golden opportunity at home, only drawing 1-1. They then slumped to a 2-0 defeat in the replay, bidding adieu to the FA Cup once again. As for Lawson, the dream rapidly died. He was eventually transferred to Leeds United in 1962. His final League and Cup tally for the club was fifteen goals, of which eight had been scored in just three successive cup matches.

Blackburn Rovers came close once again, their fourth-place finish being just two points short of promotion. The goals certainly flowed and Tommy Briggs continued his unstoppable form. Johnny Carey virtually rebuilt the side. Youngsters Roy Vernon and Peter Dobing replaced Crossan and Quigley and he raided Goodison Park to sign Matt Woods and Harry Leyland to replace the ageing Elvy and Kelly. Langton retired to be replaced by Ally MacLeod from St Mirren and Ken Taylor made the right-back position his own. It was a side with potential, with talent and ambition, but on occasions the defence would go walk-abouts as when conceding six at Leicester and seven at Fulham. When the points were calculated at the season's end, it was the losses to two poor sides, Lincoln City and Port Vale, that consigned them to another year in Division 2. It was a tough FA Cup Round 3 away draw at Everton and although it was close, the Merseyside Blues won 1-0

1957-58

Team	Pos	Played	Won	Drawn	Lost	GF	GA	Pts
Burnley	6	42	21	5	16	80	74	47
Blackburn Rovers	2	42	22	12	8	93	57	56

Blackburn Rovers		Burnley	
Most Appearances	Harry Leyland, Matt Woods, Mick McGrath (all 42)	Most Appearances	Brian Pilkington 42
Most Goals	Peter Dobing 20	Most Goals	Jimmy McIlroy 16

Alan Brown was flattered by the interest from Sunderland and he returned to his roots to take over that sleeping giant. Bob Lord was chairman by now and thus began the policy of appointing from within the club. The veteran trainer Billy Dougall had been involved with the club as a player and coach since 1926, so he was a natural replacement to take over the managerial reins. But in no time, he was so seriously ill that he resigned the post and in January 1958, back came Harry Potts, the former blue eyed boy who had been managing Shrewsbury Town. It was the best appointment that Chairman Bob ever made and the Clarets were on the fast track to glory. Consistency returned to the side, Leicester City were thumped 7-3 and a run of seven wins and two draws in their last ten fixtures clinched an impressive sixth position. Jimmy McIlroy scored twice as Swansea Town were pushed aside in the FA Cup 3rd Round, but after drawing 2-2 at Division 2 Bristol Rovers, they truly messed up in the replay, going down 3-2 after leading 2-1.

Any club finishing third, sixth, fourth and fourth in consecutive seasons deserves to be promoted and this is exactly what happened to Blackburn Rovers the following campaign. It was a close-run thing and the Blue and Whites had to put together an unbeaten run of seven games at the sharp end of the term to push their chests over the line. Mick McGrath, a Republic of Ireland wing half had moved in as Ronnie Clayton's partner and Tommy Briggs' wonderful run was coming to an end. Peter Dobing came through the youth system to take over his mantle and was top scorer, including a four timer at home to Bristol City. And for the second half of the season, there was a cameo performance from Tom Johnston, signed from Leyton Orient on transfer deadline day. Carey wanted a steadying influence up front to guide them to promotion and the veteran provided just that, his eight goals in eleven games coupled with his overall team play instantly repaying his transfer fee. On the last day of the campaign, West Ham were certain to be promoted, but Charlton Athletic (who needed a draw), the Rovers and Liverpool could all go up with the Hammers. The fixture list had paired Charlton and Blackburn at the Valley and 56,435 turned out to witness a classic game of football. After conceding an early goal, a couple from Dobing and a screamer from Vernon had given them a comfortable interval lead. After Douglas converted a penalty following a foul on Johnston, it looked all over after sixty-five minutes. To their credit, Charlton battled back with two more goals and the last few minutes were nail-biting in the extreme before the final whistle gave the Rovers those two essential points. After ten years in Division 2, Blackburn Rovers were back in the big time. The derbies would return and these games would be difficult. But with both of the East Lancs sides once more able to go head to head, there were some exciting matches in prospect.

The Blackburn Rovers side that were promoted from Division 2 side in second place in 1957-58 (started over 15 games, max 42) was; Harry Leyland, Ken Taylor, Bill Eckersley, Ronnie Clayton, Matt Woods, Mick McGrath, Bryan Douglas, Roy Stephenson, Peter Dobing, Roy Vernon, Ally McLeod.

The supporters of Blackburn Rovers were at fever pitch because of the 1957-58 league campaign, but little did they know in January that the FA Cup trail was to lead to even more excitement. Dobing hit a hat-trick at Rotherham in Round 3 and he was on target again as they squeezed through 2-1 at Everton, a most unexpected result. A replay was required in Round 5, Cardiff City eventually going down 2-1 after a goalless draw in Wales. I was most unhappy when my mother put her foot down and banned me from the quarter final home tie against Liverpool. A full house was predicted and her opinion of Merseyside football supporters was low indeed. I was not the biggest of twelve year olds and so I had to listen to odd snippets on the radio as two of the Division's finest locked horns. The attendance was 51,000 and Liverpool struck first, but a stunning diving header from Ronnie Clayton and a fierce strike from Ally Macleod sealed their place in the last four. The opposition was to be Bolton Wanderers; a local derby and Maine Road, Manchester was chosen as the neutral ground. There was good news from the Bolton camp. Nat Lofthouse was injured and without the power, strength and goal scoring ability of the "Lion of Vienna", I honestly believed that the Rovers would win. Ralph Gubbins replaced Nat, a journeyman footballer, more frequently a reserve. But everyone is famous for fifteen minutes and in an instant, the understudy became the star as he scored twice and the Rovers were out.

Burnley's Colin McDonald [pictured] was one of the unluckiest of players. An outstanding goalkeeper, he made eight successive international appearances in 1958, but received an horrific injury in a Football League representative game and never again played at professional level. At Ewood Park, Bryan Douglas and the classy inside forward Roy Vernon both made their international debuts for England and Wales respectively. The 1958 FIFA World Cup was held in Sweden, all of the four home nations qualifying for the final stages. Jimmy McIlroy played in all five of Northern Ireland's matches before they were eliminated by France in the Quarter Finals. England failed to reach the Quarter Finals, but Colin McDonald of Burnley was in goal throughout their four games. The Blackburn Rovers pairing of Ronnie Clayton and Bryan Douglas also travelled to Sweden. Douglas played in all three group games whilst Clayton had lost his place to Eddie Clamp from Wolverhampton Wanderers and remained on the bench. It was necessary for England to play the Soviet Union in a play-off game which the Three Lions lost 1-0. Clayton was re-instated for this game, but Chelsea's Peter Brabrook replaced Douglas on the right wing. Roy Vernon made one appearance for Wales in the group stages against Sweden, an eventual finalist. Bryan Douglas talked about the aspects that few are privy to with regard to Internationals.

BLACKBURN ROVERS BACK ROW: Mulvey, McGrath, Daly, March, Smith, Jervis. THIRD ROW: Busby, McEvoy, Kirkup, England, Dorgan, Taylor, Cairns. SECOND ROW: Clayton (K.), Woods, Rainford, Leyland, Briggs, Heron. FRONT ROW: Douglas, Dobing, Eckersley, Mr. J. Carey (manager), Clayton (R.), MacLeod, Kennedy.

"My first international call up was early in 1956 when I played for the England B side against Switzerland at the Dell, Southampton's ground. It was all new to me but Ronnie Clayton helped me out. He was a big mate of Duncan Edwards; in fact the United player was due to be his best man at his wedding but he sadly died in the Munich air disaster just weeks before. Duncan was playing at the Dell and he waited for me, showed me round and introduced me to the players. I think I was the only one from Division 2 so I was overawed at first, meeting all these top players. Tommy Cummings from Burnley was playing at right back and we won 4-0. My Under 23 debut was in Copenhagen against the Danes and Ronnie played in the same game. At the end of the 56/57 season, I was chosen to go on to the U/23 Summer Tour. We went to Communist countries and I played in all three games. We lost in Bulgaria but beat Rumania and Czechoslovakia, but they were all close. In those days we shared rooms, but the management picked who was with who. On this tour I had to room with Brian Clough. That was an experience! My international debut was at Ninian Park in Cardiff. The FA never let us know personally, they just let the club know. I was walking down to the ground and I bumped into Bill Eckersley coming the other way. It was he who told me. He had heard it on the nine o'clock news on the radio. Ronnie by this time was an established international and he played every game. Tom Finney was winning his 68th cap and it was my first, but he really took me under his wing. 'Now that you are an international, there will be some who would be out to hurt you, to show who is boss. Never ever retaliate, just ignore them and keep your mouth shut. They will call you soft, they will call you a coward and they will swear at you as well, but what it means is that they are scared of you. If they thought you were no good, they would ignore you. You will be a target but deep down they will respect your ability and this is why they need to try and kick you.' There were lots of things that went on in a game that the public didn't know about. Nasty sly comments, quick punches when the ball was miles away and treading on you when you were trying to get up after a tackle. Tom knew this well. He had received this treatment all of his career and he had come through it to be such a marvellous player. I really listened to him and tried to do what he said, but there were times when the treatment was so bad that I had to retaliate, either verbally or physically. I admired Tom as a player but I admired him even more as a man. He was so kind to me. We won this game 4-0 and I then played ten on the trot. We also won 4-0 at Hampden Park against the Scots and I scored my first international goal and had a blinder. The press made a big thing about my performance and I was selected for the World Cup squad in Sweden. I played in all the group games, drawing all three. We had to play Russia in the Play-Off to decide who went through to the quarter-final, but they left me out of that. We lost but we had struggled in all of the games. On the English coaching staff in Sweden was Jack Marshall. We all found him easy to get on with. He was really down to earth and I was really pleased when he came to the Rovers. I enjoyed my time playing for him and I think he was the best manager I played under".

Since the conclusion of World War 2, life had been enjoyable for fans of Burnley Football Club. But apart from the excitement generated by promotion, Wembley and a totally unexpected third place finish in the 47-48 season, there had since been little to be intoxicated over. They were now accepted nationally as a Division 1 side. It was quite a snug feeling, nothing ever to worry about and complacency was becoming the by-word. In the last ten years, their final league position had fluctuated between fifteenth and sixth. They were being recognised as the "Steady Eddies" of English football, but would the fans have wanted something akin to a bare-knuckle ride. This was exactly what their counterparts in Blackburn had grown to love over the last five years. Of course they were a division below and there was a difference between playing host to the "Wolves", Manchester United and Arsenal rather than welcoming Doncaster Rovers, Lincoln City and Grimsby Town. Legends of the game, Tom Finney, Stan Matthews and Billy Wright could be admired at close quarters, whereas the opposition at Ewood Park was almost always of the journeyman variety. Comparing average crowds over the previous eight seasons gives a figure of around 23,750 for the Rovers and 25,600 for the Clarets. Not a great difference, in fact somewhat disappointing from a Burnley perspective, when top clubs were strutting their stuff fortnightly in the town. All of this leads to a question which could be debated for hours. What do supporters want from a game of football? Even as a septuagenarian, I can sulk with the best of them if my side loses, irrespective of the opposition. First and foremost I want them to win. I want the bi-weekly thrill of waking up on a Saturday morning, going down to the ground and watching "us" come away with a victory. A stack of goals in our favour is heaven, but a 1-0 win will send me home happy. Winning generates excitement which generates anticipation, whichever the division in which your clubs plays. So is it better to be supporting a Division 2 side hell-bent on promotion or watching your side struggle to hold on to a mid-table Division 1 place? As much as the fans of the Clarets would have smugly looked westwards at this time, content with a secure position in a superior league, might there have been twinges of jealousy at the "ride of your life" which was annually being enacted in front of the Blue and White followers week in, week out? It is such an intriguing question.

The Pride, Passion and the Prejudice 1958 – 1966

Pride: a feeling of pleasure and satisfaction that you get because you or people connected with you have done or got something good.
Passion: A strong or powerful emotion.
Prejudice: an unfair and unreasonable opinion or feeling, especially when formed without enough thought or knowledge
Cambridge English Dictionary

As of the present day, there have been three eras incorporating a lengthy run of derby games. In the 1888-1900 seasons, the clubs clashed twice every season with the Blackburn side generally coming out on top. The 1913-1930 campaigns, interrupted of course by the Great War, saw intense rivalry, caused mainly by a levelling out of the ability across the two clubs. As the 1958-59 season kicked off, no-one knew that this would be the third and final era. Nor would they know that the period would provide a combustible mix of action which would draw in the fans, grab the attention of the Southern based national media and put football on to the agenda of so many conversations in East Lancashire.

Burnley were a settled side, very much a potential top side whereas the Rovers, having at long last broken free from Division 2, had many points to prove. Many would say that Wolverhampton Wanderers were the country's top club in the late fifties. But Tottenham Hotspur would often play a game that was a stratosphere apart from their rivals, there was a football revolution on its way out of Merseyside and Manchester United were in the process of rebuilding after Munich. Could our two mill towns possibly compete against these giants of the game? The crowds were there, smaller perhaps than in the big cities, but full of pride for their club, passionately exhorting them on to greater things. Pride is good. Do we not all puff out our chests that little bit more when we can tell strangers that X has always been our team? And if a sport fails to engender passion, is it really worth playing? Even in sports such as the game of golf where demeanour is strictly monitored, there is passion throbbing through the veins of all who play and watch. It has to be kept in check of course, but unless it is against the Americans in the Ryder Cup after holing a ten footer, no golfer will dance with the flag à la Roger Milla, the Cameroonian striker in the 1990 World Cup. Prejudice is a different animal. Of course you want your team to play well, you desperately want them to win and losing can often spoil a weekend. But prejudice only clicks in when at the same time, you totally hate the opposition, will cheer if their star player is carried off and will mock them should they lose. Prejudice joining forces with pride and passion became the hallmark of sixties football in Europe.

1958-59

Team	Pos	Played	Won	Drawn	Lost	GF	GA	Pts
Burnley	7	42	19	10	13	81	70	48
Blackburn Rovers	10	42	17	10	15	76	70	44

Blackburn Rovers		Burnley	
Most Appearances	Matt Woods 41	Most Appearances	Bobby Seith 42
Most Goals	Peter Dobing 24	Most Goals	Ray Pointer 27

Burnley's league performances over the last six seasons bore a passing resemblance to an old gramophone. From time to time it would stick and continue to play the same old song. In this instance however, it was a song that the fans had grown to like. Their league position had scarcely moved during this period and for a seventh campaign, they occupied a slot between sixth and tenth. This time it was seventh yet again, and for those on the Longside, that was always a good result in Division 1. The big advantage that the Clarets held at this time was that they spent no money on players. Players stayed at a club for much longer periods of time in the fifties. It was partly down to loyalty and partly due to a contractual system of employment which tied players far more rigidly to clubs. Nonetheless there were plenty of selling clubs who would willingly release a player from his contract if a sizeable cheque was produced. Manchester City and Tottenham Hotspur had often paid out money to buy the finished product in the late fifties and there was much wheeling and dealing which went on in the game whilst the Clarets were developing their youth programme. Only Bolton had gone down a similar route and it is said that their '58 FA Cup winning eleven cost £110, this being eleven times the ten-pound signing on fee the clubs had to hand to the Football League when a youngster signed professional forms.

This was Ray Pointer's breakthrough year. The blonde bombshell was extremely mobile, combining pace, agility and technical ability with a lust for goal. Burnley had been short of a genuine number nine since they sold Bill Holden to Sunderland. McKay had been a penalty area pick pocket but Pointer was a leader of the attack. Also fast off the production line was John Connelly. His pace, crossing ability and goal scoring talent quickly cemented his grip on the number seven shirt. The young John Angus played for much of the season at right back and Adam Blacklaw, a Scot from Aberdeen, proved an able replacement for Colin McDonald. The Clarets have produced a regular supply of top-class goal minders over the decades but the Tottington born McDonald is the all-time number one. There were plenty of goals, Pointer scoring in eight successive games from November into the new year. Connelly and Robson, the latter now the regular number 10 following Cheeseborough's transfer to Leicester City, were scoring regularly but it had been a low profile start to Potts' first full season in charge. It took the Clarets nine games to reach six points, but as Bill Shankly once said, "the Football League is a marathon not a sprint". By Christmas they were tenth and with six to play, they rested third. The title was out of range but a frustrating run dropped them to seventh.

Blackburn Rovers' return to Division 1 produced "Fantasy Football" long before the concept was invented. A 5-1 win at Newcastle on the season's opening day was followed by a Monday evening cake walk against Leicester, 5-0 in front of the disbelieving fans at Ewood. A crowd of 41, 830 turned up the following Saturday and returned home in raptures as five more without reply were dished out to Tottenham Hotspur. I remember telling my dad that evening that if it continued like this, they would hit the 200 goal mark for the campaign. Being a very realistic type of fellow, he just smiled but even he must have been shocked by the turnaround in fortunes. The next forty-two days, which included a 6-1 thrashing at the home of Manchester United and a lively 6-3 defeat by West Ham at Upton Park, brought eight games, no wins and just ten goals. But there were other problems at the club. There was Littlewoods Football Pools cash behind Everton and their manager's chair was vacant. Johnny Carey was hot property, was tempted and he left. The side he had built at Ewood became known as "Carey's Chicks" and he raced to the top of the "next manager wanted" list. When a predator like Everton appeared, it was impossible for the Rovers to hold on to him and he was Goodison bound in the autumn of '58.

Ironically, the Blue and Whites lost just once in the next eleven games and Christmas saw them sitting safely above midway in the table. Dally Duncan, who had found success at Luton, guiding then into the 1st Division, was Carey's successor. Peter Dobing was again the leading marksman and Tommy Johnston, who returned to Leyton Orient just after Christmas, had already notched fourteen. Roy Vernon, capped by Wales against Scotland, was prolific also and Mick McGrath was capped by the Republic of Ireland, the first of his eighteen international appearances.

The derby games

The first derby game was in mid-October. Ten and a half years before, the Rovers had travelled to Turf Moor and, in spite of being relegated, managed a goalless draw. History would repeat itself this time. The sides were near neighbours in the league table, Burnley in ninth, three places above their rival.

Ronnie Clayton

They were unbeaten in the last five games, whereas the Blackburn side, having been through a sticky patch, had hammered Preston North End 4-1 in their previous game. A crowd of 41,961 packed into Turf Moor, hoping for a memorable occasion, but both sides struggled to find some rhythm and a goalless draw was a disappointment all round. Only Ronnie Clayton on the Blackburn side was not making his derby debut, having played in the '52 FA Cup game. Of the Burnley eleven, both Cummings and Adamson had played in the same game. The cast re-assembled at Ewood Park in early March with a much reduced attendance of 27,071. The form of both clubs was of the up and down variety, each still occupying mid-table positions. The home side was forced to draft in Roy Stephenson, ex of Burnley, to fill the attacking role which had been unclaimed since Johnston's return to Leyton Orient. Ally McLeod was injured and Jack Airey made his debut at outside left. A future star made his derby debut in the Claret and Blue shirt, Brian Miller in the process of consolidating a regular position in the half back line. A close game was expected, but the result must have come as something of a shock to the Turf Moor side, accustomed to being East Lancashire's number one. Pointer scored the opener after twenty minutes, but goals from Dobing and Stephenson gave the home side the interval lead. Jack Airey scored again for the Rovers and Vernon put them out of sight, a 4-1 victory giving so much pleasure to the Ewood Park crowd. This was the biggest home victory by the Rovers in a derby game since the 1929 goals bonanza when they won 8-3.

18 10 1958	Burnley	Blackburn Rovers	0-0	
07 03 1959	Blackburn Rovers	Burnley	4-1	P Dobing, R Stephenson, J Airey, R Vernon. R Pointer

Blackburn Rovers, for the first and only time in their history, won the FA Youth Cup. To bring home this silverware, they had to overcome the next class of youngsters from Old Trafford in the last four and then defeat the red-hot favourites in the final; a West Ham side which contained both Bobby Moore and Geoff Hurst. The crowds flocked down to the ground to watch the semi-final where the young Rovers disposed of the Busby Babes. In the first leg of the final in London, Alan Bradshaw equalised West Ham's opener. Over 28,500 spectators were present at the second leg of the final at Ewood Park. Goalless for ninety minutes thanks to a marvellous Barry Griffiths penalty save, the Rovers dominated the latter stages of the game and in the one hundred and first minute, Paddy Daly, an Irish inside forward, raced past Bobby Moore to knock the ball into the net. Fred Pickering, Keith Newton and Mike England all went on to have long and successful careers, each one representing their country at senior level. Barrie Ratcliffe made thirty-seven appearances without ever really being considered a first team regular and the same could be said of Alan Bradshaw who made just eleven starts. The Blackburn boy however went on to make almost three hundred appearances for Crewe Alexandra, somehow combining a full-time role as Head of PE at Shadsworth school in Blackburn and playing as a part time pro for the Alex.

Both East Lancs clubs cruised through the 3rd Round of the FA Cup. Blackburn Rovers were drawn at home to Division 2 side Leyton Orient, Tommy Johnston scoring against his old club in a 4-2 victory. Burnley travelled to Division 3 Stockport County, a Pointer double securing the win.

The derby FA Cup game

The draw then paired the East Lancashire clubs at Ewood. There was snow in Blackburn on January 24th and by half time it started to freeze. There had been no first half goals and after an extended interval, the referee abandoned the game. It was the first time I had witnessed an abandoned match, but we trudged away, determined to be back for the re-run. The following Wednesday, the pitch was fit and both sides were at full strength. In front of 43,752 spectators, Dobing opened the account for the Rovers. The second half was a battle, but McIlroy equalised and then controlled the game. It was heading for extra time when Jimmy Robson popped up with the winner. This was only the third cup meeting between the clubs and following their victory, Burnley led the series 2-1.

24 01 1959	Round 4	Blackburn Rovers	Burnley	0-0	**Match abandoned, icy pitch.**
28 01 1959	Round 4	Blackburn Rovers	**Burnley**	**1-2**	P Dobing. **J McIlroy, J Robson.**

Portsmouth competed well at the "Turf" in Round 5 but a rare Jimmy Adamson goal guaranteed an away tie at Aston Villa. The Midlanders were struggling, eventually being relegated at the end of the season, but Burnley were organised and it ended goalless. Burnley were now favourite to reach the semi-final but they reserved the replay at the "Turf" to produce their poorest performance of the year, losing 2-0.

1959-60

Team	Pos	Played	Won	Drawn	Lost	GF	GA	Pts
Burnley	1	42	24	7	11	85	61	55
Blackburn Rovers	17	42	16	5	21	60	70	37

Blackburn Rovers		Burnley	
Most Appearances	Matt Woods 41	Most Appearances	Ray Pointer, Brian Miller, Jimmy Adamson (all 42)
Most Goals	Peter Dobing 18	Most Goals	John Connelly 20

It may have been less instantaneous, less dramatic and probably less life changing than the conversion of St Paul on the Damascus road, but I was certainly converted this year. Converted to the belief (the fact even) that an intense rivalry between Blackburn Rovers and Burnley was real, it existed and it mattered. Like the great apostle, I too could point to an exact spot and say, "that's the place, that's where it happened". But more of the events of March 12th, 1960 later.

What the previous season had shown was that the Rovers belonged in English football's top league. Everyone knew that Burnley did, but their rival had given them a run for their money. But not even the most optimistic of supporters from either side of the "Great Divide" would have predicted such a roller coaster ride.... at both clubs. Slowly but surely the southern cognoscenti began to realise that the Burnley production line was no flash in the pan. Could they come through to challenge? No-one took the Rovers challenge seriously, but they had a new centre-forward; an Irish international and a real character by the name of Derek Dougan. Waiting in the wings were the starlets from the Youth Cup winning side. Could any of these make an instant breakthrough?

In retrospect it was clear that Harry Potts had been slowly assembling his first eleven over the previous season and a half. He paid £5,000 for another promising youngster from Glentoran, thrusting Alex Elder into the first team at just eighteen years of age, a position he would hold for the next eight years. Wing half Bobby Seith had given sterling service for ten years, joining as a youngster in 1948 and making 211 appearances, but he could no longer make the team and he returned north to Dundee. In a season where fifty-five points won you the title and thirty-four sent you down, results were unpredictable. The Clarets for example lost at home to the soon to be relegated Leeds United and yet comfortably raced past eventual runner-up Wolverhampton Wanderers 4-1; it was that type of season. Up to Christmas they hovered around 6th position in the league, generally winning at home. There was a Saturday afternoon to remember against Nottingham Forest when Jimmy Robson crashed home a five timer in an 8-0 victory. The County Durham born inside left was tall and, compared with the forwards around him who simply oozed talent; he seemed to be a workmanlike type of player, but nothing more. The one thing he did however as well as anyone in English football at the time, was stick the ball in the net and thinking back, he was obviously some player. Jimmy was one of football's humble men. He would sooner talk himself down rather than brag about his exploits. I got to know him when I was looking at young talent in the club around the turn of the millennium. Without realising it, he would embarrass me at games. I would try so hard to spot any future talent before

him but after five minutes he would quietly tell me to watch number so and so. "How the hell does he know that" I would mutter to myself and after about half an hour, I knew he was right. He once told me the story about his first team debut. Not having faith in football clubs, Jimmy's mother had told the Burnley club when he went down to Turf Moor at fifteen, that they must ensure that he learned a trade. They apprenticed him to an electrician and one of his earliest games was the inaugural lighting up of the floodlights. In mid-afternoon, he was miles high, attaching the bulbs into the lights and at 7.25 he was running out to play for the first team. Not the type of story you would read in a Cristiano Ronaldo biography.

John Connelly gained his first England cap this season and he went on to score a hat-trick at Highbury, as Arsenal went down to a 4-2 defeat. A 2-1 Boxing Day triumph at Old Trafford was followed by a real let down for the fans two days later as Manchester United gained emphatic revenge at the "Turf", knocking in four. Into the New Year it was a different story and there were just three defeats in the last eighteen games. Following such a good run, they approached the last two games still never having topped the league. They were now without leading goal scorer Connelly with twenty to his name. He had been injured and was replaced by a young Trevor Meredith. The penultimate fixture was at home to Fulham, a mid-table side, but the inconsistency of the early season returned and the Cottagers held on for a goalless draw. Both the Wolves and the Spurs had completed their fixtures, but the Clarets, back in third place had one more to play. A win at Maine Road against the

masters of inconsistency would seal the title and after a tense ninety minutes, goals from wingers Brian Pilkington and Meredith were sufficient, Manchester City losing 2-1. It was their first title since 1921 and a sweet moment for manager Harry Potts who could now forget about the 1947 FA Cup Final defeat to Charlton Athletic. Some things are indeed worth waiting for. The manager certainly trusted his squad and only eighteen players were used throughout the forty-two league games. Potts had an undisputed hierarchy of eleven players; all eleven being iconic names in the history of Burnley FC. They also equalled the 1946-47 record of achieving eleven victories away from home, this time against the elite of the country, Interestingly Harry Potts was involved both times, being a leading light in the immediate post-war side and now managing this magnificent squad.

The Burnley Division 1 title winning side 1959-60 (started over 22 games, max 42) was: Adam Blacklaw, John Angus, Alex Elder, Jimmy Adamson, Tommy Cummings, Brian Miller, John Connelly, Jimmy McIlroy, Ray Pointer, Jimmy Robson, Brian Pilkington, David Smith.

An interesting aside here concerns the demeanour and attitude of footballers. Many of those who hit the headlines nowadays are so concerned with their self-importance and their desire to be in the limelight; what in a child you would call attention seeking. But in my limited experience of talking with ex-professionals, there are many who are humble, are embarrassed and self-conscious about their one-time fame and really need pushing to talk about themselves. Mike Duffy reminded me about this when discussing the title clinching win at Maine Road.

> "Years later when my son was playing in a school game at Preston, I thought I recognised the referee. I asked him where I might know him from, spoke about football, asked him if he had played and he answered, "a bit". Almost reluctantly, he eventually told me that he was Trevor Meredith, the scorer of the winning goal in that historic victory, arguably the most important goal ever scored in a Claret and Blue shirt."

Meredith was a good player, but John Connelly, certainly one of Turf Moor's finest, was barring his way. Given limited first team opportunity, thirty seven starts in six and a half seasons, he moved closer to home and played well over two hundred times for Shrewsbury Town before becoming a teacher. He could have dined out for years on that fleeting moment of glory on a May evening in Manchester, but like so many of his contemporaries, that was not his style. John Connelly was a real headache for the Rovers' defence during this period and he certainly was grateful for the advice and support he received from the manager. As Phil Webster told me.......

> "In later years, John talked to me regularly about how Harry had helped him with his game. He consistently told him to make sure he could receive the ball from either Jimmy or John Angus, fly down the wing and knock over the crosses. There will always be someone in position to bury it, whether it be Ray Pointer, Jimmy Robson or later on, Andy Lochhead. As John used to say, 'it was simple advice, nothing technical or tactical, it was just what a winger should do. He knew my strengths and he told me to play to them.' It fits in with something Harry used to say when we discussed the game on a Sunday. 'Whoever we are playing, we only think about what we are going to do. We never make it complex, we play our way and most of the time it works".

A few miles further west, Blackburn Rovers had to endure a rocky ride in Division 1. The Rovers made the brightest of bright starts to their second campaign at the top level and with Peter Dobing scoring goals for fun; they topped the league after five games. From then on in it became a dog fight. December was a good month with Dougan on fire. He was now capped as a Rovers' player for the first time, partnering Jimmy McIlroy in the Northern Ireland attack. The controversial striker scored four against West Ham United and the winner in each of the games against Blackpool and Leeds. That was the end of the good times. They managed just three wins in their final nineteen games, dropping down the league like a stone. Thankfully Luton Town struggled to find the net whilst Leeds could not stop conceding, both sides being relegated. But the Rovers only escaped by a three-point margin, locked in a four way tie for seventeenth place. Bill Eckersley was reaching the end of the road, bedevilled with injury, and Dave Whelan, tough and quick from the Wigan area but the very antithesis of the classy ex-international star, replaced him at left back. Roy Vernon, extremely talented in a wide right position or as a goal scoring inside forward, was eventually sold to Everton mid-season for £27,000, becoming a hero at Goodison Park. From the terraces, we thought he was moody but it later came out that he was constantly at loggerheads with the manager. At least his absence forced Duncan to move Douglas into a scheming role at inside left, a position from where he was later able to completely dictate games.

Modern pundits talk about mid-field players who can break the lines. Douglas, with a swivel of his hips, could do just this, leaving the opposition behind with his pace over a few yards. Vernon was replaced by Louis Bimpson. The Merseysider, bought for a "song" from Liverpool, was a strong running forward, but had none of the technical ability of the departed Welshman. Losing Vernon probably pleased the manager, but there was another bad apple in the dressing room. Derek Dougan, the leggy Northern Ireland striker eventually proved to be one of the Top Tier's ace marksmen. He later became recognised as one of football's deepest thinkers, chairing the Professional Footballers' Associa-

Rovers 3-Burnley 2 in the 1959-60 league fixture at Ewood Park. Bryan Douglas finds the back of his home net despite Leyland's efforts

tion and later being chairman of the Wolves, but that was long after he had left Ewood Park far behind. He was sufficiently strong to be a presence in the penalty area, particularly in the air, had an eye for goal, pace to burn and at times, mesmeric skills. Unfortunately, all four of these attributes rarely seemed to turn up at the same time during his days in the blue and white halved shirt. He seemed far more interested in being theatrical, showing more elation over nut-megging an opponent than laying on a goal for a team mate. His off the field antics also gathered more column inches in the local newspaper than his performances on it. He dated a Miss World and had more changes of hair style than a 1980s pop star.

Fortunately, there were hard working souls in the squad to keep them afloat. My particular favourite of the day was Ally MacLeod. Several of us worshipped him so much that we had furious arguments at school over the relative abilities of the Scottish winger and Douglas. In retrospect, it was a one-horse race. Douglas was in a different league. But there was something special about MacLeod, nicknamed "Noddy" for his peculiar head movements when running at speed. He was a trier, a very personable trier. When attempting to obtain autographs as our heroes reached the Players Entrance. "Noddy" had a pleasant word with everyone, signing our books and chatting to the fans. He was the darling of the Riverside and he later became manager of Scotland. In some respects, the highlight in this roller-coaster season was the selection of Ronnie Clayton as captain of England. He was able to emulate the feat of Bob Crompton, some forty five years before and the first time he led out the Three Lions, an eleven which included Burnley's John Connelly, was at Ninian Park, Cardiff where the sides drew 1-1. After five games, the FA then preferred Fulham's

Johnny Haynes to be their leader as Ronnie lost his place in the team, but you have to be some player to achieve 35 caps.

The derby games (League)

Going into the season's first derby game, Burnley were fifth whilst the Rovers occupied sixth position in the league, two points behind. But the Clarets had been thumped by Blackpool 4-1 in their previous home game, whilst the Rovers has won at Leicester City. It was certain to be close, far too close to call and that is how it threatened to turn out. A crowd of 33,316 packed Ewood Park and hardly had the referee blown his whistle when the home side scored through Dougan. Within ten minutes, Pilkington had equalised but Dobing's effort after 26 minutes meant I could digest my half-time Wagon Wheel, free from immediate worries. This state of contentment lasted exactly sixty seconds before Douglas bizarrely knocked one past Harry Leyland, his own keeper and for so long, a draw seemed inevitable. But with nine minutes remaining, Roy Vernon clinched the game for the hosts, making it 3-2 and the Blackburn side took over fifth spot from Harry Potts' eleven. The local press blamed Adam Blacklaw in the Burnley goal for the defeat, but it had been a thrilling game, one that lived up to the local derby tag and both clubs were still in the hunt to challenge for the top spot.

An own goal scored by an attacker was such an unusual occurrence in the days when diverted shots were credited to the player who made the initial strike on goal and not the defender who makes the last contact as per now. Equally surprising at that time was that it was Bryan Douglas who made the mistake. He had already gained 12 England caps and was a third of the way through his international career. Along with Clayton, he was the most respected of this Rovers' side, having a reputation akin to that of Jimmy McIlroy at Turf Moor. When I interviewed him, there was no doubt that it had caused him some embarrassment but Vernon's late winner was the headline maker, allowing "Duggie's" error of judgement to be quietly forgotten.

Much then happened between the October and March fixtures. Burnley had crept up to third, three points behind leaders Wolverhampton Wanderers but their arch rivals Blackburn Rovers had slid down to eleventh, having lost seven on the bounce. Preston North End had bamboozled their defence in what was Tom Finney's final season, the North End winning 5-3, whereas the previous Tuesday evening, the Clarets had beaten Tottenham Hotspur, a place above them in the league by a 2-0 margin under the Turf Moor lights. This time the pundits were confident they had the right result. A home banker was the projected result across all of the morning papers. In front of 33,321, they were right, although it was another tight affair. In actual fact, the game never quite caught fire. Perhaps the Burnley players were too conscious of not losing the two vital points after a Jimmy Robson header put them ahead after twenty-seven minutes and so they were unprepared to go for all-out attack. Whatever

Another near miss for Burnley as they dominate the first 75 minutes of the 1960 FA Cup Tie at Turf Moor

the reason, 1-0 was the way it stayed and for the visitors, it was now eight successive defeats and they were looking over their shoulders towards the relegation candidates. Burnley, on the other hand, sensed that there was something special around the corner and that thirty-nine years since their last notable triumph, silverware could be returning to North-East Lancashire.

17 10 1959	Blackburn Rovers	Burnley	3-2	B Douglas, P Dobing, R Vernon. B Pilkington, o.g.
05 03 1960	**Burnley**	Blackburn Rovers	1-0	J Robson

Normally such a poor season at Ewood Park would have merited a couple of paragraphs in this book, but this turned out to be no ordinary season. The FA Cup was its saviour. Blackburn Rovers and Burnley both defeated 2nd Division opposition in replays, the Rovers at home to Sunderland and the Clarets at Lincoln City. Both sides also needed replays before safely navigating the 4th Round. A two-timer from Jimmy Robson saw them through to the next stage against Swansea Town. A very, very late Mick McGrath equaliser scored from (at most) three yards out following a scrum involving twenty one players which would not have looked out of place at Twickenham, rescued a 1-1 draw against Blackpool. The Rovers, helped by a Dobing double in the replay, sailed through to the 5th Round. Here, in the middle of a dreadful league run, they were drawn away at table toppers Tottenham Hotspur. I sat by the radiogram, pessimistically waiting for Sports Report and danced around the house when the announcer said, "Tottenham Hotspur 1" and then, raising the intonation in his voice as they still do to pronounce an away victory, "Blackburn Rovers 3". Matt Woods, somehow scoring from the half way line, and a rare Louis Bimpson double were responsible for this massive upset. An away trip to Third Division Bradford City ought to have been a walk in the park for Burnley, but for eighty minutes, the "Bantams" certainly rained on their parade. Thankfully John Connelly was on hand with a late double to force a draw and with doubles from Pointer and Robson plus a fifth from Connelly; the Turf Moor side romped through the replay and into the last eight.

The derby game (Cup)

At lunch time on the Monday before Burnley's replay, the news shot round the yard at Darwen Grammar School. It was Burnley away in the 6th Round if they could find a way past Bradford City in mid-week. Then one of the lads worked out that on the Saturday morning of the game, our Under 14 side was due to play St Theodore's, a strong footballing school in Burnley. We could not wait and we had to make plans to stay on in Burnley for the cup tie. It was not easy persuading my parents but there were chip shops to provide lunch and a couple of willing parents promised to fill up their cars and ferry us home. In the morning, we ground out a draw in Townley Park and stood outside Turf Moor with our bags of chips wrapped in newspaper, waiting for the turnstiles to open. I swear I was the first to enter the stadium, our shouts of "C'mon the Rovers" echoing round the empty ground. Our team had lost 1-0 on this very ground just seven days before and was in the middle of a dreadful run. We were thrilled to be there, full of excitement, yet deep down believing we were on a hiding to nothing. We were amongst a crowd of 51,501, and talk about a game of two halves......although it was actually a seventy-five, fifteen minute split. The Blue and Whites had their moments before the break but they could not handle Connelly. Time and time again, McIlroy would find him with a pinpoint pass and the winger would fly down the right wing and cross with precision. The combined efforts of Woods and Clayton kept them at bay until half time, but when they turned around and the Clarets were attacking the covered end where we were stood, McIlroy took over. Within fifteen minutes, the maestro opened up our defence on three occasions and Pilkington, Pointer and inevitably John Connelly put the hosts three up. Being a Blackburn fan was sheer agony and it seemed game over as the minutes ticked by without any indication of a Rovers' revival. Then suddenly, Alex Elder went to clear the ball in his own penalty area. The ball must have hit a small divot and it deviated slightly, slicing off the full back's foot and hitting his hand. Thinking back, it was never a penalty. This was ball to hand, not hand to ball as decreed in the law. But we didn't care and when Douglas slid the ball home from the spot, a glimmer of hope appeared on the horizon. The conductor's baton had suddenly passed from "Jimmy Mac" to "Duggie". He played in Dobing and the inside forward did what he did best, hammering the ball home from twenty-five yards. Sensing that the game was no longer lost, Clayton smashed in a shot, the ball ricocheted off a defender and from what appeared like point blank range to our watching eyes from the other end of the ground, McGrath completely miscued the ball. Fortunately it flopped against the post and somehow crept home. It was the second time in this cup run that the Irishman had scored a vital very late equaliser, feet from the goal line.

> We talked non-stop in the car on the journey home, recounting time and again those magical last fifteen minutes, but there was a replay to be endured. On the following Wednesday evening, we gulped down our teas and arrived at Ewood Park at 5.30, two hours before kick-off. We were going to be first on the ground again, but unfortunately half of Blackburn was blessed with the same ambition. The queue for the "Boys" turnstile (did girls ever watch football in those days?) stretched halfway round the ground. We finally went through at 7.25 and the police directed us to sit on the pitch side of the wall, inches from the playing surface. Many of us were actually sat on the grass and when the likes of Ronnie Clayton wanted to take a long throw, we had to shuffle to one side to give him room for his run up. It was a close encounter but the Rovers always held the edge. Roared on by a crowd of 53,892, the game was still goalless after ninety minutes. The home side then took total control and goals from Dobing and MacLeod took them safely into the semi-final. I arrived home hoarse, tired out yet overjoyed until my mother informed me that I still had my homework to complete.

12 03 1960	Round 6	**Burnley**	Blackburn Rovers	3-3	**B Pilkington, R Pointer, J Connelly.** B Douglas, P Dobing, M McGrath.
16 03 1960	Replay	Blackburn Rovers	**Burnley**	2-0	P Dobing, A McLeod.

Bryan Douglas gave his views on the penalty, the game in general and his derby memories.

> "I never stopped to think if it was a penalty or not. If the ref said it was, it was and I was thinking about how I was going to beat Adam Blacklaw and get us back into the game. Football is an instinctive game most of the time and you rarely have the chance to think about what you are doing. You just do it and so nerves don't play a part. Penalties are different. I took a lot and missed a few but I was not one of those who grabbed the ball and said it's mine. Others could take them but even the best of ball strikers like Peter Dobing didn't want to take penalties. So that's how I came to take so many, but it's at these moments when the nerves really kick in. And when there's fifty odd thousand watching and it was probably our last chance to get back into the game, I did feel the stress. I was so relieved that it went in but we still had a massive job in front of us. I wouldn't say I hated Burnley. I had come across some of their players like on international duty and they were ok, but there was always that little bit more aggression on the field in a derby game. It was the crowd that really wound all the players up

Harry Leyland tips one over the bar as Burnley win 1-0 at Turf Moor in March 1960

and although I don't know why, I always thought that the Burnley supporters were more desperate to beat us than ours were to beat them. In later years John Connelly came to play at Ewood and we welcomed him as one of ours and he had been a rival for my number seven England shirt at one time. And when I retired I became very friendly with a number of their ex-players. The other year I went to Jimmy McIlroy's funeral and I actually had tears in my eyes. He was once one of my deadliest opponents and here I was crying at his funeral. It just shows the respect that we all had for each other".

There is no doubt that winning promotes a much preferable reaction to losing. There was so much happiness in our Darwen house that night but over in Nelson, it was a different story at the home of Mick Duffy.

My worst recollection of that season when the double was a distinct possibility was the sixth round of the FA Cup, when the Rovers' come-back was precipitated by a cruel decision by Mr Hunt of Portsmouth for a penalty for handball when the ball ricocheted off Alex Elder's foot and struck his hand. It was never a penalty in a million years. The law stated that the hand must move deliberately to the ball. It certainly did not on this occasion. The Clarets were leading 3-0 at the time but Douglas's penalty began the come-back that led to a 3-3 draw. We were robbed by the referee. The replay at Ewood is painful for a number of reasons. I had a double detention, the first on the night of the replay for wearing my duffel coat to school, the second the night after for "borrowing" the school bell, which did no good at Ewood as we lost the replay. The defeat by two goals to nil completed my misery.

Ray Pointer makes it 2-0 for the Clarets in the epic 1959/60 FA Cup Tie at Burnley

It was Sheffield Wednesday at Maine Road, Manchester in the semi-final and we journeyed first by train and then by bus, clutching our tickets tightly because this was an all-ticket affair. My sandwiches and bottle of pop were in my school satchel but for some long-forgotten reason; my ticket was in a different part of the ground to my mates. The Yorkshire club would be tough opposition, in fact they finished fifth in the league, but the mis-firing outfit which turned out in the blue and white halved shirts for league games bore no resemblance to the cup fighting heroes.

It was another tight affair and the 75,000 spectators saw a real end to end battle. Douglas set up Dougan to put the Rovers in front and then the Owls had a goal disallowed for offside. When Dougan scored a second, he was reputed to have turned to Peter Swan, the Wednesday and England centre half and said, "do you want a cup final ticket?" The Sheffield club battled to the end but in spite of a Fantham goal, it was the Rovers who were on their way to Wembley. I somehow found my way home from Maine Road to Darwen on my own and when I entered the house, I was scalded by my mother for leaving my school satchel on a Manchester Corporation bus.

For the final stage of the cup run, I will let David Elliott tell the story. He is a Rovers fan from birth and although he emigrated to Tasmania at the end of the sixties with his newly wedded bride, he has never lost his passion for the Ewood boys, watching live games in the middle of the night and whatever else it takes to follow your club from the other side of the world. And whenever he has returned on holiday, taking in a Rovers' game has always been at the top of his agenda.

I went to both Burnley games and I've got to say the first at Turf Moor was the best game I ever remember, not just for the excitement and the drama but also the quality of the football. Outside the ground afterwards. I have never seen such celebrations from Rovers fans, including the win over Newcastle that virtually won us the Premiership. I also went to the semi-final, great result but the start of disillusionment from Rovers fans about how they were treated in terms of ticket sales. The preparation for the Final must have represented the worst scenario you could dream up. Ticket sales were a shambles. Season-ticket holders were short-changed massively, fans of decades with the most expensive season tickets, fobbed off with standing tickets for the game. Non-season-ticket holders applied by mail. Anyone could get the few available, fans who never missed a game had the same chance as anyone who had never been. A lad I remember from school got a ticket by making 10 applications via his relatives and did get one but rarely went again. So, great unhappiness at the Club and its management of what should have been one of the great days. The players' preparation mirrored the admin side of it perfectly! No way were they prepped for the game. They spent the fortnight leading up to it exploiting the occasion for their own personal advantage. No question, they were badly paid and many knew there would probably never be an opportunity like this again. I've personal knowledge of this. I idolised the Club and the players so on a Tuesday before the game, I went down on my own to watch the players train. I was the only one there! That includes the players, none were training, they were all at Woolworths in Blackburn, selling their autographs for sixpence a go! I know that for a fact too because I went down to "Woolies" myself after the non-training sessions. Hard to imagine now. Only Ronnie Clayton was at Ewood, training in a six a side on Little Wembley with the Youth team. I recognised Pickering and England but that's all. You remember Little Wembley, ash-laid little pitch behind the ground at the Blackburn end.

Now for the Great Day that never was! We set off very early, think special train left Blackburn about 6am, a special - straight to nearest station to Wembley, no stops. Had full cooked breakfast on board. Packed with incredibly excited and confident Rovers fans. Remember the cuttings being thronged with kids cheering us on as we left Blackburn but becoming increasingly negative the closer we got to the Midlands! We seemed to have been held up by every signal for some reason and we were very late getting to Wembley. Instead of having about 2 hours to peacefully stroll up to the stadium and take in all the sights and sounds, we were rushing pell-mell to get there in time for the kick-off! My abiding memory of that part of the day is how incredibly hot it was. I remember thinking that the players will struggle with this. As for the game—we were down to ten men within the first 10 seconds. Everyone knew Dougan shouldn't have played and Wolves certainly did. Straight from the kick-off Flowers went for him and slammed into his thigh with his knee. Dougan wheeled around in agony and was a passenger for the rest of the game. He probably wouldn't have done much anyway. We had one chance to go ahead when Dobing was clear with a one on one with their goalie.

He smashed it at him instead of placing it and that was that. Can't remember any other chances. Then came the calamitous few minutes when McGrath scored his own goal and Whelan broke his leg. We were one down with effectively 9 men and no hope. The second half was torture, stinking hot, nothing to play for but we had to watch it. "Noddy" MacLeod had his best game ever for Rovers that day. He was always a trier without much else going for him but he lapped up the miles that day, tearing up and down that left-wing. I think I spent the journey home with my head in my hands. I can't remember any atmosphere on the train at all, just a crushed silence at the 3-0 defeat. The recriminations started the next day when it was revealed Dougan had put in a transfer request on the Friday. Attendance plummeted the next season, many vowed they would never go again. Not a happy note to end on! I'm sorry I couldn't have been more uplifting but every fan who was there would say the same. It was such a tragic day.

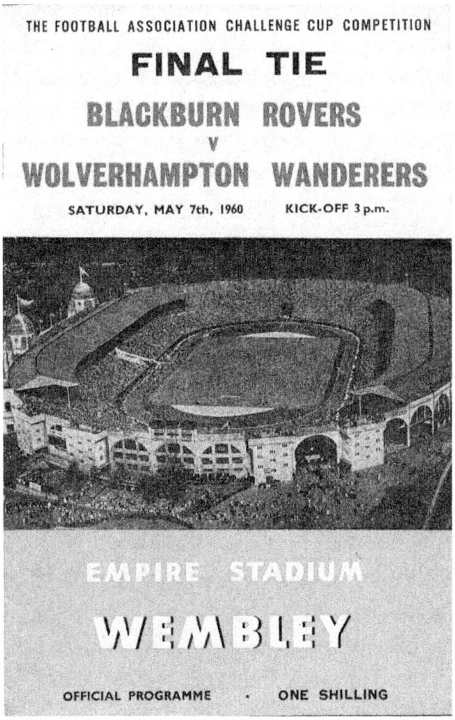

I also do not remember missing a home game all season but I had no chance of acquiring a ticket for the game. There was an avalanche of letters to what was then the Northern Evening Telegraph, complaining about a most unfair distribution. My dad told me of several of his wealthier customers, coming into his shop and openly boasting about obtaining tickets. He told me how one gentleman had said that it would be the icing on the cake for a lovely weekend in the capital with his wife. "And is your wife going to the game?" my dad asked meekly. "Of course. It will be the first time she has seen the Rovers; she is really looking forward to it" was the reply. "I felt like throwing a cabbage at his head" said my dad in a rare show of anger. Football tickets falling into what we would call the wrong hands is commonplace sixty years on in this celebrity prawn sandwich era, but this practice certainly stirred up much anger in working class Blackburn in 1960.

The Blackburn Rovers 1960 FA Cup Runner-Up side who lost 0-3 to Wolverhampton Wanderers was; Harry Leyland, John Bray, Dave Whelan, Ronnie Clayton, Matt Woods, Mick McGrath, Louis Bimpson, Peter Dobing, Derek Dougan, Bryan Douglas, Ally MacLeod.

Bryan Douglas gave me the inside story on that forgettable day for football in Blackburn.

> "The players travelled down to London a couple of days before the game and there were doubts about Derek Dougan's fitness. Nowadays he would have been given a thorough investigation and a hard work-out, but in those days it was far different. We trained at a school in the London area on the Friday morning and Derek was given a fitness test. He ran up and down in straight lines for a couple of minutes, said he felt ok and so he was declared fit. My wife was actually heavily pregnant at the time but the midwife said that it was not due for several more weeks. The official party; directors, staff and wives, travelled down on the Friday and suddenly my wife knew that the baby was coming. They thought about taking her off the train at several stations on the way down but eventually she reached London and was rushed into hospital. We (the players) had all gone to watch a film that evening and when we arrived back at the hotel, I was greeted with a "Congratulations Mr Douglas." "What have I done" I replied and they told me that I was the proud father of a son. On the Saturday morning, whilst all the other players were taking it easy and relaxing, I was visiting my wife and son Graham in the University College hospital. It was always going to be a tough match because the Wolves were a very good side, but I knew within five minutes that we would be playing them with ten men. I made a break with the ball, looked up and placed a perfect pass in front of Dougan. He was normally lightning quick and would have been clean through, but he never got anywhere near it. He shouldn't have played and I have never really forgiven him for not being honest. I also blamed Dally Duncan because he should have been strong enough to insist that he had a really thorough fitness test. When Dave Whelan was carried off before half-time, we were 1-0 down and effectively had nine men on the field. We tried really hard but did well only to lose 3-0. I had won back my place in the England team and we had to meet up in London after the Cup Final, playing Yugoslavia at Wembley where I scored in a 3-3 draw and Ronnie Clayton played his final game for England, being replaced by Bobby Robson. We then travelled to meet Spain in Madrid and Hungary in Budapest. It was a couple of weeks before I returned home and got to see my wife and baby son. I have never properly got over the defeat at Wembley because we could have given Wolves a tough game, but I have rarely watched a Cup Final on TV since. It brings back so many bad memories for me."

A new decade beckoned; the swinging sixties. For Blackburn Rovers, there were problems galore, not least with a manager who was sacked during the summer, but Burnley, with its enviable youth policy, was well set for another ten years. The 59-60 season had shone a spotlight on this small town club which would blaze across Europe. The question to be asked is …… was it the best ever season for the Clarets? It is either this or the 1913-14 season, but the answer is "who knows". And those that supported the club in 1960 would probably say "and who cares?" It had been a marvellous achievement and the town was absolutely buzzing.

1960-61

Team	Pos	Played	Won	Drawn	Lost	GF	GA	Pts
Burnley	4	42	22	7	13	102	77	51
Blackburn Rovers	8	42	15	13	14	77	76	43

Blackburn Rovers		Burnley	
Most Appearances	Matt Woods 42	Most Appearances	Adam Blacklaw 41
Most Goals	Peter Dobing 18	Most Goals	Jimmy Robson 25

Fuelled with the optimism of a Division 1 title win just months before, Burnley started the new season knowing that they could potentially win five trophies. They had qualified for the FA Charity (now Community) Shield and eligible, as champions of England, to play in the European Cup (now Champions League). The Football League introduced its new baby, The Football League Cup, and the two long running competitions, the FA Cup and the League Division 1 title, made up the five. Wolverhampton Wanderers as reigning FA Cup holders provided the Charity Shield opposition and the result was a 2-2 draw and a shared trophy; each club displaying it in their Trophy Room for six months.

Burnley's attempt to retain their title was virtually over as soon as it started as they lost three of their first five games. From then on in, Burnley began to find their title winning form. Robson scored a hat-trick at home to Preston North End and the number ten repeated the feat against Fulham and at Stamford Bridge. Connelly was twice on the scorecard in a thrilling 5-3 home win against Manchester United and Pointer made sure that the goals were shared out, particularly when knocking in a hat-trick at home to Arsenal. Newcastle United were downed by the Lancashire side's superior fire power, 5-3 on New Year's Eve, but the most memorable goal fest however was reserved for White Hart Lane. The league leaders produced a tour de force for thirty-six minutes, by which time they led 4-0. Their defence however was severely tested for the remainder of the game as those Three Musketeers in the Claret shirts gave them a dose of their own medicine, Connelly twice with Robson and Pointer one each. It was not only the match of the day but the game of the season. They set a record of 102 goals during the campaign, but although Harry Potts had three executioners in his side, it was the craft of Adamson and McIlroy in the middle of the park which constantly provided the ammunition. By the turn of the year they were handily placed in third position but unfortunately, the Spurs had lost just once up to December 31st and were unstoppable. Then suddenly, like a tap had been turned off, the Clarets' goals dried up. Robson scored just one more league goal during the rest of the season and the post-New Year period was a stop-start affair. Gordon Harris had now replaced Brian Pilking-

ton on the left wing and the diminutive Lancastrian was sold to Bolton Wanderers for £27,000. He had made 300 league appearances and scored sixty-seven goals. Results then improved steadily to the end of term and they won their last three, which included a sparkling second half performance against the champions Tottenham Hotspur where they came from behind to win 4-2. It was disappointing when compared with the previous season, but the fans had certainly received their money's worth. Because of injuries, Walter Joyce, a combative wing half who had come through the ranks at the Burnley training ground at Gawthorpe, actually started thirty games. Angus and Miller, each won their solitary international cap for England at the end of the season and Alex Elder's [pictured] long career in the green shirt of Northern Ireland had well and truly started.

Four of the extra fixtures were involved with their European Cup campaign. In November 1961, the Clarets played their first ever game at this highest of levels against French champions Reims (pronounced "Remms"). Veterans Raymond Kopa and Just Fontaine, two of the greatest French internationals of all time were in their side. Goals from McIlroy and Robson gave Harry Potts' side a two-goal advantage from the home leg and the game in Paris was extremely tight, the Burnley boys just managing to hang on to an aggregate lead. Adam Blacklaw was forced to concede three times as the French side, mixing theatricals and outstanding football skills, threatened to overrun the English champions, but they were thwarted by goals from Connelly and Robson which gave the Lancastrians a 4-3 aggregate win. The Quarter final draw paired the Clarets with West German champions SV Hamburg, Uwe Seeler and all. Once again, Burnley claimed a two-goal home victory. On this occasion, Brian Pilkington scoring twice. Jimmy Robson added a third, showing a poacher's instinct to tap home from three yards out but SV Hamburg managed a consolation goal that was ultimately to prove crucial. They were confident heading to Germany but Hamburg were simply explosive on their home terrain and in spite of a Gordon Harris goal and Jimmy McIlroy hitting the post in the final moment; Hamburg won the leg 4-1, giving them a 5-4 aggregate victory. Two Seeler headers swung the game but watching grainy clips of the games on U Tube, it is remarkable how we can forget the appalling state of English pitches in those days. Turf

Moor resembled a ploughed field in the first leg, whereas the Volksparcstadion was ideal for playing a passing game.

Burnley continued to steal the show in East Lancashire, but quietly, Blackburn Rovers had a successful season. Dally Duncan had said good-bye to the club during the summer, his inability to deal with spiky characters in the dressing room possibly tipping the balance against him. He was replaced by Jack Marshall. "Jolly Jack", as he was quickly christened, was highly thought of in spite of him being something of an unknown to the public when first appointed. He was in post at Rochdale when the Rovers came calling. His tenure at Ewood spanned six and a half years, still the record for the longest single stint at the club in modern times. He oversaw the perfect start as a Dougan hat-trick saw off Manchester United at Old Trafford. Bryan Douglas returned to the right wing where he was able to torment full backs at will and this also enabled the manager to find a place for Chris Crowe, an inside forward bought from Leeds United who came with glowing references. Marshall needed time to find his best side and he was also reluctant to regularly blood the youngsters from the FA Youth Cup victory of 1959. Peter Dobing was once more top of the scoring charts for a fourth consecutive year. There was a tricky spell in October when they lost all five games and close encounters were generally the order of the day, but they managed to score four goals on five occasions. My abiding memory of this season was when Tottenham came to Ewood. They played a brand of football which could only be described as sumptuous. The Rovers simply could not take the ball from them as they were "passed silly". The final defeat was by a 4-1 margin and the 26,819 Ewood Park crowd applauded the opposition from the field after ninety minutes. But eighth place was a positive start for Marshall and Andy McEvoy, then a wing-half made his Republic of Ireland debut.

The derby games

The Blackburn Rovers side was much changed from the Wembley escapade with Bob Jones in goal and two of the FA Youth Cup stars England and Pickering occupying the full back slots. Roy Isherwood, Douglas' perennial understudy, was in because of injury to the great man and Eddie Thomas, make weight in the Vernon deal, replaced Dougan up front alongside Chris Crowe from Leeds United. It was no wonder that it was a one sided affair. They were once again tormented by Connelly's pace, the winger scoring twice in the first half. Thomas equalised half way through the first period but second half goals from the two Jimmy's, Adamson and Robson, made it a comfortable journey home for the Burnley faithful as the reigning champion won 4-1. It was ample revenge for the 4-1 thrashing two years before and for the FA Cup debacle earlier in the year. The game had suffered because McIlroy joined Douglas on the side lines, but the Clarets, who brought in Gordon Harris at inside forward, had a much stronger squad, hence their convincing victory. It had been their biggest away win in a derby since they produced a thumping 5-1 victory in 1926. The Ewood Park side had a much stronger look to it for the return at Turf Moor. Douglas and Dougan were fit, Bray and Taylor offered far more strength and experience at full back and Leyland was back in goal. Burnley fielded a talented eleven as usual with only Cummings missing and they were riding at fourth in the table. The Blue and Whites were in the middle of a long unbeaten run which lasted almost three months, so an intriguing match was forecast. It was tight and competitive but the crowd had to wait until the hour mark for the first goal. It fell to Burnley's Brian Miller, but within moments, MacLeod had equalised and the spoils were shared.

08 10 1960	Blackburn Rovers	**Burnley**	1-4	E Thomas. J Connelly 2, J Adamson, J Robson.
25 02 1961	Burnley	Blackburn Rovers	1-1	B Miller. A MacLeod.

Blackburn Rovers, with sights set on Wembley's twin towers once more, cruised through in the FA Cup Round 3 replay over Chesterfield. They thumped Bolton Wanderers 4-0 after a replay in Round 4 but there was disappointment in the last sixteen where they bade farewell to the Cup with a close 2-1 defeat at Sheffield United. With involvement in four competitions, the last thing Burnley needed was a draw and a late John Connelly goal at Turf Moor saw them through against Bournemouth. There was a replay in Round 4 however before normality was restored against Brighton and Hove Albion. The Clarets romped home against Swansea Town in Round 5 and they drew the other Sheffield side in the round of the last eight. Adam Blacklaw had a blinder between the sticks at Hillsborough, forcing a goalless draw, but it was easier in the replay at the "Turf" as Potts' eleven sealed a semi-final slot. Unfortunately the all-conquering "Spurs" side came out of the hat in the semi-final draw. The press wrote of nothing but the first double of the twentieth century and the London club certainly justified favourite's tag, being far too good on the day and winning 3-0. It was disappointing, but this was one of the Twentieth Century's great teams and there was little Burnley could do to stem the tide.

As if there was not enough football, the clubs also played for the Football League Cup, the brainchild of Alan Hardaker, the Football League secretary. The fans voted with their feet and the attendances were poor. Blackburn Rovers won 3-1 (a Dougan double) at York City and edged through 2-1 at Swansea Town to meet up with Rochdale at Ewood Park in Round 3. Here a brace from Chris Crowe saw them through to Round 4. Blackburn Rovers were at their frustrating worst against Wrexham. There was a 1-1 draw at Ewood but at the Racecourse Ground, the Welsh Dragon roared its way to a 3-1 victory. Burnley thumped Cardiff City at Ninian Park, Gordon Harris scoring a hat-trick. They then defeated Third Division Brentford at home in a replay which they won 2-1. Potts had played a complete reserve eleven in the original tie. A 2-1 win at home to Nottingham Forest took them to Southampton in Round 4 where a couple from reserve team forward Ronnie Fenton helped them on their way to a 4-2 victory. Aston Villa provided the semi-final opposition over two legs. It was 1-1 in Burnley, 2-2 at Villa Park and in the replay at Old Trafford, Jimmy Robson's seventy first minute goal kept them in the game before the Villa's eighty eighth minute winner eliminated the Clarets. It was their fifth and final exit from competitions in one very long season in which Jimmy Robson had scored thirty-four goals in forty-nine games.

1961-62

Team	Pos	Played	Won	Drawn	Lost	GF	GA	Pts
Burnley	2	42	21	11	10	101	67	53
Blackburn Rovers	16	42	14	11	17	50	58	39

Blackburn Rovers		Burnley	
Most Appearances	Keith Newton 41	Most Appearances	Adam Blacklaw 42
Most Goals	Ian Lawler 14	Most Goals	Ray Pointer 25

If you finished above the likes of Tottenham, Everton, the two Manchester clubs, Sheffield Wednesday and the Wolves in the early sixties, you deserved to be Division 1 winners. This is what happened to Burnley but from out of nowhere, Ipswich Town, in their first ever season in the top flight, pipped the lot and were crowned champion. It was masterminded by Alf Ramsey who took over in 1955 when the club was in the Third Division South. He brought them all the way through to Division 1 and they came from a long way back, overtaking Burnley in late April and taking the honours on the last day of the season. It was the stuff of fairy tales, but sadly a horror story in Burnley.

Bob Lord withdrew the club from the Football League Cup, a move copied by several other top clubs, citing that it was an unnecessary drain on the stamina of the players. It is true to say that Potts' team was virtually unstoppable for most of the season. There had been an early season shock when hammered 6-2 at Ipswich, but seven consecutive wins in September swept them to the summit of the league, opponents being contemptuously brushed aside in an avalanche of another century of goals. Birmingham conceded a seven and a six and there were other six goal hauls against Leicester City, Manchester City and West Ham, with doubles from Robson and the young winger Ian Towers. Yet again the front five all reached double figures in the annual goals competition, this time Ray Pointer [pictured] topping the list. There were setbacks but they ran Manchester United silly at Old Trafford and thumped the consistent Sheffield Wednesday 4-0. After a March 24th 2-0 victory at Aston Villa and, with a healthy lead coupled with games in hand, it was all but game over. Then, inexplicably, the wheels dropped off. They drew five of their last ten games, scoring only three times in the process and even worse, lost another four to hand the title to the Tractormen on a plate.

Blonde-haired goal machine, Ray Pointer, had made his England debut and in all he was selected three times. For his final appearance against Portugal at Wembley, he joined up with Connelly and Douglas and the Burnley pair made the score sheet in a 2-0 World Cup qualifying win. It was rare for both Douglas and Connelly to play in the same eleven, both being right wingers. For these two games however, the Blackburn star was moved inside, but it was an experiment that was never repeated. They both were picked for the World Cup squad in Chile the following summer, Douglas playing in all four games with Connelly keeping the bench warm.

In all honesty, Blackburn Rovers were poor this season. There had been three major exits from the club during the summer. Peter Dobing left for Manchester City after a transfer fee of £37,500 was agreed. He had scored 88 goals in 179 league games, placing him in eleventh place in the club's all-time scoring charts. The Manchester born inside right was quick, his touch and technique quite perfect and the power and precision in his shooting accounted for so many of his goals. Derek Dougan was allowed to move on to Aston Villa. In spite of all his talent which included scoring a number of vital goals, he was a major disappointment at the club. The genial Ally McLeod fell out with the Blackburn Board because, on the abolition of the maximum wage, they chose not to increase his take home pay. He signed for Hibernian and was a big loss at Ewood. Joe Haverty, his replacement bought from Arsenal for £27,000 was another huge disappointment and he left after a single season having represented the Republic of Ireland twice in his one season in Blackburn.

Fred Else had been signed from Preston North End for £20,000 as a solution to Jack Marshall's goalkeeping worries. He was a fine keeper, if ever so slightly on the small size. Keith Newton broke through to make the left back shirt his own and Taylor regained the number two shirt from Bray. Chris Crowe was Wolverhampton bound in mid-season but Northern Ireland striker Ian Lawther had been bought from Sunderland for £18,000. He formed a strike partnership with Fred Pickering, another local boy and in a season when goals were scarce, Lawther was leading scorer. The season had started badly, losing 6-1 at Old Trafford on the second Saturday. There was a slow but general improvement and one highlight away from home was a 3-0 victory at West Ham where "Boy Byrom" as the local paper called him, fresh from the Reserves, scored the season's only hat-trick. With safety well and truly secured, the Rovers then put together an embarrassing run of five consecutive defeats to end the year in sixteenth place. Douglas played in the three group games in the World Cup in Chile as they squeezed through to the quarter final. There they met a great Brazil side which contained a number of legends but were without the injured Pele. They were too strong for England, going through 3-1. Mike England became a regular in the Welsh side before doing so at the Rovers, making his debut this season. Ian Lawther was capped twice more at Ewood Park.

The derby games

Bryan Douglas told me that he thought that Blackburn Rovers generally competed well in the derby matches in this era. Statistics tell us that Burnley actually had the edge but considering that the Clarets were far more successful on a season to season basis; much the stronger squad, Douglas is correct in his assertion. The games over this eight year period were far closer than one would have expected. The 1961-62 matches were both played in the latter part of the season, in February and April. Harry Potts' side was actually at the top of the table when they travelled to Ewood Park. It was a full strength side apart from Ian Towers standing in for Harris. Jack Marshall was able to send out his best eleven and there were derby debuts for left back Keith Newton and left winger Barry Ratcliffe, both of whom had impressed in the FA Youth Cup winning side plus Ian Lawther, the summer signing from Sunderland. A crowd of 33,914 was in attendance, the highest gate at Ewood this season. Burnley, playing like champion's elect, took the lead through Pointer, but were sunk with goals from the Rovers' new strike force of Lawther and Pickering. This was a setback, but they retained their lead at the top of the table and put together another unbeaten run. They lost at home to Manchester United immediately prior to the Turf Moor derby and slipped into second place. There was no doubt that they were beginning to struggle as they chased the double and young Ratcliffe (born in Blackburn) put the Rovers in front after half an hour. There was still an hour left to put matters right and the Burnley of a couple of months before would have passed Blackburn to distraction, creating sufficient chances to win the game. But this time they could only huff and puff, failing to break down the Blue and White resistance. A final placement in any league is of course dependant on the results of all games played, so it is inaccurate to claim that the Rovers prevented the title returning to Turf Moor. But these were two games that the Clarets ought to have won and when you consider that Ipswich's winning margin was three points, and that Burnley had a far superior goal average (1.5 as opposed to 1.3), even a win and a draw against their local rivals would have been sufficient. As for the Blackburn side, this result confirmed their Division 1 status for another year and was their first derby double since the 1925-26 season.

24 02 1962	Blackburn Rovers	Burnley	2-1	I Lawther, F Pickering. R Pointer.
17 04 1962	Burnley	Blackburn Rovers	0-1	B Ratcliffe.

In the FA Cup, Blackburn Rovers had a long trip to Brighton where all three goal scorers were Blackburn born, Byrom, Pickering and Ratcliffe. A Douglas penalty saw them through against Division 2 Stoke City in Round 4 and a victory over Second Division Middlesbrough at Ewood Park in Round 5 qualified the Rovers for a last eight place. The Rovers had a potentially favourable encounter, a home tie against a struggling Fulham side. They drew 2-2 at home, but the replay produced a disappointing result and they travelled back to the North on the back of a 1-0 defeat. Burnley continued their prolific scoring in Round 3 of the FA Cup, savaging Division 3 Queens Park Rangers 6-1 at Turf Moor, but had a real scare in the next round before going through 1-0 in a replay at the home of Leyton Orient. Burnley began to scent a long cup run, but they had to defeat a resurgent Everton, at long last living up to their reputation as a top club. It was tight, it was tense but this Burnley side performed magnificently to overcome the loss of an early goal to win 3-1. The Clarets were given a tricky tie at the home of Sheffield United, but Pointer's second half strike took them a step closer to the final. Burnley's semi-final against Fulham was scheduled for Villa Park, not the happiest of hunting grounds for them, but they managed a 1-1 draw before Robson scored once in each half in the reply at Leicester City's Filbert Street, making the Cottager's last-minute score irrelevant.

And it came to pass that England's best two sides would meet at Wembley on May 6th. Harry Potts was able to field his best eleven as were Tottenham, who had added Jimmy Greaves to the side following their double success the previous season. Greaves quickly showed why he was so highly rated, ultimately the highest ever goal scorer in top flight English football. The Cockney inside forward dribbled his way into the Burnley box after just three minutes and knocked the ball past Adam Blacklaw. Burnley remained in the game until half-time and Jimmy Robson equalised in the fiftieth minute. Disastrously, Smith quickly put the London side in front again and then Robson scored again but was ruled offside with what must have been an extremely tight decision. Cummings then handled on the line and Blanchflower stroked the ball home from the spot. There was also controversy here because the linesman had flagged for a foul on Blacklaw moments before, a signal not seen by the referee. Therefore, it was the Spurs who received the cup, whereas Burnley had to settle for runner up for a second occasion in fifteen years.

The Burnley 1962 FA Cup Runner-Up side that lost 1-3 to Tottenham Hotspur was; Adam Blacklaw, John Angus, Alex Elder, Jimmy Adamson, Tommy Cummings, Brian Miller, John Connelly, Jimmy McIlroy, Ray Pointer, Jimmy Robson, Gordon Harris.

The Trawden born Dave Timberlake has been a true Claret from being a boy and still follows the club home and away, in spite of having lived in the Midlands for many years. He was at Wembley and his story paints a picture of what it was like being a fan in those days.

> "My dad was a Corporation bus driver and he seemed to know everyone. As a result he found tickets for the big day, two in particular coming his way because the wife of an acquaintance who had two season tickets, was due to go into labour that weekend. We had an old and dilapidated Vauxhall Wyvern, a complete rust bucket. It was so bad that there were holes in the body work and my kid brother and a mate spent the journey down eating toffees and pushing the papers out through the gaps. There were no motorways and it took an age to get down there and Wembley Stadium at that time was divided into small pens. Being on the small side, we were pushed to the wall at the front and we had an excellent vantage point behind the goals that Burnley attacked in the first half. It was a great experience but Burnley were second best. They would probably say now that we just didn't turn up. Robson's goal, the hundredth to be scored in a Wembley Cup Final, brought us back into the game, but we were all dismayed when we had a close up of Blanchflower's penalty hitting the back of the net. Although we were upset, we took it on the chin. We believed we were the best side in the country and we would be here again and again. In my life time up to then, Burnley were a top side and we thought they always would be."

The Football League Cup had made a less than auspicious start the previous season and this time the competition was lacking representation from a raft of top clubs. Blackburn Rovers made their first ever visit to Peterborough United and Lawther scored twice in a 3-1 win. In the 2nd Round, having drawn at Bristol Rovers, the meagre crowd of 5,357 witnessed a remarkable performance from Eddie Thomas who scored all four goals in a 4-0 victory. Goals by Ratcliffe and Lawther safely navigated Round 3 as Nottingham Forest were beaten 2-1 and Round 4 saw the arrival of prospective champions Ipswich Town. By now the crowd had topped the ten thousand mark and, on the night, the Tractor Boys were no match for the Rovers. Two goals from Pickering were central to a 4-1 upset. Lawther's goal guided them to a 1-0 victory at Rotherham United and suddenly, Marshall's side were in the last four; with Blackpool the only other Division 1 side left in the competition. The Rovers drew Rochdale from Division 4 and the first leg was a shambles, Rochdale winning 3-1. The return at Ewood was played on a quagmire. It was a completely one-sided affair and although the Rovers scored twice, they somehow allowed Rochdale to pinch one back, thus failing to reach the final.

1962-63

Team	Pos	Played	Won	Drawn	Lost	GF	GA	Pts
Burnley	3	42	22	10	10	78	57	54
Blackburn Rovers	11	42	15	12	15	79	71	42

Blackburn Rovers		Burnley	
Most Appearances	Keith Newton, Bryan Douglas (both 41)	Most Appearances	Adam Blacklaw, John Angus, Brian Miller (all 42)
Most Goals	Fred Pickering 23	Most Goals	Andy Lochhead 19

Although matters were running less smoothly off the pitch, Burnley were still something special on it. Tommy Cummings played the first game of the season, but that was the end of a magnificent career. It spanned fourteen seasons and included 434 league games, the fourth highest ever by a Burnley player. John Talbut, a graduate from the Gawthorpe Training Ground, immediately replaced him in the heart of the defence. Andy Lochhead broke through also, providing stiff competition for both Robson and Pointer, being the leading goal scorer with nineteen strikes. But it was the sale of Jimmy McIlroy which almost caused riots in the streets. In modern times, he has been the ultimate footballing hero in the town and there was genuine anger amongst spectators when he was placed on the transfer list. The winter of the 62-63 season was one of the worst on record and even the very top level of the professional game ground to a halt during the "big freeze". Burnley did not play a single league match between December 30th and March 1st. Not playing meant no gate receipts but players still had to be paid. Many felt that Bob Lord sold "Mac" during the freeze because the club needed the money and because he knew a club would pay £25,000 for him; something Stoke City did. There were suggestions that Harry Potts felt that he was no longer as effective on the pitch, but nothing was officially said and McIlroy himself kept a dignified silence. Many swore that they would never go to Turf Moor again and apparently a number kept their promise. It was a strange and equally sad incident. Jimmy believed that Burnley was by then his hometown and he returned to live and work there when his playing days were over. His 439 appearances were second only to Dawson's, his 116 league goals place him third behind Beel and Pointer and 51 international appearances make him easily Burnley's most capped player. I asked Philip Webster if he had any first-hand knowledge of the transfer.

> "I have honestly never known. None of the supporters could understand it. Something must have gone on somewhere, but Harry told us nothing except to say that it was not of his doing. I think it could have been a row between Jimmy and Bob Lord, but I have no proof. It has been a well-kept secret, one that Jimmy took to his grave and I guess we will never know now."

MICHAEL ENGLAND
Blackburn Rovers F.C. Centre Half
Wales

On the field, little changed. They lost just two of their opening seventeen games and in turn they scored five on three occasions, against both Manchester clubs and Sheffield United. Their on-field disaster was at Wolverhampton when Lochhead scored early and Pointer late, but in between they leaked seven goals. Nonetheless they continued to chase the leaders from the blue side of Liverpool and a run of four wins and a draw when they resumed post-freeze kept them on their coat tails. They finished with a bang, winning four out of the last five to finish third, a point behind Tottenham but seven behind Everton. There was still consistency in form and team selection, two vital ingredients necessary to challenge for the top honours.

There were changes to the regular starting eleven at Ewood Park also. John Bray won back his number 2 shirt from Ken Taylor and Mike Harrison joined from Chelsea in mid-September. A speedy left winger, he could strike a ball perfectly with his left foot and he was often joined on the other flank by Mike Ferguson, ex of Accrington Stanley. This enabled Douglas to return to an inside forward position where his slide-rule passing began to set up goals for Fred Pickering. The Blackburn youngster had made the number nine shirt his own and he was top scorer with twenty- three goals. Douglas, not only the play maker and provider, was once more amongst the goals. Marshall had three players good enough to be in the side but who struggled to find their true position. Andy McEvoy was an excellent footballer but was he a wing half or an inside forward? Mike England, a supreme talent who would go on to wage war against the Clarets, had all the makings of an outstanding centre half but there was no way that Matt Woods could be omitted so the Welsh youngster played at full back or wing half if there was an injury. Finally, there was John Byrom. He could certainly finish but Pickering had the shirt and he was now scoring goals for fun. As a result, Byrom only played if Marshall was short of a forward.

It was a middling season. An eleventh-place finish with more goals scored than conceded. The campaign started in bizarre fashion. In a 3-3 draw against Ipswich Town, Bobby Craig, a scheming inside forward rather than a goal scorer who signed from Sheffield Wednesday at the end of the previous season, scored all three. He could not settle in Blackburn so he returned to his native Scotland after just eight games, being signed by Celtic. This was not the only hat-trick. Fred Pickering notched two against West Brom and Wolverhampton Wanderers and Bryan Douglas scored perhaps the greatest goal I have ever seen. Receiving the ball in his own half, he dribbled past what seemed to be every single member of the Birmingham City side before sliding the ball into an empty net. It was a crazy afternoon when Arsenal came to town and after a ten goal thriller, the points were shared. You don't see many 5-5 draws. The Rovers never quite flirted with relegation but a wonderful last five fixture finish produced five wins and nineteen goals, eight being attributed to Pickering. Bryan Douglas scored his eleventh international goal in his final England outing against Switzerland in Basle; a satisfying way to end an international career which spanned 36 games. A month prior to this however came what was possibly the personal highlight of his career. Brazil played a friendly at Wembley in front of 92,000 spectators. Pele put the South Americans in front only for Douglas to score late on to clinch the draw; not a bad name with whom to share the goal scoring honours.

The derby games

Knowing how close derby matches could be, the Clarets had to make sure that the Blackburn side could claim no credit this time for a failure to win the league. Over 50,000 in total turned up to watch the two games and the first encounter at Ewood Park featured a Burnley side which was currently on the Podium and a Rovers outfit which had beaten Manchester City the previous week and was looking to move up the gears after a shaky start. Andy Lochhead, yet another Scottish striker and a veritable goal machine in the Reserves, had finally replaced Jimmy Robson and John Talbut took permanent ownership of Tommy Cummings' number five shirt. Bobby Craig would be playing his last game in a blue and white halved shirt, his disappointingly short stay coming to an end and Mike Harrison was making his derby debut in East Lancashire. Lawther put the home side ahead but the visitors hit back with two goals in three minutes from Harris and Lochhead to give them the interval lead. Douglas equalised from the penalty spot just after the break but the big Scottish striker sent the Burnley fans home happy with a winner just past the hour mark. The Rovers slipped closer to the relegation zone but the win enabled the Clarets to remain close to Everton and the Spurs. The return at Turf Moor was equally well attended, the first of nine games that the home side had scheduled for April and it was again keenly contested. The result was vital for Potts' side with Everton threatening to pull away from the field. Arthur Bellamy had replaced McIlroy, Adamson was now struggling with injuries and local boy David Walker replaced him. McGrath was injured again and Mike England had the opportunity to cement a regular spot in the team. McEvoy had replaced the departed Craig and local lad John Byrom was currently favoured over Lawther. The game was settled with a first-half penalty, Gordon Harris once more on target, but the Clarets could never relax, eventually seeing the game out at 1-0. The win kept them in the hunt but the overall performance acted as a confidence booster to Marshall's side, as they lost only two of their remaining eleven games, enabling them to achieve a top half finish. History has shown us that completing derby doubles is far from easy and it was the first one for the Clarets since the 1926-27 season.

06 10 1962	Blackburn Rovers	**Burnley**	2-3	I Lawther, B Douglas. G Harris, A Lochhead 2.
02 04 1963	**Burnley**	Blackburn Rovers	1-0	G Harris.

The 3rd Round of the FA Cup was postponed so many times due to the freezing conditions and was finally played on March 5th. Middlesbrough were the visitors to Ewood Park for the second consecutive season and the North Yorkshire side escaped with a 1-1 draw, winning the replay on Teesside 3-1. Burnley managed to play their first game as early as January 16th, but they had a huge task on their hands. In a re-match of the previous year's final, they travelled to White Hart Lane and achieved one of the club's greatest victories, Harris, Connelly and Lochhead combining with a goal apiece to shatter any illusions that the London club may have had of winning the trophy for a third consecutive year. A home draw against the newly promoted Liverpool, now moving relentlessly upward under Bill Shankly, produced a 1-1 draw. In spite of Alex Elder giving them the lead in the replay, the game finally moved into extra time, the Reds winning it with the last kick of the match after 120 minutes.

Blackburn Rovers progressed well in the League Cup. After a 3-1 home victory over Derby County, Leeds United were despatched 4-0 at Ewood in Round 3. For the second year running, they were paired against Rotherham United, this time in Blackburn. It was another four-goal bonanza, the Rovers winning 4-1. A trip to Sunderland, now playing in the 2nd Division loomed in the last eight, but they had the edge on the Rovers, winning through by a narrow 3-2 margin. It would be another thirty years before the Blues would better this performance in the League Cup.

1963-64

Team	Pos	Played	Won	Drawn	Lost	GF	GA	Pts
Blackburn Rovers	7	42	18	10	14	89	65	46
Burnley	9	42	17	10	15	71	64	44

Blackburn Rovers		Burnley	
Most Appearances	Ronnie Clayton, Bryan Douglas, Mike England and Mike Harrison (all 41)	Most Appearances	Adam Blacklaw 42
Most Goals	Andy McEvoy 32	Most Goals	Andy Lochhead 11

The year that Liverpool last won the 1st Division crown in 1947 was the last year that Blackburn Rovers had featured in a higher position in the Football League pyramid than Burnley. For the following sixteen seasons, they had struggled along in the wake of their East Lancashire rival but suddenly, the sun started to shine on Ewood Park, bringing cautious optimism to the success

ANDY McEVOY
Blackburn Rovers F.C. Inside Right
Eire

starved spectators. The five successive wins at the end of the previous term had laid the foundations for a shot at the big boys. Jack Marshall had found the right blend at last and it was based on the inside forward partnership of Douglas and McEvoy. Like McIlroy at Burnley, "Duggie" had all the tools to conduct the play. His touch, his dribbling skills and his ability to not only pass the ball accurately but also to time the pass and weight it to perfection, was a skill that few have possessed. When Marshall moved McEvoy forward to join Pickering, Douglas always had two options every time he moved forward and the opposing defences could only guess as to the ball's final destination. Harrison on the left wing now provided pace and power, adding to "Fergie's" trickery on the opposite flank. For half a season, they were the finest Rovers side (including the 1995 version) that I have ever seen. There was one other major change. Matt Woods bade farewell after seven seasons and 260 league appearances. His contribution to the club over this period was immense and while we were all sorry to see him sail away to Australia to complete his career down under, we were excited at the thought that Mike England would seamlessly step into this vital position. The Welshman had waited for this opportunity and this super-talented athlete let no-one down.

The first sign that something special was about to happen was when Tottenham Hotspur came to Blackburn in early September. It was a hot afternoon in late summer and the ageing Spurs side was run ragged. Blanchflower and company chased shadows all afternoon and it was sad to see such quality players being overrun so easily. Douglas was masterful, the Spurs half backs could not take the ball from him and McEvoy helped himself to four goals as the Rovers won 7-2. The Wolves were slaughtered 5-1 at Molyneux and from October 28th when they drew 2-2 at Old Trafford until the glorious 26th of December, (which has gone down in history as the most amazing day in English football, but more of that later) they were unbeaten in ten games, winning seven. In this run, they won 4-2 at Goodison Park and 2-0 at Anfield. The final game of this majestic two-month period took place at West Ham on Boxing Day. It was a lunch time game and the brother of one of my mates was taking us to see the Burnley v Manchester United game at Turf Moor. His new car was fitted with a radio and we could not believe the score which the BBC broadcasted. It was West Ham United 2 Blackburn Rovers 8. Pickering and McEvoy each scored hat-tricks whilst master puppeteer Douglas pulled all of the strings. Boxing Day was on a

Thursday and two days later the fixtures were reversed. On that Saturday afternoon, we congregated behind the goal at the Darwen end, expecting double figures. What we saw shocked us as much as the result from Upton Park two days before. A young wing half called Eddie Bovington virtually occupied Douglas' jock strap. He followed him every single step of the way and without its master technician, the Rovers were reduced to firing blanks. Bobby Moore looked after the Rovers' twin strike force and the Hammers' centre forward Johnny Byrne, so effective playing in a slightly withdrawn position, gave Mike England plenty to think about. He also had a young Geoff Hurst playing alongside of him and the London side followed the tactics set out by their Burnley born manager Ron Greenwood, lethally attacking with pace on the break. It was football for a future era and the Rovers simply could not cope, slipping to a 3-1 defeat.

The dream did not actually end on that day. They had led the table after the Boxing Day game, but they managed to stay in contention until early March. They won 5-2 at Leicester City, "Andy Mac" notching his third four-timer of the campaign. Pickering was being talked of as an England player and he asked for a transfer. Everton offered £85,000 and the Board bit their hand off. He had already scored twenty-three goals that season but without him, the Blackburn club's season fell apart. They used some of the money to buy George Jones from Bury, a young striker with apparently lots of potential, but he achieved very little at Ewood Park. They failed to win for seven games, but it had been a thrilling journey at times. One thing however was clear. The Board of Directors were not prepared to speculate in the transfer market. Over the last few years they had developed a number of quality young players, sold them on for good money and spent far less on replacing them with to be frank, far inferior players. With this philosophy there was only one future destination and it was downwards. Seventh place is a very acceptable reward but with a Jack Walker at the helm, I suspect that they would have run Liverpool extremely close. What was even more worrying was that Newton and England were earning rave reviews in the press. How long would they keep hold of these two jewels? But it was Andy McEvoy's season. The Irishman's total of thirty-two strikes was just three behind Jimmy Greaves, the league's leading scorer. It was also the highest at the club since Tommy Briggs' thirty- three, nine seasons previously but the highest in Division 1 since Ted Harper scored thirty-five goals in 1927. I asked Bryan Douglas why it had all gone wrong in the second half of the season.

> There is absolutely no doubt that it all went wrong after we sold Fred Pickering. Fred was a tremendous centre-forward. He could smash in the goals, was decent with his head and always made himself available. I could understand why he left. Everton was a bigger club and they must have paid him a lot more than the Rovers did, but he was happy here, his mates outside the game were here and he wasn't as successful at either Everton or Birmingham as he was with us. I believe we could have won the title if he had stayed. He and Andy McEvoy were a wonderful pair to have playing in front of you. They were constantly making

runs but often Fred's were to move the defenders about. Andy went late into the gaps that Fred had created. He was direct and was certainly the best finisher I played with at the Rovers. Tommy Briggs was great to play with because he was so strong and scored goals with his head, his feet and with his knees and backside if needed. But he hadn't the class of McEvoy who could score with either foot and he struck the ball so cleanly. His shots were not necessarily rockets, but they were placed to perfection. I have to say though that he wasn't the best I ever played with. That had to be Greaves. He was a wizard in the penalty area, the best I have ever seen. No defenders could keep him quiet. As far as defenders were concerned, I always thought that Bobby Moore was a little bit over-rated. He was classy and he always looked the part but he never worried us too much. Burnley's best player was Jimmy McIlroy without a doubt, but I felt that Tommy Cummings was their most difficult defender to play against. Alex Elder was good, but he was more of a nuisance. Tommy was a real defender. Leeds United were the team I most disliked playing against. The aggression used to come out when we played Burnley but that was because the rival fans stirred us all up in the derbies. It was different against Leeds. You felt that they came out on to the field to win at any cost and if they could seriously hurt you, they would. It was hard to have any respect for them because they were forever trying to verbally wind you up as well in the nastiest way possible.

The success story that was Burnley FC still had more distance yet to run. They would ultimately extend their occupation in the top level of English football to twenty-four years but from the end of the 1962-63 season until the present day, they would challenge for the highest honour on just one more occasion. Their success however since promotion in 1947 was worthy of a Hollywood script. This was and still is a small town, a conurbation beset by economic problems and at times looked upon as one of the very poorest in the country. Compared with its rivals nationally, their fan base footprint has always been miniscule. The side had been put together at a total outlay of £12,000, managed by a former player who had also been brought to the club for nothing shortly after leaving school and owned by the local butcher. It is a story that would not be out of place alongside Roy of the Rovers, a story you would be reluctant to make up for fear of micky-taking. But Burnley FC had been amongst the best teams in the country for sixteen seasons, with only one non-top ten finish in the previous fourteen.

What caused the beginnings of the deterioration this season? The time was up on a number of Burnley's quality players. McIlroy and Cummings had left the club, Adamson was nearing the end of the road and injuries were catching up on those twin strikers, Pointer and Robson. Burnley's success was built on the production line at Gawthorpe. If youngsters ceased to come through, they would have to rely on the cheque book, but this was not a wealthy club. There was no particular sign of panic; some said it was a temporary blip, but there was certainly an unaccustomed tetchiness apparent in both the manager's office and the Board Room.

The highpoint of the season was reached following the derby victory in October which pushed them up to fourth in the table. Arthur Bellamy, the replacement for McIlroy, was immediately prominent early season. He was a talented mid-field player who would go on to have a long career at the club, but he was no "Jimmy Mac", although he had scored a hat-trick when reigning champions Everton came to Burnley early in the campaign and were turned over 4-3 after a most thrilling encounter. Lochhead was certainly building a reputation as a centre forward who could look after himself, one of the 1960's renowned hard men. From that point on, the performances dipped and the club hovered around mid-table, a couple of late victories edging them to yet another top ten finish. One of these was a 7-2 thrashing of Tottenham Hotspur ("anything the Rovers can do, so can we") with doubles from Harris, Willie Irvine and Brian O'Neill. The latter two had moved up from the reserves and would both make exceptionally good professionals. Injuries to Adamson, Elder and Connelly restricted Harry Pott's team selections. There were opportunities for youngsters to show their wares. Willie Morgan impressed on the wing enabling Harris to move into the McIlroy role and both Ian Towers and Sammy Todd were given opportunities. The fans were crying out for a marquee signing but Bob Lord's cheque book stayed firmly closed.

The most emphatic win came on Boxing Day, Lochhead proving far too tough for the Manchester United defence when bagging four of the goals in a 6-1 victory. Morgan scored the other two and generally led the "Reds" a merry dance. I saw the game on one of my rare visits to Turf Moor and the Clarets' performance, coupled with the result at Upton Park, made it a memorable Christmas. Burnley travelled to Old Trafford two days later on the Saturday, thus becoming part of the craziest weekend in English football history. The result in Manchester, as at Ewood, was a complete turnaround, a 5-2 home victory, most notable for George Best's first ever league goal. Around the country, extraordinary reversals abounded, none more so than Ipswich Town losing 10-1 at Fulham on Boxing Day and then winning 4-2 at Portman Road. The Boxing Day games also saw Chelsea score five at Blackpool, Liverpool knock six past Stoke City at Anfield, the Potters reversing the result when winning 3-1 on the Saturday and two high scoring draws; 4-4 at West Brom where Spurs were the visitors and 3-3 in the Notts Forest versus Sheffield United game. There were sixty-six goals in 10 games. With apologies to Frankie Valli and the 4 Seasons, "Oh what a....... day, Late December back in '63".

The derby games

Both derby games were played in the month of October, eighteen days apart. The Turf Moor game was on a Tuesday night, with the Clarets ninth in the table after recovering from an iffy start. Elder had broken his ankle, Walter Joyce deputising. Harris and Adamson were both injured and Pointer was struggling to reach peak fitness. Brian O'Neill made his derby debut to start a long run of games which would see this talented but sometimes controversial wing-half establish himself in the game. The Blackburn side had made a slightly better start and were a place above their rival. McGrath was once more unfit and Ferguson had a knock, but with Byrom and Ratcliffe coming in, this was a strong side and opinions varied as to which one would prove victorious. The game was notable for the war of attrition waged on each other by Andy Lochhead and Mike England. With two tall men, both strong and ruthless in their approach to the game, the physicality was brutal, resembling two stags locked in combat in a Highland Glen. Both trod a fine line between what was fair and what was unacceptable, but when England, out of sheer frustration, smashed into the Scot, the line had been crossed and the Rovers were down to ten men. With the Rovers now struggling, it became something of a cakewalk for the home side and the goals came from less recognisable sources, namely Walter Joyce and an Arthur Bellamy double. Both sides remained unbeaten between the derby games and the Rovers were certainly beginning their push for honours. England was suspended and young Chris Sims from Clitheroe made his debut at full back, Newton playing centre half. With Elder, Adamson, Robson and Pointer all out with injuries, it was a less than familiar Burnley line up, but the gate of 26,740 expected a far closer contest than had taken place at the "Turf". It was a contest to remember. Pickering gave Marshall's side an early lead. But that man Connelly was once again their hero, scoring twice as they ground out a 2-1 win. For the second consecutive year, Burnley had completed the derby double. It was their first double-double since the "Golden Years" of the immediate post First World War period, a feat not accomplished by the Rovers since the 1888-90 era when the Blue and Whites won six on the bounce.

01 10 1963	**Burnley**	Blackburn Rovers	3-0	A Bellamy 2, W Joyce.
19 10 1963	Blackburn Rovers	**Burnley**	1-2	F Pickering. J Connelly 2.

In the FA Cup, Blackburn Rovers comfortably defeated a poor Grimsby Town side 4-0. Marshall played his best eleven which was customary in all cup ties in those days and McEvoy banged in another hat-trick. Rotherham United was a well-established Division 2 side in the fifties and sixties and they gave Burnley all sorts of problems in the Third-Round clash at Turf Moor. Lochhead scored for the home side in a 1-1 draw and in the replay at Millmoor, the Clarets had to come from behind to squeeze through 3-2. In Round 4, Newport County from Division 4 played out of their skins, but still narrowly lost in East Lancashire, Connelly and Morgan scoring the goals whilst an early Pointer goal set them up for a comfortable 3-0 win over Division 2 Huddersfield Town in the 5th Round. It was the Pickering/McEvoy one two in Round 4 at Ewood Park as Fulham failed to cause an upset, giving them an away trip to Oxford United. The club from the university town had only recently joined the Football League, replacing Accrington Stanley and was captained by Ron Atkinson, later to make his mark as manager of Manchester United. Nestling in the lower reaches of Division 4, the "Us" were in no position to cause an upset but cause an upset they did. It was not even close, the Rovers tamely surrendering and losing 3-1. Burnley's Round 6 trip to West Ham would always be difficult and the Hammers, narrowly edged through 3-2 in spite of goals from Connelly and Pointer. The Blackburn side's interest in the Football League Cup ended as early as September 2nd. Having won at Aston Villa in the league on the preceding Saturday, they somehow lost at Notts County who would finish rock bottom of Division 3 by a 2-1 margin. Such defeats are unfathomable, but fingers can be pointed at the motivation level of the Rovers. Were they interested in the League Cup? Probably not, but neither were Burnley who once more sat it out.

1964-65

Team	Pos	Played	Won	Drawn	Lost	GF	GA	Pts
Blackburn Rovers	10	42	16	10	16	83	79	42
Burnley	12	42	16	10	16	70	70	42

Blackburn Rovers		Burnley	
Most Appearances	Walter Joyce, Bryan Douglas (both) 42,	Most Appearances	Brian Miller 39
Most Goals	Andy McEvoy 29	Most Goals	Willie Irvine 22

There were no notable new additions to the Blackburn Rovers squad. Keith Newton switched over to right back, thus encouraging him to attack more on his favoured side and Walter Joyce played the majority of the season as his defensive partner. The one player however who really made progress was John Byrom. His twenty-five goals would normally have seen him easily top the scoring charts but his strike partner was Andy McEvoy and he matched the total of Jimmy Greaves at Tottenham as they shared the national honours on 29 goals. The evergreen Bryan Douglas played in every game and there were highlights of course. A 3-2 home win over reigning champions Liverpool precipitated a run of three excellent wins in early September and a similar run in October cemented their place in the top half of the table. Sunday sport was banned in Great Britain but in Southern Ireland, the national football team played their internationals on the "Sabbath". Ireland played Poland in Dublin on Sunday October 25th, just 24 hours after a full fixture list in England. Today, Sports Scientists would have a field day, producing bucket loads of statistics about "warm down days", but were the stars of the sixties particularly affected? Andy McEvoy played at Goodison Park for the Rovers on October 24th, 1964. The blue and white halves came from behind and won the game 3-2, the Irishman scoring twice. On the following day at Dalymount Park, the Republic came from 2-1 down to beat Poland 3-2 and you've guessed it: perfect symmetry. McEvoy notched another double. Did playing the day before affect his fitness... appar-

ently not? You can call modern professionals "pampered softies" or you can make the case that it is lunacy to expect highly tuned footballers to put their bodies through such rigours. The modern game is certainly higher octane than 50 years ago, but the heavy ball and muddy pitches were far more energy sapping. The carefully planned 21st century international programme prevents such fixture congestion, but did McEvoy and others suffer unduly because of a lack of duty of care by the footballing bodies? I am sure they did and sadly the genial Irishman died aged 55 although others of his generation are still going strong. It is a fascinating story but it reflects badly on football administrators of yore. The campaign at Ewood Park generally settled into a win one, lose one scenario but a place inside the top ten was maintained. Alas, a visit to Old Trafford where the United hammered them 5-0, was followed by two further defeats but a home win over the Spurs and a crazy 5-5 draw at Birmingham City gave the fans something to talk about in the close season. What they really wanted was a major signing, a star name to light up Ewood's dull skies, but the fans were clutching at straws.

Although Matt Busby developed so many star players at Manchester United, he also had a fat cheque book at the ready and it was brandished at Bob Lord, the Burnley butcher pocketing £50,000 for John Connelly. The flying winger had made 215 league appearances, scored 85 goals (eighth on the all-time list) and been capped on ten occasions for England whilst at Turf Moor. The Clarets made a dreadful start to the season. One win in ten, two in fifteen and the eighteenth slot in the league was occupied for three weeks as November gave way to December. There were injuries and a general changing of the guard as Brian O'Neill became established as the regular right half and Lochhead and Irvine took over the twin striking roles from Pointer and Robson. Jimmy Adamson, now player coach, had made 426 league appearances since his debut in 1951, a most educated footballer, a true Turf Moor legend and fifth on the all-time list of appearance makers. Pointer, the blonde bombshell, had led the attack with distinction through the glory years, amassing 118 goals in 223 league games, all in the top level of football. His three England caps were scant reward for such an energetic forward with a better than one in two strike rate. He was sold to Bury followed by moves to Coventry City and then Portsmouth, his career continuing successfully for another eight years. Robson also offered much on his release from Turf Moor. Blackpool, Barnsley and Bury were his ports of call, a combined total of 253 further games.

Harry Potts' main problem was on the left wing. Gordon Harris was the obvious choice, but as McIlroy had never been adequately replaced, "Bomber" was required to play in an inside forward role. As a consequence, five different players wore the number eleven shirt, none with great distinction. Thankfully he had the strength, reliability and experience of Mr. Dependable, Brian Miller, to play anywhere across the defence and he turned out in the three, five and six shirt through the campaign. The goals of Lochhead and Irvine turned round the season at Turf Moor. The Scotsman was never capped by his country but his twenty-one goals this season included a hat-trick at Blackpool and five against Chelsea at the "Turf" in the final game of the season. Willie Irvine scored even more. He would ultimately win seventeen caps for Northern Ireland and his twenty-two goals, with a Boxing Day hat-trick against Fulham, assured the Clarets of a respectable, if a tad disappointing, twelfth-place finish. It was the first time outside the top ten since 1952.

The derby games

Blackburn Rovers had lost the last four derby games, Could they put a stop to this dreadful run when they visited Turf Moor in October? Current form indicated that they could, being positioned in twelfth place, five above the Clarets. They were at full strength except for an injury to Mike Harrison, local boy Alan Bradshaw deputising. Walter Joyce had played in the number 3 jersey for Burnley exactly a year before in the derby and he was in the same numbered shirt this time; the only difference being that the pattern was blue and white halves. Burnley had O'Neill, Bellamy and Harris missing, Sammy Todd, Towers and the tiny winger Johnny Price taking their places. The game had a goalless draw written all over it until Douglas converted a penalty with eight to go. Not to be out done, Burnley attacked and the referee evened everything up by awarding them a spot kick which Lochhead smashed home. The game had settled nothing, except for proving that both sides were at best, mid-table material and all eyes then turned to the return at Ewood Park in late February. Burnley were without wingers Willie Morgan and Gordon Harris, Towers again being given a starting role and new boy Les Latcham playing wide left. Their fifteenth place to their opponents tenth again made the Blackburn side favourites although they had an injury to rising star Keith Newton, the young Billy Wilson making his derby debut in his place. The first encounter at the "Turf" had excitement, it had been close, but there was a different script altogether at Ewood. The game was certainly fractious, without ever quite reaching the levels of barbarism which certain recent encounters had. This was the game where Alex Elder sat on the ball and followed Douglas around the pitch, totally infuriating the home crowd. Burnley raced well clear with first-half strikes from Irvine and Elder and it was game over when O'Neill sent them three clear with ten to go. The Rovers' fans who had stayed on for the last rites at least had a Mick McGrath goal to cheer with five left, but Willie Irvine gave one last turn of the screw in the final moments to rubber stamp an extremely comprehensive 4-1 away victory. The Burnley fans remained to cheer their heroes, but those wearing blue and white favours were left to ponder on when they would finally manage their next derby win.

10 10 1964	Burnley	Blackburn Rovers	1-1	A Lochhead. B Douglas.
24 02 1965	Blackburn Rovers	**Burnley**	1-4	M McGrath. A Irvine 2, A Elder, B O'Neill.

I had moved to Leeds to continue my studies and we regularly caught the bus from Headingley down to Elland Road. Burnley arrived for an evening kick-off in early March and my mates and I witnessed football thuggery at its most savage level that damp Yorkshire evening as the home side lived up to its reputation as the dirtiest team in the league. Morgan had opened the scoring but when they were not kicking and intimidating the Clarets, Leeds United replied with five goals. Bobby Collins was the worst offender. He was barely five foot four inches tall and nearly as wide. He was a clever and talented player so why he had to break the rules with impunity is anyone's guess, but his over the top tackle on a Burnley defender was the most cynical I have ever seen. Adam Blacklaw was also badly roughed up; the injury he received snapping the big Scot's club record run of 172 consecutive league appearances. It was a most unedifying spectacle all round. There is no doubt that referees were prepared to let things go far more than now, possibly because there was far less scrutiny; only occasional television coverage and certainly no replays, but the derby games also had their moments. Interestingly however, although there was a complete absence of players faking injuries, diving or simulation as it is now referred to, it did not mean that the players had short memories. Les Latcham talked about this when referring to the Ewood Park game.

"This was only my second game in the first team and I was playing against a young lad called Wilson. There was a running battle between Willie Irvine and Mike England and at one point, big Mike flattened Willie and then walked all over him. I am not certain that he could avoid Willie as he lay on the ground, but Andy

Lochhead was certain that it was done on purpose. He raced across the pitch and yelled at Mike, saying that he would get him back for this. A few years later we were playing at Tottenham where England had been transferred to. He came up for a corner and I took one look at Mike and burst out laughing. After the game, we were all having a drink in the Players' room and he came up to me asked why I was laughing. He had a black eye and I knew how he had got it. He couldn't understand why Andy Lochhead had given it to him. I told him it was because of the incident at Ewood Park. He said that was years ago. I said "Yes, but Andy said he would get you back". "I know", said Mike, "but this is my third black eye. Why would he want to get me back three times". When I told Andy about it, he said that it was quite unfortunate because every time he went up for a header, his body would swivel and his elbow would swing round and Mike's eye had a knack of colliding with it." Mike had a reputation in Burnley for being rough, but I never thought he was malicious. Like all the Rovers' players at the time, he was easy to get on with off the pitch. And there is another story that a man I knew told me. He had been to a derby match at Ewood, parked his car in the street and after the game, he had a couple of beers in a pub. But when he went back to the car, it wouldn't start. He was wearing his Burnley scarf and he knocked at the door to ask if they had a phone so he could ring a garage. A man answered and said that his son would drive him down to one. The son came out and it was Bryan Douglas. He had been watching him on the pitch an hour before and here he was helping out a supporter from the other side."

Forty two league matches, a marathon not a sprint as Bill Shankly never stopped reminding us, can easily be thought of as a grind, particularly in the damp, wintery conditions of January and February which is why even now, the arrival of FA Cup games can be a breath of fresh air. It was abundantly clear that no league silverware would be heading to East Lancashire this season, so extra excitement was engendered by the World's oldest football competition. Burnley struggled through Round 3, Brentford from Division 3 eventually succumbing in the replay. Blackburn Rovers however were not so lucky. They were handed a home tie, but against those indomitable cup fighters Leicester City, reigning League Cup holders and twice a Wembley finalist in the FA Cup in the early part of this decade. There was a stalemate at Ewood Park, but after a hard-fought replay in the East Midlands, the Rovers returned home having lost 2-1. Burnley were presented with 3rd Division opposition once more in Round 4. The tie against Reading again needed two games before the Clarets came through to meet Manchester United. It was the toughest opposition they could possibly face and although Lochhead's early strike gave them hope, the superior "Red" firepower prevailed by the narrowest 2-1 margin.

With the top teams (including Burnley) still absent, the League Cup presented a less than onerous way to gain success. And the Rovers did make a most impressive start in Round 2. Drawn against Bolton Wanderers on a midweek evening in September and being the last week of my long summer holiday, we boarded the train at Darwen for the short trip to Trinity Street Station, close to the Burnden Park ground. Having been relegated at the end of the previous season, the Wanderers were cut to shreds by the razor-sharp Rovers' attack. McEvoy scored twice, Byrom, Ferguson and Harrison followed suit in a 5-1 win. As we celebrated the victory, a tough looking Bolton fan approached us and viciously punched one of my mates on the nose, before rushing away. There was no segregation and we were so shocked at this gratuitous savagery that we stood there and did nothing. It was my first view of the malaise to become known as football violence and sadly it was the start of an epidemic. If the Rovers touched perfection at Bolton, it was a case of total ineptitude in Round 3. The draw had given them an away trip to Workington, managed by Ken Furphy, later to hold the reins in Blackburn, Jack Marshall's side had to occasionally dig deep to achieve a goalless draw and only six thousand or so spectators turned out at Ewood for the replay. There they watched with horror as this band of journeyman professionals scored five with just one in reply from McEvoy. This was no snatch and grab affair. This was a lowly Third Division outfit completely out playing the tenth best side in the country on their own patch. Marshall had a number of successes during his six year stint in East Lancashire but his reputation has been somewhat tarnished by the three defeats in cup competitions to Rochdale, Oxford and Workington; clubs that many would say were not fit to be playing on the same pitch as a side packed with internationals.

1965-66

Team	Pos	Played	Won	Drawn	Lost	GF	GA	Pts
Burnley	3	42	24	7	11	79	47	55
Blackburn Rovers	22	42	8	4	30	57	88	20

Blackburn Rovers		Burnley	
Most Appearances	Mike Ferguson 42	Most Appearances	Brian Miller, Andy Irvine (both 42)
Most Goals	Andy McEvoy, George Jones (both 10)	Most Goals	Willie Irvine 29

The World Cup in England was played exclusively in July at the end of this season and for the Clarets, it had been a return to the form that they had displayed for a good ten years through the fifties and sixties, finishing third. They certainly looked like title winners in the first half of the season, matching their rivals every step of the way and actually topping the league on three occasions. In Morgan, Lochhead, Irvine and Harris, they had four forwards at the top of their game and the consistency of Angus, Elder, Miller and O'Neill gave the forwards a steady supply of the ball. Talbut was beginning to struggle and the experienced Miller was often moved across from left half to cover this vital posi-

tion, giving a young Dave Merrington the opportunity to start. Ralph Coates eventually made the number eleven shirt his own, adding his particular brand of magic to the mix. There was much for the fans to celebrate. Willie Irvine [pictured] set a post war record for the club with twenty nine league goals, a total good enough to see him become the first and so far only Burnley player to top the Division 1 scoring charts, sharing the award with England World Cup hero Roger Hunt of Liverpool. He also scored three league hat-tricks and there was a cracking home victory over Manchester United and doubles over West Bromwich Albion and Leicester City, both of whom were enjoying successful seasons. The season demanded a big finish and Liverpool were beaten 2-0 at Turf Moor and Tottenham Hotspur likewise at White Hart Lane by a 1-0 margin as a glimpse of final day glory flashed through their minds. The home game against Leeds United, the penultimate fixture, was vital, but Revie's uncompromising outfit ground out a 1-0 win. Their fourth top three finish in seven years would guarantee four Champions' League campaigns today, but once more Bob Lord had not speculated. I am sure however that if overtures had been made, quality players would have said "yes" to play alongside the talent already there.

In the thirteen years since football began to dominate my life, this was the first when that interest began to wane. There were reasons; there are always reasons but being in Leeds did not help. I was at a College with the second highest PE rating in the country. Top athletes flocked to Carnegie, particularly those skilled in Rugby and Football so it was extremely difficult for mere History students to break into the football teams. Putting it another way, I was not as talented as thirty or more others so I could not find a game with any of its three teams. I loved the night life in the city and I had a girlfriend there. My mates and I watched Leeds United from time to time and regularly played five a side, but something had changed and as a result I rarely travelled back to Lancashire at the weekends. When I did, the football at Ewood Park was depressing.

The 1965-66 season commenced in August, but because there had been a polio outbreak in the town, it was September before Blackburn Rovers were allowed to play at home. Mick McGrath, with 268 league appearances to his name in a career which had epitomised a strong fighting spirit, neat footwork and tough tackling skills, had clearly reached the terminus; the end of the line for this level of the game. He had been capped twenty-two times by the Republic of Ireland and after appearing just once as a substitute this campaign, was allowed to move to Bradford Park Avenue where he played on for another couple of seasons. George Sharples, signed towards the end of the previous campaign from Everton, replaced him but he lacked the Irishman's tenacity and close control. But the biggest blow were the injuries sustained by Bryan Douglas. He made just sixteen appearances and as a result, the twin strike force had no-one to supply the ammunition. There were only eight wins, six of them at home and the final points tally of twenty ranks with some of the worst ever in the top Division. Apart from the Burnley result, they scored four at home against Newcastle United, beat fellow relegatees Northampton Town 6-1, Jones scoring a hat-trick and completed the double over a struggling Notts Forest. Somehow, they managed to draw 2-2 at Manchester United, Mike Harrison scoring twice, and also at Everton, but they unbelievably finished thirteen points behind the twenty first placed club. Talk about being tailed off last. Of their last thirteen games, twelve were lost and during this run, I borrowed my dad's car and drove my College mates down to watch the Blue and White halves at Sheffield United. It was limp performance from the Rovers who lay down and lost 2-0. I felt embarrassed to drive the lads back north to Leeds. And just when it seemed that it could not become any worse, Marshall signed Martin Britt, a centre forward from West Ham for £25,000. I watched him a couple of times over the Easter holiday period and he was quite poor. After eight goalless appearances, he was diagnosed with a knee injury for which at the time there was no cure and he retired. Yet another inspired signing! Mike Ferguson started every game and Jack Marshall was able to blood a promising full back by the name of Billy Wilson, who settled in quickly and made thirty-three appearances. I felt like looking for a different hobby, a different interest but then along came the World Cup and when I finally found my way back to Darwen after a crazy European summer vacation, a group of mates with whom I had grown up were waiting for me. "We are starting a football club", they announced. "Are you interested in joining and helping out?" You bet I was and suddenly football was back at the top of my agenda.

The derby games

It was impossible to seriously compare the respective abilities of the two East Lancashire sides this campaign. Burnley were outstanding, standing shoulder to shoulder with the elite of the land. Blackburn Rovers were simply appalling, probably not even good enough to compete with the majority of Division 2 sides. The Clarets were top of the league, the Rovers at the bottom. For the initial game at Turf Moor, the home side fielded their best eleven players, whilst Newton was again out injured, Byrom dropped and Dick Mulvaney, captain of the Reserve team, in at centre-half for the visitors. This was not because Mike England was injured or dropped, he was Jack Marshall's last throw of the dice at finding a centre-forward who might terrorise opposition defenders. The game was a certain home win, the odds far too short to even contemplate a

Willie Morgan congratulates Willie Irvine as the Irishman gives Burnley the lead on New Years Day 1966 at Ewood Park

bet and the pundits were unanimous; it would be one-sided. And so it turned out, except it was Burnley that were thrashed. England was never a striker, but he was tall, he was awkward, exceedingly tough and outstanding in the air. As a result, he totally put the fear of god into the Burnley back line. Every corner, free kick or cross brought panic stations as the lambs to the slaughter turned slaughterers. England and Harrison put them two up after twenty, Lochhead gave hope to the "Turfites" with a fine goal, but McEvoy made it 3-1 before the interval. The shell-shocked Clarets could not raise their game after the interval. Douglas knocked in a fourth to dislodge them from top spot and momentarily raise the expectation levels of the previously disheartened Rovers' fans. This was "Duggie's" fourth in derby games, but surprisingly his first in open play. His three previous strikes had been from the penalty spot.

A crowd of 28,013 turned out for a spot of festive cheer on New Year's Day at Ewood Park, optimistic that the Blue and Whites would once more repeat the show of magic. The England experiment still continued, the Welshman having scored seven in eleven since his move forward. Douglas was absent and both Malcolm Darling, a young Scot and a recalled George Jones were making their derby debuts. Burnley still occupied second place but apart from an injured Lochhead, they had their strongest side out, Blacklaw having returned in goal. The Rovers' were still in the drop zone and this time they failed to find the form from the previous game. There were more nasty incidents and Willie Morgan was sent off. He had become embroiled in a clash with Mike England, but there was no excuse for him kicking out at the Welshman. Even reduced to ten men,

Burnley were able to dominate the game. Irvine scored early and Harris on the seventy minute mark, the home side, missing the inspiration from Douglas, slipping to yet another defeat. The inevitable relegation followed and there would be no more derby games for eleven years. The last eight years had provided some memorable moments and attracted large crowds.

The battles between England and Lochhead in particular were legendary and there is no doubt that there was ill feeling on the pitch whenever these two local adversaries met at this time. The passion and the pride from both sets of supporters had probably contributed greatly but we had yet to see occurrences of the crowd violence that had happened when several other clubs visited Turf Moor. It is difficult to ascertain when the "prejudice" arrived; maybe it had always been there, but as it mushroomed, it caused an unacceptable element to enter the mix. It was an element which kicked respect into touch and allowed verbal and physical abuse to flourish. Many decent folk turned their back on the game, parents became unwilling to allow children to attend and only a concentrated and combined effort by the Police, the clubs and the Football Authority, coupled with the creation of much safer environments in and around grounds, has at least (and at last) generally reduced thuggery, with battles still to be won on language and respect for the opposition.

09 10 1965	Burnley	Blackburn Rovers	1-4	A Lochhead. M England, M Harrison, A McEvoy, B Douglas.
01 01 1966	Blackburn Rovers	**Burnley**	0-2	W Irvine, G Harris.

The FA Cup was something of an interruption and an irritant to Burnley's bid to take the Division 1 title. However there was excitement and goals, goals, goals. After drawing on the south coast, Bournemouth and Boscombe were trounced 7-0 at Turf Moor. Andy Lochhead scored four times in the first half as Bournemouth stumbled into the dressing room to contemplate a five-goal deficit. Lochhead grabbed his fifth in the second half and Harry Potts' side went through 7-0. There were seven goals in Round 4 also, but sadly, Burnley only notched three of them. Drawn away at White Hart Lane, Irvine's two goals gave them a 2-1 interval lead. Spurs equalised, Irvine put the Clarets back in front before the home side, led by the double G strike force of Greaves and Gilzean netted twice more and Burnley were out of the cup. To score a hat-trick away from home and then lose is a difficult cross to bear.

So bad was the Blackburn Rovers season that one would have expected them to go out at the first time of asking to Arsenal, but they won decisively, a McEvoy double helping to send them to fellow Division 1 rivals West Ham United in Round 4. I hitch hiked down, standing on the Leeds ring road at 5.00 a.m. With the mother of all hangovers, I thumbed the lift of a life-time. Two Leeds United fans were off to London to watch the Chelsea-Leeds cup tie and they took me all the way to central London. A seriously injured Bryan Douglas stayed on the field for the full ninety, a great display from effectively a one-legged footballer. Barely unable to limp, he stood on the right touch line, always providing an angle to receive a pass and usually finding a team-mate with the ball. It was a classic wide-open game played in front of a raucous East End crowd and John Byrom scored a hat-trick for the Rovers. West Ham also scored three and at the end of this roller coaster game, I heard a Hammers' fan cursing Byrom. "The f..... always scores against us", he was saying to no-one in particular. I couldn't miss the replay. I excused myself from a lecture and thumbed my way across to watch Byrom score again and Andy McEvoy net a hat-trick. I would have loved to hear what the West Ham supporter had to say this time. A 2-2 draw at 2nd Division Norwich City in Round 5 brought the Canaries back to Ewood. I crossed the Pennines again and saw a humdinger of a game, a 3-2 home victory. Suddenly it was the last eight and a home draw against Sheffield Wednesday. Byrom scored in front of a 33,000 crowd, but without the injured Douglas, the more experienced Wednesday side were well worth their 2-1 victory. Byrom had scored seven goals in six FA Cup games. In twenty-six league games he had scored just twice. Has anyone ever been able to explain that?

In comparison, the League Cup campaign was over in a flash for Blackburn Rovers. At home to Northampton Town in Round 2 after a 1st round bye, they lost 1-0. Burnley had decided to enter this year and they thumped Doncaster Rovers at Belle Vue, Andy Lochhead at his most prolific, scoring a hat-trick. Southampton travelled north in Round 4, Potts playing a full-strength side but they were pushed to the limit before the "Saints" bowed to a 3-2 defeat mainly due to an Irvine double. Stoke City were always a tough proposition but the Clarets squeezed through 2-1 in the replay. Peterborough United away, relative Football League newcomers, ought to have been cannon fodder in the round of the last eight, but oh how the mighty can fall..... and they did 4-0.

It's total Claret domination again as the Rovers hit the depths 1966 – 1976

"In the depths of winter,
I finally learned that within me there lay an invincible summer."
Albert Camus
French Philosopher 1913-1960

It is said that you never appreciate the highs if you have never experienced the lows and although Blackburn Rovers never hit rock bottom in the next few years, their performance in the 1973-74 season was the record lowest league placing in its entire history. Thirteenth in Division 3, the 57th ranked club in the country, was way down the pecking order and to think that at Christmas exactly ten seasons before, they were the bookies' favourite to win the title.

So in the words of Monsieur Camus, they were metaphorically "in the depths of winter". There surely was optimism somewhere around the club, perhaps a budding multi-millionaire standing on the Blackburn end. That would have been sheer fantasy to those 3,520 hardy souls who gathered in small groups on the terraces to watch the last act of this outrageously awful season, appropriately a 2-1 home defeat to Wrexham. They were not to know that twenty-one years later, they would be cheering and waving as Dalglish and his boys, accompanied by the local multi-millionaire, returned to the ground with the Premier League trophy. The hope that kept them all going must have been akin to Camus' invincible summer and just as their neighbours at Turf Moor were later to learn, it is possible to return from an even more desperate situation and walk with heads held high in the sunshine, in the top tier of football.

1966-67

Team	Pos	Played	Won	Drawn	Lost	GF	GA	Pts
Burnley	14	42	15	9	18	66	76	39
Blackburn Rovers	4	42	19	13	10	56	46	51

Blackburn Rovers		**Burnley**	
Most Appearances	John Barton 42	Most Appearances	Gordon Harris 41
Most Goals	John Connelly 11	Most Goals	Andy Lochhead 18

The Burnley story over the next ten years epitomised English football at the time. The city clubs dominated and their small town counterparts scuffled and scrapped to stay at the top level. Burnley's third place finish the previous season meant that they gained entry into the Inter Cities Fairs Cup, making it a total of four competitions in which to compete. So often they started so well, but perhaps because their depth of squad was insufficient for success at this level, they would tumble back down the league as injuries and fatigue bit hard. For four successive seasons, fourteenth place was their final position. In this campaign, the second half of the year was a disaster. The Treatment Room was regularly full and over-flowing and there was a 7-0 thrashing in the penultimate game at Sheffield Wednesday. Brian Miller, that man mountain both on the pitch and later in the dug-out was Burnley through and through. The Padiham born defender had accumulated 379 league appearances in thirteen seasons and been capped once for his country. The ultimate Mr Reliable, he shored up the defence, made body-shuddering tackles and scored more than the occasional vital goal; twenty-nine to be exact. Sadly the fourth last game of the season was his last farewell to the Burnley fans at the age of thirty, being seriously injured at Aston Villa. Alex Elder also moved on during the summer. The left back had been another mainstay of the Division 1 winning side, making a total of 271 appearances. Not the tallest of defenders, he was quick and accurate in his tackles and his ball distribution was excellent. Capped 34 times by Northern Ireland, disenchantment with life at Turf Moor saw him on his way to Stoke City for £50,000. Adam Blacklaw, capped briefly by Scotland whilst at Turf Moor, lost his place at the "Turf" to Harry Thomson following what can only be described as a "stinker" when conceding three goals at Stoke during the Christmas period. He was literally "down the road" in the summer to join the enemy. And John Angus [pictured], an automatic choice at right back since 1958, was beginning to find that injuries were catching up on him.

Les Latcham explained how he came to be signed by Burnley and then how he gradually worked his way into the side.

> "I was brought up in Crook and the local non-leagues were very strong in the Bishop Auckland area. I was playing for Crook Juniors and a Burnley scout approached me and invited me down for a trial. I was seventeen at the time and vaguely a Newcastle United supporter, but the club I followed was Crook Town. On the way down with my dad, I borrowed his paper to see what league Burnley were in. I couldn't believe it when I saw they were up at the top of Division 1. My trial game was at Langho against Blackburn B and I scored a hat-trick. So Burnley signed me but it took me a few years to break into the first team. I had a set back playing against Blackburn in a Reserve game when Dick Mulvaney tackled me and my cartilage went. I was still a left winger in those days and eventually I became the travelling twelfth man and then when substitutes were brought in, the number 12. I had played the odd game, but this Burnley side was so good and so difficult to break into. Then both at home to West Brom and a couple of weeks later to Newcastle, Alex Elder came off with a groin injury. Harry Potts told me to go on and I asked him where I was playing. He said "left-back" and I told him that I had only once played at full back for the reserves and had had a stinker. He told me I would be ok and I actually played well both times. When Alex went to Stoke at the start of the next season, I was straight in at left back and stayed there for several years. This was typical of the way Burnley was run under Bob Lord. He needed the money he could get from Stoke for Alex, but he was not prepared to let him go until he had a replacement coming through from the Reserves. Once I had shown that I could play left-back, then Alex could go,"

In many respects, the headline making news in East Lancashire in the 1966-67 campaign was Burnley's European adventure. They eased their way into Round 3 of the Inter Cities Fairs Cup with a 3-1 aggregate win over VfB Stuttgart followed by an 8-1 aggregate thrashing of Switzerland's Lausanne-Sports, Lochhead hitting a hat-trick in the home leg. All the excitement came in Round 3. Naples may have beautiful views across the Bay, but the city has its dark side and the reputation of their football club at the time was similarly black. Burnley were simply scintillating in the first leg in Lancashire, convincingly winning 3-0. The return in Italy, in front of 60,000 fanatics baying for blood and without Irvine and the regular full backs, was less a football match, more a battle for survival. Somehow the Clarets hung on for a goalless draw, Harry Thomson having the game of his life. In this most Catholic of cities, the only deity in sight was the Burnley goalkeeper. Attacked and spat at, the Burnley defence somehow kept their cool against an incessant barrage of physical aggression and aggravation plus some extremely inventive play. There were scuffles amongst the players after the game, the Burnley side defending themselves against physical attack. Blacklaw rescued Thomson from a mob and was then approached by men toting guns. All the action in the quarter final was on the pitch. Miller scored in a 1-1 draw in Eintracht Frankfurt, but they were out thought in the second leg as the Germans raced into a two-goal lead. Miller pulled one back, but short of the fire power that both Lochhead and Irvine would have provided had they been fit, they went out 3-2 on aggregate. Memorable it may have been but unfortunately it would be another fifty-one years before the Clarets would see European action again. Latcham was involved in the Napoli games, playing at outside-left both times.

> "We were brilliant at home when we won 3-0 and I scored along with Andy Lochhead and Ralph Coates. When we went to Naples, Keith McNee, sportswriter on the Burnley Express, showed us the local paper which he had translated. It said, 'Lambs from Burnley come to the Naples slaughter house'. So we knew what we were up against and they kicked us and punched us all game. But Harry Thomson was never going to let a goal in, even though he had been roughed up a few times. I smacked heads with Altafini, but it was more my fault and we were both in a daze and my head had to be patched up. When the final whistle blew, their centre forward went to shake hands with Harry and Harry gave him the V sign. It all went off then. Someone chased Harry down the touch line past our subs and Adam Blacklaw tripped him up. We really struggled to get off the pitch and I saw Adam, clinging on to a window frame with smashed glass and being confronted by men in dark suits with guns. It turned out that they were something like secret police who in actual fact were trying to protect us, but Dr Iven had to put stitches in my head wound. Their medical room was a bare room with a high ceiling, nothing in but a table and about a 15 watt light bulb. I told the Doc that he couldn't possibly see to stitch me up, but he did. We had a police escort to the airport, two Land Rover type vehicles each containing four of the men in dark suits with machine guns.

Everton, reigning FA Cup holders were the opposition in Round 3 and it was goalless in Burnley, but the Toffees went through 2-1 in the replay. In the Football League Cup, the Clarets were held to a draw in Shrewsbury but thrashed the Shropshire side 5-0 back home. Sheffield United away was a 50/50 tie, but the Yorkshire side squeezed home 2-1.

Jack Marshall carried on as manager at Blackburn Rovers without a contract following the horror show the previous season. Relegation meant lots of comings and goings over the summer at Ewood Park. Fred Else moved to Barrow after 187 league games in goal, but the sickening news was Mike England's transfer to Tottenham Hotspur for £95,000. The Welshman was the best centre-half in the country, completely irreplaceable. The completely unpredictable John Byrom, one minute top class striker, next minute way off the pace, was sold to Bolton Wanderers for £25,000 and Andy McAvoy retired to the Republic of Ireland mid-season, completely disillusioned by life in the Central League. His eighty-nine league goals in 189 outings places him at number 10 on the all-time Rovers' goal scoring chart. John Barton arrived from Preston to replace Else, Marshall bought Welsh international wing-half Barrie Hole from Cardiff City for £40,000 and the former Burnley and England star John Connelly was signed for £40,000 from Manchester United, just weeks after playing v Uruguay in the World Cup Final group stage at Wembley. In their first season at Tier 2 for nine years, they were close to mid-table by Christmas, Eddie Quigley joined the management team as assistant to "Jolly Jack". There was no doubt that "Quigs" tightened up the side and just one defeat catapulted them up the league before Marshall finally left. With Quigley in charge, the clash on Easter Saturday against Jimmy Hill's Coventry City side became massively important. It was a game that the Rovers could have, should have and would have won had not Mike Ferguson been sent off. The result was a disappointing fourth place finish, a position not bettered for another twenty-six years.

Carlisle United were certainly the villains of the piece for the Rovers in Cup competitions this season. For once they were a good side and they won 2-1 in Round 3 of the FA Cup, and after Marshall's side had knocked out Barrow and York City in the Football League Cup, they travelled north and were hammered by the Cumbrians by an embarrassing 4-0 margin in Round 4.

1967-68

Team	Pos	Played	Won	Drawn	Lost	GF	GA	Pts
Burnley	14	42	14	10	18	64	71	38
Blackburn Rovers	8	42	16	11	15	56	49	43

Blackburn Rovers		Burnley	
Most Appearances	Billy Wilson 42	Most Appearances	Willie Morgan 42
Most Goals	Mike Ferguson 8	Most Goals	Frank Casper 14

The moths at the bottom of Bob Lord's pocket must have thought it was Armageddon as the Burnley chairman actually put his hands down there and brought out the cash to buy Frank Casper for £27,000 from Rotherham United. Colin Waldron, an impressive centre half from Chelsea, was brought in to replace Miller for £30,000, but the direction of player flow remained predominantly outwards. Gordon Harris was sold to Sunderland for £70,000 in early '68, a club record sale. He had made 258 appearances at Turf Moor, scoring sixty-nine goals. An extremely talented and predominantly left footed player, he had been a permanent fixture in the starting eleven since Brian Pilkington had departed the scene in 1961. And then Willie Irvine went to Preston North End for £45,000 in March. He had fallen out with the management but with seventy-eight goals in 126 games for the club, a staggeringly high 0.62% of goals per game, it seems odd that a seventeen times capped Northern Irish international was sold for a less than massive fee and to a struggling Division 2 club. Losing just twice at home but winning only twice on their travels, the Clarets ended well clear of relegation once again.

The 1967-68 season will always be remembered for the success of the Burnley youth side. The side included future stars Steve Kindon and Dave Thomas, plus Mick Docherty and Eric Probert who strongly featured in the first team. Alan West and Eddie Cliff also racked up a number of appearances. Willie Brown, a Scots born striker, made only one first team appearance but finally compiled a record of over 350 appearances and 121 goals playing in the lower reaches of the Football League. Both Manchester clubs, Everton and Sheffield United were eliminated on their way to the final where they met Coventry City over two legs. Joe Brown's youngsters lost 2-1 at Highfield Road, but a 2-0 victory at home brought the cup to Burnley for the first and only time.

They reached the quarter-final of the Football League Cup, being fortunate to be drawn at home in all rounds to reach the last eight. Willie Irvine scored three times as Cardiff City, Nottingham Forest and Queens Park Rangers were all put to the sword but it was the Arsenal games which were so exciting. Lockhead and O'Neill had put Burnley two up in ten minutes, but by half time, Arsenal led 3-2. Irvine scored the only goal of the second half to force a replay in London. Irvine was also on target there, but by then Arsenal had scored twice and it stayed at 2-1. It was a London side which eliminated them from the FA Cup, West Ham winning 3-1 at Turf Moor in Round 3.

Without a massive war chest available to Eddie Quigley in the following season, to finish eighth was not too disappointing. Adam Blacklaw and John Coddington, a centre half from Huddersfield Town were both brought in to bolster the defence. They only lost once in their first nine games and their second defeat was at Huddersfield on September 30th, 1967, the baptismal day of BBC Radio 1. Walter Joyce was sold to Oldham Athletic and Mike Harrison left for Plymouth Argyle. The elegant left winger with pace to burn and a sumptuous left foot, had lit up the Ewood stage from time to time with forty goals in 160 games over a four-year period but his career was reaching its final stage. For Dave Kennedy, then a ten year old Accrington boy, Christmas came twice in two days.

> "I was already sport mad at this age but my dad just wasn't interested in football. I kept begging my mother to let me go to Ewood Park and so as a slightly belated Christmas present, she took me down to watch the Rovers play against Derby County on Boxing Day. She had bought me a Rovers' scarf and we caught three buses to get to the ground. One from near Accy Hospital to the centre of Accrington, one to Blackburn Boulevard and the third to the ground. We had

fantastic seats on the front row of the Riverside Stand, just on the Darwen side of the half-way line. I remember the Rovers won 3-0 and I remember Barry Hole playing. It was my best ever Christmas present."

Don Martin was signed from Northampton Town, later to become a huge crowd favourite in whichever position he played and with seven games to play, a strong finish was required. Sadly their promotion effort gently subsided. and Mike Ferguson left the club at the end of the season, being sold to Aston Villa for £50,000. In six seasons he had made 220 league appearances and scored twenty-nine goals. The fans had loved him, his skills and frustrating habits and he only cost £1,500 from Accrington Stanley; a real bargain.

The FA Cup once again produced a minor shock as the Rovers travelled down to Wiltshire and lost 1-0 to Swindon Town in Round 3. They battled through to Round 4 in the League Cup, defeating Brighton and Middlesbrough at Ewood with Ferguson and Rogers both scoring twice, but a tough Round 4 draw led to a 2-1 defeat at Highbury to Arsenal

1968-69

Team	Pos	Played	Won	Drawn	Lost	GF	GA	Pts
Burnley	14	42	15	9	18	55	82	39
Blackburn Rovers	19	42	13	11	18	52	63	37

Blackburn Rovers		Burnley	
Most Appearances	Eamonn Rogers 41	Most Appearances	Frank Casper 41
Most Goals	Don Martin, Malcolm Darling, John Connelly (all 10)	Most Goals	Frank Casper 13

Burnley were beginning to struggle. Finance was certainly top of the agenda at Turf Moor throughout the 68-69 campaign and Bob Lord therefore had to finally admit that Burnley FC was now a selling club. Harry Potts lost two more outstanding attacking players. Willie Morgan, already capped on the wing by Scotland and with almost two hundred league appearances to his name, was sold to Manchester United for £117,000. And six weeks later, Andy Lochhead had packed his bags and was en-route for Leicester City. The Scot, a Turf Moor legend, had scored 101 goals in 226 league games, making him the last striker at the club to hit the century mark and is ranked sixth in the all-time list. A Thomson arrived and a Thomson departed the same season. "Mad Harry" the goalkeeper, was sacked for a "domestic matter" and Potts paid out £40,000 for Jim Thomson, a centre-half from Chelsea and ten grand less for Doug Collins, a mid-field player from Grimsby Town. Both later fully repaid the amount spent and more besides. After a promising autumn, their shaky defence on the road really caused problems, picking the ball out of their net seven times at Tottenham and Manchester City and six at Leeds as they finished fourteenth again.

The highlight of the season was a run to the semi-final of the Football League Cup when Harry Potts was still operating as boss. It was an achievement but the last four game was so disappointing. Home wins over two Division 4 clubs, Grimsby Town (7-1 on aggregate) and Workington sent Burnley through to Round 4. There Leicester City were hammered 4-0 at the "Turf" and Crystal Palace 2-0 at the same venue to ensure a semi-final berth. Swindon Town were waiting for them, a two-legged affair, and the Wiltshire side came out with a slight 2-1 advantage at home. Burnley ought to have settled the game in the second leg, but could only win 2-1, an aggregate score of 3-3. In the replay at the Hawthorns, the Clarets were behind until the last minute when Dave Thomas equalised. Casper put them in front on the re-start but they ultimately could not cope with wave after wave of Swindon attacks, finally buckling twice and losing 3-2. There was a 3-1 home win over Derby County in Round 3 of the FA Cup, Casper scoring twice, but Liverpool away was a tough one and they went down 2-1.

Blackburn Rovers had never before completed a season lower than sixteenth in Division 2. But records are there to be broken and they dropped to nineteenth, seven points clear of relegation. Keith Newton [pictured] was first choice full back for Sir Alf Ramsey's England, an outstanding achievement by a player competing at a level below his international team mates and they had started well but one win in their last sixteen games caused panic all round. The fifty-two goals scored was their lowest return for seven years. What was sad about this time in the history of the club was that the careers of Ronnie Clayton and Bryan Douglas, two of their greatest players, should end amid the turmoil of a wretched campaign. Even the most majestic of careers have to end sometime and with the inevitable happening at Ewood Park, the supporters bade farewell to Ronnie and Bryan.

Their footballing lives had been intertwined since they came through the ranks. They played together for England and of course were one-club men. Whether their likes will ever be seen again in Blackburn Rovers colours is one for the crystal ball but certainly they would make anyone's all-time top five. Ronnie made 579 league appearances, second only to Derek Fazackerley and captained his country five times whilst winning thirty-five caps.

Bryan's 438 appearances place him fifth on the all-time list and although always a provider rather than scorer of goals, he still helped himself to exactly one hundred, the sixth best career haul at the club. Only the legendary "Bob" has emulated "Duggie's" thirty-six England international appearances whilst playing at Ewood Park. Although never in the same league, Barrie Hole, capped five times for Wales during his spell at Ewood, was a Riverside favourite, but typically, the hard-up Board sold him to Aston Villa for £60,000 early doors.

There is no doubt that Bryan Douglas loved his time at the Rovers, but it was difficult for him and Clayton to reconcile themselves to lacking that pace, energy and probably waning skills. In their case, the manager did not help either.

> "At the Rovers, in my early days in the team, I roomed with Eddie Quigley and he was really good to me, but the funny thing was that when he came back to be manager and I was reaching the end of my career, we didn't really get on and I found him difficult. He was always having a go at Ronnie who never gave less than his best. He talked to us as though he knew far more than us about the game and it was difficult to put up with."

At last there was something approaching an FA Cup run. In Round 3 they beat Stockport County 2-0 and a Malcolm Darling hat-trick helped to eliminate Portsmouth. Surprisingly, this woeful Rovers' outfit had reached the last sixteen, drawing reigning champions Manchester City at home. Jim Fryatt was quickly on target, but that was the end of the celebrations as Francis Lee and Tony Coleman ran them ragged, the Sky Blues winning 4-1. Dave Kennedy, now a twelve year old, was allowed to go to the game with his mates, but it was difficult to find a good vantage point.

> "There was a massive crowd on [42,315] because City were a great side and I remember Francis Lee and Mike Summerbee playing. I could hardly see so we decided to climb up a floodlight pylon where we would see everything. Quite quickly the Rovers scored. It was a magnificent header by Jim Fryatt and we all thought the Rovers were going to win. Then we began to realise that our hands were all sticky and they were coloured red. Apparently they had just red leaded the metal and our clothes were full of it. To make matters worse, once City got going, they absolutely murdered the Rovers so it was a bad night all round.

There was a Division 1 victim, Stoke City in a Round 2 replay of the Football League Cup, Stuart Metcalfe scoring at the Victoria Ground. But drawn once more at Swindon, they again lost 1-0.

1969-70

Team	Pos	Played	Won	Drawn	Lost	GF	GA	Pts
Burnley	14	42	12	15	15	56	61	39
Blackburn Rovers	8	42	20	7	15	54	50	47

Blackburn Rovers		Burnley	
Most Appearances	Billy Wilson, Don Martin (both 42)	Most Appearances	Peter Mellor, Steve Kindon (both 42)
Most Goals	Don Martin 13	Most Goals	Steve Kindon 17

STEVE KINDON (Burnley)

As the decade came to a close, what odds could you have found on Burnley finishing fourteenth for the fourth consecutive year? This is exactly what happened but this time it was a strong finish after an abject start to the season, just one win in their first thirteen games. Harry Potts relinquished his team management role and accepted the post of General Manager. Jimmy Adamson replaced him. He had ten games to conjure up a survival package, something he comfortably achieved; finishing thirteen points clear of the drop.

Steve Kindon, with a hat-trick in the 5-0 thrashing of Notts Forest, led the revival with a glut of goals, but at the end of the campaign Brian O'Neill was sold to Southampton for £75,000. He had made 231 league appearances and he was a crowd favourite. Harry had needed all of his management skills to keep the fiery Northumbrian on the right track, but he was the complete wing half. Another wing half, the eight times capped Northern Irishman Sammy Todd, had topped the one hundred appearance mark and he was sold to Sheffield Wednesday for £40,000.

With the possible exception of John Haworth, Harry Potts was the most successful manager that Turf Moor had seen. In twelve years of his stewardship, the club had maintained its place amongst the elite of English football, becoming one of the main contenders in the chase for honours. There were eight top ten placings, including three podium finishes and the title winning side of 1960. His lowest placed position was fourteenth and the average final position each year over this period was 7th. Exceptional for such a small fish in a large pond. There was a semi-final and a final appearance in the FA Cup and two semi-final appearances in the Football League Cup. He had not spent silly money on players. He encouraged the junior side of the club, resulting in talent continually coming off its production line. There had been a recent decline, it had become a mid-table club; but one that stayed well clear of relegation. The news of his resignation came as a bombshell; completely unexpected and although there was much respect for Jimmy Adamson, his successor, the fans were upset by the thought of a Burnley FC without Potts in charge. Philip Webster, who knew

Harry better than most, offers another perspective on the man and the decision to relinquish his post.

> "It was never felt that Harry was a top coach. He let others do this job but there was no doubt that he was a top manager. He understood how to handle players; effectively how to manage them. The final say on which players to sell and when, rested with Bob Lord, but Harry often knew the best time for the club to let them go in terms of balancing their effectiveness on the pitch and the money gained from their sale. He was never cocky, never a big head, but he wanted his players to play with a swagger. So when Alex Elder actually sat on the ball during a derby at Ewood Park, this was his club saying.... "we are better than you". He also used Elder to literally man mark. It is believed that he told him to follow George Best even if he went to the toilet in a match versus Manchester United and the same tactic was used to frustrate and eventually nullify Bryan Douglas' great skills in the derby. Elder simply followed him around the pitch. Burnley were also one of the first clubs to use the short corner routine, with McIlroy being heavily involved. Harry had managed the England B side on a couple of occasions and he said that he learned a lot from a continental trip where they played Italy and Poland. Everyone talked about Adamson being his protégé and his natural successor, but although the press reported that it was an amicable change over, deep down Harry was unhappy about it. But I suppose no-one wants to come to the end of a road, particularly when the job has had such an impact on your life. Also he was still a relatively young man, not quite fifty. And the role of General Manager did not suit him. It was reported that it was his decision, but I have never been that certain although Harry followed the party line, saying that his successor was the right man for the job."

The FA Cup kicked off with a decent win in Round 3, Wolverhampton Wanderers being put in their place to the tune of 3-0 at Turf Moor. A 2-2 draw at Chelsea where Dobson scored two late goals, made them favourites in the replay, but the exciting London side came back to win 3-1 in extra-time. They also progressed in the League Cup, Stoke City and Rotherham United after a replay being beaten. The Round 4 tie finished goalless when the Old Trafford giants came to Turf Moor and the replay was equally competitive, the Manchester side edging home 1-0.

From struggling to avoid relegation the previous year, Blackburn Rovers improved considerably, only six points behind the promoted Blackpool. The improved form could be put down to Quigley's wise buys. For a total outlay of around £100,000, he signed Alan Hunter, a classy and extremely strong centre half from Oldham Athletic, Ken Knighton, a dynamic wing half and a real crowd pleaser from near neighbours Preston North End and Brian Hill, a left winger from Huddersfield Town. Hunter and Knighton were successes, Hill less so. On the debit side, the Rovers lost its best player, England international Keith Newton to Everton for £80,000. John Connelly, a great servant of East Lancashire football dropped down a division to sign for Bury. He played 148 games in four seasons at Ewood Park, scoring 36 goals. In an era when the club made a number of bad buys, he was the rare exception, adding to the stellar reputation gained at Burnley when at his peak. Adam Blacklaw had reached the end of his career, having made 96 appearances behind the Blue and White defence. He was replaced by Roger Jones, a most impressive keeper signed from Bournemouth for £30,000. This was not a free scoring Rovers side, but after twenty-four games, they were promotion contenders. Only five games had been lost and Don Martin scored a hat-trick against Millwall. From Boxing Day onwards, there was a definite decline in performance. With no obvious replacement for Newton, they began to leak goals and what could have been a promotion winning side faded to an inconsequential eighth place.

Swindon Town had now been promoted to Division 2 and unbelievably, the Rovers drew them yet again in Round 3 of the FA Cup. It was a good Wiltshire side, far too good for Quigley's outfit and they strode to a 4-0 victory at Ewood Park. An easier League Cup draw had enabled them to defeat Stockport County and Doncaster Rovers in the first two rounds, Martin scoring twice against the Yorkshire men. But another recent adversary welcomed the Blue and Whites in Round 3, Carlisle United winning at Blundell Park.

1970-71

Team	Pos	Played	Won	Drawn	Lost	GF	GA	Pts
Burnley	21	42	7	13	22	29	63	27
Blackburn Rovers	21	42	6	15	21	37	69	27

Blackburn Rovers		Burnley	
Most Appearances	Roger Jones, Alan Hunter (both 42)	Most Appearances	Ralph Coates 38
Most Goals	Brian Conlon, Eamonn Rogers (both 6)	Most Goals	Eric Probert 5

It was relegation with a capital R for Lancashire clubs in the 70-71 season, Burnley and Blackpool from Division 1 and likewise for Bolton and Blackburn in Division 2. Whichever way you look at the year from Burnley's perspective, it was diabolical; their worst since 1903 in terms of points gained, fewest goals scored, most games lost and fewest won. Amazingly, Blackpool won just four times, naturally finishing below Burnley; bottom of the heap. With Casper hampered by illness, injury and loss of form, the leading scorer award went to Eric Probert with five goals, a most damning statistic from a shambolic season. Good servants such as Dave Merrington (to Bristol City) and Les Latcham (to Plymouth Argyle) departed, but of far more consequence to the fans was the sale of Ralph Coates. At the time, he was the best player in a Claret and Blue shirt, but with a diminishing revenue, a star player had to be sold and Coates left Turf Moor for Tottenham Hotspur for a staggering £190,000. He had played a total of 214 league games and scored twenty-six goals from either the wing

or inside forward positions, being capped twice by England whilst at the "Turf".

There was sadness throughout the area when John Angus called it a day. The right back, the last remaining member of the great 1960 Champion winning side, had been bedevilled with injury for the final few seasons, but he made 438 league starts, third only to the mighty Jerry Dawson. Not even Burnley could off-load at such a rate and not make a move into the transfer market, so late in the 70-71 season but too late to save them from the drop, Paul Fletcher, a goal scoring centre-forward, was bought from Bolton Wanderers for £60,000; another sound buy. He has a theory that this was the beginning of the decline of the Burnley Football club that had been so successful in the previous twenty years or more.

> "As I joined, Jimmy Adamson was claiming that we were going to be the team of the seventies, but it never happened and it was all about money. Suddenly we were struggling to compete with the city clubs and although it probably took another ten years for the real slump to occur, you could see the beginnings of it here."

Les Latcham had started 149 league games before his move to Devon and his last few months at Turf Moor was not a happy time.

> "I was a regular at left back for most of the second half of the season, but my contract was up at the end. I approached Jimmy Adamson about it but he said they hadn't made a decision. I found it difficult to talk to Adamson so I approached Harry Potts who was General Manager by now. He was so different and I was able to ask his advice. He told me in confidence that Plymouth Argyle were after me and were prepared to pay £4,000. But Harry said I should wait to see what happened with regard to my contract and if there was not to be one, I would go for nothing but I should ask Plymouth to pay me the money as a signing-on fee. This is what happened and I was always grateful to him for the advice. Adamson had nothing to say to me at the end but I had to him. I told him that as a coach he was fantastic, but a manager he was sh.. I felt he was a bully and if he could control you, he would play you. If he couldn't, he would try to get rid of you. Dave Thomas was an absolutely wonderful player. At the Gawthorpe Training ground,

he would try out new tricks but the minute he saw Adamson coming over the bridge he was a bag of nerves, scared to try to do something different because he knew he would get shouted at if he did anything wrong."

Both Cup competitions passed in the blink of an eye. Aston Villa were comfortable in winning 2-0 at Villa Park in the Football League Cup and in the FA Cup Round 3, the Clarets travelled to meet Oxford United. This recent addition to the Football League had the Indian side on East Lancashire clubs, replacing Accrington Stanley in 1962, embarrassing a very talented Blackburn side in the FA Cup in 1964 and now rolling over Burnley 3-1.

In the same season that Burnley were relegated, the Rovers also dropped a division. And the Blackburn side was equally appalling, only twenty-seven points gathered in forty-two games. Unluckily the much vaunted Jimmy Kerr, bought from Bury for £60,000, quickly picked up a serious injury which ended his career. Fred Pickering alas was brought back to the club from Blackpool, but having lost his pace, he was unable to make an impact. The Ewood club had made a reasonably decent start but one win in their last fifteen games sealed their fate.

Off the field, Johnny Carey, brought back as administrative manager, exchanged roles with Quigley, the Irishman taking control of team affairs. As always with a relegation side, there was little to excite the fans throughout the year. The financial situation was so serious that they were forced to sell one of their few assets, Ken Knighton to Hull City. There were heavy defeats at times and so relegation was confirmed, the first time that they would compete in the third tier of English football. Of the original twelve sides that had entered the Football League in 1888, the Blackburn side was the 9th club to be relegated from Division 2, only Everton, West Brom and of course Burnley being so far saved from this ignominy. It was also the end of the line for both Quigley and Carey, the club desperately needing a fresh face on the touch line. They say that every cloud has a silver lining and a young Derek Fazackerley was the beneficiary of this particular one. A Preston boy who had arrived at Ewood Park in the summer of '68 as a sixteen year old, he talked to me about life at the club in those days.

A number of clubs asked me to come down for trials, but the Rovers were the first to make me an offer and so I signed with Eddie Quigley's boys as an apprentice. I know a number of players have been quick to criticise the boss and certainly his man management skills at times did not match up to a number of other managers I later went on to play for. He would send an apprentice to pin up the team sheet on the notice board, rather than tell someone face to face he had not been selected,, but he was a tremendous help to me. After only being there for a few months, I received a dead leg in an A team game away at Tranmere. After a long period of inactivity through not being able to shake off the injury, I was eventually sent to a specialist who diagnosed it as calcification in the muscle. I would be out for twelve months and I was like a lost soul around the place until Eddie took an interest in me. He actually sent me round to watch local professional games, filling in scouting reports on teams we would be shortly playing and then handing them in on the Monday morning. So I have lots of good words to say about the much criticised Quigley. I was thirteenth man when we played Hull City in the 1970-71 season at their Boothferry Park ground. My duty was to help the physio sort out the dressing room and help out with the kit; no kit man in those days, but the game was abandoned at half-time when the Rovers were losing, because of thick fog. When it was rescheduled, Johnny Carey, who had replaced Eddie Quigley as team manager, picked me in the starting eleven and we drew 0-0 against a side that came close to promotion. This was my professional debut and I played in the number 5 shirt. I was subsequently selected for the final fourteen games, but we were sadly relegated. The club's poor form was a disaster but in some ways it helped me. If we had been winning all the time, I would have had to wait far longer for my big chance, so bad as it was, it turned out to be a bonus for me.

Like Burnley, the Rovers quickly lost interest in both Cup competitions. Drawn away at Bolton Wanderers, they lost 1-0 in Round 2 of the League Cup and a slightly longer trip to Everton in Round 3 of the FA Cup produced a similar result.

1971-72

Team	Pos	Played	Won	Drawn	Lost	GF	GA	Pts
Burnley	7	42	20	6	16	70	55	46
Blackburn Rovers	10	46	19	9	18	54	57	47

Blackburn Rovers		Burnley	
Most Appearances	Roger Jones 45	Most Appearances	Martin Dobson, Paul Fletcher (both 42)
Most Goals	Tony Field 17	Most Goals	Frank Casper 18

Chairman Bob kept faith with Adamson, but Burnley had to come to terms with life in Division 2, their first taste of football at this level since 1947. Obviously there were fewer paying home spectators and the absence of giants such as Liverpool with their huge travelling support being replaced by clubs like Orient bringing one coachful of diehards, certainly hit the Balance Sheet. They never really came close to bouncing straight back at the first attempt in spite of scoring plenty, with Casper and Fletcher spearheading the attack. A strong finish enabled them to climb to respectability in seventh place, but ten points behind the promoted clubs. Arthur Bellamy was yet another who came through the ranks. He had been a reliable member of the first team squad for nearly ten years, making 217 league appearances before being sold to Chesterfield for £10,000 at the season's end. One final departure really upset the fans. Steve Kindon had convinced the faithful that he was the type of player to take them back to the 1st Division. Strong, quick and direct with an eye for goal, he had terrorised defenders, but when Wolverhampton Wanderers flashed a cheque for over £100,000 in front of Bob Lord's eyes, he was off to Molineux. He had a similar theory to Paul Fletcher's, but has also added reasons which, in retrospect, make sense.

> "I struggled to get on with Jimmy Adamson, this is why I left for Wolverhampton. He didn't seem to like me although I thought he was a great coach, much better than Harry Potts, but what Harry had and Jimmy didn't was great man-management skills. And when I was an Apprentice coming through, it seemed that the club never sold a star player unless they had a youngster to take his place. It was a very clever system. Lochhead and Irvine had replaced Pointer and Robson before I got there, then O'Neill took Adamson's place, Merrington replaced Miller, Coates took over from Harris, before Thomas came in to replace Morgan. This enabled Coates to replace O'Neill in mid-field and I was converted to a number nine to replace Lochhead and James came in to take my position at outside left. People ask why did they have to sell their stars but I was told that they needed to raise a profit of £100,000 from transfer fees each season to keep the club going. Bob Lord was renowned for paying good wages but when he finally retired and then died, the new Board could not believe how much went out on wages. From then on, they were cut and the slide really accelerated. By the time Martin Dobson was sold, they probably needed £200,000 a year."

A Frank Casper [pictured] goal in a 1-0 win at Division 1 Coventry City was a promising start in the League Cup and a 1-1 draw at Old Trafford, James on target, was even better. The Clarets performed heroically in the replay before going down to a late United goal. Division 1 side Huddersfield Town came to Turf Moor in Round 3 of the FA Cup and edged through 1-0.

The Board of Directors at Ewood Park did find a new manager quickly. The Directors wanted a younger figure, a track suited manager, and they plumped for Ken Furphy. He had managed Workington, master minding their shock 5-1 win at Ewood in the 1964 League Cup. Further success came at Watford, taking them to an FA Cup semi-final berth against Chelsea. For the first time, the club was faced with a forty-six-game schedule with unfamiliar opponents; Torquay United, Tranmere Rovers, Walsall et al. The new manager brought energy to the job, completely re-vamped the playing squad and off-loaded players to bring in the new blood which was so desperately required. He sold Dick Mulvaney, a centre half and captain who had made over a hundred appearances to Oldham Athletic, Northern Ireland international Alan Hunter who had represented Northern Ireland six times during his time in Blackburn and far and away their best player, moved to Ipswich Town; a bargain buy at £60,000 and Billy Wilson, who had made 246 league appearances at full back, was sold to Portsmouth to help to balance the books. Eamonn Rogers was capped fourteen times by the Republic of Ireland but in spite of playing 159 league games for the Rovers, he never resolved the conflict within regarding his exceptional talent and total inconsistency. He was eventually sold to Charlton Athletic during Furphy's first term, but a plethora of injuries caused him to retire prematurely from the game at the age of twenty-seven.

In their places came forwards Barry Endean from Charlton Athletic and Tony Field from Southport, mid-fielder Terry Garbett from Watford and defenders Mick Heaton from Sheffield United and the rock hard John McNamee, a veteran centre-half from Newcastle who had played in Division 1. The fans were shell shocked at the start of his reign, losing every game in September and being thrashed at 7-1 at Shrewsbury Town on October 2nd. Then came Furphy's make over and of the eleven who played in game 1, only goalkeeper Roger Jones, Fazackerley, David Bradford and Don Martin played in the 46th. From November onwards, progress began. Tony Field's seventeen goals led the way, but Furphy failed to achieve an immediate return, finishing tenth.

History of sorts, the wrong sort, was made in the FA Cup when In November, they lost 3-1 at Division 3 strugglers Port Vale in Round 1. It was their earliest exit from the competition since their first year of entry in 1879. Revenge was extracted from Workington for the shambolic performance in this competition in 1964, when they beat them 2-0 in Round 1 of the League Cup, but a 4-1 drubbing in the replay at Lincoln in Round 2 was just as embarrassing.

1972-73

Team	Pos	Played	Won	Drawn	Lost	GF	GA	Pts
Burnley	1	42	24	14	4	72	35	62
Blackburn Rovers	3	46	20	15	11	57	47	55

Blackburn Rovers		Burnley	
Most Appearances	Roger Jones, Derek Fazackerley (both 46)	Most Appearances	Alan Stevenson, Colin Waldron, Keith Newton, Jim Thompson, Frank Casper, Leighton James (all 42)
Most Goals	Tony Field 17	Most Goals	Paul Fletcher 15

Adamson still had enough talent at his disposal in this campaign to storm clear of the pack and win promotion back to Division 1. With a team that often picked itself, Burnley lost just four games throughout the season. They were crowned Division 2 Champions for the first time since the Jimmy Ross inspired side of 1898. To guarantee a return to Division 1, Adamson splashed

out £50,000 on a goalkeeper, Alan Stevenson arriving from Chesterfield, but the boss had to grit his teeth and watch Dave Thomas, yet another young starlet who had been at Gawthorpe since leaving school and who had topped the 150 appearance mark, be sold to their immediate Division 2 rivals Queens Park Rangers for £165,000. Keith Newton arrived from Everton and Leighton James, Geoff Nulty and Mick Docherty, all who had been at the clubs since their teens, had become automatic choices.

The Burnley Division 2 Title winning side 1972-73 (played over 15 games, max 42) was; Alan Stevenson, Mick Docherty, Keith Newton, Martin Dobson, Colin Waldron, Jim Thompson, Frank Casper, Paul Fletcher, Leighton James, Doug Collins, Geoff Nulty.

Although progress in the Cup competitions was minimal, Burnley could at least blame it on tough draws. Yet again they had to face Liverpool in Round 3 of the FA Cup and once more the Clarets pulled out all of the stops, a goalless draw being achieved at Turf Moor before the expected 3-0 defeat at Anfield. The performance at Leeds in early September in the League Cup was questionable as they went down 4-0 to an extremely strong opponent.

Much was expected of the 1972-73 season at Ewood Park, Furphy's second campaign and promotion was almost achieved. Bolton Wanderers were the class of the field, but a rare Fazackerley goal gave the Rovers a 1-0 victory at Burnden Park and with Tony Field terrorising every defence, a top two finish was easily in their grasp. It had been a disastrous start and the attendance figures had been low early doors, 5,943 for the visit of Walsall, but five figure gates became the norm as the year progressed. Three wins were required from the final three fixtures, but three draws left them an agonising two points from promotion. Tony Parkes, from non-league Buxton, was given the opportunity to partner local boy Stuart Metcalfe in mid-field, a combination which worked effectively through much of the seventies. Roger Jones played every game in goal, far and away the best player at Ewood Park.

In the Cup competitions, the Rovers played like a poor Division 3 side. They lost at home in Round 1 of the League Cup to Rochdale and although they took revenge on the previous season's 4-1 shellacking at Lincoln in the League Cup by exactly reversing the score line in the FA Cup Round 1 replay, Field scoring three, their display at home to Crewe Alexandra was so poor that they were booed off the pitch by their own supporters following their 1-0 defeat in Round 2.

1973-74

Team	Pos	Played	Won	Drawn	Lost	GF	GA	Pts
Burnley	6	42	16	14	12	56	53	46
Blackburn Rovers	13	46	18	10	18	62	64	46

Blackburn Rovers		Burnley	
Most Appearances	Derek Fazackerley 46	Most Appearances	Geoff Nulty 42
Most Goals	Tony Field 11	Most Goals	Paul Fletcher 13

Back now in the top division, if anyone had offered Jimmy Adamson a top six finish at the start of this season, he would certainly have taken it. He spent £35,000 of the Thomas fee on Peter Noble from Swindon Town, yet another inspired purchase. The Clarets performed magnificently until the New Year, occupying a top three position, and conceding just twenty-one goals in twenty-three games. They slid away from the heady heights of the table but there was still time for the Turf Moor side to seal a top three place. Unfortunately too many draws down the finishing straight contributed to a sixth-place finish. Burnley's successful season certainly lit up the town; a good job really because the country was often in darkness throughout the winter. The miners' strike, the confrontation with the Ted Heath government, caused coal shortages and consequently a lack of electricity. There was now three up and three down between the top four leagues. Paul Fletcher told me that the reason why they did not cause even more of a surprise and finish in the top three was all about finance.

> "Jimmy Adamson needed more money to strengthen the squad, because we knew that if injuries and tiredness began to take its toll, we would struggle. The players knew that he and Bob Lord were always arguing about this but one of the bonuses about having a small squad was that we had a fantastic team spirit. Colin Waldron used to say during the previous season when we won the Division 2 title how fantastic it was going on to the field knowing we weren't going to lose. But if the manager could have splashed some cash towards the end of the first year back in Division 1, we would have easily finished third."

At last, there was excitement surrounding the FA Cup as they qualified for a berth in the semi-final. This was their best campaign under Jimmy Adamson in either of the cup competitions. The Clarets had a straightforward run to the last four, all against lower placed opposition in the shape of Grimsby Town, Oldham Athletic, Aston Villa and Wrexham. Burnley had now reached their fourth semi-final since the war. Twice they had gone on to finish as runner-up at Wembley, but the fates certainly conspired against them on this occasion. Newcastle United stood in their way, a very ordinary Division 1 side. But the game came exactly one week after their epic victory over Leeds United and the scars were still showing. Casper should not have played, but Adamson took the gamble. Worryingly the striker was a shadow of the man who hit the heights the week before and the "Toon Army" had their own match winner. Malcolm McDonald had once scored five goals for England in an international fixture. On his day, he could fully live up to his nickname of "Supermac" and this was one of those days. He scored twice at the neutral venue of Hillsborough, delivering the knock-out blow to Burnley. I spoke to Brian Nelson, now a Burnley Director, about his memories from that day.

> "We really fancied our chances. Newcastle United were having a nothing sort of season and we were making good progress, having just hammered top of the league Leeds, 4-1 away. We were in the Leppings Lane end of Hillsborough, exactly where all the tragic deaths were fifteen years later. In fact the Police did exactly the same thing when we were there. All the Newcastle fans were supposed to be at the other end, but at the last minute they let in a load of them and many had drunk a lot. We hadn't been to Wembley for twelve years and we were convinced we were going back this time. We were the better team and we dominated the game but they had Malcolm McDonald and he was simply unplayable. Whenever he had the ball near our goals, we panicked. For one of his goals, both Waldron and Thompson were hanging on to him, fouling him and doing anything they could to stop him. Any modern day striker would have gone down to claim the free kick outside the box, but not McDonald. He was so strong and tough and he scored both their goals in the second-half. I had been at Wembley against Tottenham as a young teenager but I didn't feel anything like the dismay that stayed with me for days and days after the Hillsborough loss. My first Wembley was a great spectacle for a lad, win or lose, but it was a different story in Sheffield. I was absolutely devastated by the result. I was an adult by then and I believe that when you are a kid, you can quickly recover from football defeats. The older you get, the longer they take to get over. It was our last FA Cup semi-final which makes the memory even worse, even from forty-six years ago."

The League Cup was nowhere near as exciting. Eventually Cardiff City were beaten 3-2 in a replay, Leighton James scoring four of the five goals they notched over the two ties, against his compatriots of course. But the Round 2 fixture was a horror story as they bowed out 2-1 to the lowly Division 3 side Plymouth Argyle in Burnley.

The bookies were offering short odds on Blackburn Rovers reaching Division 2 as the 73-74 season kicked off, but once again it was a stuttering start. Eventually they put together a winning streak before to everyone's dismay, Ken Furphy was tempted to take the Sheffield United job and he was quickly off to Division 1. Gordon Lee was his replacement. A first team regular in his Aston Villa days, he had performed miracles to bring promotion to Division 3 for Port Vale and then keep them there. However for the rest of the campaign at Ewood Park, the air was full of frustration. There was a solitary win at home to Rochdale and by this stage, the crowd was voting with its feet, only 3,520 bothering to turn up to the season's finale, a 2-1 defeat to Wrexham and a thirteenth place finish. Kevin Hird made his debut towards the end of this season, a 0-0 draw at Watford. His early days make interesting reading.

> "I was born and brought up in Colne and was a big Burnley supporter, and although I felt I was a really good player, there were no scouts around to look at me. So my older brother told me to go down to Turf Moor, my nearest club and ask for a trial. I did and knocked on the door but the person I talked to was completely disinterested in me, saying they just didn't give anybody a trial. When I told my brother, he said go down to Blackburn and as a fifteen year old boy who had just left school, I again knocked on a door and this lady was really lovely. She took my name and address and I quickly received a letter from Johnny Carey inviting me to a trial. I went down, did well and they signed me as an apprentice."

The draw for the FA Cup was too good to be true, but the Rovers almost made fools of themselves. They needed replays to defeat two non-league sides, Willington from County Durham and Altrincham before having to face Everton at Goodison Park in Round 3. Not unnaturally, they lost 3-0. They had also been forced to a replay by Southport in Round 1 of the League Cup before Division 2 Orient defeated them 2-0 in Blackburn.

1974-75

Team	Pos	Played	Won	Drawn	Lost	GF	GA	Pts
Burnley	10	42	17	11	14	68	67	45
Blackburn Rovers	1	46	22	16	8	68	45	60

Blackburn Rovers		Burnley	
Most Appearances	Roger Jones, Tony Parkes (both 46)	Most Appearances	Peter Noble, Leighton James (both 42)
Most Goals	Don Martin 15	Most Goals	Leighton James 16

In the 1974-75 season there was yet another set-back with the sale of skipper Martin Dobson [pictured]. A stylish and complete mid-field player, he had led them to promotion and was capped four times by England. Born locally, he was a Claret through and through but £300,000 from Everton was money

that the club could not turn down and of course very little of it was spent on a replacement.

Geoff Nulty brought in £120,00 from Newcastle United around Christmas time having made 130 starts, yet another enforced sale of a player who was about to reach his peak. Burnley truly hit the wall with eighty per cent of the race run. They were lying second with eight games to go and, in this most congested of seasons at the top of Division 1, finally finished tenth. Suspensions were now becoming more frequent and Burnley, with its small squad. suffered as much as any side from this sort of nonsense. Wins over wealthy clubs such as Liverpool, Tottenham, Arsenal and Manchester City reminded the country that the small mill town was still a force to be reckoned with, especially when the front three of Hankin, Fletcher and James were on the ball. The highly talented Burnley side were leading scorers in Division 1 and if Dobson and Nulty had not been sold, would they have won the league? On the other hand, what would the financial situation have been? Bob Lord, love him or hate him, was a sound housekeeper but should he have looked outside the club to find extra finance by bringing in a couple of wealthy directors? It is the old "more questions than answers" conundrum, but forty-seven years on and counting; this has still been the last reasonable chance that this wonderful little club, which has so often punched above its weight, has had to have its name adorning the old Division 1 Trophy or the Premier League equivalent.

As Burnley were starting their final push for league glory in early January 1975, Turf Moor witnessed one of the FA Cup results which will probably never be forgotten. An upset to at least match all other upsets. There have been a number of David v Goliath contests in the history of this great competition, but Round 3 on January 4th was a pea-shooter v a Centurion tank. Wimbledon, from the Southern Premier League, had battled their way through six previous rounds to face a Burnley eleven, the fifth placed Division 1 side entering the competition at this stage. Mike Duffy tells the story.

> "I recall a bet I made with a colleague – he could have three goals and the draw – against non-league Wimbledon in the FA Cup 3rd Round. I had remembered huge victories over Chesterfield 7-0 and New Brighton 9-0 in the late fifties and thought I was on to a winner as I stood on the Longside, not far from my position those years ago with school friends. To my horror, Dickie Guy the Wimbledon keeper was the hero of the day in a 1-0 giant killing. It was an almighty upset, resonating across the football world."

ROVERS UP! BRING ON THE CHAMPAGNE

VERDICT . . . Burnley down at City

ALF THORNTON with the Rovers

Just fan-tastic!

THE Rovers are back in the Second Division again after four years in the soccer wilderness.

And they clinched promotion in style at Ewood Park with a fine victory over Chesterfield. Stuart Metcalfe got the first ...

In the Football League Cup, Burnley had fought their way past Hull City and Reading, winning both games away from home only to be paired yet again with a Division 2 Manchester United in Round 4. It was a cracker of a game at Old Trafford as Noble and Hankin gave the Turf Moor side a 2-1 interval lead. But Tommy Docherty's side, playing with such confidence, twice scored late on to end the Clarets' interest. Peter Noble had scored in each of the three rounds.

A hundred years old and playing like someone of that age. That would have perfectly summed up the performance of Blackburn Rovers during the first six months of Gordon Lee's stewardship. But 1974-75 was a new season and the manager cleared the decks and introduced their replacements to the starting line-up. He had immediately lost Field and Garbett, snatched by Ken Furphy and taken to Sheffield United and Barry Endean to Huddersfield Town. In came Graham Hawkins, a classy centre-back from Preston, Ken Beamish, a popular striker from Brighton and Hove Albion, Graham Oates, a quality wing-half from Bradford City and Andy Burgin, a full back from Halifax Town, all of whom were instrumental in the club winning the Division 3 title, along with Mike Hickman, a striker who arrived from Grimsby Town. And from the off, they played like promotion contenders. Six wins and two draws in eight games from the start of September to mid-October set out their credentials to the rest of the competition. There was a blip around Christmas time and what was required was an unbeaten run, but no-one expected it to last for ten weeks and fifteen games. Plymouth were welcomed back to Blackburn and it was one of the most uplifting games I have ever seen. With Paul Mariner, a future England World Cup goal scorer leading their attack, the West Country side raced into a 2-0 lead, silencing the 17,000 plus crowd. But the never say die attitude once more came to the fore and doubles from Martin and Hickman clinched a memorable and vital 5-2 victory. With just one defeat in the last eighteen games, the Blackburn side hung on to be champions. The gap between them and Burnley had been two divisions, so this promotion was vital.

The Blackburn Rovers Division 3 Title winning squad 1974-75 (started over 18 games, max 46) was; Roger Jones, Mick Heaton, Andy Burgin, Stuart Metcalfe, Graham Hawkins, Derek Fazackerley, Ken Beamish, Graham Oates, Don Martin, Tony Parkes, Mike Hickman, John Waddington, Mick Wood.

The Cup games also kept the fans happy. In the FA Cup, wins over Matlock Town and Darlington set up a Round 3 home fixture with Bristol Rovers who proved too good on the day, winning 2-1. In the Football League Cup, they again avoided the top teams, defeating Stockport County and Northampton Town, the latter after a replay. Beamish had already scored three times in the competition and they next travelled to Hartlepool United and drew 1-1. A decent crowd of 11,121 came down to see the replay but the Blue and Whites simply failed to perform and towards the end, the crowd streamed off, letting the players know what they thought of their performance. But in truth, the cup results simply mirrored what was happening at the club. There was little money, the quality of player was inferior to what had once been the norm and the people of Blackburn expected far more.

1975-76

Team	Pos	Played	Won	Drawn	Lost	GF	GA	Pts
Burnley	21	42	9	10	23	43	66	28
Blackburn Rovers	15	42	12	14	16	45	50	38

Blackburn Rovers		Burnley	
Most Appearances	Derek Fazackerley 42	Most Appearances	Keith Newton 41
Most Goals	Ken Beamish, Tony Parkes (both 7)	Most Goals	Peter Noble, Ray Hankin 13

This season was a nightmare for Burnley fans. Victories were scarce, just four accruing by the time the Christmas festivities were concluded. Remarkably, Peter Noble scored four at home to Norwich City but failed to be on the winning side, the final result being a 4-4 draw.

Jimmy Adamson, always an honourable man, resigned with the club's best interests at heart. He had been a natural successor to Harry Potts, so typical of the continuity that had been the mainstay of Bob Lord's managerial appointments since taking over as Chairman. Jimmy had a sky high reputation in the game, almost an academic in his approach to coaching and tactics, but he was not as successful as his predecessor. His reputation was based on his coaching ability and he was Walter Winterbottom's second in command with the England squad in the Chile World Cup of 1962. But as jobs go, there can be a world of difference between coaching and managing and the "one club man" had two problems to overcome. There was still talent in the club, but less than in the days when he was dictating operations on the pitch. There was also the age old difficulty at Turf Moor. "We sell our star players to survive financially". He took them down, brought them back up again, came close to a podium finish in 73-74 which included a semi-final date, gave it a great shot in 74-75 before finally resigning.

Jim Thomson, who struggled to find a place in the Burnley starting line-up for several years after being bought from Chelsea, was an ardent admirer of Adamson's coaching technique, although he found it extremely difficult to like him.

> "I thought Jimmy Adamson was an unbelievable coach and I can understand why the FA wanted to offer him the job as coach of the England side. He seemed so clever and intelligent about football. Every training session was different which was unusual in the game at that time. We worked so hard on corners and free kicks. We scored a number of goals from set pieces because the opposition had not a clue about what was going to happen. I did find it hard to get on with him though because if you made a mistake he was on at you all of the time. Colin Waldron was a big mate of mine and I was always moaning about Jimmy. 'Waldo' thought he was fantastic and he regularly told me to shut up. "I don't know why you moan about him so much' he said. 'Doesn't he pick you every week?' This was eventually true but I had struggled like mad to get in the side and I once asked for a transfer but the club refused it. I couldn't understand why because the club was doing well without me in the side. The manager played several of the kids who had won the FA Youth Cup and I was stuck in the Reserves, but once I finally got into the side, I became a regular for a few seasons."

No bookmaker was offering odds on Jimmy Adamson's replacement and sure enough, Joe Brown, the Assistant Manager was promoted. Once more it was a case of "keeping it in the family". Brown's arrival saw a mini revival but a further run of six games without a victory sealed their fate. Finishing twenty-first, five points short of safety, they were relegated. This slide into Division 2 was the start of thirty-three years in the doldrums. Relegation seasons often bring about the end of careers or players moving away to remain at a higher level, and this was no exception. Leighton James [pictured], arguably the Clarets' best footballer since McIlroy and with twenty-two Welsh caps to his name, had started his career at Burnley and they had somehow kept hold of him through 180 league appearances and 45 goals. But the usual combination of cash shortage at the club and the ambition of their best player meant that he was sold to Derby County for a then club record of £310,000. Other loyal servants who played their final games were Colin Waldron (308 appear-

ances) who was off to Manchester United, Doug Collins (172) en route to Plymouth Argyle, Mick Docherty (149 in a career ravaged by injury) leaving for Manchester City and Frank Casper (230 and 74 goals; 12th in the all-time list) retiring after struggling to recover from the viciousness meted out by Norman Hunter. All five had given so much for the cause and will be long remembered and with the exception of Casper the retiree, each were given free transfers. Joe Brown used £100,000 of the James money to sign Tony Morley from Preston North End, but the exciting winger arrived far too late to save them from relegation.

Jimmy Adamson's final game in charge midway through the campaign was the FA Cup 3rd Round encounter with Blackpool at Bloomfield Road. Hankin was dismissed, it was a 1-0 defeat and the Clarets had exited the competition to a club somewhere in the middle of Division 2. There was a result to cherish in the League Cup. A win over Hereford United in Round 2, Flynn and Noble each scoring twice, sent them into Round 3 and totally belying their horrendous league form, a Noble penalty presented them with a 1-0 win at Liverpool in a Round 3 replay. Leicester City were unable to hold Burnley at the "Turf", Morgan and Hankins's goals earning them a 2-0 victory, but there was no reversal of form in the quarter final at Middlesbrough where they went down 2-0.

Blackburn Rovers found their first season back in Division 2 to be fraught with problems, the majority of Gordon Lee's title winning boys were Division 3 players. But an even bigger problem faced the Board of Directors.

When a manager leads a side to promotion, the bigger clubs take note and if they are in need of a new man at the helm, their pulling power is extremely strong. Once more they circled and the manager left for Newcastle United in the summer of 75 after lots of wrangling. The Board at Ewood had become well practiced in the art of finding a new "boss". For a third time they delved into the lower divisions and plucked out Jim Smith who had gained promotion to Division 3 with Colchester United. Called the "Bald Eagle" for obvious reasons, he initially found some success but struggled through the winter. Lee also came back to raid the club when he settled in the North East. He took Oates and Jones with him and Hickman moved to Torquay United. Jones had made 242 appearances in goal. Jim Smith brought along Bobby Svarc, a centre-forward from his old club and veteran wingers Gordon Taylor and David Wagstaffe arrived from Birmingham City and Wolverhampton Wanderers respectively. He did however lose a couple of extremely popular characters. Injury forced Mick Heaton, team captain and motivator supreme at right back, to retire. Don Martin returned to Northampton Town, his former club, but he will long be remembered at Ewood Park as a manager's dream. A utility player who made 214 appearances and scored fifty-seven goals.

As the weather improved, so did the team's prospects and five wins and a draw from their last eight games saw them five points clear of relegation in fifteenth place. It had been a tough baptism for the new boss but he had consolidated the club's position in the second tier. Derek Fazackerley had lots of respect for both Lee and his predecessor.

> "Ken Furphy arrived with a good reputation following his work at Watford. He tried hard and brought in several good players he could trust like Barry Endean, Terry Garbett who he had worked with before at Watford, Mick Heaton, Tony Field who was a great goal scorer at this level and John McNamee. John was an experienced centre-half who I had the benefit of learning from. Ken was well respected and popular with the players, but he just couldn't get us over the line. Gordon Lee had also worked wonders at his previous club, and he led us to promotion from Division 3 but unfortunately when a manager does well lower down, the bigger clubs want them and this is why the Rovers lost both of them."

There was an instant exit from the League Cup, Preston North End winning 2-0 on aggregate in August and Luton Town proved too good in the 3rd Round of the FA Cup, winning 2-0 at Kenilworth Road.

It's 50/50, then a 32-year run of Blue and White domination begins, 1976 - 1985

"When they were up, they were up,
And when they were down, they were down,
And when they were only halfway up,
They were neither up nor down."

The Grand Old Duke of York

Traditional nursery rhyme, origin unknown

After ten years without a derby game in sight, on occasions with a two division gap between the sides, the traditional rivalry exploded on East Lancashire once again. Historically, these encounters had taken place in Division 1; now they were one step below and although the level of football displayed on the pitch may have been inferior and the attendances lower (22,189 at Ewood on December 27th compared with the previous festive Ewood clash on New Year's Day in 66 of 28,013), the intensity of passion remained high.

It was as if the fans were saying "to hell with what division it is, it is still a derby". The levels are obviously dictated to by performances on the pitch the previous season. Burnley were on the way down, the Rovers ultimately on their way up, but like the grand old Duke of York's men, at this current juncture 'they were neither up nor down'; a holding position between where they both would have loved to be and where they were scared of falling to.

1976-77

Team	Pos	Played	Won	Drawn	Lost	GF	GA	Pts
Blackburn Rovers	12	42	15	9	18	42	54	39
Burnley	16	42	11	14	17	46	64	36

Blackburn Rovers		Burnley	
Most Appearances	Tony Parkes 42	Most Appearances	Peter Noble, Billy Rodaway (both 42)
Most Goals	Bobby Svarc 10	Most Goals	Peter Noble 13

There were mixed feelings amongst Blackburn Rovers' fans this season. The young Paul Bradshaw was a quality keeper in the making and Jim Smith also put his faith in two young full backs, Kevin Hird and John Bailey. Both were quick and loved to join in the attacks as the concept of wing backs began to appear in the game. The manager showed that he could spend money wisely when signing Glenn Keeley from Newcastle United. But the problem was in the goal scoring department; John Byrom being brought back from Bolton Wanderers, ten years after his departure. But Metcalfe and Parkes continued to perform as the ideal mid-field pairing and the latter was in the middle of a run of ninety-four consecutive league games.

After a comprehensive 3-0 victory over Bolton Wanderers in the seasonal opener, the Rovers lost four straight games before winning in style, 3-0 over reigning FA Cup holders Southampton, Waddington scoring twice. But there were red faces around Ewood Park when Dave Wagstaffe became the first player in English football to receive a red card. In spite of being reduced to ten men, they managed to win the away game at Orient 1-0, Svarc being on target. Eventually they finished twelfth, way off the pace.

Joe Brown signed Malcolm Smith on loan from Middlesbrough and Terry Cochrane was bought from Coleraine. To off-set this however, Ray Hankin, one of their few who could command a decent fee, was sold to Leeds United for £180,000 having scored 37 times in 110 starts. The supporters were heavily critical of Bob Lord of course but the club was apparently losing £4,000 a week and in debt to the tune of £400,000.

Two wins in their first eleven games quickly dispelled any illusions of an instant return to Division 1. They narrowly won twice around Bonfire Night time but their next victory arrived three and a half months later. Mike Summerbee had been released and Gerry Peyton had been sold to Fulham for £40,000, Alan Stevenson having regained his place in goal. When they lost 2-0 at Southampton to drop to twenty first in the league, Bob Lord called time on Joe Brown's fourteen-month tenure as manager and Harry Potts returned for a second spell.

The first game under Harry brought a 2-0 home win over Carlisle United and slowly, the team managed to turn the corner. In the last twelve games, they avoided defeat nine times with five wins including one against the soon to be promoted Chelsea. Malcolm Smith, having now signed a permanent contract, was on target five times during this period and Tony Morley's skill and pace was shining through. Harry Potts had taken the club from deep in the relegation zone to two points clear in sixteenth place, saving the club from the humiliation of a double relegation. The hero had returned!

With Bradshaw on the floor, it's a lucky let off for Rovers as the Clarets made a rare first half attack at Ewood in December 1976

Rovers goalie Paul Bradshaw watches the ball hit the post before rebounding to Peter Noble who fired home the Clarets first goal in the game at Ewood Park in December 1976

The derby games

I well remember the Blackburn home fixture. It was the first derby game for almost eleven years and for the first time I was aware of an antipathy, an antagonism and an atmosphere of nastiness between the two sets of supporters. You expect a set of supporters to be raucous, noisily cheering any action which may lead to a score, booing any suggestion of unfair play by the opposition and jeering every time a wayward shot or a misplaced pass materialises. This was, is and forever will be football and much of it can be amusing, even though it will infuriate the opposition fans. But suddenly derby games were different. The banter had gone; the tone was threatening and you knew for sure that every utterance from a section of the supporters came straight from the heart; a worryingly black heart. The fixture still had pulling power, 22,189 turning up at Ewood Park, the day after Boxing Day. The home side had become safely entrenched in mid-table as Christmas approached, but Burnley, with Joe Brown seemingly unable to lift them out of this desperately poor run of form, were languishing in nineteenth position, too close for comfort to relegation. None of his side had played in an East Lancashire derby before with the exception of Keith Newton, but in those days his shirt was a somewhat different colour. Back in 1966, Jack Marshall had left John Byrom out of the side which travelled to Turf Moor, but he was not going to miss this one and he cracked in two goals after half-time to the delight of the Blackburn End.

But the Burnley players refused to surrender and late goals from Peter Noble and Ian Brennan gave their fans in the Darwen End something to shout about. Noble was outstanding, the ultimate leader of men and in those closing stages, the Rovers simply could not cope with him. A top ten finish was on the cards for the Rovers as the return derby game approached. But going into this fixture, the Blue and Whites had lost their previous two games by a 3-1 margin, the second at home to a relegation haunted Carlisle United. The derby was contested on Good Friday and a respectable crowd of 17,372 came down to the "Turf". Burnley were in 20th place, it was a "fight for survival day" for them and with Harry Potts back at the helm, they certainly did. It was possibly their best performance of the season as Malcolm Smith gave them the lead only for Svarc to equalise on the stroke of half-time. The second half belonged to the Clarets and Noble and Peter Robinson were both on target to give them two desperately needed points. The derby games had returned and in spite of a difficult season, Burnley had had the better of the head to heads.

27 12 1976	Blackburn Rovers	Burnley	2-2	J Byrom 2. P Noble, I Brennan.
08 04 1977	**Burnley**	Blackburn Rovers	3-1	M Smith, P Noble, P Robinson. B Svarc.

Jim Thompson had played for the Clarets at Ewood but a nasty cartilage injury had ruled him out for a while, including the return game. Although the details of the actual game are sketchy, his memories of the surrounding days are certainly not.

> "I am a Glasgow lad, we lived in a tenement and when I left school, I started work at a shipyard on the Clyde so I was brought up on the conflicts that happened every year on Glasgow derby day. When I was playing at Chelsea in the late sixties, there was nothing special about games against the other London clubs, but when I arrived in Burnley, other players and staff would talk about the rivalry against Blackburn. There were no games for eight years because the

Rovers keeper Paul Bradshaw plucks the ball from the head of Paul Fletcher during Burnley's 3-1 victory in April 1977

clubs were in different divisions but it suddenly happened this year. I played in five in total and on the field I loved it. We used to kick lumps out of each other but there were no threatening remarks and after the game, we would talk to each other. It was the fans who were really wound up. They really hated each other and when I talked to some of them, they would tell me that they wanted us to really hurt their players. I could understand the bitterness in Glasgow because it was a religious thing as well as a football thing, but I have never fully understood it down here. But it led to a fabulous atmosphere on the ground and it was unbelievable when we ran out from the changing rooms for my first derby game. That was one of my favourite moments in football. It was difficult in the game in Blackburn when we went 2-0 down, but the Burnley fans really kept us going and it was fantastic to come back and draw. When I finished playing, I became a sales rep for John Smith's brewery for many years and Blackburn became my area. At first, when my customers in the pubs and the clubs learned that I had played for Burnley, there were several who found it hard to talk to me and one of my colleagues who was life-long Rovers supporter used to turn his back on me. Eventually it all settled down and I was welcomed everywhere, but that first year or two was difficult."

Dave Kennedy was in the Blackburn end for the first derby game and he can remember the game as if it was yesterday.

We absolutely hammered them in the first half but couldn't score. We had such a good time, giving the Burnley fans in the Darwen end so much abuse and we couldn't wait for the second half to start because we thought it was going to be such an easy win. The start of the second half was even better. John Byrom, who was a Mill Hill lad, the same as Stuart Metcalfe, scored both goals and we were certain that was it. But I do remember Peter Noble and suddenly he scored late on. The Burnley fans went crazy and just before the whistle they scored again. We couldn't believe it. How had we not won?

After FA Cup wins over Charlton Athletic, 2-0 in a home Round 3 replay and a most comfortable 3-0 victory over Orient, the Blackburn Rovers' run ended at the home of Derby County, losing 3-1 to the Division 1 side. On paper, Burnley had comfortable draws in both Rounds 3 and 4, but of course you don't play on paper. It was heavy weather when beating Division 3 Lincoln City at the second attempt. Paul Fletcher was on target in both games but the Port Vale result was atrocious, losing 2-1. A serious opportunity to make progress and sorely needed finance was lost.

The Rovers entered the Football League Cup in Round 1, Rochdale again providing the two-legged opposition. This time there were no upsets as the Rovers won 5-1 on aggregate, Svarc scoring three of the goals. Stockport County should have similarly been swept aside, but they won comfortably at Ewood Park. Things were no better at Burnley. Torquay United was a long journey from East Lancashire, but surely the Devon side could not win, could they? But they did, 1-0.

1977-78

Team	Pos	Played	Won	Drawn	Lost	GF	GA	Pts
Blackburn Rovers	5	42	16	13	13	56	60	45
Burnley	11	42	15	10	17	56	64	40

Blackburn Rovers		Burnley	
Most Appearances	Kevin Hird 42	Most Appearances	Alan Stevenson 42
Most Goals	Noel Brotherston 11	Most Goals	Steve Kindon 12

Two defenders, each of whom had compiled a record of over one hundred appearances for Blackburn Rovers, left the club at this time. Mick Wood, a left back who could play anywhere down the left-hand side, moved on to Bradford City and Graham Hawkins, a fine centre half now into his thirties, was transferred to Port Vale joining Ken Beamish. Bobby Svarc, hampered now by recurring injuries, also became surplus to requirements.

Noel Brotherston, signed from Tottenham Hotspur on a free transfer, was a revelation on either wing, and towards the end of the season with promotion on the cards, John Radford, an Arsenal legend, joined the club. He scored several important goals but was unable to avert the end of season slump which sounded the death knell to their promotion hopes in this pre-Play-Off era. Smith's side was still reliant on Metcalfe [pictured] and Parkes in mid-field but they conceded too many goals, particularly on their travels.

Paul Bradshaw had been sold to Wolverhampton Wanderers and was replaced by John Butcher coming up through the youth system. I well remember the Blackpool game. Our fixture in the Blackburn Combination on February 4th was called off at 2.00 by the referee and someone had the idea to dash over to Bloomfield Road to watch the Rovers, still on the fringes of the promotion race. We piled into a couple of cars and saw most of the match. The Ewood Park side was a regular threat going forward, at one point leading 2-1, but Blackpool seemed to score every time they went down the other end, finally winning 5-2. It was a salutary warning and sure enough there were only four other wins, including none in the last eight games. It was a sad end to what had been a most promising campaign. Twenty-nine points at the half way stage was table topping form; but in mid-March, Jim Smith left the club to become manager of Birmingham City. Jim Iley was appointed to replace him. A distinguished wing half with Division 1 clubs Spurs, Forest, and the Uniteds of Newcastle and Sheffield, he had successfully managed Barnsley for five seasons in Division 4. However, he completely failed to have a positive impact at Ewood Park. Fifth place was their highest league placing for eleven years, but with horrific performances over the final five weeks, the fans felt as though they had been relegated.

Burnley's season was a mirror image of what had transpired at Ewood Park. The Clarets were relegation bound at Christmas. With the debts mounting, their only saleable item, Brian Flynn, after 193 league games, was on his way to Leeds for £175,000. Brian Hall, who had been a medal winner at Liverpool, was signed from Plymouth Argyle for £25,000 and Potts also splashed out £85,000 on bringing back crowd favourite Steve Kindon from Wolverhampton Wanderers. Paul Fletcher dovetailed well with him and there was plenty of pace on the flanks from Cochrane and Morley, but defensively there were massive short comings. Keith Newton's career was coming to a close. He had played a total of 562 league games at the Rovers, Everton and Burnley, as well as being capped twenty-seven times by England. It surprised no-one when he left Blackburn for Everton for £80,000 and his stock rose even higher during the 1970 World Cup in Mexico where his performances really caught the eye. What was surprising however was his demise on Merseyside. After two less than average seasons, he moved to Burnley where he re-discovered his form. He knew how to defend, could move forward with intent and was so cultured with the ball at his feet. He was equally comfortable at left or right back, won many a ball in the air and was quite sublime in his distribution. He eventually amassed 209 appearances for the Clarets of which 119 were in Division 1 and he helped Adamson's side to regain their place at the highest level in 1973. He has to be the best player to have turned out for both elevens With Harry Potts, there was always a chance of a comeback. It kicked off with a goalless draw at home to Sunderland on New Year's Eve and there was only one reversal until mid-April. Ian Brennan had scored twice at Burnden Park as Bolton were defeated 2-1 and the fans could not believe the change. From the perilous situation at the turn of the year, survival was secured with a 2-0 home win over Fulham in the penultimate game of the season, Burnley somehow finished eleventh in a congested mid-table. Harry Potts had done it again, snatching survival from the abyss of relegation. But for how much longer could a club with such a limited budget, which had consistently sold every good player they had developed for the last fifteen years, carry on at this level?

The derby games

> "I have played in some fairly tasty derbies, like Birmingham City against Aston Villa, but the 45 minutes against Burnley on Boxing Day 1977 was absolute nirvana. We were 3-0 up by half-time and missed a penalty to make it 4-0. But football being what it is, Burnley fought back to make it 3-2 and we thought the whistle was never going to blow."
> Gordon Taylor in an interview with the Independent – 18th October 2009

Bank holidays were the scheduled dates for the two derby games this year. Turf Moor was the first venue and there was a gap of almost the depth of the league between Blackburn Rovers on the edge of promotion and the Clarets rock bottom with only thirteen points. Keith Fear, an attacking mid-field player on loan from Bristol City, made his derby debut and Keeley, coming back from injury, was on the bench. Harry Potts was able to send out the best side available to him and this fixture on Boxing Day was at the exact half-way point in the season. For the first forty-five minutes, Burnley's form was an accurate reflection of the previous twenty games, as goals from Wagstaffe, Fear and Brotherston were ample reward for a magnificent Blackburn team performance. Somehow Harry Potts' team talk invigorated his side and the revival was on. A goal from Morley and a Peter Noble penalty set up a grandstand finish and although the 27,427 fans (not bad for a team at the bottom of the league) trudged home from Turf Moor having witnessed yet another defeat, they were not to know that this was a seminal moment for both clubs. The Rovers' star would begin to wane whereas the Burnley season was just about to kick start into action. The Ewood side had produced several decent wins in the second half of the season but after a Brotherston goal set up a 1-0 away victory at Sunderland, the next fixture on the list was Burnley, down at Ewood Park on Easter Monday. Unbeaten in their last six games, the Clarets were a different proposition than on Boxing Day. Newton had finally succumbed to "Old Father Time, Derek Scott replacing him and Morley was missing, but the belief had

Peter Noble converts a December 1977 spot kick past John Butcher, incredibly Noble scored all 28 penalties in his Burnley career

Steve Kindon is helped from the field on Boxing Day 1977 Rovers ran out 3-2 winners at Turf Moor

Glenn Keeley and Tony Parkes (10) have words with referee George Courtney at Ewood Park in March 1978

Referee George Courtney orders off Noel Brotherston during the game at Ewood Park in March 1978

returned. The Rovers, without the injured Fazackerley and Waddington, gave a derby debut to the veteran John Radford, but the Clarets deserved to win and win they did. A 20th minute Cochrane strike lengthened their unbeaten run to seven and started the Rovers' miserable run of eight without a win. The derbies had been shared courtesy of two away wins, only the third time this had occurred, but showing that any permutation of results is possible in this fixture.

26 12 1977	Burnley	Blackburn Rovers	2-3	T Morley, P Noble. D Wagstaffe, K Fear, N Brotherston.
27 03 1978	Blackburn Rovers	**Burnley**	0-1	T Cochrane.

Derek Fazackerley's name was on virtually every Rover's team sheet for well-nigh seventeen seasons, but no-one is totally immune from injury, causing the hardiest of individuals to miss games. Ironically for one with BRFC tattooed across his heart, he only played four times against Burnley, being injured for the four other games that were played during his time in East Lancashire.

"I played in the Boxing Day game in Burnley and we absolutely dominated them in the first-half. But it was much harder in the second half and they pulled a goal back. Then as we expected the ref to blow for full time, he gave them a penalty and Noble scored from the spot. In those days, we didn't have a fourth official who counted the time to be added on. The referee usually blew just after the ninety minute mark but this one was playing on and on. We were due to play the following day at home to Sunderland and we were panicking by now. In desperation I shouted at the ref. 'For god's sake blow your f....... whistle because we are going to be late for the kick-off tomorrow.' Fortunately he did and we secured a well-deserved win. People used to tell me that I was fairly quick, but it was only after this game that I realised how quick I needed to be to be a success at this level. Steve Kindon was in the Burnley side and he was a real flier. I was tested that day to keep pace with him, but although it took such an effort, I managed to do it for long enough to for us to get a result. I received a niggly groin injury well before the second derby game and I missed the rest of the season. I was at the Ewood Park game and in the dressing room afterwards. John Bailey, our left-back, had lots of tricks and he tried one on Terry Cochrane who pinched the ball from him. The defence was caught square and Cochrane raced towards our goal and launched this tremendous shot past John Butcher. Jim Smith was livid when the players returned to the dressing room. He grabbed Bails by his throat and pinned him to the wall, screaming that he would never play for him again. Little did we know, but the manager was right. Jim actually left the club almost immediately after, joining Birmingham City who were in Division 1 at the time. I think one of the first players he wanted to sign was Bails. Typical of the wonderful volatility of the passionate Jim Smith."

Kevin Hird had similar comments to make about the Boxing Day game at Turf Moor.

> "In all of the hundred and odd games I played for the Rovers, the first half at Burnley was the best we ever played. We should have had six in those forty-five minutes and Keith Fear missed a penalty. I don't remember why he took it because it was usually my job. As we walked off, the noise coming from our supporters was fantastic. But although we scored three, we were short of a proper goal scorer. When I have thought back about it, I have said that we were a Simon Garner short of magnificent team that season. He didn't really make the team until after I left for Leeds. People ask me who was the best player I played with at the Rovers and you have to put Faz and Stuart Metcalfe up there, but David Wagstaffe was the one. He had unbelievable skills."

Jim Thompson said that the Cochrane goal was so typical of the player.

> "Terry Cochrane was a good player, quick, great ball control, but we never really knew what he was going to do next. Most players would have tried to get closer to the Blackburn goal before shooting or wait for someone to pass to. But he was afraid of nothing. Everything was so impulsive about him and without thinking, he just shot at goal. It was a fantastic effort and a wonderful goal, but very few players would have risked it. Terry came from Belfast and at times gave the impression he was the next George Best, but he could play and did well for Burnley"

Steve Kindon remembered his battles with Derek Fazackerley and agreed they were all about speed of foot.

> Scotland had always had a reputation for sprint competitions and these were professional at a time when all official athletics was amateur. People could bet on the races and they decided that they would have a race for professional footballers. I decided to enter the one at Meadowbank and Malcolm McDonald who played for England was also in it. He finished fourth and I won it easily in a time of 10.7 seconds. My brother ran for Great Britain in the high hurdles and I was quicker than him, but he was a far better hurdler. I had spent all of my early life playing rugby where my speed was tailor-made for the game so I wasn't that skilful as a footballer, but my speed definitely helped. Derek was actually a mate of mine and we had some great tussles but they were always fair ones.

Paul Fletcher always remembers the running wars he had with Glen Keeley.

> "These battles with Glen Keeley really meant so much to me, but it did to him, so you can imagine the tussles we had. He was really tall, but I did like playing against his type of player. It was a real challenge for me because I was only a

little over 5'9", yet I won so much of the ball in the air. When I was at school, I played a lot of basketball and this helped my timing, which is the secret of winning aerial battles. When I first arrived at the club, Jimmy Adamson, who was the coach then, had already told the players that I was just what they needed and that I would win everything in the air, so when I first walked in, they must have expected a giant. They really laughed when they saw me and did take the mickey out of me for a few days. I was disappointed with my final tally of goals at Burnley, although I was never dropped until my final few weeks under Brian Miller when I was reaching the end of my career. Jimmy Adamson told me always to take up a position just beyond the far post and when the crosses came over, head the ball back towards the penalty spot where the likes of Geoff Nulty and Martin Dobson were expected to win the second ball and crash it into the net. I did win my share of ball with Keeley, although it was difficult with his height and ability. In the home game of this season, when we were three down at half time but kept pushing forward all the second half, he dropped me and I won a penalty against him late on and Peter Noble scored to make it 3-2."

Derek Scott also has fond memories of the Ewood Park game.

"There was another big crowd on and if anything, Blackburn were the better side this season. Terry Cochrane scored the goal quite early in the first half and from then onwards we were under the cosh. It was like the Alamo and it was a great performance by us to hang on. Although there was only one goal, the pace of the game was thick and fast and it was exciting for the fans. There was a tremendous build up in the press in the week before the game and we were kicking lumps out of each other on the pitch. But when the game ended, we all got changed and would go upstairs to the Players' Lounge and all have a drink together. In fact I was quite friendly with several of the Rovers' players. But it has been the same in the Youth Cup games against Blackburn. Because there would be few watching, we could really hear the coaches and they were all encouraging us to really get stuck in. It was probably fiercer than playing for the first team. Dave Merrington was our coach and he really wound us up. It was like him asking us to kick a brick wall down for him.

Both Burnley and Blackburn Rovers were victorious in the 3rd Round of the FA Cup. The Clarets won a close affair 1-0 against Fulham at the "Turf" and the Rovers were equally pushed hard, but they came through 2-1 at home to Shrewsbury Town. The 4th Round draw was at least one step too far for both clubs who lost in London, Burnley being hammered 6-2 at Stamford Bridge and the Rovers losing 3-1 at the Orient.

Blackburn Rovers crashed out of the Football League Cup in Round 2, being thrashed 4-0 by Division 3 Colchester United (the manager's former club) in a replay after the sides had drawn 1-1 at Ewood. It has to rank as one of their worst ever defeats. Burnley's early season form was so dire that even a Football

League Cup Round 1 tie against Chester was a fifty/fifty game, but the Clarets hung on to earn a home tie following a 2-1 aggregate win. A mere 6,000 crowd came to watch First Division 1 side Norwich City in Round 2 and to their amazement, goals from Morley, Noble and Ingham led them to a 3-1 triumph. Ipswich Town came to Turf Moor in Round 3, but in spite of an early Fletcher strike, the Suffolk side won 2-1.

1978-79

Team	Pos	Played	Won	Drawn	Lost	GF	GA	Pts
Burnley	13	42	14	12	16	51	62	40
Blackburn Rovers	22	42	10	10	22	41	72	30

Blackburn Rovers		Burnley	
Most Appearances	John Bailey 39	Most Appearances	Alan Stevenson 42
Most Goals	Simon Garner 8	Most Goals	Peter Noble 14

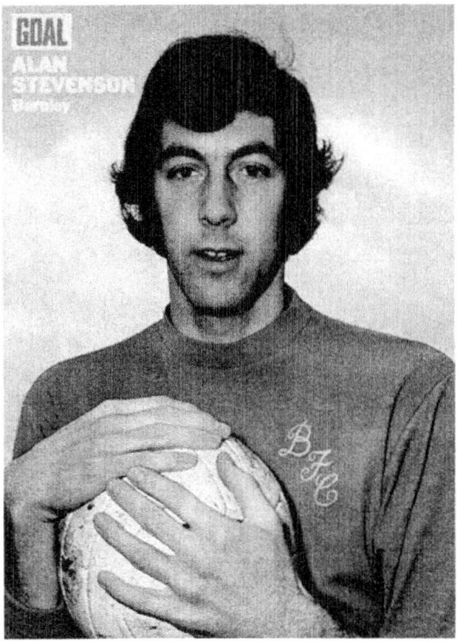

Burnley began the season with the same squad that performed so well in the second half of the previous campaign. During the seventies, both the Clarets and Blackburn Rovers had entered the Texaco Cup, later given the Anglo-Scottish label. Although not topping any club's agenda, at times it could be a money spinner. The Turf Moor club had qualified through the group stages and drew Glasgow Celtic in the 1st Round proper. Steve Kindon scored the only goal of the home leg, a score which was overshadowed by the subsequent violence that caused many injuries as a small number of Celtic fans hurled anything hard (including iron railings) into the Burnley supporters. The second leg was close again, but Harry Potts' side caused an upset as Ian Brennan smashed one in from distance and Kindon also scored to seal the tie, 3-1 on aggregate. The East Lancashire side eventually won the competition by beating Oldham Athletic 4-2 in a two legged final, but it is the Celtic encounter which is remembered. Burnley reneged on their promise that their days of being a selling club were over and sold their Northern Irish winger Terry Cochrane to Middlesbrough for £210,000. They did bring back Leighton James for £165,000 from Queens Park Rangers, but the side remained settled through much of the year. The back six of Stevenson, Scott, Brennan, Noble, Thompson and Rodaway missed only fifteen games between them.

They tracked the leaders until Christmas, meandering between fourth and seventh, a number of their results giving out a warning to the rest of the Division. Peter Noble crashed in a hat-trick in a seesaw 5-3 victory over Fulham and then suddenly there was no league football.

The snow fell, it froze heavily and a month elapsed between fixtures. Once it thawed, Burnley kept in contention. The remaining eight games were vital but they drew two and lost six. Counting cup games, Burnley had played fifty-eight times, a plausible reason as to why they finished thirteenth. Peter Noble was the leading scorer with fourteen goals, a remarkable player whom we hated and yet admired at Ewood.

It was disappointment at Turf Moor but heartbreak at Ewood Park. The Rovers won just three league games up until March 28th. Iley's stint as a manager was disastrous. Appointed with four games left of the previous season, he lasted eight league games into this campaign. With one win only to his credit, he was sacked, leaving the club in an almighty mess. The two veterans, Wagstaffe and Taylor left on free transfers and their replacements such as Johnny Aston, Joe Craig and Alan Birchenall were at the "fag end" of their careers. Embarrassing was the word when David Gregory, a loanee from Stoke City who immediately hit the goal trail, chose to play at Bury in Division 3 when his loan deal concluded.

I used to pop into the club on a regular basis on schools' football business but usually only saw the Manager on the rarest of occasions but John Pickering was different. He really put himself about. He had only played lower division football but Jim Smith appointed him Reserve Team manager and then he became Iley's assistant. In no time he was given the top job when Iley left, but the promotion came far earlier than he had expected. The side was down on its uppers, lacking talent and direction. Pickering was not afraid to blood youngsters and Simon Garner scored twice against Fulham in a rare victory, but a diabolical run of sixteen games without a win made relegation a stone-cold certainty.

When all seemed lost and Kevin Hird had been sold to Leeds United, the Board suddenly stumped up the cash to bring Duncan McKenzie, magnificently talented but an under achiever, from Chelsea for £75,000 and Mick Rathbone, a tough tackling full back, was signed from Birmingham City for £40,000. Suddenly seven wins and a draw from the last thirteen games was top half of the league form, but it was far too late. With thirty points, the Rovers finished bottom, four points short of safety. They would again be a level below their arch-rival up the road.

Pickering's efforts deserved a reward, but this was football and he was sacked to make way for Howard Kendall. The ex-Everton legend was an "A" Lister, from a different world to where Pickering had learnt his trade and he proved to be an inspired choice, but one had to feel sorry for his predecessor.

Simon Garner was from Boston in the footballing backwaters of Lincolnshire. I asked him how he came to arrive in Blackburn.

> "I was playing for Boston United as a schoolboy, a top non-league sides and Jim Smith had started his managerial career there. He had retained his contacts in the area and the club secretary rang him to let him know about me. I went up for a trial and they offered me an apprenticeship. By the time Jim had left, the club had no money so in many ways, it was a good place to start your career because promotion to the first team would be faster than at a bigger club with loads of professionals. We felt sorry for John Pickering, he was a nice guy but Howard Kendall changed things around and really improved the club. Again it was not easy for him because there has to be a line drawn between manager and players. Howard was Player Manager, but he couldn't really mix socially with the squad. I respected him, but we didn't really get on. I had banged in some goals in my first season under John, but in the following season, although Howard gave me a good run, it was Andy Crawford who was mostly on target. Back in Division 2, I had a good spell early on but goals dried up and he wanted to sign another striker. The Board said "yes" but he had to sell someone first and he chose me. Halifax Town came in with some money but I didn't want to leave and so he told me he wouldn't pick me again. Fortunately for me, Everton came after him and he inevitably moved on at the end of the season"

The derby games

With Burnley on the fringes of the promotion battle, the Boxing Day tussle at Turf Moor brought in a 23,133 crowd for the local derby. The Clarets fielded their best eleven, but Tony Parkes was missing from the Blackburn side. It was a 2-1 home victory, surprisingly close in that this was a woefully poor Blackburn Rovers side in the middle of a sixteen game run which produced just five draws. Fletcher within five minutes and Noble just before the interval, had given the Clarets a two goal interval lead, but Kevin Hird, born just up the road in Colne, was in a fine vein of form and he responded with his fifth goal in ten games, all from right back. With more than a half an hour to play, no-one in the crowd could relax, but the Claret and Blue shirts had sufficient confidence to see out the game. By the time of the return fixture at Ewood Park, the Rovers had at least managed to win three of their last six, but the locals still remained to be convinced, hence the disappointing 14,761 crowd. In truth, critics and pundits alike had totally written off their chances of avoiding the drop and their selected eleven bore little resemblance to the one that narrowly lost in Burnley, earlier in the campaign. Local boy Neil Ramsbottom was in goal, the recently signed Mick (Basil) Rathbone replaced the Leeds-bound Hird at right back and Metcalfe, Parkes and Fazackerley were out injured. Pickering chose to leave recent ageing signings such as Radford, Craig and Birchenall out of the side, and coming in was a young Simon Garner. Reserve players Paul Round, Martin Fowler and Tim

Brian Miller makes his views known to the referee after a bad tackle had floored Steve Kindon at Ewood Park in April 1979

Parkin were all presented with an opportunity to shine, and making their derby debuts were new signings Duncan McKenzie and Russell Coughlin. The Rovers' fans that stayed away probably made the right choice, although Garner gave a preview of the future when he opened the scoring in the first half. But Burnley were giving promotion one last throw of the dice. Second half goals from Morley and Hall won the points and with games in hand, it was still possible for them to catch the leaders. Unfortunately this was their last win, the nightmare end of season run followed, It was Potts' last derby game and Burnley's last victory against their rival for thirty-three years, a statistic which those returning eastwards could never have contemplated.

26 12 1978	**Burnley**	Blackburn Rovers	2-1	P Fletcher, P Noble. K Hird.
14 04 1979	Blackburn Rovers	**Burnley**	1-2	S Garner. T Morley, B Hall

Steve Kindon agreed with a number of other players that the derby game was more important to the fans than it was to the playing staff.

"There were always battles with various opponents but the ones in the derby games always had that bit more edge. John Waddington liked to dish it out when we played the Rovers and when the clubs met at Turf Moor on Boxing Day the season before, he smashed me with his elbow and there was blood all over the place. I had to go off and they wanted to replace me but I shouted and screamed that I wanted to go back on. Eventually they agreed and as I came on to the pitch, Kevin Hird, who was playing for Blackburn then, said "Kindo you look a mess." I was in such a rage that I told him "....to keep out of my f...ing way". Derek Fazackerley made a similar comment and I said the same back to him. My only aim was to get Waddington back, but he managed to keep out of the way." It was over a year after in the derby at Ewood Park that we met up again. I think everybody had forgotten the previous incident except me and unfortunately he had to go off with a bad ankle injury, the result of a non-footballing accident or an act of malice if you want the truth."

Kevin Hird played one of his final games in the Boxing Day clash this year.

"We were really struggling that season, John Pickering had taken over as manager but there was still a good crowd on Ewood. We were 2-0 down at half-time and the crowd were fed up. But I had been on a bit of a goal scoring run even though I was playing right back and just after half-time I got forward and I noticed Alan Stevenson off his line. So I didn't go for power, I just chipped it into the corner. Around this time, the papers were full of talk about me and John Bailey being sold to big clubs. I didn't want to leave, but it was inevitable because the club was really short of money. I believe Leeds initially offered £250,000 and when the Rovers turned it down, they went up to £300,000. The Rovers still thought I was worth more but when Leeds upped their offer again, I was on my way. I had to do it for my career's sake as it was a chance to play in the Big League. The irony of it was that the Leeds manager who signed me was Jimmy Adamson. I had had nine years at Ewood and I think that this was a forgotten time in the history of the club. There were seven different managers in total and we had no money. There seemed to be a lack of discipline when I started as an apprentice, but when Ken Furphy arrived, he started to fine players who arrived late and things improved from then on. Billy Bancroft was Chairmen then and he made several good choices as manager. Ken Furphy, Gordon Lee and Jim Smith all moved on to bigger clubs after the Rovers, showing what good choices they were and at the beginning of every season, the Chairman would come down and speak to all the players from apprentices to the first teamers. He always had a really posh suit on and really shiny shoes and he was a bit scary when he told us what was demanded of us. But it was this that kept the club going. He kept it on the straight and narrow and I think without him, we could have easily become a third rate club in the seventies."

Playing at a professional club is never as straightforward as it may appear. Derek Fazackerley never signed a seventeen year contract at Ewood, there would have been a number of renewals throughout this period. His contract was due to expire at the end of this season and although agents were a rarity forty years ago, there was still gossip in the papers and negotiations had to take place.

"Jim Iley came and left the club after a short and miserable period of time. He had obviously been successful at Barnsley, but his man-management skills were called into question. He rarely called you by your name, always referring to you by the number on your shirt. So he would say to Stuart Metcalfe for example, 'Number 7, pass the ball a bit quicker'. When he left, John Pickering was put in temporary charge and the club was struggling for money. John came to me and told me that Oldham Athletic had offered £100,000 and that the Board had accepted the offer. I didn't really want to leave the club and Oldham did not appeal to me, but I said that I would think about it over the weekend. It was always a non-starter with me, I told him that I didn't want to go and I preferred to stay. Later in the season, Jim Smith would ring me and say that he wanted me at Birmingham City. I liked Jim and would have loved to continue playing for him, but there was never quite a concrete offer. When Howard Kendall arrived, he almost immediately called me in and told me he was taking me out to lunch. He was very persuasive. He explained his ambitions for the club and what he wanted to do, as well as the offer to improve my contract, which helped persuade me to stay after careful consideration. Not long afterwards, I learned that Jim had signed Colin Todd to play at the back for him. He had played a lot of games for England and was a quality defender, so it came as no surprise to me when I found out about this signing."

Because of the Arctic weather, Burnley's only fixture in January was in the 3rd Round of the FA Cup against Birmingham City at St Andrews, which the Clarets won 2-0. It took forty-three days and eight postponements before the 4th Round tie was played against Sunderland at Turf Moor. Neither side wanted a draw but it finished 1-1 and Roker Park staged the replay. Burnley hit top form that night, Ingham, Fletcher and Kindon on target without reply.

Blackburn Rovers drew Millwall in Round 3 and goals from Brotherston and Radford gave the Blackburn side a 2-1 victory, the only win in the long mid-season winless run. It was Anfield next where the 1-0 loss to Liverpool was considered a magnificent performance; many had predicted a cricket score. Burnley was the next lamb to the slaughter at fortress Anfield in Round 5. There they went head to head with the country's best side, but class told after forty minutes and the Anfield side ran out 3-0 winners.

Burnley and Blackburn Rovers entered the Football League Cup at Round 2. The Rovers had to travel to South Devon to meet Exeter City from Division 3, losing 2-1. Burnley came back from the dead when they beat Bradford City 3-2 in a replay at Valley Parade. This earned them a Round 3 draw at home to Brighton and Hove Albion, but the Sussex club was enjoying a most exceptional season in Division 2 and won 3-1.

1979-80

Team	Pos	Played	Won	Drawn	Lost	GF	GA	Pts
Burnley	21	42	6	15	21	39	73	27
Blackburn Rovers	2	46	25	9	12	58	36	59

Blackburn Rovers		Burnley	
Most Appearances	Derek Fazackerley 46	Most Appearances	Alan Stevenson 40
Most Goals	Andy Crawford 18	Most Goals	Billy Hamilton 7

With the Blackburn side having been relegated back to Division 3, the derby games would be on hold for the next three seasons. In many respects, they encapsulated the history of the game in East Lancashire with the see saw working overtime. After four successful seasons at Goodison Park, Martin Dobson returned but it was a vastly different Turf Moor from the one he had left, performance wise.

> "I had been capped five times for England, four times at Burnley and once at Everton and under three different managers, Sir Alf Ramsey, caretaker Joe Mercer and Don Revie. I was a regular at Everton for the full five years I was there and we had finished fourth in the old First Division in the 78-79 season, but Harry Potts showed an interest in taking me back to Burnley. I think it was a case of my heart ruling my head because it meant dropping down a division, but I had so much respect for Harry. He had first signed me when I was nineteen from Bolton Wanderers on a free, Burnley had shown interest in me when I was at school but I went to Clitheroe Grammar School and it seemed to be a better option to take my A levels there. As soon as I finished I signed for Bolton, who were prepared to take a risk on someone who had not come through the Apprentice scheme. It didn't really work out for me there so they allowed me to leave and I went to see Harry Potts. He signed me as a full-time pro quite quickly after that and I became a Claret. My father was actually a Rovers supporter and I was brought up on Clayton and Douglas but the people in my home village of Rishton, which is exactly half-way between the two clubs, were split between the two. My father-in-law went to Turf Moor one week and Ewood Park the next. Harry resigned early on in the season, but Brian Miller took over. I was ruled out for the season after damaging my achilles in early March and we went down. We always thought of Brian as Mr Burnley, so loyal. He could have played at the very best clubs as a player but he never could leave his one and only club. But this Burnley was a different club to the one I left. It was clear it was struggling and it always had been a selling club, but whereas in the past, there was always someone else in the pipeline from Gawthorpe, now there was much less coming through."

Burnley's campaign could be divided into three segments. The initial one comprised of the first fourteen games which saw Harry Potts resign and Brian Miller take over; once more Bob Lord keeping it in the "family". There were no victories to report, just five draws and nine defeats including a 7-0 hammering at Queens Park Rangers. Harry Potts' side was ageing and when they lost 2-0 at home to Cardiff City and settled at the bottom of the league, Potts honourably resigned. He had given fourteen years and ten months across two stints in the hot seat.

His second spell was nowhere near as successful as the first, lasting thirty two months, but the world had changed since he first came on board in 1958; small mill town clubs no longer expected to laud it over the big city establishments as he and his Clarets had done in the sixties. No-one would deny Brian Miller the right to test himself in the toughest job at any football club and the whole of Burnley knew that this one-club man would give it his all and more after progressing through the coaching ranks at Gawthorpe following his most unfortunate injury which must have robbed him of at least five more years on the pitch. Looking at the second segment of the season which ran until the beginning of February, there were six wins, four draws and only two defeats; promotion form. And then it was on to the third segment, a disastrous run of sixteen games without a single win, eight points from safety.

Their total of just six wins was also the lowest since 1897. Thus Burnley were relegated to Division 3, becoming the tenth of the original twelve professional clubs to taste life in Tier 3. Only West Bromwich Albion and Everton had never fallen at that time. Three influential figures left Turf Moor during the season. Tony Morley had been sold to Aston Villa in the close season for £220,000, amazingly Peter Noble departed to Blackpool for a paltry £5,000. He had made 243 appearances since his arrival from Swindon Town and his total of sixty-three league goals from a mid-field or right-back position was outstanding. He was worth every penny and more of the original £40,000 transfer fee.

Paul Fletcher moved to the same club for £30,000. He had turned out for 293 league games and scored on 71 occasions since arriving from Bolton Wanderers as a twenty-year old in 1971. He told me possibly the main reason why he stayed so long.

> "Burnley Football Club was a family to so many of the players. After leaving school, we grew up there, put down our roots in the area and once children came along, we were in no hurry to leave. I was told that several clubs were after me over a ten year period and I actually went to look round and chat to the manager at Derby County. This was a club at the top of the tree in the 70s, but we didn't want to move house and it was a good two hours from Burnley, so I politely said, "no thanks". Portsmouth was in Division 2 at the same time as us, but they weren't as good as us and it was at the other end of the country. It came to the stage where I was no longer good enough for Burnley and so I spent my final year by the sea-side, travelling every day."

Paul also made an interesting comparison between players of his day and the current crop.

"I suspect that 50% of the players playing in my day would not have found a game in this modern age. They were not skilful enough and the skill level has gone up massively in recent times. But also I don't think 50% of modern players could have competed in the 70s because they are not hard enough. They wouldn't be able to take the hard knocks. So why are they more skilful in this day and age? Possibly because they know they are better protected by the referees and VAR. Then you really had to be able to look after yourself."

Steve Kindon was allowed to leave to join Huddersfield Town. This was the end of Kindon's second stint with the club, always a crowd favourite as he made 185 appearances and scored forty-six goals. He did not want to leave but was left with little option.

I was far happier at the "Turf" under Harry Potts than I was under Jimmy Adamson and I wasn't looking to leave. Burnley were still paying good wages but we were struggling on the pitch, Then Harry Potts resigned and Brian Miller took over. I felt that I was playing well and so I was surprised when Brian came up to me and said that the club had to sell me to Huddersfield Town. They were in the Fourth Division but absolutely flying. I asked the boss why he wanted to get rid of me but he said he didn't. He told me that the club needed the money so I had to go, simple as that.

Billy Hamilton was bought from Queens Park Rangers and the crowd instantly warmed to the Northern Irish international and he eventually topped the season's scoring chart. He won thirty-four caps in total whilst at Burnley and made the World Cup squad to Spain, He started all five games, scoring twice against Austria and returning home a green shirted hero. Having sold or dropped so many established players, the manager placed his faith in youngsters. The only consistent experience later in the season was provided by Stevenson, James and Dobson.

In their relegation season, Burnley unexpectedly knocked Division 1 Stoke City out of the FA Cup, Dobson grabbing the goal, but Round 4 was good bye for the Clarets, embarrassingly losing away to Bury 1-0. Division 1 side Wolverhampton Wanderers had been held to a draw in the Football League Cup at Burnley following a Dobson penalty, but they won the replay 2-0 back in the Midlands.

It is true that good players do not necessarily make good managers, but when the Rovers appointed Howard Kendall as manager in 1979, the excitement round the club and town was tangible. Having impressed as player/coach at Stoke City as the Potters returned to Division 1, the former Preston and Everton star was expected to do well at Ewood Park, something he easily achieved. He had no open cheque book but he bought carefully, led by example on and off the pitch at Ewood Park, stood no nonsense, stayed loyal to those who gave him everything and was comfortable and popular with the press and

fans. His start however was rocky. He did not have an initial clean out but the following left the club. John Bailey, a most promising left back, was the only one to bring in some money, sold to Everton for around £300,000. Waddington moved to Bury, John Radford into non-league football, John Aston retired and Alan Birchenall moved on to Luton Town. In return, Kendall initially brought in just one new player, Jim Arnold, an experienced goalkeeper from Stafford Rangers, who immediately replaced Butcher.

He bought Jim Branagan mid-season from Huddersfield Town, a right back with debatable ball skills but whose tackles regularly left opposition wingers on the floor. Andy Crawford was bought from Derby County for £50,000 to partner Garner, an attacking force which terrorised defenders and McKenzie was also amongst the goals. He sauntered through games, brought class to everything he did and his individual goal against Gillingham ranks with the finest I have ever seen.

After ten games, they dropped into the bottom half of the table then slowly but surely, Kendall's influence and experience on the field began to rub off on the others. He was passion, determination, ruthless in the tackle, an inspiring leader and quality on the ball. With a settled side, the performances improved and positive results flowed in with nineteen wins in the last twenty-eight games. Statistically it was a strange year. Twelve away wins is rare but it compensated for the five defeats and five draws at home.

It was the strength of the defence however which piled up the points. Only thirty-six goals were conceded, the back four bringing stability, understanding and consistency with Fazackerley once again outstanding, as the leaders were hunted down. I was at the penultimate game of the season at Gigg Lane where a Crawford double defeated Bury 2-1. The Rovers were back in Division 2.

The Blackburn Rovers Division 3 Promotion winning side 1979-80 (started over 25 games, max 46) was; Jim Arnold, Jim Branagan, Mick Rathbone, Howard Kendall, Glenn Keeley, Derek Fazackerley, Noel Brotherston, Duncan McKenzie, Tony Parkes, Simon Garner, Andy Crawford.

It was a non-league double for the Rovers as they comfortably strolled through to Round 3 of the FA Cup following wins over Kidderminster Harriers and Stafford Rangers. Two further wins over Fulham and Coventry City with Andy Crawford having scored in every round, qualified them for Round 5; exciting for a Division 3 outfit. It was Aston Villa at home but frustratingly I was on a Skiing Trip to Andorra with three other members of staff and forty pupils, the match scheduled for the day we were due back in Darwen. The coach driver reckoned we could catch an earlier ferry out of Calais and be back in Blackburn for the kick-off. He really hammered the coach on the quiet French motorways and I rang Alan Bradshaw, then on the coaching staff at Ewood, from a motorway café to order several tickets. We just made the kick-off and a crowd of almost 30,000 roared the Rovers on.

With the help of an Alan Evans own goal, the Villa were held to a 1-1 draw and I was at Villa Park for the replay. There the Rovers lost 1-0 but won many friends for their valiant effort. Following a comfortable two-legged victory over Bury in Round 1 of the Football League Cup, they drew 1-1 in the first leg of Round 2 against Nottingham Forest. But the reigning champs really turned it on at the City Ground, a 6-1 score line showing the gulf in class between sides two Divisions apart.

1980-81

Team	Pos	Played	Won	Drawn	Lost	GF	GA	Pts
Blackburn Rovers	4	42	16	18	8	42	29	50
Burnley	8	46	18	14	14	60	48	50

Blackburn Rovers		Burnley	
Most Appearances	Jim Branagan, Glenn Keeley (both 42)	Most Appearances	Martin Dobson, Billy Hamilton (both 46)
Most Goals	Kevin Stonehouse 10	Most Goals	Steve Taylor 16

The Burnley fans felt that promotion would be instant and after a stuttering start, a nine-game unbeaten run took them into the promotion zone. There were several disappointing results, but as Christmas approached, Burnley still occupied third place. There were more defeats in the second half of the season and a lack of consistency meant that they finished in eighth place, nine points from promotion.

Billy Ingham, popular with the fans, compiled a total of 181 league starts and he had left for Bradford City at the start of the season. Even more worrying was the sale of Leighton James at the same time to Swansea City for £130,000. He correctly did not consider himself to be a 3rd Division player. Jim Thompson, that solid defender, had been at the club since 1968 and 297 appearances later; it was time for the club to release him.

The season's leading scorer Steve Taylor, arrived from Mansfield Town and the Northern Ireland international Tommy Cassidy from Newcastle United added maturity to the side. Cassidy was honoured four times by his country and he was at the World Cup, but he only once came on as a substitute in the magnificent win over Spain. He and Eric Potts from Preston each cost £30,000, full back Dave Holt was signed from Oldham Athletic, but the line-up changed regularly as Miller tried to find a winning formula, only Dobson and Billy Hamilton [pictured] starting every game. Two youngsters emerged. Brian Laws had an excellent season at full back and Vince Overson had settled in at centre half, playing alongside Derek Scott for much of the campaign.

Wrexham were comfortably defeated in Round 1 of the Football League Cup before West Ham United proved too good, winning 2-0 and then 4-0 in the second leg. They failed to reach Round 3 in the FA Cup, losing in disappointing fashion to Port Vale after a replay following the defeat of Scarborough in the opening round.

The season following promotion for Blackburn Rovers was almost as triumphal and Howard Kendall's side set two club records. Never before had a Rovers' side drawn as many as eighteen games and the twenty-nine goals conceded (0.69 goals per game) was the lowest ever. Stuart Metcalfe moved to Carlisle United in the 1980 close season. Over twelve seasons, the locally born mid-field player had amassed 376 first team appearances in the Football League, giving him an appearance ranking of eighth place amongst the all-time Blackburn Rovers' elite.

Mick Speight from Sheffield United was his replacement. Metcalfe and Tony Parkes had been the Rovers' engine room, and Parkes was also reaching the end of a magnificent career which came to an abrupt end following a nasty leg break. He had made 345 appearances (tenth in the all-time list) and scored thirty-eight goals. Duncan McKenzie was off to Tulsa Roughnecks and Kevin Stonehouse was the surprise leading scorer. After a perfect start, from mid-October the wheels came off the wagon as one win and two draws were the only reward from ten consecutive matches.

The back four plus Arnold in goal and Kendall controlling midfield remained steadfast, shoring up the second most miserly defence in the four Divisions. There were two losses in the final twenty-four games, but fourteen draws. If just one goal had been scored in the nine no-score draws, they would have gained promotion, but Swansea had a plus seven better goal difference, the margin between going up and staying in Division 2. It had been a great effort by Kendall. As they say, he "got the best out of" a limited group of players, making them virtually impregnable defensively but lacking that touch of quality in the final third of the pitch. But then having almost achieved two promotions in two years, he was a dead ringer to be poached. Everton had just sacked Gordon Lee. The Goodison Park club was where Howard had played his best football and when they knocked on his door, no Division 2 manager was going to refuse them and sure enough he was off to Everton.

They reached Round 3 of the Football League Cup by beating both Huddersfield Town and Gillingham by the tiniest of margins, the former on the away goals rule. Birmingham City at St Andrews was a difficult task for Kendall's side and Jim Smith's mid-table Division 1 outfit edged the game 1-0. The FA Cup also produced a tricky tie, this time in Round 3 and it was a rapid exit, 2-1 at Notts County on their way to pipping the Rovers for promotion.

1981-82

Team	Pos	Played	Won	Drawn	Lost	GF	GA	Pts
Blackburn Rovers	10	42	16	11	15	47	43	59
Burnley	1	46	21	17	8	66	45	80

Blackburn Rovers		Burnley	
Most Appearances	Ian Miller 42	Most Appearances	Alan Stevenson 46
Most Goals	Simon Garner 14	Most Goals	Billy Hamilton 11

The 1981-82 campaign was one of mixed emotions for Burnley FC with a stupendous high of promotion and a shocking low; the death of Bob Lord, possibly the most influential figure ever to be associated with the club. Ironically there had been a feeling in the town that the Chairman was beginning to hold back the progress of the team and the local media at times made this point rather forcibly. There was no doubt that the professional game had changed out of all recognition whilst Mr Lord held office and his autocratic manner was something at odds with life in general in the Eighties.

He had been Chairman for twenty-six years, the majority being during those magnificently successful seasons when the club from the smallest town in the top level of English football went head to head with the great clubs of the land, punching massively above their weight. It is difficult to research which club introduced the concept of a youth policy, it could have been Burnley, it could have been Manchester United, but so successful was the Turf Moor variant that the club became totally dependent on the progression from Gawthorpe to Turf Moor... and how successful it was.

For this, Lord deserves much praise and there is no doubt that he was as equally successful at punching above his weight. A self-made man who never lost his Lancashire accent, he took on the high and the mighty, the Lords and Gentlemen of the FA and Football League, many of them "toffs" from public school backgrounds. Rightly or wrongly, he was in general against progress in the game (the abolition of the maximum wage, televised games and paid referees). There was no doubt that there was something of the dinosaur in him and we naturally detested him in Blackburn, a feeling sadly based on envy and jealousy because his methods worked and Burnley was a top club. We referred to him as "Lord Bob". It was supposed to be insulting but looking back it must have come across as quite complimentary. But secretly, he was suffering towards the end. He sold his shares to a consortium headed by John Jackson and Dr Iven in September and by December he had passed away, just another cancer victim.

I remember him as a friend of Schools' Football, always willing to loan out Turf Moor to the Burnley Schools for their finals and also for Lancashire Schools' FA county fixtures. I remember being entertained in the Board Room along with other officers of the County SFA after a game v Yorkshire on the "Turf". The great man had been at a football meeting in London but was expected back

at the ground later in the evening and the staff constantly asked each other for news of his whereabouts. Nervousness could be detected in their questions because the Chairman respected those involved in schools' football and they had to be royally treated....or else. Widely respected in the game, an outsider better known than many an insider, he was Burnley through and through and will never be forgotten.

I was once on the wrong end of his "Neanderthal" behaviour. My teaching career had briefly plateaued out and I had a yearning to be employed in the football industry in the mid-seventies. Still single but with a steady girlfriend, I applied for a job as an assistant to Jim Kenyon, the Secretary of the Lancashire FA. I was granted an interview and to my surprise, the chair of the panel was none other than Mr Lord. In practice he was the interviewing panel and everything went well until out of the blue, he asked me if I was married. "No," I replied to which he asked me if I was "a queer fellow". Now how do you deal with a question like that? Nowadays I would have been able to hold the LFA to ransom, taking them to the cleaners in a court of law, but in those days it was different. Bob Lord ruled the roost in local football then and he could do what he wanted. I stumbled through the rest of the questions and was eventually informed that I would not be required. In the end however, everything worked out well. I returned to school, and when I informed the Head Teacher that I would not be leaving, he was extremely pleased, saying he did not want to lose me. Not long afterwards, I was offered a promotion and I could then laugh about the time that "Lord Bob" questioned my sexuality.

Jim Thomson made several comments about the Chairman.

"When I was at Chelsea, I had never heard of Bob Lord. But when I arrived at the club, I realised just how powerful a man he was. Everyone in the game seem scared of him. They used to say that Martin Edwards, the top man at Manchester United, watched what he said to him. When Tony Morley signed from Preston, he came with long hair so the Chairman called him in and told him he wouldn't play until he had it cut. The next day he turned up with a 'Yul Brynner', completely bald. Nobody at that time had a skin head and when Mr Lord found out, he called Tony up to his office straight away. I believe he gave him a right roasting. Tony was great fun in the changing room but he had pushed his luck too far this time.

> In my last season, I had some time to run on my contract but I knew it was time to be thinking about moving on because I wasn't part of Brian Miller's plans. but the Chairman beat me to it. I was called in and told there was nothing for me there now so I had better think about leaving. I knew he was right but I didn't like the way he had told me, so as soon as my contract was up, I retired from the game."

The start of the campaign was dreadful with just two wins in the first thirteen games. There was little transfer action either in or out. Billy Rodaway moved to Peterborough which ought to have signalled the need for defenders, but Miller was confident enough to rely on the youngsters, ex-Lancashire Schools' players and local boys such as Michael Phelan from Nelson and Andy Wharton from Rossendale. It was a policy that worked this time. Positioned in the relegation zone, and with December being decimated by bad weather, they would stay dangerously close to it until early January. The crowds were pitifully low, the first gate to top 4,000 being the 2-2 draw against table topping Fulham in the sixth home match at the "Turf". Then out of the blue came an unbeaten run of twenty games which pushed them well into the top half of the league and the Turf Moor crowd rose above the 5,000 mark. They were in raptures when Bristol Rovers were hammered 4-0. They drew in the vital fixture at Fulham and draws were a feature of this successful season, seventeen in total, more than twice the number of defeats.

A final seven-match unbeaten stint brought the season to an end, a Hamilton double providing the goals in a 2-0 home victory over Preston North End. At last the town took notice of this resurgence, 13,911 attending the PNE game and with promotion secured; a draw at home to Chesterfield in front of 18,711 would make them champions, Kevin Young's second half equaliser bringing the silverware to Turf Moor along with promotion back to Division 2. It had been a magnificent performance and one richly deserved for a most under stated, reliable and loyal manager; one of Burnley's favourite sons and for the fans, there was also the prospect of two more derby matches to look forward to in the following season.

The Burnley Division 3 Title winning side 1981-82 (started over 18 games, max 46) was; Alan Stevenson, Brian Laws, David Holt, Derek Scott, Michael Phelan, Martin Dobson, Steve Taylor, Billy Hamilton, Tommy Cassidy, Kevin Young, Vince Overson, Stuart Robertson, Andy Wharton, Paul McGhee

Given a fortunate draw in the FA Cup, they twice scrambled through after replays against Runcorn and Bury. It could have been Liverpool in Round 3, but the gods continued to smile on them as Altrincham came out of the bag. It was just the cannon fodder they needed, smashing six past the non-league side's defence. Hamilton hitting three. An away tie at struggling Division 2 club Shrewsbury Town was an opportunity missed, the Shropshire side winning with the only goal of this Round 4 tie. The first leg of the Football League Cup against Tranmere Rovers on the Wirral was a real roller coaster of a game, the Birken-

head side taking a 4-2 lead to East Lancashire for the second leg. This game was equally thrilling and the two sides shared six goals, but it was the Division 4 side which progressed to the Second Round on the back of a 7-5 aggregate win.

Blackburn Rovers decided to dip into the lower divisions again and brought Bobby Saxton from Plymouth Argyle. He was a different breed of manager altogether. Somewhat taciturn and lacking the communication skills of Kendall, he nonetheless proved popular with the players. But the departure of Kendall not only robbed them of a manager but also a still extremely competent midfield player; a natural organiser on the pitch. He also took Jim Arnold with him to Everton, but Saxton bought Terry Gennoe from Southampton for £60,000 to replace him and also paid the same amount of money for Ian Miller, a quick and very traditional right winger from Swindon Town. A run of three consecutive wins in September and then a five-game unbeaten spell in October raised the hopes of the fans, but scoring goals remained a problem. Then from nowhere came a consistent run, six wins, a draw and a defeat saw them fly up the table, promotion being a faint but still possible dream.

Queens Park Rangers, a genuine top three contender, and Crystal Palace were both beaten in Blackburn and the Rovers hit Derby County for four. But as inevitably happens, the final run in was a massive let down. Just one win in the last nine games resulted in a final position of tenth, some twenty-two points away from third place in the first season that three points were given for a win. Garner and Stonehouse scored more than 50% of the goals and AFC Bournemouth paid £40,000 for Andy Crawford.

Garner was becoming a crowd favourite, his powerful runs and ability to score with either foot lifting many a grey day. Noel Brotherston also thrilled the crowd with his delicate skills and precise technique. His final tally of Northern Irish international caps was twenty seven and he appeared as a substitute in three of their 1982 World Cup games. Sadly the Rovers could only be classed as a very ordinary mid-table side; a slap in the face for a defence which deserved more. Gennoe had proved to be an excellent buy and the Branagan, Keeley, Fazackerley and Mick Rathbone [pictured] back four was as good as anything in the Division. Between them, they missed only seven games.

The FA Cup brought a 3-2 defeat at West Brom in Round 3, a brave effort against Division 1 opposition and in the Football League Cup, they were exempt until Round 2. Bobby Saxton's side squeezed past Sheffield Wednesday 2-1 on aggregate before once more drawing Nottingham Forest in Round 3. A crowd of 14,752 turned up at Ewood Park to watch quality players in the flesh, knowing that the Blue and Whites would raise their game to make a match of it. This they did and although a tad disappointed with the 0-1 result, we walked back up the road to Darwen, satisfied with what we had seen against one of the country's best elevens.

My main motive in talking to so many people in and around football has been to find extra information about the derby games for this book.. However it quickly becomes apparent that although they may have been top players, they are basically human beings, the same as all of us. They have the same hopes and ambitions, similar ups and downs, have families, have illnesses and grow old. I glean information about them which is so interesting, sometimes eye opening, exciting or sad, because inevitably, the conversation veers away from its original intention. One such conversation about Harry Potts made me smile and feel sad in equal measures and it must have been a bitter-sweet moment for the family. Philip Webster, his son in law, takes up the story.

> "Harry had two interests, football and family and he continued to work in the game after resigning for the second time at Burnley. He was never short of work because he had made so many friends, acquaintances and contacts at so many clubs. So he scouted for Chelsea amongst others for a while. I would drive him to games in his later years and in particular I remember taking him to Bradford City in the late eighties on numerous occasions to watch Stuart McCall, whom Chelsea and a number of other top clubs were chasing before he finally signed for Everton. But suddenly his health began to fail at a dramatic rate. Ultimately he had to be admitted to a Nursing Home in the Burnley area and of course we all visited him regularly. Eventually he struggled to recognise even the closest of his family which brought great sadness to his wife and daughter in particular, but when his grandson James visited with us, he would bring along one of those miniature footballs. They would go out of his room together, standing at either end of a long corridor. From that moment he would remember his grandson's name, would become animated and they would hit long passes to each other the length of the corridor. When they finished, he would return to the room and sometimes look with puzzlement at his visitors, no doubt wondering who we were. As difficult as it was at the time, we now look back fondly at the memory which summed up his twin passions so well."

1982-83

Team	Pos	Played	Won	Drawn	Lost	GF	GF	Pts
Blackburn Rovers	11	42	15	12	15	58	58	57
Burnley	21	42	12	8	22	56	66	44

Blackburn Rovers		**Burnley**	
Most Appearances	Mick Rathbone 42	Most Appearances	Mike Phelan 42
Most Goals	Simon Garner 22	Most Goals	Billy Hamilton 13

A League Cup semi-final berth, a place in the last eight of the FA Cup, an instant return to Division 3, a new manager and twice being "done" by that striker called Garner from down the road. It was certainly a crazy season at Turf Moor, one which did nothing to help fans with dodgy hearts or high blood pressure. Brian Miller was so pleased with his squad from the previous campaign that he publicly stated that he was not looking to strengthen, a massive vote of confidence if one that was to prove to be mis-placed. Billy Hamilton was quickly into his stride as the new season unfolded, on the score sheet three times as the Clarets took seven points from their first three games. But then everything went wrong.

One victory in ten games dropped them from fifth to twentieth. A home win against mid table Cambridge United when Steve Taylor scored twice was quickly forgotten as another seven games went by without a league win. Brian Flynn had been brought back to the club for £60,000 after five successful seasons at Leeds United and Willie Donachie, the veteran Manchester City left back who had been playing in America for Portland Timbers, made the long journey back to sign for the Turf Moor side. In sharp contrast to their extremely indifferent league form, Burnley had reached the last eight of the Football League Cup, but the Board, taking note of their position at the very bottom of the league, panicked and sacked Brian Miller. Assistant Manager Frank Casper took over but only in a caretaker role, the club continuing to keep it in the family.

As invariably happens, there was an immediate rebound effect and four wins and only one defeat in the next seven matches at least narrowed the gap between the club and safety. Taylor scored a hat-trick at home to Sheffield Wednesday and then came the farcical home fixture against Charlton Athletic. The "Addicks" finished with nine men, Taylor and Hamilton both notched hat-tricks and the 7-1 victory, such a rare score line in the modern game, gave hope all round. With eight games to play, they probably needed six wins to be safe.

Three wins and three draws were achieved, including a surprise 2-1 home win against Queens Park Rangers, late signing Terry Donovan from Aston Villa scoring both goals. Approaching the final game, there was still an escape route if they could win at Crystal Palace, thus sending the Eagles down. As it turned out, the South London side comfortably hung on for the last half hour after going in front and the Clarets were relegated.

In spite of the two derby wins, it was only an average season for Blackburn Rovers, eleventh in a twenty two team league. Bobby Saxton eventually filled the number 4 shirt, which had done the rounds since Howard Kendall's departure, by signing Colin Randell who had previously been managed by Saxton at Exeter City and Plymouth Argyle. Glenn Keeley missed a large chunk of the season as he became in dispute with the club, briefly being taken on loan by Kendall to

Rovers Simon Garner slots home a penalty during Blackburn's 2-1 victory at Ewood Park in April 1983

Everton. This gave a chance to a young David Mail who came to Ewood after being released by Aston Villa at the conclusion of his apprenticeship.

David Hamilton, released by Sunderland on a "free" became the utility player, operating in a variety of positions whenever the need arose. After a poor start, four defeats in five games which included a ridiculous 5-0 defeat at a struggling Grimsby Town, the Rovers became a competitive outfit, difficult to beat. The double was achieved over the soon to be promoted Leicester City and from November 6th until the end of the calendar year, they were unbeaten in nine games. Sadly four defeats in five games through March was the nail in the coffin with regard to a late promotion push. But most of all, this was Simon Garner's year. His return of twenty-two goals was the best by a Rover's player since Andy McEvoy's twenty nine in 1964-65. He knocked in doubles against Cambridge United, Chelsea, Carlisle United, Oldham Athletic, Crystal Palace and Burnley. His skills enabled him to hold up the ball in tight situations so that his teammates could play into his feet, but whenever a ball was played down the channels or simply over the top, excitement poured through our veins and the fans would erupt. Here his strength and speed were often too much for defenders and the resulting rocket shot tested the best of keepers. Why did he not move on to a Division 1 club? There was talk about his addiction to cigarettes and that he liked his beer, but I can honestly say that he never gave the impression of being anything but 100% sharp. Shearer apart (and not forgetting Tommy Briggs), he was the most exciting player I have ever seen in a blue and white halved shirt.

Terry Gennoe's penalty area goes up in smoke at Ewood Park in April 1983

The derby games

The Football League had once again scheduled the Christmas game and Easter Monday for the derby games, starting at Turf Moor. Burnley were bottom but one and had Billy O'Rourke deputising in the nets for Stevenson. The Rovers had last lost in late October and were on a seven game unbeaten run. Their side had an extremely settled look to it, with David Mail continuing to partner Fazackerley at the heart of the defence. The twenty thousand barrier was cracked once more as the supporters looked for post-Christmas entertainment. There was nothing between the sides on the day but Simon Garner scored on the half hour mark and the noose began to tighten round the Brian Miller's neck.

Frank Casper was in the hot seat as a paltry 13,434 spectators rolled up for the second derby game in Blackburn for the Easter Bank Holiday clash at Ewood Park. By this stage of the campaign, the Clarets were occupying bottom spot whereas their opponent was safely settled in mid-table. Scott and Stevenson returned to the side and John Lowey replaced Norman Bell as leader of the Rovers' attack. It was a black day both for Burnley and football in general. The simmering hatred between the two sets of supporters found an outlet and some Claret and Blue fans were a disgrace to the club, the town and themselves. Of course, they were repeatedly goaded by Blackburn fans and when the results had been going against you and too much alcohol was fuelling the emotions, the last thing you wanted to hear was incessant chanting of the "You're going down" variety. The response was predictable, the game was stopped for fifteen minutes and there were thirty-three arrests. On the field, the Rovers pulled away in the second half, Simon Garner scoring two penalties

The damage at Ewood Park in April 1983

and although Derek Scott reduced the deficit with a late goal, the Rovers had completed the double over their bitter rivals in what was to be the last derby for eighteen seasons. Garner only competed three times in derby games. Not his fault, that is the total number of games played against each other since he became a regular in 1979 until he left the club in 1992. He scored four goals in 270 minutes, 1.33 per match, a return which is up there with the very best of them. The results were not unexpected. This was not the worst ever Burnley side, but it was generally poor, although a win and a draw in these two games would have retained Division 2 status for them.

27 12 1982	Burnley	Blackburn Rovers	0-1	S Garner.
04 04 1983	Blackburn Rovers	Burnley	2-1	S Garner 2. D Scott.

The violent scenes witnessed at Ewood Park in the derby game were now par for the course. In fact you could say that this was the period of time when football violence ran amok. Derek Fazackerley played in both derby games this season and he commented thus.

> I suppose I was lucky in one sense in that I played at the back and was generally immune from the excessive verbal abuse handed out to the lads who played in the more prominent positions. If you played up front and were a regular goal scorer, you received all the praise and also the majority of the criticism if things

Derek Scott scores Burnley's consolation goal in a 2-1 reverse at Ewood Park in April 1983

were going against your side. It was easy for any opposition football supporter to insult Simon Garner, He was the one inflicting the damage on your team, but far more difficult for them to work out the contribution of a defender like myself. We were a far better side than Burnley this year. I was aware of the passion that this fixture generated, having played in them previously, but the behaviour of Burnley fans at Ewood was a disgrace. I was shocked when several of them climbed on to the roof of the Darwen End stand and started hurling down pieces of asbestos on to the pitch. The police struggled to contain it, but I think they learned a lot from this experience and were more prepared for events in the Stadium when the next matches were played.

Damian Hartley also has much to say on this matter.

It seemed that no matter which club the Clarets were playing, there was trouble at the ground. It always occurred on Brunshaw Road, usually after the game. It reached the state that we had to try and plot a route away from the Turf which would be free from violence. It certainly wasn't easy. In the Boxing Day game of 1982, a big fellow in a sheepskin jacket ran on the pitch and squared up to the Rovers' defender David Mail. He was quickly arrested by the police who followed him on. In those days there were no bans from the ground, although he went to court and was fined. At the very next home game against Sheffield Wednesday, I saw him walking up and down the Longside holding a box in front of him. Believe it or not, but he was asking for contributions to pay his fine and there were plenty willing to drop coins into it. Earlier that Boxing Day morning, several of us met up in the centre of Accrington prior to travelling to Burnley for the game. I was feeling pleased because my parents had bought me a Burgundy coloured leather jacket, exactly like the one Billy Hamilton wore to turn up to the game. I knew this because we always congregated outside the Players entrance to collect autographs and I collected his on a number of occasions. That was what devoted young fans did in that era and Billy was my current hero. As we stood talking close to the Bus Station, a large group of men walked towards us wearing Burnley scarves. They were no doubt "Accy Clarets" waiting to catch the bus to the ground. Moments later, as if it had been planned, a similar group wearing the blue and white Blackburn scarves also arrived. These were Rovers' supporters who lived in Accrington and were also waiting to catch a bus to Turf Moor. Within seconds they were all scrapping until the police arrived to sort it out. I quickly got out of the way because I didn't want any damage doing to my new jacket. Whether this was planned or just happened I'll never know, but it was typical of the time.

I was also at the return game at Ewood, in the Darwen end with the Burnley fans. After the Rovers went two-nil up, a group of our lot managed to climb on to the roof of the stand, kicked loose pieces of asbestos sheeting and started to hurl them down on to the field. After the game was stopped and the referee took the players off, Frank Casper appealed to the fans to behave themselves over the loudspeaker. He didn't really have any effect but eventually it all calmed down, possibly because the police retreated as so many fans had joined in. Then the ref re-started the game. Ever since then, Simon Garner, who scored all three of the Rovers' goals over the two matches, has been hated by a minority of Burnley fans.

Derek Scott scored the Burnley goal in the second game at Ewood Park.

"I was playing more and more in mid-field at this stage with Trevor Steven and Kevin Young because Brian Laws was doing well at right back and we had signed Willie Donachie to play at left back. We were struggling at this point in the league, but the game was fairly tight. Then the Rovers were awarded two penalties in the second half. One definitely was, the other definitely wasn't. Unfortunately they had Simon Garner on penalty duty and he could always find the back of the net. I think the dodgy penalty was what started the demolition job on the roof of the stand and the game became a shambles. We were taken off by the ref and even Frank Casper came on to ask them to behave themselves. Eventually they did and slowly we began to have more chances. With just a few minutes to go, there was a bit of a scramble in their penalty area and we had a couple of shots charged down before it came out to me and I knocked it past Terry Gennoe with my left foot.

Martin Dobson played in both derby games.

> "I don't remember any ill-feeling at the derby games between the two sets of players. Of course we played hard but we always respected our opponents. I played over 400 league games for Burnley but only two were against Blackburn Rovers. This is because we were a league or more above them for most of the time and then we were a league below for a couple of seasons. The problem this season was that we were winning all the wrong games. Our win at Tottenham in the League Cup when Billy Hamilton scored twice was one of the club's greatest wins and then in the semi-final, we actually beat Liverpool in the second leg at home. We also had a great FA Cup run, going all the way to the quarter final where we only lost in a replay, but we couldn't beat Rotherham, Grimsby and Cambridge or Blackburn Rovers twice. Brian Miller had been replaced by Frank Casper and although we were finally relegated, we all expected Frank to get the full time manager's job at the end of the season. We were all surprised when it was John Bond.

Blackburn Rovers were given the most difficult of draws in Round 3 of the FA Cup. Over twenty-one thousand spectators flooded into Ewood Park to watch Liverpool, the best team in the country, win 2-1. Garner of course was on target for the "Blues", but the crowd was happy to see the Rovers give of their best and make the Merseysiders work hard for their victory. Carlisle United were not the easiest of starts in Round 3 for Burnley, but after a 2-2 draw in Border Country, the Clarets won by a 3-1 margin. A 4th Round home tie brought exactly the same result against Swindon Town and the Clarets were expertly avoiding the big boys.

This time it was fellow Division 2 strugglers Crystal Palace in London and a late Steve Taylor winner in the replay saw them approaching the dizzy heights of Round 6. It was prominent Division 2 opposition this time, a promotion contender Sheffield Wednesday. Taylor missed a penalty but a second half Tommy Cassidy equaliser meant a replay back across the Pennines. After so many thrilling Cup displays, there had to be a "stinker" and Burnley reserved it for a March night at Hillsborough with an embarrassing 0-5 score line. It was the club's best run since the manager himself had played in the 2-0 semi-final defeat by Newcastle United in 1974.

Two legged Football League Cup ties can produce high aggregate scores and in the 1st Round this time round it was Bury, beaten 8-4 on aggregate by Burnley. The opposition in Round 2 was Middlesbrough, struggling themselves in Division 2. After the first leg at Turf Moor, the Clarets took a 3-2 score to Ayresome Park. There a Laws second half penalty, equalising an earlier Middlesbrough effort saw them into Round 3. Incapable of winning a league game, the Clarets stormed on in the Cup, triumphing 2-1 at Division 1 strugglers Coventry City. After being two up in Birmingham in Round 4, it looked like game over, but the "Brummies" stormed back to equalise before a fortuitous own goal gave Miller's boys a 3-2 victory. Even the loyal fans felt that an away trip to White

Hart Lane in the last eight would signal the end of the road, but with Casper in charge for the first time, the most unlikely of second halves ensued. Tottenham led 1-0 after forty-five minutes but Graham Roberts twice put through his own net and Hamilton with another double sealed a 4-1 victory; the shock result of the season. Liverpool in the two-legged semi-final was sadly a step too far as the Division 1 leaders swept to a 3-0 first leg lead. Burnley had only pride to play for in the second leg at Turf Moor, and the 22,228 crowd applauded them from the field after producing a battling 1-0 victory, Derek Scott scoring a memorable goal and others going close. Brentford were a decent Division 3 side and a 3-2 loss down at Griffin Park was not a disastrous result for Blackburn Rovers. The Bee's however defended stoutly at Ewood Park, there were no goals and the Rovers were out at the first time of asking. Cup football has a knack of producing unexpected results, but here was a Burnley team, not good enough to retain their place in Division 2, finding cup success only ever having been emulated by the finest of Burnley elevens in the League Cup. Football at times is both difficult to understand and explain.

1983-84

Team	Pos	Played	Won	Drawn	Lost	GF	GA	Pts
Blackburn Rovers	6	42	17	16	9	57	46	67
Burnley	12	46	16	14	16	76	61	62

Blackburn Rovers		Burnley	
Most Appearances	John Lowey, Simon Garner (both 42)	Most Appearances	Roger Hansbury, Billy Hamilton 46
Most Goals	Simon Garner19	Most Goals	Billy Hamilton 18

For the first time under Bobby Saxton, Blackburn Rovers became genuine promotion contenders. The South Yorkshire man had comfortably kept the club in Division 2 for two seasons, now it was time to aim higher. Bobby Saxton signed Chris Thompson, a centre forward from Bolton Wanderers and encouraged the promotion of youngsters to the first team squad, notably Simon Barker, a stylish and hard-working midfield player and the Darwen born Mark Patterson, a tricky left winger to whom I had the "privilege" of teaching CSE History. Goal keeper Terry Gennoe [pictured] gave so much confidence to the side and apart from injuries, one being a particularly nasty one to Mick Rathbone, we could all guess the composition of the side as we walked down to the ground.

There were some crazy results early doors. They defeated Derby County 5-1 at Ewood Park and Simon Garner scored all five. The following week they travelled to Maine Road and were hammered 6-0 by Manchester City. They then embarked on a twenty-one-game run with only one defeat. I visited an old College friend on Boxing Day and he took me along to watch the Blue and Whites at St James' Park, Newcastle. We were stood in the middle of the open Gallow-

gate end, keeping thousands of Geordies company, and when Simon Barker gave us the lead, I kept my mouth shut with great difficulty. Kevin Keegan and a young Chris Waddle helped to mount a "Toon Army" second half charge, but a 1-1 draw was certainly a satisfying result. With thirteen matches still to play, a strong run-in would have taken them close but five defeats and four draws resigned them to a sixth-place finish, thirteen points short of promotion. But in retrospect, as a group, they were not quite good enough to bridge the gap to the summit of the game.

There was a mini FA Cup run for the Rovers. The 1-0 win over Chelsea was a notable result, Noel Brotherston grabbing the goal. In Round 4 they came through 2-1 at Swindon Town. Southampton came out of the hat with them in Round 5, the Division 1 surprise packet. It was played under the Television cameras on a Friday evening in Blackburn and it was a tremendous game. Peter Shilton was in goal for the Saints and the Rovers certainly tested him but he stood firm, the Rovers being eliminated by a narrow 1-0 margin. They bowed out at Round 2 of the Football League Cup in the 83-84 season to Ipswich Town from Division 1. Both legs were competitive, but Ipswich finally triumphed 6-4 on aggregate, Garner scoring three times across the two games.

After a season which mixed stunning results in the two cup competitions with the despair of relegation to Division 3, the majority of Burnley supporters felt that Frank Casper deserved a full season, preferably with a permanent contract. But this was not Bob Lord's club anymore and for all his faults, a lack of loyalty was not one of them. And so the John Jackson led Board kicked Frank Casper down the road and brought in John Bond before the 1983-84 campaign began. Continuity of manager had always been Bob Lord's mantra but this was no longer the case. To appoint John Bond was so un-Burnley like. The previous six managerial appointments had all had strong links with the club. And they were all genuine Northerners with no bling and no bluster; certainly not Fancy Dans. Not for them the appearances on the "Panel of Experts" for televised games. Their idea of dealing with the media was talking to the Burnley Express, the Lancashire Evening Telegraph and Radio Lancashire. Bond was the exact opposite; a natty dresser, a favourite of the national media and recognisable on TV. He was a nationally known figure. An ex-West Ham United right back and late manager of Manchester City, he had built a reputation as a manager who could have an impact at a club but did not let the grass grow under his feet. Bond was known for turning clubs round but his tactic at the "Turf" was to off-load a number of popular players and replace them with well-known players from his previous club who were rapidly reaching their sell by date.

If Ewood Park was akin to a country station on a branch line in terms of players in and out, Turf Moor could be likened to a major rail terminus. There was so much movement of players and he was happy to sell the jewel in the crown, the nineteen-year-old Trevor Steven to Everton for £300,000. He also moved the consistent Brian Laws on to Huddersfield Town for £50,000 in a sale which seemed impossible to justify. He also let Lee Dixon go to Chester City. The full back, who became part of the legendary back four at Arsenal in Wenger's early years, had not quite broken through at Burnley but given time, he would have done so. Alan Stevenson had been allowed to transfer to Rotherham United.

He was yet another in the fine line of keepers who had graced the posts at Turf Moor, starting 434 league games, the fourth highest for a Burnley player. Another leaving the club after a successful spell was Steve Taylor who moved to Wigan Athletic. His thirty-seven in eighty-six was a most impressive goal to game ratio. Tommy Cassidy, approaching his mid-thirties, quit the English game to play for APOEL Nicosia in Cyprus. To replace them, he brought in veterans who had played at a much higher level, many with a Manchester City connection.

Tommy Hutchinson, the former Scottish World Cup winger came from Bulova in Hong Kong, centre forward Kevin Reeves, an England international and a £1 million man plus arrived from "City" and midfield hard man Gerry Gow from Rotherham United. All three had played in the 1981 FA Cup Final for Bond's "Sky Blues". Roger Hansbury, who had played under Bond at Norwich City, moved in from Eastern AA in Hong Kong. Later in the season came more astonishing buys. Malcolm Waldron, a centre back at Southampton, was signed for £70,000, Dennis Tueart, now in his mid-thirties who played at Maine Road for many years, arrived from Stoke City and Steve Daley, generally considered to be the worst ever £1million buy when he left the Wolves for the blue half of Manchester, arrived from Seattle Sounders. Kevin Reeves from Manchester City was the one who immediately sparkled as he and Billy Hamilton clicked straight away as an attacking partnership.

With Brian Flynn providing the spark in midfield, they were hovering around seventh place as they approached the run-in, promotion still a possibility. But Reeves failed to recover from a hip injury, retiring from professional football at the age of twenty-six. Then Martin Dobson was allowed to join Bury as Player Manager. He had made 410 starts for the Clarets in two stints (seventh on the all-time list). It was no wonder that the performances dipped and of the last twelve games, only one was won. The final twelfth place finish was so disappointing and it was not a season to remember, but there would be worse.

In the FA Cup, Burnley managed to stumble their way to Round 3, having eventually shown their superiority over Hyde United and Chesterfield, after a replay. Hamilton scored a brace at the "Turf" making this at least a par performance for a Division 3 club. Oxford United were in the process of running away with Division 3 and so the goalless draw at Turf Moor was a good result for the Clarets. Hamilton scored an equaliser in the replay at the Manor Ground but a 70th minute strike saw the "U's" through 2-1. In the 1st Round of the Football

League Cup, Crewe Alexandra, from the depths of Division 4, posed all sorts of problems to the Clarets, winning 5-3 on aggregate with the 4-3 loss in the home leg such an embarrassment to the "Turfites".

1984-85

Team	Pos	Played	Won	Drawn	Lost	GF	GA	Pts
Blackburn Rovers	5	42	21	10	11	66	41	73
Burnley	21	46	11	13	22	60	73	46

Blackburn Rovers		Burnley	
Most Appearances	Mick Rathbone 42	Most Appearances	Wayne Biggins, Tommy Hutchinson (both 46)
Most Goals	Chris Thompson 15	Most Goals	Wayne Biggins 18

The poor displays at the end of the previous campaign meant another year in Division 2 for Blackburn Rovers, a season which turned out to be much better. The club again failed to make a major signing in the summer. There was a consistency of team selection, with Glenn Keeley back to his indominable best.

The players stayed loyal to the manager who, in turn, stuck with those he could depend on. Some would say he was too loyal, but it was a season of so many "what ifs" as the Board yet again failed to put its collective hands into pockets when surely the purchase of a quality midfield player to partner Barker would have sent them up. They would surely have recouped the money and much more besides if promotion had been achieved, but this was the pre-Jack Walker era when no-one in power at the club was prepared to speculate to accumulate. Goals were not particularly a problem, three strikers each hitting the double figure mark.

One was Jimmy Quinn, an Irish international bought from Swindon Town for £32,500 and capped thirteen times during his stint at Ewood Park. He was generally third choice after Thompson and Garner for the two striking roles. They made a flying start, losing only at Fulham in the first ten games. Another unbeaten run of eight games climaxed with a memorable 2-1 home win over Leeds United on Boxing Day in front of 20,150 spectators. Thus, at exactly the halfway mark, they led the field with 46 points; promotion was on the horizon. Unfortunately, as has happened at Ewood Park on too many occasions, it was impossible to hold on to this outstanding run of form. For a time they stayed in the title chase but a trio of defeats in the first three games in March saw them lose touch with the top two. They came again with another five-game unbeaten run, seemingly cementing third place, but three defeats to Crystal Palace, Charlton Athletic and Portsmouth shattered the dream. As a result, the Rovers finished fifth, one point behind Manchester City in third. Nowadays such a finish would guarantee a Play-Off spot, but this rule change was still several years down the line. An interesting fact at the end of the season was that ex-Blackburn Rovers managers were in charge of the Champions of Division 1 and 2; Kendall at Everton and Smith at Oxford United.

In the FA Cup, the Rovers defeated Portsmouth 2-1 after a replay, Quinn scoring both goals, Awaiting them in Round 4 was a visit to Oxford, Jim Smith and all. In what was arguably their best performance of the year, the Blackburn side edged through 1-0, Jimmy Quinn on target yet again. The 5th Round brought Manchester United to Blackburn. It was a night full of atmosphere in front of 22,692 spectators but as they said at the time, "class will out" and an Old Trafford side, containing a multitude of internationals, won 2-0. The "Bald Eagle", the affectionate nickname for Jim Smith, was a familiar figure in the opposing "dug out" to Bobby Saxton during the year. His Oxford United side and the Rovers clashed five times in three separate competitions, the first time in the two-legged Round 2 of the Football League Cup. Simon Garner scored in both legs, the first at Ewood Park where they shared a 1-1 draw. In the return encounter at the City Ground, Smith's outfit showed why they were up at the top of Division 2 with a 3-1 win.

There was arguably more action off the field at Turf Moor before the season began than on it during the ensuing forty-six games. It was all centred around John Bond. He had irritated the Board of Directors by missing several Burnley games at the conclusion of the previous season, ostensibly to scout talent for the following campaign. When he finally unveiled a clutch of new signings, not all the Board members were supportive. And then came the two biggest shocks. Billy Hamilton, a crowd favourite for four seasons and out of contract, moved to Oxford United. He had scored fifty-eight goals in exactly 200 league appearances, excellent figures considering he was playing in a side which was twice relegated. "Who will score the goals now" wailed the supporters. And then came the second source of bewilderment. Bond told the Directors that he was unhappy with a seeming lack of support in the Board Room and someone had to go. It was the manager, leaving five days before the opening game and to be replaced by his assistant John Benson. He had been Bond's number two at several clubs before joining him a Turf Moor. He had a good reputation as a coach but his less than successful season in Burnley added to the catalogue of failures when asked to be the number one man. At the end of the previous season, the likes of Gerry Gow, Steve Daley and Dennis Tueart were quickly offloaded along with Willie Donachie who had at least stayed for sixty games and a couple of seasons. In their places came Neil Grewcock, a winger signed from Shepshed Charterhouse, the ex-Blackburn Rover Kevin Hird (successful at Leeds

DEREK SCOTT BILLY RODAWAY

United) and Stoke City full back Peter Hampton. All would contribute positively to the forthcoming battle for survival in Division 3. Less prominent would be Alan Taylor, once an FA Cup winning star with West Ham United. Kevin Hird is probably the most unique of the players who have turned out in both Blue and White and Claret and Blue shirts, particularly those who made a major contribution to both clubs. Not only did he play for both, but he was also brought up as a supporter of one of them.

> "When I arrived at Leeds, we were challenging for honours under Jimmy Adamson, but slowly under Alan Clarke and Eddie Gray, we slipped down the league and ended up in the Second Division. After five seasons there, I was out of contract and Burnley were interested in me. They were a big pull being my local club and I was given a great welcome by the crowd. When I had been at Blackburn, I still lived in the Colne area but although there was some banter, I never had any trouble from the local fans and although I thought I might get some stick when I first came on at the "Turf" for my debut, having been an ex-Rovers' player, there was nothing of the sort. But it was a difficult time for the club. John Bond signed me and then he was off. John Benson lasted that season and we had both Martin Buchan and Tommy Cavanagh the next season. It was as if no-one at the club knew what they were doing, but we were players and we pressed on with it even though we were relegated. I was always picked when I was fit and I was hardly ever injured so they must have thought I did all right, but at the end of my contract when I fully expected to receive another one, no-one said anything. I became totally disillusioned and decided to pack it all in. So I got a part-time job and went to play non-league football and never got to play under Brian Miller who took over that summer."

The start to the season was perhaps not as disastrous as first thought. There were only two defeats in the first nine games, but five of them were drawn. But there were problems with the two last remaining players from the Division 1 days. Derek Scott broke his leg at Rotherham and Brian Flynn, clearly unhappy at the club, asked for a transfer and was sold to Cardiff City. He had made 193 league appearances, gained thirty-four Welsh international caps whilst at Burnley and was sadly too good for Division 4. From nowhere came a 7-0 home win over Rotherham United, Hird, playing in midfield, bagging a hat-trick. Wins then became difficult to find and going into the last three matches, Cambridge had been down for a while but Burnley were just one place above them.

Relegation rivals Swansea City were now managed by John Bond and there was much rejoicing when the Clarets beat them 1-0 at home, but the Swans survived and Burnley were faced with the prospect of life in the basement of English football, having finished in twenty first place. John Benson had tried his best, respected by the fans but it was apparent that he was not the man to bring about a renaissance. Probably realising that the Burnley Board was likely to fire him, he did the honourable thing and resigned.

Derek Scott finally said good-bye to Burnley. Bolton Wanderers were interested in him and they had retained their place in Division 3 whereas the Clarets had been relegated. He had started 277 league games, a real stalwart who had married the daughter of Brian Miller. This was becoming the Turf Moor royal family. He had been an England Schoolboy international, joined Burnley at sixteen and would go on to play three full seasons at Burnden Park. In his final season at Bolton, the club had been relegated and he found himself playing against Burnley. I asked him what this felt like.

> "It wasn't just playing against my old club, my father in law was managing them also. But Bolton were paying my wages, I was expected to be professional and I played as hard against them as if they had been any other side. We actually met five times in all. Twice in the Associate Members Cup, once in the FA Cup and twice in the league. We (Bolton) won four out of the five, losing one of the league games 2-1 at the Turf. I think Burnley were glad to get rid of me for one reason. It meant that they no longer had to pay me. The club was in a real financial mess. We expected to lose our best player every season because the transfer fee would keep us afloat for another twelve months. Brian Miller once told me that he wanted to sign the keeper Chris Pearce and mid-fielder Paul Comstive (both actually ex Blackburn players) from Wrexham and the combined fee would be £8,500. Even then, this was nothing but he had to contact the bank to check that it was ok to buy them; such was the state of the finances.

Derek told me that on finishing playing, he enrolled in the Police and so I asked him, half-jokingly, if he ever had to take action against any hooligan behaviour by Burnley fans,

> "I never had to at Turf Moor. I was on traffic for a long time and I did have to escort the team coaches into the ground. But on one occasion, I was called to a domestic incident which had become a stand-off between a father and son. There were several police there and they were waiting outside. When the main offender saw me turn up, he shouted to me to go in, recognising me because he was a Burnley fan. His attitude totally changed and we chatted for about ten minutes. I told him that we would have to arrest him and he held out his hands and I

cuffed him and we walked out to the car. People have often gone on to me about the perks of being a footballer but I never expected it to help me as a policeman,"

Burnley progressed reasonably well in the FA Cup. They could not have wished for an easier Round 1 draw. Penrith finished rock bottom of the North West Counties Division 1 and they were lambs to the slaughter at their own Stadium, Wayne Biggins and Alan Taylor both notching hat-tricks in a 9-0 massacre. Halifax Town held the Clarets to 1-1 at half-time in Round 2 at the Turf, but goals from Devine and Biggins saw them through to the "Round of the Big Boys". Just ten years previously, non-league Wimbledon had shocked the football world by winning 1-0 at Turf Moor but in a role reversal situation, the Clarets were the underdogs when they travelled to Plough Lane. Could history repeat itself and the under dogs win?

Not on this occasion as "The Dons" cruised into a 3-0 lead with Peter Devine's 89th minute strike reducing the arrears. In the Football League Cup, Benson's side managed to edge through 4-2 on aggregate against Crewe, at least partially erasing the memories of the previous year's fiasco. From playing one of football's traditionally poor clubs, it was a "two-legger" against the super-rich in Round 2 and the Reds from Manchester smashed in four at Old Trafford and three at Turf Moor with never a hint of a reply from the boys in Claret and Blue. If the fans did not realise it before, this was a reminder of the reality of football. There were the haves and the have nots and Burnley were indubitably in the second category.

The attendances must have been a huge cause of concern at this time. With football violence regularly hitting the headlines (although it was a rarity at Ewood), there was a reluctance to put yourself at risk, particularly if you wished to take young children to the game. To avoid pitch invasions, clubs had constructed metal fencing and the vast majority of stadia had far more standing than sitting areas. Peering through the fencing gave a prison like atmosphere and as a result, the crowd consisted mainly of men. Just as well because the toilet facilities were Victorian and the food and drink outlets were scarce.

To put it simply, the venues were unattractive and did not encourage anyone but the diehards. Even so, it was incomprehensible that Blackburn Rovers, a club ranked twenty eighth in the country at the end of a fairly successful season, could only average 7,619 supporters per game. It must also be remembered that in the league with them were big city sides, renowned for their massive travelling support. Clubs such as Newcastle United, Sheffield Wednesday, Manchester City and Leeds United boosted the gates, but at times they were pitiful. The attendance at the final home game of the season, when Cardiff City visited in 1984, was 3,107.

Over at Turf Moor, apart from the 12,690 crowd for the Manchester United game, the highest gate was the cross-Pennine derby with Bradford City, exactly 7,000 in attendance but only 2,843 could be bothered to turn up to watch them beat Cambridge United in mid-April 1985.

Jack takes over at Ewood, but for Burnley, it's almost the end, 1985 – 1992

The sun is slowly sinking
The day is almost gone
Still darkness falls around us
And we must journey on
The darkest hour is just before dawn
Written by Ralph Stanley
Recorded by Emmylou Harris :1980

For virtually a century, there had only been two seasons when a gap of two Divisions separated Blackburn Rovers and Burnley. These had been the 1973-74 and 1974-75 campaigns when the Blackburn side competed in Division 3 and the Clarets "mixed it" with the elite in Division 1. Now, in a complete turnaround, The Turf Moor fans could only gaze upwards with hope that the two Division gap would be hastily reduced.

The story line being woven throughout this seven year period was the battle being waged at Turf Moor to right a ship which had been badly holed following those most majestic days of the fifties, sixties and seventies. They could accept that they were no longer able to comfortably compete with the best in the land, but competing with the dregs of football society (with apologies to those fine small clubs who annually struggle to survive) week in, week out was too much to bear. And when 15,696 brave souls ventured on to the "Turf" on May 9th, 1987, it was probably to say their last goodbyes. If ever there was a darkest hour, this was it, but would the club still be there to witness tomorrow's dawn spreading across the sky. All their hopes and dreams were wrapped up into one final 90 minutes; one last throw of the dice.

1985-86

Team	Pos	Played	Won	Drawn	Lost	GF	GA	Pts
Blackburn Rovers	19	42	12	13	17	53	62	49
Burnley	14	46	16	11	19	60	65	59

Blackburn Rovers		Burnley	
Most Appearances	Mick Rathbone 42	Most Appearances	Ray Deakin 46
Most Goals	Simon Garner 12	Most Goals	Alan Taylor 16

Generally speaking, five years is the maximum length of time that a side stays together and, if you compare Bobby Saxton's 1981-82 regular starting eleven to this one five years on, only Simon Barker [pictured] and Jimmy Quinn were new faces.

And nothing changed this term. Only midfielder Colin Randell moved on to Swansea City. And that was the way it stayed throughout the forty-two league games, with just seventeen players starting the games. The only competition for places were between Patterson and Brotherston at outside left and Quinn and Thompson for the number nine shirt. Results tell their own narrative and they were saying that Bobby's boys had reached their sell by date.

Being loyal, being consistent in selection works for so long, but improvements need to be made. Predictably however they did not happen although results initially were very much in their favour. I remember being there on a damp and dismal October day when our son Simon saw his first professional match. They beat Fulham 1-0 and we sat high up in the old Nuttall Street stand, Simon, myself and 5,241 other spectators. When you consider that thirty one years before, I had seen my first game on the same ground and in the same Division in front of 45,521 fans, there could be no doubt that professional football was massively in need of a make-over in the seventies and eighties.

From the end of October however when the Rovers topped the Division 2 table, there was a complete loss of form. The relegation warning lights were flashing, but part way through this dismal run, Derek Fazackerley broke Ronnie Clayton's record for most league appearances by a Rovers' player. The away fixture at Fulham resulted in a 3-3 draw and it was "Faz's" 580th start for the club. Unexpectedly on the weekend after Easter, Sheffield United were taken to the cleaners at Ewood Park. Patterson knocked in a hat-trick as they wrapped up a 6-1 victory. Safety was still not a certainty but after a convincing 3-1 home win over Grimsby Town on the season's final day, they were three points clear of Carlisle United in nineteenth position, living to fight another season two leagues above the arch enemy.

The draw for the FA Cup was certainly unkind to them, pairing them with Division 1 stalwarts Nottingham Forest at the City Ground in Round 3, they drew 1-1. Paul Cox gives a colourful and philosophical account of the replay.

> "As the seventies passed to the eighties, I managed to get myself to my first Rovers game; not my first ever match as my dad had previously taken me to the Baseball Ground. But my first Rovers game was an evening midweek encounter in 1986; Rovers v Nottingham Forest in the FA Cup. What an evening! It absolutely took everything away from me. It was almost as if I'd been hypnotised. The noise, the lights blazing out of the dark evening sky, the cold air; all of it was more than enough for me to become immediately engrossed in the life that is supporting Blackburn Rovers. Needless to say, we played amazingly, beating one of the top First Division teams 3-2 but then, in typical Rovers style, lost the next round to Everton (if my memory serves me right). Following the Rovers has led me to one of my biggest beliefs; one that has had such a serious impact on my life. It is that nothing is guaranteed for you. It is a tough world with few breaks."

And what a way for him to commence a lifetime obsession to the cause, but having the naivete of youth, Paul obviously expected the Rovers to perform at the same level on Merseyside. For those more hardened however to the knocks and set-backs that following a team can bring, the 3-1 defeat was as expected. The result against the Forest was atypical, but the performance in the Football League Cup was certainly not. A 5-0 crushing at Plough Lane by the soon to be promoted Wimbledon gave them no chance in the second leg. Patterson and Quinn were on the score sheet, but it was a 6-2 aggregate Round 2 defeat.

A regular result of relegation is the exit of some of the better players and the 1985-86 season was no exception at Turf Moor. Goalkeeper Roger Hansbury had left for Cambridge United, Tommy Hutchinson, feeling let down because Martin Buchan and not himself was given the Manager's job, joined up with John Bond again at Swansea City. Buchan had been a Scottish international defender who had impressed so many on the field in two World Cups, at Aberdeen, Manchester United and latterly at Oldham Athletic. His intelligent reading of the game hinted at his managerial capabilities but he had never managed and so this was a bold gamble by the club. Mike Phelan was sold to Norwich City for £60,000 and Derek Scott was now at Bolton Wanderers.

There were transferred players coming in the other way. Woefully short of defenders, Ray Deakin arrived from Bolton Wanderers as make weight in the Scott deal, Jim Heggarty was picked up from Brighton and Hove Albion and Phil Malley, a midfield player from Hartlepool United. To replace Hansbury, Buchan brought in Joe Neenan from Scunthorpe United. For the older Claret fans, used to seeing the best in the land performing at Turf Moor, Division 4 was a shock to the system. Virtually none of the clubs could be classed as an attraction, the only exception perhaps being Preston North End, but this was a club in deep financial meltdown. As a result, the crowds were pitifully low, ranging from a

4,279 gate in the season's opening 3-2 win over Northampton Town, to 1.988 to welcome Crewe Alexandria for the final home game of the campaign.

The start was acceptable with Burnley installed in the top seven, but after failing to score in three successive games, Martin Buchan suddenly (and sensationally) resigned. He was extremely honest, admitting after eleven league and two cup games that the role of manager was not for him. Tommy Cavanagh, his successor, was fifty-seven when he accepted what was actually his first managerial appointment. He had however been in the game a long time and had spent thirteen years as part of the training and coaching staff at Old Trafford, having been Tommy Docherty's assistant. Buchan brought him to Turf Moor as his Assistant Manager and he was given the task of saving the Claret and Blue's season, not an easy task when the club was massively in debt, losing more and more money each month and after just one game in the job, he lost his top goal scorer Wayne Biggins to Norwich City for £35,000 as the Board attempted to avert the slide to bankruptcy.

The club managed to stay clear of relegation without ever looking likely to challenge for promotion, but this was a season which was more about the financial problems and managerial crises than the on-pitch performances. In actual fact, a top eight finish was on the cards but one win in the last eight games ensured a fourteenth-place finish, the eighty second best club in the country. Bob Lord must have turned in his grave!

And the Cup competitions were equally degrading. In the FA version, they scraped home 3-2 at non-league Nuneaton before being thumped at home 4-1 by Rotherham United. It had been even worse in the Football League Cup against Bury. The Clarets nicked it 2-1 in the first leg at Turf Moor and a Taylor double and one from Hird was a tremendous effort at Gigg Lane. However, the defence was haemorrhaging goals, five to be precise and the aggregate loss was 6-5.

1986-87

Team	Pos	Played	Won	Drawn	Lost	GF	GA	Pts
Blackburn Rovers	12	42	15	10	17	45	55	55
Burnley	22	46	12	13	21	53	74	49

Blackburn Rovers		Burnley	
Most Appearances	Simon Barker 42	Most Appearances	Ray Deakin 46
Most Goals	Simon Barker 11	Most Goals	Leighton James 10

Changes had to be made in the following season and 1986-87 saw the end of an era at Blackburn Rovers. Automatic names on the team sheet were often missing, whether because of injury or age catching up with them. Bobby Saxton released Chris Thompson and John Lowey to Wigan Athletic. The ex-Bolton player had scored twenty-four times in eighty-one starts and the cultured midfield player had made 136 starts in a five year stay. Chris Price arrived from

Hereford United for £25,000. He was a favourite with the crowd who loved to see him dart forward from a right back position, causing all sorts of problems to the opposition. Another favourite was Scott Sellars, a delightfully neat and talented left sided player. He had shone at Leeds United and it was quite a coup for Saxton to secure his signature. But Terry Gennoe had suffered from injuries and illness, so Vince O'Keefe, his long-standing deputy, grabbed this opportunity to play regularly. Jim Branagan had lost the number 2 shirt to Price, but he managed to start most of the games, slotting in wherever there was a gap.

Time is the enemy of all footballers and Derek Fazackerley's career ground slowly to a halt this season. His 593 starts, commencing with a 0-0 draw at Hull City in the immemorable Division 2 relegation season of 1970-71, may never be beaten, but those who watched him during his seventeen year career will remember him for his consistency, his strength, his pace, sharpness of tackle and ability in the air. Above all, his loyalty to the club and the town shone through in everything he did. In the mid-eighties, I organised a ten-week coaching course for promising twelve-year-old schoolboy footballers in the town, one night a week after school.

Derek was the coach, giving his services for free and although quite humble and respectful to the "kids", you could see within him, a drive and determination to stay in the game after retirement. He left Blackburn part way through the season, joining Chester City as Player/Assistant Manager, the first step in a long coaching career, the pinnacle being Assistant to England Manager Kevin Keegan. David Mail, who had been defensive understudy since 1982, became first choice in the number six shirt. I spoke to Faz about those final few months at the club and his memories looking back.

> I was in and out of the side the season I left, and I was fully aware that my time at the only club I had played for was coming to an end at the age of thirty-five. David Mail and Glenn Keeley were Bob Saxton's preferred choice at centre-back, but he was extremely good to me. He asked me what I wanted to do when I left the club and I told him I wanted to stay in the game, ultimately in a coaching capacity. He said that he would look out for any opportunities and let me know straight away if he heard anything. I had played under a number of Managers whom I respected and also thought did a brilliant job in my time at Ewood. Certainly Bob has to be near the top of that list. How he kept us in the hunt for promotion with an incredibly low budget, I don't know. There were a number of bigger and far wealthier clubs who played in Division 2 during my time and we managed to compete with all of them. These included Sunderland, West Bromwich Albion, Chelsea, Tottenham Hotspur, West Ham United, Newcastle United, Sheffield Wednesday, Wolverhampton Wanderers, Manchester City and Leeds United. Each of them attracted massive gates in contrast to ours and they could afford to throw lots of money at transfers and wages. It was never easy for Ken, Gordon, Jim Smith and Howard and they all worked extremely hard to keep the club moving forward, but Bob had the hardest task of them all and still kept the

club competitive. Eventually the sands of time had caught up with me, and the lack of money, and the inability to change the squad around much led to a disappointing season. It was a struggle near the bottom of the league rather than our usual position competing at the top and eventually the Board of Directors sacked Bob and on the same day, Chairman Bill Fox invited me into the wonderfully wood panelled boardroom and told me that I could go. I knew my time was up and there was an offer on the table for me to join Chester City as player-coach, but I do think it could have been handled better. Almost immediately I was on my way to Chester, saddened to leave my second home, but realising that this was football and I would have to put those last few days behind me.

The season started with a bang, three successive wins including a 6-1 thumping of Sunderland. Simon Garner was on target four times as the fans excitedly talked about promotion but talk about the wheels coming off the wagon. As Christmas loomed, the Rovers fell to the foot of the Division. This was relegation form with a vengeance and Bobby Saxton paid the price. It was his sixth season at Ewood Park and the Board had stayed loyal to him, respecting his work ethic and knowledge of the game, but relegation could not be contemplated and he was sacked over the festive period.

Bobby Saxton's playing career had been unspectacular, his management career had been unspectacular and no-one would use the word spectacular to describe his personality, character or behaviour. But talking to several ex-Rovers who played under him, it is clear that qualities of reliability, loyalty and honesty were there in abundance. His performances with such a low budget, not only retaining their place in that division for five and a half seasons, but also challenging for honours in two of them were remarkable.

Tony Parkes took over as Caretaker Manager and almost immediately there was an improvement in results and an eight-game unbeaten run pulled them well clear of relegation. And suddenly, there was a new Manager at the helm, the Scotsman Don Mackay. He quickly returned to Scotland and brought in Colin Hendry from Dundee and Chris Sulley from Dundee United. Hendry was originally signed as a centre forward before becoming a legend at both Blackburn and in Scotland as the "Braveheart" centre half.

Sulley was an experienced left back with five successful seasons at Bournemouth on his CV prior to his time at Tannadice. Jimmy Quinn returned to Swindon Town after fifty eight less than successful games at Ewood and Mackay built on Parkes' success, the club finishing twelfth; decently mid-table.

An away trip to Portsmouth proved enough to signal exit from the FA Cup in Round 3, losing 2-0. There was a victory in the Football League Cup, now sponsored by Littlewoods. After comfortably overcoming Wigan Athletic 5-1 on aggregate, Simon Barker scoring three of the goals, they went out to Queens Park Rangers 4-3, also on aggregate in Round 2. Having failed to make any impression on the two major trophies, Blackburn Rovers found success in the third rated competition as a run in the Full Members Cup materialised. It was

something of a "Mickey Mouse" affair, introduced to fill the gap left by the non-participation in European Competitions and open to all Division 1 and Division 2 clubs. It was such a low key event when it commenced in September and even with wins at Huddersfield Town and at home to Sheffield United, only 2,843 turned up for the Oxford United Round 3 game to witness a thrilling 4-3 victory. Over seven thousand were present for the quarter final encounter as Division 1 side Chelsea were well beaten 3-0 and with the public becoming used to Don Mackay's exhortations in the press and on Radio Lancashire, 12,060 came down to watch Division 2 Play-Off candidates Ipswich Town fold, Garner, Barker and Patterson all hitting the net without reply. It had come as a complete surprise to many, but the Rovers were returning to Wembley for the first time for twenty-seven years, Division 1 side Charlton providing the opposition. Because I had driven a mini bus full of ball boys down to the Stadium from Blackburn, schoolboys from the two competing towns being on duty on the day, my wife and I were allocated seats immediately behind the Royal Box, but it was something of a dour encounter. There was a 40,000 crowd but the majority were from East Lancashire, Charlton fans from the south side of London, being somewhat indifferent to the significance of the occasion. The Addicks contributed more to the attacking side of the game, but the Rovers defence held firm with O'Keefe and Keeley in particular in imperious form. With five minutes to play, Ian Miller rocketed down the right wing and knocked over a cross which kindly fell at the feet of Colin Hendry. The blonde striker proceeded to smash it into the back of the net and Blackburn Rovers and their fans drove north on this late March evening, accompanied by the trophy.

The Blackburn Rovers 1987 Full Members Cup Winning side that beat Charlton Athletic 1-0 at Wembley Stadium was; Vince O'Keefe, Chris Price, Chris Sulley, Simon Barker, Glenn Keeley, David Mail, Ian Miller, Alan Ainscow, Colin Hendry, Simon Garner, Jim Branagan. Substitute Mark Patterson.

The managerial merry-go-round continued at Burnley. Tommy Cavanagh had undergone hip surgery and the ensuing ill-health forced him to resign. Having suffered nothing but disasters with four "outsiders" in the manager's office, the Board turned once more to Brian Miller. He needed no introduction to the fans who knew he would give his all. When he was sacked three and a half years before, the club was in Division 2, but he immediately agreed to step in and save the club he had joined as an apprentice, thirty-four years before. As ever, it was a busy time for outgoing and incoming transfers and the Colne born Kevin Hird retired after a career which encompassed a long stint at Ewood Park and eighty-three appearances for the Turf Moor club. Northern Irishman Jim Heggarty and Peter Devine drifted into Non-League football whilst Alan Taylor followed a familiar path to Bury. Predictably, Leighton James returned for a third stint at the club, signing from Newport County in Division 3.

Another returnee was centre back Billy Rodaway from Tranmere Rovers who played the full season alongside Joe Gallagher at the centre of defence. Possibly his most intuitive signing was yet another thirty something. Scotsman Ian Britton, with stacks of experience at Chelsea and Blackpool, was brought in to play in midfield. Miller steered them into fifth place by the end of September but then it all unfolded. Going into the Festive period, four points improved matters, but the next victory was on March 13th, a 1-0 win over Stockport County with the Accrington born left winger Ashley Hoskin finding the target.

Twenty first was a precarious position to occupy and four more straight defeats saw them staring up at the other twenty-three clubs with one more game to play. There was of course much merriment in Blackburn and Darwen at Burnley's plight. The Rovers could boast about silverware (albeit the Full Members' Cup) whilst the enemy was fighting for its life, two Divisions below.

I taught with an avid Claret and Blue man and he was in despair; like so many others in the east of the county, he could not believe what was happening. Worse still, salvation was not in the hands of Miller's men. They had to beat Orient at Turf Moor on May 9th, but Lincoln City and Torquay United were two and one points respectively ahead. On the day of the game, 15,696 spectators turned up to help to save the day. The media also flooded the ground and there was full coverage on BBC Radio 2. Yet not all of the faithful could bring themselves to watch the game. Mike Duffy's comment ..... "I could not face going to Turf Moor for the Orient game, instead listening nervously on the radio" summed up the feelings of so many for whom following the Clarets was a religion. And there was also the possibility of thunderous support causing the team to freeze but it certainly worked for fifty-five minutes.

Neil Grewcock scored a fine solo goal on the stroke of half-time and no sooner had the crowd settled after the break when Ian Britton, probably the smallest man on the pitch, rose to head home from a Grewcock free kick. The crowd was in a frenzy but it all helped to spur on the Londoner's response. Within ten minutes Orient had pulled one back and those with transistor radios were passing on updated reports from the games of their rivals. Conceding one more goal would have sent them down and it became a game of shooting practice for the Londoners, but somehow Brian Miller's heroes hung in there. As the clock ticked down and the support grew and grew, news came in of a Lincoln defeat. Once the referee's whistle finally sounded, the crowd invaded the pitch and Burnley were safe once more. In the early evening I was driving through Clayton-le-Moors en route to the house of my fiancée when I saw a familiar bulky figure dancing (yes dancing) down the road. It was my teacher colleague and I pulled up sharply and jumped out of the car. It was at that moment that I was pleased Burnley had won. All the mickey-taking throughout the week had been simply banter. Here was an ardent supporter whose emotions had been given a lifeline and I felt happy for him.

I vigorously shook his hand and slapped his back; men did not hug in the eighties, and I watched him going into the pub for yet another pint. Leighton James' return had certainly helped, but it will be Ian Britton who will always be remembered for the goal which made the difference between survival and, dare one say, extinction. Dave Timberlake, living in the East Midlands, was another who dare not go to the game.

> "I was actually banned by my wife from attending. She said that the atmosphere would get to me and she didn't want me to have a heart attack. She often became irritated by my obsession with the club. She once told me that I loved Burnley more than her. In retaliation, I told her that I loved Blackburn Rovers more than her. She found me something to do during the afternoon. I had to paint the garage but I was listening to every kick on the radio, Whenever something happened, I would rush out to shout the news to my son who was playing on the street. The folks around where I lived were used to it. They all call me Burnley Dave and are accustomed to me leaving at 7.00 a.m. on match days, it being a three train journey to Turf Moor. I really don't know what I would have done if Burnley had gone down"

No time was wasted on either of the Cup competitions. The 3-0 defeat at non-league Telford in the FA Cup was worse than the one v Wimbledon, unimaginable to any Burnley fan and a 4-2 aggregate loss to Rochdale in the Littlewoods Cup was scarcely more acceptable. They had drawn at Spotland 1-1 but crumpled at home, the veteran Leighton James scoring away and at home.

1987-88

Team	Pos	Played	Won	Drawn	Lost	GF	GA	Pts
Blackburn Rovers	5	44	21	14	9	68	52	77
Burnley	10	46	20	7	19	57	62	67

Blackburn Rovers		Burnley	
Most Appearances	Colin Hendry, Nicky Reid (both 44)	Most Appearances	Chris Pearce 46
Most Goals	Simon Garner 14	Most Goals	George Oghani 14

With so many regulars having reached the end of their career, at least at Division 2 level, the Manager had to bring in new blood for the 87-88 season, but there was a surprise exit for Glenn Keeley. The "man mountain" of a centre half had made 365 appearances (9th on the all-time list) and captained the side

at Wembley. As the most influential figure on the pitch, he wanted a new two-year contract, the Board offered one year so he headed for Oldham Athletic. Two more outstanding performers said good-bye this campaign. The shy Irishman Noel Brotherston had made 307 league starts since arriving, winning twenty-seven Northern Ireland International Caps and his sleight of foot and impeccable ball control always excited the fans.

Mick Rathbone, after 270 starts and so many rampages forward from left back, was signed by Preston North End. Terry Gennoe, now fully fit, regained the goalkeeping jersey and Nicky Reid was picked up on a free transfer from Manchester City where he had played regularly for eight seasons. The first month of the 1987-88 campaign brought a series of iffy results but after a five month stretch without a defeat, this had become a serious attempt on the title by the Blackburn side. And by this time, Mackay had shocked the footballing world by taking Steve Archibald on a six-month loan from Barcelona. He had won League titles in Scotland and Spain plus two FA Cup and one UEFA Cup winning medals with Tottenham Hotspur. He was a classy, modern striker and made an ideal partner for Simon Garner as the Rovers homed in on the leaders. But once again, the club faltered with the winning post in sight. Four defeats in eleven games was not suicidal, but this final flourish was not enough. Two more points would have given them automatic promotion, but in an extremely tight finish, they had to be content with fifth place. The opposition in the Play-Off was Chelsea on a Sunday afternoon and we all trooped down to Ewood Park, but the blue and whites could not quite compete with the classier Londoners, slumping to a 2-0 defeat. It was even worse in London, Chelsea going through on the back of a 4-1 win, 6-1 on aggregate.

For the second year running, Portsmouth, now in Division 1, proved to be their FA Cup nemesis. On this occasion, the Pompey won 2-1 in Blackburn. They were handed a most difficult draw in Round 2 of the Littlewoods Cup, having to welcome the all-conquering Liverpool side to Ewood Park. My older son Stephen was quietly a Liverpool supporter as were most boys of his generation but he had been to Ewood on several occasions before, watching opposition that in the main meant little to him. He was therefore naturally excited at the prospect of seeing household names on the pitch but a curious metamorphosis occurred during the game. Scott Sellars had levelled the scores at 1-1 and as the clock ticked down, the crowd was at fever pitch, exhorting the Rovers to hang on to the draw. I suddenly became aware that Stephen was also screaming encouragement and when the referee blew for full time, he was so pleased that the blue and whites had earned a magnificent draw. Was this his conversion to the cause? I probably think it was. Inevitably they went down in the replay at Anfield, but it was close again, the Merseysiders taking a slender 1-0 victory.

Reprieved from relegation to the Non-League sector at the eleventh hour with the victory over Orient, Brian Miller had a massive clear out before the 1987-88 campaign. During this season, the manager only used eighteen players, ten of whom had been drafted in during the summer. Joe Neenan moved to Peterborough United and Peter Hampton to Bury. Both had played their part in the great survival as had veteran centre backs Billy Rodaway and Joe Gallagher. Both retired from the game, the former having made 245 appearances in a Claret and Blue shirt in two stints.

Leighton James stayed on at the club as Youth Team coach, even managing to participate in nineteen first team matches through the season. A whole host of players arrived to replace them. Welsh goalkeeper Chris Pearce and Paul Comstive, both of whom had played at Blackburn, were signed from Wrexham. Peter Daniel, a defender who had played for both Wolverhampton Wanderers and Sunderland in Wembley League Cup Finals, arrived from Lincoln City and left back Shaun McGrory from Coventry City. Andy Farrell, who would become a great crowd favourite, left Colchester United to play in midfield.

Natural goal scorer George Oghani settled in from Bolton Wanderers on a free transfer where he formed a partnership with former Clarets' striker Steve Taylor, arriving for a second spell from Preston North End. The final piece of Miller's jig saw as the season commenced was Steve Gardner, a centre back who had come through the youth set up at Old Trafford. Fifteen points from the first seven fixtures placed the Clarets in fourth position, the 1-0 home win over the eventual Play-Off winners Swansea City being particularly impressive.

In early October, Steven Davis (as opposed to Stephen Davis) joined from Crewe Alexandra and made the centre half berth his own, but the performances then became somewhat topsy-turvy and there was far too much inconsistency for them to ever mount a serious promotion challenge as their league position fluctuated between third and fifteenth. Three wins in the final eleven forced them to be content with tenth place, frustratingly only three points shy of the Play-Offs. There had been a definite feeling around the club that a chance to return to Division 3 had been squandered, but compared to the previous campaign, the faithful were not embarrassed to wear the scarf and proclaim to the heavens that they were Clarets' fans.

There was also a competition specifically for Division 3 and 4 clubs. The Football League Trophy has had a variety of names, depending on the Sponsor, and this year it was the Sherpa Van Trophy. Burnley progressed through their group by beating Tranmere Rovers and Rochdale. The Round 1 and 2 ties both produced 1-0 wins for the Clarets against Chester City and Bury but the Northern

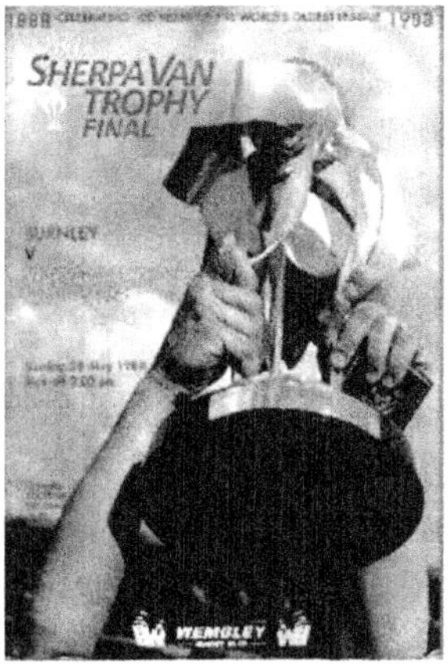

Semi- Final against Halifax Town ended in a goalless draw at Turf Moor, the home side going through 5-3 on penalties.

It was goalless in the Northern Final first leg against Preston North End in front of 15,680 fans but Burnley romped to a 3-1 victory at Deepdale, Oghani, Hoskin and Comstive scoring the goals. Cup fever gripped the town as virtually every household made plans to travel down to Wembley for the Final against another great old club; Wolverhampton Wanderers.

The Burnley 1988 Football League Trophy (Sherpa Van) Runner-Up side that lost 0-2 to Wolverhampton Wanderers was; Chris Pearce, Peter Daniel, Steven Davis, Ray Deakin, Steve Gardner, Shaun McGrory, Andy Farrell, Ian Britton, George Orghani, Steve Taylor, Paul Comstive. Substitute Leighton James.

The Midlanders had run away with the Division 4 title and were firm favourites. An enormous crowd of over 80,000 for a game between two Tier 4 sides, a record in itself, witnessed a close contest. Miller introduced the thirty-five-year-old Leighton James as a second half substitute, but the Wolves side, which had the soon to be capped England striker Steve Bull leading the line, had just too much for the Lancashire team, winning 2-0.

It was Burnley's first visit to Wembley since the 1962 FA Cup Final and a listing of the front fives from each game shows how much they had slumped in twenty-six years. Connelly, McIlroy, Pointer, Robson and Harris were household names to football fans across the land whereas Farrell, Oghani, Taylor, Comstive and McGrory were barely household names in Burnley. It was journeymen v legends, but the 1988 eleven had given of their best, had captured the imagination of the town and deserved to be remembered for transforming the spirit of anyone remotely interested in the progress of Burnley FC. Dave Timberlake, as ever, was at the game. He had waited patiently for twenty-six years to return to Wembley to support his Clarets.

> I called this the friendly final. It was Bank Holiday Sunday and there was not an ounce of acrimony between the supporters, all of whom seemed to treat it as a special occasion; a celebration of football because this was the centenary year of the Football League. The crowd was ten thousand bigger than had attended the England v Scotland game the week before. We had taken our family on a short break to Butlins at Skegness and on the morning of the match, my son and I left the camp early to drive down to London. On our way out, Security asked us where we were going at this unearthly hour. "Wembley" we replied, "we're Burnley fans" and they all had a good laugh. We strolled around before and after the game, chatting to both Burnley and Wolves supporters. It was that sort of day. The Wolves were a good side, they had stormed their way to the Division 4 title and were well worth their 2-0 win, but none of the Clarets' fans seemed to care too much. It was just a relief to be supporting the club on a special day.

Yet another 1st Round exit in the FA Cup hit Burnley, losing 1-0 to Bolton Wanderers at home. They defeated Wrexham in Round 1 of the Littlewoods, losing 1-0 across the border before three late home goals saw them through to meet 1st Division Norwich City in the Second Round. It was close, just one goal separating the clubs on aggregate, 2-1 after George Oghani had opened the scoring in the first leg at the "Turf".

1988-89

Team	Pos	Played	Won	Drawn	Lost	GF	GA	Pts
Blackburn Rovers	5	46	22	11	13	74	59	77
Burnley	16	46	14	13	19	52	61	55

Blackburn Rovers		Burnley	
Most Appearances	Mark Atkins, Scott Sellars (both 46)	Most Appearances	Steve Gardner 44
Most Goals	Simon Garner 20	Most Goals	Brendan O'Connell 13

Exactly one hundred years before, the towns of Burnley and Blackburn were preparing for their debuts in the inaugural Football League season. A century on, now in the 1988-89 season, both clubs had slipped from those lofty heights but the fans of Blackburn Rovers were convinced that they would once more be back amongst football royalty. There was much optimism that Don Mackay's side could achieve that this time around, although Chris Price was sold to Aston Villa for £150,000 and Simon Barker to Queens Park Rangers for £400,000, both wanting Division 1 action. Barker had been at Blackburn from being a schoolboy and he made 182 appearances in five seasons, a complete mid-field player.

To replace them, in came right-back Mark Atkins from Scunthorpe United, right-sided striker Howard Gayle from Stoke City, mid-field player John Millar from Chelsea and centre-forward Andy Kennedy from Birmingham City. The Rovers made a cracking start, just one defeat in eleven starts, that a 1-0 defeat at Maine Road, and they stayed in contention throughout, only losing twice more in the twelve-match run-in. The undoubted highlight was a 4-0 pounding of Manchester City. Simon Garner had closed in on Tommy Briggs' all time club scoring record and he needed just one goal to draw level. After Kennedy had opened the scoring, Garner equalled the record before half-time before scoring twice more in the second period to take the record and the match ball.

Their consistency throughout the year guaranteed a fifth placed finish and a Play-Off spot for the second successive season. In the Play-off, Watford and the Rovers clashed at Ewood Park. There was little between them and a goalless draw was a fair result. In the second leg at Vicarage Road, it was equally tight. Watford scored but Garner was also on target and they went through on the away goals-rule. In the final against Crystal Palace, in front of a 16,421 crowd, they led 3-1 after the first leg, It was a case of "Division 1, here we come".

All they had to do was keep Palace to a one goal margin of victory and an away goal of course would make it even easier. It could have happened, but Ian Miller blazed wide. The South Londoners were spearheaded by that blossoming duo, Bright and Wright. And "Wrighty" was unstoppable. He scored twice and there was a disputed penalty, but the Rovers were awful. Listening on the radio was agony and the dream died for yet another year; twenty-three years and counting without Tier 1 football

The Blackburn Rovers 1989 Runner-Up side in the Division 2 Play-Off 2-legged Final v Crystal Palace. Won 3-1, Lost 3-0. Terry Gennoe, Mark Atkins, Chris Sulley, Nicky Reid, Colin Hendry, David Mail, Howard Gayle, John Millar, Ian Miller, Simon Garner, Scott Sellars. Substitutes Alan Ainscow, Sean Curry.

They entered the Littlewoods Cup at Round 2 level and there were lots of goals as Brentford were finally beaten 6-5 on aggregate, Garner and Sellars helping themselves to two each. The performance in Round 3 was extremely commendable, holding Tottenham Hotspur to a goalless draw at White Hart Lane, forcing the classy Division 1 side to battle hard to triumph 2-1 in the replay. It was their good luck to draw Welling United in round 3 of the FA Cup, a Conference side on a once in a generation run, but a Ronnie Hildersley goal settled the tie. Sheffield Wednesday from Division 1 looked a good test for the Rovers in Round 4, but the Lancashire side was up to the task as goals from Garner and Tony Finnigan helped them to a 2-1 home "Roses" victory. Having already knocked Brentford out of the Football League Cup, the fans were beginning to dream of a long Cup run, but over fifteen thousand of them trooped home disappointed as the West London side completely tore up the form book and won 2-0.

Having walked up Wembley Way just months before in the Sherpa Van Trophy Final, the Claret fans were chomping at the bit as the 1988-89 season commenced. They must have looked westward and seen that their deadly rivals were close to snatching a place in Division 1 and while a two-league gap between the sides was a hard pill to swallow, a three Division chasm would be totally unacceptable. Brian Miller was still in charge, a symbol of stability, so surely this was the season to set Division 4 ablaze. The only player exiting in the close season was Peter Leebrook, a full back who came through the junior ranks and played over fifty first team games, including the crucial life or death game against Orient.

There were three new faces. Brendan O'Connell arrived from Exeter City, a centre forward with a reputation for finding the net. Paul Atkinson, a left winger who had come on as a substitute for Watford in the 1983 FA Cup Final, was signed on a free from Oldham Athletic and Gary Rowell, who had scored goals for fun at Sunderland prior to a serious knee injury, joined from Carlisle United to complete the trio. The Board also spent money on Winston White, a winger from Colchester United and full back Ian Meacham from Cambridge United. A legend and a hero both called time on their lengthy careers at the end of the season. The evergreen Leighton James was a Burnley legend, possibly one of their best ten players of all time whereas Ian Britton will be remembered as a hero for his "survival" goal against the Orient. Paul Comstive was transferred to Bolton Wanderers for £37,000 at the end of the campaign, Steve Taylor, after a disappointing second stint, moved to Rochdale and Ashley Hoskin, the diminutive left winger with a striking resemblance to Phil Collins, drifted into Non-League football after seventy-two league starts.

The Clarets started like the proverbial express train and a 6-0 home victory over York City, with Paul Comstive scoring twice, sent the 7,248 crowd into ecstasy as Burnley swept to the top of the table. But within weeks, defeats were out numbering victories. A drastic run of seven winless games, halted by a 1-0 win over Grimsby Town on New Year's Eve, put intense pressure on Brian Miller and two further away defeats led to him handing in his resignation.

An honourable man, he knew that he was unable to work a miracle with a low budget squad and with the side in fourteenth position, he walked away before the Board was forced to consider his future. Hopefully having learnt from previous appointments, Frank Teasdale moved for a known face and Frank Casper resigned as Martin Dobson's Assistant at Bury to move into the hot seat at Turf Moor.

The response was immediate and two wins and a draw moved them into the top ten. But then catastrophe! Eleven games without a win, albeit six were draws, sent them tumbling down the table to eighteenth, but doubles by O'Connell in a 3-0 win over Doncaster Rovers and by White in a 3-2 win at Lincoln City (quickly promoted back into the Football League) resulted in a sixteenth place finish.

Their third successive 1st Round FA Cup exit came at the hands of Chester City from Division 3, 2-0 at Turf Moor and although they exacted some revenge over Rochdale in the League Cup courtesy of a 5-4 aggregate victory, O'Connell notching three of the goals, Luton Town from Division 1 eventually proved too good. The Clarets had performed well however, being edged out 2-1 on aggregate.

1989-90

	Pos	Played	Won	Drawn	Lost	GF	GA	Pts
Blackburn Rovers	5	46	19	17	10	74	59	74
Burnley	16	46	14	14	18	45	55	56

Blackburn Rovers		Burnley	
Most Appearances	Scott Sellars 43	Most Appearances	Joe Jakub 46
Most Goals	Simon Garner 18	Most Goals	Winston White, Ron Futcher (both 7)

The fans at Ewood Park were even more convinced that 1989-90 would be the year when the long drought of Division 1 football would come to an end. Just one poor performance in South London had denied them last time, surely

it would happen this year. Ian Miller, the "Flying Scot" departed to Port Vale after eight full seasons and 252 league appearances as age began to slow him down. Mackay went for experience to finally clinch promotion.

Frank Stapleton came from Le Havre in France, but his exploits at both Arsenal and Manchester United saw him idolised in both the south and north of England. He was the Republic of Ireland's all-time leading goal scorer for a while and the manager felt that his experience could add something special to the squad. Alan Irvine also arrived from Dundee United to replace Miller as the season began, again with loads of experience of the highest level of football with Everton. The third arrival was the one who eventually made the difference.

Kevin Moran from Manchester United via Sporting Gijon in Spain, was everyone's idea of the best type of centre-back. Immensely strong, always uncompromising, a ferocious tackler, outstanding in the air and a superb reader of the game, he was to be responsible for the club's eventual promotion. He was also needed straight away because the club was unable to keep Colin Hendry and he was sold to Manchester City. The season started so well and Simon Garner hit a hat-trick in a 5-0 whitewashing of Barnsley.

Goals however were regularly being leaked until with the arrival of Moran playing alongside David Mail, they conceded just fifteen goals in nineteen games, enabling the Rovers to mount a challenge for the Play-Offs. Confidence and form went out of the window at the death but they dragged themselves over the line to achieve the vital fifth spot. Swindon Town had finished fourth and the two clubs met at Ewood Park in the first leg of the Play-Offs. The Rovers were poor on the day and they went down 2-1.

They again failed to raise their game in the second leg, again losing 2-1. Howard Gayle managed to score, but poor defending contributed to two more Swindon goals and an aggregate 4-2 defeat. It was a sorry ending to what had been an exciting and entertaining season.

Exeter City were to go on to win Division 4, but surely Blackburn Rovers would prove too strong for them in the Football League Cup. Unfortunately that was not the case and a horrendous display in Devon resulted in a 3-0 1st leg loss. Two Atkins goals gave them a chance at Ewood, but it was an aggregate result to be ashamed of, a 4-2 defeat.

After the lovely post-Christmas present of a non-league side in the 3rd round of the FA Cup the previous year, it was back to reality with a tie against Aston Villa. A fighting 2-2 draw at Ewood was much to be pleased about but a replay at a top club is not recommended and sure enough, the Rovers slumped to a 3-1 defeat.

Could Burnley improve on the previous season's lacklustre sixteenth position in Division 4 was the question on the minds of the fans as football resumed for another season? There was the usual procession of arrivals and departures at the start of the 89-90 campaign, but would they be good enough to help the club mount a promotion challenge? Frank Casper drafted in five players with experience of lower league football. The club paid £30,000 for John Deary, a midfield player with close to three hundred league starts at Blackpool under his belt. Roger Eli a striker, arrived from Bury and another striker, Tony Hancock from Stockport County. Peter Mumby was the third striker that the manager signed, this time from Leeds United and former Claret Joe Jakub, now reaching the veteran stage, was re-signed from Chester City.

They compiled a nine-game unbeaten run to reach fifth place in the table, Brendan O'Connell scoring twice in a 3-1 home win over Hereford United and this early success had been achieved despite the loss through injury of first choice centre backs Steve Gardner and Steven Davis. But when Ray Deakin was injured for a lengthy spell, the cracks began to appear. Bizarrely, a Stephen Davis arrived on loan from Southampton to play at centre back, but imagine the problems the fans had.

Two players with the same surname is complicated enough but when they both answer to Steve and both play in central defence, it becomes something close to impossible. Thankfully their first names were spelled differently. As the injured one returned to full fitness, they played together for eight games before the South Coast side recalled their Mr Davis.

Ron Futcher was the catalyst for improvement part way through the season. The Board had splashed out £65,000 to capture him from Port Vale, but he had made his name at Luton Town, playing in front of his identical twin brother Paul. He then moved to North America where he became an extremely prolific goal scorer. John Francis, signed from Sheffield United for £90,000 in February, added goals from wide positions, all preventing Casper's boys from straying into the relegation zone. Results madly fluctuated, but after a winless run of ten games, the final position was sixteenth, the same as the previous season. It was unacceptable then and was even more unacceptable a second time around.

In five seasons in the bottom Division, tenth had been the highest position. How had it come to this? With far less coming through the ranks and the spiralling transfer costs of ordinary players, the club would need something special to lift them back to anywhere close to what, for almost thirty years, had been the norm.

A battling performance in the replay against Stockport County saw them into Round 2 of the FA Cup where they met Scunthorpe United three times (no penalty shoot-outs then). After two draws, The Turf Moor side suddenly upped their game and thrashed the North Lincolnshire outfit by a magnificent 5-0 margin. Roger Eli and Futcher both scored twice but a trip to the seaside brought a 1-0 defeat to Blackpool. This was the second Cup defeat of the season by the Tangerines who brought about their elimination from the Football League Cup by the narrowest of 3-2 margins after two legs.

1990-91

	Pos	Played	Won	Drawn	Lost	GF	GA	Pts
Blackburn Rovers	19	46	14	10	22	51	66	52
Burnley	6	46	23	10	13	70	51	79

Blackburn Rovers		**Burnley**	
Most Appearances	Frank Stapleton 38	Most Appearances	Steven Davis, Joe Jakub (both 46)
Most Goals	Frank Stapleton 10	Most Goals	Ron Futcher 18

Following three years of near misses which saw the return of optimism and excitement to the terraces, years of feast as the Bible would have said, the 1990-91 campaign was a return to famine; a struggle to survive. The slump, which saw the Rovers flirt with relegation came as a massive shock to the Ewood Park fans used to Play-Offs at the season end. The squad was sorely stricken by injuries and David Mail had been released to play for Hull City. The centre half had amassed 200 League appearances at Ewood and proved himself to be quick, hard tackling and reliable. Mike Duxbury, Accrington born and an English international right back during his time with Manchester United, arrived on a free transfer, but he was reaching the end of his career.

Lee Richardson, bought from Watford for £250,000, looked like one for the future, Andy Kennedy journeying the other way. They finished thirty-six points behind Joe Royle's Oldham Athletic down in nineteenth position, just four points clear of the relegation spots. Injuries to Mackay's big three, Gennoe, Garner and Scott Sellars totally disrupted his team selection and there were only two notable imports.

Goalkeeper Bobby Mimms came from Tottenham Hotspur for another quarter of a million fee, but the best import by far was Jack Walker. The Blackburn born multi-millionaire had supported the club on the Blackburn end from being a boy and he made it his personal crusade to return the Blue and White halves to the top echelon of English football.

Having recently sold his steel empire (Walker Steel), he certainly had the money to do so. By Christmas, the side was bottom of the League. Centre forward Steve Livingstone and defender Tony Dobson were both signed from Coventry City with "Walker money" and they made a difference, Livingstone scoring the equaliser against Wolverhampton Wanderers at Ewood Park to guarantee safety in the penultimate game of the season. Until the season's mid-point, the performances were extremely poor but the recovery, aided by the first tranche of cash from Jack Walker's seemingly bottomless pockets, spread optimism across the town as they looked forward to the next season.

Rotherham United proved difficult opposition in Round 2 of the Football League Cup before the Blackburn side finally won 1-0 at Ewood in the second leg, having drawn at Millmoor. Division 1 side Queens Park Rangers down in Shepherd's Bush was not the tie that the Rovers had longed for, but they did not disgrace themselves, fighting hard but ultimately losing 2-1. Once more the draw paired them with Liverpool in the FA Cup and this time a Garner goal gave them a 1-1 draw. Inevitably the Reds turned it on at Anfield, comfortably winning 3-0.

John Pender, bought from Bristol City for £70,000, proved to be the strong man Burnley required at the centre of the defence as the 90-91 campaign unfolded. The Clarets had occupied an automatic promotion place into February and there had been plenty of goals for the fans to applaud from an attack spearheaded by Futcher and Francis. But three successive defeats, all to clubs way below them in the table and a disappointing 1-0 defeat to lowly Maidstone United consigned them to the Play-Offs. Frank Casper was able to regularly pick a settled side and in the Play-Offs, Burnley found Torquay United barring their path. The first leg at Plainmoor was a disappointing day for the Clarets. The Devon club were quick to run up a two-goal lead, one they defended for the full ninety minutes. It was all Burnley in the return match at the "Turf", but their only reward was a late Torquay own goal and another year down in Division 4 was their immediate future. But speaking frankly, it was not good enough. Torquay United have been one of the poorest clubs to operate in the Football League in modern times and, having beaten Blackpool in the final at Wembley, they were gaining promotion at the expense of Burnley FC. Frank Casper had given his all and the Board gave him another season to come up with the goods, but who, thirty years before, would have predicted a seven-year stint for the Clarets down among the basement boys. Two of Turf Moor's favourite sons said goodbye at the end of term. Ray Deakin had made 213 League appearances, propping up the defence during troubled times and captaining the club on numerous occasions.

Neil Grewcock would always be remembered for his goal in the unforgettable victory over the Orient. He had been at the club for seven seasons, the final three seriously hampered by injuries but in all, he made 202 starts, scoring twenty-seven goals from a wide right position. Ron Futcher had only spent a season and a half at Turf Moor, leading scorer for both seasons, but he chose to move on to Crewe Alexandra. Steven Davis, who had been outstanding at centre back for the four seasons since his arrival, refused the new terms offered and was sold to Barnsley for £180,000.

Non-League Stafford Rangers were defeated in Round 1 of the FA Cup and a struggling Stoke City side, making a rare appearance in Division 3, were taken out by late goals from John Francis and Winston White to earn them a home tie against Manchester City. A crowd of over twenty thousand saw the Clarets "give as good as they got" from the Division 1 side and the fans trooped home, sad about the 1-0 defeat but certainly satisfied with the performance. It had taken the might of another of the country's top teams, Nottingham Forest to knock Burnley out of the Football League Cup. A close 2-1 aggregate win over Stockport County had taken them through to Round 2 where Brian Clough's eleven dominated them 4-1 at the City Ground before strolling through 1-0 in Lancashire.

1991-92

Team	Pos	Played	Won	Drawn	Lost	GF	GA	Pts
Blackburn Rovers	6	46	21	11	14	70	53	74
Burnley	1	42	25	8	9	79	43	83

Blackburn Rovers		Burnley	
Most Appearances	Bobby Mimms 45	Most Appearances	John Deary, Stephen Davis 40
Most Goals	David Speedie 23	Most Goals	Mike Conroy 24

Football politics was centre stage throughout the previous season, with the moneyed clubs determined to flex their muscles and escape from what they saw as the strictures of the Football League. In doing so they founded the Premier League, an organisation which has become a veritable money pit for its members and which, thank God, has not become a closed shop. Relegation from and promotion to has never become an issue, therefore even the lowest of clubs can dream of matching their skills against the top teams in the land. There was a race on amongst Second Division clubs to be founder members and Jack Walker was not slow in writing cheques.

Mackay signed David Speedie, a fiery and extremely pacy goal scorer from Liverpool for £500,000. He was Scots born but spoke with a South Yorkshire accent and was certainly a firecracker at Ewood Park. The Rovers made the worst possible start. Don Mackay's side gained just one point from their first three games but this was not what Walker had in mind when he took over the club and the manager was quickly sacked.

He had been successful when in charge of Dundee and also at Coventry City. He had worked at Glasgow Rangers as Assistant to Graeme Souness. He was a lively character, a media favourite who would speak to the fans in the street and in his four and a half seasons at Ewood, he had initially guided them from relegation candidate to the safe haven of twelfth position, then achieved three consecutive Play-Off campaigns and finally overseen a mediocre nineteenth finish.

He was always chatty and generally well liked by the fans, although I distinctly remember the constant criticism from one supporter who stood close to us on the Blackburn side of the old Nuttall Street Enclosure. He would position himself by the railings to the Players' Tunnel and therefore Mackay would be comfortably in hearing range of his regular denunciations. Whenever a Rovers' player made a mistake or heaven forbid, the team conceded a goal, he would let the Scotsman know what he thought of him. "Mackay, you're a Tup Head" was repeated ad infinitum. We never understood the exact meaning of the phrase. It was certainly not complimentary but it always lightened up a grey Saturday afternoon at Ewood Park. One day he was missing and all those around us asked "where's Tup Head"?

Tony Parkes took on the caretaker role and five wins and two draws in eight games propelled them up the League. At other times, he would have been handed the job on a permanent basis, but Walker wanted the best available and he pursued Kenny Dalglish until the man said "yes". Kenny had left Anfield, having given his all and more but now refreshed, he took on the challenge in Blackburn and gave the locals the roller coaster ride they had desired for over a quarter of a century. The end of Don Mackay was inevitably the time for loyal servants to stand aside. Terry Gennoe, at the age of thirty-eight and built like a Grenadier Guardsman, had saved them on countless occasions and was much loved by the fans during his 289-game stint; a record for a goalkeeper at the club.

Frank Stapleton was thirty-five when he left, having intelligently led the line for a couple of seasons and John Millar, a tidy, hard tackling and hardworking midfield player, moved back to Heart of Midlothian after starting 126 games in four seasons. Alan Wight, a diminutive but talented left back, was bought from Blackpool, Colin Hendry returned from Manchester City, Gordon Cowans, an England international and European Cup winner, was picked up from Aston Villa and Mike Newell became the club's first million-pound player when signed from Everton.

Surprisingly Dalglish had no quick fix, losses at Swindon Town and Southend United in his first four games raising eyebrows, but when money is available, it makes life easier. As the quality players began to arrive, the club raced to the top of the table but in a February win over Newcastle United, Mike Newell broke his leg. Six successive defeats brought the fans back into the real world. The Play-Offs were now touch and go but Newell returned and Speedie re-found his golden goal touch, scoring a hat-trick at Plymouth Argyle in the final game of the season to finish sixth. It was the Rovers' fourth appearance in the Play-Offs in five years. For the home leg with Derby County, the 19,677 crowd, the biggest at Ewood Park that season, was silenced as both the flair and organisation of the Midland side shone through, taking them to an early 2-0 lead. By half-time however, goals from Scott Sellars and Mike Newell made it too close to call. But in David Speedie, the Rovers had the ace in the pack. For 45 minutes he was electric, giving an unstoppable display of pace, power and opportunism. His two goals brought the house down and gave his team mates a fighting chance in the second leg. Derby could still go through if they scored twice without reply and they almost did, but a brave Kevin Moran header was enough to send the Rovers to their second Play-Off Final with a 5-4 aggregate win; their first as a one shot knock out on Wembley's hallowed turf.

When I look back over the thousands of games I have watched from eight-year olds in a park to Internationals at Wembley, the semi-final encounter against Derby would probably make my personal top twenty. Sadly the Final against Leicester City would not. On a red hot Spring Bank Holiday Monday, better suited to sunbathing around a Costa del Sol hotel pool, the two sides put on a sterile display, neither eleven daring to make a bold move. The referee saw an infringement in the Leicester City area on the stroke of half time, allegedly against Speedie and a penalty was awarded. It was a "soft penalty" but Newell, with so much riding on this one strike, slid the ball into the Foxes' net and the

Blackburn side hung on for the next forty-five minutes.

We had to walk past an emerging mass of unhappy Leicester fans on our way back to the mini-bus and one tall character grabbed my son's blue and white hat. In fairness, there was no damage to Simon, half the size of his assailant and it was more an act of frustration than malice; a feeling that was not difficult to understand considering the result and the fact that the Rovers had generally been outplayed.

Football, whether it be a Sunday morning on a park pitch or played by young millionaires in the world's largest stadia is a results-based industry. And for the fan; yes, we want to be entertained by an exhibition of glorious football, but even more than that, we want our club to win. If it has been a long journey and the result has been to our liking, there is so much we need to talk about that we do not want the journey home to come to an end. But if we lose, we cannot wait to get back. So many Rovers fans arose early on May 25th, 1992 and I well remember the convoy of coaches on the M6 and M40. There were lots of cars with scarves fluttering out of their windows and many fans had to find ingenious methods of travel and accommodation to simply be there. Paul Cox, barely into his twenties at the time, gives his impression of the way it was that day.

> A big away trip was the Play-Off final v Leicester City in 1992. It was on the Spring Bank Holiday Monday and my mate and I had decided to hire a Ford Transit. To cover the cost, we would take a load of lads in the back. The night before we both went to watch a band in Bury. The Gig finished about 11 and because in our wisdom we must have thought that London was about a thousand miles away, we then started to pick everyone up in Haslingden about 11.30. It was of course ridiculously early, but we were young then and the plan seemed to make sense. So we loaded up with beer and passengers and made our last stop picking up Alan. He was older and had his own place with his partner. On arrival he looked in the back and complained it didn't look comfy. So we decided to take his settee and chair, plus bean bag, and load them all into the back of the van. It looked like a winner, first class travel to the big city. But back in those days with no mobile phones, his girlfriend woke up the next morning and thought they had been robbed.

No doubt Paul could have also waxed lyrically about the journey home, but back where it mattered; Mr Dalglish had done what was asked of him. The Blackburn side had been founder members of the Football League, now they were to be members of the inaugural Premier League, joining only Aston Villa and Everton in this historic and illustrious trinity.

The Blackburn Rovers Division 2 Play-Off winning side, played at Wembley Stadium was; Bobby Mimms, David May, Alan Wright, Gordon Cowans, Kevin Moran, Colin Hendry, Chris Price, Mark Atkins, David Speedie, Mike Newell, Scott Sellars. Substitutes Lee Richardson, Roy Wegerle.

The Football League Cup was such a disappointing result and probably cost Mackay his job. They entered in Round 1 and could only draw 1-1 against Hull City before an even more insipid showing at Boothferry Park where they lost 1-0. They managed to reach Round 4 of the FA Cup, courtesy of a comfortable win over Kettering Town from the Conference, but Notts County, fighting relegation from Division 1, sneaked through 2-1 at Meadow Lane.

Following a win at Wembley for the Rovers at the end of this season, there would have been a potential three Division gap between the two East Lancashire clubs, but Burnley could not allow this to happen. With perfect timing, the Clarets chose this season to take their first tentative steps away from the basement of the professional game. But there was nothing tentative about the way they eventually went about the job. Frank Casper moved quickly to replace Steve Davis by buying the other Steve Davis from Southampton. Referred to as S Davis (2) by Ray Simpson in his magnificent tome, "The Clarets Chronicles", he had impressed at the club whilst on loan and when the club secured his services for a mere £60,000, the fans knew that it had been good business. I asked him why he had left an established Division 1 (soon to be Premier League) club with the likes of Alan Shearer and Matt Le Tissier in the dressing room to join a Division 4 outfit.

> "There were many good players at Southampton and it was difficult to find a place in the starting line-up. I needed to play regularly and I had enjoyed my short stay up there eighteen months before. I was delighted that they were interested in me and I knew how big the club was. It may have been in Division 4, but it had the potential to play at a much higher level. Players used to talk about other clubs and I knew that it had a good reputation. It was exactly the right move for me at that stage in my career."

Striker Mike Conroy from Reading and winger Steve Harper from Preston North End proved to be good acquisitions and the start of the season was not disastrous. In fact Roger Eli was a hat-trick man in a 3-0 defeat of Chesterfield, but three successive defeats to Hereford United, Rochdale and Scarborough quickly provoked the inevitable chant of "Casper out" from the crowd. The manager had given his heart and soul to the club for nigh on twenty-five years but as often is the case, the fans can be quite unforgiving. Unable to take any more stick he resigned and was replaced by the ex-Blackpool manager Jimmy Mullen. As much as Frank had been loved and respected by the fans, it did not always stop them from hurling insults if the team was struggling.

Both he, and previously Brian Miller nearly three years before, had managed to steady the ship after taking over in extremely problematic circumstances, but both resigned because the crowd had convinced them that a failure to do so would result in the direst of consequences for the club. Did the Board of Directors support them sufficiently during the bad times? Very few people would be privy to that information, but they will both be long remembered as special players and managers "who did their best". Casper had offered the role of Assistant Manager to Jimmy Mullen during the previous season, Mullen having previously held the post of Manager at Blackpool for a season and he was placed in charge at Turf Moor on Frank's resignation.

To everyone's delight in the town, the Clarets hit the ground running, winning the next nine games, a run which swept them to second in the League. This included a 6-2 win at Wrexham where the youngster Graham Lancashire netted a hat-trick. They went top in mid-January when a Conroy three timer helped to sink Gillingham 4-1 and virtually stayed there until the season ended. There was an occasional blip, but the title was won at York City with two games remaining. Mike Conroy had been on target 24 times, the highest return in a season since Willie Irvine's thirty-seven in 1966. Goalkeeper Chris Pearce played his last match, his 181st appearance as the season began to wind down. It was a season for equalling records.

For the fourth time in their history, Burnley won eleven times away from home and their other record was to equal the performance of Wolverhampton Wanderers four years previously when they became the first club to win the title in all four Tiers of the Football League. It was the Clarets seventh title, two at Tier 1, three at Tier 2 and one each at Tiers 3 and 4. Is this a record to boast about? In many ways the answer has to be "yes". It shows a certain tenacity, it shows an ability to take the knocks, stand straight back up and resume the battle and all this over so many years. But to achieve this record, it is essential to have lived through the failures caused by numerous relegations.

Arsenal, relegated just once since 1893 and that for just two seasons, are commencing their ninety seventh consecutive campaign in Tier 1 and Everton, founder members in 1888, have only been relegated twice, for a total of four years. Manchester United, Liverpool, Chelsea, Newcastle United, Tottenham Hotspur and West Ham United are the only other clubs never to have ventured lower than the second tier since first being accepted into the Football League. So Burnley's record equalling feat is something to acknowledge with pride, but it should never be used to express the club's greatness. For Jimmy Mullen and everyone involved with the Burnley club, it was only the beginning of a long trek towards the summit of the football mountain. A corner had been turned, they were now in the foothills, but the peak was visible. It was a long distance away, it would take so, so long, but maybe one day they would regain their rightful place at the top of the game.

The Burnley Division 4 Title winning side 1991-92 (started over 15 games, max 42) were; Andrew Marriott, Ian Meacham, Joe Jakub, John Deary, John Pender, Andrew Farrell, Stephen Davis, John Francis, Mike Conroy, Steve Harper, Roger Eli.

There was almost another day out at Wembley for the Claret and Blues, as they reached the Northern Final of the Autoglass (Football League) Trophy. Blackpool, Doncaster Rovers, Scarborough, Rotherham United and Huddersfield Town were all brushed aside prior to the Northern Final against Division 3 side Stockport County. A 1-0 defeat at Turf Moor made further progress difficult and despite a John Pender equaliser in Stockport, they were finally edged out 2-1 on aggregate.

They scraped through Round 1 of the FA Cup in a replay against Doncaster Rovers. Rotherham United succumbed to a 2-0 defeat at the "Turf" and the draw brought the strong Division 2 side Derby County to the town in Round 3. In a cracking cup-tie, Burnley twice came from a goal down to earn a draw, but try as they did, the Midland opposition was too good at the Baseball Ground, Jimmy Mullen's side losing 2-0. Their Football League Cup campaign was over in double quick time, losing to Wigan Athletic 6-3 on aggregate.

And so another period of time came to a close and there had been no clash between the two clubs in any meaningful competition, but the ill-feeling between the fans seemed to grow each year. The singing at both grounds, irrespective of the opposition, included the most abusive of comments about their neighbours, even when there was no immediate likelihood of a fixture between them. And each club was as guilty as the other. It is easy to blame the idiot fringe but there were fans in the "posh" seats who were capable of joining in. When the half time scores were announced on the tannoy, a Clarets/Rovers negative score would be greeted with childlike glee. It is as if the local rivalry brings out an inherent malice, possibly in some cases bordering on evil, which is lodged somewhere deep in our psyche. I have to admit that I occasionally derived more pleasure seeing Burnley struggle than watching the Rovers win during this time.

It has to be a defect somewhere in our personalities but I will leave that to psychologists to explain. Thankfully from a public order perspective, no fixtures give no opportunity for these feelings to be let loose, but the vandalism, the anarchy and the vitriolic language which quickly rise to the surface are just a reflection of the malaise which hit the English game in the seventies and continued through the eighties. It would remain dormant in East Lancashire for a while yet, but the festering hatred was certain to cause a massive eruption when the clubs eventually next met.

Glory comes to Ewood Park and Burnley can only watch, 1992 – 1999

"The real glory is being knocked to your knees and then coming back. That's real glory. That's the essence of it."

Vince Lombardi

Legendary American Football coach of the Green Bay Packers who won the first two Super Bowls

Throughout the history of football, at least in the top European leagues, there have been spells when a certain club has dominated the honours, sometimes for years. Real Madrid, Juventus, Bayern Munich, Manchester United and Paris St Germain are recent examples of seemingly all conquering sides who have regularly annexed trophies, but although their time has come, it will surely go as it may be doing in Barcelona and certainly has at AC Milan, Borussia Monchengladbach, Arsenal and Lyon.

For twenty years, Liverpool dominated English (and European) football and during the summer of 2020, it was possible to understand the feeling of relief when they actually won the domestic title for the first time in thirty years even though not agreeing with the nature of their excessive celebrations which rocked a city already reeling from the Coronavirus epidemic. This comeback under Jurgen Klopp seemed much more glorious because in their minds, they had been knocked to their knees (relatively speaking) and starved of success for so long. For Blackburn Rovers, there had been years which are best forgotten. The four seasons in Division 3, particularly occupying a place in the bottom half in Gordon Lee's first campaign in the mid-seventies, need erasing from the history books, but suddenly in front of them lay their date with destiny. It had been eighty-one years in coming, but holding high the Premier League Trophy after so many years in the doldrums would be the real glory indeed.

1992-93

	Pos	Played	Won	Drawn	Lost	GF	GA	Pts
Blackburn Rovers	4	42	20	11	11	68	46	71
Burnley	13	46	15	16	15	57	59	61

Blackburn Rovers		Burnley	
Most Appearances	Bobby Mimms 42	Most Appearances	John Pender, Marlon Beresford (both 44)
Most Goals	Alan Shearer 16	Most Goals	Adrian Heath 20

Burnley left Division 4 in May and began to play in Division 2 in August. A promotion of two Divisions you may deduce, but in actual fact it was all down to the re-branding of the country's highest-ranking League. This was now to be known as the Premier League, with the three other full- time professional leagues being labelled as Divisions 1 to 3. Thus, the Clarets, now playing in the 3rd Tier, were actually competing in Division 2. The re-appearance of Blackburn Rovers at the elite level in the 1992-93 season ended a twenty-six-year absence, having been relegated in 1966. Another interesting, albeit depressing statistic, concerns those once formidable clubs from the cotton towns of Lancashire. Blackburn Rovers, Bolton Wanderers, Burnley and Preston North End had made up one third of the first Football League. They were the backbone of English football but not one of them had featured at the summit of the game since the Wanderers were relegated in 1980. Thankfully this was now remedied and Lancashire was represented at the top table once more.

As the history of these two wonderful clubs unfolds, it is apparent that the managers were using far more players in a season and that the length of time that a player stayed at a club was becoming shorter. The change of law that introduced multiple substitutions meant that squads had to be bigger and the emergence of agents has encouraged players to seek more money elsewhere, effectively causing the disappearance of one-club men. As a consequence, there was so much traffic in and out of the clubs but fewer who stayed long enough to become much loved treasures at either the "Turf" or Ewood.

If anyone doubted Jack Walker's intentions, this season made them think again. If you are going to buy, buy the best was his motto and no-one had more to offer than Alan Shearer. Featuring strongly in the backstory of Shearer was Alex Ferguson and for once the great man came off second best in his jousts with Jack Walker. When the Geordie was at Southampton, Ferguson was desperate to make him a Manchester United player, but Jack Walker's perseverance, the size of his wallet and no doubt the opportunity to work with the legend that was Kenny Dalglish lured him to Ewood Park. The £3.3million British transfer record included David Speedie making the journey to the Dell in the opposite direction. In his first season, Dalglish steered them to fourth place, their highest finish since Bob Crompton had captained the side to a third-place finish at the end of the 1914-15 season. Shearer was not the only expensive purchase. These included the dashing winger Stuart Ripley from Middlesbrough for £1.2million, Henning Berg, a quality right sided defender from SK Lillestrom in Norway and the classy left back Graeme Le Saux for £650,000 in a deal which saw Steve Livingstone travelling to Chelsea. Scottish international striker Kevin Gallacher left Coventry City for £1.5million but the club recouped most of that when the Midland side paid £1.1million for Roy Wegerle. The American naturalised striker had only been bought from Queen's Park Rangers for £1million the season before and he won a solitary USA cap just before he left, but his disappointing goals to games ratio made this particular sale good business. Scott Sellars was sold back to Leeds United for £800,000, the midfielder having made 194 appearances and scored thirty-five goals in a most productive six years and Chris Sulley moved to Port Vale on a free transfer; his 134 appearances including the Full Members Cup triumph of 1987. But by far the most tears shed were at the departure of Simon Garner. Some would place him amongst the best ten players to represent the club, and certainly as he left for West Brom, then in the new Division 2, the fans could picture nothing else but the sight of him accelerating to the ball and crashing it into the net. Powerful, quick, tenacious, talented and two footed, he should have played at the top level, but the locals were happy that he never made the move. A club record of 164 goals in 455 appearances following his arrival as a seventeen-year-old from Boston United in 1976 indicates both his loyalty and ability. Like Derek Fazackerley, it is difficult to select someone who never played at Tier 1 in your best ever eleven, but that detracts nothing from my image of him bearing down on goal, my adrenalin level still hitting the red zone as the memories come flooding back.

Simon talked at length about his years at Ewood Park.

> "I suppose my favourite period was when Bob Saxton was manager. There was very little money at the club and he was forced to pick the same team week after week. This was good for us because we knew where we stood and Saxton was a decent down to earth Yorkshireman; so easy to get on with. It was much the same also under Don Mackay who took us to three series of Play-Offs. In total, including time under Kendall and Saxton, we finished in the top six on six occasions before finally being promoted under Kenny. Towards the end of Don's time in charge, Jack Walker took over and we all sensed what would happen. He would bring in a big name manager and big name players. By then, I was struggling to hold down a regular first team place as Walker money had brought in Dalglish to manage and quality strikers like David Speedie and Mike Newell. I found the new manager to be straight and fair and he took me to one side towards the end of the season. You can see out the final year of your contract here if you want but I cannot promise you games, was the gist of what he said and I appreciated his honesty. I still felt I had several years left in me and so I wanted to play every week. That's why I dropped a division with West Brom instead of moving up one with the Rovers. So I never managed to play in the top flight of English football. I like to think that I was almost a one club man. As far as I know, no club enquired

about me when I was banging in the goals, but perhaps they did and the Rovers never told me. There were no agents then so as long as we liked the camaraderie at the club and were getting a game, we stayed. I am still ranked fourth in the all-time list of appearance makers at the Rovers and I bet that no-one catches us unless the game changes radically. I always thought that scoring was a natural habit for me. I knew I was quick over five to ten yards and I did things instinctively. I could also hammer a ball with both feet and I always worked hard to stay fit. Ossie Ardiles was the manager who signed me at West Brom. He had played a few games at Ewood under Don Mackay when he came on loan and because he had been one of the best players in world football, we expected him to be aloof. He was nothing of the sort and he was so friendly with every one of the players. He must have remembered me from those days because he was quick to sign me in 1992. We reached Wembley for the Division 2 Play-Off final and I was on the bench, but I came on as a sub as we beat Port Vale 3-0. By the end of the following season, Martin O'Neill had signed me for Wycombe Wanderers and I again played at Wembley in the Division 3 Play-Off, this time playing the full game and scoring in a 4-2 win over Preston North End".

One aspect of the game that we "outsiders" know virtually nothing about is the countless hours taken up by management to persuade players (and now of course their agents) to join their club. And even then, you never really knew if it is the correct decision that is made. Craig Short had almost signed for the Rovers in 1992 before making the move seven years later, so he had first-hand experience of this.

"I had contributed to Notts County's remarkable rise through the divisions under Neil Warnock, two successive promotions taking us up to Division 1 in the final season before the Premier League began. Unfortunately we were relegated that season, but I felt it time to move away from Meadow Lane and I must have impressed some clubs because they were chasing me. One was the newly promoted Blackburn Rovers managed by an Anfield legend and I was tempted. I spoke at length to Kenny Dalglish but in the end I chose what at the time was the safest option, moving to Derby County. They had just been pipped for promotion to the Premier League, having lost out to the Rovers in the semi-finals of the Play-Offs. I had friends there and was confident that we would be promoted next time, so I signed for the "Rams". I later realised that it was one of my biggest mistakes. Not that I didn't enjoy myself at the Baseball Ground and I am now back coaching the Development Squad at this lovely club, but if things had gone my way at Ewood Park, I could have been forever remembered as part of that marvellous journey to the top of English football. But who knows? I may not have forced myself into their starting line-up."

Sir Kenneth Mathieson Dalglish was in charge at Ewood Park at the beginning of this period and he could be the most successful "footballing man" ever nurtured in the United Kingdom. Has anyone in the last 130 years produced a CV to match that of the Scottish wizard. When one combines playing and managing, I don't believe he has an equal. He was the best British player of his generation. A legend at Celtic, a legend at Anfield and the most capped Scot of all time. He won the domestic lot several times by the Clyde and repeated the feat by the Mersey, fourteen in nine years including four European Cup wins. He was the complete inside forward, a number ten in the modern game and in the period from 1971-86, arguably only Beckenbauer, Cruyff and Platini could claim superiority in Europe and definitely only Maradona in the rest of the world. This is triple A list company and to put it simply, "the boy could play".

In management, he again achieved everything nationally, three Division 1 titles at Liverpool plus two FA Cup and one League Cup win. And remember that when the "Reds" completed the double in 1986, he was that rarity, a Player-Manager, starting twenty nine whilst also managing the side. Add to this the Premier League title at Ewood and simply regarding him as a manager, you are looking at one of the most successful of all time. Also, if it had not been for the behaviour of a tiny minority of Liverpool fans at the Heysel Stadium in Belgium in 1985, behaviour which caused the death of thirty Juventus supporters and caused English clubs to be banned from all European competitions for six seasons, it is hard to believe that his Liverpool side would not have added to their tally of European Cup honours.

And yet I do have a lingering doubt about his "stickability" in the world of football management, an ever so slight chink of vulnerability showing in his mental armour. He left Liverpool for the first time in February 1991. Liverpool were clear once again at the top, still in the FA Cup and the reigning Division 1 champion. To be fair, as well as performing miracles on the touch line, his work in supporting the families of Hillsborough victims went far beyond the call of duty.

There were ninety six funerals and he attended many of them, urging his playing staff to also become involved. Whether the combined pressure of supporting the families and the City of Liverpool in general, plus the day by day stress of keeping the football team at the top of the league had finally caught up with him, we will probably never know but certainly his resignation came as a tremendous shock to everyone outside the inner circle of the club and his family. Likewise his departure from the hot seat at Blackburn came completely out of the blue, Had he once more given his all to the cause and had nothing more to give?

Again it is difficult to find anyone who knows the answers but I do think that it slightly tarnishes his reputation. There is however another way of looking at it. For instance, we all believe that the subsequent medical problems of Muhammed Ali were caused by not knowing when to call it a day. In fact so many sports men and women have had that one last race, that one last match too many. Has this been the case with Andy Murray? Perhaps "King Kenny" really is that rare genius; the one who knows the right time to pull the plug, to pack it all in when at the very top.

The Rovers made an early impression on the league, going seven games without defeat until Everton halted their progress with a 3-2 win at Ewood. Shearer had been quick to make his mark also and both he and Mike Newell scored twice as Norwich City were crushed 7-1. He added another double as Leeds United, reigning champions, were beaten 3-1 in a home Boxing Day thriller, taking his tally to the season to sixteen in twenty-one games. Then disaster struck. He tore his cruciate ligament and took no further part in the season. Tim Sherwood was becoming a player of influence in the middle of the park, David May had given them pace and assurance at the back and they lost only twice in their last twelve games. To finish fourth was a campaign beyond everyone's wildest dreams and Jack Walker's club had certainly laid down a marker for their rivals.

The 1992-93 season was their best attempt in the FA Cup since 1966 and was not bettered for the rest of the century. Wins over AFC Bournemouth and Crewe Alexandria gave them an easy passage to Round 5 where a Roy Wegerle goal was sufficient to beat Newcastle United. They were favourites against Sheffield United in Round 6, but without Shearer there was a bluntness to the attack in the goalless draw at Ewood. The replay also ended all square, 2-2 with goals from Livingstone and Newell but the Yorkshire side triumphed 5-3 in the penalty shoot-out. The Football League Cup run had been even better as they reached the semi-final. Rumbellows had handed the sponsorship rights over to Coca Cola and the Rovers produced their best performance since 1962.

Shearer scored three times across the two legs in Round 2 against Huddersfield Town as the Lancashire side went through 5-4 on aggregate. Norwich City, Premier League podium finishers were comfortably beaten 2-0 and then Watford were hammered 6-1 in the last sixteen, Shearer and Newell with doubles. With Shearer now injured, another Newell two-timer edged them past Cambridge United 3-2 in the quarters. The Sheffield Wednesday semi-final was a real 50-50 tie, but the Lancashire side was no match for its "White Rose" counterparts over two legs. After a disastrous first half performance from Dalglish's side, they went in 4-2 down and it stayed that way. It was no better at Hillsborough as the "Owls" won 2-1.

At Turf Moor, consolidation was the name of the game in Burnley's 1992-93 campaign. For once there were no notable departures but there were a couple of significant arrivals. Jimmy Mullen signed goalkeeper Marlon Beresford to give stability to the last line of defence. He had found it difficult to break into the first eleven at Premier League club Sheffield Wednesday, but he was comfortable in Division 2 and his £95,000 transfer fee turned out to be mere peanuts as his performances at Turf Moor over the next six years made him a crowd favourite.

Adrian Heath came from Manchester City, by now at the "fag end" of a career which had seen him perform with distinction at the highest levels of club football, particularly at Everton. He immediately became a crowd favourite and his twenty goals during the season was the second highest since 1966.

He also gave the team energy and experience, all requirements that the manager was desperate for. The fear of relegation haunted Mullen for the first few weeks of the season and it took them to game 10 to register just their third victory. It was against the powerful West Brom side and leading their attack was that much-vilified striker, Simon Garner. The close to 15,000 crowd that packed Turf Moor roared with delight as Harper scored early doors but within a quarter of an hour, Garner reminded everyone that he was public enemy number one in Burnley, equalising for the Baggies. Beresford then made save after save enabling Conroy to put the Clarets back in front around the hour mark and then it was defend, defend, defend to eke out a 2-1 victory. Other notable wins followed and the defence, consisting mainly of Measham, Jakub, Davis and Pender, generally held firm. A 13th place finish was acceptable for a first season out of the wilderness and hopefully Mullen could build on this.

The Clarets squeezed past Division 3 Scarborough and Shrewsbury Town in the FA Cup to earn a passage to the round of the 'Big Boys'. Sheffield United, a mid-table Premier League team, were 2-0 down with ten minutes to play at Bramall Lane, both goals coming courtesy of Adrian Heath. It was so disappointing when the "Blades" levelled and they were never going to be so generous at the second time of asking. True to form they rattled in four in Burnley but the home side put up a stirring fight, Heath scoring early and Mark Monington late to salvage some respectability from the game. The Football League campaign was a wash-out, being easily despatched 5-2 on aggregate by Carlisle United in Round 1.

1993-94

	Pos	Played	Won	Drawn	Lost	GF	GA	Pts
Blackburn Rovers	2	42	25	9	8	63	36	84
Burnley	6	46	21	10	15	79	58	73

Blackburn Rovers		Burnley	
Most Appearances	Graham Le Saux, David May, Stuart Ripley (all 40)	Most Appearances	Marlon Beresford 46
Most Goals	Alan Shearer 31	Most Goals	David Eyres 19

Dalglish bought in a steady stream of players throughout the first part of the season. Not all of the group were headline names, but the most notable ones were David Batty, that Yorkshire terrier of a mid-field player from Leeds United, Paul Warhurst a forward from Sheffield Wednesday and a quality goal keeper in Tim Flowers from Southampton. Batty and Flowers became integral parts of their future success, but Warhurst was extremely unlucky. He was a good signing because he could play at centre-forward or centre-half with equal aplomb but a succession of injuries kept him very much on the periphery.

Having finished fourth the previous campaign, there were hopes amongst the fans that they could edge closer to the top and this is actually what happened. Two defeats in the first three months and then a run of twelve games without defeat moved them into the role of principal challenger. Manchester United had been fourteen points clear at Christmas, but after a 2-0 home win over Ferguson's boys on April 2nd, Shearer netting a double, the Rovers were sharing top spot in the Premier League.

Dalglish's simple tactic of switching from 4-4-2 to 4-2-4 as they attacked worked a treat and the fans, restricted to 20,000 maximum because of the building work, simply could not believe that they might win the title. It was not to be as the Manchester giants, more accustomed to managing a title campaign, battened down the hatches, only conceded four goals in their final seven games and won the league for the second year running; this time by eight points. Apart from another sensational season of goal plundering by Shearer, the defence also played its part, only picking the ball out of the net on thirty-six occasions. It was the best performance by a Blackburn side since the title winning 1914 eleven and talking about going one better the following year was the only conversation in the town.

The FA Cup run was a disappointment. They struggled to defeat Portsmouth in a replay and then lost to Charlton Athletic, again in a replay. Again the Football League Cup was more interesting, It was a struggle against both AFC Bournemouth and Shrewsbury Town, Newell scoring twice at Gay Meadow, but they were goalless at White Hart Lane in Round 4, the Spurs going through 1-0.

Two years before, Burnley were in Division 3, the bottom of the heap, but suddenly, as if from nowhere, promotion to Division 1 was a possibility. Warren Joyce from Plymouth Argyle and David Eyres from Blackpool for £90,000 were the prominent new arrivals, Joyce returning to his father's old stamping ground. They both contributed well, but Eyres at the age of thirty, regularly weaved his magic down the left hand side and scored thirty-seven goals in 171 league appearances. The season started slowly and after nine games they were occupying twelfth spot. Four wins and a draw in five games, and they were scurrying up to third. There were slight stumbles, but they were never again below seventh. Tony Philiskirk, signed from Peterborough United in January, notched a hat-trick against an outclassed Barnet outfit and although the final five encounters brought their share of jitters, they were safely into the Play-Offs. Marlon Beresford, John Pender and Stephen Davis formed an impregnable rear guard fortress throughout the campaign, making life so much easier for the rest of the squad.

And so to the Play-Offs. Plymouth Argyll, home and away in the semi-final was always going to be difficult, The first leg at the 'Turf' drew a crowd of 18,794, but they had to suffer a tense goalless draw. There were far more fireworks at Home Park, particularly when the Devon side took the lead but Jimmy Mullen had inspired his boys and two goals from John Francis and one from Warren Joyce booked a place at Wembley for the final. Ted McMinn was signed just before the March transfer deadline and he certainly made a difference in the later games. The final will go down as a farce in the annals of the game.

The opposition came from Stockport County and the Greater Manchester club had finished fourth, twelve points above the Clarets. Within a couple of minutes, County were a goal up and then John Francis hobbled off to be replaced by Andy Farrell. From then on in, the momentum swung back the way of the East Lancashire team. Stockport had a man sent off for spitting and then Eyres launched the ball past the County keeper. Into the second-half and Stockport had a second man dismissed for foul play and surely Burnley could not be denied. Gary Parkinson scored the winner and the 2-1 victory over nine men saw them return to the second tier for the first time since being relegated in 1983. It was a joyous return for the Clarets' fans and they cared not a hoot that the opposition finished two short. They were now only one division behind their deadly rivals. When would they catch them?

The Burnley side which won the Division 2 Play-Off at Wembley Stadium in the 1993-94 season was: Marlon Beresford, Gary Parkinson, Les Thompson, Stephen Davis, John Pender, John Deary, Warren Joyce, Ted McMinn, David Eyres, Adrian Heath, John Francis. Substitute Andrew Farrell. Dave Timberlake was there of course and remembers it as the spitting final.

> "Ted McMinn and a Stockport player had an altercation and he spat in the Burnley player's face. It was an instant dismissal. We were one down then but we had fabulous support; so much so that we could not hear the Stockport crowd. There were around forty-five thousand in the ground and well over thirty thousand supported the Clarets. The David Eyres goal was something special and when they were reduced to nine men for a stamping offence, Gary Parkinson scored and we honestly thought we would score a bag full. But nerves got to us and we were so glad to hear the final whistle because we never really looked like scoring again. You might think that we were embarrassed to have struggled to beat nine men, but we were overjoyed at the final whistle. It was Division 1 here we come."

Burnley again reached Round 3 in the FA Cup with wins over York City and Rochdale at home where Eyres completed another hat-trick. They then had to travel to Charlton where they were beaten 3-0. In the League Cup, the Clarets thumped Preston North End from the basement division by a 6-2 margin over two legs in Round 1, Eyres scoring in both games. They then played above themselves to earn a goalless draw at Turf Moor against Tottenham Hotspur in the first leg but then bowed out following a 3-1 defeat in the return.

1994-95

	Pos	Played	Won	Drawn	Lost	GF	GA	Pts
Blackburn Rovers	1	42	27	8	7	80	39	89
Burnley	22	46	11	13	22	49	74	46

Blackburn Rovers		Burnley	
Most Appearances	Alan Shearer 42	Most Appearances	Mark Winstanley 43
Most Goals	Alan Shearer 34	Most Goals	David Eyres 8

The 1994-95 Premier League campaign was a scramble. It was never going to be a runaway success, but for those Rovers' fans even with the longest of memories, it has to be the highlight of our lives as Blackburn Rovers fans. Kenny Dalglish could do nothing to prevent David May's £1.2million sale to Manchester United and Alan Wright, surely one of the shortest professionals to play for the club in modern times (and also one of the most talented), was sold on to Aston Villa for £1million after being a mainstay in the defence until Le Saux arrived. With Kevin Moran also having to bow out because his ageing body could take no more after 143 starts, a replacement had to be found.

Tony Gale was the man and he brought a wealth of experience with him as he played alongside Colin Hendry for some of the season, alternating with Ian Pearce who had been at the club since Chelsea released him in 1993. But it was Chris Sutton who made the difference. At £5million, he proved a bargain as he immediately formed a partnership with Shearer up front. Nicknamed the SAS, they terrorised so many Premier League defences. There were two serious injuries, a fractured foot sustained by David Batty and a most unfortunate double set-back for Kevin Gallacher. He broke his leg and had a repeat of the injury in his first game back, thus missing the whole of this season bar one game.

The Rovers made a wonderful start to the season, a start which refused to end until January. With only two losses in twenty three games, they were topping the table. Sutton scored a hat-trick against Coventry City and Shearer twice followed suit against Queens Park Rangers and Ipswich Town. The Old Trafford side completed the double over them, Cantona scoring the game's only goal with ten to go. From then on in, the goals dried up to some extent and it was a case of grinding out results and defeats to Manchester City and West Ham United , both in the bottom half of the table, showed that nerves were taking over. I well remember the game at Everton. Because of my role with the English Schools' Football Association, I was given three tickets, all amongst Everton supporters. I brought along a life-long fan, my mate from Australia, but because spectator behaviour had significantly changed in the last twenty-five years since he was around, I specifically told him that if the Rovers scored, he must sit on his hands and control his emotions. Within minutes Sutton had scored and the Tasmanian immediately stood up and started celebrating.

It was all we could do but drag him back into his seat and to be fair, he used his discretion when Shearer put them two up not much later. A 1-0 home win over a Newcastle United side, full of attacking flair in the penultimate game of the campaign, in retrospect won them the title. This has to go down as one of the games which I would include in my anthology of all-time favourites, end to end attacking, marvellous goalkeeping by Flowers with everyone perched on the edge of their seats. With just ninety minutes of the season remaining, an away date at Liverpool, the press boys were tentatively backing the Rovers but there was still an enormous mountain to climb. A draw would suffice at Anfield, providing the "Red Devils" did not win at West Ham. Let Paul Cox tell the story.

> For our big day out at Anfield in 1995, a lift was secured for the four of us to Liverpool. Upon arrival we looked to have a few drinks in the area around the ground. Of course, keeping a low profile was a key factor and something we were good at. However, that day we chose a pub close to the ground and found ourselves a quiet corner. But as we were having a couple of drinks, a few of the locals approached. Now I started to think that we could be in trouble here. The largest of the group leaned over and said, "you lads Blackburn fans"? Not being very bright, we said "Yes". So he turned to his mates and said "drinks for these boys, on me. We don't want that United scum winning the league." And what an afternoon developed. Shearer scored in the first half, but John Barnes nicked an equaliser around the hour mark. Everyone was listening to the United game on their radios and the news came through that McClair had made it 1-1 at Upton Park. As the minutes slowly ticked by, we thought we were the champions despite Fergie's side being camped in the Hammers' half. Then well into injury time, Liverpool were awarded a free kick which Jamie Redknapp rocketed into the corner of Tim Flowers' net. For a moment, everyone thought we had lost out but then the announcement came on the tannoy. It had finished a draw in London. So how about this for a magical day, winning the Premier League and not paying for a drink on Merseyside. We chanced our arms after the game and went back to the same pub. There was a karaoke about to start, and as we entered, they played "We are the Champions" by Queen. Great memories!

Tickets were hard to come by for the Anfield game and I had to content myself watching with a group of friends and relatives in another friend's house. The last couple of minutes were surreal. It was as if everyone amongst us had lost track of what was required and when Redknapp fizzed in his free-kick from distance, we were all momentarily deflated as the referee immediately blew for time. And then the television cameras were all centred on Jack Walker and then Kenny Dalglish and it dawned upon us that the Rovers had clinched the title after all. There were stacks of interviews, the panellists talked and talked about the game, highlights were shown ad nauseum and finally the programme ended, the credits being rolled to the accompaniment of Lou Reed's "It's such a Perfect Day". Whenever I hear it played, I tell anyone who will listen what the tune means to me. One random story which amused me concerning this era was told to me by Vicky Foy, a teenager at the time and a Rover's fan from birth.

> "My dad was a Rovers' fanatic and from being quite a small girl, I caught the bug from him. My older sister wasn't really interested so it was me that he took down on the Blackburn end. Roy Wegerle sticks in my mind as the scorer of the goal in the first game I saw which was against Newcastle. [it was an FA Cup 5th Round game which the Rovers won 1-0 in the 1992-93 season: Editor]. We were all stood up then and when we scored there was a tremendous surge forward and my dad had to grab hold of me. Nowadays it would be seen as a daunting experience, particularly for a girl just about in her teens, but it was something that everyone accepted then. I remember in those days always having a bag of chips and a can of coke during the game, but by the time I was about sixteen or seventeen, me and three other mates started going to Pleasington in the School/College holidays to watch the Rovers train. You could do that in those days because Brockhall wasn't ready, they had to train in a public space and they couldn't stop anyone coming down to watch. It was quite horrible, sometimes freezing cold or pouring down, but we got to know the players. I had a thing about Tim Sherwood and I have to admit that we were groupies. In fact you could say we were stalkers. This was the season that we won the Premier League and I have loads of photos at home of me and the players, taken as they came off the pitch from training. I used to pester Tim all the time about him letting me have his shirt. The last home game was a night match against Newcastle and after the game, we waited for the players to drive off the car park to wish them goodbye and good luck at Liverpool. As Tim drove out, he saw me and wound the window down and passed his shirt to me. I couldn't believe my luck and I dashed off home in case anyone tried to take it off me. My mate got one from Mike Newell. I still have mine at home and bring it out from time to time. We used to go to watch the Youth team and got to know several of them and when we went up to the Cavendish [a Blackburn Night Club], we used to hang out with some of them. This was probably my last year as a groupie, but was still was a regular at Ewood which was now an all-seater stadium.

The Blackburn Rovers Premier League winning side of 1994-95 (started over 15 games, max 42) was; Tim Flowers, Henning Berg, Tony Gale, Ian Pearce, Colin Hendry, Graeme Le Saux, Stuart Ripley, Tim Sherwood, Mark Atkins, Jason Wilcox, Alan Shearer, Chris Sutton, Paul Warhurst, (Both David Batty and Jeff

Kenna played in the final game at Anfield.) There was no doubt that this was a talented side. All eleven who played at Anfield were internationals. Shearer and Sutton will be long remembered for their goal scoring exploits, but there were other unsung heroes deserving of a mention. Dalglish and his Assistant Roy Harford played a rigid system which meant that wide men Stuart Ripley and Jason Wilcox had to support their full backs when the side was defending and attack with menace, supplying telling crosses when, to use the modern idiom, there was transition. So many of the goals scored by the SAS were from crosses provided by these two. And perhaps one of the reasons for a lack of attacking fluency in the last quarter of the term was the serious injury sustained by Wilcox. But the most unexpected star was Mark Atkins.

We all love the "Hollywood style" heroes, the great internationals known nationwide and beyond, but particularly in this part of the world, we have such a lot of admiration for the those who make it on pure hard work. An integral part of the triumph was Mark Atkins. Nicknamed "Super Atko" by the fans, he had been a journeyman right back for much of his career at Ewood, but when Batty was injured, he was the man most trusted by the manager to win the ball in the middle of the park.

There he sweated blood for the cause and in total he played in 257 league games, scoring thirty five times before being sold to Wolverhampton Wanderers for £1million at the end of the Premier League winning season. He was one of only two members of the squad not bought by Jack Walker money, having arrived in the pre-Walker era. Wilcox was the other, having come through the ranks of the youth set-up.

There was one great disappointment in this never to be forgotten season. Finding yourself in the rarefied air towards the summit of the English game brings rewards in Europe but their first venture in the UEFA Cup was embarrassing. Trelleborgs F.F. from Sweden were a semi-professional club, the Rovers selected a full strength side. It ought to have been a cricket score but the part-timers won 1-0 at Ewood Park. Surely they could not repeat the form in the second leg and with the 90 minute mark looming, the Blackburn side were through on the away goals rule, courtesy of leading 2-1, S and S supplying the goals. Then at the death, the Swedes stole in for a second goal. Exit the Rovers, fallen at the first fence. And to make matters worse, an opportunist Burnley fan stole out in the middle of the night and visited all roads leading in to Burnley, and where the place name on the sign says, 'Welcome to Burnley' added 'Twin Town: Trelleborgs'.

Normally, top sides receive comfortable opposition in Round 3 of the FA Cup, but a home tie against a good Newcastle United side was likely to stretch the Rovers. Sutton scored in a 1-1 draw at St James' Park and in the replay at Ewood, he scored again, but Newcastle had the edge, disappointedly knocking the Blue and Whites out by a 2-1 margin. League Cup wins over Birmingham City and Coventry City brought Liverpool to Ewood for a last sixteen tie. The Rovers had won 3-2 earlier in the season on the day the renovated stadium was re-opened on all four sides, but a sub-par performance handed Liverpool a 3-1 victory.

As Blackburn Rovers' season slowly built to the ultimate crescendo, Burnley were tentatively dipping its toes into uncharted waters; uncharted for the last eleven years that is. Whereas the 82-83 side included household names and in some cases international players such as Stevenson, Dobson, Steven, Hamilton and Flynn, the 1994-95 starting eleven included no-one of that pedigree, only keeper Marlon Beresford, that defensive stalwart Stephen Davis and the veteran Adrian Heath being known to anyone outside the town except for the true football anoraks.

Twice Jimmy Mullen smashed the club's transfer record before the start of the season, full back Chris Vinnicombe arriving from Glasgow Rangers for £200,000 and Liam Robinson, a forward player from Bristol City for £50,000 more. Neither played too long at the "Turf" and were something of a disappointment in what was a disappointing season. Two trusted servants of the club left during the season following years of sterling service. Andy Farrell, after seven long seasons and 237 starts left for Wigan Athletic and John Deary, four and a half years and 209 starts, moved to Rochdale. The support was certainly there for them, the gate falling below the five figure mark on only two occasions but the start was poor, only two wins in the first twelve games condemning them instantly to a relegation spot.

Then came a mini-revival, ten games undefeated albeit seven being drawn. From fifteenth spot, the world suddenly looked a lot brighter but a disastrous run of eight successive defeats sent them crashing to the bottom of the heap. Without a striker to lead the attack, it always looked like a losing battle. Centre-half Davis was second leading goal scorer with seven, just one behind Eyres, a statistic which says it all. They say you need fifty points to be safe in a 24 club league and forty-six was never enough in this exceptional year where at least fifty-four points were needed for survival.

The base line statistic was stark. They had been relegated after finishing twenty-second. It was a bitter pill for the manager to swallow, a case of starting over again in League 2 while they were singing from the roof tops down the relatively new M65 Motorway. One salient statistic suggests the reason for the gulf between the Rovers and the Clarets at this time. The Burnley club had spent approximately £640,000 in total on transfer purchases this season whereas the Rovers paid out £5million for Chris Sutton alone.

If a club wants to make progress in a cup competition, good advice would be to avoid serial winners like Liverpool. In the 1994-5 season, Burnley were drawn against them in both of the two major competitions. The FA Cup run actually provoked excitement in the town. Entering in Round 1, Shrewsbury Town (home) and Chester City and Cambridge United (both away) were all dismissed. Of the eight goals in total that were scored, Eyres and Heath were both on target twice.

Over 20,000 fans packed Turf Moor for the visit of Liverpool in Round 4 and the Burnley boys deserved all the plaudits, holding the Mersey giants to a goalless draw. The performance in the replay was almost as good, conceding only once but sadly failing to score. In the League Cup, after a victory over York City, the draw for Round 2, two legged once again at this time, sent them to Anfield. This time it was a more predictable result, a one sided 6-1 aggregate victory for the Merseysiders, Liam Robinson being on target twice in this competition.

1995-96

	Pos	Played	Won	Drawn	Lost	GF	GA	Pts
Blackburn Rovers	7	38	18	7	13	61	47	61
Burnley	17	46	14	13	19	56	68	55

Blackburn Rovers		Burnley	
Most Appearances	Henning Berg 38	Most Appearances	Kurt Nogan 46
Most Goals	Alan Shearer 31	Most Goals	Kurt Nogan 20

For those packed into what now was a very modern Stadium at Ewood Park, the 1995-96 season was the opportunity to erase the defeat to the Swedish minnows in the UEFA Cup by performing well in the big one, the UEFA Champions League which had previously been won by Real Madrid, Liverpool, Manchester United et al. There was also a certain Premier League title to be retained and anticipation was sky high amongst the growing band of fans. But before all that, there was the question of a new manager. Kenny Dalglish shocked the town and probably much of the British Isles when he resigned at the end of the season, although he did stay on as Director of Football.

He had been sufficiently savvy to bring in Ray Harford as his number two when he arrived in Blackburn and there is no doubt that much of the credit for the Rovers' Premier League win could be laid at Harford's door, his tactical nous, organisation and technical knowledge complementing the aura which surrounded Dalglish. He was determined to stay as a coach, but when "Uncle Jack Walker" popped the question, it was always difficult to say "no" and so Ray Harford became the twenty-second official permanent manager of this fine old club. Having played at the highest level does not necessarily make you a top manager, but there must be times when it must be an advantage.

No-one likes to be given a "bollocking" by the boss. "Bet you couldn't do that" is something you think, if not say. But when a Kenny Dalglish says "Don't do it like that, do it like this" it is a conversation stopper. You simply take it on the chin because he did it right, all of the time.

The road to managerial success is littered with the corpses of successful coaches who find it a step too far. There is no doubt that it is a different role. Coaches work extremely hard with the players on a day to day basis, but the buck stops with the manager. The final decisions, the difficult decisions that keep ordinary mortals awake at night, are with him. Now was it this part of the job that Harford found difficult, or perhaps the fact that there was less respect for him having played at a much lower level or that only the very finest of sides retain their title and this group had peaked and was on the way down? It is an interesting question and as with many aspects of professional football, a question which only those with insider knowledge can begin to answer.

But if you study the top teams which have dominated English football in the last sixty years, they all have had more than one star player at a time. Best, Law, Charlton and then later, Giggs, Scholes, Ronaldo at Manchester United, Dalglish, Rush and Hansen at Liverpool with Henry, Vieira and Bergkamp at Arsenal are just a few examples. The Blackburn Rovers 1995 side had ten good players plus Alan Shearer and history tells us that to stay at the top of the tree for even a couple of years, more than one great is required.

His replacement Ray Harford had been a centre-half at several lower Division outposts such as Colchester, Lincoln, Exeter and Port Vale. He had built up a reputation as a knowledgeable coach and had tasted success as a manager with Luton Town. He had the experience and he fully understood the game, but the Rovers were now one of the country's top teams. Was he the right man for the job? It may not have been his fault that the club quickly fell away from that small circle of clubs that dominate at any one time. Injuries, loss of form and sometimes just plain bad luck often play their parts, but whatever the reason, there was disappointment in the town as Harford's side started indifferently, then raised their game somewhat towards the end only to finish seventh. He was hampered by lengthy injuries to Le Saux, Gallacher and Sutton, plus Atkins and Gale left the club, the latter released to play at Crystal Palace and Harford splashed out money in the transfer market to bring in replacements.

Billy McKinlay from Dundee United, Lars Bohinen ex-Notts Forest, Chris Coleman from Crystal Palace and Gary Flitcroft bought from Manchester City were all good players but it was outstanding players who were needed to help the club retain its title. Mike Newell had lost his goal touch and was transferred to Birmingham City at the end of the season, having scored twenty-eight goals in 113 league appearances. For a reigning title holder, it was such a disappointing start, although Shearer was still knocking in goals. There was a hat-trick in a 5-1 demolition of Coventry City, and a 7-0 home win over Nottingham Forest was a further catalyst to their improved performances.

One defeat in twelve games saw them accelerate away from the relegation zone towards possible European qualification. There were losses in February but the campaign ended on a high with another stunning defeat of Notts Forest, 5-1 at the City Ground.

The potentially biggest ever games for the club came into focus this season, the European Champions' League. As English title holders, the Blackburn club

automatically qualified for the last sixteen, being England's sole representative. There was a tremendous responsibility resting on the shoulders of Harford and his boys but the opposition within the group appeared rather accommodating at first glance. There ought to have been little to fear from any of Spartak Moscow, Legia Warsaw and the completely unheralded Rosenburg from Norway. Reality however painted a different picture. Five of the games were closely contested, the only one-sided affair being the one that the Rovers won at home to the Norwegians. There was also a draw at home to the Poles but the Russians, who went on to top the group from Legia Warsaw, completed the double against them. Shipping three goals in Moscow was a poor result, compounded by all the bad press received when Le Saux and Batty were in trouble with the referee for fighting. Bizarrely it was with each other; talk about negative publicity. The feeling in the press was, because of this particular incident, the Rovers had let down the country and to be fair, they had. The trouble between two completely different animals from contrasting upbringings and cultures was apparently never really sorted until Batty was transferred to Newcastle United in February for £3.75million. Fascinatingly both of them were members of Glenn Hoddle's 1998 England World Cup squad in France. I wonder if there was still acrimony between them in the Argentina game in which they both played, particularly after the Yorkshireman missed his penalty after 120 minutes. The only highlight for the blue and white halves was the hat-trick Mike Newell scored against Rosenburg.

For the second year running, the Rovers crashed out of the FA Cup in Round 3. A goalless draw at Division 1 Ipswich was acceptable but a 1-0 home defeat in the replay after extra time certainly was not. Their performance in the League Cup was also less than adequate. They defeated Swindon Town 5-2 on aggregate in Round 2, Shearer inevitably scoring four of the goals. A trip to Watford in Round 3 brought a close 2-1 win but another away journey saw their elimination in the last sixteen, a poor Leeds United side edging through 2-1.

Fortunately for the fans of Burnley Football Club, the trials and tribulations which combined to produce a disappointing season in Blackburn, did much to hide the fact that their campaign was far, far worse. Back in Division 2, two tiers below their neighbours, there was a feeling at Easter time that a second successive relegation was on the cards. And yet the season began promisingly, fifth place being attained after a comprehensive 3-0 victory over a poor Brighton side in mid-October. Stephen Davis had been sold to Luton Town for £750,000 and replaced by Peter Swan, a £200,000 buy from Plymouth Argyle. He would partner Mark Winstanley at the heart of the defence and Kurt Nogan, signed from Brighton towards the end of the previous season, led the attack, mainly alongside Andy Cooke, a new arrival from Welsh football.

There were two crazy early 4-3 results at Turf Moor. Notts County being the victors in one of the matches, Stockport County the victims in the other. It was all very entertaining but equally worrying and then it was free-fall time. Sixteen games yielded just one win and the Clarets were twentieth, one place above the dreaded drop zone. Mullen departed during this run having guided them to two promotions, unceremoniously "dumped" with the club, albeit on a losing streak of four, in mid-table.

Clive Middlemass, Jimmy Mullen's assistant, was promoted to the post of temporary manager but one point in three games meant a permanent replacement was required and Adrian Heath, "Inchy" as he was known in the game, had been released in the December to become Assistant Manager to Howard Kendall at Sheffield United. He quickly returned to become the club's first ever Player-Manager. He had been a hero at Turf Moor, but the difference he made this time was marginal, although sufficient to comfortably stay up, six points clear of relegation. In actual fact, he only appeared on the pitch three times, but his experience helped to grind out the victories over Peterborough and Shrewsbury Town which ensured safety, compiling exactly a point a game in the sixteen played following his appointment. Winstanley was a tower of strength at the back but Nogan was the recipient of the praise from the stands, his twenty goals being the major factor in their drive towards the safety of seventeenth position. The understanding of the fans in determining if it is a good sale or purchase and the criteria used by the Board and Manager can be quite different. Steve Davis' sale made good business sense to the Board but the fans saw it as weakening the side. Spending only £200,000 for Peter Swan as a replacement also made sense to those in high office, but the fans knew he would not match the quality of his predecessor. Warren Joyce, who had worked hard for the cause in mid-field, left for Hull City at the end of the campaign whilst John Francis, scorer of thirty seven goals in 143 games was also released. But looking at it from a wider perspective, the gap between the two East Lancashire clubs had widened once again. Jimmy Mullen had been appointed in October '91 and he engineered two promotions in three seasons; his four years plus stint certainly being action packed. He was having to operate when the finances at Turf Moor were far from secure and he deserves much credit for what he achieved. Interestingly in his playing career, he skippered Sheffield Wednesday, Rotherham United and Cardiff City to promotion, all from Tier 3, so what he achieved at Burnley should not have come as a surprise.

Steve Davis explained why he moved away from a club where he had enjoyed two promotions in three years, before they quickly fell back down one rung of the ladder.

> "My first three years at Turf Moor were tremendous. To achieve two promotions was something special but we struggled in Division 1. We conceded too many

goals and scored too few. This is not a good recipe for a successful season but I was still looking to extend my contract. I thought I had done really well in my time there and I was at the top of my game, but what they offered me, in my opinion, was not good enough. I found out that Luton Town were interested in me and that David Pleat had recommended me. That was good enough for me. There was a disagreement between the two clubs as to how much the transfer fee should be and a Football League Tribunal had to make the decision. I think Luton were shocked when the verdict came in, but they paid out the £750,000."

A home tie in the FA Cup against Division 2 side Walsall ought to have gone in the Clarets' favour, but a 3-1 defeat typified the season. There was a smidgeon of success in the Football League Cup as Mansfield Town were defeated 4-1 on aggregate in Round 1, Nogan scoring three of the four goals. But the run quickly stalled in the second round as they lost 2-0 home and away to Leicester City.

1996-97

	Pos	Played	Won	Drawn	Lost	GF	GA	Pts
Blackburn Rovers	13	38	9	15	14	42	43	42
Burnley	9	46	19	11	16	71	55	68

Blackburn Rovers		Burnley	
Most Appearances	Jeff Kenna, Tim Sherwood (both 37)	Most Appearances	Gary Parkinson 43
Most Goals	Chris Sutton 11	Most Goals	Paul Barnes 24

During the summer break, an extremely serious problem surfaced at Ewood Park. Alan Shearer, it was rumoured, wanted to leave. Newcastle United was famous for its number nines, all the way back to the 1920s, heroes who all topped the hundred goal mark in the famous black and white shirts. Now, having come close to winning the title in the previous season, they desperately needed an iconic figure who would bulge the net week in, week out. There was no-one more iconic in the English game than the Rovers' centre forward and just to add a touch more romance to the story, he had been born in Gosforth on the outskirts of the city. There are stories of tea time telephone calls between Lancashire and Jersey as Shearer and Jack Walker talked serious money, of Walker making a stupendous offer and then changing his mind, but there was a feeling that whatever was offered, the legend had worn the blue and white halved shirt for the last time. By July 30th, 1996, Blackburn directors had refused to sell to Manchester United. Ferguson and David Gill, the United Chief Executive at the time, have both admitted this in print, and so he was off to St James' Park with a world record £15million price tag on his head. Was he worth it? I think every Geordie would say he was. Would they be able to replace him at Ewood? Sadly, not a hope in hell. He quickly became the most recognisable face on Tyneside, possibly their greatest ever player, but his Pre-

mier League medal from his Blackburn days remains the only one on his mantel piece. Now had he been allowed to join the "Reds"...?

In the subsequent season, 1996-97, the Republic of Ireland international full back Jeff Kenna had become a regular in the side. Signed by Dalglish for £1.5million towards the end of the title winning season following an injury to Jason Wilcox, he stayed at Ewood Park for seven seasons, amassing a total of 157 appearances, but heads were drooping in the stands as they lost 2-0 to Tottenham Hotspur in the opening fixture at Ewood and they dropped a lot further as the first eleven games provided just four points. One, completely out of the blue, came from a 2-2 draw at Old Trafford but it was clear where the problems were. They had conceded only sixteen goals in this period but scored a paltry seven.

Predictably, Harford could not find a replacement for Shearer and his only purchase was Georgious Donis, a lightning quick winger from Panathinaikos. Quick he may have been, but in terms of end product there was scarcely nothing. With the side at the bottom of the league, Harford tended his resignation. Dalglish had already quit his post as Director of Football and with Shearer and now Harford moving on, some wags claimed that the rats were leaving the sinking ship. "Mr Reliable", aka Tony Parkes accepted the offer to take over on a temporary basis. As so often happens, the "new manager bounce" worked for him. A 3-0 win over Liverpool, Sutton scoring twice, turned the tide and kicked off a series of small unbeaten runs.

Kevin Gallacher scored a hat-trick as Wimbledon went down 3-1 at Ewood and by this time, relegation was no longer on the agenda. Then typically, one win in the last nine games had them looking anxiously over their shoulders, but Parkes had done what he set out to do, safety being ensured by a two point margin and a thirteenth place finish. The problem had been a lack of imagination going forward which restricted the quality of service to Sutton and Gallacher, hence the goals for column boasting a total of forty-two from thirty eight games, the lowest since relegation from Division 2 in 1979.

At last there was an FA Cup victory. They eliminated Port Vale but disappointedly went out to a poor Coventry City outfit in Round 4 at Ewood Park, Sherwood scoring the goal in a 2-1 defeat. In the Football League Cup, Brentford were beaten home and away, a 4-1 aggregate win in Round 2. There was a real low in Harford's final game however, Stockport County from Division 2 winning 1-0 in Round 3. No wonder the manager quit.

The 1996-97 season was one of those "might have been years" at Turf Moor. Adrian Heath brought in Damian Matthew (from Crystal Palace) and Nigel Gleghorn (from Stoke City) for the 1996-97 campaign but neither of these two midfield players made a lasting contribution. Paul Barnes from Birmingham City however certainly made an impression. He was a centre-forward with a strike record of one in every two games over the last four seasons and he continued that form in Lancashire after Burnley paid a club record £375.000 fee for him. Interestingly, his son Harvey now plays for Leicester City in the Premier League. It had been many years since a footballer of note left Glentoran to join Burnley (McIlroy and Elder being the two everyone remembers) but Glen Little followed the same path this year, £100,000 changing hands. He would prove to be a bargain buy.

As was so often the case with Burnley during this period, there was a topsy-turvy nature to the campaign. Two wins, three defeats then two wins and a draw saw them in eleventh place after ten games, Nogan being the principal goal scorer. Then suddenly Barnes exploded. He scored all five in the 5-2 win over Stockport County and the fans had a new hero. It was the first five-timer by a Burnley player since Andy Lochhead performed the feat against Bournemouth in the FA Cup in 1966. Cooke and Barnes shared four of the five goals as Gillingham suffered a 5-1 hammering over the Christmas period and approaching St Valentine's Day, the Clarets occupied fifth spot. After Barnes' hat-tricks at Blackpool and home to Peterborough, visions of promotion flitted across the town. But just when a big finish was called for, the response was muted.

Four defeats and two draws in the final eight games saw them slither down to ninth spot. Burnley had scored seventy-one goals, the highest in the league but finished five points off a Play-Off place. Not to finish in the top six was a sin and Adrian Heath, perhaps realising this, moved to Everton to become Howard Kendall's assistant once again. Heath was always popular with the paying public. When the Board turned to him as manager, a move much approved by the fans, he saved them from another relegation and promotion the following year was a strong possibility, but when it never materialised, he resigned. The Burnley post possibly came too early in his coaching career for him, because he has since gone on to be successful managing and coaching in the MLS in North America over the last twelve years.

The 1996-97 version of the FA Cup also brought excitement to Burnley. New signings Gleghorn and Matthew were on target as Lincoln City were beaten 2-1 and the crowd certainly got their money's worth in the replay against Walsall at the "Turf". It was 1-1 after extra-time, but the Clarets won the shoot-out 4-2. Unbelievably, it was Liverpool at Anfield again in Round 3 and Burnley once more played above their station, going down to a solitary Stan Collymore strike. It was a game which meant a great deal to the young Paul Weller.

"When you are down in Division 2 and the draw for the FA Cup sends you to Anfield, it is the most exciting time in a footballer's life. Adrian gave me my instructions; mark John Barnes out of the game. It seemed like a tall order until he came on to the pitch. He was fat and 'here's my big chance' I thought. I knew I was far fitter than him and that I could harass him and nip in and win the ball, but it sadly turned out far different. He never tried to run past me, but he simply passed the ball round me. He could really play. His touch was brilliant, just one and two touches all night. Even marking him tightly, I couldn't get near him and although he was nearing the end of his career, he was by far the best player I ever came directly up against."

In the Football League Cup, Burnley easily handled Mansfield Town for the second consecutive year in Round 1 but Charlton Athletic from Division 1 were a different proposition and Heath's side was easily defeated, 6-2 on aggregate. David Eyres scored three of the club's seven goals in this mini-cup run.

1997-98

	Pos	Played	Won	Drawn	Lost	GF	GA	Pts
Blackburn Rovers	6	38	16	10	12	57	52	58
Burnley	20	46	13	13	20	55	65	52

Blackburn Rovers		Burnley	
Most Appearances	Jeff Kenna 37	Most Appearances	Neil Moore 38
Most Goals	Chris Sutton 18	Most Goals	Andy Cooke 16

Poor Tony Parkes. He was the "Mr Fix It", but never became "Mr Permanent" because a top European coach was now on Jack Walker's radar. When Sven Goran-Eriksson shillied and shallied, he switched his attention to Roy Hodgson, a football academic if there ever was one. Although very much an Englishman, his managerial career blossomed in Europe where he was very much a nomad, moving on after a couple of years at a club. He was in charge at the likes of Malmo in Sweden, Grasshoppers Zurich, the Switzerland National side with which he qualified for World and European finals and Inter Milan.

When at Inter, he was approached and he quickly said "yes". It was a big coup for Jack Walker to bring this most intellectual of coaches to the north of England. There was great excitement around the club and Hodgson certainly made a difference. To bring in new players, he had to sell Henning Berg to Manchester United and Graeme Le Saux to Chelsea. Having managed regularly in continental Europe, it was no surprise that a number of foreign players were brought in. We expected Martin Dahlin to become the new poster boy but along with Tore Pedersen, Patrick Valery and Anders Andersson, they made little impact; the only one becoming an established player was the stylish Swiss centre-back Stephane Henchoz signed from Hamburg, who slotted in alongside Colin Hendry. It was still the Dalglish/Harford signings who played regularly and Chris Sutton and Kevin Gallacher had magnificent seasons.

One defeat in fifteen games was a measure of Hodgson's style of play, a run that was brought to a jarring halt with a 4-0 defeat at Old Trafford. But a second place at New Year and a 7-2 thrashing of Sheffield Wednesday gave so much hope before two defeats in February, two in March and four in April saw them plunge down the table. By defeating Newcastle United 1-0 on the final day of the season, they edged Aston Villa out of sixth place, enabling them to qualify for the UEFA Cup.

The "in play" form in the League Cup was impressive, less so from the penalty spot. Preston North End were smashed 6-1 on aggregate, Martin Dahlin making a rare appearance on the score sheet with a brace. But then a difficult draw at Stamford Bridge in Round 3 was the platform for both a battling 1-1 stalemate but also a dismal display in the art of penalty taking, scoring just once with Chelsea sailing through. In the FA Cup campaign, Gallagher scored twice as Wigan were beaten 4-2 and Sheffield Wednesday were similarly disposed of, 3-0 at Ewood. In Round 5, following a 2-2 draw in London and still no winner after 120 minutes of the replay, Hodgson's side again failed to pass the penalty test, West Ham sneaking through 5-4.

Once more it was managerless Burnley. Harry Potts had initially sat in the hot seat for twelve years before he had decided to step down in 1970 having kept the club close to the top of the football tree throughout that period. Since that date, thirteen different appointments had been made in twenty-seven years. It cannot be said that if a club stays with the same man, everything will be fine, but looking at Burnley's journey in that two and a half decades, it does suggest that if the Board could have shown a little more patience, then the results may have been somewhat better. Other questions to be asked surround the quality of the men chosen and whether the Board "did their homework" before making the decisions. But the issue prior to the start of the 1997-98 season was once more to find the right man. They plumped for Chris Waddle, one of the best footballers that this country has produced. His appointment was greeted with a frenzy of excitement but the question few people asked was "can he manage"? The swift answer was "no-one knows". Had the Board been captivated by his name alone?

It quickly became apparent that they had. The start to his reign was abysmal, their first victory arriving on October 11th at home to Carlisle United. And the struggle continued until the very last game of the season. In a twenty-four club division, the Clarets only spent four weeks higher than twentieth. They even spent fifteen weeks in bottom spot. He considered himself to be a player-manager and actually made an appearance in thirty-one of the games, many in the starting line-up. The fans could not believe what they were seeing early doors, six goalless games flashing by before Paul Barnes found the net in a 3-1 defeat at York City. Then Gerry Creaney arrived on a two-month loan from Manchester City and his eight goals in nine games turned it around and lifted them away from the drop zone. But after his departure, there were four more blank games, no goals and a single point from the home game against Chesterfield on Boxing Day. David Eyres left for Preston North End and Paul Barnes was Huddersfield bound in a swap deal with Andy Payton, a local boy whom the Clarets had released at sixteen but who went on to score 131 league goals at Hull City, Celtic, Barnsley and Huddersfield Town prior to joining his hometown club. These two departees shocked the faithful but at least there seemed some logic in the Paul Barnes case. Andy Payton possessed a proven track record of finding the net. I asked Andy why he had returned to Turf Moor when his career was flourishing elsewhere.

> I was at Huddersfield Town in Division 1 and in my first season there I had knocked in seventeen league goals. At the start of the new season I had scored in the League Cup and then I heard talk of this swap with Paul Barnes. I looked at the league table and it meant me dropping down a division but worse than that, Burnley were at the very bottom of the league. At first I thought it was a stupid idea but then I started to remind myself that this was Burnley. It was my home town club and I had supported them all my life, so I said yes. I like to think that my goals kept them up and then Stan came in at the end of the season. I knew him well because he had managed me at Hull City. He had then gone to Bury and performed miracles there, taking them up two divisions and actually keeping them up in Division 1. Anyone who could do that is a marvel.

Chris Brass, a dependable defender had worked his way through from being a trainee at Gawthorpe but he was now a first team regular and Andy Cooke found the net twice against Watford, the Payton-Cooke combo beginning to pay dividends. The home crowd was stunned when York City were put to the sword, a 7-2 win followed by a 3-2 victory at Deepdale once more lifting them out of the twenties. Cooke hit a hat-trick against York but once again the inspired form was transient and another seven winless games took them to the very bottom of the league. Payton however was now in the groove and he scored the winning goal in four games to give them a chance of survival if they could defeat Plymouth at home in the final game of the campaign. The Argyle was a fellow relegation candidate, and Waddle's side had to depend on Brentford not winning at Bristol Rovers. A crowd of 18,811 turned up for either a wake or a celebration and two Andy Cooke goals gave them a 2-1 win, sending the fans home with a huge sigh of relief. It had all been too much for Chris Waddle, management obviously was not for him and he resigned from his post. One crazy side line in this crazy season was that with twelve games still to be played, Marlon Beresford had been sold to Middlesbrough after making 240 appearances in goal. Chris Woods had been brought along as goalkeeping coach on Waddle's arrival and the boss had no compunction about throwing this veteran international into the spotlight at the age of thirty-eight where he made a major contribution to Burnley's survival battle.

Paul Weller gave me his summing up of the Waddle year, his life under other managers and the difficulties encountered in this profession which are not always apparent to those not directly involved in the game.

"I had found it wonderful to play in a team managed by Adrian Heath and was so disappointed when he moved on to Everton. But imagine my excitement when Chris Waddle was appointed. As a Spurs fan from being a boy, he was one of my big heroes and I have to admit that I was overawed at the prospect of being in the same dressing room as him. In pre-season training, he still had the tricks and touches and he was determined to be a player-manager. It didn't help that his initial impression of me was that I wasn't good enough and both myself and Glen Little didn't even make the bench for the first game of the season. He slowly came to appreciate what we could both give to the team and I eventually became a regular in the starting line-up. It took us a while to get on, but as the season progressed I began to feel that he was growing into the job and by the end of the season, he had got it right. I was therefore surprised when he left. I think if he had stayed for another year, he could have done something. But I also think that managing in the lower divisions is completely different to being involved at the top of the game. And this is why I think he was a bad choice. He was thrown straight in and at first he had no understanding of what the game was about in Division 2. We needed someone with experience at this level, someone like Stan Ternent and when he took over, he really took the club up a step. In his first two seasons there, I had a terrible time health wise. In total I spent sixty days in hospital, seriously ill for a long while. The manager was fantastic with me, visiting me in hospital to keep me updated and showing so much patience as it took so long to return to full fitness. He told me that I had no chance of being in the side until I was completely well, but when I was, he would want me involved. I was so happy playing for Stan but four years later in 2004, my contract was due to run out and the club was short of money. They wanted me to stay but I would have to take a cut in wages. I refused the offer but Stan told me not to worry and he would see what he could do as the season ended. Unfortunately, the Board made the decision to change manager, Steve Cotterill came in and as many do, decided that he could bring in men who would do a better job than those at the club. I was due to be married in the close season and on the eve of the wedding, Cotterill rang me and told me I was surplus to requirements. I couldn't believe that I had been treated so thoughtlessly after twelve years at the club and from that moment on, I fell out of love with the game. I moved to Rochdale and after five games, Steve Parkin offered me a contract, but it was basement wages at a basement club. To his amazement I walked away, totally disillusioned with the game."

There were to be no heroics in the FA Cup this season. The 1st Round draw sent them to Rotherham United and the 3-3 draw hinted at better things to come, but a 3-0 defeat at home in the replay was as unfathomable as it was appalling. The Football League Cup saw them manage to stumble through against Lincoln City and a Round 2 pairing with Stoke City. In a case of the least said the better, the Potters blazed through 6-0 on aggregate.

1998-99

	Pos	Played	Won	Drawn	Lost	GF	GA	Pts
Blackburn Rovers	19	38	7	14	17	38	52	35
Burnley	15	46	13	16	17	54	73	55

Blackburn Rovers		Burnley	
Most Appearances	Stephan Henchoz, Callum Davidson (both 34)	Most Appearances	Gordon Armstrong 40
Most Goals	Kevin Gallacher, Ashley Ward (both 5)	Most Goals	Andy Payton 20

The 1998-99 campaign was most disappointing for the Blackburn club, in particular for Roy Hodgson. He lost Colin Hendry, replacing him with Christian Dailly. Stuart Ripley and James Beattie, a promising local striker, both signed for Southampton and Hodgson made a move into the transfer market but the incoming players were either not quite up to the standard of those having left or were complete flops, the foreign imports in particular. But two of the lesser names who managed to hold down a place were Darren Peacock, a centre-half signed from Newcastle United (pony tail and all) and Callum Davidson, a left back from St Johnstone. The squad was beset by injuries and marquee players such as Sutton, Gallacher, Flitcroft, McKinlay, Dailly and Sherwood all played fewer than half the matches. Hodgson preferred the Australian John Filan to Tim Flowers in goal but the biggest flop of all was Kevin Davies.

Further down the line, he became a most respected professional, but his haul at Ewood Park was one goal in eleven starts and twelve appearances off the bench. "What a waste of money" sang the fans and they were 100% correct. Hodgson had bought Nathan Blake from Bolton Wanderers for nearly £4million, not exactly a failure but with nowhere near the potency of a Shearer.

Yet still the crowds continued to pour through the gates but two wins in their first fifteen games was sufficient to see the end of Hodgson's eighteen month reign with the Rovers rock bottom. There has always been gossip, exaggerations and no doubt fake news leaking out of dressing rooms, some you can take with a pinch of salt, but there is no smoke without fire as my grandma used to say. Back in the old days, a footballer would train in the morning and go to the betting shop or have a game of snooker or golf in the afternoon. The life style of the players had obviously changed in the preceding twenty years, but it was still the case of morning training and then have the rest of the day to themselves. Roy's twice a day sessions were probably acceptable to professionals such as Sherwood when they were winning but when results were going the wrong way, they needed something to blame. Was disharmony and divisiveness the reason why Hodgson ultimately failed at Ewood? ... Possibly!

Unfortunately, Roy had also been unable to conjure up a decent run in the UEFA Cup. For the third time this decade, Blackburn Rovers found themselves in Europe where they were drawn against Olympique Lyonnais in the 1st Round. More commonly referred to as Lyon, this was a club which would dominate French football in the first decade of the new century but at this time, they were one of the better French teams, but certainly not the best. Only 13,646 turned up to watch an insipid performance from Hodgson's side at Ewood Park which the visitors won 1-0. By the time of the second leg two weeks later, the Rovers still only had that solitary win over Leicester City to their name. There was an improved performance, but sadly the 2-2 draw was still not good enough. Goals from Perez and Flitcroft had held out hope but at the very first hurdle, they said au revoir to a run in Europe.

Jack Walker knew his target and nothing was going to stop him. His replacement again seemed the perfect choice. Brian Kidd's reputation as Alex Ferguson' assistant was immeasurable. He was the hero of Wembley 68, the first English victory in the European Cup. His apprenticeship had been long. Surely this was his moment. He arrived in double quick time from Old Trafford and the fans were elated. But the truth was that the playing staff simply was not good enough. The old brigade was either over the hill, needed a change of scenery or had just given up. The recent buys were not up to standard and for the talented youngsters coming through (Duff, Dunn and Taylor), it was at least a season too soon. There was the usual improvement of form on the arrival of a new man at the helm, six games unbeaten and "Uncle Jack" pulled out the cheque book once more. Keith Gillespie and Ashley Ward, two Republic of Ireland internationals Jason McAteer and Lee Carsley plus Matt Jansen added up to £18million of expenditure, but they finally lost Sherwood to the Spurs and his presence in the middle of the park was sorely missed. The newcomers were all decent players but at this stage of the season, none were good enough to inspire a revival. Kidd's side drew eleven of their final twenty three matches, but only five wins was insufficient to avert the drop. In the end they failed by six points and were relegated in nineteenth position after seven years of residency in Division 1.

Matt Jansen shared an interesting insight into the wheeling and dealing that goes on in the days leading up to a transfer.

> "I had been sold to Crystal Palace for £1million when I was still quite young and I managed to knock in a fair number of goals in the eighteen months I was there.

Anyone who scores goals in the Premier League for a struggling side is instantly targeted by bigger clubs and believe it or not, Juventus, amongst others, wanted to sign me. The asking fee was reputed to be £5million but they all wanted to pay in instalments which is the norm. Then along came Jack Walker who said he would pay it all up front. Palace actually asked me if I would choose Blackburn, because they were desperately in need of the money. In actual fact, the final fee was £4.1million but for me, I was happy to go there and scoring against Tottenham Hotspur in my first game in front of almost 30,000 at Ewood certainly endeared me to the fans. I was so sorry that we were relegated and in some ways it was Brian Kidd's fault. He believed that the fittest sides won matches and he was guilty of trying too hard in this respect. That was over twenty years ago and now although managers believe exactly the same, Sports' Science has come into its own. We were tiring rapidly after seventy minutes because we had worked so hard all week and that was when we were conceding goals. Nowadays there is far more structure to fitness, but then it was slog, slog, slog. I have been asked if having a price tag on my head affected me. It did, but very positively. I suppose I was super confident in those days and that I had quite a large ego. The club paying that amount of money for me told me that I was worth every penny and that enabled me to take risks on the pitch without a negative thought in my mind. I knew I had the skill to go past defenders at speed. I was a dribbler; that was my game and you need lots of confidence to play like that."

There were wins in the Football League Cup, a charge to the last eight. Exempt until Round 3 because of UEFA Cup commitments, a win at Crewe Alexandra and at last, a penalty shoot-out win over Newcastle United, sent them to Filbert Street where they lost 1-0 to Leicester City. The 3rd Round FA Cup home win over fellow relegatees Charlton Athletic (Kevin Davies and Jason Wilcox on target here) gave them a Fourth round tie against Sunderland. Over 30,000 crammed into Ewood and they witnessed a Keith Gillespie goal and the last sixteen beckoned. It was yet another trip to Newcastle and after a draw, the Geordies hung on for a 1-0 victory in Blackburn. They had drawn the "Toon" four times in Cup competitions this decade, winning two and losing two.

The Chris Waddle affair was a relatively dark moment in the history of the Burnley club, but in the long term, no damage was done. As a player, he was one of the very best. A major player in the 1990 World Cup, he was a mainstay of the Marseilles side which reached the final of the 1991 European Cup and had been worshipped at Newcastle and Tottenham before transforming a Sheffield Wednesday side and taking them to two Wembley finals in 1993. Paul Weller expresses the opinion that as a manager, he probably could have made a second career there eventually, but I think everyone agrees that his complete lack of experience, particularly lower down the pyramid, made it an untenable position. The comparison with Stan Ternent who followed him was a cheese and chalk scenario. Stan was born to be a manager, Chris was born to be a super player. Ternent was used to handling players, in all shapes

and sizes, mentally, physically and emotionally whereas for Waddle, the consummate left sided attacker, he had only been called upon to think about his own condition and his own game. Stan Ternent had managed Bury to two divisional wins in succession and then helped them to survive in Division 1. That showed outstanding management skills and it was no wonder that the Clarets called upon him to work his magic there. He had played for the club in the mid-sixties, but he could not break into the first team. But now he had found his forte in the game and Burnley would benefit from his experience.

The thirty-eight players used in the 1998-99 campaign usually hints at relegation form, and for much of the season, Burnley hovered just above it. Stan Ternent quickly informed the public that he was not happy with his squad and within days of the season starting, four players including Mark Winstanley were given free transfers. He brought in Paul Crichton in goal and Steve Morgan to replace Winstanley. These were quickly followed by two incoming Bury players, Peter Swan and Gordon Armstrong. But no matter how much Stan rang the changes, wins were hard to find. By the turn of the year, only six had been achieved. From fifteenth position on January 9th, a run of ten games with only one win saw them entrenched in the relegation zone. Every now and then, the defence had a stinker. Bournemouth and Gillingham both knocked in five and as winter gave way to spring, the sky blues from Manchester went one better without a single response from the Burnley side. Thankfully Stephen Davis returned from Luton Town for his third spell at the club and three players who would give excellent service in the next couple of years also arrived. Stan Ternent's signings during the season were quite predictable, almost sculpted in the image of the manager himself. Paul Cook and Graham Branch from Stockport County and Micky Mellon from Tranmere Rovers were uncompromising, competitive and experienced. They were able to stiffen the side and also provide some support for the twin strikers, Payton and Cooke. The former again showed what a goal poacher he was with twenty goals, a tremendous haul in a struggling side. The Turf Moor side remained unbeaten in the last eleven with two notable victories. Stoke City were beaten 4-1 at the Victoria Ground and then champions-elect Fulham lost 1-0 at the Turf. Payton missed the last three games through injury but the veteran Ronnie Jepson stepped up to fire the winner against the Londoners. In the end, a fifteenth place finish was acceptable. The manager had shown that he could make a difference and there was optimism around the ground once more. Graham Branch gave me an insight as to what it was like playing under Stan Ternent.

> "They all told me that there were turbulent times at Turf Moor before the Gaffer arrived. This is Stan Ternent I am talking about and he will always be the Gaffer to me. I still phone him up from time to time and I always say, "Alright Gaffer". This is because I have so much respect for him. And the reason why he was able to turn it around was because the players he chose also had loads of respect for him. He was really tough, but he was never arrogant. And he was honest with the players. You always knew where you stood. I suppose I wasn't the easiest of players to manage because I always said what I thought and we could fall out but it was always over with quickly. He didn't always pick me and when he did, I was often moved from position to position. I am quite versatile and so he could push me in anywhere but I always tried my hardest. The players he signed on were similar. So many were experienced pros who had been around a bit and he would watch them and could usually pick the right ones out. I had fallen out with Gary Megson at Stockport because he tried to bully us and I was stuck in the reserves. The Gaffer came along to watch me and on the strength of what he saw, he signed me. He made me captain of the club because I like to think he had faith in me and that was a real honour for me. It was fantastic playing in the promotion winning side and he kept us in Division 1. We gave the Play-Offs a good crack a couple of times and I think if we had a bit more depth in the squad, we could have done it. But when we had a poor season, he was given the push which I thought was unfair. I do feel that he gave the club a bit more belief in themselves and the position the club is in now I think had its foundation in the Gaffer's days."

Three separate stints at a club is not unique, but it is rare and so I had to ask Steve Davis the question once more……. "why".

> "Luton by now was a mid-table side in Division 2 and I heard that Stan Ternent, the new manager at Burnley, was looking to take me back. Barry Kilby had taken over as Chairman from Frank Teasdale and the story was that there was now some money on the table. The rumour was that a fair amount was earmarked for me, but they had to pay out £800,000, £50,000 more than Luton had paid for me. Stan said he wanted to build a team around me, a team which would obtain promotion and then challenge for honours in Division 1. I believed him, it was an attractive move to go back and so I signed. The fact that I cost a lot of money never made any difference to me. I settled so quickly at Burnley. I had been lucky with injuries, rarely missing a match for years and I felt comfortable back in Lancashire. I had always been in the manager's plans wherever I played and it seemed that this would continue under Stan Ternent. At no time did the crowd say that I was a waste of money. There was no doubt that centre-half was my position, but I did like scoring goals and I knocked in quite a few wherever I played. Many were headers from set-pieces, some were direct free-kicks but

there is no finer feeling in football than scoring a goal. Unfortunately, the opportunities rarely come your way when you are playing in the centre of defence."

Tranmere Rovers were in Division 1 at the time and so I asked Micky Mellon why he was content to take what initially appeared to be a downward step.

"I had had two really enjoyable seasons at Tranmere Rovers. John Aldridge was manager and he was having to operate with extreme financial constraints in Division 1. At the end of the season, John came to see me and told me that Burnley had offered good money for me, money which would see them survive the next season. I didn't really want to drop a division but promised John that I would go to talk with Stan Ternent and Sam Ellis, his assistant. They really sold the club to me, talking about its long history and traditions. He also talked about his plans for the coming season and that he was sure they could achieve promotion. So sadly, I said good-bye to Birkenhead and it turned out to be a great move for me. I really respected Stan and he was so good to us at that time."

The Football League Cup, the Worthington Cup, as it was now known, paired Stan Ternent's current club with his previous one. Sadly for the manager, the Gigg Lane side comfortably cruised through 5-2 on aggregate. The FA Cup run was even shorter. Darlington away in November rather lacks appeal, but the Quakers were in Division 3 and ought to have been an easy victim. Andy Payton put them two ahead, but three Darlington goals in the last ten minutes saw the Clarets leave red faced.

There's an average Premier League side at Ewood, but Burnley still cannot catch them, 1999 – 2009

Here they come again, mmmm-mm-mm
Catch us if you can, mmmm-mm-mm
Time to get a move on, mmmm-mm-mm
We will yell with all of our might
Catch us if you can, Catch us if you can,
Catch us if you can, Catch us if you can

CATCH US IF YOU CAN

(Dave Clark / Lenny Davidson)

Having tasted the ultimate glory, Blackburn Rovers had to come to accept that this was a once in a generation achievement and it was necessary to initially work hard to return to the Premier League and then comfortably stay there. This they eventually managed to do and the talk in the game at this time was that the Rovers were an extremely competitive and combative side who would always be a difficult foe.

Burnley also had rid themselves of the stigma of the struggle to stay in the Football League and under Stan Ternent they would gain a similar reputation, but usually a league below. It was Stan's ambition to catch the Ewood Park side, but until the Board of Directors could find the resources necessary to attract Premier League players, it was not going to happen. Therefore the Blackburn fans could smugly look down their noses at their rivals below and the words of the Dave Clark Five classic were only too appropriate. Interestingly memories of Dave Clark carry on in football, Crystal Palace continuing to walk out to the London group's even bigger hit, "Glad all over".

1999-2000

	Pos	Played	Won	Drawn	Lost	GF	GA	Pts
Blackburn Rovers	11	46	15	17	14	55	51	62
Burnley	2	46	25	13	8	69	47	88

Blackburn Rovers		Burnley	
Most Appearances	Christian Dailly 44	Most Appearances	Paul Crichton 46
Most Goals	Lee Carsley 10	Most Goals	Andy Payton 27

Half way through this season came an event of such magnitude that it was celebrated throughout the world. It was of course the new millennium and Stan Ternent and his boys were determined that the fans would have a second celebration at the beginning of May. For the Blackburn Rovers' fans, they would have to be content with just the one. There was an avid Burnley fan who worked with me. Totally dedicated to the cause, he was a season ticket holder at Turf Moor and a regular traveller to away games with his daughter. We would snipe at each other every Monday morning, mainly good-heartedly on the surface, but if the results had gone the wrong way at weekend, I had to grit my teeth and put up with his smirking face in the staff room.

Because of the strong finish to the previous campaign, Burnley fans were looking forward to something special. Ternent introduced two new defenders, Dean West from Bury and Mitchell Thomas from Luton Town who had played for Tottenham Hotspur in the 1987 Cup Final. There was a settled feel to the starting line-ups which brought a calmness on the field and terraces. After two games, the Clarets occupied sixth place and it got better and better.

Andy Payton [pictured] hit three against Colchester and they briefly topped the table, but until the last four games of the season, their median position was fifth. There was a John Mullin double against Wrexham and Payton claimed the match ball yet again after a narrow 3-2 home win over Oxford United. Four defeats at home were more than counteracted by seven wins on the road. In February the Manager made his third and fourth purchases of the season.

Ian Cox, a right back from Bournemouth and to the amazement of the football world, Ian Wright rolled up at the "Turf". Although at the tail-end of his legendary carer, Ternent felt that he could give them that extra impetus in the run-in. Stan managed to sign him because he was Assistant to Steve Coppell at Crystal Palace whilst "Wrighty" was learning the trade, prior to his promotion to Arsenal. It was here that the friendship was formed.

With four to play, the Clarets had to win all four matches to gain automatic promotion and hope that Gillingham dropped points. Here Wright's experience told. Since his arrival, he had only started four games but came off the bench eleven times, scoring four goals. But each time he came on, the energy level on the pitch seemed to rise. Mickey Mellon gave me the inside story from the Changing Room.

> "We were preparing for an away game at the Gawthorpe Training Ground, feeling confident about making the Play-offs but wondering if we could reach an automatic place. Then I noticed this guy walk in and thought "he looks like Ian Wright". It was an experienced bunch of professionals that Stan had brought together, so none of us were starstruck when Wrighty walked in, not that he would have wanted us to be. He settled in so quickly and on the field, he certainly made a difference. At thirty-six, he struggled playing the full ninety but he lit up the pitch as soon as he came on. He had that extra bit of magic, scored several vital goals and everyone was talking about him. He put a few more thousand on the gate at Turf Moor and even the away grounds reported improved attendances. It was as if everyone wanted to see the Circus. What was more, he was such a decent guy."

There were panic stations however when Millwall thundered back from a 4-0 deficit to score three times in the last half hour. Wright was on target as Brentford were defeated 3-2 at Griffin Park and a Payton double was enough to overcome Cambridge United in Burnley. The final game was at Scunthorpe United and Burnley had to win and hope Gillingham lost at Bristol Rovers. The "Iron" went in front at Glandford Park but goals from Mellon and then Glen Little meant that the fans were biting finger nails for the last twenty minutes. Fortunately the Gills lost in Bristol and Burnley were back in Division 1. Although Ian Wright had stolen the limelight, Andy Payton was the real hero. His twenty-seven goals saw him presented with the Division 2 Golden Boot award and the best news of all was that the derby games were back. Roll on August!

The Burnley side promoted as runners-up from Division 2 in 1999-2000 (Started over 18 games, max 46) was; Paul Crichton, Dean West, Mitchell Thomas, Stephen Davis, Micky Mellon, Paul Cook, Glen Little, John Mullin, Graham Branch, Andy Cooke, Andy Payton, Gordon Armstrong, Lenny Johnrose.

The Clarets, given the worst of all draws in the Worthington Cup, quickly lost interest after being hammered 6-0 on aggregate by Manchester City. The FA Cup however gave the fans plenty to cheer. They saw off Barnet and Rotherham United and their Round 3 performance was arguably the best of the season as the Premier League's Derby County lost to an Andy Cooke second-half goal in the North Midlands. Unfortunately they could not repeat their form in the last thirty-two trip to another Midland Premier League club, going down 3-0 to Coventry City.

This was the opportunity for Brian Kidd to attack Division 1 with intent. The manager had too many players but insufficient quality and Kevin Davies returned to Southampton in a swap deal for Egil Ostenstad. Kevin Gallacher was sold to Newcastle United after six years at Ewood Park. His time had been bedevilled by injury although he still managed to compile a record of forty six goals in 144 games. Others moving out were Stephan Henchoz (70 appearances) to Liverpool, Tim Flowers (175 games between the sticks) to Leicester City and Chris Sutton (47 goals in 125 starts) to Chelsea. With money in the bank, Kidd replaced them with Republic of Ireland international goalkeeper Alan Kelly Jr from Sheffield United, centre-back Craig Short from Everton and Simon Grayson from Aston Villa.

The Danish international Per Frandsen moved a few miles north from Bolton Wanderers for close to £2million, but had left by the end of the season. It was a worrying time for the fans as by the time Queens Park Rangers had taken all three points from Ewood, fourteen games had elapsed with only three wins to boast about. Defensively they were fairly sound, but it was at the other end of the pitch that the problems lay. Ostenstad scored a brace against Norwich City, but goals were scarce. With the club resting in eighteenth place, Jack Walker could take no more. Kidd's contract was terminated and he again turned to Tony Parkes to perform his usual Houdini act. I asked Craig Short what it was like playing for a manager when the rumour around the club was that the day of his sacking was imminent. We also talked about what a player felt like when he knew his time was up.

"It was difficult for everyone and it was difficult for me. I felt that I had not shown my full potential in this season so far. I had played better at Everton and even though I was now thirty-one, I knew I could play better here. Kiddo came to talk to me during this bad run and started to apologise for letting us all down. I told him this was nonsense. He had signed me to do a job and I had underperformed. In actual fact I told him in no uncertain terms that I and the rest of the players had let him down. I believe he tried extremely hard, but the club was in a mess and a change was needed. In football, there are times in your career when you begin to realise that you are surplus to requirements. I believe that Brian Kidd was beginning to go through that thought process and in the final stages of the 2004-05 season, it eventually came to me. Looking back I was so pleased that I could still be playing in the Premier League at the age of thirty seven. I had originally been given a four year contract and then John Williams (Chief Executive at the club) had offered me two more. In the middle of this season they signed the New Zealand centre half Ryan Nelsen and as soon as I saw him in training, I knew he was going to take my place. It was one thing knowing it but another accepting it. I still felt fit and competitive and could do a job but my first instincts were proved to be correct. I had honestly believed that I would spend my final days at Ewood Park, but my old boss Neil Warnock came calling and he offered me a two year contract at Sheffield United, then in the Championship. I played over twenty games that first season and we were promoted into the Premier League. It was my third promotion out of the Championship."

To some extent, Parkes succeeded and the Rovers looked more impressive at home. Jason Wilcox from the Premier League winning squad was sold to Leeds United for close to £4million, but it was Fortress Ewood until the struggling Crewe Alexandra somehow secured a 1-0 win. Relegation by now was off the agenda and Lee Carsley was strong in mid-field and scored goals, but Jack Walker yearned for the glory days and he wanted a manager with a reputation. Graeme Souness certainly fitted that description. As a player he was outstanding; creative, technically excellent and an extremely hard man.

These characteristics shone through in his managerial performances and he was often in trouble with the authorities. In his own words he could be obnoxious but his charisma acted as a magnet to quality footballers. When he arrived, promotion was a faint hope, but still possible. With youngsters Dunn, Duff and Jansen given carte blanche to perform, they certainly gave it their best shot, but an away 2-1 defeat to Play-Off rivals Wolverhampton Wanderers scuppered any possible chance, having to be content with an inauspicious eleventh place. It was disappointing and as with the news of Burnley's accession to Division 1, the fans simply had to take it on the chin. But confidence was in the air about the forthcoming season and hardened supporters rubbed their hands in anticipation of two local derbies.

Portsmouth were blown away with a 6-1 aggregate win in the Worthington Cup, Jansen scoring twice in a 3-0 win in the away leg, but In Tony Parkes' first game in charge, an away trip to Premier League side Leeds United in Round 3 produced an expected 1-0 loss. In the FA Cup, the Rovers survived Round 3 after defeating West Bromwich Albion after a replay and Round 4 produced their finest performance for some time. There was a full house to greet the arrival of Liverpool.

A slightly faded Merseyside outfit no longer bestrode the football world like a colossus, but Gerard Houllier's side was still good enough to finish fourth in the Premier League. But in Parkes' finest hour, he conjured up a magical display from the boys in blue and a late Nathan Blake goal saw them through to the last sixteen. Newcastle United ought to have been an easier task in Lancashire, but the Geordies progressed by a 2-1 margin. And who should score the two Newcastle goals? A certain Alan Shearer of course.

2000-01

	Pos	Played	Won	Drawn	Lost	GF	GA	Pts
Blackburn Rovers	2	46	26	13	7	76	39	91
Burnley	7	46	21	9	16	50	54	72

Blackburn Rovers		Burnley	
Most Appearances	John Curtis 46	Most Appearances	Stephen Davis 44
Most Goals	Matt Jansen 23	Most Goals	Andy Payton 9

I had still not come to terms with the Rovers' relegation and as it had coincided with promotion at Burnley, there were a couple of derbies to contemplate. And because of this, I had a "moment". It had always been the Rovers for me; no-one could question my loyalty. When I became involved in schools' football, particularly at Town Team level, a strong relationship grew between the club and our organisation. At that time, the office of the club secretary John Howarth was on the other side of Nuttall Street in one of the terraced houses. Every season I would be in there, organising a couple of our matches on the ground itself plus the end of season schools' finals. I felt I could walk into the ticket office, the ladies in there all knew me and were most welcoming.

But it was not just a one-way arrangement. The Rovers in those days trained on Pleasington Playing Fields during the week and if the weather was wretched, Alan Bradshaw and later Jim Furnell would ring me at school and ask me if the team could come up and use the Darwen Vale High School Sports Hall. Our PE staff always agreed, the quid pro quo being that the school was given twenty free tickets per home game to distribute amongst our pupils. It was when I was elected to the Council of the English Schools' FA that things changed.

I simply did not have the time to continue as the Blackburn and Darwen Schools' FA secretary and thus I also lost some contact with the club. This coincided with the Jack Walker revolution and when I went down three years later to ask for permission to stage an English Schools' international at Ewood, I was shocked by what I saw. I had watched games during this period and was abreast of all the ground development changes. But the office, having once been tiny, was now massive, populated by so many dividing screens, each with a secretary and computer. It was as if a cottage industry had turned into a multi-national concern overnight. I had such a positive feeling, seeing the club keeping in step with all the latest technology, a well-oiled machine at work, but somehow the cosiness had gone. But this was the age of the innovative Premier League and full marks to the club for ringing the changes.

The pressure of work at school and from the family was the reason for my resignation from ESFA, but Jeff Taylor fortunately had a word with me, asking if I fancied using a little of my spare time to scout for Burnley at under 16 level. I knew and respected Jeff, whose job was almost mission impossible. During the Harry Potts era, the Clarets were renowned for their scouting system and youth policy which went hand in hand together. But swingeing cuts at the club through the seventies and eighties meant that the youth set-up below the age of sixteen was run on the proverbial shoe string. It was in fact a one man band when I first became involved in the late nineties. Jeff had to do everything, although the arrival of local businessman Barry Kilby as chairman saw that more than lip service was given to the youngsters. It was a strange time in my life in that I was loving the part time work I did for the Clarets, scouting for youngsters.

At the Academies of the big clubs there were boys playing their final few games, being released at the age of sixteen for failing to meet the sky high standards of the Premier League sides. And talk about the spy in the bushes.

It was all so secretive, sliding in incognito to the training grounds at Euxton (Bolton Wanderers), Brockhall (Blackburn Rovers) and Platt Lane (Manchester City), being friendly to parents in the hope that they might let it slip that such a boy would not be taken on at the end of the season. These boys were good players and so they interested Burnley and if a big club was shedding potential professionals, Jeff Taylor at Gawthorpe wanted to be the first to know. My heart was still at Ewood but I had certainly gained an affection for their rivals up the motorway. My contacts with schools' football were useful and being able to talk to the likes of Vince Overson, Terry Pashley, Jimmy Robson and Brian Taylor gave me more of an insight into the workings of the club.

I was excited by the work, although what the club gained from it is debatable. I organised several trial games and brought a number of boys down to the Centre of Excellence. A few were taken on as scholars/apprentices but not a single one remained beyond the age of eighteen and none made the first team squad. Was it because I was inept or was it a hopeless task? I would like to think the latter because it was akin to searching for the needle in the haystack. And to make it even more difficult, there were scouts from up to fifteen rival clubs in the region, hoping for the next Wayne Rooney to turn up. Only a miniscule percentage of young footballers see the process through to the first team and with the influx of more and more foreign players, the number dwindles every year.

So what has this to do with my moment? I never watched the first team at Burnley, but I was beginning to feel an empathy for the Clarets. The derby game was approaching fast. Everyone at Gawthorpe was talking about the game and I could have asked for a ticket, but I was unsure if I wanted to sit amongst the Burnley fans. A friend of mine asked me to pop round to his house and watch it on Sky and I swear that as I sat down in his lounge, I was genuinely uncertain as to which side I wanted to win. Then the referee blew the whistle and suddenly I knew. Suddenly I had no doubts and that moment of uncertainty was crushed by the great weight of forty-seven years of loyalty to Blackburn Rovers. At that moment it was ...... "Come on the Rovers" and I felt so relieved.

Burnley had added to their squad in the close season, bringing in mid-field muscle in the shape of the experienced Kevin Ball from Fulham, although it was at Sunderland where he had honed his reputation over a number of years, captaining the side through a mainly successful decade. Although possibly nearing the end of his career, he was exactly what Ternent needed. Lee Briscoe was signed from Sheffield Wednesday to fill the left-hand side role and Nik Michopoulos came in from PAOK Thesaloniki to replace Paul Crichton between the sticks.

The Rovers had started the season well, comfortably beating Crystal Palace at home , but then came the tragic news. Jack Walker had died at his home in Jersey. The great benefactor had singlehandedly funded the club's rise from a non-descript Tier 2 side to the Champions of England, spent over £20million on completely rebuilding the ground and heaven knows how much on the state of the art training facilities at Brockhall. He was a "Blackburner" and a "Blackburn ender" for many years, Importantly he was no lover of Burnley FC.

The club and the citizens of Blackburn all found his passing hard to take and the affection of so many people was demonstrated by the sea of flowers, almost on a par with the tributes paid to Princess Diana at Kensington Palace, decorating the stand named after him. Burnley had Bob Lord, their Blackburn counterparts had Jack Walker, both giants in the world of football, both long remembered even far away from their small town roots.

Graeme Souness quickly off-loaded Lee Carsley to Coventry City and Christian Dailly to West Ham United, the Rovers losing out on both deals. Matt Jansen however was prominent on the goal scoring front as they remained unbeaten in the first five games, but then after a min-slump, southern clubs Fulham and Watford were threatening to run away from the rest; was it going to be another of those seasons?

But Souness was shrewd, he still had Walker family money and he speculated well. Two new defenders were brought in, John Curtis from Manchester United and Stig Inge Bjornebye from Liverpool with Henning Berg returning from Old Trafford. Craig Hignett's arrival from Barnsley would add attacking options and six successive victories were the aperitif to a nineteen game unbeaten run. The crowds rolled in to watch the action. over 20,000 spectators watching a clinical 4-1 win over rivals Bolton Wanderers. They lost again 2-1 to Fulham, their only defeat in their final ten fixtures and finished in second spot, but ten points behind the Craven Cottage club. Promotion had been sealed at Preston, Jansen scoring the vital goal. He later said that this was right up there with his finest moments on a football field. He was the first to top the twenty mark since Alan Shearer left the club. It had been a grand old season for Lancashire's traditional clubs, with the Clarets, the Rovers, North End and the Wanderers all competing in the same league for the first time since the 1977-78 season when it was Burnley, Bolton, Blackburn and Blackpool, all in the second tier.

Burnley's season prior to this game had generally been acceptable to the Turf Moor faithful. It had been more top half than bottom half with a seven game unbeaten run as Autumn kicked in. This was followed by a minor blip when Notts Forest cracked five past them, but there was a thrilling 2-1 home victory over Fulham which was cheered to the rafters. Burnley also finished the season strongly, raising hopes of a more successful promotion run the following season. Five wins, two draws and a solitary defeat at Sheffield United ought to have enabled the fans to go away on holiday in an upbeat frame of mind, having finished in seventh spot. However, it was a case of mixed feelings.

Finishing just two points behind sixth placed and Play-Off candidates West Bromwich Albion was hard to bear and they were left to rue the 1-1 draw at Turf Moor against the same "Baggies" side, whose late goal made the difference to their respective fates. It was the lack of goals scored which was the Clarets' downfall. Andy Payton, eighteen starts but a further twenty-two as substitute, was leading scorer with nine goals. During the season, the manager had purchased two new strikers, Ian Moore and Gareth Taylor. Both would score goals in the future but the fifty goals in this season were shared amongst fifteen players plus two own goals, an extremely salient statistic.

The derby games. Match one.

> "Another desperately disappointing performance in the derby game saw Clarets poor form in big games continue." Clarets Mad by Dave Clark – opening sentence 17th December 2000

The first derby game was scheduled for December at Turf Moor, and coming into the game, Burnley held ninth place in the league. The Rovers were the form team of the competition, having lost only once in their last eleven games. Homing in on the Play-Off places, the club was now being tipped for promotion back to the Premier League. Looking at the line-ups, it was obvious that the Blue and Whites had the players of greater pedigree and experience, a number with elite clubs. Souness had secured the transfers of Brad Friedel from Liverpool, Henning Berg and the newly signed Mark Hughes from Everton. Each had a drawer full of international caps and another goal scorer, Marcus Bent, came from Sheffield United for over one million pounds. Add to that the exciting youngsters Duff, Dunn and Jansen and it was an eleven brimming over with talent. But the Burnley fans had waited so long for this day. They trusted the manager and they knew the starting eleven would give everything, putting their bodies on the line for the shirt.

The first half of the lunch-time televised game was fiercely competitive. Burnley had their moments with Ian Moore, the club's first one million pound signing from Stockport County, causing trouble with his pace and Andy Payton always looking like he would sniff out a goal. Heading for the half-time whistle it was goalless until the Burnley defence made a complete hash of a long Bjornebye throw in. They were unable to deal with the bounce of the ball and Jason McAteer nipped to score a simple headed goal. The Rovers dominated the second half and somehow Hughes missed from four yards out, a goal my grandma would have scored, as we used to say. Jansen came on and with his skill, combined with Duff's pace, a second goal seemed inevitable. And the tackles started raining in. Davis was booked for hauling down Duff and then Dunn gave the impression that the ball was tied with string to his foot. He turned effortlessly, Ball came in like a man on a mission and the Blackburn playmaker took off horizontally. To say the tackle was high was an understatement. "Wild and reckless" was the comment from the Sky commentator. Ball had worked hard throughout to help the Clarets keep their defensive shape but there was no question that it was a red card and "the walk of shame" was his last contribution to the game. Another fracas broke out with half of the twenty-one players involved and as the final whistle loomed, Jansen turned the defenders to set up Bjornebye who rocketed in a goal bound shot. Michopoulos saved brilliantly but Marcus Bent was on hand to nod in the rebound from close range. There was still time for Payton to sneak in behind the Rovers defence but Friedel was so quick off his line and Payton's raised boot caught him late. The referee was happy to blow for full time before any more physical damage could occur, with the Blackburn side well worth its 2-0 victory.

17 12 2000	Burnley	Blackburn Rovers	0-2	J McAteer, M Bent.
01 04 2001	Blackburn Rovers	Burnley	5-0	C Short, o.g., M Jansen 2, C Hignett.

I spoke to Kevin Ball and asked him if "the tackle" was pre-meditated.

Hahaha no! I think it's very difficult to pre-meditate a tackle but one thing's for sure I would have never turned down an opportunity! Football's a physical game and I always went in hard and in the main fair. You have to if you want to win the ball and if the opponent is not up to it, then he can always pull out. They talk about going for ball and man and this is what happened in the Dunny incident. He had caught me late earlier on in the game and I just got on with it, but the crowd was so worked up and this does come down on to the pitch. As hard as we had tried, we were losing the game so there would have been some frustration in us all as we wanted to beat our nearest rival badly. Dunny turned with the ball and I allowed him to do it, as this gave me the perfect opportunity to tackle him hard. He went flying through the air like an acrobat and within seconds the Rovers' players were all around me. Souness was on the pitch having a go at me and Ternent was having a go at him for having a go at me. Looking back, Stan's mantra of " all for one, one for all" certainly was evident in this case. Stan was class!

You have to respect the referee's decision so I quickly walked away. But it was a long walk back to the dressing room, located behind our goal. Nik Michopoulos was very supportive of me as I walked past and told me not to worry, I replied with, "I thought I got the ball". The Burnley fans all applauded me off, but the Blackburn fans behind our goal were apoplectic with rage. As I approached, they started spitting on me and I had to tell myself not to react. After the game I was asked to talk to Sky to say my apologies for the tackle; I politely refused. On the way back to the North East after the game I rang home. Our son has always supported me incredibly well over the years when we spoke about my performances and he answered the phone. "I thought it was a fair tackle dad." My wife then came on and I asked her if the ref was a bit harsh on me. "A bit harsh? It was awful. They should have arrested you". I felt no remorse for the tackle but for my sins, I missed two games and a fortnight's wages.

I refused to watch the video for a few years until I was in charge of the Sunderland Youth Team and we were on our way to London to play a game in The FA Youth Cup. We travelled by train and I became aware that several of the lads were watching something on their tablets, making "shock type" noises and then glancing at me. I had this feeling it was the tackle and when I went over, I saw that sure enough it was. They said that if they did one like that, I would ban them for a fortnight. "It's disgraceful boss," they told me and I had to agree. I also said they were right; I would ban them and fine them, just like I was.

Sometime later, Dunny and I met up and we talked about the incident. I bought him a drink and we ended up laughing about it. We have since bumped into each other on a number of occasions and there is no acrimony between us and I would not expect anything else of him. He did what he could for his team and I did what I did for mine. We will always say "hello". Whenever I am at Turf Moor, the crowd gives me a rousing reception but on the odd occasions I am at Ewood, I turn up my collar just in case the gloves need to come off!!

I still believe I did not intend to hurt him, only give him a reminder, but this is football and you have to make the most of the ability you have. I became pigeon holed as a supposed hard man and nothing else, which I think is a little unfair. Sure I was very competitive and wanted my team to win at all costs, but I was two footed and could pass a ball well. Ok, I could not drop my shoulder and go past a man so effortlessly like Glen Little could, who I have to say was outstanding. My other assets seem to have been forgotten by people, but they are as important to an eleven as the cultured craftsmen who get the headlines. But whether giving or receiving the hard knocks, I always made sure that I shook hands with my opposite number at the full-time whistle; just not Dunny on that occasion!!.

David Dunn was quite phlegmatic about the whole affair when discussing the game with me, but we need to remember that he was still a relatively inexperienced youngster at twenty-one whereas Kevin Ball had turned thirty-seven. This was well into his vintage years as a footballer, but one laden with experience.

"I had made my Rovers debut at eighteen in a goalless draw at Everton and what a shambles that turned out to be for me. The manager brought me on after 70 minutes and shortly afterwards, Martin Dahlin was sent-off. The side had to be re-jigged and a sub came on and I was the one taken of in the 81st minute. Subbed as a sub on your debut is not the dream way to start your professional career. By the time this derby came along, I had played almost fifty games for the first team. I was seen as the local lad in a local derby and so the press made a big deal about me playing. Bally's tackle was a foul, but this is football and although it could have really hurt me, it didn't and I quickly got up and got on with it. Both sets of supporters were going crazy about it but I have seen Kevin a number of times since and we can both smile about it. I have been asked questions about his tackle so many times but I have no problems with it. The press went even crazier over the Ewood derby game and all because we had been in Dubai immediately before it. They thought that we had gone on a holiday and that we were saying that we would beat Burnley whether we trained or not. We actually trained hard over there and we absolutely hammered them.

For Andy Payton, it was one big disappointment.

"As a Burnley fan when I was young, my secondary school was a few hundred yards from the Gawthorpe training ground and it was my dream to play for the club and score against the Rovers. I managed to do this four times in my career, but all were with other clubs. I never scored in this derby match. In the week before the game, the local press took me and Dunny up to the Crown pub in Accrington for photographs. I was the local Burnley boy and Dunny was the local Blackburn lad. They gave me a dart with the Burnley badge on it and the same sort of thing for him. The photos all appeared in the papers. This was all to stir up even more interest in the game. This was rivalry rekindled. I felt that we matched them in the first half and only a defensive mistake gave McAteer the goal bang on half-time. At half-time, Stan Ternent made sure we were ready for anything and that's why tackles were flying in. But twenty years ago, refs tended to play on and let the players sort it out in their own way. We were more determined than ever. That was the way it was then, a good old fashioned derby. Now it is a different game. For the neutrals, derbies are often disappointing but for the committed, they are the ultimate. But Blackburn were a good side with some Premier League players and when Bally was sent off, it made it even more difficult. Then Marcus Bent nicked another and I had that late chance. Brad Friedel was out like a flash and I did catch him. It was unintentional, he was just that fraction quicker than me. The funny thing was that I did something to my groin and I ended up more hurt than him. Brad and me had a word after the game and everything was ok between us, but the game was a big downer for me. We were a good side that season and I honestly thought that we could win."

Mickey Mellon was optimistic in the days leading up to the game, believing that there was sufficient quality in the side to gain a result.

"We were in the top ten going into the game and although we knew Blackburn had a number of players with Premier League experience, Friedel, Berg, Hughes, Flitcroft, Short and McAteer, and promising youngsters like Dunn, we knew we could do it. The first half was so close and when you have played the game for a long time, you start to have the feeling that the game was going to be won or lost on a mistake. And so it was, but without the sending off, I am sure we could have found an equaliser from somewhere."

Paul Weller talked at length about the physical approach that Burnley used to try to gain an advantage over their more sophisticated neighbour.

"The previous season we were in Division 2 and the Rovers were in the Premier League, a gap of two divisions. Suddenly, with our promotion and their relegation, we were in the same league. Stan Ternent reckoned that we could rough them up, play in a physical manner which would off-set the advantages they may have had in quality. "Win the war, then win the match" was one of his phrases and he motivated us with words such as "you lot are paid in fivers, they're paid in millions". I was not considered to be a dirty player. In fact my only sending off was in my last season in a 5th Round FA Cup tie at Millwall. Dennis Wise kicked me, I pushed him back and the up and coming Howard Webb saw it as an opportunity to make his name and red carded me. But I was certainly willing to get stuck in against Blackburn and it was a really niggly match. It meant so much to the fans. When we went out to warm-up, maybe an hour before the start, the Longside was already packed. We thought the game would have meant more to us than them, but to be fair to the Rovers, they gave as much back. There were things going on behind the ref's back but everyone goes on and on about Kevin Ball's tackle. It was definitely a foul, but Dunny got straight back up; he wasn't hurt."

Matt Jansen said that from a Rovers' point of view, there was so much riding on this derby game, but not necessarily for the right reasons.

"This was really a hatred thing....from both sides. Our aim was to win a promotion that would take us back to the Premier League, but to people in and around the club, the thing that mattered most was that we beat the Dingles. We had grown used to playing at grounds that had decent changing facilities, particularly in the Premier League, but at Turf Moor, the away dressing room was down a narrow corridor and it was like entering a box room. It really was quite intimidating to opposition players."

Dave Timberlake's main memory was all about coaches.

"I try not to remember games we lost, but I will always remember the Blackburn Rovers' coaches. We were trying to cross the road to the ground before the match and this enormous procession of Shearings Coaches all suddenly appeared. There were so many and we were stood there for an age until they passed. There were stacks of police all around but what got me was that their lot were travelling in style and apparently for free. When we played at Blackburn later in the season, we were all bussed in, but our transport was a load of rackety double decker buses and the worst coaches and mini-buses they could find. On top of that we were charged £4 each. Thirty odd years before when we went to a derby game at Ewood Park, we caught the train to Mill Hill Station and sauntered down to the ground. This time we were jeered at, the coach spat upon and every Blue and White fan wanted to give us the V sign. I obtained my ticket through London Clarets and I still do. Their theory is that if we are losing by three goals, it's best to leave the ground. On this occasion we were three down in an hour but there was no way we could leave. The Police made us stay in our seats until well after the final whistle. It was one thing being hammered by five but another having to sit there afterwards for an eternity in their Stadium."

The second derby game

With All-Fools Day on the horizon, it was still possible for Burnley to attain a Play-Off position from tenth place. Glen Little was fit again and Gareth Taylor had arrived from Manchester City, these being the only changes from the December fixture. The major Blackburn Rovers change from Turf Moor was Jansen replacing Hughes as Bent's strike partner. With almost a quarter of the games to play, there was no guarantee that Souness' side would be promoted, so it was essential that another three points would be collected here.

Craig Short explained how seriously Graeme Souness took the game in particular and his reflections on playing his first derby game in general.

"We had been to Dubai for warm weather training immediately prior to the game and we all came back with suntans. The boss however was keen to dispel any rumours that this had been a holiday. He worked us hard and impressed on us how a victory in the derby match would keep us on track for promotion. I had missed the Turf Moor game through injury and before I came to Blackburn I had no idea the East Lancashire derby existed. Having sat amongst the crowd in the first game, I quickly realised just how much was riding on the game and there was a crowd of 23.442 for the second fixture. I couldn't believe it when I was first credited with both opening goals. I didn't really deserve praise for either of them. In the first incident, Dunny shot and the ball hit my foot and flew in and the second was definitely an own goal. I just smashed a cross in the direction of the six yard box, it hit the Burnley defender and the goal keeper had no chance. Thankfully the second one is now officially an own goal."

Steve Davis spoke about his introduction to the East Lancashire derby and his take on the own goal, one he felt was quite bizarre.

"Craig Short somehow found himself on the bye line, a strange position for a centre back. It looked as if the ball was going out of play but somehow Craig knocked it in with pace. I was stood just outside the post, the ball hit me and heaven knows how from the acutest of angles, the ball flew into the corner of the net. We were second best in this game but just before half time, Morro (Ian

> Moore) had a goal chalked off for off-side and I had a chance from a header which just missed. If we could have gone in only one down, the second half may have been different. But as at Turf Moor, the second half belonged entirely to the Blue and Whites. They had great quality for this division and the crowd was treated to some excellent football. This was in contrast to the whole of the first game and the first half at Ewood Park where it was all about blood and thunder. There were so many hard tackles as we all tried to impose ourselves on the game, but back then, twenty years ago, the players accepted it far more. The tackle on David Dunn for example in the first game, if made in the current climate, would have been followed by Dunny rolling over and over and staying down until the ref had made a decision. Full marks to him, he got straight up."

Matt Jansen was unstoppable, scoring twice, the second following a lovely one-two and to rub salt in the wounds, substitute Craig Hignett cracked in the fifth. David Dunn had dominated the game, perhaps fate repaying him for the pain of the tackle four months previously. It was the highest winning aggregate margin (7-0) since the 1889-90 season when the aggregate score was 9-2 to Rovers.

For some long-forgotten reason, I was not at the game, but I remember watching it on television. My lasting memory is of the post-match interview with the managers. Both were smartly dressed but the contrast in choice of attire somehow encapsulated the divide between the clubs. Stan Ternent was old school, smart sports jacket and slacks. Graeme Souness' sharply cut suit on the other hand looked as if it had been sewn by a couturier in Milan's fashionable Galleria Vittorio Emanuele II.

And the words of Ternent further exaggerated the gulf between the two clubs at that time. "We're a million miles away financially from Blackburn Rovers and that shows on the football field." Andy Payton agreed.

> "The second game we were dead and buried at Ewood. I was on the bench and it was 4-0 when I came on. Blackburn deserved to go up that season. I was thirty three by this stage and coming to the end of my career. I was content with what I had achieved, apart from not scoring in a derby match, but I wonder what would have happened if Burnley had not released me when I left school."

Like Craig Short, Matt Jansen felt that much was made of the Rovers' trip to Dubai before the game.

> "Before this time, clubs taking their players away during international breaks was extremely rare. The accusation made against us was that we had been on a jolly in Dubai and because we had recently played in the top tier of football, we thought of ourselves as "Big time Charlies". All this unwarranted criticism from the Burnley press really spurred us on and by winning the second game so convincingly, we really answered our critics. It was a great season for me and only Louis Saha at Fulham scored more in the Championship. I do know that he

took the penalties but Dunny wouldn't let me take ours, so perhaps I could have won the Golden Boot."

The Blackburn Rovers side promoted from Division 1 in 2000-2001 (played over 18 games from a maximum of 46) was; Brad Friedel, Henning Berg, Stig Inge Bjornebye, John Curtis, Craig Short, Damian Duff, David Dunn, Gary Flitcroft, Jason McAteer, Marcus Bent, Mark Hughes, Matt Jansen.

Blackburn Rovers made progress in each of the two cup competitions. Entering the Worthington Cup at Round 1, Rochdale were thrashed 6-1 on aggregate, David Dunn setting a Rovers record, a hat-trick of penalties. In the two-legged tie against Portsmouth, they coasted through 5-1, but in the last thirty-two encounter at Premier League side West Ham, the Hammers won 2-0. The FA Cup was far more productive. The Rovers had too much for Chester City in Round 3. Premier League side Derby County came out of the hat for a record tenth time in this competition as Rovers' opponents in Round 4. After holding the Rams to a goalless draw, they trounced them 5-2 in the replay, Marcus Bent scoring twice. A 1-1 draw at their close Division 1 rival Bolton Wanderers followed and a brace from Craig Hignett contributed greatly to a 3-1 win in the replay. A peak form Arsenal at Highbury in the last eight was a step too far, the Gunners cruising to a 3-0 victory which indicated the gulf between the top clubs in the Premier League and the Championship. Nevertheless it was the best FA Cup run since 1993 by the Blue and Whites,

For the first time since the 1982-83 season, Burnley entered the FA Cup in Round 3. The game against Scunthorpe United threatened to be a marathon. A 2-2 draw at Turf Moor, a 1-1 draw at Glanford Park after extra-time and so to penalties. The Clarets missed one and Scunthorpe netted the lot; a quick exit for the Lancashire side. In the Worthington Cup, a hat-trick from Andy Payton in the home leg set them on the way to a 6-4 aggregate win against Hartlepool United and it was draws aplenty against Crystal Palace, 2-2 at Burnley, 1-1 draw at Selhurst Park. The new ruling for the League Cup only, was that drawn ties should be decided on away goals, so Burnley left the competition in Round 2.

2001-02

	Pos	Played	Won	Drawn	Lost	GF	GA	Pts
Blackburn Rovers	10	38	12	10	16	55	51	46
Burnley	7	46	21	12	13	70	62	75

Blackburn Rovers		Burnley	
Most Appearances	Brad Friedel 36	Most Appearances	Lee Briscoe and Dean West 43
Most Goals	Matt Jansen 10	Most Goals	Gareth Taylor 16

With no derby games with which to concern themselves, Blackburn Rovers set about re-establishing their place as a Premier League side. They were still only one of three Premier League winning clubs, they had a manager whose fame was known across Europe and a number of young and talented players intermingled with experienced professionals who could return the club to the summit of the game. The manager would not countenance the Rovers as a selling club, only allowing players to leave who were surplus to requirements. Money was raised from the sale of Marcus Bent to Norwich City, Jason McAteer to Sunderland, Aussie goalkeeper John Filan to Wigan Athletic and Nathan Blake to Wolverhampton Wanderers. Finally, both Damian Johnson and Jeff Kenna, the final member of the 1995 Premier League winning side, were allowed to leave for Birmingham City. Players of this quality needed replacing and Souness was quick to splash out £1.3million on Tugay Kerimoglu from Glasgow Rangers. He had worked with the Turkish international whilst managing Galatasaray and although he was now past his thirtieth birthday, he proved to be one of the greatest bargains of all time. He had consummate control of the ball, could pick passes that others simply could not see and the rocket-like quality of his right foot when shooting for goal was a gift to behold. When I was living in France, the noted weekly magazine "France Foot" showed a caption to his picture stating, "Tugay, le Zinedine Zidane de Turquie"; praise indeed. The manager looked to strengthen the side at full back and £1million was spent on the combative Aussie, Lucas Neill from Millwall. Swedish left back Nils-Eric Johansson was bought from FC Nurnberg in Germany for £2.7 million, but the largest fee (and the biggest waste of money) was reserved for Corrado Grabbi, another of the legion of non-scoring centre forwards who have populated the home dressing room at Ewood Park. His two goals over a thirty month period worked out at £3.375million per strike; work it out. Souness spent even more money over Christmas, £8million to be exact on Andy Cole from Manchester United. He was no longer the superstar that had previously set alight St James' Park and Old Trafford, but his goals nevertheless helped to keep the Rovers competitive over the next thirty months.

The fans expected a flying start but unfortunately indifferent was a more appropriate adjective. The start was steady enough, one of the highlights being a David Beckham own goal at Ewood as they drew with the reigning champions 2-2. By the time Corrado Grabbi grabbed his goal in a 1-0 home win against Everton, they were positioned sixth and three weeks later, West Ham were destroyed 7-1, each goal being credited to a different player. David Dunn scored twice in the following fixture at champions-elect Arsenal in a stirring 3-3 draw, but then the rot set in. At the turn of the year they occupied fifteenth spot and after a five game winless run, the arrival of March saw them in the relegation zone. And then suddenly, Andy Cole remembered why so much money had been spent to secure his signature. He scored seven in the last eleven and Duff and Jansen joined the party. Six wins and three draws in the last twelve games enabled them to rise up the table and over 30,000 packed into Ewood Park in the final game of the season to see two more strikes from Cole. The 3-0 victory over Fulham enabled them to make the final jump into tenth spot; their

sixth top ten finish in the eleven years since their elevation into the Premier League.

But if the regular league season was something of a roller coaster ride, it was the Worthington's League Cup for which this group of players will be remembered. Given a bye into Round 2, the competition started quietly as Oldham Athletic succumbed at Ewood. Another home tie against Middlesbrough brought a 2-1 win, and although struggling in the league, they still had enough in the tank however to beat the Manchester City 2-0. Drawn at home again in the last eight, what a shock it was when they knocked four past Arsenal without reply, Jansen taking home the match ball after his hat-trick. Suddenly this was a competition to be taken seriously and the two legged semi-final was a Battle of the Roses against Sheffield Wednesday. The Owls were now a Division 1 club and it was the red rose which triumphed, winning 2-1 at Hillsborough and 4-2 at home. Craig Hignett and Cole each scored in both legs.

With Wembley closed for renovation work, the final was played at Cardiff's Millennium Stadium and the opposition would be Tottenham Hotspur. As the day of the game dawned, the Rovers were in eighteenth place in the league whereas the Spurs were sitting pretty just behind the Champions' League places. They had an under-rated but outstanding centre-back in Ledley King, two veteran strikers, Sheringham and Ferdinand, each of whom was still a quality Premier League player and who should be running their mid-field but one Tim Sherwood, the last Rovers' captain to pick up a trophy, back in 1995. The Blackburn side was short of four of their better players.

Lucas Neill was cup-tied and Tugay, Short and Flitcroft suspended. The pundits could only see one winner; the Londoners of course. Souness however played a master stroke. Mark Hughes had been one of the finest centre forwards to play in the English league. By now, aged thirty-eight, he was mainly used as a substitute striker but as well as possessing all the skills required to play at the highest level, he was also phenomenally hard. So who better to play in Tugay's role in the middle of the park. If nothing else, the Tottenham players would know they had been in a game.

Cole strike stuns Spurs: Blackburn lifted the Worthington Cup for the first time and booked themselves a UEFA Cup spot next season with a deserved win over Tottenham at the Millennium Stadium. Matt Jansen gave Rovers the lead, before

Christian Ziege restored parity for Spurs in the first half. But Andy Cole scored the winner with 22 minutes remaining to give Blackburn their first cup triumph for 74 years in what was a thrilling encounter. Tottenham will feel aggrieved not to have been awarded a penalty in the dying seconds when Teddy Sheringham was brought down in the area. And Brad Friedel made several outstanding saves to thwart Spurs...... But victory was no less than Graeme Souness' side merited for a determined display - and on the day they showed the greater hunger - that should serve them well in their battle for Premiership survival.
BBC Sports Website February 24th, 2002

It was the first time that the Rovers had won the trophy, (they have now won each of the three domestic competitions), and it was Henning Berg holding the cup aloft as captain. There was no doubt that nationally, this was an upset. Stuart Reilly, a long time Rovers' supporter was at the game and he travelled back immediately after the game.

"We were listening to a Football Phone-In in the car and virtually all the calls were from Tottenham fans. It was obvious that they had regarded the Trophy as theirs before the ball was kicked, judging by their comments. All the calls started the same way 'I'm gutted mite (mate), absolutely gutted. Can't believe we lost. We're all gutted.' We couldn't stop laughing all the way home.

The Blackburn Rovers 2002 Football League Cup Winning side that beat Tottenham Hotspur 2-1 was; Brad Friedel, Martin Taylor, Henning Berg, Nils-Eric Johansson, Stig Inge Bjornebye, Keith Gillespie, David Dunn, Mark Hughes, Damian Duff, Matt Jansen, Andy Cole. Substitutes Craig Hignett, Yordi.

This was one of the most memorable moments in David Dunn's football career.

"There was one disappointment with the day and that was that it should have been Wembley. It means that I never got to play at the great Stadium because when I made my debut for England against Portugal, that was played at Villa Park. Not many people expected us to win. Our captain Gary Flitcroft was suspended and Tugay, Craig Short and Lucas Neill were all missing. I had been Tim Sherwood's boot boy when he was captain at the Rovers and now I was playing opposite him in a Cup Final and we won it. I believe it was the first ever final to be played indoors because they closed the roof at the Millennium Stadium. This made it a fantastic atmosphere to play in."

Blackburn Rovers also gave the FA Cup their all, beating Barnsley after a replay in Round 3. Millwall were challenging hard for promotion in Division 1, but an Andy Cole strike was sufficient to see Souness' side through to Round 5. An away trip to Middlesbrough was always going to be tricky and the Teesside club took revenge for their elimination in the League Cup with a tight 1-0 win.

There is no doubt that luck plays its part in football and looking at a career in a considered way, it is fair to say that if luck is around, you cannot complain if the good and bad balance each other out. There are some careers however where fate deals a most unbalanced hand. Take the case of Matt Jansen. I interviewed him by telephone whilst stationary in the car at a Motorway Services. My wife was with me and the phone on speaker. By the time Matt had finished, there were tears in her eyes, so sad was the story.

"I always felt I was lucky as my professional career took off. At only nineteen, I was surprised to be given a place on the Carlisle United bench at the Football League Trophy final at Wembley Stadium. Not only did we beat Colchester United to lift the trophy, but I actually came on as a sub in the later stages. I had played at the old Wembley Stadium, the classically designed Wembley Stadium with its large bath in each changing room. I had no complaints about my time at Crystal Palace and then a recent Premier League title winning side paid a lot of money for me. There was a relegation but we came straight back up and even though Wembley was now closed for renovation, it was magical to go to the Millennium Stadium at Cardiff to win another trophy. The Spurs side was littered with stars but I was on the score sheet. I also briefly felt lucky to have been partnered with Andy Cole, even for only a half season. He was an out and out centre forward, occupying the defenders and this gave me, as a number ten as they now say, many loose balls to pick up and run at the opposition; my natural game."

"From that moment on, it all began to go wrong. In the run up to the World Cup, England played Paraguay at Anfield. We had trained the previous day at Wrexham, Sven Goran Eriksson paired me up front with Michael Owen in training and I later learnt that this was how we were to line up. In the changing room prior to the game, I began to feel desperately ill. It turned out to be a serious strain of gastro-enteritis and I was rushed home and placed on a drip, obviously missing the match. The manager came to watch me again and I was measured for my suit and invited to David Beckham's pre-World Cup party. I was told to make myself available for the week's stay at Baden Baden in Germany with wives and girlfriends prior to flying out to Seoul. My girlfriend was due to sit her finals at University but her father managed to persuade the Authorities to allow her to take them at a later date so that she would not miss the trip of a life time. Eriksson turned up to watch our penultimate league game of the season against Liverpool and he told Graeme Souness that he hoped I would not be injured because they were announcing the squad the following morning and I was in it. The announcement came and there was a late change. They had decided at the eleventh hour to take Martin Keown, an extra defender and I was out."

"I could not believe my ill-luck and so as soon as the season ended, my girlfriend and I decided to go on a short break to Rome. We hired a scooter; I was stationary at a junction and a taxi hit us at speed. My girlfriend received a few bumps and scratches but I was in a coma for six days. Miraculously I recovered physically and although the Rovers medical staff suggested I should take the season off, I was determined to start playing and was back before Christmas. What I hadn't realised was that although I was physically fit, my mental fitness was way, way behind. My skills were in running at defenders, playing it off the cuff; all built on confidence. My decision making, which had always been intuitive, now needed thinking about and I began to only take a couple of touches, something which cut out mistakes but which made me a far less potent player.

The club was good to me in many ways, being patient and offering to send me to see psychologists but this was something unprecedented in football. Although the PFA and Gordon Taylor made every effort to help, the assistance for depression and other mental illnesses, now thankfully common place, did not exist in the game at that time. At my peak, if I made a mistake, it was never my fault. Now I constantly blamed myself and a psychological battle was raging inside me. Over the next six years I regularly tried to make a fresh start, training with different clubs, but I was finished as a player at the top level. I had tried so hard in short stays at Coventry City and Bolton Wanderers amongst others, but I could no longer hack it. It took me a number of years to accept that but now I have managed to put it behind me and get on with my life with the girlfriend, now my wife, and our two children."

Having come within two points of a Play-Off spot the previous season, the fans at Turf Moor felt that they could improve on that performance. They did, but still failed to reach the knock-out stages at the season's end. Stan Ternent made few changes from the year before, only Arthur Gnohere was signed from Caen in France to bolster the defence and Alan Moore, a mid-fielder arrived from Middlesbrough. With only a defeat at title favourites Manchester City in the first eight games, the other seven were won, the Clarets had made a scintillating start. At this stage they could look down from the top of the league table and Glen Little had twice scored a brace against Bradford City and Birmingham City. They slipped back a touch but an unbeaten run of ten games took them back to the top for Christmas. Gareth Taylor enjoyed a purple patch, scoring in five of six successive games and Tony Grant, a stylish mid-field player was signed from Manchester City. It was this opponent which halted the winning run. The Clarets travelled to Maine Road and were walloped 5-1, a preamble to a less than distinguished run of games. Marlon Beresford returned from Middlesbrough to replace Michopoulos in goal and as a last throw of the dice, Ternent presented Paul Gascoigne to the national press as his latest signing. Ever since the defeat in Manchester, Burnley had managed to stay in the Play-Off places but a disastrous 3-1 defeat at lowly Grimsby Town in the penultimate game put tremendous pressure on the final fixture. Basically they had to win the home game against Coventry City by a greater margin than Norwich City against Crewe Alexandra. Approaching the last minute, Norwich were winning

2-0 whist the Clarets were only one up. In those final crucial seconds, Gascoigne twice came within inches of converting free kicks but he was denied twice by exceptionally brilliant saves by the Coventry keeper. For the second year running, the Clarets had finished seventh and the margin of difference this time between Play-Offs and also rans was one single goal after over 4,000 minutes of football. The season had produced excitement for the fans and they were longing and expecting more from the following term, but in actual fact, this would be the last season for six years before the club would mount another challenge on the summit of Division 1.

In the FA Cup, Burnley ought to have benefitted from favourable draws. They were far too strong for non-league side Canvey Island in Round 3, winning 4-1 at Turf Moor, Ian Moore notching a hat-trick. Round 4 was a disaster, losing 2-1 at Cheltenham Town from the fourth tier of the pyramid. Their performance in the Worthington's Football League Cup was even more ignominious. Rushden and Diamonds from a Northamptonshire village came to Burnley as rank outsiders. Stan was probably over-confident, playing a much weakened side. The Division 3 side grabbed a first half lead and the Clarets could never quite catch them, losing 3-2.

2002-03

	Pos	Played	Won	Drawn	Lost	GF	GA	Pts
Blackburn Rovers	6	38	16	12	10	52	43	60
Burnley	16	46	15	10	21	65	89	55

Blackburn Rovers		Burnley	
Most Appearances	Brad Friedel 37	Most Appearances	Dean West 41
Most Goals	Damien Duff 9	Most Goals	Gareth Taylor 16

With the trophy for the Football League Cup in the cabinet for the first time, Blackburn Rovers became the thirteenth club to have won all three major English competitions. Pre-season at Blackburn Rovers was scarred by the near-fatal accident which happened to Matt Jansen. Mark Hughes had already announced his retirement so Graeme Souness was soon into action with his cheque book. Andy Todd, a central defender like his father Colin who played a number of times for England, was signed from Charlton Athletic.

He was the very antithesis of his cultured dad, being extremely rugged and possibly the "dirtiest" player, along with John McNamee, that I have ever seen in a Rovers shirt The club then handed over £2 million to Manchester United for Dwight Yorke. He and Andy Cole had started the 1999 Champions' League final against Bayern Munich and the manager hoped they could re-discover their highly effective strike partnership. Stig Inge Bjornebye received a fracture to his eye-socket pre-season which forced him to retire from the game, half-way through the season.

It was a season where the blue and whites never dropped below fifteenth spot and their finishing position was a season-high sixth place. This equalled their best post-1995 performance, gained under Roy Hodgson's managership. The start was nothing more than steady until an unbeaten autumnal run of four games. This included a 5-2 home win over Newcastle United, both David Dunn and Martin Taylor scoring twice and a shock 2-1 away win at Arsenal, Dwight Yorke notching the winner. This run lifted them into the top ten and by this time, they had bought David Thompson from Coventry City for £1.5million. This diminutive ex-Liverpool mid-field player was as tough as they come and his control and passing ability quickly made him a crowd favourite. A Gary Flitcroft first-half goal was an early Christmas present as Manchester United were beaten 1-0 at Ewood on December 22 and a Cole equaliser a week later at Anfield launched them on to an unbeaten six game run. There were defeats, but the imperious form of Brad Friedel, surely the Premier League's top keeper, helped to keep them solid at the back and doubles over Fulham and Leeds United offered them the opportunity of a top six finish if they could win in London against the Spurs in the final game. Not only did they win, they outclassed the opposition with a 4-0 victory. "The Rovers were back where they belonged", stated the fans. An established Premier League side capable of testing any opponent.

By winning the Football League (Worthington) Cup the previous season, Blackburn Rovers qualified for the UEFA Cup. The draw for Round 1 paired them with CSKA Sofia from Bulgaria and the home leg resulted in a 1-1 draw. In the second leg, the Lancashire side stormed to a three goal lead after an hour, Thompson, Ostenstad and Duff hitting the target, before the Bulgarians roared back with three of their own, enabling the Rovers to scrape through on the away goals rule. The Round 2 draw was fascinating with an initial away tie in Glasgow's east end against Celtic. The hoops were reigning Scottish champions, managed by Martin O'Neill, but the Rovers battled to the end, going down to a late Henrik Larsson goal. The return leg was eagerly anticipated but the Glaswegians' class told and another goal from Larsson and one from ex Rovers' favourite Chris Sutton saw them comfortably through.

Far more exciting for the Blackburn club was their adventure in trying to retain the Football League Cup. Exempt until Round 3, it needed a penalty shoot-out to beat an unheralded Walsall side. They then crushed Rotherham United 4-0 in Round 4, Yorke scoring twice. An away trip to Wigan in the last eight produced a 2-0 win, Cole completing a double strike, and it was Manchester United in the two leg semi-final. A late David Thompson strike cancelled out a Paul Scholes effort at Old Trafford, but in spite of Cole grabbing an early lead for them in the return, a couple from Scholes and a third from van Nistelrooy at an almost full house at Ewood, squashed any dream of a return trip to the Millennium Stadium. The FA Cup campaign was short, full of goals and featured ties against two other Premier League clubs. Aston Villa were simply rolled over in Round 3 at Villa Park, Jansen, in a rare outing, and Yorke each scoring twice in a 4-1 victory. It was a 3-3 score line in Round 4 against Sunderland which included a brace from Cole and Flitcroft was also on target twice as they drew 2-2 back in the North-East. The old saying "they couldn't hit a donkey's bum with a banjo" would have been most appropriate for the Rovers in the penalty shoot-out. Three successive penalties were missed and the Wearsiders ran out 3-0 winners.

One point from the first five fixtures is without doubt relegation form, but such was the topsy-turvy nature of Burnley's season that any result was possible in any game as their free-scoring forwards knocked in goals for fun on occasions but the gossamer thin defence, without the retired Kevin Ball to provide cover in front, was even more likely to "go missing" at any given time. There were no incoming transfers in the close season and the fans asked "why?" after such a poor start. But then, as if the storm clouds had blown away, they were unbeaten in their next ten. The Clarets serenely sailed up the league table to eighth place as Robbie Blake, bought from Bradford City, and Ian Moore began to knock in the goals. Then the crazy season began in earnest, losing 6-5 at bottom club Grimsby Town, 6-2 at home to Rotherham United and when Reading visited the "Turf" on February 1st, they too were unstoppable, winning 5-2. Ternent's side had slumped to sixteenth and alarm bells were sounding.

Three clean sheets moved the club into the top half again, but the last fourteen games yielded just eight points as they twice conceded seven at home to Watford and the already relegated Sheffield Wednesday. The sixteenth place finish came as a relief to so many. Ternent initiated a clear out as soon as the season ended. Stephen Davis, a total of 321 appearances and a surprising forty-two goals, was off-loaded to Blackpool. Goalkeeper Marlon Beresford, so many vital saves over 286 games was on his way to Bradford City and Ian Cox returned south to Gillingham, Paul Cook was down the road to Accrington Stanley and Lee Briscoe to Preston North End, both of whom made in excess of a hundred starts. Finally Gareth Taylor was sold to Nottingham Forest for £0.5million, having scored thirty six goals in eighty-eight games. It was the end of a generation but the manager had to find quality replacements.

It was interesting to hear from Steve Davis just what goes through the head of a professional when he is reaching the end of a long career.

"Having been so fortunate with injuries over such a long period, my body began to let me down from around thirty-three onwards. I began to have trouble with my calf muscles in my last two seasons at Burnley, followed by damage to ligaments in my knee. Whereas I could guarantee over forty appearances every year, I was suddenly down in the twenties. Every time I tried to put a decent run of games together, another injury would crop up. Burnley talked about offering me a further one year contract but the new ITV Digital channel, which was set to be the saviour of football below the Premier League, suddenly collapsed. Instantly clubs had to re-assess their budgets for the following year. Belts were tightened and at the end of this season, I knew it was time for me to leave Turf Moor. I moved to Blackpool and had a reasonable season there but whenever I played, I was looking forward to the ref blowing for full time instead of loving every minute as I had for so many years. I ended up at York City in the Conference and I was even struggling physically at that level. I spent the year looking forward to retirement and my body was completely shot. But now I can look back at the positives, all of my good memories. I enjoyed twenty-one years of football, many as captain plus three promotions and one Football League Trophy win (at Blackpool). I am listed in the all-time top twenty appearance makers at Burnley, this wonderful historic club which I now feel is my team, although I always look for the Sunderland result first. If someone had told me at sixteen that I would be playing until I was thirty-seven, I would have laughed at them."

The highlight of Burnley's season came in the cup competitions. In the Worthington's Cup, both Blackpool and Huddersfield Town from Division 2 were defeated. Then came the stand out performance. Drawn at home to Tottenham Hotspur, the Londoners opened the scoring but goals from Blake and Davis helped them through to the 4th Round. Twenty-two thousand spectators packed Turf Moor for the visit of Manchester United but lightning did not strike twice.

The Clarets however did not disappoint and the 2-0 score line against them was a reasonable result. The FA Cup was even more exciting and the draw much more favourable. Grimsby Town were thrashed 4-0 in a replay, Ian Moore scoring twice and they then turned it on in West London, winning 3-0 at Division 2 Brentford. Premier League Fulham away were next up in Round 5 and after an early Alan Moore goal, Fulham equalised but the "Turf" once again acted as a lucky charm with another clean sheet and three goals from Taylor, Ian Moore and Drissa Diallo in the replay. It was as reasonable a last eight draw as they could expect but unfortunately the performance by the Clarets at Watford disappointed and they stumbled their way to a 2-0 defeat.

2003-04

	Pos	Played	Won	Drawn	Lost	GF	GA	Pts
Blackburn Rovers	15	38	12	8	18	51	59	44
Burnley	19	46	13	14	19	60	77	53

Blackburn Rovers		Burnley	
Most Appearances	Brad Friedel 36	Most Appearances	Brian Jenson 46
Most Goals	Andy Cole 11	Most Goals	Robbie Blake 19

Graeme Souness had to face the upcoming season at Blackburn Rovers without one of the crowd favourites. Local boy David Dunn had allegedly fallen out with the manager and he wanted away. The Rovers were initially unwilling to sell but they eventually accepted an offer from Birmingham City for £5.5million and Dunny was gone. He told me that he later regretted the move.

"Looking back I should have been more patient. But I was too quick to make decisions in those days and I was Birmingham's record buy. The whole thing turned into a nightmare because I had a bad deal with injuries. I had so many problems with my hamstrings and I missed too many games. I eventually had to have an operation on my spine and I never had anything wrong with my hamstring again, although I started to have problems with my calves which made me wonder if the operation didn't just move the problem downwards. I was at Birmingham for three and a half seasons, but I was only fit enough to start fifty-eight games."

Henning Berg, seven seasons in total in Blackburn collecting exactly one century of Norwegian international caps, left for Glasgow Rangers, but the biggest star to move on was Damien Duff. The club was adamant that they would not sell, but when Chelsea, now backed by Abramovich money, offered £17.5million for his services, it triggered a release clause in his contract and he too was gone. Three players moved to Leicester City, Keith Gillespie, Craig Hignett and John Curtis. Lorenzo Amoruso was signed from Glasgow Rangers for £1.4million to replace Berg. He had earned a reputation as an indestructible defender, extremely useful in the opposition box at set pieces.

Marcus Babbel arrived on a season-long loan from Liverpool and Republic of Ireland international mid-fielder Steven Reid joined from Millwall. But perhaps Souness' best signing was wide right player Brett Emerton, an Aussie bought from Feyenoord in Holland. After a 5-1 winning start against Wolverhampton Wanderers, Amoruso scored his second, this time at home to Manchester City but his lack of pace was quickly put to the test when Nicholas Anelka gave him a ten yard start over twenty, won the ball and cracked it past Friedel to earn the Sky Blues a 3-2 victory. With a lengthy injury, he played only occasionally over the next two years.

The season resembled a game of snakes and ladders, falling and rising between mid-table and the relegation zone before a four game winning streak as the season edged to a close saved them from relegation. Jon Stead scored a late goal to defeat Manchester United 1-0 and the ex-Huddersfield Town centre forward's six goals since signing in February were probably the principle reason why they stayed up, their final placement being fifteenth. Barry Ferguson, the Scottish captain, had earlier signed from Glasgow Rangers for £7.5million and Michael Gray, a cultured left back arrived initially on loan from Sunderland prior to the move becoming permanent. There had been little to be excited about, the reputation of Souness taking a nose dive.

When competing in three different cup competitions, the law of averages will suggest that you have at least one decent run. But there is always an exception to every rule. Gaining entry to the UEFA Cup, Genclerbirligi SK came out of the hat with the Rovers in Round 1; a Turkish outfit whom no-one had heard of, let alone could pronounce their name. They were better than we thought, winning 4-2 on aggregate. The Carling (Football League) Cup paired them with Liverpool at Ewood and Yorke put the Ewood side one up but this was a Rovers side completely bereft of form and helped by an Emile Heskey double, the Merseysiders led 4-1 with ten to go. From nowhere, the home side started to compete and goals from Ferguson and Yorke again made it a close run thing; close but not

quite close enough. Could the FA Cup be something of a saviour? The draw was once again relatively unfair, away at fellow Premier League club Birmingham City, but the answer to the question was an unequivocal "NO". The Lancashire club was second best throughout and lost 4-0.

There was re-construction work to be done at Turf Moor, and re-construct is what Stan Ternent did. In total, fifteen players made their debuts during this campaign, although only five played more than twenty games. A goalkeeper was his number one priority and the Dane, Brian Jensen, joined on a free transfer from West Bromwich Albion. Nicknamed "The Beast" for obvious reasons, the Burnley fans immediately took to him and in total he made 271 league appearances over a ten year period, his speciality being saving penalties. Lee Roche arrived from Manchester United to play at right-back and left back Mo Camara moved north from Wolverhampton Wanderers. Luke Chadwick, a Manchester United starlet came on loan to play for the full season in mid-field and David May, the ex-Rovers and Manchester United central defender, played out the final season of his career in the Claret and Blue shirt. Did Stan have contacts at Old Trafford?

It was said he did and his purchases and loans provide the evidence. After a shambles of a start, three wins followed and after Walsall were beaten 3-1 at the "Turf" in the twelfth fixture, eighth place in the league was being occupied. Delroy Facey, who arrived from Bolton Wanderers on a short term loan, scored a hat-trick in this fixture. From then until Christmas, only two out of the next fourteen games were won and relegation was on the cards, but thankfully Robbie Blake was scoring goals. Although there were several more embarrassing performances, four victories in the last nine games allowed them to avoid the drop by just two points.

Defensively they suffered, conceding six at Ipswich, five at Deepdale and at home to Norwich plus a 4-0 loss at Coventry City. Glen Little had started 246 league games and scored thirty two goals in a Claret and Blue shirt, a long remembered right winger, probably Burnley's best player over the last seven seasons with his pace, sleight of foot and football brain but when his contract ended, he was allowed to sign for Reading on a "Bosman". Paul Weller also said goodbye at the end of the season. He had come through the ranks at Gawthorpe and gone on to make 199 league starts, playing at right back, in mid-field and out wide on the right. Dean West, bought by Stan Ternent at Bury and at Turf Moor had been an attacking full back, making 145 league starts before moving back to Lincoln City where his career began.

Both cup competitions gave the fans something to cheer. In the Carling Cup, Burnley went through at Chesterfield on a penalty shoot-out and battled their way to a 3-2 victory at Division 3 Scunthorpe United. Round 3 was a visit to Wolverhampton Wanderers from the Premier League and that extra ability told, the Molyneux side winning 2-0. The FA Cup 3rd round draw saw an Ian Moore brace in a 2-0 victory at Mansfield Town and Gillingham next went down 3-1 at Turf Moor in the 4th Round, Blake scoring twice. Millwall was the last sixteen opponent at the New Den but the South London side proved too strong on the day, winning 2-0 before successfully moving on to the final.

It would be remiss of me not to mention Stan Ternent's contribution to the cause at Turf Moor. Born in Gateshead, he inevitably followed the trail to Gawthorpe, joining Burnley as an apprentice. He struggled to break into the first eleven of a team riding high at the top of the pyramid in English football, not easy when O'Neill, Miller and Todd was the resident half-back line and Merrington was ahead of you in the queue. He was sold to Carlisle United where he played regularly for six seasons. He quit playing to take up coaching at the age of thirty and after stints in management at Blackpool, Hull City and most successfully at Bury, he returned to Turf Moor at the age of fifty two. In six seasons he took the club from Division 2 to Division 1 and twice narrowly failed to reach the Play-Offs for the Premier League. Burnley at this time was a parsimonious club, the chairman Barry Kilby being determined (probably quite rightly) never to spend money the club did not possess; a situation which made Ternent's contribution even more notable.

His sacking was announced in the run up to the final home game against Sunderland. The crowd of 18,852 was the highest of the season and they came to say their goodbyes and give their thanks to a manager who had worked so hard to retain Burnley's place in the second tier of English football. Was he Burnley's most successful manager? No has to be the answer because John Haworth and Harry Potts achieved much more, but Stan Ternent is in hallowed company, where he deserves to be, after a six year stint beset by problems on and off the field, and still leaving the club in a stronger position than when he arrived.

2004-05

	Pos	Played	Won	Drawn	Lost	GF	GA	Pts
Blackburn Rovers	15	38	9	15	14	32	43	42
Burnley	13	46	15	15	16	38	39	60

Blackburn Rovers		Burnley	
Most Appearances	Brad Friedel 38	Most Appearances	Mo Camara 45
Most Goals	Paul Dickov 9	Most Goals	Robbie Blake 10

If you cannot average at least a goal a game, you are in trouble; the exact scenario at both Ewood Park and Turf Moor this season. If however your defence holds firm, life is not that exciting for the fans, but reasonably safe and secure. If therefore you think that this is a campaign which can be quickly forgotten, think again because the FA threw a spicy substance into the mix. It was all to do with the 5th Round draw for the FA Cup, but more of that later.

Following the previous season's non-event, Graeme Souness knew he had, as my grandmother used to say, "to pull his socks up". Known for an ability to fall out with players, the manager lost Andy Cole to Fulham and Dwight Yorke to Birmingham City over the summer. Yet again, other players were brought in. The two most notable were Paul Dickov, an extremely combative and tempestuous striker who had scored goals in abundance at Leicester City and Morten Gamst Pedersen, signed from Norwegian side Tromso for £1.5million. He was an exciting left sided player with tremendous power in both feet.

After five games, the Rovers were second from the bottom of the league with two points. One of these had been gained at home to Manchester United, the Reds equalising in time added on (Fergie time) after the Rovers had hung on to a 1-0 lead for most of the game following Dickov's early opener. By this time, Souness was being head hunted by Newcastle United and it would be interesting to know the reaction of the Board to the Geordies' approach. My guess it was one of relief. Mark Hughes, not long retired from playing at Ewood and who had earned many plaudits for his work as manager of the Welsh team, was quickly brought in. From being rock bottom at the end of November, they slowly but surely improved as Hughes worked on the general level of fitness. The turn of the year saw them up to fifteenth and the manager then dipped into the January sales, buying the impressive New Zealand captain and central defender Ryan Nelsen from DC United on a free transfer. Aaron Mokoena, a mid-field player who would later captain South Africa, was signed from the Belgian side KRC Genk and £3million was spent on securing the services of the ultimate action man, Robbie Savage from Birmingham City. The principal outgoing transfer was that of the disappointing Barry Ferguson back to Glasgow Rangers. For the rest of the season, the Ewood Park club fluctuated between thirteenth and sixteenth, always indicating that they were clear of relegation. They impressed on Merseyside in consecutive games, winning 1-0 at Everton and holding Liverpool to a goalless draw. There was an identical draw at Old Trafford and after a shaky run-in, safety was comfortably secured in fifteenth spot. Mark Hughes had come up with the goods and although goals were at a premium, they were never really taken to the cleaners.

Although it was a very long evening, their Football League Cup campaign which started in Round 2, was over virtually before it began. It was one of those crazy attack at all costs games against AFC Bournemouth from Division 1. It was 2-2 after ninety, 3-3 after extra-time and a marathon penalty shootout which ended in a 7-6 victory for the south coast side, Tugay of all people missing the final penalty. By contrast the FA Cup was a lengthy adventure for the blue and white halves. Cardiff City were finally defeated 3-2 in a replay at Ewood and Colchester United from the third tier travelled north but subsided to a 3-0 defeat. And then came the draw for Round 5; Burnley v Blackburn Rovers on February 20th in Burnley.

The number one task in the close season at Burnley was to find a new manager. After much speculation amongst the press and fans, Steve Cotterill was the Board's choice, young, energetic and track suited; someone equally at home on the training ground as behind a desk. He had brought Cheltenham Town out of non-league football and into Division 3 and he had certainly been in demand as a coach. He needed replacements to match the reliability and talent of Little and Weller. David May retired but in his place came three defenders; Michael Duff, a Northern Ireland international from the manager's old club who would repay his £30,000 transfer fee time and again, John McGreal, a centre back who had played in the Premier League with Ipswich Town and the Jamaican international Frank Sinclair who had won medals at Chelsea and Leicester City. Another Jamaican international to sign this summer was midfielder Micah Hyde from Watford.

It was the first year of the Championship and Burnley started reasonably, with only two defeats in the first fourteen games and tenth place was the league position at this time. In fact tenth place was the highest they would achieve all season, as defeats started to dampen any talk of promotion. The defence was solid, but goals were hard to come by with only Blake regularly finding the back of the net. After a 2-1 defeat at Sunderland, the Board could no longer say "no" to a £1.25million offer from Wigan Athletic for the striker and he left a gap that was never satisfactorily filled for the rest of the term. Worse was to follow. Richard Chaplow, a fine prospect in mid-field, was sold to West Bromwich Albion for £1.5million, a new club record. Ian Moore was sold to Leeds United for £50,000, having made 192 starts and scored thirty seven goals. A £600,000 fee was spent on Ade Akinbiyi, a giant of a man from Stoke City to replace Blake. The London born Nigerian had a debut to forget, coming on as a substitute against Sunderland and head-butting an opponent within two minutes; an instant red card. He was soon on the goal trail, but the goalless draw at Millwall in the final fixture summed up the season. Cotterill's signings had shored up the defence, helped by a successful loan signing half way through the season, the young Gary Cahill from Aston Villa whose form suggested he was one for the future. And so the season ended with Burnley in a disappointing thirteenth spot.

The Carling (League) Cup gave the fans reasons to be cheerful. A Blake double saw off Bury in Round 1 and he also scored the equaliser against Wolverhampton Wanderer, a game which the Clarets eventually won 4-2 on penalties. Premier League Aston Villa were the visitors in Round 3 and they surprisingly folded, the Clarets winning 3-1. Blake was not on the scoresheet this time but he set up Branch, Camara and Jean-Louis Valois to put the result beyond doubt. It was another home draw in the last sixteen, but Tottenham Hotspur were three up on the hour mark and that was how it ended. It was a less than full strength Liverpool side in Round 3 of the FA Cup and there was typically freezing winter weather which swept in from the Pennines. On the night there was no doubt that the Turf Moor side was better equipped, better prepared, better motivated and ultimately able to outfight a tentative opponent; a group of journeymen professionals who fully deserved their 1-0 victory courtesy of a bizarre Traore own goal. The packed house roared its approval at the final whistle as Benitez was left to rue his team selection. Ian Moore, left to lead the attack without his recently departed sparring partner Robbie Blake, then scored twice on the south coast in a 2-0 win over AFC Bournemouth to set up what could only be described as the mouth-watering prospect of the first FA Cup derby game since 1960.

The derby FA Cup games

And so to the derby game. There was excitement galore at Turf Moor as the two local rivals clashed. It was a game which dominated conversations for days after but no-one much mentioned the football. But first of all, here is a question. If you pair a side that struggles to score goals all season with a side that struggles to score goals all season, what do you get? The answer is usually a game without goals and this is exactly what happened in Burnley, Yes there were exciting moments, but these were mainly off the field and those that occurred on the field centred round a streaker, a mindless individual who strolled on the pitch at half-time waving a flag and far more seriously, a Burnley fan who wanted to knock out Robbie Savage.

The Rovers perhaps had more of the game, the Clarets seemed content to defend strongly and show no interest in attack and the Police must have been the most stressed group in the vicinity. A number of Burnley supporters certainly did not cover themselves with glory but the lunacy was definitely not one-sided. The game had to be stopped at one point when the Clarets' winger Jean-Louis Valois could not take a corner because of the shower of coins raining down on him from the stand where Blackburn fans were seated. For those who had turned up to watch a game of football, there was little to discuss; hopefully the replay would display better fare, but for those turned on by sirens, flashing blue lights, riot vans and circling helicopters, it was "top of the bill" stuff.

The police had been criticised by all and sundry after the initial tie and they knew they had to formulate more effective plans for the replay. Officers were drafted in from all over Lancashire and what worried the Police the most was that there had to be a winner. That alone would cause all sorts of problems post-match. Apparently 400 of the "boys in blue" were deployed and it needed a small army to supervise the off-loading of eighty coach loads of fans, all having to be kept separate from the goading Roverites who would have desperately liked to have been given access to the enemy.

In all, 7,000 from up the M65 packed the away (Darwen) end and the cacophony of noise from all quarters filled the night air. The game itself was far more interesting and exciting, but it was a typical derby from the off. Robbie Savage immediately set the tone, being booked within three minutes and Mark Hughes wisely hooked him off at half-time. Burnley played far more positively, as did the Rovers and the capacity crowd was treated to three spectacular goals. The Rovers saw far more of the ball in the first-half and when Jensen was forced to deal with a Savage free-kick, he punched with authority, finding good distance. The ball fell to Tugay, perhaps twenty five yards out and his shot took a wicked deflection and flew into the opposite corner, leaving the Burnley defence helpless. The Clarets began to push forward and were rewarded with a goal of outstanding quality from Micah Hyde. Mick Duffy tells it thus.

> "Four years after the previous clash, the two teams met in the fifth round of the FA Cup in the 2004-05 season. Probably the best goal ever scored in an encounter between the two rivals was scored at Ewood Park – the first time Burnley had scored on the ground for twenty-two years. Micah Hyde took a throw-in on his thigh, close to the touch line. In a single motion, he swivelled and launched his goal of the season into the top corner past Brad Friedel to level the scores. Quite correctly, the American keeper was slightly off his line but not only was there so much pace on the ball, it dipped at the last moment prior to crossing the line. I do not believe that any goal keeper in the world would have saved it."

The second half was closely contested and just when the crowd was thinking about extra time, Morten Gamst Pedersen attempted to cross the ball from the right. His effort was charged down, but he was the first to react and he simply smashed the ball past (or was it through) Brian Jensen to seal the game for the home side. Once again it was a case of the keeper being in the right position but the Norwegian's shot came with such venom that no-one chalked this up as a goalkeeping blunder. Yet again the Burnley side had come off second best in a derby game. Their last win had been in December 1979 but that was nearly twenty five years ago and in that time, a whole generation of Burnley folk had been born, got married and had their own children.

Would the see saw ever swing back? In terms of public order offences (the Police label not mine), forty were arrested over the whole evening. It is of course forty too many, but there had been no pitch invasions, no major incidents and the town of Blackburn appeared to be relatively unscathed the following morning. The Rovers were in the 6th round of the FA Cup, the town of Burnley was able to hold its head high after a gallant performance and the Police had probably learnt a lot more about how to handle such a potentially dangerous situation.

Date	Round	Home Side	Away Side	Score	Scorers
20 02 2005	5	Burnley	Blackburn Rovers	0-0	
01 03 2005	Replay	Blackburn Rovers	Burnley	2-1	Tugay, M Gamst-Pedersen, M Hyde

Morten Gamst Pedersen celebrates after the Cup replay

Graham Branch was on the bench for both cup ties in spite of making thirty-nine starts in league games that season.

"The Micah Hyde goal is one you would never forget. I was sat with the subs and it really got us back into the game. And the second half was so close. Steve Cotterill sent me on with about ten to play and we were thinking about going for the winner although it could have gone to extra-time. We lost the ball as we pushed forward and it came to Pedersen who smashed it in and we were out of Cup. Afterwards, we felt we were unlucky to lose."

Damian Hartley was at the Turf Moor game.

The policeman on duty just in front of me was someone I vaguely knew. He was stationed at Burnley but was in fact a Rovers' supporter. When the hooligan ran on to the pitch to confront Savage, he was the first "copper" to reach the incident. Somehow or another he ended up on the floor but the next moment the invader met his match. Ryan Nelsen, the Rovers' centre-half, was a very big man and a most imposing and hard looking individual. He dived in to protect his team mate. There would have only been one winner and the Burnley fan decided to make a run for it. As he reached the touchline, he was collared by two policemen, both of whom he assaulted, knocking off one of their helmets. He was then marched off to a mixed reception; a cascade of boos from the sizeable Blackburn contingent but volley after volley of cheers ringing out from the Claret and Blue supporters. By this time, football violence had become a much more serious offence in the eyes of the law and the man was actually jailed for five months and given a banning order.

Dave Timberlake remembers it for the logistics involved in watching a night match so far from home.

"A close friend of mine who lives in Newark is also a Clarets' fanatic. He worked with someone who lived in Doncaster but who was equally fanatical about the other lot. My boss let me have the afternoon off and said I could come in late the following morning. So I caught a train to Newark and my mate drove me to Burnley via Doncaster. Altogether there were five us in the car, three Clarets and two Rovers' supporters. We then had to be bussed down to Blackburn for the game. After the game ended (and it was close) we had much to discuss, but we were held back on the ground again. We then returned to Turf Moor by bus, met up with the two from Doncaster and then had to set off back south. It was late by this time and as we hit the M62, we decided to stop at Birch Services for a coffee. Three of us were wearing claret and blue shirts, two of us in blue and white halved shirts. Then all of a sudden, a small group of Police walked in. When they saw us, they dashed over to check that there was no violence about to break out. Apparently they had been at the game, all police leave being cancelled all over the North West and they had just worked their socks off separating rival supporters all evening. On their way home, they had stopped for a break and a drink. It took several minutes for us to convince them that we were actually good friends who happened to support different clubs. When the penny dropped, the coppers couldn't stop laughing."

Mark Hughes now had to focus on a home last eight game in twelve days' time against Leicester City. It was a difficult afternoon, but a late Paul Dickov penalty was sufficient to send the Blue and Whites to their first FA Cup semi-final since they beat Sheffield Wednesday in 1960. Facing them was Arsene Wenger's Arsenal, Premier League runner-up. It was always going to be an uphill struggle at the Millennium Stadium in Cardiff; Wembley had still not re-opened. Hughes' plan was to try and stifle the attacking flair of the Gunners and if that meant committing many fouls, so be it. The plan worked for most of the first half, Arsenal players repeatedly hitting the deck after a whole succession of rough tackles. But after yet another free kick, Robert Pires put the Londoners in front just before half-time, meaning that the manager's interval talk had to centre on a Plan B. This seemed to be to foul even more but when Robin van Persie came off the substitutes' bench it was soon game over; the Dutchman scoring two exquisite goals to send the dispirited Blackburn fans home empty handed. The press was quick to criticise the Hughes approach; in particular the off the ball elbow chop by Andy Todd on van Persie which was missed by the referee but no-one else in the Stadium.

2005-06

	Pos	Played	Won	Drawn	Lost	GF	GA	Pts
Blackburn Rovers	6	38	19	6	13	51	42	63
Burnley	17	46	14	12	20	46	54	54

Blackburn Rovers		Burnley	
Most Appearances	Brad Friedel 38	Most Appearances	James O'Connor 46
Most Goals	Craig Bellamy 13	Most Goals	Ade Akinbiyi 12

In the ever-changing world of the ups and downs of professional football, a stay of four years in the league hints at longevity and Blackburn Rovers were about to commence their fifth season amongst the elite, Burnley their sixth in Tier 2. A part of a manager's brief is to avoid relegation, another to make a concerted effort at promotion or winning silverware. So to sum up, a place in a European competition had to be Hughes' goal and for Cotterill, a serious tilt at the Play-Offs.

The life of a footballer in this new millennium had become far more mobile, both geographically and employment wise. Of the regular starters at Ewood Park this term, only Todd, Gray and David Bentley were English. Hughes' signings were Georgian, Kosovan, Welsh, English and a Frenchman on loan. Those leaving were Craig Short (134 league games in four seasons), Nils-Eric Johansson and Jon Stead. And as the revolving door swings players away from a club, it also brings in the next generation. To boost fire power, Craig Bellamy from Newcastle United was the perfect solution. Renowned for his speed of foot and quickness of temper, he certainly knew where the net was. He had built up a reputation for never allowing the grass to grow beneath his feet and he holds the record for having scored Premier League goals for seven different clubs, a statistic which indicates both his ability on the pitch and his inability to settle anywhere. The Georgian Zurab Khizanishvili came from Glasgow Rangers, Shefki Kuqi, a Kosovan via refugee status in Finland, from Ipswich Town and David Bentley, a talented winger. Unable to break his way into the super-gifted Arsenal starting eleven, he initially came to Blackburn on loan; a deal which was quickly made permanent. He remains the last Rovers' player to be capped for England whilst at the club.

Public apathy was one of Mark Hughes' main problems, evident from the first home game. After a 3-1 defeat at West Ham, less than 17,000 turned up to watch them edge past Fulham 2-1. Those that stayed away missed one of the finest goals ever seen at the famous old ground, Morten Gamst Pedersen volleying home from at least thirty yards at an angle, the ball almost ripping the top left netting from its mounts. I was with my two sons that afternoon, sat in the Riverside immediately behind the trajectory of the shot, but those who missed it had many opportunities to relive the moment because it was voted "goal of the month" on BBC TV's Match of the Day. And for those wanting icing on their cake, Tugay smashed home the winner from a similar distance, albeit from a more central position. We reminisce about the occasion whenever the talk turns to football on family get togethers.

After this one win in their first six games, they next played at Old Trafford and overturned the United side by a 2-1 margin. Pedersen was the hero with both; probably his finest hour in his long career in Blackburn. Craig Bellamy hit the goal trail with four in three games but Gary Flitcroft, ex captain and a fine mid-field player, left the club around this time for Sheffield United, his 248 league appearances and fourteen goals spanning ten seasons. From a relatively stable mid-table position, five wins and a draw over Christmas and through January gave them a "perchance to dream". This run culminated in a thrilling 4-3 win over Manchester United; a double over the "big time Charlies", a David Bentley hat-trick sending them into the top ten. Often remembered as the low point of Rio Ferdinand's on-field career, the classy centre back had been involved in giving away the softest of goals which gifted Bentley his hat-trick, gently heading the ball back to van der Saar without knowing the Dutch keeper had raced out beside him to collect the ball. Ferdinand was also sent off for a wretchedly high tackle on Robbie Savage, scuppering any chance of a complete "Reds" comeback after being 4-1 down. For those with anorak tendencies, the previous time that the double was achieved against the United was in 1931 when heroes from so long ago, Puddefoot and McLean, were on the scoresheet. Bellamy hit four doubles, propelling them to fifth with a Champions' League spot now a possibility. But a touch of inconsistency saw them conclude the season in sixth place, in spite of a big finish; three successive wins. Over 25,000 turned out to witness the final home game, showing that Hughes had won over the fans. It was a 2-0 win over Manchester City and the goal scorers were Khizanishvili and Kuqi. What my grandfather would have made of two such named players scoring for his club is anybody's guess, but it does show the international influence on a league which was once the preserve of United Kingdom players. Sixth place was no mean achievement, the third time since the glory days of 1995, but sadly the last time to date they would feature in such a high position.

The Carling League Cup caught the fan's imagination from autumn through to winter. Two West Yorkshire clubs were quickly eliminated at Ewood Park in the second and third rounds, Huddersfield Town and Leeds United, a shadow of their former self. The next two rounds produced close victories over Charlton Athletic and Middlesbrough to qualify them for a semi-final battle with

Manchester United. With a re-scheduled league game in between, the two sides would wage war three times within a three week span. And wage war they did. The first leg was as close as could be, Pedersen equalising Luis Saha's opener to send them back to Manchester all square. The Old Trafford game was simply an old-fashioned cup-tie, no quarter given and none asked. Ruud van Nistelrooy was outstanding but in Brad Friedel he found an opponent just as unyielding. The Dutchman put the "Reds" in front, driving the ball past the American keeper from fifteen yards. Nicky Reid's equaliser was equally clinical and the second half was a pulsating forty five minutes of thrust and counter thrust, flying tackles and sheer physical endeavour on a less than perfect pitch. Friedel saved a van Nistelrooy penalty in magnificent fashion and another save from the United striker's header was Gordon Banksesque. As time ticked away, Tugay was pushed off the ball by Fletcher, surely a foul but Graham Poll shook his head, and Saha volleyed home in spectacular fashion; Gallic flair and technique of the highest order. It had been the Rovers' third League Cup semi-final in five years, one win and two defeats, but with a fit Craig Bellamy on the field, it may just have been a different story. The Blackburn Rovers FA Cup campaign started in fine style; the Championship club Queens Park Rangers going down 3-0 with Bellamy bagging a brace. However, the Round 4 tie at Upton Park, surely the country's most uninviting venue in those days, was no happy hunting ground as they went down 4-2 to West Ham.

It does not take an Einstein to work out that if you continue to sell your best players, you will weaken your side. I am certain that Barry Kilby and co in the Burnley Board Room were fully aware of this, but as they had no intention of running up losses each season, then sell they must. This time in mid-term, Steve Cotterill had to say good-bye to another star striker, Ade Akinbiyi leaving for Sheffield United. The Blades bought to strengthen their side prior to a successful tilt at the title whereas the Clarets, in a top ten position at the time, sold even though it virtually signalled the end of their Play-Off chase. A "speculate to accumulate policy" can work, but the road to failure is littered with clubs who tried to live beyond their means. Perhaps if the Board had followed a similar policy, would Burnley FC have been able to establish themselves in the Premier League a decade earlier? No-one knows of course. The Guinean international Mo Camara to Celtic, right back Lee Roche to Wrexham and Tony Grant, after four years and 141 games full of hard work, to Bristol City were the departees. Replacements were required and Steve Cotterill travelled down to the south coast for a smash and grab raid on three AFC Bournemouth players, Wade Elliott, Gareth O'Connor and John Spicer. Gifton Noel-Williams, a tall striker from Stoke City who had a reputation for scoring goals, arrived on a free and the £75,000 spent on left back John Harley from Sheffield United proved to be an astute investment.

Apart from Akinbiyi's double in the 4-0 thumping of Coventry City, the start was lamentable; one win in ten. Questions were asked of the manager but the Board had faith in Mr Cotterill and a run of four victories which included an Akinbiyi hat-trick at Luton Town proved how quickly fortunes can change. Ten games later, the Clarets occupied a Play-Off spot with the odds on a Clarets' return to the big time rapidly shortening. But Neil Warnock, the Sheffield United manager had set his sights on Akinbiyi. The press knew all about it and the resulting publicity caused all sorts of upset and anxiety within the camp. Suddenly it became all about defeats and after a particularly heavy one at Cardiff, the striker was gone. After a Boxing Day high of fifth, they won one game from the next thirteen as they fell down the table to a worrying eighteenth spot. The search for a striker ended when Andy Gray, the next generation of the famous family who contributed so much to Leeds United's success in the seventies, was signed from Sunderland. He was immediately successful and his goals contributed to a finish in seventeenth spot, twelve points above the drop zone. It had been another disappointing campaign at Turf Moor, but their purchases were in the hundreds of thousands whereas their rivals talked seven figure numbers. Cotterill had tried his best with what little was at his disposal and next season however would be their seventh in the second tier. Cotterill was still there and as twenty-first century professional football is all about money, for clubs like Burnley there is much merit in simply staying put.

In Rounds 1 and 2 of the Carling League Cup, A late winner gave them a 2-1 winning margin over Carlisle United, but Barnsley were comfortably beaten 3-0. A trip to Villa Park in the last thirty-two was their reward. It was close, but the Premier League side, as expected, won 1-0. The draw for Round 3 of the FA Cup took them to Derby County. It was a game Burnley could have won, but it came at the height of the Akinbiyi debacle and at the beginning of the club's slide down the table. A 2-1 defeat was therefore a par score.

2006-07

	Pos	Played	Won	Drawn	Lost	GF	GA	Pts
Blackburn Rovers	10	38	15	7	16	52	54	52
Burnley	15	46	15	12	19	52	49	57

Blackburn Rovers		Burnley	
Most Appearances	Brad Friedel 38	Most Appearances	Jon Harley 44
Most Goals	Benni McCarthy 18	Most Goals	Andy Gray 14

Mark Hughes said an immediate good-bye to his number one goal scorer, unable to do anything about Craig Bellamy's departure. Written into the fiery forward's contract was a clause enabling him to leave for a side which had qualified for the Champions' League. Liverpool came in with an offer of £6million and the Rovers had to say "yes". He was quickly replaced by one of the top front men in Europe, Benni McCarthy, a South African from FC Porto at a knockdown fee of £2.5million. Jason Roberts, a Grenada international from Wigan Athletic and Shabani Nonda on a season-long loan from Roma also checked in.

Stephane Henchoz returned on a free, having also last played at Wigan and the Board paid out £2million to PSV Eindhoven for multi-capped Dutch centre-back Andre Ooijer. It was a dire start, one goal and two points from the first four games. But ten points from the next four, including a 1-1 draw at Liverpool, were instrumental in a rapid rise into the top ten. Four successive defeats and a draw dropped them to seventeenth but by the time they won at 3-0 at Wigan on New Year's Day it was back to eleventh, in spite of a 6-2 crunching against Arsenal at the Emirates. And give or take a position or two, they firmly remained in mid-table, helped enormously by a big finish which garnered twelve points in the last six outings. Pedersen had netted doubles in a 3-0 victory at Manchester City and a 2-1 win at home to Sheffield United, but McCarthy was scoring throughout the season and his total of eighteen was second only to Chelsea's Didier Drogba. But it was Hughes' dabble in the transfer market over the January window which made the difference. He lost Lucas Neill, having made 188 league starts, to West Ham United for £1.5 million but left-back Stephen Warnock arrived from Liverpool for £2.5 million and bargain buy Christopher Samba, a giant of a centre half, was brought in from Hertha Berlin for £450,000. But the move which most pleased the fans was the return of David Dunn from Birmingham City for £2.2million. All three would certainly give value for money.

There was a run of sorts in a European competition. They overcame Red Bull Salzburg 4-2 in the First Round of the UEFA Cup and in the Group Stage, Wisla Krakow, FC Basel, and Nancy were all beaten and Feyenoord held to a goalless draw, thus qualifying them for the last thirty-two. Bayer Leverkusen was a cut above the previous opposition but although the Rovers lost 3-2 in Germany, they had two away goals in the bag. Unfortunately the stubborn German side held on for a 0-0 draw at Ewood and the cup run was over. Qualification for this competition meant an exemption in the Carling Football League Cup to Round 3 but Chelsea was the opponent. The Londoners had so much quality, winning 2-0. The fans, however had plenty to cheer in the FA Cup.

On fire in Rounds 3 and 4, they smashed their way past Everton 4-1 at Goodison and then won 4-0 at Luton Town. There were no goals in the 5th Round tie at Arsenal, but a McCarthy strike won them the replay in Blackburn. An almost full house witnessed a 2-0 win over Manchester City and it was off to the Old Trafford, the neutral ground for the semi-final against Chelsea. The two sides had already clashed three times this season, all victories for Jose Mourinho's side. The fourth game was no different, but at least the Lancashire side managed a goal this time, Jason Roberts equalising Lampard's opener before Michael Ballack grabbed the winner in the second period of extra-time. Mark

Hughes had taken his side to a cup semi-final in three successive years and in each case, they were knocked out by the eventual winners.

Earlier on in the decade, Jeff Taylor had sent me to cast an eye over Matt Derbyshire, a fifteen year old Darwen lad playing in a local final. "He's quick" I reported "but he is small, not strong enough and only wants the ball over the top; basically not good enough for Burnley". Several years on, he scored four times in this cup run for the Rovers and is still plying his trade years later in Europe. What do I know about football?

Steve Cotterill went for continuity and the only summer signing was Steve Jones, a striker with Crewe Alexandra. By the time Bonfire Night had passed, a podium finish was on the cards, having lost just three times in sixteen games. A hat-trick from Gifton-Williams and doubles from Jones and Gray made people take notice but like someone switching off the light, there was only one more win before the end of March. Gray missed ten games with a broken foot and with a blunted attack, the Clarets became cannon fodder. Cotterill's loans were uninspired but he bought Steven Caldwell from Sunderland for £200,000, a strongly built and tough tackling centre back who quickly became a fans' favourite and Akinbiyi returned from Sheffield United but he was not the player that had left the previous campaign. Then with relegation staring the club in the face, Plymouth Argyle were thrashed 4-0, Gray quickly regained his goal touch and the Clarets pulled away to a safe fifteenth place, eight points clear of the drop.

Three of their standout defenders over the years came to the end of the road. Frank Sinclair was loaned out to Huddersfield Town and John McGreal retired; each having played almost a century of games. Graham Branch, a magnificent servant who could play anywhere down the left hand side was also released to Accrington Stanley, having started 208 league games with over fifty appearances as a substitute. Branch was ultimately glad to be away.

> "After the old Gaffer, I found it more difficult under Steve Cotterill. He was what I classed as arrogant and the dressing room was not as happy a place. He had played me regularly for two seasons, but in my final year, I was often not even a sub. As a result I left under a cloud even though I still felt fit enough to be playing at this level. But it didn't spoil my memories of the club. I will always feel that Burnley was my club and I always love going back to the area."

The cup competitions passed with the blink of an eye. The kids were still on their summer holidays when Hartlepool United came down and sneaked a 1-0 Football League Cup win. And the kids were still on their Christmas holidays when they visited the Thames Valley in Round 3 of the FA Cup, performing well against Reading from the Premier League, but losing 3-2.

2007-08

	Pos	Played	Won	Drawn	Lost	GF	GA	Pts
Blackburn Rovers	7	38	15	13	10	50	48	58
Burnley	13	46	16	14	16	60	67	62

Blackburn Rovers		Burnley	
Most Appearances	Brad Friedel 38	Most Appearances	Wade Elliott 45
Most Goals	Roque Santa Cruz 19	Most Goals	Andy Gray 11

Year by year, the elite clubs dominated the Premier League a touch more. The top six this campaign were all from the large conurbations, so there was no disgrace in finishing seventh. And if three successive top ten finishes could be achieved by one of the lesser lights, there you had a successful club. Therefore Mark Hughes at Blackburn Rovers could feel proud of his contribution to the once capital of cotton in the first decade of this new millennium. A League Cup winner's medal, saving them from relegation in his first year in charge and now three very acceptable finishes. It may not have quite reached "Freedom of the Borough" status, but it was damned impressive. There were only two notable outgoings in the summer. The club sold Andy Todd to Derby County and Shabani Nonda returned to Roma after his loan deal was over. Hughes made an immediate move to replace Nonda, paying Bayern Munich £3.5million for Paraguayan striker Roque Santa Cruz.

Whereas some seasons have had a very up and down footprint, challenging for honours and fighting against the prospect of relegation in the same campaign, this in contrast was a staid affair. They briefly touched sixth spot and had almost as briefly been eleventh, but for the rest of the campaign, the ongoing league position was somewhere between the two. The early fixture list was tough and these first eleven games could have put them on the back foot, but just one defeat, albeit alongside four draws, stirred the imagination of the fans.

Cristiano Ronaldo dampened the spirits with a double for Manchester United in a 2-0 Ewood reversal and there was an embarrassing 4-0 home defeat to Aston Villa. There was also a crazy 5-3 loss at Wigan a couple of days before Christmas. Incredibly there were two hat-tricks in the game; Marcus Bent for Wigan and one from Santa Cruz. But there were impressive results with doubles over Newcastle United, Bolton Wanderers and Derby County and through it all, Santa Cruz was banging in the goals. His total of nineteen was the highest by a Rovers' striker in the Premier League since the halcyon days of Shearer twelve years before.

The giant South American had given them an early home lead against Manchester United and only an extremely late Tevez goal snatched a point for the "Reds". The Blackburn club had quietly shown that they were still a force to be reckoned with in the week to week grind for vital points. Fans favourite Robbie Savage, the mid-field assassin with the long blonde locks, was sold to Derby County in January for £1.5 million, after keeping the on-field tempo high at Ewood during three successful campaigns.

The Blackburn club had qualified for the Intertoto Cup, way down the list of prestigious UEFA tournaments. They were exempt until Round 3, after which the winners would proceed to the UEFA Cup. As early as July 22, they eliminated FK Vetra from Lithuania and then came through against another household name....not, MyPa 47 from Finland in Round 2 of the UEFA Cup Qualifying Section. Progress ground to a shuddering halt when Larissa won in Greece in Round 1 and then hung on to their lead in Lancashire, only going down 2-1 for a 3-2 aggregate win. Confused? So was I but the Rovers were out of the competition. Could the Rovers repeat the Carling Cup run to the semi-final? Exempt once more until Round 3, a home win over Birmingham City and another victory at Portsmouth, both fellow Premier League clubs, gave them a home tie versus Arsenal in the last eight. Was this going to be another "semi-final here we come night"? Two goals down in half an hour, Santa Cruz scored twice as the Blue and Whites rallied, taking the game into extra-time. There an Eduardo goal was the knock-out blow. The FA Cup was such a disappointment for the Rovers. In the middle of a decent run of form, they were drawn at home to Championship strugglers Coventry City. It ought to have been the prelude to something special but the Midlanders caused the upset of the round, winning 4-1. So for the first time in four years, Mark Hughes' men failed to reach a cup semi-final. Interestingly, the Rovers played forty-eight matches this season and 'twixt the posts each time was Brad Friedel; a testimony to his greatness.

Steve Cotterill had completed three full seasons at Turf Moor without making a concerted charge towards promotion. It was steady but lacking in excitement although in some respects, he deserved praise for retaining their Championship slot on such a low budget. There were many in the town however thinking that a change of manager was needed. Robbie Blake returned to the club for a £250,000 fee from Leeds United and the prospect of Akinbiyi and Gray teaming up with Blake was instantly mouth-watering. Goalkeeper Danny Coyne was released to Tranmere Rovers and Cotterill brought in Gabor Kiraly from Crystal Palace. The Hungarian keeper would go on to win 100 international caps. He sold full back Wayne Thomas for £1.2million to Southampton and signed three defenders, the experienced Scottish international Graham Alexander from Preston North End, the academic Clark Carlisle from Watford and David Unsworth, formerly a stalwart at Everton, from Wigan Athletic. All would play a part in keeping Burnley in the Championship this season.

The season started brightly, a 2-1 home win against champions elect West Bromwich Albion and ten points from the first five games. After eleven fixtures, they were occupying tenth position and Andy Gray had found the net seven times. A plunge to fifteenth following two home defeats forced the Board to listen to the clamour from the fans and Cotterill was gone. Into his shoes stepped Owen Coyle. The Scot knew the English game, having played at Bolton Wanderers, but on retirement had been extremely successful as manager of St Johnstone, taking the Perth club into the Scottish Premier League.

And what a start he made. Four wins and two draws saw them reach a season's high of seventh, but a run of four defeats and two draws dropped them back to twelfth with Play-Off hopes almost extinguished. Andy Gray had scored eleven times in twenty-five games and the Board, showing that old habits die hard, sold him to Championship rivals Charlton Athletic for £1.5million.

Andy Cole now in the veteran stage, was taken on loan from Sunderland to score goals. There were good team performances to follow and Cole hit a hat-trick at Queen's Park Rangers. Blake scored twice in a 2-2 draw at home to Watford and a safe league position was achieved. The defence had generally held up well until the final two games, a 3-3 draw against FA Cup finalists Cardiff City and a 5-0 thrashing at Crystal Palace in the curtain closer. To languish in thirteenth place, a sixth consecutive "teen finish", was once more disappointing. And as for the changes in management in this period? Ternent, Cotterill and Coyle, had these changes made any difference. "Plus ca change, plus c'est la meme-chose" as they say in France.

Burnley reached the last thirty two of the Carling Football League Cup. They went through Round 1 at Grimsby on penalties. Blake, Gray and Akinbiyi all played against Oldham Athletic in Round 2 and all three scored in a 3-0 victory. A visit to the south coast to play Premier League club Portsmouth was a trip too far and they lost 1-0. The draw for the Third Round of the FA Cup was interesting, hopefully exciting but it could have been many times easier. They were drawn at home, but the opposition came from Arsenal. It could have been a banana skin for the London giants, but that was not in the script and the Clarets went down 2-0. It was their third successive exit at the first hurdle.

2008 - 2009

	Pos	Played	Won	Drawn	Lost	GF	GA	Pts
Blackburn Rovers	15	38	10	11	17	40	60	41
Burnley	5	46	21	13	12	72	60	76

Blackburn Rovers		Burnley	
Most Appearances	Stephen Warnock 37	Most Appearances	Graham Alexander 46
Most Goals	Benni McCarthy 10	Most Goals	Martin Paterson 12

When Burnley were relegated to what was then Division 2 back in 1976, even the most pessimistic of supporters would not have believed that thirty-three years would pass before the club would once more grace the finest stadia in the land. In fact their exclusion from this elite grouping of clubs was almost biblical in terms of time. It was only seven years short of the period that the Moses-led Israelites wandered through the wilderness until they came across the land flowing with milk and honey. And with regard to their competition with the neighbours down the road, it surpassed the record of the Rovers who, from 1966-1992, were denied access to England's foremost division for twenty-six years

Listening to Owen Coyle on Radio Lancashire, there was no doubt that he talked a good game. But to be fair to the loquacious Scotsman, not only did he talk the talk, he also walked the walk, returning the Burnley club back to football's "promised land". With over half a season's experience of working with the players, he knew who he wanted to stay, who he wanted to go and with whom to replace them. This was the club's ninth successive season in the Championship, a lengthy stay in this most competitive of leagues.

The out of contract James O'Connor and Jon Harley were allowed to leave on a free to Sheffield Wednesday and Watford respectively, O'Connor having made 148 league starts and Harley 119. But the sale which netted Burnley the most money was when Glasgow Rangers paid £3.5million for Kyle Lafferty, a Northern Irish international centre forward who had graduated through their Centre of Excellence. Christian Kalvenes and Kevin McDonald arrived from the Dundee clubs, the Norwegian from United and McDonald from the Dens Park club. Two £1million transfer fees secured the services of Martin Paterson, a striker from Scunthorpe United and Chris Eagles, a winger who was signed from Manchester United. Another striker, Scottish international Steve Thompson, was signed from Cardiff City on a free.

Coyle had made it clear that Brian Jensen was his number one choice between the sticks and Joey Gudjonsson, the Icelandic international mid-field player, signed from AZ Alkmaar eighteen months previously, was now being regularly involved.

And as for the actual league matches, it was all about mini-runs of victories and defeat. It was fourth spot by Christmas, with the scent of promotion in the air. Paterson was banging in the goals, Blake was providing assists and whenever there was a penalty, Graham Alexander stepped up to the spot and converted. It would have not been Burnley of course, if they hadn't slumped to tenth place, conspiring to lose five on the bounce. "We've seen it all before," were the thoughts racing through the minds of the suddenly disillusioned fans. But all of us who have been involved in any sporting contest know that form, whether good or bad, can be transitory, short lived and definitely impermanent. One defeat in thirteen games and suddenly, the sky was blue, the birds were singing and most importantly, so were the fans. Wins against Sheffield United and a comprehensive 4-0 victory over Bristol City in the final game were sufficient for fifth place with the Play-Offs to follow. The goals were shared around as the Clarets notched up seventy-two, the highest tally since the seventy-nine strikes in the promotion year of 1991-92.

The Carling Football League Cup run was equally thrilling. The fourth round was reached without conceding a goal; Bury 2-0, Oldham Athletic 3-0 and then a 1-0 victory over Premier League Fulham at Turf Moor. Chelsea away in Round 4 was a mountain to climb and Ade Akinbiyi scored a rare goal to take the game into extra-time, it ending 1-1. The Clarets certainly kept their nerve in the penalty shoot-out, edging it 5-4 and it was Arsenal at home in the last eight. Scotsman Kevin McDonald popped up with a goal in each half and Burnley had equalled their best ever performance. Tottenham Hotspur provided the opposition in a two-legged semi-final and after a convincing 4-1 win at White Hart Lane, it looked game over. But football, as they used to say, is a funny game and ninety minutes later, goals from Blake, McCann and a young Jay Rodriguez made it 4-4 on aggregate and the Turf Moor crowd had to pinch themselves, never expecting to see extra-time. For twenty eight further minutes, it seemed as though the Lancashire side was going through on the away goals rule, but as the fans whistled for full time, Spurs scored twice. It was the Clarets' fourth losing semi-final in the competition. The FA Cup run was equal in excitement if not in length. In Round Three, a Jay Rodriguez goal against Queen's Park Rangers saw them through. Round Four also went to a replay, a brace from Thompson winning the tie against West Bromwich Albion. Arsenal away in the last sixteen evoked recent memories of their League Cup victory but this time at the Emirates, there was only one winner; the Gunners 3-0.

And so to the Play-Offs. The league season had kicked off nine months before; talk about value for money for the fans. Reading was the opposition in the two-legged semi-final. The Burnley defence was outstanding throughout this mini-series, enabling them to take a narrow lead back to Berkshire, Graham Alexander's late penalty being the only goal of the game. The Clarets' defence refused to give an inch in the second-leg, goals from Paterson and Thompson taking them to Wembley. Since the Play-Offs had been introduced in 1987, this was the third that Burnley had been involved in, but never in an attempt to win their way back to the highest echelon. It was Burnley's first visit to the "New Wembley" and they played in light blue shirts and socks with claret shorts. Over eighty thousand watched a nerve wracking and action packed game with a sensational early goal from Burnley's Wade Elliott; a real screamer from twenty-five yards. Burnley were the better side, wasting a number of chances to increase their lead, but when Mike Dean blew the final whistle, the Clarets had defied thirty-three years of history to return to the summit of the English game. There was jubilation across the town and the number one topic of conversation was the Blackburn Rovers' fixture. Dave Timberlake described it as a tense game.

> "I was a bag of nerves. That's the trouble when you score early. It had been a great strike by Elliott from well outside the penalty area, but it was in the thirteenth minute. He should have scored it in the eighty-ninth. It reached the point late on where I could not dare to watch any more. For the last couple of minutes, I turned my back on the action and prayed for the final whistle. Sheffield United were a good side and they were capable of scoring at any time but we were experienced and after the game, it was a fantastic feeling to know we were back in the big time again."

The Burnley side which won the Championship Play-Off final at Wembley Stadium was; Brian Jensen, Michael Duff, Clark Carlisle, Steve Caldwell, Christian Kalvenes, Wade Elliott, Graham Alexander, Chris McCann, Robbie Blake, Martin Paterson, Steven Thompson. Substitutes Chris Eagles, Joey Gudjonsson, Jay Rodriguez.

Totally eclipsed by the events up the road, there was consternation in Blackburn when Mark Hughes left for Manchester City. Now an extremely rich club, their potential was far greater than that at Ewood Park. The question was, who would replace him? The Board of Directors opted for Paul Ince, a multi-capped mid-field player in the nineties for England whilst playing for three of Europe's top clubs. He had already tasted success as a manager, orchestrating the promotion of MK Dons from the fourth to the third tier as champions. Whether his CV was sufficient for a top ten rated Premier League side was debatable. The subsequent six months proved that it had come too early for him. Brad Friedel had been sold to Aston Villa to be replaced by Paul Robinson from Spurs and Stephane Henchoz had retired.

The London club however was soon to pay back the money received for Robinson and lots more when they signed David Bentley for £15million. There was a feeling in the town that the Walker family was losing interest in the club. Would they sell if the chance came? Certainly Ince had been informed that he did not have the open cheque book that Jack had presented to predecessors. Nonetheless, he brought in the Aussie international Vince Grella from Torino and the Irish mid-fielder Keith Andrews from MK Dons plus loanees Danny Simpson from Manchester United and Carlos Villanueva from Chilean football.

All were competent footballers but only Robinson won over the Rovers' faithful.

After wins at Everton and Newcastle, the warning bells were ringing when they shipped four goals at West Ham and at home to Arsenal. Then suddenly, the wheels were off the wagon completely and the club plunged down the table as they collected just three points from eleven games. The goals from Santa Cruz and McCarthy which had lit up previous campaigns had dried up; this was relegation form. The Board acted quickly and Ince was sacked. Work to install a new boss had obviously been carried out, because the day after he was sacked, the club announced the arrival of Sam Allardyce. "Big Sam" had built a reputation at Bolton Wanderers as a manager who could deliver the goods in the Premier League with a Championship budget. He was the man to save the Blackburn club from relegation.

And save them he did, immediately grinding out results as he lifted the club away from the bottom three. He somehow motivated McCarthy, the South African scoring five times in Allardyce's first six games. There were defeats on the road and the defence twice capitulated, shedding four at the Emirates and also at home to Liverpool. He had paid Sunderland £2million for the Senegal and former Liverpool striker El Hadji Diouf and his pace from wide helped them to win several games and gain fifteenth position, well clear of relegation. It had not been pretty; a typical Allardyce performance, but when safety has to be the priority, the fans will accept a style of football which is less than free-flowing. Forty goals is a paltry return on a season and some felt that Allardyce would have to work hard and wheel and deal if Premier League status was to be retained after the following campaign.

During Paul Ince's stay, there were at least some Carling League Cup wins to rouse the spirits. Grimsby Town were brushed aside 4-1 with Derbyshire scoring twice. A big scalp was taken in Round 3, Everton losing 1-0 at Ewood Park and in the last sixteen there was a commendable 2-1 win at Sunderland. The last eight brought a trip to Old Trafford and it was certainly some game. Carlos Tevez was on target four times but two strikes from McCarthy kept the Rovers in the hunt before the United big guns finally fired them to a 5-3 success.

By the time Blackburn Rovers entered the FA Cup in Round 3, Allardyce was in charge. They made hard work of a 1-0 win at Blythe Spartans and a second North-East win followed in Round 4, defeating Sunderland 2-1 in a replay at home. The 5th Round is usually when it starts to become interesting and the Rovers really missed a trick, only drawing 2-2 at home to Coventry City from the Championship. It was a chance that had gone begging, because the West Midlanders were strong enough to score after an hour and hold on for a 1-0 victory in the replay.

See-saw time again... Burnley now on top, 2009-2022

(Oh) Life is like a see-saw, it has its ups and downs.
Sometimes it brings us happy smiles, sometimes it makes us frown.
When you're up, you're up and when your down your down.
So when you're up, you know what, you really go ta town.

Richie Kavanagh Irish singer/songwriter

In this book, the see saw metaphor is regularly used to describe the juxta positioning of Burnley and Blackburn Rovers since league football began in 1888. Being "up" is the dominant position, "down" is subservient and there is no doubt that supporters of the club that has Premier League status for example, feel so superior to its rival in the Championship. It is not the only way to gauge supremacy over your neighbour, the derby games can also be used as a measuring tool, but as they have only been contested in 50 of the 123 completed seasons, it is not as accurate an assessment as comparing league positions, Therefore fans, although yearning to win a derby game whenever one comes along, more commonly use the see saw method to claim "bragging rights".

It had been in the 1979-80 season that fans of the Clarets had last been able to make that claim, a dark period in the history of this fine club, but during the next few years, the old see saw would begin to tilt in the opposite direction. The supporters of Blackburn Rovers, having enviously looked upwards and felt so anxious and frustrated for ten seasons, could now look forward to competing on level terms again with the enemy, winning the derbies and assuming a superior league position.

2009-10

	Pos	Played	Won	Drawn	Lost	GF	GA	Pts
Blackburn Rovers	10	38	13	11	14	41	55	50
Burnley	18	38	8	6	24	42	82	30

Blackburn Rovers		Burnley	
Most Appearances	Paul Robinson 35	Most Appearances	Brian Jensen, Tyrone Mears (both 38)
Most Goals	David Dunn 9	Most Goals	Steven Fletcher 8

Burnley's last game in the then Division 1 (the Premier League equivalent of its day) was on April 24, 1976. A crowd of 11,675 had turned up to watch a most mediocre performance from the Clarets, losing 3-1 at Turf Moor to Coventry City. Joe Brown had been in charge and Derrick Parker scored early doors, before the inevitable second half capitulation. The last time they had met Blackburn Rovers in the elite division was in January 1966 watched by a 28,013 crowd. The highflying Claret and Blue outfit, managed of course by Harry Potts, had coasted to a 2-0 victory at Ewood Park; the opposition a worse than mediocre Blue and White side managed by Jack Marshall. Willie Irvine and Gordon Harris had been on target, responsible in part for the relegation of the Ewood Park club.

Sam Allardyce had saved Blackburn Rovers from relegation the previous season, virtually with a group of players signed on by other managers. Now it was his turn to construct a squad with his stamp upon it. Some decisions were taken out of his hands. The Jack Walker Trust was not the generous benefactor that its founding father Jack had been and certain players had to leave. Andre Ooijer, Aaron Mokoena and Tugay, multi-capped internationals all, were reaching the latter stages of their careers and had no doubt been on good money. Tugay, an idol of the Turkish nation, was thirty eight and had started 233 games at Ewood over eight seasons. He announced his retirement having been one of the club's all-time standout players; who could replace him? Ooijer returned to PSV on a free and Mokoena signed a three year deal at Portsmouth.

Matt Derbyshire moved to Olympiacos in Greece with £3million changing hands, Roque Santa Cruz's transfer to Mark Hughes' Manchester City was accompanied by an invoice for £17.5million and the talented left back that was Stephen Warnock signed for Aston Villa for £4.5million. He was replaced on the same day by Pascal Chimbonda from Tottenham Hotspur for £2million less. The club had already spent £650,000 on Steven Nzonzi, a future World Cup winner from Amiens in France's Ligue 2. Two foreign international strikers were imported. Franco de Santo on loan from Chelsea and Croatian Nikola Kalinic from Hajduk Split for £6million. Massive potential yes, but In terms of delivery, no. Finally the veteran Real Madrid right back Michel Salgado, a serial collector of medals and with over fifty Spanish international caps, was signed at the age of thirty-three.

So Allardyce had sold well, bought frugally and now had to earn his wages. The early prognosis was bleak, with two solid thumpings on trips to the capital, 6-2 at Arsenal and 5-0 at Chelsea. Seventeenth spot in a twenty club league is always a worrying situation, but there was a slow climb up the table with Ewood a safe haven for much of the season, only losing three matches there throughout the campaign. Most of the victories were against clubs that would finish below them but only one defeat in their last nine games unbelievably saw them finish tenth; back in the top ten. It was a remarkable achievement considering their under-performing, under par strike force. Only twice did anyone score more than one goal in a game, Jason Roberts and David Dunn notching a brace each against Portsmouth and Birmingham City respectively. Team selection was inconsistent, a sure-fire indicator of a lack of quality in the ranks. The French international left sided defender Gael Givet arrived from Marseilles on loan, part way through the previous season and the Rovers paid £3.5million to make the deal permanent. Benni McCarthy left for West Ham United for £2million mid-season having scored thirty-seven goals in 109 starts. The Rovers' back line was generally solid and much of this was due to the strength of the centre-backs, Ryan Nelsen and Christian Samba; both formidable figures.

Their nemesis in cup competitions this season was Aston Villa. The Carling Football League Cup was becoming something of a speciality for the Blue and White halved shirts. After Gillingham, Nottingham Forest and Peterborough United were comfortably disposed of, the quarter final was at home to Chelsea. It was frenetic, full of goalmouth incidents and goals. The Rovers led 1-0 at half-time, within twenty minutes the visitors were 2-1 up before an Emerton goal sent it to extra-time. There a McCarthy penalty looked to have sealed the game but the Londoners equalised with the last kick of the 120 minutes. Paul Robinson was the hero of the hour, twice saving spot-kicks as the home side went through on penalties. In the semi-final at Ewood, Aston Villa took home a 1-0 advantage. The second-leg was even more exciting than the Chelsea game.

Two Kalinic goals gave Allardyce's side the lead after twenty-five minutes but it was all square at the break. Three Villa goals soon after half-time spelled game over but the Lancashire side fought back with strikes from Olsson and Emerton and they pressed hard for the equaliser before Ashley Young made it 6-4 well into time added on; the final aggregate score being 7-4. It was the Rovers' fourth semi-final of the decade and earlier in the month of January, they had travelled to Villa Park in the Third Round of the FA Cup. This however was a more mundane affair, the home side winning 3-1.

For Owen Coyle, taking Burnley back to the highest level of English football was special, but keeping them there would take far more. His squad of decent Championship players definitely needed strengthening with players from the Premier League; no Brian Miller, Leighton James or John Connelly coming off the Gawthorpe production line as in the good old days. He lost none of his regular starters but to compete for players in a multi-million pound industry, Coyle needed to flash the cheque book. Unfortunately, the Board was again unwilling to go into debt to both buy and pay a top Premier League calibre of player and the manager had to be satisfied with the £3million splashed out on Scottish international forward Steven Fletcher from Hibernian.

Tyrone Mears was bought from Derby County, much travelled striker David Nugent came on what turned out to be a season-long loan from Portsmouth and Cameroon international Andre Bikey was signed from Reading for £2.8million. None of these were A listers but Coyle had created a winning mentally the previous season from a group not over blessed with talent, so the hope was that he could do it again. And to be fair to the Scottish manager, miracles were on the menu for a short time. They produced two sensational 1-0 home victories over Manchester United and Everton, the crowd going wild as Robbie Blake and Wade Elliott produced the goals. There were other wins and other defeats but the defence was leaking goals, twelve in three visits to London. Nugent scored a couple in a 3-1 home win over Sunderland and Fletcher was beginning to find his shooting boots. A three game unbeaten run (Alexander was on the score sheet twice in a 3-1 win over Hull City) briefly took them to ninth in the table. It then became hard work. There was a welcome 1-1 home draw with Arsenal but by the turn of the year, it was fourteenth position and serious doubts were being cast on the strength of the squad. Perhaps Coyle had a crystal ball, but when Bolton Wanderers showed interest, he was off like a flash. You could praise him, arguing that he achieved what he was brought in to do or you can accuse him of betraying the town, club, players and fans, leaving at the first sign of trouble.

But this was, still is, professional football and loyalty and integrity may be words that have lost their meaning in the modern game. As it was, the Clarets needed a new hand on the tiller and that man turned out to be a former player, the much praised ex-full-back Brian Laws. He had been a success at Scunthorpe United for nine years and had recently managed at Sheffield Wednesday, but here he was on a hiding to nothing. Danny Fox was brought in from Celtic but the club was in free fall, the squad ill-equipped for a sustained run of decent performances and Laws had never before managed at this level. Fifteen defeats in eighteen games was nailed on relegation and their decent home form had evaporated. Nothing sides began to win at Turf Moor and there were totally embarrassing defeats to Manchester City (6-1) and Liverpool (4-0). In the very last match, Tottenham Hotspur were clouted 4-1. The Turf Moor faithful did not know whether to laugh or cry at the irony of it all. Defensively poor, they conceded eighty-two goals, relegation form from whichever angle one looked. It had taken thirty-three years to climb back to the summit and one to fall back down again.

The Derby Games

The 18th of October 2009 was a date which had been engraved on the minds of Burnley supporters' since the fixtures were released in June. It was a day to delete all those doubts, forget those frustrations and go to Ewood Park and fight like underdogs. There was an enormous pre-match police presence in the areas surrounding the ground and Police horses and dogs were used to keep the rival fans apart. It was virtually impossible for Burnley fans to travel other than on special buses; in fact any tickets bought were in the form of a package deal which included transport on official Burnley Supporters' Club coaches and double-decker buses. Almost frighteningly in terms of English football, only two members of the Rovers' starting eleven were eligible to play for this country, Paul Robinson from Yorkshire and David Dunn from the Red Rose county.

The statistic from the bench was even more unpalatable. Sub-goalkeeper Jason Brown was born in Bermondsey, South London, but his international caps were earned for Wales. And as for the others, you would need a world atlas to identify their places of birth. The Clarets had made a decent start to their Premier League campaign, but had yet to even score a goal away from home. Even so, their tenth position prior to the game placed them five positions higher than their opponent which, in the eyes of some folks, made them favourites.

And what a start they made. Within five minutes, Robbie Blake had broken clear and smashed an unstoppable twenty-five yard shot past Paul Robinson to open the proceedings. The lead lasted just three minutes before Di Santo produced a rare touch of magic to set up David Dunn, who swept a first time left foot shot past Brian Jensen. Di Santo himself was next to score, taking advantage of a defensive mix-up which Jensen failed to take command of, leaving the on-loan striker the easiest of headed goals. When Chimbonda and Pedersen then combined beautifully to set the Frenchman up to score on the stroke of half-time, the Burnley contingent in the 26,689 crowd knew there was a mountain to climb. The Clarets had more of the ball after the interval, but it was the Rovers who looked most like adding to their lead. As the final whistle approached, Chris Eagles scored with a neat finish, but it was far too late to affect the result. In spite of intense provocation, the Police kept their cool and generally kept control, but there could have been a most serious incident at the end of the game. Damian Hartley told me the following story.

> "A group of perhaps a dozen Burnley men travelled to the Cherry Tree area of Blackburn in mid-afternoon, had a drink in the Station pub and proceeded to march with intent towards the ground. There was violence on their minds, but the Police must have been tipped off because they were waiting for them as they approached. There was furious fighting but the Police quickly gained control and arrested the "invaders" who, between them, were sentenced to a total of thirty-two years in prison."

Between this game and the return encounter in March, much had changed concerning the respective form of the two protagonists. Burnley had slumped to nineteenth, looking dead ringers for relegation and the Rovers had attained a relatively safe mid-table placing, tenth in actual fact. The "Turf" was packed to capacity and everyone knew that only a victory here would give them any sort of chance to escape to safety. Brian Laws was now in charge and Leon Cort, a defender who cost £1.5million from Stoke City and a young Jack Cork on a half season loan from Chelsea, had been added to his squad. Martin Olsson was the star of the show, running riot down the Rovers' left hand side and when he was tripped by Jensen when bearing down on goal, David Dunn knocked in the penalty. Was it a foul or did he dive? Even the most partisan of Blue and White supporters had their doubts, but it was the decisive moment in the match. The Blackburn side dominated much of the game and their 1-0 win made life so

Robbie Blake scoring Burnley's first Ewood Park goal at the elite level since Gordon Harris scored on New Year's Day, 1966

much more difficult for the Clarets. Olsson's performance was admired by the travelling fans but it was Dunn who was the villain of the piece in the eyes of the Burnley supporters. He had scored at Ewood, been influential and knocked in the "dodgy" penalty at Turf Moor and no self-respecting Claret and Blue fan had forgiven him for his theatrical dive (in their eyes) which caused the dismissal of Kevin Ball back in 2000. Hated by the whole of Burnley, he had once more broken their hearts, their dreams of victory over the enemy and only God knew how long it would be before the next opportunity would arise.

18 10 2009	Blackburn Rovers	Burnley	3-2	D Dunn, F Di Santo, P Chimbonda. R Blake, C Eagles,
26 03 2010	Burnley	Blackburn Rovers	0-1	D Dunn.

David Dunn actually said that the Ewood Park encounter was one of his favourite all time matches.

> "Not only do I remember so much about the game but the goal I scored was also one of my favourites. Franco Di Santo's pass picked me out but it was fractionally behind me. I didn't have time to take two touches so I had to hit it first time and I did this by leaning my body away at an angle so that I could swing my left foot at it and it flew in. That got us back in the game and we were brilliant for the rest of the first half. Burnley's second was scored far too late to cause us any problems. When we went to Burnley later in the season, it was fairly easy for us. The Burnley crowd were so angry about the penalty decision and they let me know how they felt when I took the kick, but it went in ok."

Graham Alexander became the oldest player to make his debut in the Premier League this season. And when he knocked in a penalty against Sunderland in September, he was the fifth oldest to notch a Premier League goal; all rather magnificent at the age of thirty-seven. These are his thoughts on the one year he played at the top level of English football.

"I was fortunate to captain Burnley at this time and the combination of playing against some of the world's greatest players and at so many iconic stadia, was a most thrilling experience. When we played Man United, I shook hands for the toss-up with Ryan Giggs in the first game, Gary Neville in the second and the Everton captain who greeted me was Phil Neville. Just over eight years later I shook their hands again, when I was confirmed as manager of the club owned by the Class of 92, Salford City. We all thought Owen Coyle was a wonderful manager, so exuberant and enthusiastic and for the first half of the season, when performances were probably good enough to keep us up, we all really tried for him. The first derby game came in this period at Ewood Park. We had started well at home, but away from Turf Moor, we were poor. There was such a long build up to the game in the press and David Dunn and I were photographed together for some charity event. When you studied the quality of the two sides, all the Premier League experience was with the Rovers and we were all Championship players except Robbie Blake. He could score goals from anywhere and he did in the first few minutes here at Blackburn. We only knew one way to play at that time and that was to attack and so we were very vulnerable to counter attacks. I made a mistake on a cross, jumping slightly too early and the ball bounced off the top of my head and we conceded a goal from that. By half-time we had been battered, down 3-1, but the manager stirred us up and we gave it a good go in the second half. In fact we won that session 1-0 with a very late goal, but in spite of all our efforts, we had lost 3-2. Owen Coyle decided to leave after Christmas. From a professional point of view I didn't blame him, but the fans really did. He was called all sorts of names like Judas and Traitor, and even now, there is still ill-feeling about him in the town. Brian Laws replaced him and I felt sorry for him. We just weren't good enough to stay up and he was given stick from the terraces. The second game is all of a blur to me. When you play over a thousand games, it is difficult to remember them all and although I know we lost 1-0 and that it was a Dunn penalty, I can't remember why it was given. But I think that our minds obliterate the bad memories eventually and losing twice to Blackburn still is a bad memory. I do remember that their experience of playing in big games was the difference between the sides. They knew how to waste time, slow the game down, keep possession and fall down whenever anyone just touches you so that the free-kick will waste even more time. People like Diouf in the Rovers side was good at this. But no-one could have kept us up that year, although I think the thing that hurt most was not earning at least one win for the fans in these derby games. The Burnley supporters deserved better than two defeats. It was a wonderful

David Dunn celebrates the win over Burnley, his goal clinching the victory at Turf Moor in March 2010

experience to play in the Premier League, if only for one season, a memory that ranks up there with playing for my country forty times and scoring an equalising goal for the North End with my very last kick in the very last minute of the very last game of football I ever played in against Charlton Athletic at Deepdale.

Entering the Carling Football League Cup at the Round 2 stage, Burnley disposed of Hartlepool United, Fletcher scoring twice but Championship side Barnsley at Oakwell edged past them, 3-2. Milton Keynes Dons from Division 1 also proved tricky opposition in the Third Round of the FA Cup but the Clarets hung on for a 2-1 win. It was an away tie again, this time at Championship side Reading in Round 4 and the 1-0 defeat meant it was journey's end in cup competitions for the Clarets.

2010-11

	Pos	Played	Won	Drawn	Lost	GF	GA	Pts
Blackburn Rovers	15	38	11	10	17	46	59	43
Burnley	8	46	18	14	14	65	61	68

Blackburn Rovers		Burnley	
Most Appearances	Paul Robinson 37	Most Appearances	Tyrone Mears 44
Most Goals	Jason Roberts, Junior Hoillet, Nikola Kalinic (All 5)	Most Goals	Jay Rodriguez 14

What Sam Allardyce probably suspected in the close season, but what the public was unaware of at the time, was that this year saw the start of a fairly rapid decline in the fortunes of Blackburn Rovers, brought about by the change of ownership and the meddling of an unscrupulous agent. It was no secret that the Jack Walker Trust wanted to sell. To be able to make the commitment required to run a football club, your heart has to be in it. It is not a job and certainly not a sure fire way to make money. You have to eat drink and absolutely love the club, twenty-four seven. Jack Walker did, but somehow the passion appeared to disappear over the next few years. It is alleged that the club was valued at £23million and there were debts of over £20million.

When an Indian firm of poultry farmers, which had successfully diversified into pharmaceuticals and health products under the "Venkys" brand, bought the club on November 19th, 2010, there was many a joke circulating through football and the town itself, but also fears that they would not understand the game and how it is run in England. They quickly took on advice from Jerome Anderson, an agent who had been heavily involved in bringing foreign players into top clubs such as Arsenal and Manchester City. There is no doubt that the Venky's relied heavily on his knowledge and of course he wanted to bring players from his own portfolio to Blackburn. Allardyce reputedly wanted no such interference and was no doubt forthright in his comments.

Going into the away game at Bolton Wanderers, the Rovers were in eight position in a highly congested mid-table, but by losing 2-1, dropped down to thirteenth. Big Sam, undoubtedly the best manager in the business in club survival, was sacked and the job given to his first team coach Steve Kean, a former first team coach under Chris Coleman at various clubs. He had no experience of managership however and his playing career was limited to one game for Alloa Athletic in Scotland, four at Swansea City in Division 4 and several seasons in Portugal playing in their second tier. It was no kind of preparation for life in the Premier League, but he did just happen to be a client of Jerome Anderson.

Having lived on a permanent basis in France during this period, I have always been somewhat in the dark with relation to the absolute truth about what happened at Ewood as the club was sold. I spoke to Geoff Bury, a friend from childhood when we used to kick a ball against the gable-end wall of my house from the age of seven. He moved to Northwich on marrying in the early seventies, but has continued to journey up the M6 on many occasions to watch his favourite team. He became involved in the protests that hit the club at this time and I wanted him to check the accuracy of what I had written.

> "I was a very disgruntled Rover's fan in this period and joined the Rovers Trust about this time. Your account is probably more accurate than my feelings of the way the club was managed with Keen and Anderson as we only saw it as a dismantling of a sound well run club. It was difficult to sort fact from fiction at this time. I believe your account probably represents as true a picture as we will ever get."

But back in the summer months, Sam Allardyce was putting together a squad which hopefully would be able to compete and ensure some success for Blackburn Rovers. With negotiations ongoing to sell the club, there was no money available to buy players. So the manager stayed with the squad he had, the only departees being Pascal Chimbonda to Queen's Park Rangers, the disappointing full back Lars Jacobsen to West Ham United and Steven Reid (113 appearances) to West Bromwich Albion. The only additions of note were the season long loan of Mame Biram Diouf, a Senegalese international striker from Manchester United and the capture of Benjani, a Zimbabwean international striker who was out of contract at Manchester City.

The squad made a reasonable start and were competing and holding a steady league position just below the half way mark. They lost 4-2 at Spurs, but after Pedersen became the first Rovers' player to score more than once in a 2-0 victory over Aston Villa, Manchester United smashed seven past them at Old Trafford, Dmitri Berbatov scoring five. Following a thrilling 3-0 win over the Wolves and the subsequent narrow defeat at Bolton, Sam Allardyce was out of the door, clutching his P45. He had won thirty-two and drawn twenty four of his ninety games in charge, a win percentage of 35.6%. It is about average, but considering the circumstances he had to deal with, he had done the business at Ewood Park and most importantly, they were still members of the Premier League. Would his successor be as successful?

Kean did have a reputation as a good coach and there are examples of outstanding managers never having played the game at any decent level; Jose Mourinho and Lawrie McMenemy come to mind. So, although the fans were puzzled and in many cases annoyed by Allardyce's exit, they were prepared to give the Scotsman a chance. One advantage of being an agent to a club is that it is easy to then place the players on your books at the same club. Would this mean you were paid by both the club and the player? I suspect the answer is yes and certainly the case of Ruben Rochina was thoroughly investigated by a number of diligent fans, but sadly not the football authorities. The Spaniard was signed from Barcelona B having never played in the first team for a fee of £400,000 plus the agent's fee of an alleged £1.65million.

It is not part of this book's remit to look in detail at such matters, but if the Rovers' debt spiralled in the early Venky years, one does not have to look far to spot one of the reasons why. Kean claimed Mauro Formica, bought from Newell's Old Boys, one of Argentina's top clubs for around £3.5million, was a very special talent, but then never played him for the rest of the season. And there were two interesting arrivals on loan until the end of the campaign. Roque Santa Cruz returned from Manchester City where he had been something of a flop and the veteran mid-fielder Jermaine Jones, an American international, from Schalke 04 in Germany's Bundesliga.

There was no indication of a performance drop over Kean's first few matches in charge. Kalinic scored twice in a 3-1 victory at West Brom and Benjani notched a brace in front of over 25,000 fans against Liverpool. Steve Kean had lifted them to seventh and Europe became a distinct possibility. But then came the crash. Ten games without a win saw a steep decline in both performance and league placing, but a fighting goalless draw at Arsenal was commendable and thankfully eight points from the last four games saved their skin. Forty-three points and a fifteenth final placing, four points above the relegation line, could have been so much worse. The goal scoring chart said it all. Three players shared the award, Roberts, Junior Hoilett and Kalinic ...... all with a measly five goals.

For the second consecutive season, Aston Villa knocked Blackburn Rovers out of both cup competitions. Mame Biram Diouf scored a hat-trick in Round 2 of the Carling Football League Cup, a 3-1 win over Norwich City, but three second half goals eliminated them in Round 3 at Villa Park. Steve Kean was in charge for the FA Cup ties which started well with a 1-0 home victory over Queen's Park Rangers, but it was a 3-1 defeat again at the hands of the Villa in Round 4.

It had been a season at Ewood Park which left those who cared shaking their heads in dismay and disbelief. We were living permanently in France at this time but phone calls and emails to friends and family left me in no doubt that so much appeared to be wrong with the club. You live in hope of course but it was beginning to be apparent that the imaginary see saw that has always connected us with our neighbours was unquestionably tilting back. History ought to have taught us that these shifts in fortune could last a generation or more. We hoped it was just a temporary blip.

It had been a nightmare start for Brian Laws. Was he to blame for the fiasco of the previous season, was it the man they called Judas, now operating in Bolton or was it the Board of Directors; reluctant, said some, to dip their hands into their pockets? There was many a debate about the strategy of Barry Kilby and co but it has always been a stick or twist situation. Is it "speculate to accumulate" or "steady as we go"? The subsequent years have proved that sound thinking and a steady hand can bring dividends but with a more cavalier approach, could they have been challenging for honours with City, United, Chelsea etc? The answer in fact is "who knows". Laws needed to build a squad ready to hit the ground running in August, fully equipped to mount an immediate return to the Premier League.

Steven Fletcher wanted to stay at the top level and he was quickly sold to Wolverhampton Wanderers for £6.5million. It was good business, a case of doubling your money but he had to be replaced. Steven Caldwell, who had captained the side at Wembley and had made over one hundred starts, was out of contract and released on a free to Wigan Athletic. Similarly Stephen Jordan had contributed well at left back in spite of being dogged by different injuries. He too was released, to Sheffield United at the end of his contract. Coming in through the ever-revolving door was Dean Marney from Hull City, Chris Iwelumo, a striker from Wolves, Ross Wallace, a left sided midfield player from Preston North End and Lee Grant, a goalkeeper from Sheffield Wednesday, all for around the £1million mark. Jack Cork's loan period from Chelsea was extended and the manager had made a profit on his wheeler dealing during the break.

The Championship has always been competitive with few easy games and this was the case through the first half of the season. The away trip to Reading was a disaster, shipping four goals but in contrast, Hull City failed to offer much resistance at the "Turf", Chris Eagles scoring twice and Chris Iwelumo also bagging a couple. A thrilling game against Preston North End ended in a 4-3 home victory for the Clarets. Iwelumo took home the match ball after his hat-trick but the last minute winner was scored by Jay Rodriguez, proving to be the find of the season. There were more wins than losses, but Laws' side failed to sustain a run of victories which would have moved them alongside the front runners. In the last game of the calendar year, after a miserable 2-0 home loss to a very poor Scunthorpe United side, the Board sacked Brian Laws. It was surprising in many respects, notably because the club was in ninth position, close enough to challenge for a Play-Off place. Two weeks later, Eddie Howe was brought in from Bournemouth. He was a young, fresh manager with lots of modern ideas, particularly adept at dealing with the media, and he was quickly into his stride.

One defeat in nine games took them to seventh. Rodriguez was scoring the majority of the goals, and although the Board paid around £1million for Charlie Austin from Swindon Town, his niggling injuries and the form of the youngster meant he only started in two of the remaining nineteen games. There was a loss of form and then a resurgence and they overcame the Play-Off winners Swansea City, Middlesbrough and Derby County; three in three for Eagles. There was still a slight chance of reaching the top six, but a 1-0 loss at Leeds sentenced them to another season of Championship football; their final position being eighth. No-one was critical of Eddie Howe but once again you have to wonder if change for change's sake is worth the effort, the upheaval and of course the compensation that is paid out to the departing manager and his staff. One player saying goodbye at the end of term was the influential, honest and reliable midfielder Wade Elliott. He made 252 starts, averaging forty games for each of his seven campaigns and scored the only goal in the Championship Play-Off final. He moved to Birmingham City.

Under Brian Laws, Burnley had a mini Carling League Cup run, starting with a 3-1 win at Morecambe; the first time the two sides had met competitively. Bolton Wanderers were next, undone 1-0 at Turf Moor in Round 3, and the 4th Round draw paired them with Aston Villa, conquerors of the Rovers, at Villa Park. And it was the Clarets who came closer to an upset, a Clark Carlisle equaliser in the closing moments sending the game into extra-time where the Midlanders nicked it 2-1. In the Third Round of the FA Cup, Port Vale at home was relatively easy, a 4-2 win being the ensuing result. It was a 3-1 win over Burton Albion in Round 4, Chris Eagles snatching another brace but then they came a cropper in the last sixteen, going down heavily at West Ham by a 5-1 margin.

2011-12

	Pos	Played	Won	Drawn	Lost	GF	GA	Pts
Blackburn Rovers	19	38	8	7	23	48	78	31
Burnley	13	46	17	11	18	61	58	62

Blackburn Rovers		Burnley	
Most Appearances	Morten Gamst Pedersen 37	Most Appearances	Kieran Trippier 46
Most Goals	Yakubu 17	Most Goals	Charlie Austin 16

There was a general foreboding in Blackburn about the direction in which the club was heading, with owners who simply did not seem to know what they were doing, a manager out of his depth and an agent who was introducing his clients who were equally not good enough. As ever, the football fan hopes for the best as each new season begins, but the omens were not good. Five players of note left Ewood Park in the close season. Zurab Khizanishvili, at the end of his contract, signed for Kayserispor in Turkey. Benjani and Kalinic, two strikers who had flattered to deceive, left for Portsmouth and FC Dnipro respectively, the latter for a fee reported as £7million. Brett Emerton, capped ninety-five times by Australia and with 247 league starts for the Rovers under his belt in eight seasons, was allowed to walk away from his contract and return to Sydney. Finally the nineteen year old central defender Phil Jones, who had impressed so many clubs in his first full season, was courted by Manchester United and he was off to Old Trafford for an initial £16.5million. To replace them, Steve Kean brought in David Goodwillie, a striker from Dundee United who had just been awarded the Scottish Young Player of the Year trophy, Partisan Belgrade's Radosav Petrovic, a Serbian international midfield player plus Simon Vukcevic, a Montenegron midfield international from Sporting Lisbon. Each cost around £2million and added to these outgoings was another £1.5million paid to Everton for Nigerian international Yakubu, a goalscoring striker and the experienced centre back Scott Dann was signed from Birmingham City for around £7million.

The season was as bad as many had predicted. The only win in the first thirteen games was at home to Arsenal, a 4-3 extravaganza which thrilled the fans and contained a double from Yakubu as well as two own goals by Gunners' defenders. Yakubu had scored another brace in a 3-3 draw at Wigan Athletic and he knocked in all four in their second victory, 4-2 against Swansea City. There was an amazing 3-2 win at Old Trafford on New Year's Eve, with yet another Yakubu two-timer, but hammerings by Manchester City (4-0 at Ewood) and Arsenal scoring seven in London were too much for the fans to bear. There was a bundle of transfers in the January window, more out than in. The club said good bye to two stalwart centre halves. Ryan Nelsen, who made 172 appearances and was a veritable rock of a defender, moved to Tottenham Hotspur on a free and Chris Samba to Anzhi in the Russian Professional League for £11million. He had made 161 appearances, scored sixteen goals and was one of the most energised and exciting centre halves I have ever seen. Jason Roberts was sold to Reading for £0.5million. He scored twenty-four Premier League goals in 134 starts over a six year period and Keith Andrews, the Republic of Ireland international, left for West Bromwich Albion. Marcus Olsson, out of contract at Halmstads BK in Sweden, joined his twin brother Martin in Blackburn. Right back Bradley Orr was bought from Queen's Park Rangers and in mid-March, there was the briefest flicker of hope when they recorded two victories, but three points from their last seven matches slammed that door shut and they were relegated in nineteenth spot, seven points short of survival. Also relegated with them were the two Wanderers, Bolton and Wolverhampton, meaning that three of the original twelve founder members of the Football League faced the drop on the same day. Yakubu's seventeen goals were an excellent total for a relegated club, but only Morten Gamst Pedersen came close to starting every game. It was their seventh relegation in their 124 year history and the following season would not just be about fighting their way back. Facing them once again would be their deadly enemy from just up the road.

Just reading the above list of transfers both in and out brings about a state of exhaustion and, being philosophical for a moment, do the fans really want to see so many new players in such a short period, bearing in mind that a number are of the here today, gone tomorrow variety? Oldsters like myself have to accept that the days of the same starting eleven week in, week out are well gone. But as well as being excited and uplifted, fans also need to feel comfortable and "getting to know" the current crop lends a familiarity which builds a feel good mentality. Sides have to develop, changes have to be made, but if it can be done gradually, it surely enhances the stability of the team and of course the club generally. The sudden influx of players, often when a new manager arrives, must cause havoc in the dressing rooms.

The league form of Blackburn Rovers may have been abysmal but from somewhere, they conjured up a decent Carling Football League Cup run. The star performer was Ruben Rochina whom the fans, once they had reconciled themselves to accept the "dodgy" stories around his transfer, recognised as having quality on the ball. They won three games to take them into the Quarter Finals and the Spanish midfielder scored in all three against Sheffield Wednesday, Leyton Orient and Newcastle United. The Geordie game was a thriller in the tradition of several other recent cup-ties and this time the Rovers, going into time added on, were in complete control at 2-0. From out of nowhere, the Geordies produced two goals before the referee could blow his whistle and then, as the end of the extra thirty minutes loomed, it was 3-3 with everyone expecting penalties. But with the last kick of this enthralling tie, Gael Givet snatched the winner sending them to Cardiff City in the last eight. Here the Lancashire club reverted to type and insipidly lost 2-0. The FA Cup was over in a trice. It was Newcastle's chance for revenge. A rare Goodwillie goal put the Rovers ahead but with the north-east side having equalised, it once more looked like extra time. But with the clock at ninety-five minutes, Jermaine Jenas snatched the winner, the game was over and the Rovers were out.

Having failed at the first time of asking, could Burnley climb back into the Premier League this time? Eddie Howe set about revamping the side. A number of players had put their roots down at Turf Moor, but the boss was quick to uproot them. Two Scots were the first to be released. Kevin McDonald for Sheffield United and Steve Thompson to St Mirren. Graham Alexander and Clark Carlisle moved across the county to Preston, the latter on a season-long loan. The veteran Alexander, the penalty king, had been a favourite at Turf Moor, starting 154 games and his was a return journey to his previous club. For Carlisle, whose brave battles against depression and addiction have been well documented, it was a case of literally moving home to the town of his birth, having made 131 starts at centre half for the Clarets. Chris Iwelumo left for Watford, Tyrone Mears and Chris Eagles, both of whom had made major contributions, left together for Bolton Wanderers for a combined fee of £3million. The Burnley Board received a very lucrative offer from Southampton for left back Danny Fox (£1.8million) and he left along with fellow defender Leon Cort, moving to Charlton Athletic on a free transfer. With such a long list of departees, Howe had to move fast to replace them. With the quality of player moving into Manchester City, neither Ben Mee nor Kieran Trippier could find a place in the first team starting line-up, so they came to Burnley on season long loans. They were so effective however that the Clarets' Board signed them both for nominal fees in the January window. The striker Danny Ings arrived from AFC Bournemouth, the manager's old club, Sam Vokes was loaned out from Wolverhampton Wanderers for two months and Junior Stanislas, a lively left-winger was bought from West Ham United. Howe certainly showed that he could pick a player, all of the above going on to make their names in the game. Now he had to blend a winning team together.

The first decision Eddie Howe made was to give Charlie Austin the responsibility to lead the attack. The Former Swindon striker was quickly into his stride and he found the net five times in the first seven games but unfortunately, the results did not follow. The games were as tight as ever in the Championship, but one win in the first seven, a 2-1 win at Derby County, was simply not what the fans demanded. It became a case of win two, lose two until four successive defeats saw them hurtling towards relegation. This squad was far too good to go down however and doubles from David Edgar at Hull City to earn a 3-2 win and skipper Chris McCann in a comprehensive 4-0 victory over Ipswich Town were part of a purple patch with the Play-Offs beckoning. The new year was less kind to Howe's men but Rodriguez was suddenly the striker on fire and he notched eight in ten games, but the Clarets could not buy a win, seven games yielding three points from drawn matches. The spell was broken as an Austin hat-trick turned over Portsmouth 5-1 down on the south coast, but a series of average results brought an end to a disappointing campaign, thirteenth not being close to realising the potential of this squad. Austin claimed the title of leading scorer over Rodriguez by just one goal. As anti-climactic as the previous nine months had been, there was a feeling in the town that Eddie Howe was the right man for the job and with the local derbies back on the fixture list, there was plenty to look forward to in the immediate future.

The Carling Football League Cup brought along all sorts of thrills. Jay Rodriguez scored four in a 6-3 thriller over Burton Albion which went to extra-time. Barnet from the depths of Division 2 also surprised and it took an extra time winner from McCann to enable Burnley to squeeze through to Round 3. It was a third home tie and a third encounter with a club from a lower league, MK Dons from Division 1. And again it was ridiculously close, an eighty-ninth minute winner from Andre Bikey (sometimes listed as Andre Amougou) clinching a 2-1 victory. Cardiff City were pushing hard for promotion from the Championship and it was down in the Welsh capital that the cup run came to a grinding halt in Round 4. For for the second consecutive year, the Bluebirds won 1-0. The FA Cup Round 3 tie was a predictable result, Premier League Norwich City winning 4-1 in East Anglia.

2012-13

	Pos	Played	Won	Drawn	Lost	GF	GA	Pts
Burnley	11	46	16	13	17	62	60	61
Blackburn Rovers	17	46	14	16	16	55	62	58

Blackburn Rovers		Burnley	
Most Appearances	Scott Dann 46	Most Appearances	Lee Grant 46
Most Goals	Jordan Rhodes 26	Most Goals	Charlie Austin 25

This was Burnley's big chance. The hope was for Eddie Howe's side to hit the ground running, challenge for promotion and win their first derby match since April 1979, a mere thirty-three years before. That was also the same year that the Clarets ended a season higher placed than their rival; a statistic that really hurt. Could both these hoodoos be consigned to history in the forthcoming months? Compared with a number of recent seasons, there was very little movement of first team players during the summer. Unfortunately one of the two to exit was Jay Rodriguez. Southampton's £7million offer gave him Premier League football and also helped to balance the books at Turf Moor. Just prior to me leaving for our new life in France when I was still working for Burnley FC, Jay was the subject of a number of interesting discussions. The local born forward was an outstanding footballer but he was slow to grow. As a result, he failed to make the Lancashire Schools' Under-Sixteen side and there were doubts as to whether he was physically strong enough to make it as a "pro". The Clarets gambled upon him and now looking at the strapping 6'1" front man, it was a good call by Terry Pashley, Jeff Taylor and co. Andre Bikey also left on a free to Middlesbrough. Coming into the club were Sam Vokes, signed on a permanent basis this time, from Wolverhampton Wanderers and Jason Shackell, a centre half from Derby County.

Once again the Clarets made an indifferent start. In the first ten league games, they won only three and drew two. Charlie Austin had twice netted in a 5-2 home win against Peterborough United and he actually knocked in eleven in ten, the highlight being a hat-trick in the 3-3 home draw with Sheffield Wednesday. And then came a bombshell. Eddie Howe announced he was going back to Bournemouth where he had been successful prior to his move north. It was a drop of a division, but his mother had recently died, his wife and young family were still on the south coast and he literally felt the need to return home. Terry Pashley took over as interim boss, but within two and a half weeks, the new man was in place. It was Sean Dyche, a "hard as nails" centre back in the lower leagues who once scored a goal in an FA Cup semi-final, a penalty for Chesterfield in 1997 against Middlesbrough. He arrived having had some success at Watford and then been unfairly treated by the arrival of new owners. He strode into Turf Moor with the persona of Clint Eastwood in a spaghetti western, looking tough, speaking tough and leaving no-one in doubt that he was the boss. They had lost 4-0 at champion-elect Cardiff City just days before he arrived, but the inevitable "new manager bounce" gave him two wins. Over a period of two months however, there was no real improvement under the new regime until three successive wins in January took them to seventh place. The next twelve games brought regression, only one win and six draws, but a big finish starting with a creditable 1-1 draw at home to Cardiff courtesy of David Edgar's injury time equaliser and wins over Wolverhampton Wanderers and Ipswich Town scraped them into the top half, finishing eleventh. Martin Paterson, something of a blast from the past, had returned to the first team after two years in the shadows and his goals were crucial to the late flurry of points, although Charlie Austin's return of twenty-five goals was the best since Andy Payton in the 1999-2000 season. Once again, the change of manager naturally created some uncertainty in the dressing room and one had the impression that this was a squad which had once more under-performed. But the final league table never lies and to finish six places above your neighbour makes the season so sweet, particularly as it last occurred in 1980.

If the previous season at Ewood Park was calamitous, this could only be described as an absolute shambles. Wolverhampton Wanderers were to suffer a double demotion and the same fate , dropping from the Premier League to Division 1 in two campaigns, could easily have befallen the Rovers. Five different managers occupied the hot seat, three on permanent contracts, two in a

Jordan Rhodes of Blackburn Rovers celebrates his opening goal at Turf Moor

temporary capacity, one of whom held this latter post twice. The phrase "they don't know what they're doing" was never so apt when sung from the terraces. In fact a lawyer representing the club at a compensation hearing for one of the deposed managers actually admitted that the club was out of control. There was also the saga of the six Portuguese players, all signed on at least two year contracts and including Nuno Gomez, a Portuguese international legend who scored twenty-nine times for his native country.

In total throughout this season, the six started twelve games. The initial outlay was minimal, which is perhaps an indicator of their talent (Gomez apart), but how much money was lost on that deal is probably in the realms of the unknown, taking into account wages paid added to the agent's fees. Suffice it to say that three of them were out on loan in the January window, but it will be safe to add that some agent somewhere made a killing. They did actually make one staggeringly successful purchase. Jordan Rhodes cost £8million from Huddersfield Town but his eighty-three league goals repaid every last penny and more. Other notable in-coming transfers were former Liverpool and England midfield player Danny Murphy from Fulham, Leon Best, a striker from Newcastle United costing £3million, and Dickson Etuhu, another midfield player from Fulham. Murphy played regularly, Etuhu irregularly and Best hardly at all during this season, although he did suffer an anterior cruciate ligament injury and was out for months. Of the ten incoming loanees, probably Colin Kazim-Richards, a striker from Galatasaray, made the most impact. In terms of the players who left the club, Radosav Petrovic was off to Genclerbirligi in Turkey, Steven Nzonzi to Stoke City for £4million, Junior Hoilett to QPR for £3million, Yakubu to China for £1million, Michel Salgado retired and Vince Grella flew off to Melbourne Heart on a free transfer.

And yet the campaign had started so well. After six matches, Blackburn Rovers sat atop of the Championship. Next up was Middlesbrough at home with Jordan Rhodes now finding the net but a crowd of barely thirteen thousand was a cause of concern. The truth was that the people of Blackburn were deeply suspicious of the Venkys and could not take to a manager, whose spin on the previous season's debacle when interviewed post-match on programmes such as Match of the Day, seemed far detached from reality. And what happened that evening, when the "Boro" cruised to a comfortable 2-1 victory, Grant Hanley's last minute consolation goal papering over the cracks, left those watching in no doubt that something was wrong at the club. The following weekend, Steve Kean travelled down to Charlton Athletic in charge of the team and then at a hastily convened press conference pre-match, announced that he could no longer carry on, citing his position as "untenable" and suggesting that he had been "forced to resign". For a month, his assistant Eric Black carried on as temporary manager until, as everyone expected, the Board would presumably appoint an experienced man to the post. In a shock move, Henning Berg, a former outstanding defender at the club but one scarcely acquainted with management, became the new man in charge. Unsurprisingly for a club in such turmoil, the results told their own story. Under Black, the goals had dried up (four in six games) but the defence stood firm and he had successively performed a damage limitation exercise. When Berg arrived, the Rovers occupied fifth spot. When he was sacked on Boxing Day, ten games into his managership, they were seventeenth. The sole win had been at Peterborough United, Rhodes scoring a hat-trick in a 4-1 romp.

Gary Bowyer, a type of latter day Tony Parkes, was put in temporary charge and seven points from three games, with the goals suddenly springing from nowhere, lifted the gloom, Rhodes and Rochina dominating the goals for column. Michael Appleton had only been manager at Blackpool for a few months, but he had impressed the Bloomfield Road crowd and he was "pinched" by the Rovers. He was young, full of potential but inexperienced.

Where was the big name so craved for by the fans? After a stuttering start, they put together an unbeaten run, Rhodes scoring for seven successive matches. The combined efforts of Bowyer and Appleton had taken the club back into the top ten, but once again it all went wrong. Seven games without a league win, even Peterborough joined in the fun, winning 3-2 at Ewood, caused Appleton's downfall. Ironically, following a last gasp draw in the home derby game, Appleton was sacked after sixty-seven days. Three managers down the road in one season; being married to Henry V111 must have seemed a safer option. Gary Bowyer was ushered in again, hopefully to defend a shaky eighteenth spot. They momentarily slipped into the bottom three, but home wins over Derby County and Huddersfield Town plus a tremendous away win at Millwall saw them into a safe haven; seventeenth place, four points clear

Sam Vokes (far right) out jumps Ryan Nelson in the final moments to equalise for Burnley at Turf Moor in the December drawn derby of 2012

of the drop. The Rovers were indebted to Bowyer and also to Jordan Rhodes. His twenty-six league goals was half of the club's total for the campaign, with no other goal scorer topping five strikes. So many players had come in and gone out on loan that any attempt at team bonding must have been difficult. And with no manager at the helm and Burnley taking over the title of King of East Lancs, what did the future hold? Gary Bowyer said that he tried to take everything that happened to him this season in his stride, but that it was a crazy time.

"I was enjoying my role as Reserve Team coach when we suddenly received the news the day after the Boxing Day defeat at Middlesbrough that Henning Berg and all of his senior staff had been sacked and I was asked later that night to take the team for the next game against Barnsley. I actually continued for four games in all, wins over Barnsley and Notts Forest plus a draw with Wolves and an FA Cup win over Bristol City. Michael Appleton was appointed and I went back to coaching the Reserves. When Michael was sacked I was asked again to be the interim manager. Relegation was a real possibility and although we immediately lost a couple, one defeat in the last six saw us to safety. It was tense and credit goes to everyone who was pulling in the right direction. The 2-1 win at Millwall, which effectively saved us, was a memorable night. We were a touch lucky because the penalty the ref gave us after Grant Hanley raced sixty yards with the ball before falling down, was extremely dubious. VAR would not have allowed it. And then the club offered me the manager's job full time after the season ended."

Charlie Austin getting up close and personal with Sam Vokes after his extremely late equaliser in the Turf Moor derby.

The Derby Games

This was the season where those habitual early departees were denied their money's worth. Two close games were decided by two extremely late goals. The last time Burnley won a derby game at Turf Moor was back on Boxing Day 1978. Now back to the current year, it was a Tier 2 skirmish again, it was December again and the Rovers were six places above their hosts. Two issues dominated the pre-match speculation. Would the Police have a "get it right this time" policy, using all their resources at their disposal including horses, helicopters and every available copper in the county to keep the peace. Secondly, who would win the battle of the in-form strikers, Rhodes, the £8million man for the visitors or Burnley's Charlie Austin, a forward on fire with sixteen goals already to his name by the end of November. And it was the lad in a Blue and White shirt that almost won the game. The goal was a long time coming, but when Mauro Formica crossed the ball in the 67th minute, Jordan Rhodes knocked it into the net. With freezing cold conditions and the wind sweeping down off the Pennines, it looked as if this was to be the defining moment in the game, particularly with Paul Robinson imperious in the Rover's goal. It was time for Sean Dyche to shake things up and two substitutes made the difference. The 21,341 crowd was thinking about shuffling home, dejection ingrained on all Claret and Blue faces when Sam Vokes came on with five minutes remaining to join Junior Stanislaus for one last concerted effort. Dyche claimed that a cynic just behind the dugout screamed "what can anybody do in five minutes", but as Brian Clough used to say, "it only takes a minute to score a goal". With two left on the clock, Stanislaus knocked in a free kick and Vokes rose and headed in the equaliser. A draw had been the predicted result so contentment could be equally shared. There was contentment amongst the Police also. Their presence had been considerably increased since the shenanigans of 2009, their plans to "bus in" every single Blackburn fan had worked to perfection and from a respecting of the law perspective, the game had run smoothly.

The last time Burnley won at Ewood was in 1979, and on this occasion, the Clarets were safely ensconced in mid table, the Blue and Whites teetering on the brink of relegation. Michael Appleton gave Leon Best an opportunity to kick-start his career, but he was whisked off after forty-five minutes of inaction. This was the game where a chicken first waddled on to the pitch after a few minutes, obviously an impolite reference to the Venkys (How does anyone smuggle a fully grown hen into a modern stadium?). Jason Shackell re-paid his £1million transfer fee at a stroke by putting the Clarets in front after half an hour. It was a one-two with a difference, his header from a free kick hitting the post and he knocked the rebound in with his foot. It had been one-way traffic for the first fifty-five minutes, but the game changed on a referee's decision. Ben Mee's name had already entered the official's notebook and when he hauled down Hanley, he was dismissed for a second bookable offence. Burnley were forced to defend for the remainder of the match, but just when it appeared that their rear-guard action had been successful, and many in the crowd of 20,735 were streaming away, who should strike but the Burnley nemesis himself. Cameron Stewart, a loanee from Hull City, produced a touch of magic and David Dunn swept in the equaliser with his left foot. It was a goal that looked perfectly legal on first viewing but it was one which VAR would have subsequently disallowed. There was a slight touch by Jason Lowe on its way through to Dunn. He was onside when the ball was initially played in, but became offside when Lowe made minimal contact. How the Burnley fans hated the Blackburn boy. You can imagine pubs in Burnley pinning a photo of him to the dart board, with the customers hurling the "arrows" with venom. He had already replaced Simon Garner as public enemy number one and this latest goal simply added to that legacy. Dunn's goal ensured that their record over their rival continued to grow, it enhanced his reputation but it did nothing for Michael Appleton. Within a couple of days, his bags were packed and he was looking for new employment. An interesting footnote was that David Jones, on loan from Wigan Athletic, started for the Blackburn side. He would move to Turf Moor during the summer where he donned the Claret and Blue shirt in subsequent games against the enemy, joining the list of those who played for both clubs in derby fixtures.

02 12 2012	Burnley	Blackburn Rovers	1-1	S Vokes, J Rhodes.
17 03 2013	Blackburn Rovers	Burnley	1-1	D Dunn, J Shackell.

David Dunn was booed from virtually start to finish by the large contingent of Burnley fans who made the trip to Ewood Park.

> "Because I had scored in the last two derby games that I had played in, the Burnley crowd in the Darwen end seemed out to get me. Every time I went near the ball they would boo me which never really put me off, but they never let up. So you can imagine how pleased I was when I managed to score the equaliser when they were convinced that they had beaten us. After many re-runs on the TV screen, they finally came to the conclusion that I was off side but it was a shock to me. I didn't move until the pass was played and I was not aware that Jason Lowe might have slightly touched it. Neither the ref nor his assistant saw Jason's touch, but the goal stood and we had drawn again. Back in the changing room, I was so incredibly elated. We liked to think that derby games were just another chance to obtain three points, but this felt like the winning goal in a cup final."

Ross Wallace played in both games, staying out wide as a left winger who tracked back. He had started his career at Celtic, managed by Martin O'Neill at the time with John Robertson, the ex-Notts Forest winger as his assistant. Roy Keane played for the "Hoops" for six months at the end of his career, playing alongside Wallace from time to time. Ross talked to me about his early footballing life and then about the two derby games of the 2012-13 season.

> "Although I never reached the same level as the great John Robertson, he was very much my role model and he helped me when I was at Celtic, particularly in the skill of crossing the ball. Martin O'Neill was all about work, work, work and this set me up for the rest of my career. When Roy Keane became manager of Sunderland, he must have remembered me from Celtic because he signed me and I managed to play a season in the Premier League. He must have had a soft spot for me because he never really had a go at me. After two seasons I moved into the Championship with Preston and again played two full seasons, but they were short of money and they sold me for close to £1million, which was good for them at the time. Burnley under Eddie Howe were a great team to play for. He brought in some excellent youngsters like Trippier, Mee, Ings and Stanislaus and Charlie Austin was there plus experienced players like Michael Duff and Dean Marney. Eddie loved us to attack but when Sean Dyche arrived, he gave us more structure defensively. All we heard this season was the constant boasting coming from the Blackburn fans, reminding us of how many years it was since we last beat them. We knew we were the better side at this time, but when the first derby came along, I was quite shocked at just how much hatred there was between the fans. When we were at home, the coach used to pick us up from Gawthorpe and drive round the back way to Turf Moor. The closer we got to the ground, the more the town started to come alive and the closer we were to the atmosphere. It was a funny feeling but we just wanted to get on with the game and beat Blackburn. Both games were close this year with very late equalisers in both matches. We

scored at the very end of our home game and David Dunn got the last minute equaliser in Blackburn. He was definitely off-side. Some said slightly offside. To me he looked about ten yards off."

In the Capital One Football League Cup, Eddie Howe guided them to two wins over Division 2 opposition, Port Vale and Plymouth Argyle. Charlie Austin had scored in both ties and he did so again against Division 1 Swindon Town, but the Wiltshire club, with home advantage, were too good for the visitors, winning 3-1. For the second consecutive season, The Clarets were eliminated from the FA Cup first time up, losing 1-0 after an away trip to lowly Championship side Barnsley.

Any chance of a decent run by the Ewood Park club in the Capital One Football League Cup was blighted by team selection in Round 2. Kean sent out something akin to a Reserve side with four Portuguese starting. It was an away day at MK Dons and the Rovers lost 2-1, with David Goodwillie's late strike proving to be in vain. Gary Bowyer was temporarily in charge at the commencement of the FA Cup and in front of a paltry 5,504 crowd, Bristol City were sent packing 2-0. It was an even better performance in Round 4, Appleton now being in charge of a 3-0 win at Derby County. Round 5 had to be game over, Arsenal away at the Emirates.

It was one way traffic until completely out of the blue, Kazim-Richards stunned the Gunners and the Rovers hung on for a memorable 1-0 win. A hard fought goalless draw at Millwall in the last eight made them favourites in the replay, but the crowd was a woeful 8,635 and the home team's performance even more woeful as they went down 1-0. In better days, an expected crowd of 20,000 plus for a Round 6 game would have roared them on to victory, but these were the worst of the worst days. There has been a poorer quality of player before at Ewood, notably in the seventies, but from top to bottom, the club had lost its respect in the town and a paltry crowd was all it deserved.

For the second time in my life, football slipped towards the edge of my radar. There were no football teams close to the beautiful and historic village in the Dordogne where we lived. Rugby Union ruled in this part of France, the nearest big club was at Bordeaux, a good two hours plus away by car and I saw a couple of games there and several at Bergerac down in Tier 4, but watching the Issigeac XV became my Sunday afternoon past time. We watched all the Champions' League games on the TV screens which featured an English club at the local bar but it was more of an excuse to knock back the beers than to appreciate the football on view.

I could feel myself drifting away from the Rovers, staying in touch via the internet and phone calls, but it was such a dismal period in their history, not one to reignite my passion. Whenever we had a week or two back in England, I would always take in a game, but suddenly, and for the saddest of all reasons, it changed once more. My mother, ninety three by now and fairly independent, took a turn for the worst, health wise. We came back on a semi-permanent basis until she finally died in the summer of 2014. Whilst over here, my son and I watched them every home game and once again, football became such an important part of my life. We began to summer in France and wintered here until in early 2019, we sold up in Issigeac to live permanently back in Lancashire. From that moment on, the Rovers has been the only show in town.

2013-14

	Pos	Played	Won	Drawn	Lost	GF	GA	Pts
Burnley	2	46	26	15	5	72	37	93
Blackburn Rovers	8	46	18	16	12	70	62	70

Blackburn Rovers		Burnley	
Most Appearances	Jordan Rhodes 45	Most Appearances	David Jones, Tom Heaton and Jason Shackell (all 46)
Most Goals	Jordan Rhodes 25	Most Goals	Danny Ings 21

It had been a general rule of thumb that whenever the symbolic see saw creates a change in direction, it would normally last for a number of years. The gap between the two clubs had been small at the end of the previous season, but did it mean long term change? The Burnley fans could only pray that it did, whilst the supporters from Ewood Park were none too confident that this was a mere bump in the road. Sir Alex Ferguson had just retired as manager at Old Trafford after twenty-six long years and Blackburn Rovers had sacked three in a year. Simply pondering over the comparison renders me speechless.

Sean Dyche had been in post for nine months, long enough to have summed up the situation at the "Turf". There could now be no excuses, not that Sean is the man to ever fall back on that tactic, but the home supporters dreamed of and demanded success. Dyche knew that he needed to make changes but he also knew that to achieve anything, he had to off-load players. Five players who had given sterling service were released, four of them on a free transfer. The "Beast", Brian Jensen (271 starts in ten seasons) moved to Bury. Martin Paterson (29 goals in 130 appearances) was snapped up by Huddersfield Town.

Goalkeeper Lee Grant (114 games) returned to Derby County and former skipper and Gawthorpe trainee Chris McCann, a loyal servant for eight years and 238 appearances, left for Wigan Athletic. Charlie Austin however, the striker with the superb record of eighty-two games and forty-one goals, was sold to Queen's Park Rangers for £4million. These were all good players and would need replacing with similar or better. Goalkeeper Tom Heaton gained a magnificent reputation at Bristol City and Burnley were glad to sign him. Scott Arfield, Scottish born but who has captained Canada because of his father's nationality, was signed on his release from Huddersfield Town and David Jones joined from Wigan Athletic. So with no money spent and Austin's fee in the bank, the Board were happy, but was there sufficient depth in the squad?

A manager would love to play the same side every week and Sean Dyche was so lucky that all of his chosen first eleven this season were available for most of the games. So the phrase "same team as last week lads" must have often reverberated round Turf Moor's home dressing room. Little change was needed with one defeat in the first sixteen games, 2-0 at Brighton. Danny Ings scored twice against Birmingham City and Vokes likewise against Charlton Athletic. Ings snatched another brace as QPR were beaten 2-0 and for seven solid weeks, the Clarets topped the table. A draw at eventual champions Leicester City was a telling result and Vokes and Ings were becoming the Starsky and Hutch of the Championship, taking it in turn to smash in the goals; another sixteen matches going by without defeat. Ashley Barnes had arrived from Brighton in the January window to add his power to the front line but the run ended at the end of March, a match which decided the destination of the title. Leicester won 2-0 and try as hard as Dyche's side did, they proved uncatchable. There were only five defeats during the season and Danny Ings and Sam Vokes both hit the twenty goals mark. This was last achieved by Irvine and Lochhead in the 1964-65 season. All of Dyche's first eleven started a minimum of thirty-eight matches, with the exception of Michael Kightly on thirty-two.

Their final league position was second, nine points behind the champs but eight points above Derby in third. It was automatic promotion, one that was fully deserved. A consistent set of performances from a settled side wins matches and in this case, equals records; eleven wins on their travels was last accomplished in the 1991-92 season. It was a side which had cost little money and the defenders signed on free transfers from Manchester City, Kieran Trippier and Ben Mee were surely going to prove that they could comfortably compete at elite level.

The Burnley side promoted as Championship runners-up in 2013-14 (played over 18 games, max 46) was; Tom Heaton, Kieran Trippier, Michael Duff, Jason Shackell, Ben Mee, Dean Marnie, Dave Jones, Scott Arfield, Michael Kightly, Sam Vokes, Danny Ings.

For the seventh successive year, Burnley made good progress in the Third Round of the Capital One Football League Cup, beating York City, Preston North End and Notts Forest. Round 4 saw them play host to West Ham United. It was a scrappy game with the Hammers winning 2-0, courtesy of two penalties. In comparison, the Turf Moor side failed to win an FA Cup game for the third successive season. They travelled to Premier League Southampton and what a game it was. The Saints made the early running and led 2-0 at the break. The Clarets roared back with inevitable goals from Ings and Vokes before Jay Rodriguez knocked one in against his old mates. The home side went 4-2 up but Kevin Long kept the game alive as Burnley did everything except draw level, eventually losing 4-3.

Gary Bowyer was appointed first team manager at Blackburn Rovers at the start of the close season. It was fully deserved, having twice stepped up the previous season to provide stability as the Rovers spewed out managers on a regular basis. He came across as an ordinary guy, not bombastic and prepared to speak thoughtfully to the media. The fans, having seen what he did in trying circumstances to successfully save the side from relegation, welcomed the move. As usual, Ewood Park resembled Euston Railway Station during the summer, players moving out, others coming in. Nuno Gomes was released from his contract a year early and retired from the game. He had scored international goals for Portugal all over the world, but only four for the Rovers. Danny Murphy also hung up his boots at the age of thirty six. He contributed more than Gomes, but like the Portuguese, he was close to his sell by date when he arrived in Blackburn. Martin Olsson, who had come through the Youth Academy making 117 appearances, wanted Premier League football, so he moved to Norwich City for £3million.

The release of Morten Gamst Pedersen was much mourned. He was allowed to move to Karabukspor in Turkey on a free transfer, having delighted the fans for nine years and 288 starts. He had so many different qualities; the real deal. Finally Gael Givet was released to Arles Avignon on a free transfer at the age of thirty-two, having made 101 appearances. Gary Bowyer commented on the close season where he was determined to rebuild the side.

> "We invested the money on young hungry players who would develop over time. We had to spend money on Ben Marshall, a wide player from Leicester City, the Northern Irish midfield player Corry Evans from Hull City along with Tom Cairney on loan. Defenders Matthew Kilgallon and Tommy Spurr from Sunderland and Doncaster Rovers, as well as loanee Todd Kane from Chelsea, joined Grant Hanley in the back four. In January we were allowed to spend money bringing in Rudy Gestede and Craig Conway from Cardiff City and Tom Cairney's move from Hull City became permanent."

Burnley, for one, certainly appeared to have a stronger squad and from the very start of the season, it was unlikely that Blackburn Rovers would gain promotion. Having made that point however, it has to be said that this was a far better campaign than the previous two and they really gave it their best shot. The start to the season was shaky but an unleashed Jordan Rhodes scored five in three, settled the nerves and the team certainly looked good in the offensive phase of the game. On New Year's Day, they won 2-1 at Leeds, but defensively however, cracks occasionally showed and they conceded three at Brighton and Ipswich and also in a 3-2 reverse at home to Birmingham City. A 1-0 home win over Doncaster Rovers sent them up to eighth, but Rhodes had been very much on his own at Ewood, not that it seemed to affect his scoring prowess. When the strong and tall Rudy Gestede joined from Cardiff City, there was an extra body for the opposition to fear, especially when the ball was in the air. On the debit side, the club lost its captain Scott Dann to Crystal Palace for an undisclosed fee, but as this defensive strong man was still under contract, it must have been for a sizeable amount of money. There were inexcusable blips,

Junior Stanislas puts the Clarets in front at Turf Moor in September 2013

a 4-1 thrashing at Notts Forest and 4-0 at Bolton, but after losing three on the bounce, they were unbeaten in their last twelve matches. Six wins and six draws restored them to an eighth place final position with Rhodes scoring a hat-trick on his return to his old stamping ground at Huddersfield. Gestede followed suit in a thrilling 4-2 encounter at Birmingham City and on three occasions, they were involved in 3-3 draws. The final game of the campaign at home to Wigan Athletic was a magnificent affair, full of attacking football from each side, the Rovers nipping it 4-3, with Rhodes of course nicking the winner. This final flourish guaranteed eighth place, two places and two points behind Brighton in the final Play-Off spot. If they had defended better, and they had not sold Scott Dann, it would have been a given. Rhodes' final tally of twenty five league goals (fifty-one in two seasons) showed what a valuable asset he was at this level. Always on the move, making excellent runs, he had that knack of anticipating where and when the ball would arrive and the skills with head and feet to make full use of any opportunity that came his way.

Sometimes managers have to gamble, particularly in the early rounds of cup competitions and this is what Gary Bowyer did away to Carlisle United from Division 2 in Round 1. With only four regulars in the starting eleven, the gamble failed as the Cumbrians won on penalties. He could not gamble in the 3rd Round of the FA Cup when Manchester City came to Ewood, and yet the Rovers put on a show to remember. Tom Cairney was arguably the best player on the field and they caused the Etihad giants all sorts of problems in a 1-1 draw. If football history teaches us anything, it is that a minnow gets one chance and one chance only against the big boys. And sure enough, after holding the opposition for forty-four minutes, the flood gates opened and City waltzed to a 5-0 victory in the replay. Dann was on his way to Crystal Palace, Robinson limped off injured at half-time and Rhodes did not travel. It was a disappointing but inevitable defeat.

The Derby Games

The first derby game arrived early this season at Turf Moor, six games into the campaign. Burnley were third in the table with their rivals back in eleventh, but having won their previous two games in cavalier fashion. The Turf Moor fans knew to look out for master goal scorer Jordan Rhodes, but what would give them confidence was that in Vokes and Ings, they had punch and power to spare and their defence had conceded just four in five. This Burnley eleven was a stronger looking side than Coyle had taken up; surely this would be the day when that thirty-four year curse would finally be broken. A slightly disappointing 15,699 crowd turned up to see the spectacle and the home fans must have been pleased that Dunn was absent injured. What they saw was an excellently crafted goal, a piece of opportunism from a striker in form and an undeniable act of cheating during a tense, frenetic and exciting encounter. There was no score at half-time, but in the 76th minute, Junior Stanislas played a couple of one-twos in the centre of the park before beating Jake Kean with a crisp finish from outside the penalty area. It was a technical goal of the highest calibre, a move no doubt practiced down at Gawthorpe; an example of how quick movement of the ball can make it so difficult for defenders. With time ticking on past the eighty-five minute mark, a loose back pass from Scott Arfield was seized upon by the ever alert Jordan Rhodes. The angle was tight and as he turned inside on to his right foot, Michael Duff tried to knock the ball away for a corner but it spun off Rhodes' foot and looped into the net. It looked like being the third derby draw in a row until Danny Ings sped clear, chased by Lee Williamson. The Rovers substitute had been on the field a matter of moments, but there was only one winner and so the Blackburn player rugby tackled Ings outside the penalty area. It was a clear, professional foul, a straight red card but only a free kick... which came to naught. The referee blew for time and the home fans were enraged by Williamson's blatant cheating, whereas those sporting blue and white colours talked rather portentously of him "taking one for the team". The Clarets' fans, in my opinion, had every right to object, but the referee interpreted the situation according to the rules of the game and so for another six months at least, Dyche and his Clarets, modern day Jason and the Argonauts, would continue their search for the Golden Fleece.

By the time the return at Ewood Park came around, Burnley had been securely locked into second place for a month, with only Leicester City above them. There were however twelve more games to play and "many a slip......." and all that was holding back too many premature promotion celebrations. But with the last defeat a distant memory, almost three months before, it was difficult to stay calm. Blackburn Rovers, safe in tenth place, but still with ambi-

Rovers fans celebrate as a blue flare billows smoke around Ewood Park in March 2014

tions around a Play-Off spot, had been battered 4-0 the week before at Bolton and desperately needed a home win to stay in the hunt. Their fans were circumspect about the result, Rhodes had not scored for nine games, but those in Claret and Blue were certain that this was their day of destiny. David Dunn and Paul Robinson were back in the Rovers' starting line-up and they had taken a fine young prospect on loan from Old Trafford to fill the gap left by Scott Dann. His name was Michael Keane, later to become a huge favourite at Turf Moor.

As for Sean Dyche, he once more played his first eleven. The crowd of 21,589 was the season's highest but the start was delayed when another chicken was released on to the pitch. Burnley started brightly but the Rovers then assumed control and when, in the twenty-fourth minute, Lowe set up Rhodes, the striker made no mistake. It could have been worse just before the interval when Ben Mee cleared a Lowe effort off the line and then after the interval, Rhodes was clear, one on one with Heaton, but this time the striker hit the post.

The last twenty minutes belonged to the Clarets as first, Jason Shackell nodded home a free kick from substitute Ross Wallace and then Danny Ings reacted fastest in the box to put them ahead. The Burnley fans had packed the Darwen end and the noise as the referee blew for time could have lifted the roof. The jubilation, the released tension after thirty four years of misery, flooded out and they sang themselves hoarse all the way up the M65. In retrospect, a win here would have ultimately sealed a Play-Off spot for the Rovers, but for Burnley, now eight points clear of the chasing pack, automatic promotion was just around the corner. As Gary Bowyer said in a post-match interview, "it's all about fine margins".

14 09 2013	Burnley	Blackburn Rovers	1-1	J Stanislas, J Rhodes.
09 03 2014	Blackburn Rovers	**Burnley**	1-2	J Rhodes, J Shackell, D Ings.

Geoff Bury, still annoyed three or more years on from the debacle surrounding the sale of the Blackburn club, provided me, no doubt through gritted teeth, with this amusing story......from a Burnley point of view that is.

"I have found a reference to a plane which flew over Ewood sponsored by Burnley fans which may be of interest."

"Burnley fans found a way to taunt Blackburn Rovers supporters on 9th March this year despite not beating their rivals for 35 years. Burnley were sitting 20 points above Blackburn, who are owned by Indian poultry group Venky's, and their supporters flew a plane over Ewood Park with a banner saying "35 Years Who Cares? 20 points. Venky's 4ever." Needless to say Blackburn fans, who resent their owners, were not amused."

Ross Wallace played in the second game at Blackburn, having come on as a substitute and the whole day is still clear in his mind

"We knew we could beat Blackburn in spite of the recent drawn games where we felt that luck had really favoured the Rovers. We also knew how important it was to the Burnley fans. To the players, it was a bit more than an ordinary game but for the fans it was massive. Several told me that they would sooner beat Blackburn than get promoted. Driving down the hill from the motorway with a huge police escort, we quickly became aware of their fans and as we passed the pub just before you turn into the Stadium, we were getting all sorts of stick; rude signs and bad language. It does make the players laugh and I had been involved in Glasgow derbies when I had been at Celtic and played in the Sunderland/ Newcastle derbies but you could really feel the atmosphere here. The butterflies started in the stomach and you couldn't wait for the game to kick-off. The Rovers started well and Rhodes scored. We began to get back into the game after half-time without scoring and then with about just twenty-five to go, Sean threw me and Ashley Barnes on and he told me to start getting crosses in. We were given a free kick out wide left, I knocked it in and Jason Shackell won the header and the ball flew in. A few minutes later I managed to cut the ball back and Danny Ings knocked it in. The last few minutes were so tense as they threw everything at us but we were so happy when the final whistle went. Happy that we had another three points to help us to promotion but also so happy for the fans who had waited so long for this. I have now lived in Lancashire for the last twelve years and I consider myself a Lancashire-Scot. Having played at Preston, I have good feelings for them and of course Burnley, which was a superb five years. But there are so many good clubs in the Lancashire area and I now want them all to do well, even Blackburn Rovers."

David Dunn talked sadly about the club's first loss in a derby for so, so long.

"I suppose Burnley were going to beat us eventually but on this occasion we had played really well. We could have been well in front and we were holding on to our lead quite comfortably. Burnley made two substitutions and within a couple of minutes {the 71st minute;- Editor} the manager pulled me off. I wasn't happy because whenever I had the ball, I was occupying two of their players and I still felt strong. Liam Feeney came on for me and within eight minutes we were losing 2-1. I don't know if we would have won if I had stayed on, but I really felt as if I had more to give and that we could have stopped them from breaking their losing spell. It was my final derby game and I felt so annoyed about it."

Gary Bowyer talked about the perils of international weekends, the positives and the negatives, particularly if they were immediately before an important game like a derby match.

"The first derby match this season came immediately after an international weekend. In some ways they were a nice respite, giving you time away from football and my wife and I flew off to Majorca for a couple of nights to make sure the batteries stayed charged. We were relaxing in a bar on this Saturday evening when my phone rang. It was Jordan Rhodes and I wondered what he wanted. He was away with the Scotland side and so I answered and he told me that someone had trod on his wrist and that it would have to go into plaster, making him extremely doubtful for the Burnley game. When I returned home, we worked hard on the injury and then persuaded the referee to allow him to play with a plaster cast on his lower arm. Fortunately he agreed and Jordan rewarded us with the late equaliser. By the time the return game came around, we had sold Scott Dann to Crystal Palace and we needed cover at the back in case of injuries. I managed to persuade Manchester United to loan Michael Keane to us for the rest of the season and he went straight into the team and performed well. In the week leading up to the derby game, Michael was playing in an Under/21 international and I sent Craig Short along to watch him. Just before the kick-off, he rang me to say that Keane had disappeared. He had taken part in the warm-up and was listed in the starting line-up, but when the players came out, someone else had the shirt. I immediately thought that he had picked up an injury in the warm-up and we needed his strength at the back. Thankfully much later, we learned that it had been a registration problem and that he was fully fit to play. In both cases the situation was nowhere near as serious as I first thought but that was what these games did to you. I was so disappointed at the end of the second derby game. We had played well in the first half and should have been two up at the break. Then Jordan hit the inside of the post and the ball came out and we were beaten by two late goals."

Vicky Foy loved the derby games for their atmosphere and anything other than a defeat away from home pleased her so much.

> As I got older, I had to look out for my dad because he would argue with anyone about football and sometimes as we were walking home, we would come across some opposition supporters, certainly when it was a derby before they started to bus them all in. Then I had to grab hold of him and guide him away from any potential confrontation. Sometimes we would travel to away games. You can't beat a derby game for atmosphere and my best memory was when we played Burnley away. [September 2013: Editor]. In the last few minutes of the game, a Burnley forward was clear and Lee Williamson chased him. He was never going to catch him so he hacked him down from behind. They didn't score from the free kick and so we escaped with a draw. We were so happy on the way home.

2014-15

	Pos	Played	Won	Drawn	Lost	GF	GA	Pts
Burnley	19	38	7	12	19	28	53	33
Blackburn Rovers	9	46	17	16	13	66	59	67

Blackburn Rovers		Burnley	
Most Appearances	Marcus Olsson 41	Most Appearances	Tom Heaton, Kieran Trippier, Jason Shackell (all 38)
Most Goals	Jordan Rhodes 21	Most Goals	Danny Ings 11

The historic county of Lancashire was once the mightiest in the whole of the United Kingdom. With two giant cities and a host of industrial towns all around, it was not only in football that it held its head high, but in 1974, with the precision of a surgeon's knife (or should it have been a butcher's cleaver), it was decimated. The county is now less than a quarter the size of its predecessor in terms of population and at least five of the country's famous football clubs were shunted into newly formed counties with absolutely no tradition whatsoever.

The current county of Lancashire was then reduced to four professional clubs (it is now seven) and Burnley and Blackburn Rovers plus PNE and Blackpool were all that remained under the Red Rose banner. In the ensuing forty years (up to the end of the 2013-14 season), the Rovers had occupied Tier 1 for nineteen seasons, Burnley for three, Blackpool once and Preston North End none at all. It was clear that the Ewood Park club was the undisputed king of the county, but here was an opportunity for Sean Dyche's side to play catch-up.

His side had performed magnificently to gain promotion but it is always a giant step into the Premier League. Was this squad good enough to compete at the highest level? Dyche retained all of his eleven heroes from the previous campaign, only Junior Stanislas, his "go to" twelfth man moving away to

AFC Bournemouth. He had made ninety-three appearances in three seasons. George Boyd was his principal signing, the long haired midfielder from Hull City arriving for a possible £3million fee. Three other incoming transfers of note were Matt Taylor, a veteran midfield player from West Ham United, Lukas Jutkiewicz, a striker from Middlesbrough and Republic of Ireland left back Stephen Ward from Wolverhampton Wanderers.

And what a baptism of fire it was for the newly promoted club. Scott Arfield put them in front in the fourteenth minute of their opening fixture against Chelsea at the "Turf" and their next goal was 565 minutes later, a Michael Kightly strike at Leicester City. They had managed a goalless draw to Manchester United, but understandably they were down in nineteenth place. Following three further defeats, they hit rock bottom after losing 3-1 at home to Everton. They dragged themselves up to seventeenth but there was nothing better on the horizon. Ashley Barnes had replaced Vokes as Ings' strike partner and the few goals scored came from this pairing. Apart from an early 4-0 thumping at West Brom, they were never embarrassed. Michael Keane, came on loan from Manchester United in September, a deal which was made permanent in January for around £2million, and he certainly bolstered the defence.

There were occasional moments which lifted the faithful fans. A 2-2 draw at the Manchester City Etihad Stadium and a subsequent 1-0 victory in the home game (Boyd scoring in both encounters), brought a spring to their step, but goals were so much at a premium. Following the winner over Man City, another 541 minutes elapsed before Danny Ings found the net in a 1-0 win at Hull, their only double of the season. There were a number of 1-0 defeats and the season ended with Ings giving them a 1-0 win over Aston Villa in Birmingham, but although conceding fifty-three goals is mid table form, twenty eight goals scored in a season would relegate you in any league in the land.

No-one was entertained and free-flowing football was off the menu, but no-one suggested a lack of effort or that the manager should be shown the door. It was simply a case of the squad not being good enough at this level. Thankfully, seven points from their last three games saved them from the ignominy of holding up the rest of the league but for the second time in five seasons, Burnley's stay in the Premier League was of the minimum duration, Hopefully Sean Dyche, a young manager with a growing reputation, would not be tempted by pastures new and would come up with a strategy, not just for instant promotion, but for a stable future at the height of the English game. And for consolation, there would be derby games next time round.

The cup competitions brought no salvation for the supporters. The home tie against Sheffield Wednesday, a mid-table Championship side, in the Capital One Cup Round 2 proved to be another powder puff performance, going down 1-0. The Third Round of the FA Cup gave them another home tie and a 1-1 draw with Tottenham Hotspur, Sam Vokes scoring a rare goal. The replay in North London was entertaining and for once full of goals, the Spurs overcoming an early two goal deficit to win 4-2.

Gary Bowyer must have been happy with his squad from the previous season because the summer months were far quieter with regard to transfers, both in-coming and out-going. Several names from the past left the club, but these were players on long contracts, now surplus to requirements. The Portuguese contingent had already disappeared and Alan Judge moved to Brentford for £350,000. The rest were all free transfers and these included David Goodwillie (Aberdeen), Dickson Etuhu (AIK Stockholm), DJ Campbell (Maidenhead United) and Ruben Rochina (Granada). The most important signing was Shane Duffy from Everton. Uncultured he may have been but he was a solid rock of a defender, a "thou shall not pass" character. He would make the perfect partner for the fleet of foot Grant Hanley who was now captaining the side. Jason Steele came on loan from Middlesbrough, a rated goalkeeper who had actually represented Great Britain in the 2012 Olympic Games. Finally Alex Baptiste, an experienced right back, came on loan from Bolton Wanderers.

They hoped to follow Burnley's example the previous year and make a flying start following their twelve successive unbeaten games at the end of the previous campaign, but Blackburn Rovers were the masters of inconsistency. For the first dozen games, it was a case of win one, draw one and then lose one. They went a goal up through Tom Cairney in the first minute at Norwich, but lost 3-1. Several days later they welcomed champions in waiting AFC Bournemouth and won 3-2. Defensively they were struggling and league position wise, they were hovering mid-table. Then from out of nowhere came an unbeaten run of nine games which rocketed them into the Play-Off positions. Three second-half goals saw off Notts Forest at the City Ground, Gestede scored twice as Reading were comfortably beaten 3-1 at Ewood and there was a satisfying 2-1 home win over Leeds United. But December and January were as barren as the soil and by now, the Play-Offs were receding into the distance and inconsistency continued to rule.

Three wins on the bounce in March, including another Rhodes brace against Charlton were off-set by consecutive home defeats to Brentford and Brighton. The busiest man on the pitch at Elland Road was the referee, who needed a spare pencil after the names of so many Leeds players entered his book. The Rovers won 3-0, their best away performance and it was the prelude to an unbeaten run of seven games (three wins and four draws), but the gap was far too wide to close as they finished ninth. Rudi Gestede finished with twenty goals, one behind Jordan Rhodes. It was the first time that two Rovers players had reached twenty goals in the same season since 1964-65; McEvoy and Byrom in the old Division 1. Part of the secret to Burnley's 2013-14 success was the settled side, but Gary Bowyer came nowhere near to achieving this. Again it was disappointing, because there were a number of quality players in the squad, but for the third year running, the Clarets had the upper hand.....and it would only get worse.

Division 1 Scunthorpe United on a Tuesday evening at Ewood Park in the First Round of the Capital One Cup, ought to have been a stroll, but for the second season in a row, Blackburn Rovers bowed out at the first hurdle. The FA Cup was a different story. Charlton Athletic were edged out 2-1 at the Valley in Round 3 and Premier League Swansea City rolled over 3-1. The Welsh side made it easy for the Blue and Whites by finishing with nine men and had been poor throughout, but not as poor as Stoke City, Premier League visitors in Round 5. They defended abysmally and could not cope with the pace of Josh King. The Norwegian international, who had under-performed for the whole season, scored a hat-trick, three of his grand total of four goals for the campaign. And when the draw came out, sending the Rovers to Anfield, there was suddenly interest in the world's oldest football competition. Liverpool were far from their best, Bowyer's side was well organised, and it was a dour contest which produced a 0-0 stalemate. The replay filled Ewood to the rafters, a crowd of 28,415 watching a very close and tense affair, until Philippe Coutinho scored a magnificent 70th minute goal to send the Mersey side into the semi-finals.

2015-16

	Pos	Played	Won	Drawn	Lost	GF	GA	Pts
Burnley	1	46	26	15	5	72	35	93
Blackburn Rovers	15	46	13	16	17	46	46	55

Blackburn Rovers		Burnley	
Most Appearances	Grant Hanley, Ben Marshall (both 44)	Most Appearances	Tom Heaton, Ben Mee, Scott Arfield (all 46)
Most Goals	Jordan Rhodes 10	Most Goals	Andre Gray 23

There are a number of obvious problems with a relegation, but one of the most serious is the loss of star players. Having played on the highest stage, some players don't want to drop down a level and having been impressed when they play against you, it is only natural for the big clubs to try to lure these players away. During the 2015 summer recess, Kieran Trippier, the quality right-back who had missed just six games in four years at Turf Moor, signed for Tottenham Hotspur for £3.5 million. Similarly Danny Ings had been the leading goal scorer at Turf Moor for the last two seasons and had gained international recognition. No-one doubted his ability to play at the top and when Liverpool come calling, you go. The fee set by a tribunal was £6.5million. Jason Shackell, the club captain, departed in a sideways move, back to Derby County.

He had only missed two games in three seasons and Sean Dyche simply had to replace this trio. Eleven new faces arrived over the summer of whom four were to make immediate and valuable contributions. Matthew Lowton arrived from Aston Villa, an experienced right back to replace Trippier, and Ben Mee was moved across to fill the gap at centre back. Chesterfield's Zimbabwean international left-back Tendayi Darikwa was brought in and then Dyche paid out a club record £6.5million for Brentford goal scorer Andre Gray. Finally he took a huge gamble on signing the notorious Joey Barton from Queens Park Rangers on a free transfer. Football's number one "bad guy" was reaching the veteran stage, but he could still play and the manager hoped his experience would be the cement that would hold his mid-field together.

It was not the start the fans had waited all summer for. Two points from three games raised doubts; doubts that were quickly dispelled as they roared to four straight wins. Gray was beginning to find his feet, working in tandem with Vokes, and a 2-1 home defeat against Reading was a mere hiccup. Another six without defeat followed and after Gray scored consecutive home doubles against Huddersfield Town and Fulham, they were occupying second spot. Clubs can momentarily go off the boil at whatever level but seven points collected from eight games through November into mid-December was reminiscent of relegation form. A Boxing Day 3-0 reversal at Hull City was not the long awaited Christmas present, but what followed certainly was. A Gray hat-trick with Arfield chipping in with a fourth, brought in the New Year in style.

Bristol City were the victims at Turf Moor and the ball was rolling. Twenty-two games later, they still had not lost another match. Successive comprehensive wins of 5-0 (MK Dons away), 3-1 (Brentford away) and 4-1 (Derby County at home) had moved them up to third and then Vokes netted five times in a six game winning streak which saw them assume league leadership. Although there was a mini-blip of three draws either side of April Fools' Day, five wins and a draw climaxed the season. Middlesbrough had been kept at arms' length when Michael Keane equalised well into time added on in the vital top of the table battle at the "Turf" and the Clarets were crowned champions of the Championship, their first Tier 2 title since the 1972-73 season when Martin Dobson captained the side.

Tom Heaton had kept twenty clean sheets, a factor which no doubt helped to keep them clear at the top. For the sixth time in their 128 year history, Burnley had won eleven away league games and the Premier League with all its glitz, glamour and riches awaited. Their last two attempts had quickly evaporated. Would it be more permanent this time?

The Burnley Championship winning side of 2015-16 (played over 18 games, max 46) was; Tom Heaton, Matthew Lowton, Michael Duff, Michael Keane, Ben Mee, Stephen Ward, Tendayi Darikwa, Scott Arfield, Joey Barton, David Jones, George Boyd, Andre Gray, Sam Vokes.

The downside to the campaign occurred in the Football League Cup Round 1. Port Vale were a struggling Division 1 side and it should have been declared a no contest at half-time. Burnley had the potential to field a team full of quality players but managers often make difficult to understand decisions when planning for these fixtures. For the minnows, it is their Wembley, a chance to briefly hit the headlines, so they play out of their skins. It also needs to be remembered that the competition draws in the crowds in the later rounds, has a Wembley final and is a passport to a European competition. So when a manager as capable as Sean Dyche leaves out a number of his best players, you have to ask why. Inevitably the Staffordshire side gave it everything, the

Clarets were a touch circumspect and Port Vale won 1-0. The FA Cup Third Round paired the Championship's top two clubs and Burnley pulled off a thrilling away win, beating Middlesbrough 2-1. The German striker Rouwen Hennings, bought from Karlsruher FC in the summer for around £2million, but who was more accustomed to sitting on the bench started here and scored the vital goal to take them down to Arsenal in Round 4. Vokes hit the target at the Emirates, but inevitably, the Gunners won 2-1.

A long and illustrious career came to an end at Ewood Park this summer, David Dunn moving to Oldham Athletic as player-coach. The local lad had made 316 appearances in the blue and white halved shirt over two periods of time and scored fifty goals. In days gone by he would have been the archetypal inside forward, a play maker who could also score goals. Injury had restricted his appearances over the last few years, but at thirty-six, it was time to look at coaching. I remember taking him to an English Schools' FA course in Cheshire which I had organised, the purpose being to look at North West fourteen year olds who may make the England Schools' side the following season. As the players walked off the pitch at the end of a long day of being coached and playing, the England manager had a word with me. "This lad Dunn," he said "is going to make a proper player, but it won't be this next year. But when he grows, look out for him." Wise words from a man who knew his football.

One of the problems the Rovers had this summer was with the "Fair Play" system and for a short time, the books were imbalanced. In other words they were spending far more than they earned, As a result, Tom Cairney was sold for £3million. The Scot had scarcely missed a game in his two seasons at the club and at Fulham, he has looked a Premier League player. The prolific scoring Rudi Gestede signed for Aston Villa for £6million and the disappointing but highly talented Josh King was sold to AFC Bournemouth. Paul Robinson, multi capped by England, had performed well at Ewood over seven years and come back from a serious injury. At thirty-six, he needed a life in the slow lane and he moved to Burnley as cover for Tom Heaton and at long last, they were able to take Leon Best off the payroll. Signed from Newcastle United by Steve Kean for over £3million, he was another in a long line of non-scoring centre-forwards who have graced (or disgraced) Ewood Park.

In three full seasons, he scored twice in fourteen appearances, spending the rest of his time on either the medical table or on loan at places such as Yeovil Town. To compensate for these losses, Gary Bowyer was forced to look for players either out of contract or free transfers. Unfortunately none of the likes of Hope Akpan, Danny Guthrie, Nathan Delfouneso or Bengali-Fode Koita were of a similar calibre, quality wise, to the players who left, and this showed as the campaign was underway.

The start was abysmal, four points but no wins in seven games. Rhodes however was slowly finding his form and his brace in a 3-0 home win over Charlton Athletic was their first win. He repeated the feat in another home win against Ipswich Town but when a side loses 3-0 at MK Dons, there is something seriously wrong. Although there was a splendid 2-0 win at Leeds United, we began to think that Gary Bowyer was on borrowed time. Two draws later, he was on his way, replaced almost immediately by Paul Lambert. Bowyer had managed the club for 131 games with a percentage win of 35.9, not bad at a club with little money. His honesty and lack of ego made him popular with the fans and no-one could doubt his loyalty. But he had been dealt a succession of bad hands and this latest transfer embargo was the last straw. As Burnley had found in the late seventies and eighties, you cannot keep selling your best players without the money being used to invest in equally good replacements. If you do, the trajectory is downwards. I asked Gary what it felt like to be suddenly sacked.

> "I honestly thought that in the circumstances, we were doing as well as we possibly could do. The players tried their best, but the Championship is an unforgiving league and to comfortably stay there, you need to have access to a decent amount of money. We had drawn two and won one of our last three games and I was totally shocked when Derek Shaw came to me and told me that changes had to be made and that I was to be sacked along with my coaching staff. The conversation was that short. I had to phone the family to let them know before the decision was announced, say good bye to friends and colleagues I had worked with over the last eleven years, clear my desk, collect my belongings and leave. My feelings were a combination of sadness and anger on that drive home; so many different emotions within my body."

The Scottish born Lambert was a Champions' League medal winner at Borussia Dortmund, as a manager he had produced a successful Championship side at Norwich City and kept Aston Villa in the Premier League, but this was to be no picnic for him. Short of ability on the field and short of money in the Board Room, he had one thing in mind. Save this club from relegation. And the "new manager bounce" certainly worked its magic. Three wins coupled with several draws and to everyone's amazement, it was eight unbeaten. Four 1-0 defeats out of five over the festive period dampened any anticipation of reaching the Play-Offs and then more bad news hit the club. Jordan Rhodes was to be transferred to Middlesbrough for £9million. He had scored ten goals in twenty four games, way in front of anyone else, so who would score now? There was other disappointing news also on the transfer front in the January window. Marcus Olsson was sold to Derby County for £1million and the quick and clever left back would also be missed. But on the good news front, Elliott Bennett, a strong, experienced and athletic midfield player came from Norwich and Danny Graham, another experienced practitioner, came on loan from Sunderland to lead the attack along with Jordi Gomez, an extremely talented ball playing midfielder, but now on the wrong side of thirty. There were more creditable wins over Fulham and Middlesbrough, both beaten at Ewood Park and they exacted revenge for the defeat at MK Dons in October. There was

Andre Gray's penalty seals a 1-0 win for Burnley at Turf Moor in the March 2016

a memorable 1-0 win at Brentford, with a Hanley dismissal and six bookings before Shane Duffy stole a late winner. The last four games brought two wins, two draws and four goals for Danny Graham as the Rovers finished fifteenth, fifteen points clear of danger. Paul Lambert had achieved his objective, but he was most unhappy with the hierarchy of the club, its lack of money and lack of ambition, so he handed in his resignation. In spite of missing the second half of the season, Jordan Rhodes was still top goal scorer.

He had occupied this position for four campaigns, the first one to do so since Alan Shearer and his total of eighty-three goals places him at twelfth in the all-time list at the club. On the goals per game ratio, he stands sixth on the all-time list at 0.52 strikes per game. Only Southworth, Shearer, Briggs, Harper and Quigley sit above him in the Pantheon of legendary goal scorers. It had been a disjointed season and although the financial situation had been sorted, there was no mood of optimism around the club. They quickly needed a new manager and several quality players if next season was to be better.

The start of the season had been poor, as was their performance in the Capital One Cup, going out in Round 1 for the third successive season when they lost 2-1 at home to Shrewsbury Town from the lower reaches of Division 1. There was more to cheer in the FA Cup, although the Round 3 tie at Division 2 Newport County was a victim of the weather. Paul Cox was amongst a number of fans who made the long journey to South Wales only to be told on arrival that the pitch they shared with the local rugby club was waterlogged. The re-scheduled game was closely contested but the Rovers went through 2-1. Oxford United were one of the leading teams in Division 2, but the Blue and Whites turned it on, winning 3-0 in the university city. West Ham United in

Round 5 was a challenge and there was confidence in the town, but only for the first twenty-five minutes. Ben Marshall scored a fine individual goal to put the home side ahead but then Dmitri Payet took over, scoring two sublime goals and making a third. Chris Taylor was sent off for a second bookable offence and although West Ham were also later reduced to ten men, there was no stopping them as they ran out 5-1 winners.

The Derby Games

The media pundits prefer big matches to come around after a number of league games have been concluded because they have so much more information on which to base their predictions. But in this case, where the first derby game was in late October, you did not need to be a football "egghead" to know that Blackburn Rovers would have their hands full, even with home advantage. Playing at centre-back for Burnley was Michael Keane, another of the few who have played East Lancashire derby games in both colours of strip.

With twelve fixtures completed, Sean Dyche's men had won six and drawn four to occupy fifth place whereas the Rovers had won two and drawn five. Eleven points and fourteen places separated the sides; it was an away banker. But Jordan Rhodes had already scored seven times, the strength of Duffy and Hanley had contributed to four successive clean sheets and the game attracted 19,897 spectators, the vast majority sporting blue and white colours. So as ever in football, you never know. The game had everything expected from a local derby. It was hotly contested, fractious and enthralling.

And for those expecting one-way traffic, it was an open game, one in which the Blue and White halved shirts enjoyed more of the possession. In Craig Conway, they had the potential key to success as he teased the Burnley right flank, sometimes cutting back on to his right foot to fire in shots, at other times knocking in teasing crosses. But Burnley had Joey Barton, not averse to clattering into the opposition and then playing telling passes when in possession. Neither Gray nor Rhodes were given too many opportunities to add to their goal tallies, but it was Scott Arfield, hardworking and tireless who finally unlocked the Rovers' defence.

With sixty-five minutes on the clock, a Burnley corner was only partially cleared and there was the Canadian Scot, all technique and precision, perfectly placing the ball into the top corner of the net. He then sprinted all the way back to the Burnley fans at the other end of the ground, to join in their celebrations, followed by the rest of the team. Conway deserved to equalise minutes later when, with a dip of the shoulder, he smashed the ball against the woodwork with Heaton totally beaten. And that's how it remained; another derby win for Burnley. Was it becoming a habit? Gary Bowyer told me just how devastated he was with this result.

Burnley's Scott Arfield (Number 37) scores the only goal in the 2015 Ewood Park derby

> "Once again the derby game was so full of passion, the crowd was so volatile and the players all gave their all. We really attacked them and there was a moment when Jordan Rhodes and Tom Lawrence combined to cut the Burnley defence open. Rhodes finally played Lawrence clear and from ten yards out, he blazed the ball over the cross bar. In tight matches, you just have to take your chances and that was what Burnley did. At the other end, I have to admit that Arfield struck the ball so well when it came to him after we half cleared a corner and that was game over."

Gary Bowyer had been long gone by the time the return game was scheduled at Turf Moor. Paul Lambert was left with the task of conjuring a miracle. Having said that, his new club had won three of their last four, the stand-out performance being a 2-1 win over the Clarets' nearest rivals Middlesbrough in their most recent fixture. But Sean Dyche's men were unbeaten in eleven which included eight wins and they were looking down at the rest of their rivals from their lofty perch at the head of the Championship. With a dozen games still to play, the Blackburn side was odds on to survive the drop, but it surely had to be a home win. Lambert was cagey in his team selection, opting for Danny Graham up front on his own. Dyche in contrast, started with Vokes and Gray up, a sign no doubt of the confidence flowing through the squad. The game attracted 20,478 fans and once again, the Rovers had more possession and had more shots at goal. Elliott Bennett saw a thunderous shot brilliantly saved by the magnificent Tom Heaton and there was no doubt that they deserved a draw at least, but it was all decided as early as the sixteenth minute from the penalty spot. Boyd nipped in front of Duffy as the defender was about to smash the ball away, but the only contact made was with the Burnley player's calf muscle; a stone cold penalty. Steele dived left as Andre Gray smashed it down the middle at shin height.

Sean Dyche admitted at the end of the game that his men were far from their best and added, "That's my sixth Lancashire derby and I've not seen a decent one yet. It was cagey and awkward but obviously I'm delighted we came out on top and it is fantastic for the town and the fans. For me it's three points and another win but for the town it is a different thing." Sound words from a sound manager who, although not hailing from these parts, has become acquainted with its traditions and folk-lore. It had been thirty-eight years since they had won a derby at home but this was their sixth such match without defeat.

This has been the last league derby up to the time of writing this book, but they will return in the 2022-23 season. The balance of power had changed, the pendulum swung and the see saw was definitely tilted the other way. Whichever cliché or metaphor you wish to use, it was a fact that the cock of the walk in East Lancashire was Burnley FC.

24 10 2015	Blackburn Rovers	**Burnley**	0-1	S Arfield.
05 03 2016	**Burnley**	Blackburn Rovers	1-0	A Gray.

2016-17

	Pos	Played	Won	Drawn	Lost	GF	GA	Pts
Burnley	16	38	11	7	20	39	55	40
Blackburn Rovers	22	46	12	15	19	53	65	51

Blackburn Rovers		Burnley	
Most Appearances	Jason Lowe 43	Most Appearances	Stephen Ward 37
Most Goals	Danny Graham 12	Most Goals	Sam Vokes 10

Whenever an ex-Burnley player turns out at Ewood Park for the opposition, he is instantly booed. It is a tradition and the transfer of players between the two East Lancashire rivals are rare, but until this fateful day, no-one had ever managed both clubs. Many fans of the Blackburn club could not believe their ears and eyes when, on June 2nd, the club announced its new manager. It was the ex-Burnley boss Owen Coyle, who, simply by association, they had to boo. For those who took a more considered view of events, there were plusses and minuses to the appointment. He had managed low budget clubs in the Premier League, having taken the Clarets up, initially kept Bolton Wanderers safe from relegation for two seasons and then appearing to be unfortunately dismissed at Wigan Athletic when still in mid-table. He had skipped off to the USA for eighteen months to manage Houston Dynamo, being eventually sacked after a reasonable set of results, so there were positives to this Scotsman but his arrival failed to generate the excitement and expectancy of some of his predecessors.

One had to feel sorry for the reception he received from the fans in Blackburn. He was a professional coming to do a job. The people who ought to have been criticised were the Board of Directors and I ask a question. Would Bob Lord have ever appointed Johnny Carey or Jim Smith to a managerial role at Burnley and likewise, would Jack Walker have ever appointed Harry Potts or Stan Ternent? "Not until hell freezes over" would have been a polite and appropriate response from those two great Chairmen/Owners. They knew their club, they knew their town, they understood what fans were thinking. The Venkys may receive more criticism than they deserve, having loyally kept hold of the club, but there is no doubt that if the people in charge know the area and the people, they are more likely to be more successful at running the club.

A number of players with first team experience were released on frees at the end of the season. These included Tommy Spurr to Preston North End, Matthew Kilgallon to Bradford City, Chris Taylor to Bolton Wanderers and Lee Williamson to Burton Albion. Each had played his part but, Spurr apart, without making a position their own. To replace them, Coyle had the same problem as Bowyer and Lambert; frees or loanees. Danny Graham was signed on a permanent contract from Sunderland and Liam Feeney, a right winger from Bolton the most well known. To raise money and balance the books, Grant Hanley was sold to Newcastle United for £5.5million and Shane Duffy to Brighton and Hove Albion for £4.2million.

The Scottish international had made 183 appearances and scored eight goals, developing through the Academy at Brockhall whilst the Republic of Ireland regular made sixty-three starts and scored five times for the club. This pairing had kept the club afloat defensively the previous season. Selling them was a disaster. A smidgeon of that money (£250,000) was paid out to buy Derrick Williams, a defender from Bristol City. The ageing, but quality laden defender Charlie Mulgrew came from Celtic on a free and Sam Gallagher, a young striker from Southampton, was taken on a season-long loan.

To indicate the appalling nature of this direst of seasons, Blackburn Rovers never found themselves in a league position which was higher than twentieth. The aperitif was three successive defeats, including Shane Duffy's last game, a 2-1 defeat at Cardiff, where the defender went out with a bang; two own goals, booked and finally sent off. They finally won at the eighth time of asking, 4-2 to Rotherham United with Marvin Emnes (on loan from Cardiff) scoring his third in three games and Mulgrew's winner in the only goal of the game at Newcastle lifted them above the relegation zone. Six more games without a win dropped them back into trouble. And although yet another Mulgrew strike completed the double over champions to be Newcastle United, the crowd had become so anti-Coyle. At Barnsley on Boxing Day, a ground similar in shape to Turf Moor; the dressing rooms under the stand occupied by away supporters, we saw a most undistinguished 2-0 defeat. The manager had to endure a post-match walk of shame to a crescendo of boos from many disgruntled fans who had travelled in the hope of a belated Christmas present. Ben Marshall left for Wolverhampton Wanderers for £1.2million at the end of the January. He had made 126 appearances and scored eleven goals, but for someone with so much ability, he ultimately underachieved. The Board listened to the fans' demands for change and Coyle was sacked, thirty-one league games producing just twenty-nine points and marooned in twenty-third position.

Like Lambert last year, Tony Mowbray was employed to save the club from relegation. His task however was more difficult; far fewer games with the club close to being stranded. A quality central defender with Middlesbrough, Celtic and Ipswich Town, he had also gained managerial success with Hibernian, West Brom and Middlesbrough. The good old "new manager bounce" immediately set the club on a seven game unbeaten run, but with a growing gap to safety, they needed wins and five of these matches were drawn. With five games left, I constantly told everyone that ten points were required for safety. They actually earned eleven; a racing certainty to escape?

A crowd of 21,884 turned up at Ewood and cheered a 1-0 win over an automatic promotion chasing Aston Villa and then on a game televised live on the final day of the season, we sat in a local pub and watched them play out of their skins to win 3-1 at Brentford. It should have been celebration time, but we all remained seated, heads bowed in total silence, mourning the fact that relegation rivals Birmingham City and Notts Forest had both won their final game. Relegation with fifty-one points is rare, but go down they did.

The Rovers under Mowbray had garnered twenty-two points from fourteen games, decent mid-table form, but the poor start and the once in a generation vagary of the league table (Charlton had finished twenty-second with forty points the previous season) combined to relegate them to the third tier for the first time since 1979. Danny Graham, often left isolated up front, was leading scorer and the young Darragh Lenihan made the break through at centre back. Division 1 would not necessarily be easy next year, but Mowbray's valiant performance which had almost produced a miracle, gave hope and anticipation to the fans.

The draw for the sponsorship-less Football League Cup sent them to Field Mill at Mansfield in Round 1 where they sauntered through 3-1. A home draw in Round 2 paired them with Division 2 Crewe Alexandra in Blackburn. It was a humdinger of an encounter, 3-3 before Shane Duffy notched the winner in extra-time. It was an away trip to Leeds United in Round 3 but that was the end of the run as the Yorkshire side edged it 1-0. An away day in London was on the agenda in Round 3 of the FA Cup and Liam Feeney clinched the tie with the winning goal, Queens Park Rangers losing 2-1. Round 4 gave the Rovers the chance to welcome back Gary Bowyer and his Division 2 Blackpool side and the home side was able to demonstrate the gulf between the respective divisions with a comfortable 2-0 victory. There is nothing more thrilling in the game than a mouth-watering cup-tie against the very best opposition and on your own patch. It was Jose Mourinho and his Manchester United and 23,130 turned up to witness the spectacle. It was actually destined to be Owen Coyle's last game in charge, but his players certainly did not let him down.

In the seventeenth minute, Danny Graham finished off an excellent move and although Marcus Rashford equalised before half-time, the home side continued to battle after the break. But undeniable class, like cream, usually rises to the surface and Jose made a double substitution, bringing on Paul Pogba and Zlatan Ibrahimovic. Within minutes, the French midfield player hit a thirty five yard pass of such exquisite pace and accuracy which was instantly controlled by the Swede who, shifting to his right, lashed the ball past Steele. It was a moment of sheer quality and it won the game for the Old Trafford side.

To prevent Burnley FC from being tagged serial one year wonders, Sean Dyche had to find a way to keep the club in the Premier League at the end of the term. This meant obtaining a final total of forty points, as the so called experts like myself were saying. July 1st is always the date when clubs say goodbye to a number of players and Joey Barton had made a major contribution to Burnley's promotion charge but his one year contract had terminated and he chose to join Rangers in Scotland. Michael Duff called it a day at the grand old age of thirty-eight. He had played at Turf Moor for twelve seasons, compiling 342 games at either right back or centre half. Never a star but always totally dependable, this Northern Ireland international could be held up anywhere as a role model.

Dave Jones was another who would battle all day in the trenches and his 124 first team appearances helped the club through two promotion pushes before being signed by Sheffield Wednesday. To replace these three and to make the squad more Premier League competitive, Sean Dyche signed the Icelandic right winger Jóhann Berg Guðmundsson from Charlton Athletic. He had helped his country to knock England out of Euro 16. Two midfield players, Republic of Ireland's Jeff Hendrick, imported from Derby County and Belgian international Stephen Defour from Anderlecht cost a total outlay of £21million.

A surprise 2-0 win over Liverpool in the second game of the season, Vokes and Gray both scoring, gave a false impression about the next nine months and very quickly, the Turf Moor faithful knew they were in for another war of attrition. There were three comprehensive defeats on the road in the first third of the season at Chelsea, Leicester City and West Brom, but they held firm in mid-table with Vokes scoring four times. After a worrying run of five defeats in six, the defence began to tighten up and when both Middlesbrough and Sunderland were beaten at Turf Moor, the message was ringing out loud and clear. Be sure of winning the games against the weaker opposition and try your damnedest to pick up any scraps against the big boys. An Andre Gray hat-trick against Sunderland certainly helped and midfield player Ashley Westwood and left winger Robbie Brady, both with Premier League experience at Aston Villa and Norwich City, joined the Clarets on January 31st for £5million and £13 million respectively.

But February and March made the fans shiver, the loss of form rather than the weather as they collected a mere three points from seven games and with four to play, they were still four short of the mythical forty points. But they won at Crystal Palace, and when Sam Vokes scored twice to give them a 2-2 draw at home to West Brom, they were safe with two to play. Sixteenth was always going to be about par for the course and there were huge celebrations, as it would be their first stay at the top for more than one campaign since relegation in 1976. Dyche had been unable to keep the same settled side this year, apart from the back five where titanic performances from Heaton, Lowton, Keane, Mee and Ward kept the ship afloat. They say that promotion is hard but staying up even harder, but Sean Dyche was proving to be the master at breaking hoo-doos. He had already won derby games and kept the Clarets up. Next on the agenda would be to better the Jimmy Adamson side's three successive years in the top flight from 1973 to 1976. Could he start this potential "run" by repeating the trick next season?

Unfortunately Sean Dyche's cup record is bleak in comparison. This season proved to be no exception, two-fold embarrassment tumbling on top of the club. Entering the Football League Cup at the second round stage, the Burnley fans reacted with amusement at the draw. An away tie at Accrington Stanley would surely end up with a free pass into Round 3. It turned out to be nothing of the sort, principally because the manager virtually selected a second eleven. For the Stanley, this was their cup final at their own Crown Ground. It was extremely close and it seemed that a goal would never arrive. When it finally did, it was in the 120th minute, scored by Accrington's Matty Pearson. Lessons had to be learnt in the FA Cup and for a while, it appeared that they had. They eventually knocked out Sunderland in a replay at home. In Round 4 it was another 2-0 home win against the Championship's Bristol City and it was beginning to look promising with a 5th Round home tie against Lincoln City from the National League (ex-Conference). There were bearers of doom and gloom amongst some fans, reminding the younger ones of a similar scenario against Wimbledon which ended in tears, but this was laughed off and scarcely anyone commented on the fact that this one time Football League club opposing them was running away with their league. Burnley had the majority of the play but created little and as the clock ticked by, the Imps became more adventurous as frustration grew in the Clarets' ranks. It still came as a shock when the visitors scored in the eighty-ninth minute, a goal not without controversy as Heaton and co questioned whether the ball had crossed the line. But it did count and Lincoln City became the first non-league side to reach the last eight since Queens Park Rangers in 1914.

2017-18

	Pos	Played	Won	Drawn	Lost	GF	GA	Pts
Burnley	7	38	14	12	12	36	39	54
Blackburn Rovers	2	46	28	12	6	82	40	96

Blackburn Rovers		Burnley	
Most Appearances	Richie Smallwood 46	Most Appearances	Jack Cork 38
Most Goals	Bradley Dack 18	Most Goals	Chris Wood 10

There was now a two division gap between Burnley and Blackburn Rovers. This is the first time it had occurred since the 1998-99 season when the Rovers were in the Premier League and Burnley down in Tier 3, the old Division 2. The last time the Clarets held a two division margin over their neighbours was in the 1974-75 campaign when Jimmy Adamson's side tangled regularly with the country's elite. Sean Dyche, of course, had no control over what Tony Mowbray may or may not achieve; his mind was totally concentrated on a minimum of survival and perhaps a little bit more.

Burnley bade farewell to five influential players, two for big money. Andre Gray had scored thirty two times for the club in seventy-three games, Watford paying £18.5million for his services. Even more money was collected when Michael Keane moved to Everton, the "Toffees" handing over £25million. The English international centre-back had formed part of the backbone of this robust Clarets side and counting a previous loan spell, had made exactly 100 appearances for the Turf Moor club. Tendayi Darikwa signed for Nottingham Forest, George Boyd, having clocked up 115 starts and twelve goals from midfield, was released to Sheffield Wednesday, as was Michael Kightly to Southend United.

The clubs careful husbandry continued when the manager was allowed to spend 75% of the incoming amount. Charlie Taylor, the talented Leeds United left back moved across the Pennines for a fee decided by a tribunal, said to be around £6.5million. Jonathan Walters, a veteran striker signed from Stoke City for £3million and Jack Cork, whose father was a member of Wimbledon's "crazy gang and who had already made over fifty appearances for the Clarets when a youngster on loan from Chelsea, signed permanently from Swansea City for £8million. Phil Bardsley, an experienced right back, also arrived from Stoke and Dyche raided Elland Road for a second time, this time taking Kiwi international striker Chris Wood for a record £15million. Another striker, another £5million, was paid to Huddersfield Town for Nakhi Wells, concluding the spending spree which netted a profit of £10.75million.

One defeat in their first eight games was a start beyond the wildest dreams of the fans. The first game had been a match to remember, 3-0 up at Stamford Bridge against the previous champions Chelsea at half-time (Vokes scoring twice) and then hanging on for a 3-2 win. A 3-0 loss at Manchester City (everyone seemed to lose at the Etihad) was followed by three successive wins and there were whispers about participation in European competitions circulating in the town. For once, there were wins on the road, at Everton, Southampton and AFC Bournemouth. But football has always been a game of fine margins and from the pre-Christmas week to beyond St Valentine's Day, a win was off the table. The walls were crumbling at fortress Turf Moor as Tottenham Hotspur, Manchester United and Liverpool all returned home victorious.

The top six were galloping ahead but the rest could make no inroads into Burnley's entrenched position. Ashley Barnes had replaced a mis-firing Vokes as partner to Wood and the vastly experienced Aaron Lennon was signed for £1.5million from Everton to give some width to the attack. Five delicious and successive wins appeared as if from nowhere yet still the Clarets stayed seventh and even a dreadful late run, where two points were obtained from the last five games, still had no effect on the league position as they finished in the same position.

The defence had held up all season, conceding just thirty-nine goals in spite of Heaton's serious injury after four games. Nick Pope, bought for £1million from Charlton Athletic ostensibly to warm the bench, made it a seamless transition to the extent that he went to Russia in the twenty-three man England World Cup squad the following summer.

Similarly James Tarkowski, signed from Brentford, stepped up to replace Keane and made the shirt his own. Buy them cheap, buy them early and develop them had been the mantra of Shankly and Paisley at Anfield in the glory years. Dyche was going down exactly the same road here and so successfully. The big problem in the club was a lack of goals. Thirty-six in thirty-eight games would normally have been relegation form, the least scored since the 1902-03 season apart from the abysmal showing when last relegated three years before. Once again it had been difficult for the manager to select a settled side, but the seventh place finish was the best since 1973-74.

Thinking back forty-four years, there is no doubt that the Lord, Potts and to a lesser extent Adamson days had created a dynasty, since when the club wandered without direction, lost in a maze. Older, fanatical supporters dragged themselves to the far outposts of the land, standing to watch their favourites play at outdated grounds in Torquay, Aldershot, Scarborough, Hereford, Halifax and Darlington and surviving on a half time cup of Bovril and some type of local pie at clubs no longer in the Football League.

Now they had to become accustomed to visiting magnificent stadia, sitting in comfortable seats with alcohol and non-alcohol beverages on tap plus a choice of food at the interval, piped pre-match music and instant replays on giant screens. Were chairman Mike Garlick and Sean Dyche about to set off down the same path that Lord and Potts took in the late fifties?

The Carabao Football League Cup second round offered them the opportunity to turn the screw a little more on their neighbours, one they took with an easy 2-0 victory at Blackburn. The Championship side Leeds United, no longer a fearsome foe, came to Turf Moor in Round 3 but caused something of an upset, winning 1-0. Manchester City away was a must to avoid in the FA Cup 3rd Round but no luck for Dyche's boys, the result being Sky Blues 4 Clarets 1. The cup competitions were proving an achilles heel for the Burnley club, the last quarter final in the League Cup, apart from in 2012, was in 1983 and the last in the FA Cup in 2003. But this is now a Premier League club and they should be doing better.

It is a different world playing three divisions down. Firstly the opposition lacks the quality of the Championship, secondly entry to the two major cup competitions is always at Round 1 and thirdly, you are forced to play in the EFL Trophy, a sort of Micky Mouse competition for the bottom two leagues plus

Development squads from some of the clubs in the Premier League and the Championship. There were the usual comings and goings during the summer as Tony Mowbray rid Blackburn Rovers of what he considered to be dead wood, replacing them with players fit for purpose to support the immediate assault back into the Championship. Jason Steele left for Sunderland, having kept goal in 113 games over a two and half year period.

An excellent shot stopper, he was often criticised for his poor distribution. Connor Mahoney, an exciting young winger, was released to AFC Bournemouth for a fee of £425,000 as agreed by a tribunal. The other outgoing players all left on free transfers. They included Hope Akpan (60 appearances) to Burton Albion, Danny Guthrie to Mitra Kukar in Indonesia, Welsh international Adam Henley (80 starts) to Real Salt Lake and surprisingly, Jason Lowe to Birmingham City. He had made 173 appearances and was admired by the fans for his whole-hearted effort for the full ninety minutes. The manager made four key signings. Bradley Dack, a goal scoring midfielder, was bought from Gillingham for £750,000, the veteran Peter Whittingham arrived from Cardiff City to add class and experience to midfield, Richie Smallwood, a ball winning midfield player, also arrived from Rotherham United and Dominic Samuel, a striker with great potential, from Reading. Mowbray also used the loan system to strengthen his squad, three being signed on season-long deals. They were Paul Downing, a centre half from MK Dons, Harry Chapman, a winger from Middlesbrough and Marcus Antonsson, a striker from Leeds United.

The squad ought to have been sufficient to take the league by storm. Not one of their opponents had the pedigree of Blackburn Rovers, but the start was mundane mid-table form when it ought to have been electrifying. But after a 3-0 home win over Portsmouth on October 21st, the whole picture changed. Sixteen games later, they finally lost again, 2-0 at Plymouth Argyle on February 4th. As they kept pace with the early pacesetters Wigan Athletic and Shrewsbury Town. Bradley Dack was beginning to knock in the goals, as was centre back Charlie Mulgrew, a dead ball specialist. A 1-1 draw at Shrewsbury kept the brakes on the Shropshire side and Danny Graham was once more finding the net with a double in a 3-1 win over Walsall. Downing's loan from MK Dons was made permanent and Amari'i Bell, a talented left back was signed from Fleetwood Town in the January window. Adam Armstrong, a young striker, had arrived on loan from Newcastle United, and with power and pace to burn up front, they put together another fourteen game unbeaten run. With spring in the air, they played out a thrilling 2-2 draw with Wigan, the Latics coming back from two down to snatch a deserved point. By this stage, the Rovers were topping the table and promotion a certainty, it was a race to the line with Wigan. But unfortunately they had to settle for the runner-up spot. But it was back to the Championship after one year, emulating the feat of Howard Kendall's side in 1980. Bradley Dack was the undoubted player of the season and David Raya, the young Spanish goalkeeper who had come through the ranks made the keeper's jersey his own. Having failed to keep them up at the death last season following a heroic effort, it was good to see Tony Mowbray rewarded in such emphatic fashion.

The Blackburn Rovers side promoted as runners-up from Division 1 side in 2017-18 (played over 18 games, max 46) was; David Raya, Ryan Nyambe, Derrick Williams, Charlie Mulgrew, Paul Downing, Richie Smallwood, Bradley Dack, Corry Evans, Elliott Bennett, Craig Conway, Dominic Samuel, Danny Graham, Marcus Antonsson.

Blackburn Rovers were quickly into action in the Carabao Football League Cup, winning 3-1 at Coventry City with two from Samuel. Any hopes of further progress were then quashed by Burnley in Round 2. It had been thirty eight years since the Rovers had been forced to enter the FA Cup in Round 1 and Barnet, plus the abject Ewood gate of 3,710, somehow combined to reflect this fall from grace. The Crewe Alexandra Round 2 game was as crazy as it comes. The Cheshire side was simply useless early doors and the Blue and Whites led 3-0 after twenty minutes. Could it be a record score? Any thoughts of that however flew out of the window when Rakeem Harper, on loan from West Brom, and Bennett were both sent off either side of half time.

The last forty minutes saw an Alamo style siege as Crewe gradually reduced the deficit and there were gasps of relief all round as the game finished 3-3. Mowbray's side sneaked through courtesy of another Danny Graham goal in the replay and it was another home draw. Premier League Hull City were the Third Round visitors and after an even game, they progressed to the last thirty-two after a 1-0 victory.

The Football League Cup Derby

There was something odd about a derby match in August, but 16,313 abandoned their barbecues in favour of this Carabao League Cup tussle. What the fans of each club ought to have being doing was linking arms and sipping champagne together, but there was no evidence of that in what was the 100th meeting between the sides in official competition; a century of derby games. It had taken almost 129 years, or 119 seasons subtracting the years when the wars intervened. The Turf Moor side was the heavy favourite, particularly as the Blue and Whites had won just one of their three opening league games whereas the Clarets had won at Chelsea on the opening day of the campaign. As ever in a derby match, the atmosphere was electric and the five thousand plus Burnley fans had come to enjoy the party. The Rovers made the early running, but the gulf in quality (and transfer fees paid) soon began to show.

It was two recent arrivals at Turf Moor with a combined value of £23million who did all the damage. Robbie Brady sent over an inviting cross in the twenty-seventh minute and the head of Jack Cork obliged. Sean Dyche's men then proceeded to batter the home defence and in the run up to half-time, Cork sent Brady clear and the winger smashed home from an acute angle. To add insult to injury, Burnley introduced their new £15million man Chris Wood,

Burnley fans celebrating during the 2017 League Cup game at Ewood

whilst Dominic Samuel, a £0.5million purchase came on for the home side. The second-half was closer as Burnley tended to sit on their lead, but the Blackburn side never gave up. Mulgrew twice threatened with his wicked free-kicks and Samuel actually had the ball in the net but it was ruled off-side.

At the other end, Raya had made two sensational saves from Wood and Arfield and the Premier League side was the comfortable winner after ninety minutes of this Centenary match. It was the first League Cup encounter between the sides after close to sixty years of the competition and it added further evidence to what fans from both sides already knew; Burnley were in total ascendancy in East Lancashire.

Date	Round	Home Side	Away Side	Score	Scorers
23 08 2017	2	Blackburn Rovers	**Burnley**	0-2	J Cork, R Brady.

2018-19

	Pos	Played	Won	Drawn	Lost	GF	GA	Pts
Burnley	15	38	11	7	20	45	68	40
Blackburn Rovers	15	46	16	12	18	64	69	60

Blackburn Rovers		Burnley	
Most Appearances	David Raya 41	Most Appearances	Ben Mee 38
Most Goals	Bradley Dack, Danny Graham (both 15)	Most Goals	Ashley Barnes 12

The consolation for Blackburn Rovers was there was now only a one division gap to their rivals but at Burnley, all the talk centred on Europe. The Clarets had qualified for the Europa League, the latest version of the UEFA Cup. This meant an incredibly early start to the season because they entered the competition in the Second Qualifying Round and the date scheduled for the first leg was July 26th. It was their first European engagement since the 1966-67 season.

Two of Burnley's well established midfield players left in the summer, both on free transfers. Scott Arfield's contract had ended and he joined Rangers, having made 177 appearances and scored twenty-one goals at Turf Moor. Dean Marney had been signed way back in Brian Law's time. He started 202 games and joined Fleetwood Town.

There were three incoming signings who would challenge for first team places. Sean Dyche desperately needed a fit goalkeeper following long term injuries to Heaton and Pope and he managed to sign Joe Hart, one time England number one, from Manchester City for £3.5million. The other two were, by Burnley standards, extremely expensive purchases. Ben Gibson, a highly rated centre back arrived from Middlesbrough for £15million and Czech international Matej Vydra from Derby County for £11 million.

In one respect, playing in a European competition was such an achievement for this small town club, but it almost ruined their season. The players were given a much shorter summer break and their first game was way up north in Aberdeen. The "Granite City" club is generally ranked at number three in Scotland, but a late Sam Vokes goal gave the Clarets a 1-1 draw to take back to Lancashire for the second leg. It was another close encounter, the scores being level at 1-1 after ninety minutes, but extra-time goals from Cork and Barnes earned them a place in the Third Qualifying Round at Basaksehir in Istanbul. This was even closer, a goalless first leg and then a Cork strike in extra time in Burnley, the only goal of the two legs, sent the 16,583 crowd home happy.

A win over the Greek club Olympiacos would have earned them a place in the Europa League group stage, but it was not to be. A Chris Wood penalty was the only consolation from a 3-1 reverse in the first leg and Vydra's equalising goal at Turf Moor was too little and far too late, the Greeks going through 4-2. It had been an experience for the East Lancashire club, but it took its toll physically on the players and Dyche had to mix and match his team selection with it running alongside the Premier League fixtures from the Basaksehir away game onwards.

The start to the league season was a disaster, gaining just one point from the first five fixtures and the Clarets were propping up the other nineteen clubs. It was taking an eternity for their bodies to recover from the travel as much as the exertions of playing, and although they won their next two, a whole avalanche of defeats followed. They were struggling, especially against the attack-minded top clubs and six times they were clobbered.

Although Huddersfield Town were beginning to be tailed off, at eighteenth, the Clarets were definitely in the mix for the drop. Tom Heaton had regained full fitness and he replaced Hart after the Everton debacle on Boxing Day and then, possibly because they had eventually rid themselves of the extra trauma of the European distraction, they commenced a run of eight games without defeat.

Wood scored six times and Barnes four in this period, five wins and three draws and a mid-table place brought so much relief. A 2-2 draw at Old Trafford and a 2-1 home win over Tottenham Hotspur were the highlights, and during this run, Sam Vokes was sold to Stoke City for £9million. The Welsh international had started 238 games and scored fifty-eight goals, placing him amongst the top thirty scorers ever to represent the Burnley club. They dangled in seventeenth place; still only thirty points on the board. But in a season full of "swings and roundabouts", three successive wins, including a double from Chris Wood in a 2-0 win at the "Turf" over Cardiff City, their nearest rival, moved them to the cusp of safety. A week later on Easter Monday, a 2-2 draw at Chelsea, (Hendrick and Barnes amongst the goals) took them to the magical forty points mark and safety was assured with three to play.

A fifteenth place finish was quite admirable, considering they played forty-seven fixtures and Sean Dyche's side had now retained their position amongst the aristocrats of English football for three seasons and counting. Ever since the arrival of Sean Dyche, no opposition club, even the best in the land, had ever relished the trip to Turf Moor. The main reason has been the strength and toughness of the defensive line and paramount to this has been Ben Mee. Making his breakthrough from the Academy at Gawthorpe was winger Dwight McNeill who started nineteen games.

It had been a difficult campaign and the manager, coaches and players all deserved credit for keeping their heads and continuing to be motivated until safety was assured. It is an honour to play in Europe, but if you qualify in seventh place as the last counter, one has to doubt whether the advantages of sneaking in as Burnley did, outweigh the disadvantages of travel, of a shorter break and an overload of games.

Because of Europa League commitments, Burnley entered the Carabao Football League Cup at Round 3. The away tie at Division 1 Burton Albion represented a golden opportunity to make progress, but Dyche, probably because of squad fatigue, again picked a weaker side and to no-one's surprise, they lost 2-1. The FA Cup did at least provide them with a win. Barnsley were beaten 1-0 in Round 3, but for the second consecutive season, they were drawn away to Manchester City. It was an even worse result this time, losing 5-0. City were an outstanding outfit, once again the best team in the land and the Clarets were undone by the fickleness of the draw.

Blackburn Rovers now had the opportunity to push on and make their presence felt in the Championship. With no money coming in from transfers, the only acknowledged out-going was £1.75 million to Newcastle United to make the Adam Armstrong deal permanent. Joe Rothwell arrived for "an undisclosed fee", an attacking midfield player from Oxford United. Peter Whittingham had retired at the end of the previous season and Mowbray was forced to use loanees, including the once highly touted Jack Rodwell from Sunderland plus midfield players Kasey Palmer from Chelsea, and Harrison Reed from Southampton, both on full season loans. Ben Brereton, a young striker came from Notts Forest until Christmas. This was not the transfer market to whet the appetite of fans and the feeling was that safety was the number one objective.

There was a good start even if the following forty-seven games would prove to be insipid. After wins at Hull City and at home to Brentford, the league position after five games was fifth. Then once again, inconsistency ruled, victories over Stoke and Leeds, but Bristol City knocked four past them and Sheffield United won comfortably in Blackburn. Consecutive defeats to local rivals were upsetting, 4-1 at Preston, 3-1 at Wigan, but Graham smashed home a hat-trick to bring down Sheffield Wednesday in an Ewood Park thriller. Ben Brereton finally put pen to paper on a permanent deal costing around £7million, but the manager was loathe to start with him, coming off the bench twenty-one times but scoring just once; not what is expected of a number nine.

Fifteenth place at Christmas was depressing but if their new year's resolution was to start winning matches, it certainly came true. Four wins on the bounce lifted them to eighth and the talk was of Play-Offs. Seven games later, the question was "are we going down"? The PNE game attracted a gate of 21,577 and the majority trudged home disappointed after losing 1-0. With relegation still an issue, Mowbray somehow was able to find a system, provide the motivation and it all looked so easy as four successive wins saw them roar past the fifty point barrier. Ultimately fifteenth place and a total of sixty-one points was safe and secure.

Bradley Dack had proved to be a special player at this level, operating mainly in the number ten role whilst Danny Graham is an old school number nine; the type whom defenders must hate playing against as he physically terrorises relentlessly. Corry Evans has long been a mainstay of the Northern Ireland side and has now passed the forty mark in terms of international caps gained during a stay at Ewood Park. So with the return journey to the Championship accomplished and safeguarded, the progress next term had to be upwards.

The Carabao Football League Cup started well for Blackburn Rovers with big wins against lowly Carlisle United (5-1) and Lincoln City (4-1). A trip to AFC Bournemouth then produced an exciting encounter as the Rovers pulled back a two goal deficit, only to go down 3-2, thwarted by the winner four minutes into time added on. The draw for the Third Round of the FA Cup sent them to Newcastle United and they nearly came back with a win, Dack putting them in front only for a late penalty to force a replay. This was a thrilling affair with four goals by half-time. The second half was goalless and the final two goals arrived in extra-time, sadly both scored by Newcastle players to send them through to Round 4.

2019-20

	Pos	Played	Won	Drawn	Lost	GF	GA	Pts
Burnley	10	38	15	9	14	43	50	54
Blackburn Rovers	11	46	17	12	17	66	63	63

Blackburn Rovers		Burnley	
Most Appearances	Christian Walton 46	Most Appearances	Nick Pope, James Tarkowski 38
Most Goals	Adam Armstrong 16	Most Goals	Chris Wood 14

The Premier League season started on 9 August 2019 and concluded on 26 July 2020. The Championship season was even longer, commencing on 2 August 2019 and ending 368 days later on completion of the Play-Off final at Wembley Stadium, although the final Blackburn Rovers game took place 13 days earlier. In the history of professional football in this country dating back to 1888, no season has progressed for such a length of time and the cause, which has continued to rampage across the world, is now correctly titled Covid 19.

Initially it was referred to as Coronavirus, the collective name for a series of similar viruses. The season was suspended on 13 March and re-started on Saturday 20 June. This is only the second time that Football League fixtures have been suspended, the previous one being in early September 1939 on the outbreak of World War 2. Inevitably that suspension quickly became an abandonment and the game did not resume until 1946.

After the initial outbreak kicked off in the south-east of England, it was the North West which next bore the brunt of this lethal epidemic. The Government regularly updated us with statistics and a top ten of most affected Boroughs regularly featured both Blackburn with Darwen and Burnley. It was no surprise that this part of Lancashire was particularly susceptible to what has become a Pandemic. Poorer areas are generally less immune to disease across the world and there is no doubt that this, compared with much of England, is a poor area. Once heavily industrialised and consequently offering decently paid work to all of its adults, the decline in the cotton industry and the later closing down of coal mines prompted a slump, one that the area has since struggled to escape from. We quickly understood that this virus was completely impartial, attacking indiscriminately without fear or favour and to some extent, irrespective of age, gender, race and even vulnerability.

Generally the population followed the strict Government Guide Lines, staying indoors, working from home wherever possible. Our social lives were reduced to watching TV and Blackburn and Burnley became ghost towns as all forms of entertainment closed down. This included football and for over three months, none was played. As the threat from the virus appeared to be receding, the game started up again with the clubs following a strict protocol. By cramming in fixtures twice a week, the season was completed, although fans were banned from stadia. The only consolation was that every game was televised on one platform or another and strange as it was to watch games without spectators in settings totally devoid of atmosphere, we were at least able to follow our favourites.

Sean Dyche's Burnley commenced their fourth consecutive season in the Premier League, their best performance since the marathon 24 season stint which ended in 1971. As usual, it was a case of the budget dictating any new signings but to the delight of the fans, £10million clinched the return of local boy Jay Rodriguez from West Brom via Southampton. A proven goal scorer at the highest level, he had also gained an England cap against Chile. The experienced left-sided defender/midfield player Eric Pieters joined from Stoke City with Republic of Ireland international left back Stephen Ward moving in the opposite direction. Such was the faith that the boss had in Nick Pope that he sold international goalkeeper Tom Heaton (188 appearances) to Aston Villa for £8million. He had been so instrumental in the Clarets' rise to the Premier League and to them remaining there. He was also still at the top of his game.

To add cover between the sticks, Northern Ireland international Bailey Peacock-Farrell joined from Leeds United for £2.5million. Belgian international Steven Defour was released from his contract following a series of injuries, moving home to Royal Antwerp and Bermudan international Nakhi Wells, who had disappointed since his £5million transfer from Huddersfield Town 30 months before, was sold to Bristol City.

Two of Burnley's three previous Premier League campaigns had been a struggle from start to finish, but this was more like a stroll in the park. Twice they held fifth spot and for two weeks at the turn of the year, they slipped down to fifteenth, but they occupied a top half position for more than half of the season, eventually settling in tenth place, indicative of being an established Top Tier club.

An Ashley Barnes double gave them a flying start in a 3-0 home win over Southampton but five points from the first five games was worrying. Home wins over Norwich City, Everton and West Ham United however enabled them to end November in eighth spot. A four game loss over the Christmas period dropped them to fifteenth, but a seven game unbeaten run took them back into the top half before the suspension arrived in March. By this time, Josh Brownhill had arrived from Bristol City for a substantial but undisclosed amount of money. This midfield player had consistently performed well in the Championship. The Kiwi Chris Wood had been amongst the goals and he and Rodriguez both netted in a memorable 2-0 victory at Old Trafford.

On the resumption, a 5-0 thrashing at the home of Manchester City was a most definite wake-up call because another seven game unbeaten run, which included a Rodriguez goal in a stirring 1-1 draw at Anfield against the runaway Premier League champion, ended the campaign in style. With more wins than defeats, there was a feeling around Turf Moor that the club now deserved to be thought of in terms of Premier League stalwarts and fast approaching was a minor milestone; a fifth consecutive season in the top flight.

Another landmark was reached at the end of the campaign. Ben Mee reached the 300 mark in terms of league games played for the club, being the 22nd Claret to achieve this feat, tying with the fifties left winger, Brian Pilkington. As had become something of a trend, their cup results were disappointing. Their performance in the Carabao (Football League) Cup was quite pitiful, losing 3-1 to Division 1 Sunderland first time up in front of just over 7,000 at Turf Moor in late August. In the FA version, a Rodriguez double gave them a comfortable 4-2 win over Peterborough United in Round 3 before they succumbed to a 2-1 home defeat to bottom of the table Norwich City.

Having finished as low as 15th in their first season back in the Championship, Blackburn Rovers knew that they had to make more of an impact in this so competitive of a league. Tony Mowbray lost goalkeeper David Raya to Brentford for an undisclosed fee. The young and talented Spaniard had been nurtured through the youth set up and had played 108 times for the first team. Craig Conway, the veteran Scottish international winger had given his all to the cause at Ewood for five and a half seasons, scoring 19 times in 178 games and he moved to English Football's newest club, Salford City.

Charlie Mulgrew moved to Wigan Athletic on loan and to plug the gaps, the manager initially brought in two loanees. The experienced Christian Walton, who would start every league game, arrived from Brighton and Hove Albion and Tosin Adaraboyo, an exceptionally talented and young centre back joined from Manchester City, both being for a one year duration. Sam Gallacher who had been in Blackburn on loan a couple of seasons before was signed from Southampton for around £6million and two extremely experienced out of contract midfield players were brought into the squad; the much capped Stewart Downing from Middlesbrough and Bradley Johnson from Derby County. Finally in September, Lewis Holtby, a German international forward signed on a free transfer from Hamburger SV in the German Bundesliga.

The start was so typical of the team, win some, lose some over the first eight games where Bradley Dack was on target three times. A scary run of six games where they conceded 13 goals produced just two points, including a 3-2 defeat at Preston where they were two up within ten minutes. Fears of relegation were immediately quashed when one loss and one draw in the next eight followed as they flew up the table. Dack and Armstrong were finding the net but two drawn home games over the Christmas period brought bad news. Dack, having already scored nine times, injured his anterior cruciate ligament against Wigan Athletic which ruled him out for the season and probably more and Corry Evans suffered severe head injuries against Birmingham city, ruling him out for months.

Strong man Darragh Lenihan and the fleet of foot Adaraboyo had gelled well in the centre of defence and Ryan Nyambe at right back, Stewart Downing, Lewis Travis in midfield and Armstrong started regularly. The next ten games brought just one defeat to the talented Fulham side which would be promoted and when the government called a halt in early March, the upward momentum had offered hope of a Play-Off spot. The highlight of this period was a 5-0 win at Sheffield Wednesday, Holtby twice making the score sheet.

But after the break, the results were frankly disappointing. With nine to play, anything was possible, but six defeats and three wins was more like relegation form and two of the defeats were at Luton and Barnsley, both sides in the bottom three at the time. Armstrong had continued to bang in the goals but Dack was certainly missed as they just crept into the top half of the league, seven points short of the Play-Offs. Progress in the cup competitions was also limited. They were fortunate to eliminate a poor Oldham Athletic side in the 1st Round of the League Cup, coming from two down and scoring twice in time added on to squeeze through 3-2. Round 2 was a difficult draw and they went down 2-1 at Sheffield United, one of the better Premier League outfits this season. The FA Cup sent them to the Midlands in Round 3 where they performed listlessly in losing 2-1 to a less than talented Birmingham City from the Championship.

2020-21

	Pos	P	W	D	L	GF	GA	Pts
Burnley	**17**	**38**	**10**	**9**	**19**	**33**	**55**	**39**
Blackburn Rovers	15	46	15	12	19	65	54	57

	Blackburn Rovers	Burnley
Most Appearances	Thomas Kaminski 43	Ashley Westwood 38
Most Goals	Adam Armstrong 28	Chris Wood 12

With the previous campaign ending at the end of June, the new Premier League season did not kick-off until September 20. For Blackburn Rovers however, playing yet again in the Championship, it was a September 12 start. But because their name was in the 1st Round draw for the Football League Cup, action commenced on August 29, offering scarcely a month's break for their truncated summer holiday. The 2019-20 campaign had concluded in spectator free stadia and with Covid 19 continuing to spread, this season was played almost exclusively at empty grounds. This was the Turf Moor club's 58th season in total in the top division. There was kudos also for Sean Dyche who became the Premier League's longest current serving manager.

For the Ewood Park outfit, it was the 50th season that the club had competed away from the bright lights of Tier 1 football. It was Tony Mowbray's third Championship term in charge in East Lancashire (his fourth in all) and such is the rate of managers losing their jobs in this Division, he featured at third on the Championship managers' longevity chart. It is this stability at the managerial helm which can help clubs such as the Clarets and Rovers to weather the storms and compete against far wealthier rivals.

We need to make such an important point at this juncture. This was the Clarets' fifth consecutive season in the top strata and anyone predicting that following their promotion in 2016, would have been a candidate to be sectioned under the Mental Health Act. Burnley is a small town club with such a relatively low budget. How has Sean Dyche achieved this miracle? Yet again, the chains were tightly fastened round the club's money chest and the only signing of note in September was the vastly experienced Brighton and Hove Albion midfield player, Dale Stephens. Going out of the door, all because their contracts were at an end, were Joe Hart, the ex-England goalkeeper to Tottenham Hotspur, Republic of Ireland regular Jeff Hendrick to Newcastle United and veteran winger Aaron Lennon to Kayserispor in Turkey.

The previous season had, by Burnley standards, been relatively stress free but this one was far more difficult. With just two points from the first seven games, relegation was very much on the cards. They had failed to score in four successive games, but suddenly there appeared a ray of hope when, apart from their annual thrashing at the Etihad by the Sky Blue money bags, four games without defeat, including a 1-0 win against the Arsenal in London, had lifted them above the relegation zone. Fortunately for the Burnley boys, Fulham, West Bromwich Albion and Sheffield United in particular, struggled to gain many points.

By the turn of the year, they had settled in 16th spot with breathing space below them and there were more outstanding performances to follow. The country was stunned when Liverpool's 68 game unbeaten home record was shattered, an Ashley Barnes late penalty proving the difference between the sides, although they had the heroics in goal by Nick Pope to thank for the clean sheet. They knocked in three at Selhurst Park against the "Palace" and it was their rock solid defending which was keeping them safe. From the end of February, the defence took on a more porous appearance and Spurs hit them for four at their new ground. Liverpool also took ample revenge with a 3-0 victory at the Turf but after a Chris Wood hat-trick in a 4-0 win at Molyneux, the home of the "Wolves", they were racing certainties to stay up once more. This was easily achieved, the margin being eleven points, although three final defeats removed the icing from the cake as they finished 17th.

Compared to recent years, there was some improvement in the cup competitions, reaching the last sixteen in both of them. In the Carabao League Cup, the Premier League strugglers Sheffield United drew 1-1 at Turf Moor, but lost 5-4 on penalties. A 2-0 win at Millwall in Round 3 gave them a home tie but against the worst of all opponents. And on the night, Manchester City were far superior once again, winning 3-0. At least Sean Dyche had put out a potentially competitive side, something he failed to do when they reached the same stage of the FA Cup. They had struggled past Milton Keynes Dons in Round 3, Matej Vydra scoring with the last kick of the 90 minutes to level the scores. It went to penalties after a further goalless thirty minutes, the Clarets eventually edging the penalty shoot-out 5-4. Two Jay Rodriguez goals gave them an outstanding 3-0 win at Fulham, hinting at the promise of further success against Championship side AFC Bournemouth in Round 5. But the manager picked a virtual reserve side and was rewarded with the result he deserved, a 2-0 defeat. The only first team regular to start was Dwight McNeil but to be fair to the manager, with Burnley's limited resources, he cannot possibly fight a campaign on more than one front. A long cup run would have the fans dancing in the streets, but Premier League survival each year has to be his first concern at all times.

Ben Mee, the current Burnley captain

If one wants to find common ground between these two East Lancashire enemies, one need look no further than finance. The Clarets may have been more successful in this area over the last dozen years, but the end product is somewhat similar; little to spend on incoming players. There have been hopes however that since the takeover by Velocity Sports Partners in December 2020, the sports arm of the American management firm ALK Capital, the company with Alan Pace recently appointed as Chairman of the club, will make a substantial difference, at least financially. What Bob Lord would have made of Americans in the Board Room makes for interesting conjecture, but we are in different times. It is a different world and perhaps sadly, clubs like Burnley have to follow the trend. For Tony Mowbray, it was a case of off-loading those surplus to requirements and generally picking up the best loanees around. It can work for the immediate future but with regard to long term planning, his job must be so difficult.

Sadly it was time to say goodbye to one of its favourite sons. Danny Graham returned to Sunderland in League 1, leaving a legacy of 45 goals but more importantly, the heartfelt thanks of thousands of supporters who had warmed to his battling qualities and his leadership of the front line. Dominic Samuel, who had failed to deliver on his undoubted potential and Richie Smallwood, one of the heroes of the 2018 League 1 promotion side, left for Gillingham and Hull City respectively. Two regular starters also inevitably returned to their parent club. Regular goalkeeper Christian Walton to Brighton and Hove Albion and the outstanding centre back Tosin Adarabioyo to Manchester City. To replace Walton, Thomas Kaminski, a member of Belgium's international squad, was signed from Gent for a substantial sum. Daniel Ayala, the experienced centre back from Middlesbrough was brought in to partner Lenihan at the heart of the defence and Tyrhys Dolan, a wizard on the ball but lacking any sort of 1st team experience, arrived from Preston North End. But it was one loanee that captured all of the headlines. Arriving from Liverpool at the age of just seventeen was Harvey Elliott and anyone who saw him knew that the midfield player was one heading for the very top tier of the game. He was joined by Tom Trybull from Norwich City and Barry Douglas, a left back from Leeds United. Both were on season-long loans and they helped to plug gaps in a much depleted squad.

It was a crazy season. There were times when the Play-Offs were a distinct possibility, times when the club appeared to be descending like a stone towards relegation, but fortunately the season was all about Adam Armstrong. Having lost narrowly at the newly relegated AFC Bournemouth in the season's opener, they crashed in five against Wycombe Wanderers, and four at both Derby County and Coventry City. After seven games, the Geordie striker had seven goals to his name. There was a memorable 3-0 win at Deepdale, young Dolan scoring against his former club and a battling draw at the very impressive Brentford, somehow surviving in spite of Lenihan being sent off in the 37th minute. This was the final game of a seven game unbeaten stretch but suddenly it was all downhill. Six defeats (all by one goal) plus a draw in seven took them close to the nether regions. Armstrong's goal output had stalled but there were problems at the heart of the defence. Ayala just could not shake off his injuries and Lenihan had so many different centre back partners. Bradley Dack finally returned over the Christmas period and just when he appeared to be rediscovering the form that had made him one of the most feared Championship number 10s, he tore his anterior cruciate ligament on his other leg and was out for another season. But yet another young loan player, Taylor Harwood-Bellis, came in from Manchester City and he forged an outstanding partnership with Lenihan and only four games were lost in the final thirteen. Elliott was always looking to be creative and Armstrong roared back to form with two hat-tricks, seven in his last three games. His final total of 28 league goals was the best return since Alan Shearer in 1996. In fact only he, McEvoy, Briggs and Harper are above Armstrong in the all-time seasonal chart. And just to put it into context this season, Sam Gallagher with eight and Elliott and Ben Bretherton with seven came next on the list.

So the Rovers eventually finished 15th and here is a real random stat. It was the thirteenth occasion that the club has finished in this position in either the old Division 1, the Premier League, the old Division 2 and the Championship, way more than in any other league position. But as for the cup competitions... forget them. Division 1 Doncaster Rovers are a club I once saw the Rovers crash seven past in the Christmas period of 1954, when Charlie Williams, later turned comedian whom many older readers will remember performing on TV, played at centre half. The Rovers managed to squeeze past them on this occasion in Round 1 of the League Cup at Ewood, but a first half goal saw them exit at Round 2 in Newcastle. The draw against Doncaster in Round 3 of the FA Cup was surely one they could win again, coming in the middle of a decent post festive run, but the South Yorkshire outfit bullied them out of the game; the result, an extremely disappointing 1-0 defeat.

2021-22

	Pos	P	W	D	L	GF	GA	Pts
Burnley	**18**	**38**	**7**	**14**	**17**	**34**	**53**	**35**
Blackburn Rovers	8	46	19	12	15	59	50	69

Blackburn Rovers		Burnley
Most Appearances	Lewis Travis 45	Nick Pope 36
Most Goals	Ben Brereton-Diaz 22	Maxwel Cornet 9

Burnley commenced the season, their sixth in succession at the top level of English football since winning promotion in 2016. Sean Dyche was still in control and he would pass the nine year mark in October. Ask anyone in the town how the Clarets had survived for so long in the Premier League and his name would be a racing certainty to exit their mouths. With a pub named after Dyche a couple of hundred yards from the ground, there is no doubt as to his standing in the folk lore of this industrial East Lancashire town. As usual, the fans were hoping for the "ride of their life, but would be satisfied once more with survival. There was some movement in the transfer market, although the new American owners ignored the calls for marquee signings. After four years of plying his trade down the left side of the attack, Robbie Brady was out of contract and he dropped a division to AFC Bournemouth. Permanent "sub" goalkeeper Bailey Peacock-Farrell, first choice in goal for Northern Ireland, was loaned to Sheffield Wednesday for the season, having no chance of dislodging Nick Pope from the number one spot. To replace him, Wayne Hennessey, a veteran multi capped Welshman, was brought in from Crystal Palace to keep the bench warm. Nathan Collins, a young defender with potential, was bought from Stoke City for an undisclosed fee, as was Welsh international right back, Connor Roberts, from Swansea City. Aaron Lennon, an extremely experienced winger returned to the club a year after his transfer to Kayserispor in Turkey, but the most exciting buy was when £15million was paid out to top French club Olympique Lyonnais for Maxwel Cornet, an Ivory Coast international wide player.

The start was demoralising, four draws and five defeats anchoring them in the bottom three. Cornet, however, was displaying his skills, three goals across a couple of 2-2 draws against Leicester City and Southampton and again in their first win, 3-1 at home to Brentford. There were seven draws in the next ten, but the elusive second win did not arrive until after St Valentine's Day, 3-0 at Brighton and Hove Albion. By this time, Kiwi international Chris Wood had signed for Newcastle United for £25million. His 49 league goals in 144 games in a Claret and Blue shirt was a very decent return at a club not overly blessed with the attacking options which, at some clubs, automatically create chance after chance for the front players. Dutch international striker, Wout Weghorst, who signed in January from VfL Wolfsburg in the German Bundesliga for £12million, was on target at Brighton. Shortly after, totally dependable defender Ben Mee suffered a serious injury, but fortunately Collins was able to step in alongside Tarkowski in a back line renowned nationally for its strength and durability.

Four straight defeats in March preceded the news that rocked the football world. Sean Dyche had been sacked! It was universally condemned, even though the Clarets were odds on favourites for the drop. On cue, enter the "new manager bounce". The ex-Preston North End and Blackpool player, Michael Jackson, now in charge of the Under 23 squad, was given the job on a temporary basis and they defeated Southampton, Wolverhampton Wanderers and Watford. With four to play and Leeds United in free fall, another escape was on the cards, but one point from two encounters with an underperforming Aston Villa, plus a predictable 1-0 defeat at Tottenham Hotspur, meant that only a home win in the Newcastle United game would definitely save them. Leeds won at Brentford and even though Nick Pope had performed heroics all season long, even he was unable to save them in front of a packed house at Turf Moor. They went down 2-1 to the Geordies and their adventure amongst the elite was at an end.

In the thirty years since the formation of the Premier League, the Turf Moor club have only been in membership for eight seasons. When they were relegated under Brian Laws' management in 2010, they gained only 30 points (35 this time), lost 24 games (17) and conceded 82 goals (53). In 2015, when Sean Dyche's side lasted just one term in the highest echelon, their seven wins equalled this current season's low total, but that eleven scored a meagre 28 goals (34). Thus there is statistical evidence that this particular campaign was definitely not the worst overall on record.

And talking of records, I cannot pass this point without paying homage to the man who, on pure statistics alone, is the third best amongst all 28 permanently appointed managers who have graced the hallowed "Turf". In terms of pure longevity, Sean Dyche was in charge at the club for 425 games and almost nine and a half years. Only John Haworth (464 games) and Harry Potts (605 + 123 across two stints) have totalled more, although attempting to compare anyone in any walk of life across generations, is a virtually impossible task. Both Haworth, active in the period either side of the Great War, and Potts, from the late 50s into the 70s, achieved more trophy wise, but a manager can only deal with what he has at his disposal. Haworth benefitted from a Board of Directors who paid out money to bring in star names such as Bert Freeman, Tommy Boyle, George Halley, Ernie Mosscrop and Joe Anderson. In Potts' time at the club, the production line of talented youngsters coming from the Gawthorpe training ground guaranteed a couple of generations of stars, costing nothing but a £10 signing-on fee. He had nurtured the talents of Pointer, Angus, Robson, Connelly, Miller and Harris and had bought Elder for "peanuts". In later years, he oversaw the progress of Lochhead, Hankin, O'Neill, James, Thomas, Coates, Morgan, Irvine and Kindon who were sold for top money to keep the club out of the red.

But by the time the former journeyman centre back arrived at Burnley in 2012, it was only the careful money management of Chairman Barry Kilby and his

Both Rovers and Burnley would be left searching got a new full time manager following an eventful 2021/22 season

Board that had kept the club afloat. With wealthy neighbours on Merseyside and in Manchester, plus just down the road in Blackburn, enticing all the young talent to their Academies, Sean had to resort to carefully recruiting players who could perform in trench-like conditions, competing initially against far wealthier Championship opposition and then meeting some of the world's most affluent clubs head to head. That he defied the odds each season to keep the Clarets in the Premier League and that Guardiola, Klopp, and which ever super star manager was currently residing at Old Trafford, White Hart Lane, the Emirates or Stamford Bridge, would regularly make guarded comments about their prospects when visiting Burnley, speaks volumes for the quality of Dyche's work. He constantly produced starting line-ups which would fight until the very last whistle. He may have been raised as an East Midlander, but it was his reliance on northern grit that worried the top teams. Both Haworth and Potts fully deserve their place in the pantheon of great Burnley managers, but although the only honours on Sean Dyche's CV relate to two promotions from the Championship, his achievements with threadbare squads surely have to be carefully measured against those of his more illustrious forefathers at Turf Moor.

Someone else responsible for their six year tenure in the Premier League was Ben Mee. He had been the rock on which the manager had built his side. Partnered initially by Northern Irish international Michael Duff, and in more recent times by James Tarkowski, he reached 351 league appearances for the Clarets.

Before departing for Brentford he sat in eleventh spot on the all-time table – 20 behind George Waterfield, the international left back from the 20s and 30s and just another six short of Brian Miller's total. Mee will be missed at Turf Moor.

The Football League Cup (to be correct now the EFL Cup), brought a touch of joy. With replays on the back burner following the Covid 19 problems, these games can be something of a lottery if scores are level at the end; some penalty shoot-outs you win, some you lose, almost irrespective of the opposition. It was a win in Round 2, the tie finishing 0-0 at St James' Park, Newcastle, but the Clarets knocked in the penalties whereas the North East club missed twice. Round 3 was a game of two halves. Division 2 Rochdale led immediately after the break, but a Jay Rodriguez four timer within 26 minutes, quickly redressed the balance at Turf Moor. Even in Burnley, Tottenham Hotspur can be difficult opposition and a second half goal enabled them to creep through to the last eight, with Burnley having never reached that marker during Dyche's time in Lancashire. His record in the FA Cup was no better, once again never having set foot in a quarter final. In fact it is now 40 years since a Claret's side last accomplished that feat. This time they were knocked out after 90 minutes. In fairness, Huddersfield Town had an excellent season in the Championship, but Dyche's side was at home and Rodriguez put them ahead. Sadly the foot came off the gas in the second half, the Terriers scored twice and Burnley had fallen at the first hurdle.

The one common factor as this season kicked off, was that both East Lancashire clubs topped their Divisional list for currently employing a manager for the lengthiest period of time. In the case of Blackburn Rovers, Tony Mowbray had been in charge for four and a half years, the longest spell since Don Mackay, thirty years before. Several experienced players moved away from the club, the majority at the expiry of their contract. The biggest loss, and the one which was most expected, was Adam Armstrong to Premier League Southampton. His goal scoring feats had lit up Ewood Park and although Newcastle United were entitled to a considerable percentage of the fee, it was rumoured that the ballpark figure was around the £15million mark. Others who left were Charlie Mulgrew to Dundee United, Corry Evans to Sunderland, Amari'i Bell to Luton Town, Lewis Holtby to Holstein Kiel in the 2nd Tier of the Bundesliga, Elliott Bennett to Shrewsbury Town and Stewart Downing who retired. Mowbray also had to say good bye to four loan players whom he had depended upon the previous year. They were Harvey Elliott, back to Liverpool, Tom Trybull to Norwich City, Taylor Harwood-Bellis back to the Etihad and Barry Douglas to Leeds United. Left back Harry Pickering signed from Crewe Alexandra and also arriving was Tayo Edun, a left sided player who cost £400,000 from Lincoln City. There were interesting season long loans also. Both Jan Paul van Hecke and Reda Khadri moved from Brighton and Hove Albion, the former an outstandingly athletic centre half and the latter, a fleet footed wide attacker. Ian Poveda, a box of tricks in wide positions, left Leeds United, but he was seriously injured early doors and missed most of the campaign. One bonus was that Scott Wharton, who had been loaned out to several clubs from the lower divisions, enhancing his reputation all of the time, was now considered to be ready for Championship football.

Ben Brereton Diaz celebrates with Bradley Dack after scoring at London Road, Peterborough, in April 2022

With the threat of Covid 19 receding, the crowds returned, albeit gingerly at first. With only one defeat in the first nine games, it was clear that the goal scoring mantle had passed to Ben Brereton. His is a story with a difference. Mowbray had paid around £7million to Nottingham Forest for him as a youngster and in the eyes of the fans, he was far too light weight; therefore a complete waste of money. The Chile FA, however, discovered that his mother was Chilean and he was invited to join their national squad. He was an overnight sensation, scoring in FIFA World Cup qualifiers and the Copa America; flying backwards and forwards across the Atlantic. His success in South America coincided with a massive boost of confidence and also a strengthening of the upper body which, allied to his natural speed, suddenly made him so much of a handful to defenders. He added his mother's name to his surname, as is the norm in Spanish speaking countries and as Brereton-Diaz, he became the darling of Ewood Park. Following their promising start, which included a 5-1 crunching of Cardiff City (Brereton Diaz knocking in a hat-trick), there was the inevitable slump as they lost away at Huddersfield Town, Blackpool and Queens Park Rangers. Shortly afterwards came the Fulham debacle. The Cottagers were the best team in the Championship and they came to strut their stuff one Tuesday evening in November. After 30 minutes they were two up and then van Hecke was sent off. The uphill battle became mission impossible and Kaminski had to pick the ball out of the net five more times.

Only twice before, in 1891 and 1947, had Rovers conceded seven at home, but on both occasions, against Notts County and Middlesbrough, they had scored once. This, therefore, was an embarrassing record defeat, making them briefly made laughing stock across the country. But as a motivating tool, it worked perfectly. They won eight and drew two of their next ten games, conceding just three times, briefly occupying an automatic promotion slot. Both Peterborough United and Birmingham City were hit for four and by the turn of the year, Brereton Diaz had reached 20 league goals. But from then on it was slowly downhill. The main striker was injured and missed a number of games. They felt the loss of Khadri's blistering pace when he was also out for a while and Sam Gallagher was left to soldier on up front. Kaminski's quality in goal and the three regular centre backs, Lenihan, van Hecke and Wharton, always made it difficult for the opposition, but with the goals drying up, there were a number of narrow defeats. Late January to late April saw only two victories and although they had an exhilarating 4-1 triumph at Preston and won at Birmingham on the final day, they ended six points short of a play-off spot. There had been so much hope mid-season but to finish eighth was such a disappointment. The two cup competitions were easily forgotten. Morecambe, at home in Round 1 of the EFL Cup, produced a shocking performance. Tyrhys Dolan put Rovers ahead but they then lost control of the game in the second half and were defeated 2-1 by a side which would struggle all season in the league below. The Round 3 FA Cup game was far more competitive against a Wigan Athletic side which would be crowned champion of Division 1. It was 2-2 approaching the final whistle but the Latics snatched the winner in the 94th minute.

Tony Mowbray's contract ran until this June 2022 and there were two conflicting rumours. One was that the Rovers wanted a change at the top; the other was that aged 58, he felt it time to move on, or retire, after more than 40 years in the professional game. We may never know which rumour was true, but both Tony and the club announced that he would be leaving after the final match of the season. His total number of games at the Rovers was 267, with an above average win percentage of 40.4. Of the 38 permanent appointees, only Robert B Middleton (605) from either side of the Great War; their most successful period as a league club and Jack Marshall (329), from '60-67, have been in post longer. Mowbray took over in 2017; the club being stuck at the bottom of the Championship and almost pulled off a miracle, before they were relegated on what is normally a safe total of 51 points. Promotion immediately followed before retaining their place in the country's most competitive league for four campaigns. This has been the joint best performance since they dropped out of the Premier League in 2012. Mowbray has not always pleased the fans but a manager is always the first to receive "stick", should they lose even a couple of games consecutively. Even the most thoughtful of supporters have believed him to be too conservative at times, but this season, he changed from a possession based outfit to one that breaks fast from deep and was rewarded with the long unbeaten run. Above all, he is regarded as a decent, loyal man who has defended his players from criticism. With all of his twenty years of management experience, he was of great value to the club, the owners clearly trusting him. But we all have a sell by date, and for a football manager, five years is certainly a long stretch. The old proverb, "like trying to make a silk purse from a sow's ear" perfectly summed up his predicament at Ewood. In other words, without the available money of a number of Championship sides, particularly those receiving parachute payments from the Premier League, it is so difficult to pull clear of the pack and make it to the "Promised Land".

And so the seasons come and then they go, and it is now 134 years since the East Lancashire derby was first officially played. With Mowbray's five year stint in Blackburn at an end and Jackson's spell as temporary "boss" at Turf Moor consigned to the history books, both sides have found themselves short of a manager. The last time that each club had started a season with a new man in charge prior to 2022-23 was in the summer of 1997, when Burnley appointed Chris Waddle and Roy Hodgson took over in the hot seat at Ewood Park. In that year however, the Clarets occupied a place in Division 2, down in the 3rd Tier whereas the Rovers were looking down from on high, firmly entrenched in the Premier League. Never before has there been a season when both clubs, competing in the same Division, have simultaneously commenced a new campaign with a new hand on the tiller. Vincent Kompany, much loved and respected at Manchester City, moved back to his native Belgium after eleven success-filled seasons at the Etihad. He joined Anderlecht, and eventually became the full time manager in 2020, guiding the club to third position in the 2021-22 Belgian First Division A. He is the first non-UK manager in the history of Burnley FC. On exactly the same day, Blackburn Rovers announced Jon Dahl Tomasson as manager. The 112 times Danish capped striker played at Newcastle United and then AC Milan, where he was one of only two Milanese players to score against the inspired Jerzy Dudek in the memorable penalty shoot-out when Liverpool won the Champions' League in 2005. He was later an assistant coach of the Danish national side and, in the last two seasons, guided Malmo FF to successive Allsvenskan (Swedish League Tier 1) titles. He follows Henning Berg as the second non-British Isles born manager at the club.

Both clubs therefore will be something of an unknown quantity, Burnley desperate to regain their place amongst the elite and the Rovers to build on the foundations laid by Tony Mowbray and at least reach the Play-Offs. As always, the Championship will be difficult and both clubs will have lost several key players who were regular starters last season. We all know that football is a funny old game and will no doubt throw up shocks and surprises with hopefully the supporters of each side embarking on positive seasons. It is what we all hope for at the commencement of every campaign and there is the drama of the first league derby for six and a half years to ratchet up the excitement levels. By November 12th, the date of the first encounter ahead of any TV change announcements, we may have a better idea of where the bragging rights are heading, but as I write, I can honestly state that I have no idea whatsoever as to how this season will pan out; surely an ingredient which makes this "contest within a contest" so magical for the committed. Then, but the time of the return derby clash, scheduled for March 18th, fans of both sides will have a better idea as to whether the clash is a spicy as we all know it can be. I wager it will be!

Bragging Rights; so which is really East Lancashire's finest?

Bragging rights; A temporary position of ascendancy in a closely contested rivalry"

Oxford English Dictionary

Bragging rights have probably been in evidence since Day 1 of the simmering rivalry between East Lancashire's top two football clubs. Such statements, such discussions ought to have a base in logic but as we all know, when passions rise, logic is out of the window. So a fan of Burnley FC may well have stated last season that the Clarets are best because they are a Premier League team and the supporter from down the road will emphatically counter that with "what did you last win?" And being honest here, without such partisanship, football would be the poorer and in particular during bad times, it is often only this type of stubborn belief that keeps the club afloat. Psychologically there is much mileage in what, to outsiders, may be looked upon as wooden-headed attitudes, but without them, the fan base would dramatically decrease, even disintegrate. Over the decades, it has been such ideology which has helped to build the great traditions that have spawned the songs and ultimately given the right to wear the shirt and kiss the badge.

The trophies gained, the memories of great players from the past and the stadium all help to support our presumptions, but there is a time for evidence based logic; evidence which is not difficult to find. One of the few absolute truths in this great game is the league table. Luck and dodgy refereeing decisions can play their part, but it is universally accepted that after thirty-eight or forty-six games, luck and decisions even themselves out; the best team finishes first; the worst one ends up with the wooden spoon.

There is a detailed table in the Statistics section which, in all its simplicity, has a truth which may send followers of the Blue and White shirt into raptures of delight but which may be unpalatable to the fans to the east.

It categorically states that Blackburn Rovers have been the more successful side for the majority of the 123 completed seasons, with Burnley lagging well behind. The advantage of using this system is that every single league game is accounted for, irrespective of whichever Division the clubs may be in.

Burnley fans having a good laugh at the Rovers' expense

Years with bragging rights (i.e. higher league placing at the end of a season)

Blackburn Rovers	Burnley
76	47

The figures from the head to head derbies in some respect better reflect the passion in the games and in the very short term, are even more instant and compelling evidence of which club is the top dog. With regard to this rivalry, they tell a different story, but unfortunately the flaw here is that this system does not cover every single season as the two clubs have only competed against each other in league fixtures in 45 of the 123 seasons of official football. There is an argument to say that this doesn't matter but when the clubs are in different divisions, the higher placed one must surely have the bragging rights.

The results of cup ties may be the only exception to the rule, but only twice, in 1913 and 1952, has the side from the lower league won such a game. Also, using the result of the last derby game alone to ascertain bragging rights over a length of time when no games are being played because of a subsequent promotion or relegation, massively mitigates against the club from a higher division. This happened in 1930 when Burnley won the second derby prior to be being relegated and could claim bragging rights until 1936, even though a division below.

Flaws apart, the derby games are so important; in many ways the most exciting aspect of local football, and irrespective of league tables over the ages, Burnley have been far more competitive in such encounters. In fact taking away the first three years when the Blackburn side were totally dominant, statistics show that the Clarets have had more successes. It is also interesting to note just how many of the games have been closely contested, although as a derby game usually only takes place when both clubs are in the same division, this is not surprising. There has been the occasional walloping since 1892.

Tom Nicol's hat-trick game in 1896 (6-0 to the Clarets), Percy Dawson's four-timer in 1914 (6-0 to the Rovers) and the near tragic injury to Billy Down in '29 when the Burnley keeper tried to stay between the sticks for the full game in spite of his near death condition (8-3 to the Ewood side). But since then, only the rampant Souness side in 2001 has triumphed by a five goal or more margin. If you take the cup ties and Test matches into consideration and even starting from the very beginning, the Turf Moor side has caught up and the two clubs cannot be separated using this method of testing after exactly one hundred contests.

All Official games in Total

Club	Played	Won	Lost	Drawn	GF	GA
Blackburn Rovers	100	41	41	18	176	166
Burnley	100	41	41	18	166	176

The trophy count is another established method of ranking clubs. When added together, it can produce an order of merit from the day competition began in the 1871-72 season. Manchester United, Liverpool and Arsenal in that order, top the list and the Rovers can be found in ninth position. You have to trawl down to twenty-third place to find Burnley. That may appear to be game, set and match to Blackburn Rovers but when you consider that five of their FA Cup victories were achieved by 1891, it would indicate a much closer battle with their rival since that date.

Honours gained by Blackburn Rovers and Burnley

Team	FA Cup	Top flight titles	FL Cup	Total	Ranking Position
Blackburn Rovers	6	3	1	10	9th
Burnley	1	2	0	3	23rd

The quality of player that has performed at the club is a difficult criteria to use when establishing bragging rights, as is the number of internationals that have been on their books. No disrespect to the Caribbean Islands, but a cap for Jamaica will carry less kudos than one for a FIFA Top Ten rated country. Equally a Jimmy McIlroy with his fifty-one caps at Turf Moor puts him way in front of so many who have collected a mere handful. But looking back at the list of players can certainly be a strong indicator of the respective merits of the club, highlighting many of the undoubted stars that have graced East Lancashire. But even just selecting a small group is difficult. They surely have to be internationals and had to have been recognised by all football supporters of the day across the whole country. So in for a penny, in for a pound, here we go in alphabetical order.

Captain Crompton, consummate and commanding, the King of football in the Cotton Capital. Duggie and Ronnie, always inseparable in loyalty and longevity, ability and achievement. Alex Elder, a classical footballing left back and a complete irritant; even Bryan Douglas struggled to rid him from his back. Jack Hill, the centre half who captained England no less. "Taffy" James, Mr Boomerang himself, an outstanding and electrifying attacker who kept coming back. Bob Kelly, the finest inside forward nationally of his generation. Jimmy Mac, midfield maestro, supreme tactician and as intellectual a footballer as you will ever find. Southworth and Shearer, the ultimate S.A.S, separated by generations but the most deadly destroyer of defences. So who is the best of all? No way dare I answer that so perhaps an even more fascinating question to put to avid fans of both clubs is "which of your rival's players would you want to have played for your club?" Surely not even the most partisan of supporters would have turned their noses up at any in the above list.

But as interesting as it is to compare players from across the great divide, it is well-nigh mission impossible to use this particular criteria as a gauge to the respective merits of either club. You can never really compare players across generations. It therefore comes down to league positions, head to head results and trophies gathered. There, football historians and "anoraks" will immediately point to the evidence and state the obvious; Blackburn Rovers, historically speaking, are the most successful club in East Lancashire (and in the current county of Lancashire).

But are there other valid ways at looking at the "bragging rights" issue? Many football fans will ask what is the point of looking at the distant past. How can performances in the nineteenth century possibly have any relevance to today's game. And the same can be said of all the generations leading up to the twenty-first century. Bob Crompton may have been the best player in England during the Edwardian period, Jimmy McIlroy could toy with and ultimately out-think all opposition in the fifties, but does that matter today? Being the consummate fence sitter, I would say "yes and no".

"Yes", because without the tradition which stars of the past have helped to build, support for clubs could become transitory; a here today and gone tomorrow commodity. Football is not pop music. There have been musical phenomenona such as the Bay City Rollers who swept the nation in the Seventies but apart from perhaps a number of ladies, now into their sixties who can still remember swooning over them as they danced round their handbags, they have completely disappeared from the country's gaze. Football clubs were a work in progress from the day they were formed. And the Jerry Dawsons and the Derek Fazackerleys are the building blocks which have helped to continue that process. As one generation slips away, another one follows on. And with a few sad exceptions, Bury being the latest example, they have lasted the course.

A club from Accrington has twice been wound up, completely disappeared, but like the proverbial phoenix from the ashes, the local community has ensured that a replacement has risen up. And club and the community go hand in hand, each making enormous contributions to the other. When we arrived in France and we were having conversations with the locals, they would usually ask where we lived in England. When we said "Blackburn", several would say "et oui, Blackburn Rovers". Is there any other reason why someone in deepest France should have heard of the town? So please don't discount tradition or kick it into the gutter as if it is a total inconsequence. I suspect that without it, without it having been handed down from your grandparents to your parents, then to yourself (or perhaps from a parent of a mate) and, I suspect, is currently being handed down by you to the next generation, the club would be no more.

But harping back to the original question, I can understand why many think that the answer should be "no". A Martin Dobson or a Bryan Douglas can obviously contribute nothing now to the performance on the field and even stars of the recent past, David Dunn and Robbie Blake for example, both still relatively young men, have hung up their boots.

So bragging rights can now only be influenced by the current side. And this is what bragging rights are about, the here and now. Until the end of last season, Burnley were in the Premier League, Blackburn were not. End of story, full stop, move on. And it is difficult to contradict this view point, but the order will change eventually. A change by next May is a possibility and as long as the

A female Rovers fan celebrates the opening goal in March 2010

game continues, they will take it in turns to have precedence over the other. As history has shown, the length of precedence may be thirty plus years or it can turn around after one season. This is the nature of the beast and would we really want it any differently? Because that wonderful feeling of satisfaction in knowing that we are better than the lot down the road can only happen if the opposition stays relatively competitive. If Burnley had dropped into non-league in 1987 and become a Northwich Victoria or a Gainsborough Trinity, both former Division 2 clubs who have struggled unsuccessfully to regain their place in the professional leagues, where would we have found that nail-biting, stomach fluttering, adrenalin rushing excitement that has crashed into our senses on a number of occasions since the turn of the Millennium.

And for Blackburn Rovers fans who have sulked since their relegation in 2012 because, without a doubt, Burnley have had the bragging rights, there is one lesson that they can learn from the enemy. As Claret fans did over many a year during the Eighties, Nineties and into this century, the Rovers have to be patient, because eventually their time will return. When it does, they can let "t'other lot" know with a venom that they once more have possession of the bragging rights; once more top dog in East Lancashire. This surely is what this rivalry is all about.

Can it, should it, will it ever end?

"Goodbyes are not forever
Goodbyes are not the end
They simply mean I miss you
Until we meet again"
Source;- worldofdtcmarketing

Blackburn Rovers and Burnley began their league fixtures at the same time and in the same league; the Football League in 1888, the year that the world's first football fixtures saw the light of day. From the start of the 2022-23 season, they have re-located in different divisions on twelve occasions, sometimes one being relegated, sometimes one being promoted. On each of these twelve dates, they have metaphorically said goodbye and on each occasion, ultimately welcomed the other one back. This chapter eventually looks at the current situation and although it is impossible to estimate when they will meet up again, it attempts to answer the "can it, should it, will it ever end" question.

I can immediately think of four popular sports which officially pre-date 1888. All five of the English horse race classics had become established by 1814, the British Open Golf Championship was first played for in 1860, the Wimbledon Championship followed in 1877 and cricket's Ashes series was inaugurated in 1882. But the early days of these sports were enjoyed by the toffs and gentry and just briefly, football threatened to follow the same pattern. John Lewis and friends who founded Blackburn Rovers came from the privileged area of the town, their education being at elite public schools followed inevitably by time spent at the ultimate finishing school, either Oxford or Cambridge University. But within a decade, it was all change. Jimmy Forrest, possibly the finest footballer of his generation, had left school at twelve and was working as a tape sizer in one of the local mills when "persuaded" to join the Rovers. The social gap between him and the rest of the team would have made for difficulties, but having such exceptional skills would have been a passport to acceptance at any club in the land. And as professionalism grew, the individuals who began to participate were certainly not toffs. Football was not only attracting working class support on the terraces, it was becoming the first sport available to any male, regardless of wealth, education, family history and eventually race; something which even today, golf and tennis are still struggling to achieve.

Derby celebrations – Jason Shackell is mobbed in March 2013

The introduction of the five and a half day working week and the links with the community quickly gave an identity to these emerging clubs whose names gave the strongest of clues as to their location. Thus it became natural for the people of Burnley to associate themselves with Burnley FC, playing close to the Burnley Town Centre. Lancashire, north of Manchester, became a hot bed of professionalism and the concept of local rivalry, later to become known as derbies, made the Saturday afternoon trip to the ground an occasion to remember. For many men, it was a welcome break from the weekly grind of the cotton mill or pit and with every year passing, another group would pass on to adulthood, having been taught to read at schools, attendance at which was now compulsory. With a growing potential readership, the newspaper industry began to feature football reports and more importantly previews, giving a publicity to the game which had been missing in earlier years.

Football became a game of the people, the crowds soaring into five figures with the onset of the new century. In spite of working and living conditions scarcely showing signs of improvement, there was football to look forward to, a weekly dose of medicine to stimulate the emotions and the chance to dream of glory, albeit vicariously.

This may well have been the catalyst for those early spectators to begin to attend football matches, a chance to get away from whatever life threw at them, but as the quality of life has improved, can it be a pertinent reason in this modern age? Possibly "yes", because life can still be full of hardship and with a lack of harmony at home, it has always given an opportunity to "get things off the chest". I remember in years gone by when we used to laugh at some of the older spectators who would scream insults at referees, make nasty comments at the players and turn on the manager should the score line not be in their favour. "They behave like that because they are hen-pecked husbands" was the gist of our argument. "They daren't swear at their wives so they take it out on their own players." Now there may have been (and may still be) some truth in those assertions.

So why does the modern day fan watch Blackburn Rovers or Burnley? A family tradition, peer pressure, loyalty to the shirt or the town, a desire for excitement, the drama, the nail-biting finishes, the adrenalin rush when your team wins, the group identity, the feeling of belonging or even just a habit? There will doubtlessly be other reasons, and some have already been examined carefully in Chapter 2. In different ways, they all add to the quality of our life, each bringing benefits to our well-being once we have been converted to what some consider the latest religion, "footballism". But we have all experienced the down side of supporting our team. The woeful performance, the crushing defeat, the apparent lack of effort which ruins our evening. And supporters from both East Lancs clubs have had far too many of those in our lifetimes. The angry mutterings of "never again" as supporters stomp away early when their side is 3-0 down, is in most instances a hasty reaction and one, which following further reflection at home, will result in being back in their seat next time.

Having said that, there are probably two types of football fan. The one who will be there whatever, whether promoted, relegated or just staying put in the league. The other will be enticed into the ground following a sequence of good results, a push for promotion and perhaps by the quality of the opposition. Liverpool do not just help to fill the away grounds with their hordes of travelling support, there will be many "occasional" home fans who brush off the cob webs and make an appearance simply to watch the stars, albeit cheering on the home side in the process. But when results turn, relegation is threatened and the opposition is not sufficiently strong to tempt them to leave the warm house on a cold afternoon or evening, these will be the first to drift away.

Andy Mitten, writing in the FourFourTwo magazine in April 2005, makes the point so well in his article "Blackburn v Burnley: More than a Game". It is majestic football journalism if too denigrating of the area, making East Lancashire appear shoddy, outdated and Victorian in outlook. But one of the Blackburn Rovers supporters he interviewed admitted that the 1995 success brought in the "Baddiel and Skinner post-Euro 96 type fans". It is a racing certainty that they were the first to leave as the Jack Walker dream died with him.

As much as disillusionment can set in, it would never change my allegiance but I do admit that there have been odd occasions when I wished I had been born and brought up on the west side of Manchester for example. There, within earshot of the cheers ringing out from Old Trafford, I would have had no option but to be a Manchester United fan. In my dotage, I could reminisce about the day I was in Barcelona in '99, argue with friends about the respective merits of Best versus Ronaldo, Charlton v Cantona, reclining comfortably in the knowledge that we are England's most successful team domestically, with the majority of the honours being gained in our life time. I could even slump into a depressive state because we lost in three semi-finals in the '19-20 season. Then last season we finished as low as sixth. Heaven forbid, what a catastrophe!!! But the moment would quickly pass, because it is easy to be "United 'til I die"; far more heroic to be a "Claret forever" or a "Rover 'til it's over". It may have cost far less, but it took far more guts to be on Turf Moor on May 9th 1987, a life or death situation if ever there was one, than to be in the Camp Nou twelve years later and the taste of the beer in one of the pubs Under't Culvert would have tasted just as sweet as the glasses of Rioja in La Rambla following the game. And for the Roverites like myself, there is a part of me that believes that the winning of the Premier League in '95 means more than the thirteen successes gained under Ferguson alone. In the clear light of dawn, it is a nonsense statement, one possibly fuelled by that inverted snobbery, prevalent in so many smaller working class Northern towns. "We may not win much, but by God we are proud when we do. Just take a look at us, we've nought really but we are damned well sure we don't want to be like you who have been given it all on a plate". Of course it leaves us wide open to "green eyed monster" jibes; that it is just a defence against jealousy, but I am sure many Clarets and Rovers supporters revel in the position of underdog. If there are any true Manchester

Colourful smoke and language swirls around Turf Moor in 2013

United fans reading this book, please don't think that this is a swipe against you personally. I have several good friends who regularly attend games at Old Trafford and I admire them as much as I do any other loyal fan, but this is me telling it like it is from our perspective, through thick and thin, the bad times and the occasional good times.

So, soap box put back under the stairs, there is a point I want to make about measuring the quality of a supporter. Let me say that many supporters of a club are also supporters of football itself. They love the game and will watch it in whatever shape or form it comes along. How many of us have been dragged away by our partner for stopping to watch a group of kids kick a ball around in the street or in the park, just hoping it comes our way and we can pass it back to them? But every now and then, you come across a supporter who has not missed a game for X number of years and I had to feel sorry for them when the Covid 19 outbreak allowed their clubs to play but they were banned from attending the game. I do raise my hat to them. Theirs has been a commitment beyond belief and they are truly the best of all supporters. But for so many of us, life gets in the way. The vast majority of football fans also want to play and for many, it is impossible to combine playing at the best level you can and faithfully watching your team. The life span of a football "career" for most of us could be from the age of eight through to the mid-thirties, considerably less than half of our stay on earth. As I once told a boy at a school where I taught.... "please don't waste it". He was a decent player in the early seventies, a pupil in his last year in Secondary School when the Rovers were in Division 3. One day he came to tell me that he could no longer play for the school on a Saturday morning because he wanted to travel to all the away games that season. I tried hard to make him change his mind, saying that he could watch every week when he was too old to play. He was a polite boy but I could not change his mind. He was on the coach to Chesterfield the following Saturday morning and did not play for school again, instead watching the Ewood Park side storm to a Division 3 title success. I believed (and still do) that he made the wrong decision. We ought to take every opportunity to play whenever we can. Then we go back to following our favourites later in life, because we are a long time retired from playing.

The demands of family and work commitments also have to take precedence and there are of course so many wonderful people who commit to helping others to play, either as a coach, match official, club official or simply to help to put up the nets, collect the subs, sit at the gate to take the admission fees or serve refreshments after the game. These may be lifetime supporters of one of the two East Lancashire teams, who wait with bated breath for the result at five o'clock and yet may only be able to see a handful of games per season. And what if you move away from the area? You do not cease to be a supporter overnight. The commitment of the heart is as strong as it is for those on the ground, but you simply cannot make it to the match. For the women, growing into adulthood often means children and as Vicky Foy says, they have to come first.

> I am married now (to a Rovers' fan) and have two daughters aged six and eleven but I can't get them interested in football. They are both very active and I spend so much time at weekends driving them to dance sessions; that is their hobby. It's my ambition to get them both to Ewood someday but I suppose it was easier for me growing up because the Rovers were on the way up and the Premier League was so exciting. At the moment, they are not really good enough to attract my daughters' attention. I occasionally go down to Ewood now whenever I can, but whereas in the past, it was so easy to get into the ground, now everything is so organised, stage-managed by the Police and you never come into contact with opposition fans after the game or the players for that matter. It was different when I was younger, but then the Rovers was my only obsession and I had no-one else to think about."

For all of us, particularly those willing and able to watch regularly, success for the club means so much, particularly against opposition you may despise. These are not always the traditional derby foes and can change from year to year depending on the league situation and position of your club. If you are pushing for promotion, a rival close to you in the table can, for one year only, be the deadly enemy. Sometimes your club can have had a bad experience , possibly being on the wrong end of a referee's decision in their pre-

A Leon Best and Jason Shackell aerial duel in the 20112-13 season vious encounter, so when those opponents next come to your home park, you desperately want matters to be put right. But generally it is your closest enemy which is the recipient of all your darkest thoughts. On this matter, Paul Fletcher had some interesting comments to make regarding the East Lancashire derby.

"The derbies are for the fans more than for the players. The players want to win every game so a derby in that sense is no different, But what happens is that the players realise what the fans want and then probably put that little bit more into their performance to make the fans happy. When we went back to the ground after a weekend game, the only people there were all like-minded. They were all from the club so there is no banter about the result, but it is different for the fans. They may work with supporters of the Rovers so if we have let them down, they have to take the stick. So if the players can squeeze out a result, it certainly helps the fans on a Monday morning."

He also talked about the philosophy of Jimmy Adamson and his own views on the links between footballers and fans.

"Burnley fans fully understand that they can only be Burnley. They cannot be Manchester United or Liverpool so they do understand if the club does not win all the time. Jimmy had a motto which he regularly preached to his players and which I believe still stands in football today. 'Bad results are acceptable to the fans but lacking effort never is. The Burnley fans are working class people. They work hard all week and when they watch us, they expect us to work hard. They want to see sweat whatever the result.' Linked with that is an acceptance that you will pick up injuries. I know that certain footballers of the past have suffered badly from dementia, particularly those that have headed the ball a lot. If it was wet, the old type of leather football would become far heavier. And we didn't just head it during a game. Every week we would have heading practice and I was the one usually on the end of it. And footballers, always looking to have a laugh at someone's expense, would often take one of the training balls out of the sack and leave it in a stream which ran alongside Gawthorpe Training Ground for a few minutes. Then they would float balls over and I would have to head them past the keeper. It was impossible to spot which was the heavy one, the football that felt like a medicine ball, and when I headed that, it nearly knocked my head off. The response from the rest of the lads was predictable. They would burst their lungs laughing. I am fortunate not to be affected by dementia yet, but I do believe that heading was just part of the job. So if footballers or their families take their cases to court, I don't think they should be able to claim compensation. There were still miners working in the Burnley area when we played and their job was far more life threatening and far less well paid than that of a footballer. Other industries have similar problems and we are all aware of the risks when we start work. Football could be extremely violent from time to time. Chelsea had a giant centre-half called Micky Droy and he clattered me throughout the first half of one of our games. At half-time I told Alan Stevenson, our goalkeeper, to aim for the penalty

> spot in their half when he was kicking out of his hands. He did and as Droy was steadying himself to head the ball back, I charged at him and knocked him flying. Unfortunately as he fell, his foot caught me square in the mouth. I was helped off and Doctor Iven stitched me up, fourteen stitches in all and I was back on the field. This was 70s football, nothing sanitised then. It made the supporters day when I came back on. They knew it was all part of the game; a part of the game they loved. They knew all about hard knocks and if we could come back from one, they could empathise with that."

The unruly behaviour of the fans in the East Lancashire derby has sadly provided as many column inches in newspapers as the footballing incidents on the pitch. This is a crying shame because there have been so many closely contested affairs, so many magical moments and outstanding performances. There is no doubt that the tradition of the games has contributed to the rise in passion and the fear of losing as much as anything. I suspect that the blood pressure of the most level headed of fans goes up a level or two on derby day but I also fear that it can attract a small minority of characters more interested in the prospect of a punch-up.

Every barrel has a bad apple or two and unfortunately, the infamy that attracts itself to such characters can also act as a magnet to others who, particularly when there is too much alcohol in the system, join in. It is the responsibility of the authorities, both within the club and amongst Police Forces to seek out the unwanted and they have certainly made inroads into the gratuitous violence that was a feature of football generally through the seventies and eighties but which still occasionally raises its ugly head in more modern times.

I accept that it is the duty of the media to report the facts, but there is a balance required, and I often wonder if, in the interest of a good story, they are happy to fan the flames and their headlines and opening lines do not always cover the journalists and editors with glory. Even the less headline seeking publications such as the Independent fall into this category from time to time.

> Welcome to Hell: The mills may have gone but there is still something dark and satanic whenever Burnley and Blackburn Rovers meet in perhaps the most savage rivalry in British football.
> Independent 18th October 2009

Burnley produced a text book performance when winning 2-0 in the Carabao League Cup at Ewood Park in 2017, but the Sun led with...

> Five people were arrested and a nine-year-old boy injured amid unsavoury scenes at Blackburn's Carabao Cup derby with Burnley.

And followed up with...

There was a heavy police presence for the second-round clash between the East Lancashire neighbours, which ended in a 2-0 victory for Burnley at Ewood Park... After Jack Cork put the visitors ahead in the 27th minute, two Blackburn fans ran onto the pitch, with one confronting a number of Burnley players. The supporter had his hand on Ashley Westwood's throat before he was tackled to the ground by the Burnley midfielder. Lancashire Police confirmed a man was arrested and is being held in police custody on suspicion of assault and pitch encroachment. Meanwhile, a nine-year-old boy suffered minor burns after a flare thrown from among the Burnley fans towards the pitch landed on his back.

The Daily Mail also preferred to lead with the following headline instead of concentrating on a thrilling game at Turf Moor in 2010, finally decided by a David Dunn penalty.

Child's terror as violence returns to the football stands: More than 40 football fans were arrested today following a match between two bitter rivals. The East Lancashire derby between Burnley and Blackburn Rovers at Turf Moor resulted in the arrests, made up of both sets of fans. Superintendent Terry Woods from Lancashire Police said: "A major policing operation has been in place throughout the day to prevent any disorder. "Unfortunately, we have had to deal with some disorder inside and outside the ground. However, the operation that is in place has enabled us to successfully deal with those pockets of disorder rapidly."
Daily Mail website 29th March 2010

There is a picture which portrays what was happening amongst the crowd, but which had nothing to do with the events on the pitch and the caption read...

Terror: A young Burnley fan is pulled from the crowd after police clash with fans during a match between Burnley and Blackburn Rovers

In no way shape or form am I looking to condone or even ignore the shameless behaviour and if it is not safe to take our children to games, then we have to ask deep-rooted questions about the future of professional football, but the reporting in this fashion can make heroes out of the true villains and only stir the pot even more. The songs also are an embarrassment to the vast majority, hurtful and often quite despicable. The Blackburn chants are obsessed with Dingle connections, the supposedly inbred and dysfunctional family from ITV's award winning soap, Emmerdale.

"Your mum's your dad; your dad's your mum.
You're interbred, you Burnley scum".
Your granddad is your brother, your sister is your mother,
you're shagging one another, the Dingle family".

Since Jack Walker's death, there has been a similar obsession from the Burnley choir regarding his sad demise.

"Who's that lying on the carpet,
who's that lying on the floor?
It's Jack Walker on his back
And he's had a heart attack
And he won't be going to Ewood any more".

There is a possible five out of ten for creativity and those of us who are worldly wise find it hard not to smile, but the crowd participation has moved far away from the original meaning of the word support. The Cambridge English Dictionary defines support in a sporting context as to give encouragement to someone or something because you want him, her, or it to succeed. Now it is more of let's slag off the other lot and that will help our boys, the cruder and viler the better. The chant at Ewood park in the fifties was:

One, two, three, four, Who d'ya think we're shouting for.
R O V E R S Rovers.

It is fair to say that football crowds are now far more pointed in their songs Everything concerning derby games, from conversation, media attention and the ninety minutes itself, is now divided into two parts. The action on the field and that off it. I am sure that the on-field rivalry has not changed much since 1888. So many players, from different generations, have told me that for them, it is close to being just another game, just another search for three more points. They say it only stands out that touch more because of the media hype and of course the extra passion in the crowd. And there is also the theory that it is the second part which has developed and developed, bizarrely much more following a period without games. Kevin Hird's comments possibly back this up.

"You would have expected that it could have been a nightmare for me living in Colne in the seventies and playing for Blackburn Rovers, but apart from a few jokes, there were no problems. And when I later signed for Burnley, no-one had a go at me for having been at the Rovers for so long. Of course I don't know what would have happened if I had turned up at Ewood in a Claret shirt but there was never a derby game then. But since I retired over thirty years ago, I have recently begun to notice bits of nastiness against me. It has not been so nasty that it has bothered me too much, but there have been innuendoes that I was a traitor to sign for the Rovers in the first place. This is especially when I have been in a pub and perhaps some have had too much to drink. It might be because the rivalry has grown so much more in recent years."

Females at football grounds are now a more common sight and the ones who do turn up certainly have their points of view and deserve to be heard.

Burnley fans mocking the owners of the Rovers during their 2013 visit to Ewood Park

Natalie Smith was introduced to life at Turf Moor as a girl, going down with her family for a number of years and being a regular in the Bob Lord stand.

> "There was always an edgy feel to an afternoon watching the Clarets, but this added to the sense of excitement. I never felt scared because I always wore the Claret and Blue scarf and I had the protection of my father and much older brothers, even when exiting the ground. In those days the ground was rarely close to being full, but nowadays, there is even more passion, so much atmosphere with the singing making it more like an international rugby match. Some Burnley folk call the ground 'The Church' and I can see why. The match was such a big deal to everyone. And the atmosphere grew and grew and you became carried along with it. When the ball hits the back of the net, it's party time and you just have to stand up. I now live with my fiancé who just happens to be as avid a Rovers' fan, with a dad as crazy on the Rovers as my dad and brothers are on the Clarets. I have been to several games at Ewood and I honestly feel that the atmosphere there doesn't compare with Turf Moor. The singing is more subdued and the fans more refined. It's as if Blackburn Rovers are a touch more posh. Burnley is more urban, perhaps a bit rougher and it was interesting that when they filmed 'The Inbetweeners', they had them singing 'We love you Burnley, we do' as they were bussed in a drunken state to the hotel from the airport. The film isn't really about Burnley or the club and the real fans don't sing this song, but the Film Director obviously thought that the viewers would understand the connection between

> the name of the club and the loutish behaviour of these young men. I believe that the club means so much to the town and there was a poster going round saying 'Our Turf, our Town' which says it all. The ground is virtually in the town centre and this helps to really make the football club the team of the people of Burnley. I don't believe that generally speaking, there is a day to day problem in Burnley with Blackburn and its people, but as soon as football is mentioned, it is a different story".

I am certain that in virtually every instance, Natalie's assumption that Burnley and Blackburn folk have a decent relationship apart from in a footballing context is correct. From my experience, there is often banter, but that can often enhance a relationship. There are so many similarities between the towns and people and there is an ironic similarity in the choice of song that expresses the hatred for each other. Compare the following two choruses.

And it's no nay never
No nay never no more
Will we play Burnley B***ards
No never no more

And it's no nay never
No nay never no more
Will we play B***ard Rovers
No never no more

Having lived with this project for a couple of years, my admiration for both clubs has grown and grown. Size wise, they ought to be down in Tier 3, possibly even competing with the likes of Stockport County and Rochdale in Tier 4. That they are not says so much for them both, a determination to compete with the best, as underdogs of course, but to remind everyone that they pack a punch. Burnley have just completed a total of 59 years in the top division which places them at 21st in the all-time list, behind Everton in first place. Their adversary down the M65 has been able to complete at the top level for 72 seasons, thirteenth on the list.

In fact in all of the 123 seasons of league football, either the Clarets or the Blue and Whites or both have occupied a seat at the top table for all but 26 of them. In the 2020-21 season, of the twenty Premier League clubs, only Burnley and West Bromwich Albion did not represent an area with city status. In the Championship, only Watford and Barnsley had smaller populations than Blackburn. I have used the phrase before but here it is again because it is so apt. These two clubs have really punched above their weight.

So can the derby games survive for another chunk of years to add to the 134? First of all I believe there is no evidence to suggest that football itself is on a downward spiral at professional level. There certainly is however in terms of

A Rovers' fan leaving no doubt as to what he thinks about Burnley participation in local leagues, with far fewer Saturday and Sunday adult teams, therefore far fewer divisions, although with the arrival of Sport's Centres with floodlit courts, five a'side leagues have proliferated.

But at the top, football has never been so high profile, with sponsors and television companies throwing millions at it on a weekly basis. There is also so much more junior football than when I was a child. The exception to the rule is schools' football which has completely nose-dived since a combination of Margaret Thatcher, Trade Union Action and the professional clubs/FA began to smash it to pieces in the mid-eighties. But if recent trends continue, there is absolutely no reason why professional football cannot flourish for the foreseeable future.

There are also many reasons why it should continue. The health of the nation depends heavily on its physical fitness and playing football certainly keeps you fit. It also provides mental stimulus as well as other essentials to our wellbeing such as excitement, loyalty, friendship, working together and commitment to a cause. Any parent wanting to bring up a child with a positive ethos and in the right surroundings needs to look at football as a possible way forward. Of course there are the occasional spanners in the works. The wretched serial paedophile Barry Bennell, at both Manchester City and Crewe Alexandra, committed crime after crime of a sexual nature on young boys and then there were the left-wing intellectuals of the seventies who argued that competition is certainly not good for the soul because it has to have a winner and therefore losers.

They may have cast the occasional shadow across the minds of parents, but the great majority see the benefits of the game. Professional football encourages children of either gender to play, which in turn keeps them off the streets as they develop into teens. For those in particular who are brought up in difficult and sometimes dangerous surroundings, professional football can offer positive role models and be the spur to help them better themselves, because the game offers a wide variety of career pathways to young people. So for the good of society, the nation's health and the wellbeing of so many, the professional game should continue.

It is the "will it" which is more problematic. The world of football is awash with money but it tends to rest with the few. Fortunately promotion and relegation continues and believe it or not, there is a route which could take local clubs such as Mill Hill or Burnley Belvedere from the depths of Tier 14 in the East Lancashire League to the very heights of the Premier League. It is of course highly improbable, but the route is there and if Burnley had only drawn with Orient and dropped into the Conference in 1987, I am sure they would have returned. There were rumours that Colne Dynamos could replace them and move into Turf Moor, but it was surely paper talk. Lincoln City were relegated and they made an instant return. As long as this free movement can take place from Tier to Tier, then there will be opportunities for the derby games to continue.

There is a history of longevity in the game. Of the nineteen clubs fighting it out with Burnley last season in the Premier League, they have all been in the professional leagues since 1920. Looking at the situation from the opposite angle, of the original twelve, only Accrington are no longer with us. There are doubts about the length of existence of Stoke City, but the club has certainly been a permanent member of the League since 1919. Sadly Notts County, reputedly the country's oldest existing club, were relegated from Division 2 in 2019, ending a 131 year stay. These statistics however certainly suggest that clubs with long histories are generally immune from collapse, which indicates that the future of both East Lancashire clubs is sustainable.

However there have been nagging doubts about the ownership of other clubs in recent times. Wigan Athletic have somewhat miraculously got their act together after the setbacks caused by a change of ownership in 2020, resulting in Administration, a 12 point deduction and relegation to Division 1. Macclesfield Town were unceremoniously dumped out of the League after the unfathomable behaviour of its owner. The tragedy of Bury FC has unfolded and a Phoenix Club is having difficulty in replacing it and playing in the town because its owner, whilst seemingly unphased by the demise of his club, has made life extremely difficult with regard to releasing his grip on Gigg Lane. The saga surrounding the misfortunes of the once mighty Bolton Wanderers would make an interesting movie, as points' deductions and "alley cat scrapping" between owners and potential buyers brought embarrassment to the club and the town as they plunged into the depths of Tier 4. And who could have predicted the nonsense at fellow original member of the Football League, Derby County. As I write, there is still no certainty that they will kick-off at the start of the 2022-23 season, yet another example of a prospective owner making promises but slow to show the colour of his money.

These clubs are close enough to East Lancashire to sound out warning bells, but fortunately the only charge that could be laid at the door of the Burnley Board of Directors is one of being too sensible with its money. The new American owners have yet to make an impact in terms of signing Premier League players and there are rumours that the Parachute payment will be used to pay off the money that was borrowed to pay for the club, so the jury is still out on Alan Pace and his friends from ALK Capital. The situation in Blackburn has certainly changed during the last few years, I believe for the better. The Venkys were met with a hail of criticism after their early years of ownership at Ewood Park, but they are showing that they are in for the long haul and have not used the club as a money pit to enhance their own bank account. Someone, who until recently had been at the club for a while, told me that it is time that they received their overdue praise for having stabilised the club over the last few years. So fingers crossed, the current prognosis for both clubs is far from dismal, and although it is difficult to predict a triumphal return to glory in the short term, their futures seem safe and the derby games will continue for as long as football retains its popularity with the people of this nation.

Supporting either the Clarets and Rovers has been difficult at times. But we are a traditional lot in East Lancashire, stoic to the end. We have withstood diabolical seasons such as in 1970-71 when our two clubs between them scored a total of 66 goals, lost 43 games and collected a mere 54 points in finishing 21st in their respective leagues, relegation ensuing of course. If one adds the cumulative positions within the ninety-two club pyramid, nothing has yet surpassed the 1986-87 season when the combined position totalled 124, the Rovers being 34th and the Clarets 90th. Collectively, the best season was 1914-15, the Burnley side 4th, their rivals 3rd, a combined total of just seven. The derby games were shared that year, and there is no doubt that it is this fixture which continues to enthral the crowds, stirs the emotions and often produces the fireworks, sometimes sadly off the pitch. We long for our team to come good on derby day but also through the annual weekly slog of close to nine long months, where hope is always paramount.

I once saw a quote (and I have no-one to attribute it to) which said, "It's the hope that thrills us but it's the hope that inevitably kills us". It is so true as we become excited with a four game unbeaten run before we lose the next three. Mick Duffy hit the nail on the head when he said that when you support Burnley, "you hope for the best, fear for the worst". A neighbour of mine called Duggie Hargreaves is a Rovers' fan and he knows his football. His wife suffered a nasty injury and he was reduced to becoming chief cook and bottle washer and everything else at home for several months. My wife, being sympathetic, said, "you must be a patient man, Duggie", to which he replied, "when you have supported Blackburn Rovers as long as I have, you learn to be patient."

So many of us love this game, we love this rivalry, and receive such a buzz from it. My wife is in the opposite camp. She does not like football, is totally disinterested in it, but being married to me and having borne two sons, she has become accustomed to being bombarded with it morning, noon and night. She rarely mentions it, but when she does, Lesley Hodkinson is also worth listening to. And because I fully know where I stand in the hierarchy of our house, I will as usual, let her have the final word.

> "Life is very hard these days in Northern towns, people can be quite depressed, especially in the middle of a pandemic. For many, it is a case of surviving from one week to the next and struggling through the best we can. And for a lot of people football is everything. It is the game that keeps them going. If the club is doing well, the town gets excited, gets positive. It helps them to forget about their own misery. I believe that football is essential to many people's lives and if it means that occasionally we have to put up with awful behaviour from a few hundred so called fans whenever we have a derby match, then so be it if it gives the rest of us that bit of a lift."

Acknowledgements

Let me say that this is the first book I have ever written and if I ever write another one, I will first of all construct a plan of action. Most people, in whatever enterprise they are involved, will probably have a plan B should anything go wrong, but in this case there was not even a Plan A. I liken myself to Forest Gump; you will remember the magnificent Tom Hanks film. He thought he would embark on a short jog from his home in Georgia on America's east coast but ran on and on, finally criss-crossing the country a number of times coast to coast before ultimately resting after three years of non-stop running.

My preliminary planning was on a par with that of Mr Gump. Consequently over a two year period, there have been several partial re-writes which prevented the book going head to head with Leo Tolstoy's great tome, "War and Peace", in terms of length rather than literary genius I hasten to add. Part way through, the late Jenny Suggitt suggested that I should talk to someone with experience of writing football books and introduced me to Roy Cavanagh. He convinced me that the way forward was to make contact with Dave Lane of Legends Publications.

At the same time, I had a chance meeting with Ronnie Jepson in the "Swan with Two Necks" in Pendleton near Clitheroe. A former pro with Burnley and Huddersfield Town amongst other clubs, he has been better known for being the side kick of Neil Warnock, the saviour of so many clubs in the relegation zone. Ronnie suggested that I contact certain ex-professionals who have played in derby games. He spoke to them initially, and when they agreed to talk to me, he passed on their numbers. Andy Bayes, anchor man with Radio Lancashire Sport was similarly helpful and Veronica Simpson, who is the contact at Turf Moor for all their ex-players, supplied me with further introductions. I knew Steve Douglas, which enabled me to contact his father Bryan, an all-time Ewood Park legend and Richard Stoddart, a neighbour of one of my sons, gave me the intro to Derek Fazackerley. Also Philip Webster, son-in-law of Harry Potts, gave me so much insight into the thoughts of the great man.

Only two players refused to talk to me but I found all of the others listed below to be so obliging and with just a little prompting, prepared to delve back into their pasts and reminisce, reminisce and reminisce. They were Graham Alexander, Kevin Ball, Gary Bowyer, Graham Branch, Stephen Davis, Martin Dobson, Bryan Douglas, David Dunn, Derek Fazackerley, Paul Fletcher, Simon Garner, Kevin Hird, Matt Jansen, Lenny Johnrose, Steve Kindon, Les Latcham,

Micky Mellon, Andy Payton, Derek Scott, Craig Short, Jim Thomson, Ross Wallace and Paul Weller. I was in contact with Morten Gamst Pedersen, but we somehow lost touch with each other when he returned to Norway. Due to Covid 19 restrictions, every single interview was conducted over the telephone, except for the one with David Dunn.

My two old colleagues from the Lancashire Schools' FA, Mick Duffy and Mike Timberlake, were extremely helpful. Mick has made a number of contributions to the text and Mike introduced me to Veronica Simpson, Brian Nelson, at the time a Burnley FC Director and then his brother Dave Timberlake. He is a Burnley fan with a bottomless pit of wonderful stories from following his beloved club round the country and whose house is allegedly painted Claret and Blue. Two massive fans, Damian Hartley and Paul Cox, had so many interesting tales about their escapades as true supporters of the Clarets and the Rovers respectively, and there was much interest and support from old friends of mine, Stuart Reilly, Jamie Haddow, Geoff Bury and Dave Haworth. Dave Elliott, a resident of Tasmania for fifty years but still blue and white to the core, helped me out with a first-hand account of the 1960 Cup Final.

Dave Kennedy and Duggie Hargreaves, both from the border town of Accrington, could offer an extra dimension with their comments. Vicky Foy and Natalie Smith opened up about the life of a football fan from the female perspective and I was grateful for the support and interest shown by my two sons, Stephen and Simon, the former introducing me to Andy Bayes. Simon was particularly useful as a sounding board for a number of my ideas and, together with his fiancé Natalie, came up with the title of the book.

As hard as it was to write the book and proof read it, the search for photographs was even harder. In normal times, the local libraries and newspapers would have been a fertile source, their archives no doubt being packed with photographic memorabilia, but with the pandemic raging, these areas were locked down. Fortunately we found a number of people who were able to help.

Mary Painter from the Blackburn Central Library allowed me to search through micro films containing old newspapers and Shirley Ashton from Burnley Library gave me an introduction to Edward Walton from the Burnley Civic Trust, a voluntary organisation which worked so hard to find photographs for the book. Dan Black, with help from his colleagues on the Burnley Express was able to source numerous photos from the paper's back collections.

Scott Sumner from the Blackburn Rovers Fanzine "4,000 Holes" was most interested and through him, I was able to have some wonderful chats with Bernie Horne, a truly dedicated Rovers' fan and supporter who has a most magnificent collection of memorabilia regarding the Ewood Park club. Similarly, Shaun Borman, the Burnley FC historian, was most helpful and he gave me the name of Adam Riding at Turf Moor who found so many photos for me.

Equally Rob Gill at Blackburn Rovers came up with a collection of photographs from derby games and from wondering how we were going to find any, we have been most wonderfully swamped. It is as if there is a "football family" out there, dedicated to help anyone interested in publicising the game, irrespective of the colour of the shirt and we are so grateful to all of the above. Finally the local media have worked hard to help in publicising the book and it would be remiss of me not to mention Rich Sharpe of the Lancashire Telegraph, Dan Black from the Burnley Express and Andy Bayes from Radio Lancashire, each of whom has shown so much interest and been so helpful.

Finally my wife Lesley deserves so much of my gratitude for simply putting up with me for much of the last two years when, as well as being the driving force behind our house sale in France plus a removal to Lancashire where a new home had to be set-up, she was forced to be the grass widow to a husband for whom the writing of the book became a total obsession. I am sure that many men will have been divorced for less.

And then came the publicity and selling. Neither are my strong points but fortunately Dave Lane has taken on the brunt of the work, working his magic on Facebook as well as continuing to encourage and guide me. But even such an experienced publisher needs local help and I have received support from lots of quarters; friends, acquaintances and friends and acquaintances of friends and acquaintances. Graham Ainslie at Darwen Cricket Club, an outstanding cricketer and half decent footballer in school teams that I ran many years ago, has shown me that it is all about networking and he has certainly done that for me.

I have also learned about a whole clutch of mainly voluntary organisations who support their clubs and they in their turn have publicised the book; podcasters, club radio, fanzines and chat lines. These include: Rovers Chat, Rovers' Radio. No, Nay, Never Podcast.

Finally thanks to James Forsyth at the Burnley FC Club Shop, to Tina Neil at the Blackburn Rovers Club Shop and Dave Thomas, author of a much earlier book entitled "No, Nay, Never" for permission in allowing us to use a similar title. To all those mentioned and others whom I apologise to for momentarily having no doubt forgotten, I thank you all.

In terms of references, I wish to thank the following.

The Clarets Chronicles, the definitive history of Burnley Football Club, 1882-2007 by Ray Simpson and published by Burnley Football Club.

Blackburn Rovers. A Complete Record, 1875-1990 by Mike Jackman and published by The Breedon Books Publishing Company Limited.

The Essential History of Blackburn Rovers by Mike Jackman and published by Headline Book Publishing.

Burnley Football Club, The Complete A to Z by Dean Hayes and published by Sigma Leisure

Wikipedia, the Free Encyclopaedia.

The Football Club Historical Database, Richard Rundle.

Spartacus Educational. The history of Blackburn Rovers by John Simkin.

Association Football in Victorian England by Philip Gibbons

The facts and figures of the East Lancashire derbies

Lies, damned lies and statistics

Publicised by Mark Twain, inaccurately attributed to Sir Benjamin Disraeli and most likely first used by Sir Charles Dilke, a late 19th Century Liberal politician.

During the 1998-99 season, the Blackburn Rovers squad in the Premier League included twenty players who had either gained international honours whilst at the club or later in their careers with other teams. For those interested, they were...

Jason Wilcox, Tim Flowers and later David Dunn, plus Tim Sherwood when at Tottenham Hotspur and Kevin Davies when at Bolton Wanderers, all represented England. Winning Scottish caps were Kevin Gallacher, Billy McKinlay, Callum Davidson and Christian Dailly. The Wales team featured Nathan Blake whilst Alan Fettis, Keith Gillespie and Damien Johnson played for Northern Ireland. The Republic of Ireland were well represented by Jeff Kenna, Damien Duff, Jason McAteer and Lee Carsley and the final three were the Swiss defender Stephane Henchoz, the Swedish star Martin Dahlin and John Filan who had previously played for Australia. In the same period, no Burnley players played for their country.

Such a statistic can provide justification for two completely different lines of argument. This is typical of stats, being able to be used in whichever way suits. Political parties and major industries pay out huge chunks of money to strategists to massage figures and then spin them to their advantage. You can do that with this information. An overzealous Blackburn Rovers fan could say that with twenty internationals on their books, the Rovers were twenty times a better club than their neighbour. What rubbish they must have been without a single capped player. Equally, the Burnley fan who digs just a little deeper and discovers that the Blackburn club managed to just compile thirty-five points, win seven matches, score a meagre thirty-eight goals and were obviously relegated in nineteenth position that season, could comment that, "you had twenty internationals and still went down, what a rubbish club you are." In point of fact, both clubs were "rubbish" that season because Burnley, although avoiding relegation from Tier 3 (Division 2 at that time), finished in fifteenth place.

Irrespective of the above, I do believe that football statistics are at least interesting and can often give a true picture of a player, a manager and the club and I have inserted the following, all relevant to the performance of the two clubs vis-a-vis each other. They are presented without spin or comment and I do hope you also find them interesting.

Derby Games Since Officially Started: 1888-89

	League	P	W	L	D	F	A
League	Blackburn Rovers	90	38	36	16	162	150
	Burnley	90	36	38	16	150	162
Test matches	Blackburn Rovers	2	0	2	0	1	5
	Burnley	2	2	0	0	5	1
League Cup	Blackburn Rovers	1	0	1	0	0	2
	Burnley	1	1	0	0	2	0
FA Cup	Blackburn Rovers	7	3	2	2	11	8
	Burnley	7	2	3	2	8	11

Derby Winning Run

Blackburn Rovers	6	1888-90 & 1982-2010	Burnley	5	1915-21

Derby Sequence Without Defeat

Blackburn Rovers	9	1982-2013	Burnley	6	1962-65 & 2012-21

Season Completing In A Higher League Position

(i.e. club with bragging rights) Blue = Blackburn Rovers Claret = Burnley

1888-89	1889-90	1890-91	**1891-92**	**1892-93**	1893-94
1894-95	1895-96	1896-97	1897-98	**1898-99**	1899-00
1900-01	1902-02	1902-03	1903-04	1904-05	1905-06
1906-07	1907-08	1908-09	1909-10	1910-11	1911-12
1912-13	1913-14	1914-15	**1919-20**	**1920-21**	**1921-22**
1922-23	1923-24	1924-25	1925-26	**1926-27**	1927-28
1928-29	1929-30	1930-31	1931-32	1932-33	1933-34
1934-35	1935-36	1936-37	**1937-38**	1938-39	1946-47
1947-48	**1948-49**	**1949-50**	**1850-51**	**1951-52**	**1952-53**
1953-54	**1954-55**	**1955-56**	**1956-57**	**1957-58**	**1958-59**
1959-60	**1960-61**	**1951-62**	**1962-63**	1963-64	1964-65

1965-66	1966-67	1967-68	1968-69	1969-70	1970-71
1971-72	1972-73	1973-74	1974-75	1975-76	1976-77
1977-78	1978-79	1979-80	1980-81	1981-82	1982-83
1983-84	1984-85	1985-86	1986-87	1987-88	1988-89
1989-90	1990-91	1991-92	1992-93	1993-94	1994-95
1995-96	1996-97	1997-98	1998-99	1999-00	2000-01
2001-02	2002-03	2003-04	2004-05	2005-06	2006-07
2007-08	2008-09	2009-10	2010-11	2011-12	2012-13
2013-14	2014-15	2015-16	2016-17	2017-18	2018-19
2019-20	2020-21	2021-22			

Blackburn Rovers 76 **Burnley 47**

Most Appearances In Derby Games

Blackburn Rovers

Ronnie Clayton	1952-66	18

Burnley

Jerry Dawson	1913-26	19

Played For Both Clubs In Derby Matches

There have been a small number of players turning out for both clubs, several with great distinction. Jack Bruton, Adam Blacklaw, Keith Newton and John Connelly are the ones we all remember, but only the ten listed below have actually taken part in derby games for both clubs.

Name	Club	Apps	Derby Years	Club	Apps	Derby Years	Total Apps
Jack Bruton	Burnley	9	1925-29	Blackburn Rovers	5	1930-38	14
Keith Newton	Blackburn Rovers	8	1962-66	Burnley	3	1976-78	11
Walter Joyce	Burnley	4	1960-64	Blackburn Rovers	3	1964-65	7
Peter Turnbull	Burnley	4	1893-95	Blackburn Rovers	1	1895	5
Levy Thorpe	Burnley	1	1915	Blackburn Rovers	4	1920-22	5
Dave Jones	Blackburn Rovers *	1	2013	Burnley	4	2013-16	5
Robert Haresnip	Blackburn Rovers	1	1889	Burnley	3	1889-91	4
Peter O'Dowd	Blackburn Rovers	3	1928-29	Burnley	1	1930	4
Peter Whittingham	Burnley *	2	2004-05	Blackburn Rovers	1	2017	3
Michael Keane	Blackburn Rovers *	1	2014	Burnley	2	2016-17	3

* = On Loan

Double Derby Wins In A Season

Blackburn Rovers

1888-89	1889-90	1890-91	1896-97	1921-22
1925-26	1961-62	1982-83	2000-01	2009-10

Burnley

1898-99	1919-20	1920-21	1926-27	1962-63
1963-64	1978-79	2015-16		

Leading Goal Scorers In Derby Games

Blackburn Rovers

		Goals	Matches
Jack Southworth	1888-92	11	10

Burnley

		Goals	Matches
Benny Cross	1921-28	6	13
Andrew McCluggage	1925-30	6	9

Most Individual Goals In A Derby Game

Percy Dawson	Blackburn Rovers	Ewood Park	1914-15	4	Division 1

Highest Attendances in Derby Games

At Ewood Park

1959-60	53,839	6th Round FA Cup Replay

At Turf Moor

1959-60	51,501	6th Round FA Cup

Biggest Wins In Derby Games

Blackburn Rovers
Home – Blackburn Rovers 7 Burnley 1 1890-91 Division 1,
Away – Burnley 1 Blackburn Rovers 7 1888-89 Division 1
Burnley
Home – Burnley 6 Blackburn Rovers 0 1895-96 Division 1,
Away – Blackburn Rovers 1 Burnley 5 1926-27 Division 1

Burnley's Ben Mee is shown the red card in 2013

Dismissals in Derby Games

No.	Name	Club	Venue	Season
1	Joe Lofthouse	Blackburn Rovers	Turf Moor	1891-92
2	Alex Stewart	Burnley	Turf Moor	1891-92
3	Sandy Lang	Burnley	Ewood Park	1892-93
4	Jack Southworth	Blackburn Rovers	Ewood Park	1892-93
5	Mike England	Blackburn Rovers	Turf Moor	1963-64
6	Willie Morgan	Burnley	Ewood Park	1965-66
7	Noel Brotherston	Blackburn Rovers	Ewood Park	1977-78
8	Kevin Ball	Burnley	Turf Moor	2000-01
9	Ben Mee	Burnley	Ewood Park	2012-13

Supporters Roll Of Honour

Chris Johnson
Michael Ormerod
Gary Wiswell
David Eastwood
Tim Marsden
Catherine Guy
Ian Futter
Jason Maxwell
Stewart George
Douglas Wilkinson
Aaron Wright
Brian Jardine
Mark Joseph Jardine
Darrel Jardine
Vince O'Keefe
Douglas Hargreaves
Anthony Payne
Jack Payne
Kathleen Payne
Paul Clarke
Leslie Wooler
David Ritson
David Fielding
Jordan Fielding
Lewis Fielding
Damien Pickup
Deborah Farrell
Ian Eddleston
Janet Eddleston
Paul Wogden
David Fielding
Andrea Johnson
Harold Heys
Duncan Greenwood
David Marsden
Mike Jackman
James Moorcroft
Bernie Horne
Mark Atkinson 50
Steve Birtwell
Daniel Furness
James Moorcroft
Jon Denney
Keith Cassidy
Ian Machin
Stuart Warner
Matt Taylor
Martin Hollings
Ashlynne Elliott
Martin Hollings
Andie Fitch
David Elliott
Sarah Elliott
Daniel 'Mash' Ashworth
Heather Gray
Matt Boulton
Steven Townsend
Ashley Townsend
Peter Townsend
Evelyn Parks nee Whittaker
Kev Hibbert
Kenneth George
Daniel Carroll
Leslie Wooler
Michael Abrams
Steve Sargison
Peter Briggs
Tom Briggs
Chris Briggs
David Hutchinson
David Chadwick
Barry Faulkner
Nicola Faulkner
Stuart Reilly
David Briffett
Darin Albert Williamson
Paul Hodgkinson
Danny Bloom
Richard Baker
Barry Phillips
Steve Allen
Mark Sinnett
Vince O'Keefe
Peter Anslow
Calvin James Anslow
Matthew Slade
Bryden Holden
Simon Case
Mick Thexton
Don Higgs
Steven Barker
Mike Ryan
Richard John Baker
Michael Whittle
Barry Seddon
Kevan Shaw
Ivan Hickmott
Peter Elliott
Luke Johnson

Gary McCrae
Wayne Heaton
Joe Kay
Andrew Goodwin
Leslie Wooler
Bruce Mackie
Joe Hartley
Martin Evans
Alan Birdy Birkbeck
John Mitchell
Chris Rawson
Richard Bradford
Paul Banks
Luke Johnson
William Greenwood
Eric Greenwood
Andrew Greenwood
Darren Taylor
Paul Walmsley
Christopher Thomas Hartley
Nick Mckeown
Paul Haworth
Rodge Davies
David Hall
Kieron Altimas

Peter Toner
Mark Jepson
Geoff Bury
Daniel Bury
Denis Neale
Jon Neale
Richard Neale
Matthew Neale
Colin Wiggans
Peter Jones
Valerie Duckett
Wayne Duckett
Keith Riley
Graham Oxer
Jack Robinson
John Sutcliffe
Hendrik Nieuwenhuizen
Alan Aspinall
Jacqueline Holmes
Walter Andrews
Steve Ball
Wayne Curtis
Craig Smith
Andy Young
Gary Slinger

Stephen Townley
David Wilkinson
Matthew Campione
Jamie Box
Stephen Smith
David Whittaker
Anthony Horne
David Haworth
Robert Coar
Grant Furness
Christopher Monkhouse
Louis Fielding-Smith
Lindsay Hepworth
Anthony Culshaw
Arthur Ashworth
Graham Ainslie
Graham Hall
David Smith
Cliff Henshaw
Paul Laxton

Thanks to those fans named above who pre-ordered the book and helped support our project.

NO NAY NEVER NO MORE

Printed in Great Britain
by Amazon

53607175R00275